W9-CFC-118

THE OFFICIAL® PRICE GUIDE TO

ACTION FIGURES

STUART W. WELLS III
AND
JIM MAIN

FIRST EDITION

HOUSE OF COLLECTIBLES
NEW YORK

Sale of this book without a front cover may be unauthorized. If this book is coverless, it may have been reported to the publisher as "unsold or destroyed" and neither the author nor the publisher may have received payment for it.

Important Notice. All of the information, including valuations, in this book has been compiled from the most reliable sources, and every effort has been made to eliminate errors and questionable data. Nevertheless, the possibility of error, in a work of such immense scope, always exists. The publisher will not be held responsible for losses that may occur in the purchase, sale, or other transaction of items because of information contained herein. Readers who feel they have discovered errors are invited to *write* and inform us, so they may be corrected in subsequent editions. Those seeking further information on the topics covered in this book are advised to refer to the complete line of *Official Price Guides* published by the House of Collectibles.

Copyright © 1997 by Stuart W. Wells III and Jim Main

All rights reserved under International and Pan American Copyright Conventions.

HC This is a registered trademark of Random House, Inc.

Published by: House of Collectibles
201 East 50th Street
New York, NY 10022

Distributed by Ballantine Books, a division of Random House, Inc., New York, and simultaneously in Canada by Random House of Canada Limited, Toronto.

http://www.randomhouse.com

Manufactured in the United States of America

ISSN: 1093-2631

ISBN: 0-676-60080-8

Designed and produced by Stuart Wells

Cover design by Kristine V. Mills-Noble
Cover photo © George Kerrigan

First Edition: June 1997
10 9 8 7 6 5 4 3 2 1

THE OFFICIAL® PRICE GUIDE TO

ACTION FIGURES

CONTENTS

CREDITS AND ACKNOWLEDGMENTS

The authors extend their heartfelt thanks to the following individuals, without whose assistance this book would not have been possible:

Rob Rintoul, Brian Brick, Ezra Harris, Bob Sodaro, David Kruseski, Steven Bryant of Heroes Comics & Cards; Castle Comics, Tim Frederick, Morgan McClain, Wats Wacker, Tom Wheeler, Jim Makowski, Lenny Lee, Rich Maurizio, Bob Brought, Brendan Faulkner, Mike Van Plew, John McGonagle (*Rest in Peace, Buddy*), Danny Fuchs, Connie, Jimmy and Joey Main, Mike Tuz, Kirk Bozigian, Linda Baker, Mary Wordsworth, Ron Antonette, Karen Trachtenberg, Frank Oviatt, Steve Goodrich, Scott Fleming, Shawn Nagle, the Selti Family, the Clark Family.

INTRODUCTION

This book covers action figures sold in the United States from 1964 (the year the first action figure, G.I. Joe appeared), through the end of 1996. While the focus of the book is on the action figures, the book also covers the vehicles, accessories and playsets associated with them. Premiums, like trading cards, rings, comic books which are included in the same package as an action figure, are noted, but not separately listed or priced.

Listed prices are the retail price of the figure in MIB (Mint in Box) condition, i.e., mint figures, complete, in their original packaging. The packaging should be "near mint," which is generally the condition of the packaging when new. A price sticker may be present, or, may have been removed, as long as this was done without damage to the package. Any in-pack premium must be present. A cut-out proof of purchase is a defect, as is more than nominal wear to the package. Any such defects reduce the value of the item somewhat, while an exceptional, mint package increases the value a little.

A "loose" price is given for some figures. Generally, a loose figure is worth about 40 percent to 60 percent of a figure in its original packaging. However, common figures from recent years which can easily be found MIB are worth only a dollar or two at most, because most collectors want a packaged figure. Loose figures are complete if they include all accessories and weapons included in the original package, plus the base, if any. Prices for loose figures do not include the premium, which is a separate collectible once it is removed from the package.

Our listings are as complete as we can make them and feature the actual name of the figure as used on the header card or package, rather than the popular abbreviation seen in many magazines, i.e. "Lieutenant Worf in Ritual Klingon Attire" rather than "Worf-Klingon." Additionally, we have included the UPC code and "action feature" for every figure we could. All of this information is included to give the reader a positive match between the listing and the toy in his hand.

For selected series the figure's equipment is listed as an aid to collectors who wish to purchase a loose figure. Where this is done, the list from the package is used when one is available. We prefer not to make up our own description, if possible. Unfortunately, for many series, a description of the accessories is not sufficient to avoid uncertainty and anything less than a color photo won't do the job completely. In other words, we can tell you the figure comes with "a helmet and a spear," but you will have to check further in order to make sure the figure you are considering buying has the correct original helmet and the correct spear. Any collector buying loose figures for more than a few dollars each should research the accessories by checking a figure in its original package.

Series are listed alphabetically, except that some related series are listed under a group heading, with later series in chronological order. This mostly affects Batman, Star Trek and Star Wars. For example, Star Wars is followed by The Empire Strikes Back and then Return of the Jedi, while Batman is followed by Batman Returns, Batman The Animated Series and Batman Forever.

Within each action figure line, figures are grouped by batch or series, in chronological order, followed by large figures, multi-figure packs, vehicles, accessories and playsets. This is done because figures in the same batch were shipped in the same box and have similar packaging, etc. and this is an important element in value. This listing method preserves this vital information about the figures and allows us to note things such as in-pack premiums that are shared by all figures in the group. In addition, different batches have different distribution patterns. For instance, major toy stores may get the figures produced in years one and two but not the "Tail-in" figures from year three, which went to other toy outlets.

Within each group or batch, figures are listed in numerical order, if known, or alphabetical order if the UPC code number is not known. Groups or batches of figures usually consist of approximately five to eight different figures, so locating the listing for a particular figure in the batch is quite simple. In addition, the index in the back lists every figure name in alphabetical order and notes the page(s) where a listing for that figure may be found.

We have made every effort to eliminate questionable information, or to put it another way, we would rather err on the side of omission than commission. There are, undoubtedly, some toys and some variations of toys that we do not list. We hear rumors all the time, same as you do. We have tried to run them down as best we can and we list only the ones we have seen ourselves or in a published picture. You can't see everything.

Definitions:

Retail Price: For figures which are no longer available in toy stores, the value listed in this book is our best estimate of the price you will be quoted by a dealer at a toy collector show or in an advertisement. All prices depend on supply and demand and dealer prices for a toy will always fall in a range. Where supply seems to be adequate, our value estimate is below the middle of this range. Where only a few dealers seem to have the toy for sale, our price is about in the middle. Frequently, you can. Of course, if you are trying to sell rather than buy the figure, you won't get this much from a dealer because he has to sell at a profit to stay in business.

For recent figures which can be found at retail prices in toy stores, we use that retail price, unless the figure is harder to find than others from the same batch. Dealers will be selling these "scarce" recent figures at a premium price. Our guide uses a value between the toy store retail price and the dealer price that reflects our estimate of the actual scarcity of the figure. If it can be found at retail with a little effort, its value is close to the retail price, while if the figure is nearly impossible to find a retail, its value is close to the dealer price.

For recent figures which might be found as red tag specials at the end of 1996, original retail price is used, because by the time this book is bought and read most of these figures will be sold off. Generally the secondary market price goes back to original retail price after the red tag stock is absorbed.

No Price Found: The item is believed to exist, but we have insufficient information to assign a price with any confidence.

Not Seen: If used with a recent item, it means that the figure was listed in the manufacturers' catalogs, but was possibly not produced. Not all figures scheduled are actually produced. Some are cancelled or delayed.

If used with an older item, it means that we doubt the figure exists, despite its appearance in catalogs and even dealer lists and price guides. Sometimes the figure was never produced and the only actual examples are prototypes. Rumors are not toys, show us the toy. If we see an actual toy, and not just a rumor, we will list it in another edition.

Action Figure: An articulated figure commonly sold as an action figure rather than a collectible figure or a doll. Usually it's sold as a boy's toy. The judgment is

Mini Comic, Masters of the Universe (Mattel 1984)

made on the series as a whole, since certain monsters, etc., have different articulation than the "human" figures. Note that what is commonly known as an action figure has changed over the years. Original G.I. Joes had 21 points of articulation. Many action figures today have relatively few points of articulation. The *action* is provided by a specific action feature or accessory such as a weapon. Size is a factor as well since a larger figure can have more points than a small one.

Doll: As used in our descriptions, doll means an action figure that wears removable clothing. This is generally used for early action figures such as G.I. Joe, Captain Action and the various series done by Mego, plus the recent reincarnations of these types of figures and helps to differentiate them from recent large size figures which are all plastic.

Vehicle: Anything that an action figure rides on or in, including a car, boat, plane, horse, etc. It does not include such things as spaceships which are not to the same scale as the figure.

Accessory: Anything that the figure uses, such as a large weapon, communication or radar station, or playset. All such items are made to the same scale as the figures.

Lee's Action Figure News & Toy Review; White's Collecting Figures; Wizard's ToyFare

Header Card: The hanging card with series logo and art work, also known as a backer card.

Carded: Packaged in a plastic blister on a header card.

Try-Me Pack: One with a hole so you can push a button and hear the figure's sound feature.

Window Box: A box with a plastic window over a cut-out hole so you can see the figure.

Open Box: Similar to a window box, but with no plastic window.

Mail-in Figure: A figure acquired by sending money and/or proofs of purchase in the mail to the manufacturer (actually to a "fulfillment" company).

Two-Pack: A pack with two equal status figures such as Batman and Robin.

Role-Play: A toy such as a sword or helmet which fits the child, not the action figure. Role-Play items from a given action figure line are not covered in this book.

Abbreviations:
   Asst. = Assortment
   Anniv. = Anniversary

You should naturally try to find the figure in a store first, before paying a premium dealer price, be-cause you might get lucky or more of the figures may have shown up in stores since the dealers grabbed all the first ones and jacked-up the price. If you still can't find the figure in a store, you can pay a dealer price if you wish, or wait until the next scarce, hot figure appears that everyone is chasing and see if you can find a dealer that still hasn't sold off his stock of the one you want. His price should be a little softer then.

If figures that you want are still available as red tag specials, you should obviously buy them that way and not pay retail price to a dealer. After all, red tag specials are where many dealers buy the figures "at wholesale" and if you can find a figure at red tag price you may have a bargain too.

One last word about prices for action figures—they change. The prices listed in this book are as accurate as we can make them, but there is no such thing as the "last word on prices." Fortunately, there are several fine magazines that publish the current prices of your favorite action figures every month. Naturally, they can't list every action figure and their price lists are hardly identical, but just about every dealer and collector that we know uses one or more of them. They are pictured above. Look for them where books and magazines are sold and in comic book stores. Maybe someday toy stores will have the sense to carry them too.

THE HISTORY OF PLAYMATES TOYS, INC.

by Jim Main and Stuart W. Wells III

Playmates Toys, Inc. is one of the most prominent producers of collectible action figures. In less than ten years of manufacturing these figures, they have produced several of the most respected and most collectible lines, including the Star Trek series and, the figures that put Playmates on the map, the Teenage Mutant Ninja Turtles series. Their innovative marketing ideas have helped connect the word "collectible" to the words "action figure."

Playmates Industrial, predecessor of the current company, was founded in 1966 by Sam Chen as an original equipment manufacturer for retailers and toy companies in both the United States and Europe. Many important changes took place in the 1970s, including the establishment of a new toy division and the creation of its first United States subsidiary. In the early 1980s, Playmates Toys, Inc. was created, United States operations were consolidated in California, and Playmates Industrial, now called Playmates Toys Holdings Limited, went public in Hong Kong.

The year 1986 marked a turning point for Playmates. Richard Sallis joined the company as vice president for marketing. He played a major role in giving the green light to the "Green Guys" who took the world by storm as the Teenage Mutant Ninja Turtles. Playmates began production of this line in 1988 and the rest, as they say, is history! The Turtles have made Playmates the force to be reckoned with in the action figure industry that it is today.

The Turtles, the four green, gritty humanoid characters and their friends and foes, surprised us as toys. The simple black and white comic on which the toys were based also surprised the comic industry. The comic had only a two-color cover and was produced by two young men from Northfield, Massachusetts, Kevin Eastman and Peter Laird, just for the fun of it. In a very short time the Teenage Mutant Ninja Turtles became a major force in the independent comic marketplace with, of course, the help of Richard Sallis.

The Teenage Mutant Ninja Turtles figures were introduced in 1988. Playmates' Turtle sales were $23 million that first year, $115 million the second year, and by 1990 they were the #1 selling action figure line with worldwide sales of an unbelievable $525 million.

April O'Neil, Teenage Mutant Ninja Turtles (Playmates 1989)

The initial batch of Turtles figures that were produced in 1988 came complete with forms to fill out to join their fan club. They were Donatello, Raphael, Leonardo and Michelangelo or simply Don, Ralph, Leo and Mike to their fiends and fans. This first batch of Turtles are very rare, but not as rare as the first April O'Neil figure. April, their human female reporter friend, has been a hot collectible each year she was produced, but 1988's original April is the hottest of all. Shredder, the villainous enemy leader, along with his foot soldiers and dimwitted assistants, Bebop and Rocksteady, also made the scene in toy stores in 1988 and are avidly collected. All in all, from 1988 to the present, over 300 different Turtle action figures have been produced based on characters from the comic book, from the animated cartoon series and from the three live-action feature films along with some figures created by Playmates as toy line original characters.

Playmates, like all manufacturers of plastic poseable playthings, has had its share of misses along with the hits. Generally, however, they have been able to bank on the hits and weed out the failures before they can do too much damage, sometimes even prior to production.

One miss came in 1989, when Playmates acquired a license to produce action figures and vehicles from a series called Barnyard Commandoes. The figures were based on the animated series of the same name which involved two fighting anthropomorphic factions—the P.O.R.K.S. (Platoon of Rebel Killer Swine) and the R.A.M.S. (Rebel Army of Militant Sheep). (Don't blame me, I only report the facts!) Either Playmates was looking for what they thought might be another Turtle-like series hit, or the license was a bargain. Whatever the motive may have been, the series lasted only a year and was quickly forgotten. But by now Playmates could afford to acquire major licenses for well-known properties.

Breathless Mahoney 18" figure (Playmates 1990)

The first major licensed toy from Playmates came in 1990 when they produced a series of 5" action figures and vehicles based on what they thought was going to be a very successful feature film—Dick Tracy. Why would they think otherwise? The film starred Warren Beatty and Madonna plus many other big

screen notables and was based on a very popular comic strip character that appealed to millions of readers worldwide. Thirteen figures and two vehicles were produced and Dick Tracy was the #2 selling toy line that Christmas, but many collectors thought that the rather cartoonish design of the figures (they all looked like they were bow-legged) wasn't really their cup of tea. Collectors set their sights on the two larger 18" figures of Dick Tracy and Breathless Mahoney (Madonna's character) that were more realistic looking than the smaller action figures. The figure of The Blank, the fourteenth figure in the line, was the true collectible, as it was never made available in stores outside of Canada. Some enterprising individuals did, however, manage to get their hands on some and collectors with disposable income were finally able to add this Madonna/Breathless Mahoney secret identity figure to their collection.

In 1991, Playmates introduced three new lines to their ever expanding family of action figures—Darkwing Duck, Tailspin and Toxic Crusaders—but none of them, for some unknown reason, achieved the same kind of staying power as that of the "heroes in a half-shell."

Tailspin and Darkwing Duck were two brand new Disney animated television efforts so how could **they** fail as action figures? Heck, even I collected Darkwing Duck. Many fans and collectors were dismayed when second series figures from Tailspin and Darkwing Duck were announced in Playmates' 1992 catalog, but were never produced. Key figures, too, like Darkwing Duck's love interest, Morgana Maccawber, four of his popular villains and two of his associates. How can you have a collection of Darkwing duck without these figures?

Toxic Crusaders was another new animated effort, based on a pretty lame cult film offering from the B-film producers, the Troma Group. Many collectors already had a pretty good idea where this line would be headed. All the announced figures and vehicles were produced or it certainly appeared that way, but even if they weren't, the question remained … would anybody really care?

Despite a dismal 1991, Playmates still had the Turtles and the year to follow would bring about Playmates' next biggest licensing deal and second longest lasting line ever, when they produced their first line of action figures based on the "Star Trek" franchise.

"Star Trek: The Next Generation" figures had been done by the Lewis Galoob Company in 1988 but the license had been dormant ever since. The way Playmates handled the figures made collectors almost forget there ever had been Galoob figures. The figures were now 5"

Captain Jean-Luc Picard, Star Trek (Playmates 1992)

instead of 4" and the sculpting, as with the majority of action figures from Playmates, was first rate—they had the likenesses down pat. In addition, Playmates introduced a whole new collectibility factor ... sequential numbering.

A different number was actually printed on a sticker on the bottom of the right foot of each "Star Trek" character Playmates produced, supposedly in sequence as they rolled off the assembly line. Actually, we understand that the number is applied in the order the right feet are made, not the order the final figures are assembled. But who cares? Collectors to this day pay good money to acquire figures with numbers under 100—even more for numbers under 10. Collectors should note that not all of these low number figures were distributed in normal toy store assortments. Some were held for special distribution, such as giveaways at Playmates press conference during the 1997 International Toy Fair.

A number of interesting, and very collectible, figure variations occurred with this first series of "Star Trek" figures. Early releases of the Borg figure featured a picture on the back of the package that was reversed. Gowron, the Klingon, came both with and without gold trim and the Ferengi came with and without black coloring on his boots. The most significant variation

was on the Lt. Geordi LaForge figure. It first appeared with a removable visor, but this was quickly changed to a glued-on visor, presumably because the loose visor presented a small parts danger to younger children. Collectors quickly stepped forward to save the nation's youth by buying every one of the scarce removable visor figures they could find.

With the 1992 acquisition of the "Star Trek: The Next Generation" property came another Paramount license, "The Addams Family." The action figure line came out sometime during the run of the film, which starred the late Raul Julia as Gomez and Angelica Houston as Morticia. The figures, however, were sculpted to resemble the characters in the animated series. In any case, the figure line didn't have much staying power even with the production of a second film. It was cancelled before the original line was completed, leaving the collectors of the series missing planned figures of Wednesday, Cousin It and Thing.

Properties from MCA/Universal were acquired by Playmates for the first time in 1993. ExoSquad was launched and became a favorite of many fans and collectors during its three-year run. It was based on a finely animated and intelligently written television series from the Universal Cartoon Studios. The premise of the series is a continuing battle for the future of mankind in the 22nd century. Humans have settled the homeworlds of Earth, Mars and Venus using Exo-technology, but their genetically engineered Neosapiens have turned against them and mankind is brutally conquered and enslaved. Only the ExoSquad stands in the way of the Neosapien's permanent domination of the human race. Playmates did an excellent job on the figures, the E-Frames that they controlled, and the packaging they came in—so much so that when awards were given via the various toy collectible publications, ExoSquad won more than once.

In its last year, ExoSquad was merged with another man and machine science fiction series of popular note, Robotech. The two story lines were inconsistent and many claim that the lame effort to merge them helped cause the ExoSquad line's downfall. It's obvious that Playmates was not out to destroy the series but was probably looking for a good launching point for Robotech. It remains a favorite with collectors, and many of them hope that Playmates will one day bring back the ExoSquad series.

October 1993 marked the fifth anniversary of production for the Teenage Mutant Ninja Turtles. United States sales for the line reached 247,347,000 units, an incredible number of figures sold within a five-year period.

Playmates produced action figure lines for the two remaining MCA/Universal Properties it acquired in 1993, but these series did not appear until 1994. "SeaQuest" was a Steven Spielberg–created network undersea sci-fi series and Monster Force was a syndicated animated series which was an attempt to combine the famous monsters of Universal and bring them to the attention of a newer, younger audience. Monster Force didn't fare too well and the line was cancelled before two announced figures, Shelly Frank and HoTep the Mummy, could be produced. "SeaQuest" figures used the individual numbering system that we all thought was reserved just for the "Star Trek" toys, and the most requested and most collectible figure of this series turned out to be the dolphin, Darwin. He appeared briefly in the summer, was bought up immediately and never resurfaced afterwards.

Alec DeLeon with Field Communications E-Frame,
ExoSquad (Playmates 1993)

Several 1994 developments gave the "Star Trek" franchise a further boost, starting with Paramount's introduction of the new syndicated television series, "Star Trek: Deep Space Nine," which first began in 1993. Figures were produced for this series in early 1994, as well as for its sister show, "Star Trek: The Next Generation." This was its final season on the air (not counting reruns) but the first "Star Trek: The Next Generation" film, *Star Trek: Generations* was eagerly awaited by fans of all ages. The film included char-

acters from this series and the classic "Star Trek" program. Naturally a line of figures was produced. 1994 also marked the year that Playmates launched a series of 9" articulated figures in cloth outfits based on popular "Star Trek" characters. Appropriately enough, they began with the Command Edition featuring the three captains: Kirk, Picard and Sisko.

In addition to all this, another new action figure line, Skeleton Warriors, based on a fabulous animated television series, was introduced in 1994. While the evil skeletal characters were plentiful, the humans were not. And the best figure that was announced, that of Princess Talyn, was never produced!

In the world of the Turtles, Playmates tried to combine a couple of licenses in 1994 and brought out Universal Monster Turtles (actually two different batches, with the first beginning in late 1993). The Turtles were converted into the Mummy, Frankenstein, Dracula, the Wolfman, the Metaluna Monster (from the 1955 film *This Island Earth*), The Creature from the Black Lagoon, The Invisible Man and, the best of the bunch, April O'Neil as The Bride of Frankenstein. Then they combined their two biggest licenses and produced the Trek Turtles (Captain Leo, First Officer Don, Doctor Ralph and Chief Engineer Mike).

Playmates produced their very first series of action figures based on the exploits of costumed super heroes when they picket up the license for WildC.A.T.s, created by Image comic book co-founder, superstar Jim Lee. An animated series debuted on CBS, which soon found its way into syndication. The figures came available in standard 5" size and three of the characters were also made in 10" versions. Four different groups were produced up until the summer of 1996, all with trading cards.

The year 1995 brought us two new lines of action figures with a Japanese/Shogun warrior/martial arts theme—Ronin Warriors and Superhuman Samurai Syber Squad. Both were picked up during the time when many companies were acquiring shows based on Japanese themes of this type. They typically contain 20 percent new American content to 80 percent re-dubbed Japanese action. Many interesting creatures, robots and crafts were produced in large and small scales and these sometimes can still be spotted in discount aisles.

Earthworm Jim was introduced by Playmates in 1994 as the star of the company's award-winning 16-bit video game. A 1995 cartoon series was produced based on the adventures of the main character and his friends and foes which is still shown on the UPN network. Jim got his start as an action figure line that same year. Princess What's-Her-Name has been popular with collectors, but the rest of the figures have red tags on them at the moment.

"Star Trek: Voyager," a new "Star Trek" series was launched in 1995 on the UPN network and Playmates produced its first series of figures for the show. More Deep Space Nine figures were made that year, as well as four larger Space Talk figures from "Star Trek: The Next Generation" and a series of Classic Star Trek Movie figures, which brought characters and outfits from films I, II and VI to many collectors.

Jim Lee, popular for his WildC.A.T.s comic, show and figures, designed a signature series for the Turtles that featured Mike, Don and Ralph in superheroesque battle outfits. The Savage Dragon, a series created by Erik Larsen, also of the Image Comics group was incorporated into the Jim Lee Turtles line. Savage Dragon had his own syndicated animated show and can still be seen there. The Dragon's and Jim Lee Turtles all came out in early 1996 rather than the announced 1995 date.

The final year of action figure production covered in this book is 1996, a year which produced some interesting new lines from Playmates and one incident that disillusioned many collectors in the "Star Trek" community.

Raphael, Jim Lee's TMNT (Playmates 1996)

General Lynch, Flash Gordon (Playmates 1996)

Flash Gordon marked his debut as a Playmates action figure line in 1996. However, the figures were based on the newer, younger Flash from the animated series that appeared the same year. The younger market didn't care for this new version and it was despised by older, "baby boom" collectors. The only "flash" in this series was the speed with which it went from initial release to bargain bin to close out bargain bin at two for $5.00

The gritty, hard-edged great-looking action figure series Primal Rage appeared in 1996. It was based on the video game of the same name and contained no human characters at all, but who cared? The line is still going strong to this day, with some electronic sound enhancement and larger figure versions.

Michael Jordan and the Looney Tunes crew got together for the 1996 box-office hit *Space Jam* and Playmates inked a deal with Warner Bros. to produce figures from the film. The figures are not a big hit in the collectibles market, but they are a cross-collectible and appeal to many fans of animation aa well as sports enthusiasts.

The "Star Trek" line was still doing well but many collectors were stunned that Playmates was not doing anything really spectacular to mark the 30th anniversary of the original series. A new series called Starfleet Academy (figures of Picard, Riker, LaForge and Worf as cadets in training, each with a CD Rom adventure disk) came and went quickly, or more accurately, came and now linger around unsold, mixed in with other "Star Trek" figures which do sell. An Original Star Trek series was also produced. Many of these figures were based on the pilot episode, "The Cage."

The big announcement from Playmates during 1996 was made at the 1996 International Toy Fair. Playmates said that as a "thank you" to many collectors of the Star Trek figures, they would manufacture three special figures: Picard from "Tapestry," Tasha Yar from "Yesterday's Enterprise" and Lt. Barclay from "Projections." Each figure would have a run of only 1701 figures, based on the serial number for the *U.S.S. Enterprise*, NCC-1701. For the most part, collectors did not benefit from this special "thank you" from Playmates. A few lucky toy store stock boys and their dealer friends certainly cashed in. Collectors either had to pay many hundreds of dollars for the figures or live with the knowledge that they could never complete their collections. To them, the "thank you" felt a lot more like another two-word phrase ending in "you." At least when they came to producing the Barclay figure they at least upped the production run to 3,000.

The new Star Trek movie *Star Trek: First Contact* was announced at the very same Toy Fair, but nothing was available to be shown. The figures did appear in late 1996 and, to make them special, they were produced in a 6" size rather than the regular 5" format. A series of five special 9" figures based on the film were also produced.

What's in store for Playmates in 1997 and beyond? I attended the 1997 International Toy Fair where Playmates announced the advent of Venus de Milo, the big Teenage Mutant Ninja Turtle surprise. She will be showcased in a new live-action series on the Fox network called Ninja Turtles: The Next Mutation. Star Trek will indeed continue with new figures from the classic Trek, "Next Generation," "Deep Space Nine," "Voyager" and the Star Trek films. Both Primal Rage and Space Jam will continue on into 1997 as well with

Space Jam continuing until Spring '97 and Primal Rage continuing into Summer. New lines announced for this year are Looney Tunes (a continuation of their license with Warner Bros.), National Hockey League Pro Zone (a series of 12½" Hockey Star action figures), World Wrestling Federation (stretch figures, 2" figures and 14" talking figures plus 9" figures as well), Zorro (based on the classic as well as new small and big screen versions of this popular character), Soldiers of Fortune, Inc. and Tom Clancy's NETforce.

Playmates has had two big hits: Teenage Mutant Ninja Turtles and Star Trek. These two series account for 350 and 210 different figures, respectively, not counting reissues and variations. Playmates has produced only 250 different figures in all their other series combined! Of their other series, only ExoSquad and WildC.A.T.s lasted long enough to be considered successful. Many of their other series were D.O.A., D.S.A.A. (Dead Soon After Arrival), or, in the case of 21, D.B.A. (Dead Before Arrival).

Star Trek looks good for 1997 and beyond, but it's not anywhere near as hot a property as Star Wars. Maybe Venus de Milo will revive the Turtles line, maybe not. Collectors will like Zorro, but will it sell to kids? Hockey action figures are a good idea, but will Playmates even be able to get the licenses for the other three sports, all of which have greater sales potential than hockey, and will collectors get excited about these figures or will they stick to Starting Lineup?

The company's attention to detail and quality are legendary and have elevated the standards for the whole action figure industry. Collectors love Playmates for this, enough to forgive them for Picard Tapestry and Flash Gordon. Some of Playmates' most creative items, such as the Skeleton Warriors, should have done better and maybe another undersea series will come along on television so they can use their great seaQuest vehicle designs. The toy market is fickle and fast changing. Mego was on top of the world in the mid 1970s, but a number of bad television show licenses put them out of business a few years later.

ACTION FIGURE SCULPTING: A CONVERSATION WITH SHAWN NAGLE

Conducted By: Jim Main

The sculpting of action figures has changed drastically since the 1960s, when they were like poseable mannequins. Today they have evolved into an articulated form of art!

Shawn Nagle has consented to supply us with key information on the subject. He is a rising star among action figure sculptors. His credentials include sculpting Marvel characters for Toy Biz for toy store distribution as well as sculpting characters for publishers like Event and Harris, who produce their own comic book figures primarily for collectors. He has also sculpted a considerable number of model kit figures for major companies such as Polydata and GeoMetric, as well as for smaller outfits, including his own.

JM: Shawn, what does a company look for in an action figure sculptor?

SN: Well, they look for a person who has good ideas for design and concept, especially detailing. Right now, the biggest thing in this whole industry is to try to get something that has a lot of detailing to it because it captures your eye and has an instant appeal.

JM: I would imagine a new person in the field would have to go through the proper channels, make appointments and have his portfolio looked over before he is given an assignment by one of the companies.

SN: The way I did it was to meet with a few companies at different shows and send my portfolio in to them with my business card and hope to get a call. But it's always good to call them later to check if they did receive your portfolio because you may receive work then; a follow-up call never hurts.

JM: Do the action figure companies have sculptors working in-house or do they use free-lancers?

SN: What I've found is that it's not so much that they have "in-house" sculptors but rather that they have certain sculptors that they work with quite a bit and

that they are very comfortable with. Probably the hardest part of breaking into the industry is breaking the boundaries of them wanting to work with only these particular people. The hardest thing for me was to try and convince them that I *could* do an action figure; they thought I might be kind of restrained having only done vinyl and resin model kit sculpting previously. They assumed I couldn't handle the articulation aspects of the figure.

JM: Obviously you've managed to prove them wrong. Shawn, is there any major difference between the sculpting of a figure model and that of an action figure?

SN: Only the fact that the companies like you to sculpt action figures a little more clunkier in style, not quite as sinewy or realistic as a model kit—more of a thicker kind of design ... a little bit more heavily built. This has to do with the playability of the figure once it's produced.

JM: So the nature of the actual finished product isn't so fragile?

SN: Right ... so the knee joints wouldn't be so small that a kid playing with it would break it. Basically, if you scaled down a model kit to the size of an action figure, it would probably have very small knees and all the joint areas would be very small and fragile.

JM: I imagine that the companies provide the sculptor with all the various sorts of reference materials he needs?

SN: Usually they send you 3-point perspectives—front, side and back shots. Lately, some of the companies I've been involved with have hired very talented illustrators to highlight detailed parts of characters to give you an idea of their proportioning, the intricate parts of costumes, the shapes of their skulls, etc.

JM: Well it's certainly more to their benefit to let you get good visuals of those details to allow you to incorporate them into your work. Now when you work original figures, what materials do you begin with?

SN: Normally I'm supplied with an armature, which is nothing more than cylinders with pegs that fit in to the shoulders and hips. Sometimes they supply you with hinged joints for the elbows and knees. Basically it's the same joint for either one and you can actually whittle them down so that they're not so big; you don't want to ruin the center part, however, which is actually three circles.

JM: What do you use to sculpt over this armature?

SN: I use a material called Pro Mat, which is a type of sculpty but a bit more resilient. I like it better because it's harder, where the regular sculpty is too mushy for me. With the Pro Mat you have to really press it to make it move, which I think is better than something that moves too easily.

*Sculpture of **Beast** figure, for Battle Brigade series by Toy Biz*

JM: Where do you go from there? What do you do after you've finished your sculpture?

SN: When I did my work for Toy Biz, they had me ship the original to them and, after they looked it over, they wrote a few notations as well as making a crude drawing to point out parts for corrections, where they wanted things changed or altered. There are also

revisions, which is a scary thing; they want you to do one figure and then they say, "Well, let's do it like *this* now," i.e. and they go and change the whole concept.

JM: With a company like Toy Biz, where the majority of the action figures are based on Marvel Comics characters, by the time your sculpture is finished the same character in the comic could have gone through a major change altering his or her entire body structure or costume!

SN: You're right, that does happen. They know way in advance what's going to happen, as do many of the comic book fans.

JM: I imagine there are also approvals you have to go through at various stages before you complete your sculpture.

SN: That happens too.

JM: It's my understanding that all action figures are sculpted in a size that's known as "two-up" which means that it's roughly double the actual size of what's produced.

SN: Exactly. This means that if it's going to be a huge character of 6" you sculpt it at 12", but the majority of action figures are sculpted at 10" and shrunk down to 5".

JM: So those 10" figures from Toy Biz are produced from the actual sizes of the original sculptures?

SN: Yes, those are pretty much the same as the originals, with only some slight changes here and there. They can do magical things with computer dies. Let's say that when they shrank the figure down to 5" there was something that they didn't like; they can actually change it. If you take some of those 10" figures and compare them to the smaller 5" figures, you'll see the slight changes that they made, such as enlarged hands or other little things you'd have to look carefully to see. However, all the figures I've done for Toy Biz have been sculpted in the size that they were sold at! This could be because they were pressed for time and didn't want to shrink them down, going right from my original to the finished product.

JM: As far as the actual molds go for action figures, if a figure has 12 points of articulation (points of poseability), does that mean that 12 separate molds have to be made as well?

SN: That's right. Wherever there's a point of articulation there has to be a separate mold made for that particular piece. And, being the sculptor of said piece, I would actually have to sculpt every single point of articulation before they do their magic at the company with their mold making. I think this is one of the reasons why they get scared when they hire a guy like me who had no prior experience working on articulated projects of this nature. They may have had horror stories in the past of employing a really great sculptor who then tells the company he can't do it … this might be the reason why!

JM: So your sculptures are done in pieces, rather than as one figure to be taken apart later.

SN: Right, but there *are* those who do sculpt their subjects like figure model kits and then cut them up, make a mold from that, and make wax copies. Then they add the articulation later. I've never tried this, but there are those who prefer it.

JM: I guess this process might also vary from company to company as well. Some outfits might dictate the way they actually want it done.

SN: There are some companies that won't even work with those who do their work in sculpty! They want everyone to sculpt in wax. That's another problem I've run into. If I want to branch out into other companies I have to learn to sculpt in wax because they expect it that way.

JM: It appears that today you don't even have to be a major toy company to produce action figures. There have been smaller comic book publishers who have done or are in the process of doing action figures based on their characters. Among them are Antarctic Press, Kitchen Sink, Event, and Harris.

SN: I'm actually working for another company right now called No Mercy Comics. It has these characters called "Sisters of Mercy" and wants to have action figures based on them.

JM: I'm sure there's quite a difference in production runs here!

SN: I think the only limitation is money! They have to wait a little longer to get their production done because they don't have the pull or the weight that somebody like Kenner or Toy Biz has. And from what I've heard about Toy Biz, they even have their own factory.

JM: I have a question that's not really sculptor related, but you are in the business so, here goes …. Do you feel that there's more collectibility with the smaller production run action figures that these companies are producing, rather than with the figures that the major players are manufacturing?

SN: There's no doubt about it. They're all done in such a smaller scale run. I've heard that the one figure that I recently did of the character Ash, from Event Comics, has a 20,000 unit production run. This is nothing when you compare it to a Toy Biz run which is usually 100,000 or even 300,000 for a popular character like Wolverine.

JM: The more popular the character the larger the production run.

SN: And I think they've probably done 15 different Wolverines since figure #1!

JM: That doesn't surprise me … look at all the Batmans out there as well! If given the opportunity, what characters would you like to sculpt?

SN: I'm an old-hearted fan as far as the characters go and I like the older style Hulk … all the 1960s-styled Marvel characters the way Jack Kirby did them … those are my favorite kinds of characters. I'd love to get the chance to sculpt them that way … in that style.

JM: Is there anything you'd like to add in closing?

SN: Just that some people don't understand that when a certain guy sculpts a piece there could be a chance that the piece was changed at the factory. Please don't put all the blame on the guy who sculpted it if there's something about the figure that you don't like.

JM: So what you're saying is things can change from what you've done.

SN: You can hear many horror stories to this effect. Any guy can tell you about things the companies have done in toy production. When you see what they end up selling, you say "Wait a minute! What about this and that and this?" The worse thing is that people find out you've sculpted the figure and say "what the heck was he thinking?!," when the problem wasn't even yours! It's a Catch-22 situation but one I can live with since I really love what I'm doing.

JM: And, in the long run, that's really all that matters. Shawn, thanks for your time in answering these questions and good luck in your many various sculpting fields.

CUSTOMIZING YOUR ACTION FIGURE: A CONVERSATION WITH SCOTT FLEMING

Conducted By: Jim Main

Believe it or not, dear readers, there are many action figure collectors out there who do not purchase these products simply as potential investments! They buy them, take them out of the package, and display them. And, in an act that would probably make any dealer cringe, some even (GASP!) alter a figure's appearance and/or change it into a totally different character!

No, these individuals are not barbarians but very talented artists known in the hobby as action figure customizers. This pastime is so accepted and enjoyed that action figure customizing contests are held at certain toy shows, with prizes given to the top-ranking winners.

Scott Fleming, who operates Scooters Custom Works, has been customizing action figures for years, both for his own pleasure and for those who commission his talents. Mr. Fleming has been kind enough to answer a few questions on this hobby for those of us who are unfamiliar with it.

JM: Scott, why do people feel the need to customize action figures?

SF: The obvious answer to that is that their favorite characters aren't represented in the lines that they collect and they don't feel that the companies are going to create them.

Another answer that I've encountered more often is that people don't like the version that has come out of a particular character. The collectors are aware of what toy companies can do and they expect more from them. When their expectations are not met, the customizers will step in and make it for themselves.

JM: Is the overall process of customizing a very detailed one?

SF: It can be. With the advent of more figures out there to choose from to use as your base figure, it has become easier to find a figure that looks close to what you're going to create and go from there. It can be as detailed as sculpting a statue to as easy as doing a paint job.

JM: So there are various points of involvement here depending on how detailed the person wants the figure to be?

SF: Yes and depending on who the figure is. Case in point: A few years back, one of my customers wanted a figure of Deathstroke, a character from DC Comics. At the time a figure was available of the Marvel Comics character Deadpool, which was startlingly similar to it, so it was a pretty easy transformation. It was nothing like trying to create Batgirl from Wonder Woman. It varies from character to character.

Customized Action Figures: Colosso Boy, Bouncing Boy, Supergirl and Element Lad

JM: Let's go into the technical aspects of creating one character from another. I'd like to have an action figure done of say, the Hanna-Barbera intergalactic superhero Space Ghost. How would you go about it?

SF: Space Ghost is a good frame of reference because it's definitely a character a lot of people are interested in. The only negative aspect of making a Space Ghost figure is that it doesn't fit into any line of characters out there. You have any choice you want for a figure to start from, such as an 8" Mego-type doll, a 12" figure or a 5" plastic action figure. If we narrow it down to an action figure you have seen on a card, you would choose a figure that is animated, and, because of that, you want to choose a base figure that resembles the character. Now I've made Space Ghost before from the Animated Batman, which seemed to be a natural. I've got friends who made theirs before the Animated Batman came out, using some Super Powers figures. So you want to find a character that resembles Space Ghost as closely as possible and in my opinion Batman seems to be it. Using a base figure from which you're going to build *up* the character is best, because adding is easier than subtracting for most people. You should get a character that doesn't have a lot of weapons attached to its body or a lot of belts, one that's the size you want, and, hopefully, one that closely resembles the character you want.

I started with the regular series Animated Batman which has no accoutrements on his body and he has that cartooney look to him. I took the X-acto knife and began the subtracting process. I removed the ears and took the points off his gloves. Then I took some sandpaper and wrapped it around a pen or the handle of the X-acto knife to give myself a curved surface. I sanded away the lines where his boots came up and the lines where his short pants meet his legs. You might also want to smooth out where you take the horns off his head and the points off his gloves. Basically that is it for the subtractive process right there. Then, if there's anything on any other figure you want to add, it depends on what you favor. In an action figure, I favor doing everything the way the factory would have done it, which in this case would be to make his belt and the weapons on his gloves out of plastic. I would use Friendly Plastic, a product you can find at any craft store, or I would use some simple vinyl tape or anything that's going to give a raised ridge look when I finally primed over it. For Space Ghost, I would actually hold back on doing the belt and use colored sign vinyl tape instead. This is a Scotch product that is used to make outdoor signs. There's really not too much in the additive process for Space Ghost, but I do use the Friendly Plastic to build up the little controls on his gloves. And then I'll mask off the face and prime the piece. *Remember this stage and do it!* Many people run into painting problems because they simply forget to prime the piece first. I use an automotive primer, usually white or light gray.

JM: Well, wouldn't that make a lot of sense to prime it first?

SF: Yeah, but a lot of people don't. Many people want to customize, but the last time they did anything was with an Aurora model.

Batgirl, Extra Powers customized figure (Scooters)

SE: How do you come up with some of your ideas? Do you brainstorm with others or come up with ideas yourself?

SF: If you're someone new to this hobby I would definitely suggest networking with other customizers. People such as myself aren't afraid to give out secrets about how we go about doing this and that. Communicating with other customizers is the best way to pick up tips and hints. I've never talked with another person in this hobby whom I haven't learned a new technique from. So, it's definitely an innovative process, and, as they say, necessity is the mother of invention. Every time I talk to people they're always giving me hints I've never thought of.

An example is, when I made the 1980's comic book version of Batgirl, she has this bat-shaped belt buckle, and there are probably three or four ways to go with that. The way I chose at the time was to take Shrinky Dink material, which is still available, and then find a bat illustration three times larger than the belt buckle. When you bake it, it shrinks down to the perfect size for the belt buckle. Then, while it's hot, you bend it around so it curves to her midsection, and then just glue it down.

Those kinds of things are hard to think of and you have to get some inspiration first.

Something I've worked with lately is an idea that another customizer, Chris Longo, gave me. I was working on pieces for the 1960s Captain Action figure. Now, as you may recall, Captain Action costumes never came with gloves, so we've finally come up with a way to make gloves for these costumes. I use this material you can purchase at a regular hardware store that is used to coat the handles of tools; it's called Plasti-Dip. It's a coating that you would use, say, to dip the handles of pliers into to form a rubber-like coating. So I take a newer Hall of Fame type G. I. Joe with those big bulky hands and rub Vaseline all the way up to the forearms. Then I dip each and arm into the Plasti-Dip and let it drip off and dry. I repeat the process about three times to get a 1/8" thickness. Then when it hardens, which is usually over a period of a night, I take an X-acto knife, slit up the middle on the wrist area, gently pull it off the hand in reverse, and then flip it over. I've then got a perfect glove for a Captain Action that will fit right over his hand. I seal up the slits by simply putting the piece over a pen or X-acto knife with more of the same goop. And it's molded in red as well.

JM: What would you find to be the hardest part involved in customizing?

SF: Staying patient! When I started this I had no patience whatsoever, which was probably what kept me from being a good modeler when I was young. Look at any of the materials you're working with and add 20 percent to the curing time; walk away from something you've just painted and leave it for about a day and a half. Don't go back to it after four hours and work on it again just because it feels dry, because chances are it's not and you'll get fingerprints all over it!

Also, it is a good idea to try to visualize everything you need to do, step by step, ahead of time, and write it down. Otherwise, you could get halfway through a project and then realize you should have done something in reverse; then you've wasted all that time, material, and effort.

Tedium is also a hard part of this business as well, such as when you have to sand or cut a piece. I don't think there's really anything that's truly hard, except when you have to sculpt. There are times sculpting does enter into this hobby, but not too often. Basically, you only have to slightly fix this or improve on that.

JM: I imagine one point of frustration might be for a customizer to work on a character that is not available from a major company, only to have one of those companies announce that this character will be produced, after the customizer has completed his or her version.

SF: This has happened to me. I don't know if you could describe this as arrogance or not, but with the visibility I have in this hobby I actually believe I've provided the prototypes for at least a couple of characters. Every time I talk to somebody who works at a toy company they're always aware of me or of others who are doing similar things. They're aware of what's out there. I did a Tim Drake Robin way before it was produced in the Batman Returns line, and that was the first time I noticed it looked a lot like the one I had done. It also happened with the Superman characters I did of Steel and Cyborg Superman and I have a feeling it's going to happen with the Harley Quinn figure I did as well. Now, it wasn't frustrating to me because I was made these for a commission, but I'm sure it was frustrating for the people who bought them. This all goes back to patience. If there's an active toy line out there, you've simply got to wait, and, who knows, the character you've been waiting for might eventually appear. People called me up two years ago to have me do "Star Trek" modifications for, say, Klingons wearing battle outfits and I'd tell them to simply hold their breath for a day and as I was sure it would be out by then. I've done commissioned figures that, while I'm working on them, are announced as upcoming releases. So, yeah, this can be frustrating.

JM: Do you see action figure customizing as being here to stay?

SF: At least as long as there are action figures to customize. I have more and more people calling me that are interested in getting involved in the hobby. This has to be a reflection of the production of action figures in general. My feeling is that the action figure world is probably going to glut a bit if it already hasn't. I think there are a lot of adults who have jumped in and given it a second wind boost. The industry certainly met the demand in the last year and probably eclipsed it. I would guess by this time next year we're going to see a different size. This is the first time in a long time there are so many different action figure sizes. If action figure collecting stays the way it is, then yes, the customizing will stay that big. There are worlds of characters that no one's tapped into yet to be released, but then again the more characters they do release the less demand there will be for that special figure.

JM: But then again there might be a demand because the company might not do the figure to everyone's expectations.

SF: That's true, too. I'm a big Animated Batman series fan and was happy with everything they did up to the Rā's Al Ghūl figure, so that was the first one I really changed.

JM: Any closing comments you'd like to add?

SF: Like I said before, talk to those already involved in the hobby. People can call or write to me; I'm always willing to talk to anybody about customizing, especially to people that want to do it on their own and don't have too much experience. Try everything you can. As I'm fond of saying, "There are no rules." It's whatever you expect from your final product that you have to adhere to. And anything can be used to make the transition. I try to use as much plastic as possible and nothing different from what a company would use. To each his own, and everybody should do whatever they can to get a good looking figure.

JM: And also remember that you've got to learn to be patient when going through all the steps of customizing. If you haven't learned to be patient, you will.

SF: And that's certainly the case with painting and gluing. And for the kids that are doing this, please be careful with those X-acto knives and be very, very careful with all the materials you're using. The sharper the knives the better, but I've been missing tips of my fingers for years now!

For those wishing to correspond with Scott Fleming you can contact him at:

Scooter's Custom Works
843 Rocklyn Dr.
Pittsburgh, PA 15205
(412) 921-0459

ACTION FIGURES

A

THE A-TEAM
Galoob (1984–85)

This toy line was based on the popular 1983 to 1987 NBC television series starring George Peppard as Col. John "Hannibal" Smith, leader of the team, Dirk Benedict as Templeton "Face" Peck, Dwight Schultz as "Howlin' Mad" Murdock, and Laurence Tureaud as B.A. Baracus. Mr. Tureaud is much better known as the gold-chained star of screen, toy, comic book, trading card and motivational speech, "Mr. T." Galoob must have had a good thing going with these toys as they did them in both 3¾" and 6½" sizes. These figures don't show up very often at toy shows and the rarest of them all is the last of the 6½" line, Amy A. Allen, based on the female character portrayed by Melinda Culea.

3¾" Figures

The A-Team "Soldiers of Fortune" 4-figure set (#8456) $30.00
    B.A. Baracus, loose 5.00
    Face, loose 5.00
    Hannibal, loose 5.00
    Murdock, loose 5.00
The Bad Guys 4-figure set (#8457) 25.00

Cobra, loose 5.00
Python, loose 5.00
Rattler, loose 5.00
Viper, loose 5.00

Vehicles and Playsets

Tactical Van Play Set, 9" with **B.A. Baracus** figure
    (#8450) 35.00
Motorized Patrol Boat, 10" with **Hannibal** figure
    (#8451) 35.00
Interceptor Jet Bomber with **Murdock** figure (#8452) . 40.00
Armored Attack Adventure Set with **B.A. Baracus** figure
    and 12" plastic tank (#8453) 35.00
Combat Headquarters Set with 35 pieces including all
    four A-Team figures, tent, assault boat, sand bag
    bunkers, machine gun, weapons, etc. (#8454) . 50.00
Action Corvette Play Set with **Face** figure (#8455) . . 35.00

6½" The A-Team Figures (Asst. #8500)

John "Hannibal" Smith 12.00
B.A. Baracus (Mr. T) 15.00
Templeton Peck 12.00
Murdock 12.00
Amy A. Allen, scarce 20.00

Hannibal, Face, Murdock and **B.A. Baracus***, The A-Team (Galoob 1984)*

6½" The "Bad Guys" Figures (Asst. #8519) Unnamed
(Python) 15.00
(Cobra) 15.00
(Rattler) 15.00
(Viper) 15.00

Vehicles (1984)
Off Road Attack Vehicle (#8513) 25.00
Combat Attack Gyrocopter, with **Murdock** figure
    (#8516) 25.00

Sproink & Groink, Aaahh!! Real Monsters (Mattel 1995)

AAAHH!! REAL MONSTERS
"DARE TO SCARE!"
Mattel (1995)

These toys are based on the very bizarre Nickelodeon cartoon series of the same name. The toys look just like their animated counterparts—a true compliment for any sculptor. They were red tag specials at the end of 1996 and haven't drawn much collector interest.

4–5" Figures (July 1995)
Scarfer (#13142) $5.00
Werfel (#13146) 5.00
Sproink & Groink (#13147) . . . . 5.0⊛
The Gromble (#13589) 5.00
Krumm (#13590) 5.00
Ickis (#13591) 5.00
Oblina (#13592) 5.00

Inside/Out Monsters
Haluga (#13150) 5.00

Kaluga (#13151) 5.00
Poomps (#13152) 5.00
Splug (#13154) 5.00

ACTION HEROS/ACTION HEROES
Early Light (1985–86)

There are several different series of these unnamed, cheap, drug store military figures. Collectors have shown no interest in them.

ACTION JACKSON
Mego (1974)
You've got to hand it to the Mego company; they certainly knew how to cut costs when it came to production. The 8" articulated Action Jackson figure was either Caucasian or African American, either bearded or clean shaven and came in almost as many hair colors as Dennis Rodman does now. None of these varieties required an expensive new body mold. With his clothing accessories, Action Jackson assumed a variety of military and sports roles. Many of the accessories showed up in other Mego figure lines as did the mold.

8" Figures in window box
Action Jackson, blonde hair $20.00
Action Jackson, black hair 20.00
Action Jackson, brown hair 20.00
Action Jackson, blonde beard 20.00
Action Jackson, black beard 20.00
Action Jackson, brown beard 20.00
Action Jackson, black 30.00

Military Outfits
Aussie Marine (#1101) 15.00
Air Force (#1102) 15.00
Navy (#1103) 15.00
Frogman (#1104) 15.00
Ski-Patrol (#1105) 15.00
Army (#1106) 15.00

Adventure Outfits
Rescue Squad (#1107) 15.00
Western (#1108) 15.00
Scramble Cyclist (#1109) 15.00
Jungle Safari (#1110) 15.00
Secret Agent (#1111) 15.00
Snowmobile Outfit (#1112) 15.00

Sports Outfits
Fisherman (#1113) 15.00
Hockey (#1114) 15.00
Baseball (#1115) 15.00
Karate (#1116) 15.00
Football (#1117) 15.00
Surf and Scuba Outfit (#1118) 15.00

Vehicles
Mustang horse (#1119), 10" long, 8¼" high, battery
    powered 30.00
Rescue Helicopter (#1120), 18" long, 9¼" high, battery
    powered, remote control 50.00
Scramble Cycle (#1121), 8¼" long, 6" high, battery
    powered 40.00
Snow Mobile (#1122), 10" long, 7" high, battery

powered 40.00
Safari Jeep (#1123), 14" long, 6¼" high, battery
　　powered 45.00

Accessories
Strap-On Helicopter (#1124) battery powered 25.00
Parachute Plunge (#1125) 20.00
Water Scooter (#1126) battery powered 25.00
Fire Rescue Pack (#1127) with water gun 20.00
Formula Racer (#1140) 30.00
Campmobile (#1142) 50.00
Adventure Set (#1145) with figure 75.00
Dune Buggy 40.00

Playsets
Lost Continent playset 90.00
Jungle House 45.00

ACTION MAN
Kenner (1996)

Action Man is billed as big and tough enough to handle any mission and keep the world safe from the evil Dr. X. The best feature of this whole series may be putting Dr. X in his box upside down. Anyway, the figures have been around since about July 1996 and no one seems to have noticed because there has been only minimal comment in the collector magazines.

12" Figures in narrow box
Tiger Strike Action Man (#12762) $10.00
Kick Boxer Action Man (#27549) 10.00

12" Deluxe Figures in wide box
Karate Combat Action Man with "Ninja Star Launcher"
　　(#12807) 25.00
Scuba Diver (#16155) 25.00
Power Arm Ninja Action Man with "Spinning Wrist
　　Action" (#27553) 30.00
Dr. X with "Flowing 'Toxic' Cut" (#27559), figure in box
　　is upside down 25.00
Swimmer (#27560) 25.00
Snow Board Raider (#27575) 25.00

Vehicles
Mission Raft (#12750) 30.00
4X4 (#12751) 40.00
Scuba Ski Mobile (#27563) 30.00

ACTION PIRATE
Soma (1991)

These were Woolworth's exclusives and there are at least four different, unnamed figures. Collectors have shown no interest in them.

ADDAMS FAMILY
Remco (1964)

Remco had quite a foot in the door on popular television licenses in the 1960s. It only produced three of the Addams Family figures. Gomez was never produced, but he did show up as a Remco–produced hand-puppet. The televi-

sion show was based on the popular cartoons by Charles Addams that appeared in the *New Yorker* magazine and many spin-off books. The characters never had names until the 1964 to 1966 ABC television show on which these figures were based, starring John Astin as Gomez, Carolyn Jones as Morticia, Ted Cassidy as Lurch, Jackie Coogan as Uncle Fester and Thing as himself.

Figures
Lurch $400.00
Lurch, loose 150.00
Morticia 400.00
Morticia, loose 175.00
Uncle Fester 500.00
Uncle Fester, loose 200.00

ADDAMS FAMILY
Playmates (1992)

These figures came out at the time of the first Addams Family live-action movie, although they are modeled after the animated characters from Hanna-Barbera. They were not successful and the final three figures (Wednesday, Thing and Cousin It) were never made.

5" Figures
Morticia (#7001) $9.00
Gomez (#7002) 7.00
Pugsley (#7003?) 8.00
Uncle Fester (#7005) 7.00
Granny (#7006) 8.00
Lurch (#7007) 7.00

(Official) ADVANCED DUNGEONS & DRAGONS
LJN (1983–84)

Based on the popular role-playing game of the same name by TSR and the cartoon series which debuted in the fall of 1983. The original header cards say "Fully Articulated Player Characters," while later header cards say "Poseable Player Characters."

3¾" Figures (1983) on square header card
Warduke Evil Fighter (#1441) $40.00
Kelek Evil Sorcerer (#1442) 40.00
Zarak Evil-Half Orc Assassin (#1443) 40.00
Ringlerun Good Wizard (#1444) 40.00
Melf Good Fighter Mage Elf (#1445) 40.00
Peralay Good Fighter Mage Elf (#1446) 40.00
Strongheart Good Paladin (#1447) 40.00
Mercion Good Cleric Female (#1448) 40.00
Elkhorn Good Dwarf Fighter (#1449) 40.00

Battle Masters (1983) on square header card
Young Male Titan (#1481) 35.00
Northlord Great Barbarian (#1482) 35.00
Ogre King (#1483) 35.00

3¾" Figures (1984) with "New Battle-Matic Action," on round-topped header card
Battle Heroes
Strongheart Good Paladin 40.00

Bowmarc Good Crusader, on blue card 45.00
Bowmarc Good Crusader, on red and black card . . . 40.00
Deeth Good Fighter 40.00
Elkhorn Good Dwarf Fighter 40.00
Hawkler Good Ranger 50.00
Valkeer Norseman . . . . not produced

Evil Battle Renegades
Warduke Evil Fighter 40.00
Zarak Evil Half-Orc Assassin 40.00
Zorgar Evil Barbarian 50.00
Grimsword Evil Knight 50.00
Drex Evil Warrior 50.00

5" Battle Masters (1984)
Mandoom with "Shield Shooter Action" 90.00
Mettaflame Evil Fire Giant with "Shield Shooter Action" 90.00
Northlord Barbarian with "Shield Shooter Action" 60.00
Ogre King with "Shield Shooter Action" 60.00
Young Male Titan with "Shield Shooter Action" on
    square header card 60.00

Mounts (1983) in window box with hanging flap
Evil Nightmare Flying Horse-Like Creature 30.00
Good Destrier Mighty Battle Horse 30.00
Bronze Dragon Good and Powerful "Flying" Dragon . 30.00

Gift Sets (1984) in window box with hanging flap
Good Destrier and Strongheart 40.00
Good Bronze Dragon and Strongheart 40.00
Evil Nightmare and Warduke 40.00

Monsters in window box with hanging flap
Dragonne Half Dragon/Half Lion Monster 20.00
Hook Horror Vulture/Human Monster 20.00

Large Monster
Tiamat Five Headed Evil Dragon (#1455) 125.00

Playset
Fortress of Fangs playset 50.00

Wind-Ups (1984)
Cave Fisher wind-up Power Creature 15.00
Pernicon wind-up Power Creature 15.00
Terrasque wind-up Power Creature 15.00

Bendable Monsters on square pink header card
The Carrion Crawler 20.00
The Chimera 17.00
The Five-Headed Hydra 20.00
The Raging Roper 20.00
The Neo-Otyugh Rubber Monster 30.00

2" Solid PVC Figures
Evil Monsters (2-packs) on square blue header card
Troglodyte and Goblin 20.00
Bullywugs of the Bog 20.00
Bugbear and Goblin 20.00
Sinister Spectre and Lich 20.00

Large Monster on square green header card
Terrible Troll and Goblin 20.00
Shambling Mound and Treasure Sack 20.00
Odious Ogre and Book of Magic 25.00
Fire Elemental (Magic) and Crystal Ball Treasure . . . 20.00
Deadly Grell 25.00
Minotaur and Crown Treasure 20.00

Umber Hulk and Dungeon Treasure 20.00

Human/Monsters on square red header card
Heroic Men-At-Arms (2-pack) 20.00
Stalwart Men-At-Arms (2-pack) 20.00
Steadfast Men-At-Arms (2-pack) 20.00
Dwarves of the Mountain King (3-pack) 20.00
Elves of the Woodlands (2-pack) 20.00
Skeleton Soldiers of Sith (2-pack) 20.00
Orcs of the Broken Bone (2-pack) 20.00
Sarken Mercenaries (2-pack) 20.00

ADVENTURES OF INDIANA JONES
SEE: INDIANA JONES

Air Raiders (Hasbro 1987)

AIR RAIDERS
"THE POWER IS IN THE AIR"
Hasbro (1987)

"Imagine a world where everything runs on air … a world where air is more precious than gold. Enter the world of Airlandia, where the evil Tyrants of Wind have seized control and forced everyone to pay tribute to their corrupt and iron-fisted monarchy." Naturally the Air Raiders are determined to "make air free for everyone in Airlandia." Of course, if air were actually more precious than gold, how would you get enough of it to make it free for everyone?

Another television toon tie-in line from Hasbro that didn't fare too well! The figures were 2" tall and were available with vehicles and in figure packs.

2" Figures (Asst. #5511, 1987)
Air Raiders Fighters 5-pack figure assortment $20.00
Tyrants of Wind Sky Troopers 5-pack figure
    assortment 20.00

*Figures from **Aladdin and the King of Thieves Action Figure Gift Set**, Aladdin (Mattel 1993)*

Air Raiders Vehicles (1987)
Thunderclaw Battle Dasher vehicle with 2 soldiers and
    air cannon (Asst. #5515) 20.00
Storm Dagger Battle Dasher vehicle with 2 soldiers and
    air cannon (Asst. #5515) 20.00
Twin Lightning vehicle with individually launched twin
    missiles, pilot, and soldier (#5525) 30.00
Thunderhammer vehicle with 3 air launch features,
    officer and 3 soldiers (#5535) 36.00
Command Outpost playset with launchers, general, and
    5 soldiers (#5545) 60.00
Man-O-War vehicle, battery powered, various launch
    missiles, admiral, and 7 soldiers (#5550) 60.00

Tyrants of Wind Vehicles (1987)
Wind Razor Battle Dasher with 2 soldiers and air cannon
    (Asst. #5517) 20.00
Wind Seeker Battle Dasher with 2 soldiers and air
    cannon (Asst. #5517) 20.00
Hawkwind with double rocket missiles and pilot and
    soldier (#5527) 30.00
Dragonwind with 3 air launch features, officer, and 3
    soldiers (#5537) 45.00

ALADDIN
Mattel (1992–94)

Another example of the fine quality that Mattel puts
into its Disney-based toy license. These figures may well
have great collectibility since they are Disneyana as well as
action figures, but this hasn't happened yet. Some of these
figures and playsets were still available as red tag specials at
the end of 1996. They are based on the 1992 movie starring
the voice of Robin Williams as the genie.

5" Movie Figures (Asst. #5302)
Aladdin $6.00
Aladdin & Abu 6.00

Genie 6.00
Jafar 6.00
Jafar & Iago 6.00
Jasmine & Rajah 6.00

Second Batch (Asst. #5324)
Baseball Player Genie 6.00
Frenchman Genie 6.00
Top Hat 'n' Tails Genie 6.00

Third Batch (Asst. #5302R)
Prince Ali 6.00
Princess Jasmine 6.00
Parade Leader Genie 6.00
Sultan 8.00

Fourth Batch (Asst. #5350) with "Battle Action"
Aladdin 8.00
Jafar 8.00
Evil Genie Jafar 8.00
Palace Guard Rasoul 8.00

Multi-Pack
Aladdin and the King of Thieves Action Figure Gift Set,
    Collector's Edition (#66348) 15.00

Playsets
Cave of Wonders playset 10.00
Aladdin Once Upon A Time playset (#5301) 9.00
Jasmine, Rajah & Genie action figure playset (#5303) 15.00
Aladdin & Jafar action figure playset 15.00
Final Battle playset 9.00

Large Dolls
Aladdin 11½" doll (#2548) 15.00
Jasmine 11½" doll (#2557) 15.00
Aladdin Water Jewel Magic doll 15.00
Jasmine Water Jewel Magic doll 15.00
Arabian Lights Jasmine doll 15.00

ALADDIN
Mattel (1995)

After the Disney movie, Aladdin starred in a continuation CBS television show which started in 1994. These figures are based on the show and come on a generic header card, which saves printing costs but is less desirable to collectors. We expect that the movie series figures will have more potential for appreciation.

5" Figures

Aladdin & Abu with magic carpet	$5.00
Aladdin & Abu in purple tunic	5.00
Prince Ali	5.00
Jafar and Iago	5.00
Genie	5.00
Parade Leader Genie	5.00
Jasmine with cage	5.00
Jasmine and Iago	5.00
Sultan	5.00
Captain Murk	5.00
Abis Mal	5.00
Mekanicle	5.00
Fashoum	5.00

ALIEN
Kenner (1979)

Alien, the first movie in the series featuring the visual concepts of H.R. Giger, was directed by Ridley Scott. It is considered one of the best (and scariest) science fiction movies of all time. The movie starred Tom Skerritt as the captain and John Hurt, who gave birth to the baby alien (at dinner, out of his chest). The movie made unknown actress Sigourney Weaver, the only survivor, into a Hollywood star.

Kenner made only one figure based on this movie and it is not truly an action figure. It is poseable, but has only a few points of articulation. We have included it because it's a famous (and expensive) toy collectible. The clear plastic brain case, which covers the Alien's head, is often missing from loose figures.

18" Figure

Alien (#70060) boxed	$500.00
Loose, with clear plastic brain case	200.00

ALIENS
Kenner (1992–96)

The Aliens line from Kenner is based on the *Aliens* and *Aliens vs. Predator* comic books from Dark Horse and on *Aliens*, the excellent second movie in the series, which was released in 1986. That movie featured Sigourney Weaver again as Lt. Ripley, Michael Biehn as Corp. Hicks and Lance Henriksen as Bishop, leading a company of future marines in a battle against a horde of Aliens. Forget the lousy third movie, *Aliens 3*, because nothing is based on that movie. The second movie gave Kenner the best group of figures to draw from, and they did a wonderful job!

1992 Figures

The Space Marines appeared before any of the Aliens. The most popular figures with collectors were the various Aliens and Lt. Ripley. Bishop (the Synthetic Human who was a major character in the movie) was scarce at first, and the other three humans—Drake, Corp. Hicks and Sgt. Apone—were common. The Scorpion Alien was the scarcest Alien. Each of the early figures comes with a special 16-page Dark Horse ashcan comic. The Aliens each have a "Face-Hugger" colored to match.

The Alien Queen came out later in 1992, but it was well worth the wait! It is a wonderfully detailed figure on a larger card than the other Aliens and sold for a few dollars more.

The Power Loader, which Lt. Ripley used to battle the Alien Queen, was the first vehicle produced. Next came the Stinger, a wheeled ground vehicle which includes an alien trapper snare and takes a space marine in the driver's seat, and the EVAC Fighter, which is designed to evacuate your marines and fly them to safety. Of course, if you saw the movies, you realize that there was very little safety and that you never wanted to catch an Alien rather than kill one.

1993 Figures

The year 1993 brought the Space Marine ATAX, which is basically a redheaded space marine with armor that makes him look like an Alien. The theory seems to be that the

Space Marine ATAX, Aliens (Kenner 1992)

Lt. Ripley, Bishop (Android) and *Corp. Hicks, Aliens (Kenner 1992)*

Aliens are too dumb to tell the difference (or maybe it's that marines are dumb enough to think so), but it makes a neat toy.

One problem is that there are a few characters from the movie that have never been produced. Kenner never came out with a Newt figure for the Aliens to encase in slime and use for an egg implant. Mothers might think this encouraged some very strange thinking about a teenager's younger sister. We'd like to suggest that Kenner have the Aliens invade earth and capture some politicians.

Finally Kenner produced the first-ever Predator figures! They battle each other in the comic book series, but not (yet) in the movies. The Alien vs. Predator two-pack is the kind of thing that becomes a collector's item, but it was never scarce. In 1996, Kay-Bee/Toy Works stores distributed leftover foreign versions of the Alien vs. Predator figures, reducing the collector value, at least temporarily. Predator figures are listed later, in their own section.

Four of the 1993 Aliens figures came with a mini comic on a header card whose reverse pictures seven Aliens figures in the first row. The Killer Crab Alien and the Panther Alien have no comic and come on a new display card which lists the Aliens vs. Predator figures. This card also lists three space marines (O'Malley, Hudson and Vasquez) which only appeared overseas. Their prices are speculative because so few are available in this country, but Vasquez (the female) is the most highly sought by collectors.

1994–96 Figures

Four additional Aliens appeared in 1994 and one electronic figure was added in 1995. The inevitable red tag sales let collectors fill in any missing figures. Local Kay-Bee/Toy Works stores had most of the leftover figures, and some were still available at the end of 1996.

Just when it seemed this popular line was all through,

in October and November 1996 new figures appeared. First was the 12" Alien vs. Predator set and then the five 10th Anniversary Alien vs. Marine two-packs. These included the first U.S. issues of figures for O'Malley, Hudson and Vasquez.

The Future

There are packaging variations on many of the Aliens figures, and package back numbers are given below in [brackets]. Most variations involve the presence or absence of a small parts warning. In general, the earliest packages have no warning, while later packages have a printed warning. Some of the early packs can also be found with a warning on a sticker, which was applied to existing stock before new header cards were printed. The popular Lt. Ripley figure had a change in the name of her action feature as well as the addition of a small parts warning.

Packaging variations of this type usually have an impact on the after-market price of a figure and we expect this to be reflected in the price for these figures once all the red tag stock is exhausted. The appearance of additional special and foreign figures in the United States has kept this line alive and there are frequent rumors of another Alien movie. And finally, Lance Henriksen, who starred as Bishop, now has his own popular television show—"Millennium." All these factors could boost prices on these figures in the future.

4¾" Space Marines with mini comic book
Drake with "Smart Gun with Rapid Fire Sound" (#65750, 1992) no warning $10.00
  Reissue, warning on sticker [0500-310-00] 9.00
Corp. Hicks "Fires 2 Alienator Missiles" (#65760, 1992)
  no small parts warning 10.00
  Reissue, warning at top [0500-311-00] 9.00
  Reissue, warning bottom left [0500-311-01] 9.00
Bishop (Android) with "Real Gatling Gun Action and
  Sound" (#65770, 1992) no warning 12.00
  Reissue, warning at top [0500-312-00] 10.00
  Reissue, warning bottom left [0500-312-01] 9.00

Sgt. Apone with "Grenade Launching Action" (#65780, 1992) no warning 10.00
　Reissue, warning at top [313-00] 9.00
Lt. Ripley "With Real 'Turbo Torch' Action" (#65790, 1992) no small parts warning 15.00
　Reissue, warning at top [314-00] 12.00
　Reissue, now with "Turbo Torch with 'Real' Flame Action" (#65790) [314-01] warning bottom left 12.00

"Special Deluxe Marine" without mini comic book
Space Marine ATAX (Alien Tactical Advantage Explorer) with "Alien Disguise Gear and Helmet-Mounted Missile" (#65711, 1993) warning upper right [504-285-00] 12.00

Aliens vs. Marine 10th Anniv. Two-Packs (Nov. 1996)
Drake vs. Alien Arachnid (#27818) 12.00
Corp. Hicks vs. King Alien (#27819) 12.00
Vasquez vs. Night Cougar Alien (#27820) 15.00
Hudson vs. Scorpion Alien (#27823) 12.00
O'Malley vs. Queen Face Hugger (#27824) 12.00

Foreign Issue Space Marine Figures
O'Malley with "Extending Capture Claw" (1993) (overseas only) 35.00
　With trading card (UK only) 35.00
Hudson with "Backpack Turbo Launcher" (1993) (overseas only) 35.00
　With trading card (UK only) 35.00
Vasquez "Rapid Fires 3 Missiles" (1993) (overseas only) 75.00
　With trading card (UK only) 75.00

Aliens (1992)
Alien Queen with "Deadly Chest Hatchling" (#65710) no warning 15.00
　Reissue, warning lower left [0500-356-01] 12.00
　Foreign issue with "Attacking Double Jaws ... Whipping Spiked Tail" (#83570) with trading card 10.00
Gorilla Alien with Face Hugger, "Grabs and Squirts

Victims," and comic book (#65720) no warning [6157-017-00] 13.00
　Reissue, warning at top 11.00
Scorpion Alien with Face Hugger, "Explodes When Hit," and comic book (#65730) no warning 10.00
　Reissue, warning at top [6148-021-00] 9.00
　Reissue, warning bottom left [6148-021-02] 9.00
Bull Alien with Face Hugger, "Skull Ramming Action," and comic book (#65740) no warning [6306-022-00] 12.00
　Reissue, warning on sticker 10.00

Aliens (1993)
Queen Face Hugger with "Grabbing Tail and Crushing Legs" and comic book (#65701) warning bottom right [506-358-00] 9.00
Snake Alien with "Snap-Attack Jaw ... Constricting Tail" and comic book (#65702) warning bottom right . 10.00
Killer Crab Alien with "Dual Launching Chest Busters" (#65705) no warning [508-911-0000] 10.00
　Reissue, no warning [508-911-0002] 8.00
Panther Alien "With Flying Attack Parasite" (#65707) no warning [508-913-02] 9.00
Flying Alien Queen with "Grabbing Claw and Flapping Wings" (#65712) warning bottom right [506-578-00] 10.00
　Foreign issue (#91261) with trading card 10.00
Mantis Alien with "'Bone Crushing' Arm Action" and comic book (#65721) warning bottom right [507-413-00] 10.00
　Reissue [507-413-01] 8.00
Rhino Alien with "Power Ramming Action" and comic book (#65741) warning bottom right [507-416-00] 10.00

Aliens (1994)
Alien Arachnid with "Sneak Attack and 'Venom' Spray Actions" (#65714) no warning [516792-00] 10.00
Wild Boar Alien with "Hidden Power-Attack Spikes" (#65715) no warning [514285-02] 10.00
　Reissue warning bottom right [514285-00] 9.00
King Alien (Deluxe Alien Leader) "Traps in 'Crushing' Grip and Sprays 'Acid'" (#65726) [516789-00] . 15.00

*Space Marine Power Loader, Aliens (Kenner 1992) and **Drake vs. Alien Arachnid**, Aliens (Kenner 1996)*

Night Cougar Alien "With Attacking Kamikaze Parasite"
(#65728) no warning [515-269-01] 8.00

Aliens (1995)
Swarm Alien, Electronic with "Attack Cry and Piercing
'Laser' Eyes" 20.00

Two-Pack
Warrior Alien (vs.) Renegade Predator 2-pack (#65840,
1993) with comic book 15.00
Foreign issue (#247149, 1994) 10.00
*Note: The foreign issue Alien vs. Predator 2-pack was dist-
ributed in U.S. by Kay-Bee/Toy Works in late 1996.*

Oversize Two-Pack Figures (1996)
Aliens vs. Predator, The Ultimate Battle, 10" figures in
window box (#27790) 35.00

Vehicles
Electronic Hovertread Vehicle with 3 electronic weapon
sounds (#65713, 1992) 10.00
Space Marine Power Loader with "Alienator Missile and
Grabbing Claws" (#65800, 1992) 10.00
Space Marine EVAC Fighter (#65802, 1993) 20.00
Space Marine Stinger XT-37 with "Alienator Missiles and
Trapper Snare" (#65810, 1993) 10.00

Playset (1993)
Queen Hive Playset with deluxe Mother Alien "Traps and
Oozes Unsuspecting Prey" and bonus reusable
Aliens Ooze in 15½" x 10" x 6" box (#65835) . . 25.00

AMERICAN DEFENSE
Remco (1986)

These are small G.I. Joe–size knock-off military figures
sold in drug stores in packs of one or two. There are at least
25 different ones. Remco keeps making them, so they must
sell okay. After this they became U.S. Forces and U.S.
Military and then Desert Storm and Desert Patrol. The series
name keeps changing almost as fast as "The Artist" formerly
known as "The Artist formerly known as Prince" formerly
known as "Prince" changes his name. Collectors have shown
little interest in them.

AMERICAN GLADIATORS
Mattel (1991–92)

Any toy company can have an off product and this is
certainly the case with this figure line. Mattel was probably
looking for a license to rival that of Kenner's Starting Line-
Up and Hasbro's WWF series. Many of the characters from
this line have come and gone from the program which is,
curiously enough, still on the air! The hardest to find figure
is of the lone female—Zap.

5" Figures
Gladiator Gemini $5.00
Gladiator Laser 5.00
Gladiator Nitro 5.00
Gladiator Turbo 5.00
Gladiator Zap 10.00
Red Challenger 8.00
Blue Challenger and Gladiator Laser 2-pack 10.00

Vehicles and Playsets
Gladiator Joust (#4036) 13.00
Gladiator Atlasphere 13.00
Gladiator Assault 13.00
Gladiator Wall 13.00
Gladiator Eliminator 15.00

(OFFICIAL) [WORLD'S GREATEST SUPER HEROES:]
AMERICAN WEST SERIES
Mego (1973–75)

"Hey, let's do a western series!" "Okay!" And so
Mego, who was doing everything else at the time, decided to
do one. These figures are very rarely seen at toy shows.

Don't look for the name "American West" on the boxes
and header cards. They all have the same "World's Greatest
Super Heroes" logo as Mego's popular super heroes series,
but it's obviously a separate series and probably should have
been called "World's Greatest Western Heroes" in line with
Mego's Super-Knights and Super-Pirates series. But it was
listed as the "American West" series in Mego's catalogs and
that's what everybody calls it today, so it's the name we
used.

8" Figures, boxed
Wyatt Earp (#51360) $90.00
Cochise (#51361) 90.00
Davey Crockett (#51362) 90.00
Buffalo Bill Cody (#51363) 120.00
Wild Bill Hickok (#51364) 90.00
Sitting Bull (#51365) 90.00

8" Figures on header card
Buffalo Bill Cody 120.00
Cochise 90.00
Davy Crockett 90.00
Sitting Bull 90.00
Wyatt Earp 90.00
Wild Bill Hickok 90.00

Vehicle and Playset
Shadow, horse, battery powered 60.00
Dodge City playset, vinyl 225.00

ANNIE
Knickerbocker (1982)

In 1982, the Broadway musical *Annie* was made into a
movie directed by John Huston and starring Albert Finney,
Carol Burnett, Bernadette Peters and Edward Herrmann, as
well as Aileen Quinn in the title role. All this is based on the
comic strip "Little Orphan Annie" which was drawn by
Harold Grey and originated in 1924.

6½" Figures
Annie with locket $15.00
Annie without locket 10.00
Daddy Warbucks 12.00
Miss Hannigan 10.00
Molly 10.00
Punjab 15.00

Vehicles

Limousine 25.00

APOLLO 13 ASTRONAUT
Hasbro (1995)

Based on the Academy Award–winning movie directed by Ron Howard. Only the one figure was produced and many were available at discount at the end of 1996.

12" Doll

Apollo 13 Astronaut doll (#27508) boxed $18.00

ARCHIES
Marx Toys (1975)

One of the last items produced by Marx was this groovy series of figures based on the popular characters from "Archie" comics. Rumor has it that Reggie was quite dismayed they never did a figure of him, while Jughead was elated that Marx never produced one of Ethel.

Figures

Archie $50.00
Betty 60.00
Jughead 50.00
Veronica 75.00

Vehicle and Accessory

Archie's Jalopy Car 80.00
Carrying Case 30.00

ATTACK OF THE KILLER TOMATOES
Mattel (1991)

Man-eating tomatoes, each with a hapless human victim. The series was a poor decision on Mattel's part. Action figure equation ... bad animated television series equals equally pathetic toy line! The television series ran from 1990 to 1992 on Fox and featured John Astin as Dr. Gangreen. It was based on the 1980 live-action film, which had developed a small cult following, and a 1988 sequel, *Return of the Killer Tomatoes*.

Figures

Wilbur Finletter vs. Beefsteak (#2044) $6.00
Dr. Gangreen vs. Ketchuck (#2049) 6.00
Igor vs. Fangmato (#2052) 6.00
Chad vs. Tomacho (#2053) 6.00
Whitley White vs. Phantomato (#2067) with feet 6.00
Tara Boumdeay vs. Missing Tomato Link (#2079) with feet 6.00
Ultimato vs. Officer Bookum (#2117) with feet 6.00
Ranger Woody vs. Zoltan (#2484) 6.00
Fireman Hoser vs. Mummato (#2485) 6.00

Attack of the Killer Tomatoes (Mattel 1991)

B

THE BAD GUYS
"THE ULTIMATE ENEMY"
Remco (1982–84)

These are 3¾" figures, the same scale as the small G.I. Joe figures. Once Sgt. Rock, which Remco also produced, had obliterated their legitimate opponents, they could take on these guys. They came with code names and a header card picturing a large hooded cobra. Gee, we wonder where that idea came from .... Remco went on to produce Department of Defense, U.S. Forces, Desert Storm, etc. figures from the same molds. There is nothing wrong with these figures, but collectors are only interested in G.I. Joe.

3¾" Figures
Code name Snake $8.00
Code name Hawk 8.00
Code name Shark 8.00
Code name Scorpion 8.00
Code name Wolf 8.00
Code name Vulture 8.00
Code name Grizzly 8.00
Code name Hammer Head 8.00

Code name Buzzer 8.00

Weapons and Accessories
Battle Action Amphibious Destroyer 15.00
Big Bad Chopper 15.00
Assault Raft Invasion set 12.00
Guerrilla Enemy Camp set 15.00
Power Anti-Aircraft Weapon 12.00
Rocket Attack Mobile Unit 12.00
Hidden Ambush Gunner's Nest 12.00

BARNYARD COMMANDOS
Playmates (1989–90)

In this animated television series–based toy line, the Platoon of Rebel Killer Swine (P.O.R.K.S.) and the Rebel Army of Militant Sheep (R.A.M.S.) battle for control of the family farm. The animals are only 2½" high, but the large backpack weapons they carry make them bigger overall. Playmates probably acquired this license thinking they could create the same magic they did with their Teenage Mutant Ninja Turtles series. Wrong!

Barnyard Commandos (Playmates 1989)

2½" Porks Figures (1989) with secret code book
Private Side O'Bacon (#5914) $5.00
Captain Tusker Chitlins 5.00
General Hamfat Lardo 5.00
Sergeant Shoat N. Sweet 5.00

Second Batch (1990)
Staff Sergeant Blaster McBacon (#5915) 5.00
Corporal Hy Ondahog 5.00
Major Piggyback Gunner 5.00
Captain Hogg Wilde 5.00

2½" Rams Figures (1989) with secret code book
Major Legger Mutton 5.00
Commodore Fleece Cardigan 5.00
Sergeant Wolly Pullover 5.00
Pilot Fluff Pendleton (#5933) 5.00

Second Batch (1990)
Master Sergeant Cornelius Cannonfodder 5.00
Private Bull Bellwether (#5935) 5.00
Commander Misiles Muttonchop 5.00
Lieutenant Sureshot Shearling 5.00

The Joker, Batman (Toy Biz 1989)

BATMAN
Toy Biz (1989–90)

The very prolific action figure giant, Toy Biz, got its start with this 1989 line based on the first Tim Burton–directed Batman film, starring Michael Keaton. True to form, this series has the first Toy Biz variations, with the "four

faces of Batman" plus the curl or no curl Joker. The Joker with hair curl is the more valuable of the two Joker versions, but there is little difference in value between the various Batman faces. Bob, the Joker's Goon, which was plentiful at the time the series was in the stores, is now one of the rarer figures. He's usually called just "Bob the Goon" in advertisements and collector magazines. All of these figures were shipped mixed in with the DC Comics Super Heroes line which is listed later. Robin, who did not appear in the movie, and traditional Batman villains The Penguin and The Riddler, are all in that series. The packaging of the two series is similar, but the series had different logos and are treated as different series.

Batman loves his expensive cars, planes, and boats and Toy Biz produced quite a few of them for this series. Two have variations of note. The Batmobile came in two versions, the more valuable of which included a cocoon. The box says "includes Cocoon as seen in the movie." The less common and more valuable version of the Batwing has a plain white back to its box. The more common version has black line art on a purple ink pattern.

4¾" Figures (1989–90)
Batman with "Bat Rope" (#4401, 1989)
    Keaton Face $12.00
    Round Face 12.00
    Square Jaw 15.00
    Big Lip 12.00
The Joker with "Squirting Orchid" (#4406, 1990) without
    curl 15.00
    Variation, with hair curl 25.00
Bob, the Joker's Goon with "Power Kick" (#4407,
    1990) 20.00

Vehicles (1989–90)
Batmobile with "Concealed Rocket Launcher" in large
    box, no figure (#4416, 1989) 45.00
    Variation, "includes Cocoon as seen in the
    movie" (#4416, 1989) 70.00
Batwing with "Villain Cruncher" (#4418, 1989) 40.00
    Variation, with white back package 50.00
Batmobile with "Turbine Sound" (#4432, 1989) in box
    with flap 20.00
Batcycle with "Drop Down Wings" (#4436, 1990) in box
    with flap 15.00
Joker Cycle with "Detachable Launching Sidecar"
    (#4437, 1989) 15.00
Joker Van with "Water Shooting Action" (#4438, 1990) 40.00

Electronic and Remote Control Vehicles (1990)
Electronic Batmobile (#4435) 15.00
Radio control Batmobile (#4429) 25.00
Remote control Batmobile (#4431) 15.00

Playset (1989)
Batcave Master Playset (#4417) 60.00

BATMAN, THE DARK KNIGHT
Kenner (1990–91)

From the movie directed by Tim Burton, starring Michael Keaton and Jack Nicholson. Oddly enough, Kenner had this great series premiere in 1990, even though the movie

Sky Escape Joker, Batman, The Dark Knight (Kenner 1990)

appeared in 1989, when Toy Biz had the license for DC figures. This is the action figure line that collectors and dealers alike have used to coin the phrase "Batman Syndrome," which is used to describe a series that is based on one figure and a myriad of color changes and accessory pieces. It's not meant as a compliment, but over 100 Batmen later Kenner is laughing all the way to the bank.

There is a color variation with the "Tec-Shield Batman" figure with an accessory piece that has changed from gold to black; this keeps it in the eye of collectors, but the entire series is in demand. The most collectible figures are the three "Deluxe Crime Master Edition" figures, which came boxed rather than on a header card, and the three 1991 tail-end figures which had only limited distribution. The Knock-Out Joker from this batch of figures is the most valuable figure in the whole Dark Knight series.

Other Batman series, based on the second and third movies and the animated television series and animated movie, follow in the order in which they arrived, rather than alphabetical order. See also Legends of Batman, listed later.

4¾" Figures (1990)
Crime Attack Batman "Uses His Batarang And Claw To
    Stop Dangerous Criminals" (#63110) $20.00
Tec-Shield Batman "Uses His Flight Pack And Shield
    Suit To Escape From Danger" (#63120) gold pull 20.00
        Black pull (scarce) 30.00
Wall Scaler Batman "Uses His Climbing Action Pack To
    Scale Up and Down Walls" (#63130) 20.00

Sky Escape Joker "Uses Whirling Copter Pack To
    Escape From Trouble" (#63140) 30.00
Iron Winch Batman with "BATARANG Winch Reels
    Criminals In" (#63160) 20.00
Shadow Wing Batman with "Cape Spreading Pop-Up
    Arms and Handcuffs" (#63170) 20.00
Bruce Wayne with "Quick Change Suit Changes Bruce
    Wayne Into BATMAN" (#63180) 20.00

Second Batch (1991)
Powerwing Batman with "Fires missiles! 'Flying' wing
    lands upside down" (#63380) 35.00
Thunderwhip Batman "Spinning Arm Makes Weapons
    Whirl" (#63390) 35.00
Knock-Out Joker with "Bazooka and 'POW'erful
    Weapon" (#63450) 60.00

Thunderwhip Batman, Batman, The Dark Knight (Kenner 1991)

"Deluxe Crime Master Edition" figures, boxed (1991)
Batman with "Claw Climber" (#63540) 35.00
Batman with "Blast Shield" (#63460) 35.00
Batman with "Night Glider" (#63470) 45.00

Batman, The Dark Knight Vehicles (1990–91)
Batcycle (#63190, 1990) 18.00
Joker Cycle (#63200, 1990) 18.00
Batjet with "Blast-Off Attack Missile" (#63210, 1990) . 48.00
Batcopter (#63220, 1990) 45.00
Turbojet Batwing "3 vehicles in 1" (#63230, 1990) . . . 65.00
Batmobile 13½" with "Launching Turbo Missile" (#63240,
    1990) 75.00
Batman Bola Bullet (#63340, 1991) 15.00
Batman Strikewing (#63350, 1991) 15.00

Polar Blast Batman, Batman Returns (Kenner 1992)

BATMAN RETURNS
Kenner (1992–93)

Yes, he certainly did return, and in a big way, too, in this series based primarily on the second movie. The movie was directed by Tim Burton and starred Michael Keaton, Danny DeVito as The Penguin and Michelle Pfeiffer as Catwoman.

The toy line made many collectors happy with the additions of Catwoman, The Penguin, and Robin (even though he wasn't in the film). Catwoman was scarce on toy store shelves, but this was due, in part, to collectors buying every one they saw. They all knew they *had* to have her in their collection. The Penguin is more valuable today because he was not collected as intensely at the time. The real surprise is the Penguin Commandos. They were not popular with the kids and every store had dozens. The collectors didn't wake up until they were finally all gone. As usual, the various versions of Batman have little to do with the movie and they are all roughly equal in value.

Collectors have concentrated on the deluxe boxed Batman figures—the two electronic figures and the three Toys "R" Us exclusives. None were produced in anything like the quantity of the carded figures and all five have increased substantially in value. Don't go away, because there's a lot more to follow.

4¾" Figures
Air Attack Batman with "Camouflage Artillery Gear"
    (#63610) $15.00
The Penguin with "Blast-Off Umbrella Launcher"
    (#63640) 30.00
Deep Dive Batman with "Torpedo Launching Scuba
    Gear" (#63790) 10.00
Laser Batman with "Missile Firing Radar Dish"
    (#63810) 18.00
Arctic Batman with "Polar Armour and Ice Blaster

Weapon" (#63820) 15.00
Powerwing Batman with "Flying Wing Can Hang Upside
    Down" (#63880) 15.00
Thunderwhip Batman with "Turbo Weapon Spinning
    Arm" (#63890) 12.00

Second Batch (1992)
Robin with "Launching Grappling Hook" (#63630) . . . 16.00
Penguin Commandos with "Mind Control Gear and Firing
    Missile" (#63860) 15.00
Catwoman with "Whipping Arm Action and Taser Gun"
    (#63870) 25.00
Bruce Wayne with "Quick Change Batman Armor"
    (#63970) 16.00
Crime Attack Batman with "Firing Claw and Batarang" 18.00
Shadow Wing Batman with "Pop-Up Arms and Capture
    Cuffs" 18.00
Sky Winch Batman with "Batarang Winch" 22.00

Deluxe Toys "R" Us Limited Edition (1992) boxed
Bola Strike Batman (#63102) 30.00
Polar Blast Batman (#63103) 30.00
Claw Climber Batman (#63104) 30.00

Laser Batman, Batman Returns (Kenner 1992)

Deluxe Electronic Figures (1992) boxed
Firebolt Batman (#63930) 68.00
Rocket Blast Batman (#63940) 68.00

Late Figure (1993)
Aero Strike Batman with "Ultrasonic Armor and Flying
    Rocket" (#63649) 12.00

Large Figure (1992)
Batman Deluxe 15" (#63990) 50.00

Vehicles (1992)
Sky Blade Vehicle with "Ejecting Cockpit" (#63400) . . 45.00
Bruce Wayne Custom Coupe with **Bruce Wayne** figure
    (#63550) 25.00
    Variation, with blue-shirted figure 40.00
Batman Sky Drop Airship with "Hidden Compartment for
    Surprise Attack" (#63680) 25.00
The Penguin Umbrella Jet with "Spraying Knock-Out
    Gas and Umbrella Bombs" (#63690) 15.00
Robin Jet Foil with "Shooting Batarang" (#63730) . . . 18.00
Laser Blade Cycle with "Disrupter Device" (#63740) . 12.00
Batmissile Batmobile with "Blastoff Sides" (#63910) . 80.00
All-Terrain Batskiboat with "Torpedoes and Skis"
    (#63920) 30.00
Batman Turbojet Batwing 40.00
Batmobile 65.00

Playset (1992)
Batcave Command Center 75.00

Night Climber Batman, Batman Returns II (Kenner 1994)

BATMAN RETURNS II
Kenner (1994)

One of the action figure mysteries of the decade was
why Kenner had to have a series II to this line in 1994 when
they could have just continued the previous one. Someday
the truth will be revealed, but it must have been a mystery to
Kenner as well, because they didn't do this with any of their
other Batman series.

4¾" Figures
Hydro Charge Batman with "Water Blast Missile"
    (#64046) $8.00

Jungle Tracker Batman with "Shoulder Mount Launcher"
    (#64047) 8.00
Night Climber Batman with "Quick Climbing Hook"
    (#64048) 8.00

Vehicle
Camo Attack Batmobile with **Batman** figure (#63919) 25.00

The Riddler, Batman: The Animated Series (Kenner 1993)

BATMAN: THE ANIMATED SERIES
Kenner (1993–95)

Some of the best action figure sculpting ever can be
found in this series by Kenner, based on the great Fox
animated television series! Even with the infamous "Batman
Syndrome" at work here, there are some fine pieces in this
line which can command some big prices. Most notable in
collector/dealer circles are The Penguin, Riddler, Two-Face,
Catwoman, Poison Ivy and Bane villains, as well as the
extremely scarce Robin Dragster vehicle. On the other hand,
a number of the Batman figures from several of the batches
can still be found at retail or red tag prices.

4¾" Figures (1993)
Turbojet Batman with "Firing Wrist Rocket & Pivoting
    Engines" (#64660) $15.00
Combat Belt Batman with "Firing Grappling Hook and
    Missile" (#64670) 35.00
Robin with "Turbo Glider and Drop Missiles" (#64680) 20.00
The Penguin with "Hypno-Spin Umbrella Launcher"
    (#64690) 85.00
The Riddler with "Question Mark Launcher" (#64700) 38.00
Two-Face with "Firing Roulette Wheel Gun" (#64710) 32.00

Second Batch (1993)
Catwoman with "Whipping Arm Action and Claw Hook"
    (#63652) 25.00
The Joker with "'Laughing Gas' Spray Gun" (#63966) 22.00
Infrared Batman with "Launching Bat-Signal Disks"
    (#63997, 1994) 9.00
Scarecrow with "Thrashing Sickle" (#63999) 18.00
Bruce Wayne with "Snap-on Batman Armor" (#64664) 18.00
Sky Dive Batman with "Working Parachute for Surprise
    Attacks" (#64665) 14.00
Man-Bat with "Flapping Wings and Tow Cable"
    (#64666) 20.00
Ninja Robin with "Chopping Arm Action and Ninja
    Weapons" 14.00

Tornado Batman, Batman: The Animated Series (Kenner 1994)

Third Batch (1994)
Lightning Strike Batman with "Transforming Cape Glider"
    (#64002) 8.00
Knight Star Batman with "Star Blade Rocket Launcher"
    (#64003) 8.00
Mr. Freeze with "Firing 'Ice' Blaster" (#64004) 20.00
Clayface with "Launching Spiked Ball" (#64005) 20.00
Killer Croc with "Power-Punch Arm and Pet Crocodile"
    (#64009) 20.00
Poison Ivy with "Snapping Venus Flytrap and Dart
    Weapon" (#64012) 45.00
Dick Grayson/Robin "Transforms Into Robin with High-
    Tech Gear" (#64016) 10.00
Anti-Freeze Batman with "Firing Shield Blaster"
    (#64018) 8.00

Two-Pack (1994)
Ninja Power Pack Batman and Robin with "Duo-Power
    Ninja Weapon" (#64110) 16.00

Bane, Batman: The Animated Series (Kenner 1994)

Fourth Batch (1995) in shrink bubble header card
Tornado Batman with "Whirling Weapons" (#63982) (box
    bubble) 8.00
Rapid Attack Batman with "Escape Hook and Utility Belt"
    (#63984) (box bubble) 8.00
Cyber Gear Batman with "Hi-Tech Armor and Power-
    Launch Weapon" (#64119) 8.00
Bane 5½" with "Body-Slam Arm Action" and "Venom
    Tube" (#64124) 25.00
Glider Robin with "Winged Jet Pack and Firing Claw"
    (#64133) 8.00
Bola Trap Robin with "Whirling Battle Blades" (#64134) 8.00
Radar Scope Batman with "Firing Turbo Missiles and
    Sky-Scan Radar Gear" (#64136) 8.00

Deluxe "Crime Fighter" Figures (1994)
Mech-Wing Batman with "Mechanized Soaring Wings"
    (#63653) 12.00
Power Vision Batman with "Electric Light-Up Eyes and
    Firing Glow-in-the-Dark Missile" (#63656) 12.00
Ground Assault Batman with "Motorized Turbo-Powered
    Ground Jet" (#63657) 12.00
High Wire Batman with "Quick Escape Cable Wire"
    (#63998) 12.00

Oversize Figure
Ultimate Batman 15" with "Light-Up Electric Eyes and
    Bat Emblem" plus "Double-Barrel Assault Weapon"
    (#64019) 48.00

Vehicles
The Jokermobile (#63530) 18.00
Bruce Wayne Street Jet with **Bruce Wayne** figure
    (#63551, 1994) 25.00

Batcycle with "Motorized Turbo Power, Turbo Sound and
    Wheelie Action" with **Batman** figure (#63981) on
    header card 18.00
Robin Dragster (#63995) scarce 195.00
Electronic Crime Stalker (#64023, 1994) 18.00
Ice Hammer (#64039, 1994) 22.00
Batmobile with "Launching Pursuit Jet" (#64730) 80.00
Batplane (#64740) 45.00

Mini Vehicles (1993–94)
B.A.T.V. (#63983, 1993) 14.00
Hoverbat (1993) 14.00
Bat Signal Jet (1993) 14.00
Aero Bat (#64031, 1994) 14.00
Hydro Bat (#64032, 1994) 14.00

Playset
Batcave Command Center 50.00

weeks after the film was gone from the theaters, rather than
several weeks before the movie premier, which generally
results in better sales.

4¾" Figures (1993, i.e. early 1994)
Rapid Attack Batman with "Escape Hook and Utility Belt"
    (#63965) $12.00
Retro Batman with "Spinning Battle Spear" (#63977) . 12.00
Tornado Batman with "Whirling Weapon" (#63978) . . 12.00
Total Armor Batman with "Full Body Armor and Shield"
    (#64001) 12.00
Phantasm with "Chopping Arm Action" (#64006) 35.00
Jet Pack Joker with "Capture Nozzle" (#64007) white
    face 20.00
    Variation, with green face 30.00
Decoy Batman with "Crime-Fighting Decoy Disguise"
    (#64017) 12.00

Jet Pack Joker, Batman: The Animated Series,
Mask of the Phantasm (Kenner 1994)

BATMAN: THE ANIMATED SERIES
MASK OF THE PHANTASM
Kenner (1994)

With the Fox animated series doing so well, the
producers decided to put together a feature film in late 1993.
Though it was a fine production, it didn't fare too well on
the big screen and was quickly released for the home video
market. The Phantasm figure along with the color variations
on the Jet Pack Joker are the collecting high water marks on
this line. The figures didn't appear until early 1994, several

Torpedo Batman, Batman: The Animated Series,
Crime Squad (Kenner 1995)

BATMAN: THE ANIMATED SERIES
CRIME SQUAD
Kenner (1995)

Here's a perfect example of what happens when the
"Batman Syndrome" runs amok—a sub-line is produced for
no real reason but to produce more toys. They must have
produced a lot of them, because at the end of 1996 they were
taking up a lot of space on toy store racks.

4¾" Figures
Piranha Blade Batman with "Transforming Techno-Shield
    Backpack" (#64116) $7.00
Sea Claw Batman with "Transforming Techno-Drive
    Backpack" (#64117) 7.00
Stealthwing Batman with "Transforming Techno-Flight
    Backpack" (#64118) 7.00
Air Assault Batman with "Transforming Techno-Wing
    Backpack" (#64120) 7.00
Land Strike Batman with "Transforming Techno-Claw
    Backpack" (#64121) 7.00

Torpedo Batman with "Transforming Techno-Torpedo
    Backpack" (#64122) 7.00
Ski Blast Robin with "Transforming Techno-Ski
    Backpack" (#64123) 7.00

Vehicles
Triple Attack Jet (#64662) 18.00
Batcycle, with **Batman** figure (#64672) 12.00

LEGENDS OF BATMAN
SEE: LEGENDS

*Cyborg Batman, Batman, Special Edition,
Warner Bros. exclusive (Kenner 1995)*

BATMAN
(SPECIAL EDITION)
Kenner (1995–96)

These special edition figures are sold only in Warner
Bros. stores. They are taken from the "Legends of Batman"
Kenner figures, but the header card doesn't mention the
Legends series, so they are listed here. The first series went
largely unnoticed by collectors until it was too late to find
them easily, but the collectors were ready for the second
series.

4¾" Warner Bros. Store Figures (1995)
Crusader Batman $15.00
Power Guardian Batman 15.00
Cyborg Batman (#64781) 15.00
Nightwing (Robin) 20.00
Future Batman 15.00

Knightquest Batman (#64785) 15.00

4¾" Warner Bros. Store Figures (1996)
Viking Batman (#63953) 9.00
Samurai Batman (#63954) 9.00
The Riddler (#63956) 9.00
Long Bow Batman (#63957) 9.00
Crusader Robin (#63958) 9.00
Knightsend Batman (#63959) 9.00

Two-Face, Batman Forever (Kenner 1995)

BATMAN FOREVER
Kenner (1995–96)

Batman Forever!—Truer words were never spoken!
Kenner continues on and on with figures/characters based on
the third of the Batman films, this time with Val Kilmer in
the role of Bruce Wayne/Batman and guest stars Jim Carrey
as the way over-the-top Riddler, Tommy Lee Jones as Two-
Face and Chris O'Donnell as Dick Grayson/Robin.

You could find these figures everywhere at the end of
1996 and none of them were scarce. About the only interesting figure is the **Deluxe The Talking Riddler**, which was a
late addition to the series and may have some potential for
appreciation.

4¾" Figures (1995)
Street Biker Robin with "Launching Grappling Hooks and
    Battle Staff" (#64144) $7.00
Hydro Claw Robin with "Aqua Attack Launcher and
    Diving Gear" (#64145) 7.00

Transforming Dick Grayson with "Crime Fighting Suit and Sudden-Reveal Mask" (#64146) all variations 7.00
Two-Face with "Turbo-Change Cannon and Good/Evil Coin" (#64147) 9.00
The Riddler with "Trapping Brain-Drain Helmet" (#64148) 9.00
Blast Cape Batman with "Assault Blades and Launching Attack Cape" (#64149) 7.00
Fireguard Batman with "Spinning Attack Cape Action" (#64150) 7.00
Sonar Sensor Batman with "Flying Disc Blaster and Pop-Up Sonar Scope" (#64151) 7.00
Transforming Bruce Wayne with "Quick-Change Bat Suit and Battle Blades" (#64152) 9.00
Manta Ray Batman with "Firing Sea Sled and Pop-Out Breathing Gear" (#64153) 7.00
Night Hunter Batman with "Claw Glider Wing and Night Vision Goggles" (#64154) 7.00

Second Batch (late 1995)
Power Beacon Batman with "Light Force Suit and Flashfire Weapon" battery operated (#64163) ... 7.00
Ice Blade Batman with "Quick-Deploy Ski Sled and Blade Runners" (#64164) 7.00
Batarang Batman with "Spinning Batarang and Radar System" (#64166) 7.00

Third Batch (1996)
Skyboard Robin with "Missile-Blasting Pursuit Vehicle" (#64186) 6.00
Wing Blast Batman with "Sudden-Alert Bio Wings" (#64187) 6.00

Deluxe The Talking Riddler, Batman Forever (Kenner 1996)

Neon Armor Batman with "Snap-on Armor Shield" (#64188) 6.00
Night Flight Batman with "Bat Attack Action" (#64193) . 6.00
Solar Shield Batman with "Heat Deflection Cape" (#64194) 6.00
Triple Strike Robin with "Multi-Cannon Slinger" (#64196) 6.00
The Riddler with "Blasting Question Mark Bazooka" (#64198) 7.00

Deluxe Figures (1995–96)
Deluxe Attack Wing Batman with "Power Flex Attack Cape" (#64161, 1995) 10.00
Deluxe Martial Arts Robin with "Ninja Kicking Action and Battle Weapons" (#64162, 1995) 10.00
Deluxe Lightwing Batman with "Electra-Glow Wings and Lightning Launcher" (#64167, 1996) 10.00
Deluxe Laser Disk Batman with "Flashing Color 'Laser' Launcher" (#64181, 1996) 10.00
Deluxe The Talking Riddler with "3 Real Movie Phrases" (#64192, 1996) 15.00

Deluxe Figure and Vehicle (March 1996)
Recon Hunter Batman with "Missile Firing Surveillance Drone" (#64168) 12.00
Street Racer Batman with "Missile-Firing Pursuit Cycle" (#64169) 12.00

Two-Packs
The Riddler and Two-Face, A Double Team of Fiendish Villains (#63705, 1996) 15.00
Guardians of Gotham City two-pack (#64171, 1995) . 15.00

Exclusive Figures (1996) (Target Stores)
Riddler 15.00
Tide Racer Robin 12.00
Transforming Bruce Wayne 12.00

Oversize Figures
Aerial Action Batman, 12" soft with Parachute (#27637) 15.00
Robin, 16" soft (#29417) 18.00
Electronic Talking Batman, soft (#29427) 22.00
Ultimate Batman, 15" electronic (#64177, 1995) 25.00

Vehicles and Playset
Robin Cycle with "Ripcord Racing Power" (#64156) . 12.00
Batwing vehicle (#64157) 20.00
Electronic Batmobile with "Light-Up Chassis and Firing Long-Range Missile" (#64158) 20.00
Batboat vehicle (#64175) 20.00
Wayne Manor/Batcave Compound (#63360) 65.00

[THE ADVENTURES OF] BATMAN AND ROBIN
Kenner (1996)

The villains in this series were initially scarce, but by the fall of 1996 they were fairly common and collector prices fell accordingly. By the end of 1996, Bane, Rā's Al Ghūl and Pogo Stick Joker were hanging around more than Christmas ornaments. The previous Bane figure (#64124) on the Batman: The Animated Series header card is the scarce (and valuable) one. The Rā's Al Ghūl figure is the first and only one of this character, so his price might rebound in the future. Look for one at a discount price and don't expect an

Paraglide Batman,
The Adventures of Batman and Robin (Kenner 1996)

immediate increase because most current collectors already own at least one.

4¾" Figures, shrink bubble wrapped
Bane with "Body-Slam Arm Action" and "Venom Tube"
(#63968) $6.00
Bola Trap Robin with "Whirling Battle Blades" (#63969) 6.00
Glider Robin with "Winged Jet Pack and Firing Claw"
(#63971) 6.00
Cyber Gear Batman with "Hi-Tech Armor and Power-
Launch Weapon" (#63972) 6.00
Radar Scope Batman with "Firing Turbo Missile and
Sky-Scan Radar Gear" (#63973) 6.00
Hover Jet Batman with "Body Swinging Blows"
(#64086) 6.00
Rā's Al Ghūl with "Strike Shooter and Combat Sword"
(#64088) 6.00
Paraglide Batman with "Dive Bomb Sky Wing" (#64089)
bubble box 6.00
Rocketpak Batman with "Firing Turbo Thrust Cannon"
(#64092) 6.00
Pogo Stick Joker with "Power Launcher" (#64093) . . . 6.00

[THE ADVENTURES OF] BATMAN AND ROBIN
CRIME SQUAD
Kenner (1996)

The only reason for this series is that Batman, The Animated Series had a "Crime Squad" sub-series and when that series was changed to "The Adventures of Batman and

Robin" so was the sub-series. The first seven figures are the same in both series and even have the same UPC code numbers. The price is the same too, at least so far.

4¾" Figures, shrink bubble wrapped
Piranha Blade Batman with "Transforming Techno-Shield
Backpack" (#64116) $6.00
Sea Claw Batman with "Transforming Techno-Dive
Backpack" (#64117) 6.00
Stealthwing Batman with "Transforming Techno-Flight
Backpack" (#64118) 6.00
Air Assault Batman with "Transforming Techno-Wing
Backpack" (#64120) 6.00
Land Strike Batman with "Transforming Techno-Claw
Backpack" (#64121) 6.00
Torpedo Batman with "Transforming Techno-Torpedo
Backpack" (#64122) 6.00
Ski Blast Robin with "Transforming Techno-Ski
Backpack" (#64123) 6.00
Bomb Control Batman with "Transforming Techno-Armor
Backpack" (#64137) 6.00
Fast Pursuit Batman with "Transforming Techno-Bike
Backpack" (#64138) 6.00

Second Batch (Aug. 1996)
Disaster Control Batman with "Techno-Rescue
Backpack" (#64141) 6.00
Super Sonic Batman with "Techno-Rocket Backpack"
(#64142) 6.00

Deluxe Crime Squad (1996)
Tri Wing Batman with "Techno-Glide Backpack"
(#63659) 10.00
Skycopter Batman with "Techno-Rotor Backpack"
(#63661) 10.00

Vehicles and Accessories (1996)
Nightsphere with "Auto Rotating Cockpit" and **Batman**
figure (#64139) 22.00
Triple Attack Jet (#64662) 18.00

BATTLE BEASTS
Hasbro (1987)

These were a large series of 2" anthropomorphic characters, produced by Hasbro, that had very little, if any, articulation to them. There were three different series, with the beasts randomly packed two beasts and two weapons per header card in series 1 and 2. Series 3 figures came eight weapons and eight beasts per box. A total of 63 figures are pictured in Hasbro's catalog, but they aren't named there or on the packages. Each beast came with armor and a battle emblem which revealed whether his hidden strength was Wood, Fire or Water and battles were decided by the old Paper-Rock-Scissors technique. Collectors have not shown much interest in the series.

2" Animals
Series 1, random 2-packs, each $4.00
Series 2, random 2-packs, each 4.00
Series 3, random 8-packs, each 15.00

Battle Chariots (Asst. #5310) motorized
Ram with battle beast and weapon 6.00
Reindeer with battle beast and weapon 6.00

Tiger with battle beast and weapon 6.00

Playsets (Asst. #5314) with battle beast and weapon
Shark 15.00
Wood Beetle 15.00
Firebird 15.00

BATTLE BRAWLERS
Kenner (1986)

Two very large and quite ugly action figures produced by Kenner in 1986 that were based on no known show or other source. The only concept was that they had prehistoric power from the center of the Earth.

Boxed Figures
Crackarm (#58000) $65.00
Hammertail (#58010) 65.00

BATTLESTAR GALACTICA
Mattel (1978–79)

From the late 1970s ABC television series starring Lorne Green as Adama, John Colicos as Baltar, Richard Hatch as Apollo and Dirk Benedict as Lt. Starbuck. The header cards have very attractive character-specific artwork. Commander Adama and his "rag tag fleet" searching for a shining star known only as Earth sounded like a great concept for the folks at Mattel. If the series had only been a little better and bought some scripts instead of just special effects, it, and the toys, might have lasted longer.

3¾" Figures (1978)
Commander Adama (#2868) $45.00
Imperious Leader (#2869) 25.00
Cylon Centurian (#2870), silver 40.00
Lt. Starbuck (#2871) 45.00
Ovion (#2872) 25.00
Daggit (#2873), brown 30.00
Daggit (#2873), tan 30.00

Second Batch
Baltar (#1161) 85.00
Cylon Commander (#1162), gold 100.00
Boray (#1163) 80.00
Lucifer (#1164) 90.00

Boxed Sets
Three-figure boxed set (Gold Cylon, Baltar and Lucifer)90.00
Four-figure boxed set (Daggit, Ovion, Imperious Leader
     and Silver Cylon) 75.00
Six Figure Gift Set (Ovion, Imperious Leader, Cylon
     Centurian, Daggit, Commander Adama and Lt.
     Starbuck) (#1154, 1979) 150.00

Large Figures
Colonial Warrior 12" Figure (#2536, 1979) 85.00
Cylon Centurian 12" Figure (#2537, 1979) 80.00

Crackarm and Hammertail, Battle Brawlers (Kenner 1986)

Cylon Centurian, Battlestar Galactica (Mattel 1978)

Vehicles, Accessories and Playset
Colonial Stellar Probe 100.00
Colonial Scarab 100.00
Cylon Raider 100.00
Viper Launch Station playset (#2446, 1979) 140.00

BATTLESTAR GALACTICA
Trendmasters (1997)

Trendmasters produced a series of Battlestar Galactica figures which appeared very early in 1997, just after the cut-off for inclusion in this book. They should be available at retail at a toy store near you.

BATTLETECH
"NO GUTS, NO GALAXY"
Tyco (1995–96)

Tyco produced this Robotech/Exo Squad wannabe toy series of men and robot armor suits which was based on both the 1994 animated series and the 1984 gaming line of the same name. The figures are only 2" tall and were not sold separately.

Powersuit Assortment (Asst. #1350, 1995) carded
Infiltrator with **Adam Steiner** figure $10.00
Sloth with **Franklin Sakamoto** figure 10.00
Toad with **Nicolai Malthus** figure 10.00

Powersuit Assortment (Asst. #1350, 1996) carded
Infiltrator with **Adam Steiner** figure in "Tiger Camo" colors 25.00

Sloth with **Franklin Sakamoto** figure in "Assault Force" colors 25.00
Toad with **Nicolai Malthus** figure in "Tiger Camo" colors 25.00

Light Mech Assortment (1995) boxed
Bushwacker with **Valten Ryder** figure (#13541) 12.00
Hunchback with **Pytor** figure (#13542) 12.00
Banshee with **Franklin Sakamoto** figure (#13543) (1994 box) 12.00

Banshee, Battletech (Tyco 1995)

Light Mech Assortment (1996) boxed
Bushwacker with **Valten Ryder** figure in "Tiger Camo" colors (#13541) 15.00
Hunchback with **Pytor** figure in "Assault Force" colors (#13542) 15.00
Banshee with **Franklin Sakamoto** figure (#13543) (new 1995 box) 12.00

Medium Mech Assortment (1995) boxed
Axman with **Adam Steiner** figure (#13581) 20.00
Thor with **Nicolai Malthus** figure 20.00

Medium Mech Assortment (1996) boxed
Axman with **Adam Steiner** figure in "Tiger Camo" colors (#13581) 20.00
Thor with **Nicolai Malthus** figure "Assault Force" colors 20.00

Heavy Mech Assortment (1995) boxed
Mauler with **Zack Hawkins** figure 25.00

Heavy Mech Assortment (1996) boxed
Mauler with **Zack Hawkins** figure in "Tiger Camo" colors 25.00

Trollasaurus (#7632) 12.00
Capture Net 8.00

Count Trollula, Battle Trolls (Hasbro 1992)

BATTLE TROLLS
Hasbro (1992–93)

Battle Trolls from Hasbro combined trolls, action figures, military, monster and fantasy themes all rolled into one. We liked the Trollminator, Troll-Clops and Count Trollula when they first appeared. We didn't try T.D. Troll's Rude Locker Room Smell so we don't know the accuracy of the description.

Topping the list in the second batch was Franken Troll and not far behind are Trollbot and Super Troll.

Figures
Cap'n Troll "Grappling Spear Shoots" (#7592) $6.00
Troll-Clops with "Limb Grabbing Log Snare" (#7593) . . 6.00
Trollaf "Grappling Spear Shoots" (#7594) 6.00
Count Trollula "Crossbow Shoots" (#7595) 8.00
Trollminator with "Glow in the Dark Robot Parts" (#7596) 8.00
Sgt. Troll "Crossbow Shoots" (#7597) 6.00
T.D. Troll with "Rude Locker Room Smell" (#7598) . . . 6.00
Nunchuk Troll "Crossbow Shoots" (#7599) 6.00

Second Batch
Franken Troll 8.00
General Troll 6.00
Officer PaTroll 6.00
Punk Troll 6.00
Roadhog Troll 6.00
Sir Trollahad 6.00
Super Troll 8.00
Trollbot 6.00

Third Batch
Ace Troll 6.00
Jacques Cous Troll 6.00
K.O. Troll 6.00
Quick Draw McTroll 6.00
Slapshot Troll 6.00
Thrasher Troll 6.00
Troll-timate Wrastler 6.00
Wolfman Troll 8.00

Scales, B.C. Bikers (Street Kids 1994)

B.C. BIKERS
"DINOSAURS OF THE CHROME AGE"
Street Kids (1994)

These dinosaurs appear to be the original members of the Jurassic chapter of Hell's Angels. They ride impressive motorcycles with "Pull-Back Motorized Action." Nobody collects them.

5" Figures
Tarr, The Leatherized Leader (#01931) $5.00
Revv, The Wild Rider (#01932) 5.00
Scales, The Def Dude (#01933) 5.00
Crank, The Maniac Mechanic (#01934) 5.00

SABAN'S
BEETLEBORGS
Bandai (1995–96)

The latest of the Saban live-action adventure series to invade the television screen in hopes of recapturing the audience that viewed the Mighty Morphin Power Rangers with such frenzy.

"When three average kids enter the haunted Murren Estate, little do they know that their lives are about to change forever. They accidently unleash a funtastic phasm who grants them each one wish, and they all choose to become their favorite comic book heroes, BeetleBorgs. But this phasm's magic also releases the evil Vexor and his evil Moltrons from the comic book. Now, our three heroes must use their new super powers to defeat the fiendish Moltrons and restore peace to their hometown."

Green Hunter AV, BeetleBorgs (Bandai 1995)

It's too early to tell whether these figures will generate any collector interest, but so far they have been treated as kiddy stuff, like the Power Rangers.

6" Metallic BeetleBorgs Figures
Blue Stinger BeetleBorg (#5211) $6.00
Green Hunter BeetleBorg (#5212?) 6.00
Red Striker BeetleBorg (#5213?) 6.00
Shadow Borg (#5214) 6.00

6" Magnavors Figures
Umbrella Twirling Noxic (#5221) 6.00
Double Karate Chopping Vexor (#5222) 6.00
Saber Swiping Typhus (#5223) 6.00
Sword Wielding Scab (#5224) 6.00
Whip Cracking Jara (#5225) 6.00

Figure (1996)
Mega Blue Beetleborg (#5385) 8.00

Special Edition 12" Figures with CardZillion Card
Blue Stinger Beetle Borg (#5249) 20.00
Shadow Borg (#5250) 20.00

BeetleBorg AV Vehicles with 2½" Figures
Blue Stinger AV (#5231) 8.00
Green Hunter AV (#5232) 8.00
Red Striker AV (#5233?) 8.00

Dash Racer Vehicles (Asst. #5291)
Blue Stinger AV (#5292) 12.00
Green Hunter AV (#5293) 12.00
Red Striker AV (#5294) 12.00

Vehicles
Blue Stinger AV model (#5342) 15.00
Green Hunter AV model (#5343) 15.00
Gargantis Mobile Attack Carrier (#5245) 30.00

Otho the Obnoxious, Beetlejuice (Kenner 1989)

BEETLEJUICE
Kenner (1989–90)

Based on the Tim Burton–directed movie starring Michael Keaton, Alec Baldwin and Geena Davis, not the animated series of the same name. The most collectible figure in the series is the large Talking Beetlejuice.

6" Figures
Shish Kebab Beetlejuice with Scary Skewers (#30070) $8.00
Spinhead Beetlejuice with Creepy Cockroach (#30080) 8.00
Showtime Beetlejuice with Rotten Rattler (#30090) . . . 8.00
Harry the Haunted Hunter with Terrible Tarantula
    (#30110) 10.00
Otho the Obnoxious with Loathsome Lizard (#30120) 10.00
Adam Maitland the Headless Ghost with Beakface Mask
    and Creepy Crawler (#30130) 10.00

6" Figures (1990)
Exploding Beetlejuice with Dreadful Dragon (#30170) 10.00
Shipwreck Beetlejuice with Horrible Hydra (#30240) . 10.00

Neighborhood Nasties (1990)
Teacher Creature with Apple Bomb (#30210) 16.00
Hungry Hog with Corncob Accessory (#30220) 16.00
Old Buzzard with Chicken Accessory (#30230) 16.00
Street Rat with Flyin' Eye (#30250) 16.00

Vehicles and Accessories
Vanishing Vault with Micro Beetlejuice (#30140, 1989) 10.00
Phantom Flyer/Cycle (#30190, 1989) 10.00
Creepy Cruiser (#30200, 1990) 18.00
Gross-Out Meter (#30260, 1990) 10.00

Large Figure
Talking Beetlejuice (#30060, 1989) 35.00

BEST OF THE WEST
Marx (1965–76)

These large-sized "movable" 11½" soft plastic figures of Johnny West and friends was one of the longest running action figure series in history. It was produced by Marx starting in 1965. The figures came with plastic accessories and clothing. Some very rare figures exist in this series that were available only in England and Canada, making this series difficult for United States collectors to complete.

A number of box variations were used over the years, but the figures remained basically the same. For most of the years there was no uniform logo or packaging style and series names such as Johnny West Adventure, Collection or Series appeared on some of the packages, or no series name was used at all. Unlike most other series, these packaging variations have had no effect on value. The five Fort Apache Fighters are a sub-series, but part of the overall series as well. The four 9" figures are West kids, not a smaller scale line. The last figure produced, Jed Gibson, a black cavalry scout, is the scarcest and most valuable figure in the series. There were also three figures which were only produced in Canada and/or England. It's a well-produced line and remains a favorite among many collectors.

11½" Figures
Chief Cherokee (#2063, 1965) $90.00
Daniel Boone 275.00
General Custer (#1866) 100.00
Jane West (#2067, 1966) 50.00
Jed Gibson 600.00
Johnny West (#2062, 1965) 90.00
Johnny West with Quick Draw Action 175.00
Princess Wild Flower 90.00
Sam Cobra, renegade bad man 90.00
Sam Cobra with Quick Draw Action 150.00
Sheriff Garrett 80.00

Fort Apache Fighters Figures
Bill Buck 375.00
Fighting Eagle 160.00
Capt. (Tom) Maddox 110.00
Geronimo (#1863) 75.00
(Sgt.) Zeb Zachary 250.00

9" West Kids Figures
Jamie West (#1062) 65.00
Janice West 60.00
Jay West 50.00
Josie West (#1067) 60.00

Foreign Issue Figures
Dangerous Dan (British/Canadian issue) 300.00
Jimmy West (Canadian issue) 350.00
Sheriff Goode (British/Canadian issue) 300.00

Horses
Nodding Head Buckskin horse 75.00
Commanche, cavalry horse (1966) (Fort Apache
    Fighter) 75.00
Flame The Western Range Horse 45.00
Pancho horse 60.00
Storm Cloud Pinto Horse 45.00
Thunderbolt Horse (1965) 60.00

Thundercolt 40.00

Dogs
Flack English Setter Dog 65.00
Flick German Shepherd Dog 75.00

Vehicles, Accessories and Playsets
Buckboard with Thunderbolt horse 130.00
Buffalo 90.00
Camping Set with Jeep, Tent, etc. 125.00
Carrying Case 60.00
Chief Cherokee and Teepee 110.00
Circle X Ranch 225.00
Covered Wagon with Horse 145.00
Flame and Corral Fence 95.00
Fort Apache 275.00
Indian Canoe 225.00
Indian Teepee 130.00
Jane West Set (Jane, corral, 2 horses) 170.00
Johnny West Set (Johnny, horse, jeep) 300.00
Johnny West with Wild Mustangs 160.00

BIG JIM
Mattel (1973–76)

About the same time Mego was doing Action Jackson and Hasbro was doing the Adventure Team G.I. Joes, Mattel decided to do this primarily sports adventure action figure line. This series got the ball rolling for the second chapter of Big Jim's life.

Figures
Big Jim (1973) $20.00
Big Josh (1973) 20.00
Big Jack (1973) 20.00
Big Jeff (1974) 20.00
Big Jim Gold Medal Boxer (1975) 20.00
Big Jim Gold Medal U.S. Olympic Boxing Match
    (1975) 25.00
Big Jim With Talking Back Pack (1975) 30.00
Dr. Steel (1975) 30.00
Big Josh With Talking Camp Pack (1974) 25.00

Outfits, Vehicles and Accessories
Artic Explorer (1973) 10.00
Baja Beast vehicle (1975) 20.00
Baseball (#6854, 1973) 10.00
Basketball (1973) 10.00
Big League Baseball uniform 10.00
Boat and Buggy set (1973) 25.00
Boxer (1973) 10.00
Campin' Tent (1973) 15.00
Camping (1973) 10.00
Carrying Case (1973) 15.00
Commando (1973) 12.00
Cowboy (1973) 10.00
Cowpuncher (1975) 10.00
Cycle Set (9173) 20.00
Devil River Trip with Alligator (1974) 25.00
Eagle Ranger (1974) 10.00
Eagle of Danger Peak (1975) 10.00
Fire Fighter (1973) 10.00
Fishing Trip Playset with Boat and Buggy and
    Rescue Rig (1973) 65.00
Football (1973) 10.00
Hockey (1974) 10.00

Jungle Truck (1974) 25.00
Jungle Set (1974) 15.00
Jungle Adventure with gorilla (1974) 25.00
Jungle Guide (1975) 10.00
Karate (#6857, 1973) 10.00
Kung Fu (1974) 10.00
Kung Fu Gear with Muscle Mover (1974) 20.00
Kung Fu Studio with Muscle Mover (1974) 30.00
Lifeguard (1974) 10.00
Motocross uniform (1975) 15.00
Motocross Honda Motorcycle 30.00
Muscle Mover Pro Sports Set (1974) 20.00
Pilot (1974) 12.00
Pilot uniform 20.00
Pro Football uniform 15.00
Race Driver (1973) 10.00
Race Driver uniform 15.00
Rescue Rig (1973) 50.00
Rugged Rider (1973) . . . . No price found
Safari uniform 15.00
Safari Hunter (1973) 10.00
Scuba Diver (1975) 15.00
Skin Diving (#8655, 1973) 10.00
Sky Commander Jet (1974) 25.00
Soccer (1974) 10.00
Spear Fishing (1975) 10.00
Sports Camper (1973) 45.00
Sports Fishing uniform 10.00
Terror Off Tahiti (1975) . . . . No price found
U.S. Olympic Basketball uniform 10.00
U.S. Olympic Boxing 10.00
U.S. Olympic Boxing uniform 10.00
U.S. Olympic Judo-Karate uniform 10.00
U.S. Olympic Warm Up uniform 10.00
U.S. Olympic Ski Run (1975) 25.00
U.S. Olympic Skier uniform 10.00
U.S. Olympic Soccer uniform 10.00
Warm Up (1973) 10.00
Woodswman (1975) 10.00

BIG JIM's P.A.C.K.
Mattel (1976–77)

Part spy, part superhero, part A-Team (before that concept existed), Big Jim was the leader of P.A.C.K. (Professional Agents/Crime Killers), an elite fighting group that consisted of The Whip, Warpath, Dr. Steel and later on, Torpedo Fist. Each figure had PACK logo accessories, moving features and their own specialized weapons. And who could beat packaging by comic greats like Jack Kirby and John Buscema?

Series One, in window boxes, art by Jack Kirby
Big Jim $90.00
Whip 80.00
Warpath 80.00
Dr. Steel (#7367) 75.00
P.A.C.K. carrying case 60.00

Series Two, in narrow boxes, art by Kirby, includes 16-page comic by John Buscema
Big Jim 110.00
Whip (#9060) 90.00
Warpath (#9069) 90.00
Dr. Steel 90.00

Zorak, The Enemy, Big Jim's P.A.C.K. (Mattel 1976)

Vehicles
The Howler 60.00
The Blitz-Rig (Sears Exclusive) 140.00
P.A.C.K. Dunebuggy 75.00
The Beast 90.00
LazerVette 90.00

Series Three, in window boxes, with comic strip flap
Big Jim (Double Trouble) 80.00
Zorak, The Enemy (Double Trouble) 75.00
Torpedo Fist (#9289) 60.00

Accessories
Miner/Underworld Fighter 50.00
Hard Hat/Gunner 50.00
Photographer/Master Spy Adventure 50.00
Motorcycle Cop/S.W.A.T. Adventure 50.00

Double Trouble Disguises
Ski Patrol 30.00
Frogman 30.00
Dirt Biker 30.00
Martial Arts 30.00

BIKER MICE FROM MARS
Galoob (1993–94)

The package says, "They're motorcycle masters made of muscle. And they're the baddest mamajammers this side of Mars! Throttle, Modo and Vinnie crash landed in Chicago after escaping the evil Plutarkians who destroyed their planet. Now they continue to battle Lawrence Limburger, the head

Throttle, Biker Mice From Mars (Galoob 1993)

Plutarkian on Earth, and his ruthless partners in crime." We like the title, but we are afraid that they sold better on Mars than in the toy stores. The figures go with a kids television cartoon show and there are five carded figures and five boxed figures with motorcycles.

Galoob thought the series would be "The Next Turtles." It wasn't, but we liked Dr. Karbunkle (with Fred the Mutant) because of his evil grin. Collectors initially showed some interest in Charley, the only female in the group, but she turned out to be fairly easy to find at the end. The "Sports Bro's" batch was particularly prominent as red tag specials, along with many of the vehicles and playsets.

First Series (Dec. 1993)
Throttle with "Sprocket Launcher Really Fires"
(#25511) $6.00
Vinnie with Grip Claw and "Spinning Crowbar Weapons"
(#25512) 6.00
Modo with "Real Firing Rocket Gun" (#25513) 6.00
Dr. Karbunkle and Fred the Mutant with "Pop-Out Brain"
(#25514) 6.00
Lawrence Limburger, with "Giant Working Mouse Trap"
(#25515) 6.00
Greasepit "Weapon Really Shoots Water" (#25516) . . 6.00
Charley with "Light-Up Laser Welder" (#25517) 10.00
Lectromag with "Real Magnetic Power" (#25518) 6.00
Evil Eye Weevil "Eye Really Glows, Bones Really
Collapse" (#25519) 6.00

Sports Bro's (1994)
Home-Run Throttle with "Battle Gun with Baseball Bat

Missiles" (#25521) 5.00
Slam-Dunk Vinnie with "Slam-Dunk Cannon Really
Fires" (#25522) 5.00
Touchdown Modo with "Long Bomb Blaster Launching
Missile" (#25523) 5.00

Freedom Fighters
Tail-Whippin' Throttle with "Turbo Tail with Skyclaw
Grappler" 7.00
Rad Rebel Vinnie with "Commando Backpack Launches
Missiles" 7.00
Commando Modo with "Radical Recoil Raygun" 7.00
Rimfire with "Martian Combat Clutch" 7.00

Later Batch
Napoleon Brie in Cosmic Cape 7.00
Four-By with Roto-Action Hammer Drill 7.00
Sky Commander 7.00

Biker Knights with free video
Armatron Modo 10.00
Totalizer Throttle 10.00
Invincible Vinnie 10.00

12" Mega Mice (1994), in window box
Throttle (#25591?) 15.00
Vinnie (#25592) 15.00
Modo (#25593) 15.00

Custom Cycles (1994)
Throttle's Martian Monster Bike with "Firing Tailpipe
Missiles" (#25501) 10.00
Vinnie's Radical Rocket Sled with "Secret Pop-Up
Weapon" (#25502) 10.00
Modo's Mondo Chopper with "Double-Barrel Action"
(#25503) 10.00
Greasepit's Grunge Cycle with "Pumpin' Action Grease
Barrels" (#25504?) 10.00

Other Vehicles and Playsets (1994)
Dr. Karbunkle's Transporter and Secret Lab playset with
Fred the Mutant figure (#25530) 20.00
Scoreboard Hideout playset (#25532) 25.00
Radical Rider Set with **Vinnie** figure (#25542) 15.00
Super Sidecar (#25548) 15.00
Throttle's Blazin' Cycle with **Throttle** figure (#25570) 15.00

BILL & TED'S
EXCELLENT ADVENTURE
Kenner (1991)

From the movie starring Keanu Reeves, Alex Winter and George Carlin featuring a wild romp through time with two total idiots who must pass history class. Gathering some famous persons from history, our heroes naturally form a rock band, the Wyld Stallyns. The movie and its sequel, *Bill and Ted's Bogus Journey*, are actually reasonably funny. The action figures appeared in 1991, around the time of the second movie. There was also a Saturday morning cartoon show from 1990 to 1991, with the original actors supplying the voices for their characters. Collectors must also be music critics, because the figures are not heavily collected.

6" Wyld Stallyns Figures (summer 1991)
Bill S. Preston, Esq. on guitar (#54110) $6.00

Grim Reaper, *Bill & Ted's Excellent Adventure (Kenner 1991)*

Ted "Theodore" Logan on guitar (#54120) 6.00
Rufus on keyboards (#54130) 6.00
Grim Reaper on guitar (#54170) 10.00
Abe Lincoln on keyboards (#54220) 7.00
Genghis Khan on drums (#54260) 7.00
Billy the Kid on guitar (#54270) 7.00
Napoleon on drums . . . . not produced

Vehicles, Accessories and Playset (1991)
Wyld Stallyns speaker and tape set (#54190) 10.00
Phone Booth with snapback receiver (#54200) 10.00
Wyld Stallyns Jam Session two-pack (#54210) 15.00
Historical Playset (#54230) 12.00
Boom Truck vehicle (#54240) 12.00
Most Excellent Motorcycle vehicle (#54280) 8.00
Talking Cruiser (#54290) 12.00

BIONIC SIX
LJN (1986)

The Bionic Six was a science fiction animated series from the mid 1980s. The series pitted the Bennett family against Dr. Scarab and his evil minions of destruction every Saturday morning. The program can be caught once in a while on the Sci-Fi Channel. LJN produced this extensive line of plastic and die-cast metal figures along with vehicles and accessories in 1986. You could still find a few around at discount in the early 1990s.

3¾" Bennett Family Figures
Bunji $20.00

Madame-O, *Bionic Six (LJN 1986)*

Helen 10.00
Jack 10.00
F.L.U.F.F.I. 20.00
J.D. 10.00
Eric 10.00
Meg 10.00

Dr. Scarab's Evil Minions of Destruction
Mechanic 10.00
Glove 10.00
Madame-O 10.00
Dr. Scarab 10.00
Chopper 10.00
Klunk 10.00

Vehicles
M.U.L.E.S. Van (boxed) (#3835) 30.00
Dirt Bike (carded) 12.00
Quad Runner 12.00
Electronic Laser Aero Chair (#3815) 12.00
Electronic Flying Laser Throne (boxed) (#3815) 12.00
Secret Headquarters Super Hi-Tech Bionic Laboratory
    playset (#3840) 40.00

THE BIONIC WOMAN
Kenner (1976–77)

From the television series starring Lindsay Wagner, which was a spin-off from *The Six Million Dollar Man* show. Both were very popular in the mid 1970s, so there are a lot of potential collectors, and also a lot of product available. The world's leading collector and authority on the two series is Mike Van Plew, who has written articles on the series for all the major collector magazines. The basic Jaime Sommers figure features fully rooted hair and you can hear pinging noises (from the show) when you turn her head from side to side.

12¼" Figures
Jaime Sommers, The Bionic Woman, white shirt,
(#65800, 1976) $90.00
Jaime Sommers, The Bionic Woman with Mission Purse,
blue jumpsuit, (#65810, 1977) 120.00
Fembot (#66400, 1977) 150.00

Vehicles and Accessories
Bionic Woman Sports Car (#65830, 1977) 75.00
Bionic Beauty Salon (#65850, 1976) 75.00
Dome House (#65950, 1976) 120.00
Carriage House (#65970, 1977) 120.00
Bionic Woman Bionic Cycle (#66040, 1976) 40.00
Turbo Tower of Power and Cycle Set (1976) 65.00
Jaime Sommers Classroom (1977) 250.00

Designer Fashions (Asst. #65980)
Floral Delight 15.00
Blue Mist 15.00
Gold Dust 15.00
Casual Day 15.00
Country Comfort 15.00
Silk 'N Satin 15.00
Peach Dream 15.00

Budget Fashions (Asst. #65990)
Lilac Butterfly 15.00
Party Pants 15.00
Classy Culottes 15.00
Red Dazzle 15.00
Lime Lite 15.00
Fiesta 15.00
Lunch Date 15.00
Elegant Lady 15.00

THE BLACK HOLE
Mego (1979–80)

From the forgettable Walt Disney live-action science fiction movie starring Maximillian Schell as Dr. Reinhardt, Anthony Perkins as Dr. Durant, Robert Forster, Joseph Bottoms, Yvette Mimieux and Ernest Borgnine as Harry Booth.

3¾" Figures
Dr. Hans Reinhardt (#65010/1) $16.00
Captain Dan Holland (#65010/2) 18.00
Pizer (#65010/3) 28.00
Dr. Durant (#65010/4) 18.00
Dr. Kate McCrae (#65010/5) 18.00
Harry Booth (#65010/6) 18.00
V.I.N.Cent (#65010/7) 35.00
Maximillian (#65010/8) 50.00

Later Figures (1980)
Sentry Robot (#65010/9) 65.00

Overseas Figures
Old B.O.B (#65010/10). 160.00
Humanoid 675.00
S.T.A.R. 300.00

12½" Figures (1979)
Captain Dan Holland 52.00

Dr. Alan Durant 52.00
Dr. Hans Reinhardt 52.00
Captain Harry Booth 52.00
Dr. Kate McCrae 52.00
Pizer 60.00

BLACKSTAR
Galoob (1983–85)

From a nationally syndicated cartoon show by Filmation, featuring space-fantasy adventure. There were flying beasts and spaceships, swords and a dart laser gun on the castle playset. Every figure came with a Trobbit (spelled Trobit the first year) or a demon companion so they wouldn't be lonely between battles. The Trobbits looked like old dwarfs, while Blackstar was a well-muscled hero who looked and dressed like Conan.

1984 figures had "the phenomenal new Laser Light, a safe, sparking device" which worked more like an out-of-fuel Zippo lighter than any laser.

6" Figures (1983)
Blackstar, Astronaut Defender of Freedom and Balkar,
King of the Trobits $20.00
Mara, Princess of Secret Power and Gossamer, the
Flying Trobit 25.00
Overlord, the Wizard King and Alien Demon 20.00
Neptul, Lord of Aquaria and Alien Demon 20.00
Palace Guard, Protector of Overlord and Alien Demon 20.00
Kadray, The Invincible Wizard and Alien Demon 20.00
Tongo, The Leopard Man and Alien Demon 20.00
Gargo, The Vampire Man and Alien Demon 20.00

Second Series, with "Laser Light" (Asst. #5497, 1984)
Blackstar, Astronaut Defender of Freedom and Trobbit 15.00
Overlord, The Invincible Wizard and Alien Demon . . . 15.00
Neptul, Lord of Aquaria and Alien Demon 15.00
Klone with Trobbit 15.00

Arch Rivals, with "Laser Light" (Asst. #5496, 1984)
Palace Guard, Protector of Overlord and Alien Demon 15.00
Kadray, The Invincible Wizard and Alien Demon 15.00
Tongo, The Leopard Man and Alien Demon 15.00
Gargo, The Vampire Man and Alien Demon 15.00

Third Series, with "Laser Light" (Asst. #5509, 1984)
Vizir, Ice Castle Wizard and Alien Demon 15.00
Overlord's Warrior the Devil Knight and Demon 15.00
Lava Loc Volcanic Monster and Alien Demon 15.00
Meuton The Wasp Man and Demon 15.00
The White Knight, Overlord's Warrior and Alien Demon 15.00
Blackstar Gift Set with **Blackstar**, **Overlord** and **Klone**
figures, plus Demons and Trobbit (#5498, 1984) 75.00

Trobbits and Demons (Asst. #5508)
Trobbit Balkar 6.00
Trobbit, each 5.00
Demon, each 5.00
Note: There are a total of 12 different Trobbits and Demons.

Vehicles, Accessories and Playset
Warlock, Dragon Horse of Zagar (#5501, 1983) 15.00
Trobbit Wind Machine, 26" hot air balloon with 2 Trobbits
(#5504, 1983?) 20.00
Space Ship with Rocket Launchers (#5506, 1983?) . . 25.00

Demons and Trobbits, Blackstar (Galoob 1984)

The Ice Castle with Working Gun Tower, 27" high
    (#5507, 1984) 50.00
Triton, Kadray's flying bull (#5511, 1984) 15.00
Battle Wagon, 18", battery powered (#5512, 1984) .. 18.00

BLUE THUNDER
MultiToys (1983)

The 1983 movie *Blue Thunder* starred Roy Scheider and Malcolm McDowell battling in helicopters over the streets of Los Angeles. The movie is pretty good and Roy wins. The toy was presumably made to sell to children who were too young to actually see the R-rated movie.

Vehicle with Figure
Blue Thunder Helicopter with **Astro Division Pilot** figure
    (#2430) $35.00

BONANZA
American Character (1966)

Based on the long-running (1959–73) television western series starring Lorne Greene as Ben Cartwright, Dan Blocker as Hoss, Pernell Roberts as Adam and Michael Landon as Little Joe. Television westerns were immensely popular in the 1950s and 1960s, and this was one of the best and most popular.

9" Figures
Ben $140.00

Hoss 140.00
Little Joe 140.00
The Outlaw 140.00

Figures with horses
Ben with Palomino 200.00
Hoss with Stallion 200.00
Little Joe with Pinto 200.00
The Outlaw with Mustang 200.00

Vehicles and Accessories
4 In 1 Wagon 120.00
Mustang (The Outlaw's horse) 60.00
Palomino (Ben's horse) 60.00
Pinto (Little Joe's horse) 60.00
Stallion (Hoss's horse) 60.00

BONE AGE
Kenner (1988–89)

Bone Age features "frighteningly authentic skeletons of prehistoric dinosaurs, each with its own unique artillery action feature like shooting horns or launching rock bombs … and each comes with its own caveman action figure." It's a toss-up whether cavemen riding dinosaurs or cavemen riding somehow living dinosaur bone creatures is worse science. Since there are no cavewomen in the series, the cavemen have nothing to do besides fight. The figures were still around in 1989, but nothing new was added.

Lava Clan (Asst. #42000, 1988)
Volc the Voracious $5.00

Dynacus and Auger Launcher, Bone Age (Kenner 1989)

Karn 5.00
Bull 5.00

Stone Clan (Asst. #42000, 1988)
Crag the Clubber 5.00
Lud 5.00
Kos 5.00

Ice Clan (Asst. #42000, 1988)
Tund the Thunderous 5.00
Nord 5.00
Skog 5.00

Dinosaurs (1988)
Codus with **Bunt** Stone Clan caveman figure (#42150) 14.00
Anklor with **Tuk** Stone Clan caveman figure (#42160) 14.00
Ptero with **Brog** Ice Clan caveman figure (#42170) . . 14.00
Deitron with **Brac** Stone Clan caveman figure
    (#42180) 14.00
Stegus with **Org** Lava Clan caveman figure (#42190) 14.00
Tritops with **Tund the Thunderous** chief Ice Clan
    caveman figure (#42200) 18.00
T-Rex with **Crag the Clubber** chief Stone Clan caveman
    figure (#42210) 25.00
Brontus with **Volc the Voracious** chief Lava Clan
    caveman figure (#42220) 18.00
Dynacus with **Zur** Ice Clan caveman figure (#42230) 14.00
Plesior with **Molt** Lava Clan caveman figure (#42240) 14.00

Weapons (Asst. #42110, 1988)
Club Flinger weapon 10.00
Hammer Hook weapon 10.00
Ram Bammer weapon 10.00

Deluxe Weapons (Asst. #42250, 1988)
Bola Bomber weapon 10.00
Spear Slinger weapon 10.00

Tangle Trap weapon 10.00

THE BOTS MASTER
Toy Biz (1994)

The **Bots Masters** were a line of toys from Toy Biz designed to compete for the Robot/Transformer/Power Ranger toy buyer. You will not be surprised to learn that it is based on the animated television show of the same name. Two of the figures have bonus 3-D glasses which you can use to watch the show, presumably in 3-D. There are four good "Boyzz" and four evil "Bots" in the main action figure line, plus three Evil Transforming Bots and a "Jungle Fiver" made up of five other robots. The Evil Transforming Bots change, or morph, or transform, from robot to plane or tank or helicopter, and you can combine the five parts of the Jungle Fiver to form a giant Bot. You just possibly may have heard of other toys that work about the same way.

The Boyzz
Ziv Zulander (#52101) with 3-D glasses $5.00
Twig (#52102) 5.00
Bats (#52103) 5.00
Ninjzz (#52104) 5.00

Dr. Hisss and His Evil Bots
Dr. Hisss (#52105) with 3-D glasses 5.00
Greenbot (#52106) 5.00
Humabot (#52107) 5.00
P.P.B. (#52108) 5.00

Evil Transforming Bots
Skyfighter 6.00
Chopperbot (#52212) 6.00
Tankbot (#52213) 6.00

Dr. Hisss, The Bots Master (Toy Biz 1994)

Jungle Fiver

Tank B. (#52201)	8.00
Half B. (#52202)	8.00
Hover B. (#52203)	8.00
Heli B. (#52204)	8.00
Jet B. (#52205)	8.00

BRAVESTARR
"WILD WEST ADVENTURE IN SPACE!"
Mattel (1986)

From a Filmation space-western cartoon series, of all things. Heroic Marshall BraveStarr battled Tex Hex and a lame bunch of other bad guys in a largely undistinguished television show.

The figures were a lot better than the show. They stood almost 8" tall, which was huge for action figures at that time. The Infra-red Bravestarr and Tex Hex are especially interesting as they shoot actual infra-red beams from their "Ultimate Electronic Backpacks" and have sound effects as well.

7½" Figures, with comic and poster, in window box

Col. Borobot	$18.00
Deputy Fuzz	18.00
Handle Bar (#1723)	18.00
Marshal BraveStarr	20.00
Outlaw Skuzz and Scuzz Bucket vehicle	20.00
Sand Storm (#1724)	18.00
Skull Walker (#1507)	18.00
Tex Hex	20.00

Thunder Stick	20.00

Figures, with comic, poster and beam reflector target

Laser-Fire Tex Hex (#3151)	22.00
Laser-Fire BraveStarr (#3152)	25.00

Figure and Stallion Two-Pack

BraveStarr and Thirty/Thirty	35.00

Vehicles, Accessories and Playset

Thirty/Thirty robotic stallion (#1620)	20.00
Fort Kerium, Command Center for Marshall BraveStarr playset	80.00
Laser-Fire Backpacks	15.00
Neutra-Laser	18.00
Stratocoach	40.00

BRONZE BOMBERS
Olmec (1989)

The Bronze Bombers are black and Hispanic military figures. They are 3¾" tall, the same size as G.I. Joe, but they are not just another drug store knock-off. Olmec is a minority owned and run company that exhibits at Toy Fair every year. It also sells dolls and some other action figures with a black and/or Hispanic theme. Collectors have generally ignored all 3¾" military figures, except G.I. Joe, so these figures sell for just a few dollars each.

BUCK ROGERS
IN THE 25th CENTURY
Mego (1979)

From the television show starring Gil Gerard as Buck Rogers, Erin Gray as Wilma Deering, Tim O'Connor as Dr. Huer and Pamela Hensley as Ardella. Buck Rogers was a very popular comic strip from the 1930s and a black and white serial starring Buster Crabbe (who also starred as Flash Gordon). Buck is an astronaut, thawed out after five centuries, who battles evil doers on 25th-century earth. Chief among them are Killer Kane and the sultry Ardella. He is aided by his robot friend Twiki and the pretty, but independent minded and up-tight Wilma Deering.

3¾" Figures

Buck Rogers (#85000/1)	$45.00
Twiki (#85000/2)	35.00
Tiger Man (#85000/3)	18.00
Killer Kane (#85000/4)	22.00
Draco (#85000/5)	18.00
Draconian Guard (#85000/6)	18.00
Ardella (#85000/7)	28.00
Wilma Deering (#85000/8)	50.00
Dr. Huer (#85000/9)	18.00

Vehicles and Playsets

Draconian Marauder (#85012)	60.00
Laserscope Fighter with "Simulated Lasers and Explosion" (#85014)	40.00
Star Fighter (#85016)	60.00
Land Rover (#85018)	100.00
Star Searcher (#85020)	75.00
Star Fighter Command Center (#85022)	110.00

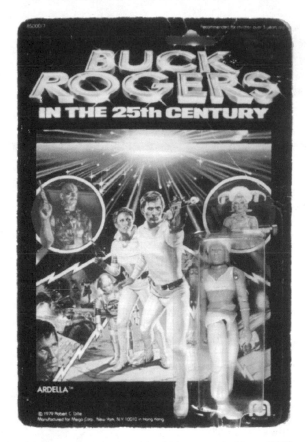

Ardella, Buck Rogers in the 25th Century (Mego 1979)

12½" Figures, in window box
Buck Rogers	65.00
Walking Twiki, 7¼"	60.00
Dr. Huer	65.00
Killer Kane	90.00
Draco	65.00
Tiger Man	90.00
Draconian Guard	65.00

BUCKY O'HARE
Hasbro (1990–91)

From the animated television show of the same name. The show was not all that successful and the series died, so no second-year figures were issued, even though a number had been shown in Hasbro's 1991 catalog. Bucky O'Hare was scarce and highly sought at first, but by the end of the series he was plentiful. Near the end of the series, most of the figures were released with different colored weapons, as listed.

5" Figures
1. Bucky O'Hare (#7281) silver weapons	$10.00
Reissue, with orange weapons	12.00
2. Dead-Eye Duck (#7291) silver weapons	10.00
Reissue, with purple weapons	12.00
3. Willy DuWitt (##7292)	10.00
4. A.F.C. Blinky (#7283) silver weapons	10.00
Reissue, with green weapons	12.00
5. Toad Air Marshall (#7284) black weapons	10.00
Reissue, with green weapons	12.00
6. Toadborg (#7295)	10.00

7. Bruiser (Berserker Baboon) (#7282) silver weapons	10.00
Reissue, with orange weapons	12.00
8. Al Negator (#7285)	10.00
9. Commander Dogstar (#7293) silver weapons	10.00
Reissue, with orange weapons	12.00
10. Storm Toad Trooper (#7294)	10.00

Vehicles (1991)
Toad Croaker vehicle with "Toad Croaking Sound" (#7287)	20.00
Toad Double Bubble (#7288)	20.00
Righteous Indignation (#7289)	20.00

BUGMEN OF INSECTA
"THE INSECT WARRIORS FROM BENEATH THE EARTH"
Multi-Toys (1983)

Cheap 4" figures not based on any television show or comic. They have drawn some interest, chiefly from monster collectors.

4" Figures (Asst. #4000)
Black Widow	$12.00
Grasshopperman	12.00
Killer Bee	12.00
Spiderman	12.00
Stag Beetle	12.00
Tiger Beetle	12.00

BUTCH AND SUNDANCE
"THE EARLY DAYS"
Kenner (1979)

From the movie starring William Katt and Tom Berenger as younger versions of the characters made famous by Paul Newman and Robert Redford.

3¾" Figures, with revolver and quick-draw feature
Butch Cassidy (#53010)	$20.00
The Sundance Kid (#53020)	20.00
O.C. Hanks (#53030)	25.00
Sheriff Bledsoe (#53040)	25.00
Marshall LeFors (#53050)	25.00

Horses, Vehicle and Playset
Bluff, Butch Cassidy's horse, with galloping feature, running sound, saddle, bridle and rifle	40.00
Spurs, Sundance Kid's horse, with galloping feature, running sound, saddle, bridle and rifle	40.00
Mint Wagon, with 4 horses, rotating gattling gun, gunner, rifleman, 2 gold chests, wagon ramp and breakaway yoke	60.00
Saloon Playset	65.00

BUTTERFLY WOMAN
Olmec (1986)

Black and Hispanic-oriented figures related to Sun-Man. This company also produced Bronze Bombers action figures. Collectors haven't shown much interest in these figures and they sell for about $5.00 each.

Hannah Dundee, Cadillacs and Dinosaurs (Tyco 1994)

CADILLACS AND DINOSAURS
Tyco (1994)

Xenozoic Tales, a popular 1987 comic book created by Mark Schultz, was the basis for the 1993–94 CBS television show on which these figures were based. In the story, Jack "Cadillac" Tenrec and his band of survivors struggle in a world gone mad. It's a world where dinosaurs of the Earth's prehistoric past coexist with men and women of the future and Cadillacs race with Wooly Mammoths. Evolution has spun out of control and humanity is in a desperate struggle for survival and the only law is Jack Tenrec, the 26th-century warrior who cruises the strange landscape of the future in an armored 1950s red Cadillac.

Hannah Dundee has been the most popular figure with collectors. The dinosaurs were recycled from the Dinoriders series.

5" Figures
Jack "Cadillac" Tenrec (#13021)	$5.00
Mustapha Cairo (#13022)	5.00
Hannah Dundee, Scientist and Diplomat (#13023) . . .	9.00
Jungle Fighting Jack Tenrec (#13024)	5.00
Hammer Terhune, Lead Evil Poacher (#13025)	5.00
Vice Terhune, Evil Poacher (#13026)	5.00

Dinosaurs
Hermes (Deinonychus) with "Dino Kicking Action" (#13027)	5.00
Zeke (Quetzalcoatlus) with "Message Carrying Backpack" (#13028)	5.00
Kentrosaurus with "Giant Lever Arm"	15.00
Snake Eyes (Triceratops) with "Giant Boulder Launcher"	15.00

Vehicles and Accessories
Jack Tenrec's Cadillac	12.50
Jack Tenrec's Glider	6.00
Hammer's Tribike (#13072)	6.00
Jack's Garage	not released

CAPITOL CRITTERS
Kenner (1992)

The six Capitol Critters from Kenner are attractive figures, as rodents and roaches go. All of them were eventually available as red tag specials.

Figures (1992) in open box
Jammet Rat (#09310)	$5.00
Muggle Rat (#09320)	5.00
Max (#09330)	5.00
Moze (#09340)	5.00
Ratso Nasty Evil Rat (#09350)	5.00
Kid Vicious Evil Roach (#09360)	5.00

CAPTAIN ACTION
Ideal (1966–68)

Captain Action was billed as the "boldest, bravest he-man hero in any hemisphere." It's hard to disagree because, for a small additional charge, he could turn into 13 different heroes and super heroes by means of his uniform and equipment packs.

As with 12" G.I. Joe figures, there were only a few basic dolls and much of the collecting action was, and is, in the costumes. This series and G.I. Joe are the two most

Captain Action (Ideal 1967)

influential, and most collectible, action figure series ever produced. They defined action figures for the 1960s and remain the most valuable items in the field. Costumes are collected loose, as well in the original sealed packages. As with any item collected in this manner, the absence of any part, however small, greatly reduces the value.

12" Captain Action Figures
Captain Action in first issue box showing 9 inset pictures, with the Lone Ranger shown in a red shirt (#3400, 1966) $475.00
Captain Action in second issue box showing the Lone Ranger in a blue shirt, including Video-Matic ring (1966–67) 600.00
Captain Action in third issue box showing 7 inset pictures and "Free! 4 ft. Parachute Inside" including Video-Matic ring and parachute (1967) 700.00
Captain Action the Super Hero in photo box "enemy of the sinister dr. evil" (1967–68) 800.00
    Loose figure, including cap, boots, gun and gun belt, scabbard and lightning sword 200.00
    Loose ring or parachute, each 25.00

12" Dr. Evil Figures
Dr. Evil, The Sinister Invader of Earth, in photo box (1967) 800.00
    Loose, with ray gun, gold chain, medallion, sandals and face mask 200.00
Dr. Evil with His Disguises and Weapons in window box (1968) 2,750.00
    Loose, with gold chain, medallion, sandals, oriental face mask, bearded face mask and lab coat, thought scanner, hypnotic eye, laser ray gun, magnifying glass, ionized hypo needle and reducing ray 1,500.00

9" Action Boy Figures
Action Boy in photo box (#3420, 1967) 800.00
    Loose, with beret, boomerang, knife, belt and boots plus Khem, his black panther, with collar and leash 400.00
Action Boy, The Bold Adventurer in photo box showing space suit (1967–68) 1,100.00
    Loose, with space helmet, spack boots, gloves, knife, ray gun, belt, black panther with collar and leash 500.00

Captain Action Uniform and Equipment Packs (1966) in window box
Superman costume with face mask and flying cape, belt, arm shackles, phantom zone projector, block of green kryptonite and boots, plus Krypto his super dog also with cape (#3401-7) 550.00
Batman costume with hood, face mask, bat-arang, bat rope and reel with grappling hook, utility belt with 2-way radio buckle, laser-beam flashlight and boots (#3402-5) 625.00
Flash Gordon costume with face mask, silver astro-suit, space helmet, space belt with holster and ray pistol, oxygen guidance "Zot" gun and silver boots (#3403-3) 525.00
Sgt. Fury costume with face mask, helmet, walkie talkie, machine gun, gun belt, bandolier, grenades, .45 pistol and boots (#3404-1) 450.00
Steve Canyon costume with face mask, 50 mission hat, helmet with oxygen mask, paratrooper uniform, parachute pack, garrison belt with holster and .45 automatic, knife and boots (#3405-8) 475.00
The Lone Ranger (**red shirt**) costume with face mask, cowboy hat, red shirt, black pants, gun belt with two holsters and two pistols, Winchester rifle and boots with spurs (#3406-6) 600.00
The Phantom costume with purple hood, face mask, belt with holster and automatic pistols, rifle with scope, knife and boots (#3407-4) 600.00
Aquaman costume with face mask, conch horns, trident spear, belt with knife sheath and knife, swordfish sword and fins (#3408-2) 475.00

Steve Canyon and Captain America outfits,
Captain Action (Ideal 1966–67

Captain America costume with hood, face mask, laser-
beam gun, ultra-sonic intensifier pistol, belt and
holster, shield and boots (#3409-0) 550.00

Captain Action Uniform and Equipment Packs (1967) with
"Video-Matic" ring, in window box
The Green Hornet costume with face mask, hat,
shoulder holster, gas pistol, watch message
receiver, hornet sting, TV scanner with phone,
shoes and ring (#3413) 4,750.00
The Spider Man costume with hood face mask, spider
light, utility belt, spider grapling hook with rope and
handle, spider saw, spray tank with hose, spider,
boots and ring (#3414) 5,750.00
Tonto costume with face mask, head band with feather,
bow, quiver and arrows, gun belt with holster and
scabbard, six-gun, knife, moccasins, an eagle and
ring (#3415) 1,200.00
Buck Rogers costume with face mask, space helmet,
space gun, gloves, space belt and harness, twin jet
packs, radio microphone with cord, canteen, space
light, space boots and ring (#3416) 1,400.00

Reissue Uniform and Equipment Packs (1967), with "Video-
Matic" ring, in window box
Superman costume with ring (#3401) 800.00
Batman costume with ring (#3402) 800.00
Flash Gordon costume with ring (#3403) 700.00

Action Boy, Captain Action (Ideal 1967)

Steve Canyon costume with ring (#3405) 650.00
The Lone Ranger costume (**blue shirt**) with blue 2-piece
outfit and ring (#3406) 1,600.00
The Phantom costume with pistols and ring (#3407) 800.00
The Phantom costume with .45 automatic and ring . 800.00
Aquaman costume with ring (#3408) 700.00
Captain America costume with ring (#3409) 700.00

Action Boy Uniform and Equipment Packs (1967) in
window box
Robin costume with face mask, cape, utility belt, gloves,
batarang launcher, batarangs, climbing grips, two
bat grenades and boots (#3421) 750.00
Superboy costume with face mask, cape, belt, super
chem lab, telepathic thought scrambler, interspacial
language translator and boots (#3422) 700.00
Aqualad costume with face mask, swordfish spear, belt,
seahorse knife, shell axe, boots and Octo the
octopus (#3423) 600.00

Accessories Packs (1967)
20-Piece Survival Kit (#3450-4) 300.00
10-Piece Weapons Arsenal (#3451-2) 300.00
Inter-Galactic Jet Mortar (#3452-0) 225.00
4-Foot Working Parachute (#3453-8) 225.00
Inter-Spacial Directional Communicator (#3454-6) . . 225.00
Anti-Gravitational Power Pack (#3455-3) 225.00

Vehicles and Playsets (1967)
Headquarters carry case with **Captain Action** doll in
Batman costume and ring (Sears exclusive) . . 500.00
Action Cave carry case (Montgomery Ward exclusive)650.00
Quick Change Chamber with **Captain Action** doll in
Batman costume and ring (Sears exclusive) . . 750.00
Silver Streak Amphibian vehicle, 21" long, in box . 1,500.00
Silver Streak Garage (Sears exclusive) 1,200.00
Dr. Evil Sanctuary carry case (Speigel exclusive)
(#8701) 2,500.00

CAPTAIN PLANET
and THE PLANETEERS
"THE POWER IS YOURS!"
Tiger (1991–94)

Originally a 1990 Turner Broadcasting television
cartoon series for environmentally conscious kids. It is still
showing in syndication in some markets. In the series,
Captain Planet and his five-kid force, called the Planeteers,
battle various polluters, like Duke Nukem and Verminous
Skumm. The trouble is, villains like this are really just fall-
guys for the corporate polluters. Anyway, the figure line
succumbed to acid rain in toy stores, but the Kmart discount
store chain arranged for a few new figures in 1993 and 1994.

5" Figures (1991) heroes include child-sized ring
Captain Planet, "flys under your control" with ring (#80-
621) $10.00
Duke Nukem "Glows-in-the-Dark" (#80-622) 10.00
Verminous Skumm with "Rat Rot Sprayer" (#80-623) . . 9.00
Planeteer Wheeler with "Real Sparking Action" and ring
(#80-624) 10.00
Dr. Blight "With MAL Evil Computer Accomplice" (#80-
625) 10.00
Linka with "Working Parachute Included" and ring (#80-
626?) 11.00
Captain Planet, color change (#80-627) 10.00

Captain Planet with "Power Commands,"
Captain Planet and the Planeteers (Tiger 1991)

Ma-Ti & Kwame, "Bonus Pack" with 2 rings (#80-628?) 12.00
Hoggish Greedly with "Water Spraying Action" (80-629) 9.00
Sly Sludge with "Instant Toxic Sludge" packets (#80-630) 9.00
Gi Planeteer with "Water Spraying Action" and ring (#80-631?) 9.00

Second Batch (1992)
Wheeler with "Grappling Hook and Launcher" (#80-639) 8.00
Commander Clash with "Satellite Backpack and Radar Monitor" (#80-640) 8.00
Light & Thunder Captain Planet (#80-641) 8.00
Captain Planet with "Power Commands" (#80-642) . . . 8.00
Duke Nukem with LED (#80-64?) 8.00
Linka Planeteer with Eco Commands (#80-64?) 8.00
Wheeler Planeteer with Eco Commands (80-645) 8.00
Gi (talking) (#80-64?) 8.00
Kwame (talking) (#80-64?) 8.00
MaTi (talking) (#80-64?) 8.00
Captain Planet with Pollution Armor (#80-64?) 8.00
MaTi with Rescue Pack "It's a backpack and a rescue vehicle" (#80-64?) 8.00
Wheeler with Tread Pack "Transform vehicle into a backpack" (#80-64?) 8.00

Vehicles, Accessories and Playset (1991–92)
Eco Disaster Bulldozer (1992) 10.00
Eco Jailor, Planotoor Vohiclo (1992) 18.00
Garbage Cannon Truck (1992) 16.00
Skumm-O-Copter, Eco-Villain Air Vehicle 18.00
Toxic Sludge Dump, Eco-Villain Disaster Set (#80-701) 15.00
Toxic Cannon, Eco-Villain Vehicle (#80-702) 10.00
Eco-Cycle, Planeteer Vehicle (#80-703) 8.00
Geo-Cruiser, Planeteer Air or Land Vehicle (#80-704) 10.00

Eco-Sub, Planeteer Underwater Vehicle (#80-706) . . . 8.00
Planeteer Copter, Air Patrol Vehicle (#80-709) 15.00
Duke's Exploding Reactor (#80-724) 15.00

All-American Captain Planet,
Captain Planet and the Planeteers (Tiger 1993)

Third and Fourth Batch Figures (1993–94)
Tornado Captain Planet with "Tornado Spinning Action" (#80636) 8.00
Argos Bleak with "Missile Launching Harness" (#80638, 1994) 8.00
All-American Captain Planet with ring (#80-652) 20.00
Arctic Captain Planet with "Camouflage Outfit for Arctic Maneuvers" and ring (#80-653) 8.00
Armor Captain Planet 8.00
Meteor Captain Planet 8.00

[THE NEW ADVENTURES OF]
CAPTAIN PLANET
Tiger (1994–95)

This was an attempt at reviving the Captain Planet series, but it basically failed, at least in the United States, as toy store chains did not carry the figures. The other Planeteers, such as Gi, Linka, etc., were listed on the package back, but have not been seen.

5" Figures
Captain Planet with Snap on Anti-Radiation Armor (#80654) $7.00
Firestorm Captain Planet (#80655) 7.00
Thunder & Lightning Captain Planet (#80656) 7.00

Corporal Pilot Chase,
Captain Power and the Soldiers of the Future (Mattel 1987)

CAPTAIN POWER
AND THE SOLDIERS OF THE FUTURE
Mattel (1987)

The package says "The Future is now! ... the late 22nd century ... Bio Dreads—monstrous computer creatures—now rule earth ... the sinister cyborg, Lord Dread, wants to eliminate all biological life forms ... humanity's only hope lies with Captain Power and the Soldiers of the Future!"

This was an attempt by Mattel to cash in on the interactive television game market, which wasn't as successful as all the hype had made it seem. Some of the toys themselves had devices that would interact during various segments of the television program that was aired during the time the toys were on the market.

The syndicated television show starred Tim Dunigan as Captain Power and David Hemblen as the chief bad guy, Lord Dread. The figures and vehicles were pretty decent themselves. Video releases were available as well, so that even when the show was off the air, you still had something your toys could interact with.

3¾" Figures

Captain Power	$8.00
Lt. Tank Ellis	8.00
Major Hawk Masterson	8.00
Lord Dread	9.00
Soaron Sky Sentry	9.00
Blastarr Ground Guardian	9.00

Second Series (1988)

Sergeant Scout Baker	12.00
Corporal Pilot Chase (#4474)	15.00
Col. Stingray Johnson	25.00
Tritor	30.00
Dread Trooper	60.00
Dread Commander	60.00

Vehicles and Accessories

Interlocker Throne/weapon (1987)	12.00
Phantom Striker evil jet (1987)	18.00
Power Base fortress set (1987)	60.00
Power On Energizer with **Capt. Power** figure (#4115, 1987)	12.00
Powerjet XT-7 heroic fighter (1987)	20.00
Powerjet XT-7 deluxe with Future Force Training Tape	40.00
Dread Stalker vehicle (1988)	12.00
Magna Cycle (1988)	20.00
Trans-Field Base Station (1988)	20.00
Trans-Field Communication Station (1988)	10.00

CAPTAIN SCARLET
AND THE MYSTERONS
Pedigree (1967)

Captain Scarlet vs. The Mysterons was a 1967 film and British television show done in "Super-Marionation," i.e. with puppets. The Mysterons are Martian invaders whom the Captain and his Spectrum organization battle to save the world. The series was created by Gerry and Sylvia Anderson.

12" Doll (1967) in window box

Captain Scarlet	$210.00
Loose	100.00

CAPTAIN SCARLET
AND THE MYSTERONS
Vivid Imaginations (1993–94)

The British television series, from Gerry Anderson, occasionally aired on the Sci-Fi Channel. As with many of Anderson's programs, it involved his "Super-Marionation" process, with high-tech marionettes. In each episode, Scarlet and his fellow agents of Spectrum took on the Mysterons, a formless intelligence from Mars, wanting nothing less than to destroy the Earth.

Vivid Imaginations tackled this action figure series in 1994 in much the same way that Matchbox handled its two Gerry Anderson properties—Stingray and Thunderbirds. These 4" figures are fine likenesses of their small-screen counterparts and there really isn't any one rare figure in the whole bunch. Collectors really enjoy the Destiny Angel figure that fits in the cockpit of the Electronic Angel Interceptor vehicle.

4" Figures

Destiny Angel (#510163)	$15.00
Captain Black	10.00
Captain Scarlet	10.00
Captain Blue	10.00
Colonel White	10.00
Lieutenant Green	10.00

Destiny Angel,
Captain Scarlet and the Mysterons (Vivid Imaginations 1993)

12" Figures

Captain Scarlet	60.00
Captain Black	60.00

Vehicles

Electronic Angel Interceptor	45.00
SPV vehicle	45.00

CAPTAIN SIMIAN
& THE SPACE MONKEYS
Mattel (1996)

From the animated television series of the same name. Charlie, who later becomes Captain Simian, was launched into space as part of the Space Program, but due to a glitch, he heads out into the abyss of space. Thirty years later he lands on a planet and is mistaken for an emissary from Earth. He is given superior intelligence, high-tech weapons and a crew of simians. His mission is to save the universe from the evil forces of Nebula, "an entity whose only goal is universal destruction," before Nebula becomes "the all-powerful Black Hole and swallows up the entire universe." When the galaxy is safe, Captain Simian will enjoy the ultimate award … a bunch of bananas."

You've heard of a "try-me" pack; these figures come on a header card which allows you to rotate the figure, i.e. a "spin-me" pack. They came out very late in 1996 and it's too early to determine if they will last for long, but one clue

Dr. Splitz, Captain Simian & the Space Monkeys (Mattel 1996)

may be the absence of any mention of this line in Mattel's 1997 Toy Fair press kit. We guess they should have offered Charlie a bigger reward.

5" Figures (Dec. 1996) in Spin-Me Pack

Captain Simian, Heroic Leader "Rifle Shoots" (#15656)	$7.00
Gor-illa, Giant Space Warrior "Bazooka Blasts" (#15657)	7.00
Spydor, Battle Scout "Battle Walker Fires" (#15658)	7.00
Dr. Splitz, Crazy Mechanic "Saw Blade Spins" (#15659)	7.00
Evil Nebula, Wicked Ruler of the Universe "Sceptor Shoots" (#15661)	7.00
Evil Rhesus 2, Sworn Enemy of Captain Simian "Brain Gun Fires" (#15662)	7.00

Large Figures and Vehicles

Speed Peeler	12.00
Gormongus	12.00
Evil Psy-Fighter	12.00

CASPER
Tyco (1995)

From the movie starring Christina Ricci, Bill Pullman, Cathy Moriarty and Eric Idle, which was based on *Casper, The Friendly Ghost* comics first published by St. Johns in 1949 and later under that and many other titles by Harvey Publications. The figures are borderline as action figures.

Figures, in window box

Casper	$12.00
Stinkie	12.00
Fatso	12.00
Stretch	12.00

C.B. McHAUL
Mego (1977)

Produced to capitalize on the Citizens Band radio fad. The figures didn't even last as long as the fad. Except for the fact that they are from the very popular Mego company, no one would even remember these figures. We are lucky this type of theme didn't catch on, otherwise we'd have "Cell-Phone McNewt" figures to worry about today.

3¾" Figures

C.B. McHaul	$8.00
Jim Oakes	8.00
Kidd Watts	8.00
Joe Marconi	8.00
Professor Braine	8.00
Bad Leroy	8.00
Sgt. Brown	8.00
Scowling Jack Jones	8.00
Speed Johnson	8.00

Vehicles

Rig Truck	25.00
Trooper Car	20.00

CENTURIONS
POWERXTREME
Kenner (1986)

"It is the 21st Century on planet Earth. A top military program is stolen from the world master computer. A program that holds the secret to the successful fusing together of man and machine. World leaders meet and discover that the notorious *Dr. Terror* and evil sidekick, *Hacker*, have escaped and have in their possession the top secret computer program! A security alert is sounded worldwide and the only weapon powerful enough to stop the evil duo is revealed—the *Centurions*!" The animated television show began in the fall of 1986.

The Centurions have Exo-Frames and lots of holes in their bodies where accessories attach. They came with Assault Weapon Systems and you could buy more weapons. A second series of figures, vehicles and weapons was offered for 1987, but were not produced.

7½" Figures (1986)

Ace McCloud, Air Operations Expert with "Skyknight Assault Weapon System" (Asst. #17000)	$18.00
Jake Rockwell, Land Operations Expert with "Fireforce Assault Weapon System" (Asst. #17000)	18.00
Max Ray, Sea Operations Expert with "Cruiser Assault Weapon System" (Asst. #17000)	18.00
Dr. Terror, Evil Genius, "Half-Mad and Half-Cyborg" (Asst. #17140)	18.00
Hacker, Dr. Terror's Henchman, "Half-Mad and Half-Cyborg" (Asst. #17140)	18.00

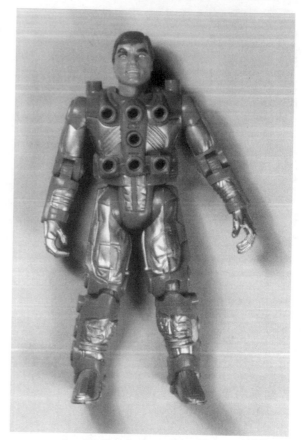

Ace McCloud, Centurions (Kenner 1986)

Assault Weapon System Vehicles (1986)

Sea Bat, Sea Assault Weapon System (#17040)	20.00
Wild Weasel, Land Assault Weapon System (#17060)	20.00
Orbital Interceptor, Air Assault Weapon System (#17080)	20.00
Tidal Blast, Sea Assault Weapon System (#17110)	20.00
Swingshot, Land Assault Weapon System (#17120)	20.00
Hornet, Land Assault Weapon System (#17130)	20.00

Deluxe Assault Weapon System Vehicles (1986)

Skybolt, Air Assault Weapon System (#17160)	25.00
Depth Charger, Sea Assault Weapon System (#17170)	25.00
Detonator Assault vehicle (#17180)	25.00

Weapons and Accessories (1986–87)

Land-Laser (Asst. #17090)	12.00
Aero-Sault (Asst. #17090)	12.00
Aqua-Blazer (Asst. #17090)	12.00

CHARLIE'S ANGELS
Hasbro (1977)

From the ABC television detective show starring Farrah Fawcett-Majors, Kate Jackson, Jacyln Smith and later Cheryl Ladd, which brought T & A to the language and made stars of these shapely young ladies. One very famous bathing suit poster of Farrah didn't hurt either. When Farrah became too big for the show and was replaced by Cheryl Ladd, the logo on the figures' header card was revised to picture "Kris" instead of "Jill." The show ran for four years, with Kate being replaced by Shelley Hack and Shelley by Tanya

Roberts in the final years. No dolls were made for those two dolls.

8½" Dolls on header cards
Jill starring Farrah Fawcett-Majors $60.00
Sabrina starring Kate Jackson 60.00
Sabrina, revised logo 65.00
Kelly starring Jaclyn Smith 60.00
Kelly, revised logo 65.00
Kris starring Cheryl Ladd 60.00

Three-Pack
Gift set of Sabrina, Kris and Kelly 200.00

Vehicles
Adventure Van vehicle 75.00

THE CHIPMUNKS
Ideal (1988)

Juvenile action figures based on *Alvin and the Chipmunks*, which was originally a 1958 song, then a 1961 cartoon series (*The Alvin Show*), before becoming a long running NBC Saturday morning cartoon in the 1980s. Brittany, Jeanette and Eleanor joined the cast in 1988 and the show title became *The Chipmunks*. There aren't a lot of collectors for these figures, but there are probably some.

3¾" "Poseable Play Pals" with clothes
Alvin in concert $7.00
Alvin up for action 7.00
Fair Brittany 7.00
Gentle Jeanette 7.00
Simon in concert 7.00
Everyday Simon 7.00
Sweet Eleanor 7.00
Theodore ready to play 7.00
Theodore in concert 7.00
Uncle Harry in His Best 7.00
Alvin in Superman-type outfit (mail-in) 15.00

Playset
Curtain Call Theater 15.00

"CHiPS"
Mego (1978–81)

From the NBC television show based on the adventures of two California Highway Patrol officers, Ponch and Jon. The series starred Eric Estrada and Larry Wilcox. Another arresting figure production by Mego, which has not proved as popular as their earlier Starsky & Hutch 8" line.

3¾" Figures on header carded
Ponch (#08010/1) $10.00
Jon (#08010/2) 10.00
Sarge (#08010/3) 10.00
Jimmy Squeaks (#08010/4) 15.00
Wheels Willy (#08010/5) 15.00

Figures with Vehicles
Ponch with Motorcycle set (#08022/1, 1979) 20.00
Jon with Motorcycle set (#08022/2, 1979) 20.00
Launcher with Motorcycle set 20.00

Vehicle
Motorcycle 12.00

8" Figures on header card
Jon (#87500/1) 18.00
Ponch (#87500/2) 18.00
Sarge (#87500/3) 18.00

Vehicle for 8" figure
Motorcycle 30.00

CHUCK NORRIS
KARATE KOMMANDOS
Kenner (1986–87)

From the Chuck Norris movies and the animated show "filled with intrigue and adventure, not to mention karate action." Chuck appeared opposite the legendary Bruce Lee in *Return of the Dragon* and has starred in quite a few films of his own. He's a long way from an Academy Award nomination, but he's stuck with it long enough to be considered an actor. The figures didn't stick around nearly that long.

6" Figures (Summer 1986)
Chuck Norris (Battle Gear) with "Dual Flashing Karate
   Chop Action" (#28220) $10.00
Chuck Norris (Kung Fu Training Gi) with "Dragonwhip
   Back Kick Action" (#28230) 10.00
Kimo with "Shogun Sidearm Thrust Action" (#28240) . 10.00
Reed Smith with "Double Flying Falcon Kick Action"
   (#28250) 10.00
Super Ninja with "Cobra Strike Kick Action" (#28260) 15.00
Ninja Warrior with "Typhoon Smash Arm Action"
   (#28270) 15.00
Chuck Norris (Undercover Agent) with "Sekitei
   Somersault Action" (#28300) 10.00
Tabe with "Earthquake Shake Action" (#28310) 10.00

Second Batch (1987)
Ninja Serpent with "Striking Back Kick Action"
   (#28450) 15.00
Ninja Master with "Power Whipping Arm Action"
   (#28460) 15.00

Vehicles and Accessories
Karate Corvette vehicle (#28210, 1986) 18.00

CLASH OF THE TITANS
Mattel (1981)

From the 1981 movie featuring Harry Hamlin with guest appearances by several famous actors slumming as Greek gods. This grand scale Greek epic was Ray Harryhausen's farewell to stopmotion animation films. The figures are popular with collectors and fans of Mr. Harryhausen, even though Mr. Harryhausen himself doesn't care too much for the toys. The Kraken sea monster figure is the most interesting and most popular collectible in the series. Don't waste your time looking for Bubo the Owl or The Lair Playset, because they were never produced, even though they were advertised.

Perseus and Pegasus battle **Kraken**,
Clash of the Titans (Mattel 1980)

3¾" Figures
Calibos, Lord of the Marsh $40.00
Charon, Devil's Boat-Man 55.00
Pegasus, The Winged Horse (#3209) 60.00
Perseus, Hero Son of Zeus 35.00
Thallo, Captain of the Guard 45.00

Figure with Horse
Perseus with Pegasus set 75.00

Large Figure, boxed
Kraken, Sea Monster (#3210) 190.00

CLASSIC MOVIE MONSTERS
Imperial (1986)

The usual Universal Studios monsters, done in an ordinary way. There are a lot of monster figure collectors, but there aren't enough kids who love these monsters to make a hot selling toy line.

8" Figures
Dracula $10.00
Frankensetin 10.00
The Mummy 10.00
Wolfman 10.00

CLOSE ENCOUNTERS
Imperial (1977)

Steven Spielberg's *Close Encounters of the Third Kind* is one of the most popular science fiction movies of all time. The Extraterrestrials didn't appear until the final few minutes of the film and have no lines. Nevertheless, Spielberg's alien design has had great influence—every nut who has seen an alien in the last 20 years remembers it looking like this one. Of course, this could be because Spielberg based his design on the accounts of actual alien abductees who returned from the spaceship hiding in the comet. Mulder and Scully have seen them and The Cigarette Smoking Man has actual killed one, although O.J. was blamed for it, but he didn't do it. We have been sworn to secrecy to protect the President, who got campaign money by holding tea parties for the aliens at the White House. We could tell you how he used the money to pay for the Black Helicopters, but then we would have to shoot you.

Figure
Extra Terrestrial bendable figure 30.00

COMBO HERO
Unknown Manufacturer (1990s)

A group of 10 cheap sci-fi/fantasy figures made in China. These figures may just possibly be worth the $1.00 we saw them selling for.

COMIC ACTION HEROES
Mego (1975–78)

These are soft plastic figures which are somewhat poseable and are borderline, at best, as action figures. However, they are superhero collectibles and were made by Mego, which makes them doubly collectible and quite valuable.

3¾" Figures
Superman (#62101-1) $80.00
Batman (#62101-2) 80.00
Robin (#62101-3) 60.00
Shazam (#62101-4) 75.00
Aquaman (#62101-5) 80.00
Wonder Woman (#62101-6) 60.00
Penguin (#62101-7) 75.00
Joker (#62101-8) 70.00

Second Series
Hulk (#62102-1) 75.00
Spider-Man (#62102-2) 80.00
Green Goblin (#62102-3) 100.00
Captain America (#62102-4) 90.00

Playsets and Vehicles
Collapsing Tower with Invisible Airplane playset with
    Wonder Woman figure 95.00
Exploding Bridge with Batmobile and Activator playset
    with **Batman** and **Robin** figures 130.00
Exploding Bridge playset with **Batman** and **Robin**,
    Joker and **Penguin** figures 175.00
Fortress of Solitude playset with **Superman** figure . 200.00
Mangler vehicle 300.00
Batman's Flying Batcopter with **Batman** figure
    (#62115) 90.00

COMMANDO
SEE: SCHWARZENEGGER COMMANDO

COMMANDO FORCE
Remco (1988–89)

These are 3¾" military figures which have not interested collectors so far.

COMMANDO RANGER
Concept (1987)

Drug store G.I. Joe wannabees, which haven't interested collectors at all, and aren't likely to.

CONAN
Remco (1984)

Conan started off as a pulp fiction character by Robert E. Howard, a grand-master of that type of story. After Howard's death, his fans reprinted the stories in books and new stories were produced. Conan remained in books until his comic book appearance, with Barry Windsor-Smith's artwork, made him famous (Smith too). Later the movies and recently the animated television series appeared.

These figures are based on *Conan the Destroyer* starring Arnold Schwarzenegger, Grace Jones and Wilt Chamberlain.

5½" Figures
Conan "The King"	$35.00
Conan "The Warrior"	35.00
Jewel Thief "The Enemy"	30.00
Devourer of Souls	30.00
Thoth Amon "The Enemy"	30.00

CONAN
Hasbro (1993–94)

The new Conan action figures from Hasbro appeared just before Christmas 1993, even though they have a 1992 copyright. They are 7½" figures and are based on the "action-packed Conan the Adventurer" cartoon television show. The figures in this line all have a pull-string motorized battle action. They didn't sell all that well, and by Christmas 1994 they were discounted. There were even a few around in mid 1996.

7½" Figure
Conan the Warrior (#08141)	$6.00
Conan (the Adventurer) (#08142)	6.00
Zula (#08143)	6.00
Wrath-Amon (#08144)	7.00
Ninja Conan (#08166)	6.00
Conan the Explorer (#08167)	6.00
Greywolf (#08168)	7.00
Skulkur (#08169)	6.00
Battle Cry Conan	8.00

Greywolf, Conan (Hasbro 1993)

Vehicles (1994)
Thunder Battle Stallion with special **Conan** figure (#08177)	15.00
Demon Hunter Battle Stallion with **Wrath-Amon** figure (#08199)	15.00

CONEHEADS
Playmates (1993)

Based on the movie starring Dan Aykroyd and Jane Curtin as Beldar and Prymaat which was based on their "Saturday Night Live" sketches. A lot of collectors were, and still are, fans of the characters from "Saturday Night Live," but the movie did not have the staying power that the SNL character-based film, *Wayne's World*, did. This means that today's kids will not consume mass quantities of these preformed polymer replicants which will, in turn, leave a lot of product around for collectors. Playmates issued all six of their Coneheads figures at the same time, and they all seemed to be readily available. All of the conical-shaped characters met their inevitable destiny at red tag sales about six months later.

5" Figures
Beldar in Suburban Uniform (#7031)	$7.00
Beldar in Full Flight Uniform (#7032)	7.00
Prymaat in Suburban Uniform (#7033)	7.00
Prymaat in Full Flight Uniform (#7034)	7.00
Connie (#7035)	7.00
Agent Seedling (#7036)	7.00

Congo, The Movie (Kenner 1995)

CONGO, THE MOVIE
Kenner (1995)

"Lost in the deepest reaches of the jungle lies a dark secret. Journey with the heroic Congo explorers to the lost city of Zinj with its legendary diamond mines. Beware the ferocious Zinj apes who viciously guard the treasure, destroying all who come near. They're hiding in the jungle—watching and waiting. In the Congo, *you* are the endangered species!"

Based on the 1995 movie from the Michael Crichton novel. The movie starred Dylan Walsh, Laura Linney, Ernie Hudson and Tim Curry, but it was not particularly successful. It wasn't a kid's movie anyway, so all of the figures were available at discount by mid 1996 and were still available at the end of 1996.

5" Figures
Blastface, Mutant Fury with "Vicious Fangs" (Eyes and
    Teeth Glow in the Dark) (#62711) $4.00
Mangler, Fearsome Guardian with "Brute Strength"
    (Eyes and Teeth Glow in the Dark) (#62712) . . . 4.00
Monroe with "Capture Claw & Surprise Attack Blaster"
    (#62713) 4.00
Amy with "Communicator Backpack" (#62714) 4.00
Peter Elliot with "Night Scope Backpack & Tracer
    Assault Weapon" (#62715) 4.00
Karen Ross, 4½" with "Ultra 'Laser' Cannon & Power
    Diamond" (#62716) 4.00
Kahega with "Battle Bazooka & Close Combat Blaster"
    (#62718) 4.00

Deluxe Figures
Deluxe Bonecrusher with "Arm Pounding and Attack Jaw
    Actions" (#62721) 7.00
Deluxe Monroe with "Firing Shoulder Cannon plus Zinj
    Attack Monkey" (#62722) 7.00

Vehicles
Trail Hacker Vehicle with "Blasting Zinj Ape Capture
    Hook" (#62701) 9.00
Net Trap Vehicle with "Aerial Ambush Net" (#62736) . . 9.00

COPS 'N CROOKS
"FIGHTING CRIME IN A FUTURE TIME!"
Hasbro (1988–89)

Bullet-Proof Vess and his lawmen battled Big Boss and his thugs in this animated televison series. The header card for the cops figures says "Cops" while those for the crooks adds "'N Crooks" but they are part of the same series. Each figure came with a "Cap-Firing Pistol" and a roll of caps. This series was fairly successful in its day and a total of 24 figures were issued, in three batches. There is some collector interest, but law enforcement figures are not as popular today as super heroes and science fiction. That could always change tomorrow.

6" C.O.P.S. Figures
A.P.E.S., Automated Police Enforcement Systems
    Officer (#7718) $12.00
Airwave, Communications Officer (#7710) 12.00
Barricade. 12.00
Bullet-Proof, Federal Agent (#7685) 15.00
Checkpoint, Military Police Officer 14.00
Highway 14.00
Inferno, Firefighter 12.00
Longarm, Patrol Officer 15.00
Nightstick, Martial Arts Expert 15.00
Officer Bowzer and Blitz, K-9 Officer and Robot Dog
    (#7687). 12.00
Powder Keg, Bomb Squad Specialist (#7717) 13.00
Sgt. Mace, S.W.A.T. Leader 12.00
Sundown, Texas Sheriff (#7683) 18.00
Taser 12.00

CROOKS Figures
Berserko, Punk 10.00
Big Boss, Crime King 15.00
Bullit, Munitions Fanatic 12.00
Buttons McBoomboom, Machine Gunner (#7684) . . . 10.00
Dr. Badvibes, Mad Scientist (#7690) 10.00
Hyena (#7720) 10.00
Koo Koo, Time Bomb Expert (#7715) 10.00
Louie the Plumber, Crooks Handyman (#7719) 15.00
Nightmare, Attack Animal (#7721) 12.00
Rock Krusher, Escaped Convict (#7686) 15.00

Vehicles
Assault Vehicle (Ironsides) with **Hard Top** figure and
　　Cap-Firing Machine Gun 18.00
A.T.A.C. (Armored Tactical Assault Car) with
　　Heavyweight figure and Cap-Firing Top Gun . . 25.00
Dragster with Cap-Activated Basher (#7627) 15.00
Highway Interceptor (Squad Car) with **Road Block**
　　figure and Cap-Firing Cannon 18.00
Air Speeder (Jail Bird) with Cap-Firing Machine Gun
　　(#7629) 15.00
Lock Up Van 27.50
Pursuit Jet with Cap-Firing Muzzle Blaster (#7646) . . 16.00
Roadster with **Turbo Tutone** figure, and with Cap-Firing
　　Double Machine Gun 20.00
Cops Helicopter (Air Raid) with Multiple Cap-Firing Rotor
　　Blades . . . . no price found

THE CORPS!
Lanard (1986)

Another group of drug store and grocery store G.I. Joe knock-off figures. No one collects them, but you certainly can if you want to. Like all such figures, they are cheap enough.

COW B.O.Y.S. OF MOO MESA
**SEE: WILD WEST
COW BOYS OF MOO MESA**

CRASH DUMMIES
SEE: INCREDIBLE CRASH DUMMIES

CREEPY CRAWLERS
ToyMax (1994–95)

Based on an animated series and produced by ToyMax, which, interestingly enough, was producing newer versions of the original Thingmaker toys at the time.

Goop Mandos Figures
C.C. (Chris Carter) $7.00
Commantis 7.00
Hocus Locust 7.00
Sting Ring 7.00
T-3 (Tick, Tick, Tick) 7.00
Volt Jolt 7.00

Crime Grimes Figures
Professor Guggengrime 7.00
2-Ugly 7.00
Rumble Bee 7.00

Shockaroach 7.00
Spooky Goopy 7.00
Squirminator 7.00

Vehicle
Goozooka vehicle 12.00

Spell of the Evil Wizard, The Saga of Crystar (Remco 1983)

(The Saga of) CRYSTAR
**CRYSTAL WARRIOR
Remco (1983)**

From *The Saga of Crystar, Crystal Warrior* Marvel comic book series which ran from May 1983 to early 1985. The series pits the Forces of Order against the Forces of Chaos.

Figures with Prisma Crystal
Crystar $12.00
Feldspar 12.00
Magma Man 12.00
Moltar 12.00
Ogeode 12.00
Warbow 12.00
Zardeth 12.00

Vehicles and Accessories
Crystal Castle 30.00
Crystal Dragon with Dragon Fly 25.00
Crystal Shatterpult 18.00
Crystal Warrior Battle Set with **Crystal Warrior** figure 28.00
Crystal Warrior Catapult Set with **Crystal Warrior**
　　figure 28.00
Lava Dragon with **Lava Dragon Warrior** figure 28.00
Lava Shatterpult 20.00
The Magic of Crystal with **Ogeode** figure 28.00
Spell of the Evil Wizard 28.00

D

Darkwing Duck, Darkwing Duck (Playmates 1991)

DARKWING DUCK
(Playmates 1991)

Darkwing Duck, "The mysterious mallard of midnight," the "super-sleuthin' secret agent of SHUSH," and his ever faithful sidekick Launchpad McQuack were the stars of a Disney animated television series in the early 1990s.

This figure series, and the companion series, *Talespin*, appeared around Christmas 1991. The Darkwing Duck figure, which was very hard to find at first, became available in quantity when the assortment mix was changed. The 12" figures of Darkwing Duck and Baloo, from the *Talespin* series, were very nice, but each set you back about $20.00 initially. The 1992 additions to these series did not appear, but the original figures were still being pushed in Playmates' 1993 catalog.

3¾" Figures

Darkwing Duck (#2901)	$6.00
Gosalyn (#2902)	6.00
Launchpad McQuack (#2903)	6.00
Honker Muddlefoot (#2904)	6.00
Tuskerninni (#2907)	8.00
Steelbeak (#2908)	8.00
Megavolt (#2909)	8.00
Bushroot (#2910)	8.00

Wind-up Assortment (1992)

Waddling Penguin (#2941)	4.00
Marching F.O.W.L. Egg Man (#2942)	4.00
Snapping Venus Flytrap (#2943)	4.00
Chomping Pizza Mushroom (#2944)	4.00
Prancing Alien Hats (#2945)	4.00

Large Figure

Darkwing Duck 12" collector figure (#2951)	30.00

Vehicles and Accessories

Ratcatcher (#2961)	18.00
Thunderquack Jet (#2962)	25.00
Darkwing Duck Quack 'Copter (#2966, 1992)	28.00

DC COMICS SUPER HEROES
Toy Biz (1989–91)

This series and the Batman series which appeared at the same time on similar header cards were the first and only DC-based super heroes produced by Toy Biz. The three Batman series figures were mixed into the assortments for this series. There were no vehicles for this series, although there were six for the Batman series. Today, Toy Biz produces hundreds of Marvel Comics–based figures, which makes sense since they are now under common ownership, while Kenner took over the production of Batman and other DC Comics figures, starting in 1991.

The rings included with Green Lantern and Superman are valuable kid size premiums, not action features of the toys. The Superman figure was scarce in the later years of this series and both it and the early versions of The Penguin do not seem to have been shipped after the first year or so.

5" Figures

Robin with "Karate Chop" (#4402, 1989) with grappling hook	12.00
Variation, with gun	18.00
Superman with "Kryptonite Ring" (#4403, 1989)	35.00
Wonder Woman with "Power-Arm" (#4404, 1989)	14.00

Wonder Woman, DC Comics Super Heroes (Toy Biz 1990)

Lex Luthor with "Power Punch" (#4408, 1989) 10.00
The Penguin "Umbrella Fires Missiles" (#4409, 1989)
    Small missile 40.00
    Variation, with large missile 30.00
The Penguin "Missile Firing Umbrella" (#4409, 1990) . 9.00
The Riddler with "Riddles & Clues" (#4411, 1989) . . . 12.00
Mr. Freeze "Changes Color" (#4412, 1990) 12.00
Green Lantern with "Water Jet Ring" (#4413, 1990) . 18.00
The Flash with "Running Arm Movement" (#4414, 1990)
    regular-sized logo 6.00
    Variation, with smaller logo (#4414, 1991) 8.00
Aquaman with "Fin Kick Action" (#4415, 1990) $18.00
Hawkman with "Flapping Wing Action" (#4421, 1990) 18.00
Two-Face with "Coin Flipping Action" (#4427, 1990) . 15.00
The Flash with "Turbo Platform" (#4441, 1991) 13.00

DEFENDERS OF THE EARTH
Galoob (1985)

The powers that be at King Features Syndicate thought nothing of licensing out their popular comic strip characters Flash Gordon, Mandrake the Magician, Lothar and The Phantom for this animated atrocity. Your heroes and their offspring help battle Ming the Merciless and his minions who are out on one of his perennial conquests. The die-hard fans of these characters had to swallow their pride to collect their favorites, since these heroes, superheroes and villains were not appearing in other series at the time.

5½" Figures, with Battle Action Knobs (Asst. #5100)
Flash Gordon, Swashbuckling Space Hero $20.00
Garax, Ultimate Evil Robot 25.00

Flash Gordon, Defenders of the Earth (Galoob 1985)

Lothar, Ninja from the Carribean 18.00
Mandrake The Magician, Master of Illusion 22.00
Ming, the Merciless 18.00
The Phantom, Powerful Mysterious Ghost 30.00

Vehicles and Accessories
Defenders Claw Copter 35.00
Flash Swordship 25.00
Garax Swordship 25.00
Gripjaw Vehicle 30.00
Mongor Slithering Evil Serpent (purple) 30.00
Phantom Skull Copter (#5110) 40.00

DEMOLITION MAN
Mattel (1993)

Hot on the heels of 1993's "really big action movie" starring Sylvester Stallone were the action figures from Mattel. It was hard for Sly to do worse than Arnold's *Last Action Hero* bomb, but he managed it. Six months later the figures were found at the red-tag sales. It's sort of unfair, because toys ought to be judged on their own merits, but action figures like this stand or fall on the popularity of the movie. Nothing else much matters. Maybe toy stores should change the "Clearance Aisle" sign to read "This Month's Box Office Bomb Aisle."

5" Figures
Battle Baton Spartan with "Baton-bashing action"
    (#11108) $5.00
Bazooka Attack Spartan "Battle-equipped! Load & Fire!"
    (#11109) 5.00

Battle Baton Spartan, Demolition Man (Mattel 1993)

Combat Cannon Spartan "Combat Ready! Load & fire!"
(#11110) 5.00
Kick-Fighting Spartan with "Smash-kick action"
(#11111) 5.00
Flame-Throwing Phoenix "Scorching torch-action"
(#11112) 5.00
Blast Attack Phoenix with "Water blaster & techno-bow"
(#11113) 5.00
Cryo-Claw Tech with "Sieze & Freeze action" (#11114) 5.00
Battle Hook Friendly with "Hook-launching Firepower"
(#11115) 5.00

Vehicles
Bolajet (#11156) 10.00
Fast Blast 442 (#11153) 15.00

DEPARTMENT OF DEFENSE
Fishel (1987)

Still more small military figures that no one collects.

DERRY DARING
Ideal (1975)

Did we really need a female Evel Knievel? Ideal
thought so, even though they had figures of the real one to
sell.

Flexible Dolls
Derry Daring Western Set $20.00
Derry Daring Action Reporter Set 20.00
Derry Daring Racing Set 20.00
Derry Daring Mountain Climbing Set 20.00

Vehicles and Accessories
Trick Cycle with figure 40.00
Wheelie Car with figure 40.00
Baja Camper 60.00

DESERT PATROL/DESERT STORM
Remco (1991)

Cheap military figures, from previously used molds,
which have drawn no collector interest, despite the name
change to capitalize on the United States war to retake
Kuwait and destroy Saddam Hussein's army. Collectors
should show more respect for United States efforts to keep
the oil tankers full. After all, action figures are largely made
from petrochemicals.

THE DEVIL WARRIORS
Unknown Manufacturer (1990s)

A group of about six cheap fantasy figures made in
China. These figures may just possibly be worth the $1.00
we saw them selling for.

DICK TRACY
Playmates (1990)

Based on the 1990 movie starring Madonna and Warren
Beatty and including Al Pacino as Big Boy and Dustin
Hoffman as Mumbles. The Blank was never sold in the

Mumbles, Dick Tracy (Playmates 1990)

United States, but was available in Canada. This factor, plus the fact that Madonna was secretly the Blank, make the figure a very hot collectible. Dick Tracy was very common and was available in quantity when the figures were finally discounted.

5" Figures
Dick Tracy (#5701)	$10.00
Sam Catchem (#5702)	13.00
The Brow (#5703)	18.00
Shoulders (#5704)	12.00
Al "Big Boy" Caprice (#5705)	18.00
Flattop (#5706	15.00
Itchy (#5707)	18.00
Influence (#5708)	18.00
Pruneface (#5709)	12.00
(Steve) The Tramp (#5711)	12.00
Mumbles (#5712)	18.00
Lips Manlis (#5713)	12.00
The Rodent (#5714)	15.00
The Blank (#570090) not issued in U.S.	175.00

Vehicles
Police Squad Car	45.00
Big Boy's Getaway Car	45.00

Large Figures
Dick Tracy 15" "Special Collector's Edition" (#5797)	50.00
Breathless Mahoney 14" "Special Collector's Edition" (#5798)	60.00

DIE-CAST SUPER HEROES
Mego (1979)

These figure are die-cast metal, with plastic heads (and cloth capes on Batman and Superman). There is no series title. The white header card/boxes have the figures logo and image in color and say "Die Cast Metal" and "Limited Collectors' Edition." Too bad they didn't make more of them. They probably would have, but this was the era of 3¾" Star Wars figures.

5½" Figures, in window box on header card
Batman (#91503)	$125.00
The Incredible Hulk (#91504)	80.00
Superman (#91505)	110.00
The Amazing Spider-Man (#91506)	110.00

DINAH-MITE
Mego (1974)

A fashion doll (with lots of outfits) articulated and poseable like other action figures (and unlike Barbie).

8" Figures
Dinah-Mite (#1400)	$20.00
Black Dinah-Mite (#1450)	30.00
Don (#1490)	20.00

Outfits
Sporting Life (Asst. #1426)
Ski Jump (#1401)	10.00
Racing Around (#1402)	10.00
Up, Up and Away (#1403)	10.00
Sport Cyclist (#1404)	10.00
Scuba Duba (#1405)	10.00
Sea Legs (#1406)	10.00

Swinging Set (Asst. #1425)
Folksinger (#1407)	10.00
Tennis Anyone (#1408)	10.00
Ridin' Around (#1409)	10.00
Roller Derby (#1410)	10.00
Wild Western (#1412)	10.00
Nightingale (#1417)	10.00

Fabulous Fashions (Asst. #1427)
Blazer Days (#1411)	10.00
Brides Bouquet (#1413)	10.00
Super Suede (#1415)	10.00
P.J.'s (#1423)	10.00
Superfly (#1431)	10.00
Brocade Beauty (#1432)	10.00

Vehicle and Playset
Dinah-Mite Camp Mobile (#1465)	35.00
Beach House playset	45.00

DINO-RIDERS
"HARNESS THE POWER OF DINOSAURS"
Tyco (1988–90)

From the animated television show. Cavemen with futuristic weapons riding their dinosaurs into battle—now why would anyone think that was an anachronism? Later, the cavemen got Ice Age creatures, like saber-tooth tigers and mammoths, to carry their weapons into battle. This is many millions of years more accurate, but we still don't know if it's good enough. Ugh to Tusk: "Keep your hairy trunk away from my phaser!" Maybe we can work this into an entry in the annual Edward Bulwer-Lytton contest for the worst opening line in a novel you would never want to read.

2½" Two-pack Figures
First Series (1988) Evil Rulons vs. Heroic Dino-Riders
Termite and Boldar	$12.00
Fang and Mercury	12.00
Fire and Mind-Zei	12.00
Demon and Nova	12.00
Six-Gill and Orion	12.00
Rattler and Proto	12.00
Finn and Quark	12.00
Krulos and Questar	12.00

Second Batch (1989)
Graff and Kraw	12.00
Hondo and Drone	12.00
Mind Zei and Sludgi	12.00
Nevtrino and Poxx	12.00
Questar and Krulos, series 2	12.00
Serena and Skwirm	12.00
Ursus and Snarl	12.00
Yungstar and Dedeye	12.00

Dino-Riders Commando
Astra, Commander	12.00
Bomba, Munitions Expert	12.00
Rok, Mountain Climber	12.00
Kameelian, Infiltrator	12.00

Brontosaurus, Dino-Riders (Tyco 1988)

Faze, Artillary Expert 12.00
Glyde, Paratrooper 12.00

Dino-Riders Ice Age (1990) Caveman vs. Evil Rulons
Tor and Gorr 10.00
Urg and Rayy 10.00
Onk and Buzz 10.00
Agga and Gill 10.00
Wizz and Gutz 10.00
Ecco and Squish 10.00

Small Dinosaurs (1:24 scale)
Ankylosaurus with **Sting** figure (1988) 12.00
Placerias with **Skate** figure (1989) 12.00
Protoceratops with **Kanon** figure (1989) 12.00
Pterodactyl with **Llhad** figure (1988) 12.00
Struthionimus with **Nimbus** figure (1989) 12.00

Medium Dinosaurs (1:24 scale)
Deinonychus with **Skye** figure (1988) 15.00
Quetzacoatlus with **Yungstar** figure (1988) 15.00
Dimetrodon with **Shado** figure (1989) 15.00
Pachycephaslosaurus with **Tagg** figure (1989) 15.00
Styracosaurus with **Tyrret** figure (1989) 15.00
Chasmosaurus with **Llava** figure (1990) 80.00
Quetzalcoatlus with **Algar** figure (1990) 80.00
Deinonychus with **Anor** figure and Rulon Dinotrap
　　(1988) 18.00
Monoclonius with **Mako** figure and Rulon Dinotrap
　　(1988) 18.00

Pteranodon with **Rasp** figure and Rulon Dinotrap
　　(1988) 18.00
Saurolopohus with **Lokus** figure and Hidden Rulon Rock
　　Bunker (1989) 18.00

Large Dinosaurs (1:24 scale)
Brontosaurus with **Ayce**, **Ion** and **Serena** figures
　　(1988) 50.00
Walking Diplodocus with **Questar**, **Mind-Zei** and **Aries**
　　figures (1988) 50.00
Tyrannosaurus Rex with **Krulos**, **Biror** and **Cobras**
　　figures (1988) 75.00
Edmontonia with **Axis** figure (1989) 35.00
Kentrosaurus with **Krok** figure (1989) 35.00
Walking Stegosaurus with **Tank** and **Vega** figures
　　(1989) 35.00
Walking Torosaurus with **Gunnar** and **Magnus** figures
　　(1988) 35.00
Walking Triceratops with **Hammerhead** and **Sidewinder**
　　figures (1988) with comic book 35.00
Walking Pachyrhinosaurus with **Atlos** figure (1990) . 100.00

Medium Mammals (1990) (1:24 scale)
Sabre Tooth Tiger with **Kub** figure 25.00
Killer Wart Hog with **Zar** figure 25.00
Giant Ground Sloth with **Ulk** figure 25.00

Large Mammals (1:24 scale)
Walking Wooly Mammoth with **Grom** figure 35.00

Dinosaucers (Galoob 1988)

DINOSAUCERS
Galoob (1988)

From an animated series with heroic dinosaucers vs. evil Tyrannos. Each one comes on a header card with an optical-action lenticular trading card. They wear non-removable futuristic torso suits so they won't have to run around naked and they carry ray guns. The smaller figures that come with the ships are either their children or their lunch.

8" Figures (Asst. #5400, 1988) with trading card

Bonehead	$8.00
Stego	8.00
Allo	8.00
Bronto Thunder	8.00
Genghis Rex	8.00
Plesio	8.00
Ankylo	8.00
Quakpot	8.00

Vehicles with 2½" figures (Asst. #5404)

Allo ship with **Allo** and **Bonehead** figures	12.00
Stego ship with **Stego** and **Bronto-Thunder** figures	12.00
Genghis Rex ship with **Genghis Rex** and **Plesio** figures	12.00
Ankylo ship with **Ankylo** and **Quackpot** figures	12.00

Playset

Lava Dome Base playset (#5402)	20.00

DINOSAURS
Hasbro (1992)

This toy line is based on the Jim Henson–created television series with Audio-Animatronic dinosaurs. The shows featured the voices of Stuart Pankin, Jessica Walter, Jason Willinger, Sally Struthers and Sherman Hemsley. The figures proved very popular in the stores for a short time. Look for the Robbie Sinclair figure, which was scarce for some reason.

Robbie Sinclair, Dinosaurs (Hasbro 1992)

4½" to 5" Figures

Earl Sinclair (#7181)	$5.00
Fran Sinclair (#7182)	5.00
Charlene Sinclair (#7183)	5.00
Robbie Sinclair (#7184)	6.00
Baby Sinclair (#7185)	5.00
B.P. Richfield (#7186)	5.00

DISNEY
Arco/Mattel (1989)

Very juvenile figures, borderline (at best) as action figures.

Figures

Astronaut Mickey	$9.00
Carpenter Goofy	9.00
Clarabelle Cow	10.00
Cowboy Donald	9.00
Farmer Donald	9.00
Fireman Donald	9.00
Fireman Mickey	9.00
Fun Time Mickey	9.00
Pirate Mickey	9.00
Pluto	9.00
Rock Star Minnie	9.00
Scrooge McDuck	9.00

Playsets

Goofy's Dune Buggy Playset	13.00
Mickey's '57 Chevy Playset	13.00
Donald's Speed Boat Playset	13.00
Wild West Goofy Playset	13.00
Mickey's Safari Adventure Playset	13.00
Dinosaur Donald Playset	13.00

DOCTOR WHO
Denys Fisher (1976)

"Doctor Who" is the long-running B.B.C. television show that was also quite popular in the United States when it was shown here in syndication. The Doctor was regenerated whenever a new actor took over the role, and the show was already on its fourth Doctor when this series came out in 1976. The show made most of its American impact in the 1980s with Tom Baker, the fourth Doctor, in his trademark scarf, battling a variety of villains with the aid of K-9, his trusty robot dog. The most famous of the villains were the Daleks, wheeled robots that first appeared in 1963, and their creator/leader Davros.

Figures
Doctor Who (4th) $200.00
Leela 225.00
Dalek 200.00
Giant Robot 225.00
Cyberman 250.00
K-9 . . . . 250.00

Vehicle
Tardis 300.00

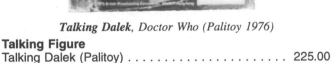

Talking Dalek, *Doctor Who (Palitoy 1976)*

Talking Figure
Talking Dalek (Palitoy) 225.00

DOCTOR WHO
Dapol (1988–95)

"Doctor Who" was still popular in the late 1980s and early 1990s when Dapol got the license to produce action figures. The series celebrated its 25th season in 1988—it's a few years older than "Star Trek" and was in continuous production for the 25 years. By then the show was on its seventh Doctor, played by Sylvester McCoy.

4" Figures
The 7th Doctor, brown coat (#W001) $18.00

Mel (pink shirt), *Doctor Who (Dapol 1988)*

Mel, blue shirt (#W002) 15.00
Mel, pink shirt (#W002) 18.00
K-9, gray (#W004) 10.00
The Tetrap 15.00
Cyberman (#W9) 15.00
Ice Warrior (#W013) 15.00
Ace (#W015) 10.00
Davros with left hand (error) 20.00
Davros, no left hand (correct) 15.00

4" Daleks
White with gold spots 10.00
Black with gold spots 10.00
Black with silver spots 10.00
Gray with blue spots 10.00
Red with black spots 10.00
Red with silver spots 10.00
Red with gold spots 10.00
Gray with black spots 10.00

4½" Daleks using Louis Marx tools, with friction drives
Red Dalek 15.00
Silver Dalek 15.00
Black Dalek 15.00
Gray Dalek 15.00
White Dalek 15.00

6" Daleks from Louis Marx moulds, with tricky-action drives
Silver finish special Dalek 20.00
Gold finish special Dalek 20.00

Vehicles, Accessories and Playsets
Tardis (#W005) 25.00
Doctor Who 25th Anniversary Commemorative Set, diorama playset with Mel (pink shirt), K-9 (green),

7th Doctor (gray coat), red Dalek with black spots, Cyberman, Tardis and battery-operated console (#W022) 125.00
The Dalek Army including seven 4" Daleks plus Davros, in box (#W021) 100.00
Gift Set with Mel (pink shirt), K-9 (green), 7th Doctor (brown coat), red Dalek with black spots, Cyberman and Tardis 100.00

Jimmy Lee, Double Dragon (Tyco 1993)

DOUBLE DRAGON
Tyco (1993)

From Tyco, by way of the video game and the television show, are Billy and Jimmy Lee, the fabled twins with the mark of the Dragon on their chests, out to do battle against the evil Shadowmaster. According to the Legend of the Dragon, "one day, twin boys shall be born who bear the mark of the Dragon. They and only they will have the ability to release the power of the fabled Dragon Sword. As long as they are united, justice shall triumph over evil and the Double Dragons shall prevail against the curse of the Shadow."

There are seven figures, most of which were readily available, and three vehicles which appeared a little later than the figures. Nothing followed and some of the figures were still lingering around as red tag specials in 1996.

5" Figures
Jimmy Lee with "Karate Kick Leg and 'Glowing' Mark of the Dragon" (#10601) $6.00

Billy Lee with "Karate Chop Arm and 'Glowing' Mark of the Dragon" (#10602) 6.00
Vortex with "Whirling Battle Spin and Hand Blaster" (#10603) 6.00
Blaster with "Super Plasma Cannon and Spare Ammo" (#10604) 6.00
Shadow Master with "Slashing Action and Combination Saber/Scythe" (#10605) 6.00
Sickle with "Evil Blades and Slashing Arm Action" (#10606) 6.00
Trigger Happy with "Laser Missile Launcher and Extra Fire Power" (#10607) 6.00

Vehicles
Double Dragon Cycle (#10701) 12.00
Double Dragon Shadow Raven (#10702) 15.00
Double Dragon Cruiser (#01082) 15.00

DRAGON BALL
BanDai (1995–96)

From the animated television series which began airing in September 1995. Goku "a brave, innocent boy with incredible powers" searches for seven magical Dragon Balls, which, when gathered together, will cause the Eternal Dragon to appear and grant him a single wish. His wish will probably be to lose his pushy girlfriend and his evil arch-enemy and spend a peaceful life with his bald buddy. There will be more of these figures in 1997. The television show is very popular in Japan and France.

5" Figures
Staff Slashing Goku (#3802) $6.00
Sword Swinging Yamacha (#3803) 6.00
Fast Kicking Krillin (#3804) 6.00

2" Collectible Figures
Twelve different, each 2.00

DRAGON FLYZ
Galoob (1995–96)

"In the distant future, humankind has risen above the Earth, creating a new world where man and dragon live—and fly—as one. When their sky world is threatened by Dread Wing, self-appointed lord of the netherworld, only one family can protect it from destruction with the aid of their mighty dragon steeds. Three heroic brothers and their valiant sister who carry the noble name of Dragon Flyz!"

There certainly is more action in these figures than most, since they really do fly from their launchers. There is an animated television series as well. So far we have not noticed much collector interest, except possibly in Apex, the female figure of the series.

Figures Without Launcher
Z'Neth with "Sky Storm Assault Gear" (#66201) $6.00
Summit with "Cloud Cover Camo" (#66202) 6.00
Peak with "Solar Blast Power" (#66203) 6.00
Dread Wing with "Molten Lava Skin" (#66204) 6.00
Dram with "Psi-Fly Power Crystal" 6.00
Apex with "Firestorm Camo" 6.00

Apex, Dragon Flyz (Galoob 1995)

Dark Z'Neth with "Windripper Flight Gear" 6.00
Fryte with "Sky Wars Tattoos" 6.00

Dragon boxed
Riptor with "Wing Master Z'Neth and Grem Wing"
   (#66240) 25.00

Figure, Launcher and Flying Grem Wing
Dark Z'Neth and Boltz (#66231) 15.00
Dread Wing and Gorejaw (#66232) 15.00
Peak and Arize (#66233) 15.00

Figure and Launcher (1996) in window box
Z'Neth 10.00
Summit (#66222) 10.00
Peak (#66223) 10.00
Dread Wing 10.00
Apex (#66225) 10.00
Fryte (#66226) 10.00
Fire Flyer Peak 15.00
Orak and Thunderfang 15.00

Battle Blazers in window box
Crystal Storm Z'Neth with Icewing (#66253) 15.00
Luminator Dram with Shock Fire (#66254) 15.00
Thunderblaze Dread Wing with Lightning Boltz
   (#66255) 15.00

DRAGONHEART
Kenner (1996)

From the May 1996 movie starring Dennis Quaid as

Bowen and the voice of Sean Connery as Draco the Dragon along with computer-generated special effects by Industrial Light & Magic. Connery was good and the movie was okay, but quickly forgotten.

According to the toys, Knights live by the Code, which says, "A knight is sworn to valour; His heart knows only virtue; His blade defends the helpless; His might upholds the weak; His word speaks only truth; His wrath undoes the wicked." The figures were discounted well before Christmas. The Knights are pretty ordinary figures. Only Kara, the female figure, has drawn any collector attention. The dragons are interesting figures and might be worth a look.

Hewe, Dragonheart (Kenner 1996)

3½" Figures (April 1996)
Brave Knight Bowen with "Battering Bola Tripod"
   (#61601) $5.00
Bowen with "Spear-Shooting War Weapon" (#61602) . 5.00
Kara with "Axe-Chopping Combat Cart" (#61603) 8.00
Hewe with "Boulder-Launching Catapult" (#61604) . . . 5.00
King Einon with "Charging Crossbow Blaster" (#61606) 5.00
Felton with "Spinning Battle Blade and Mace" (#61607) 5.00

Dragons (May 1996)
Draco with "Power-Flap Wings and Action-Ready Jaws"
   (#61608) 10.00
Medusa Dragon with "Surprise Attack Serpent"
   (#61609) 10.00
Razorthorn Dragon with "Battle-Reactive Thorns"
   (#61611) 10.00

Other Dragons and Playset (Aug. 1996)
Draco Dragon with **Bowen** figure (#61612) 35.00

Draco, Dragonheart (Kenner 1996)

Evil Griffin Dragon and **King Einon** figure (#61613) . 35.00
Electronic Draco (#61614) 45.00
Dragonheart Castle playset (#61616) 20.00

DRAGONRIDERS OF THE STYX
DFC (1984)

This is a fantasy series of generally mediocre quality, with He-Man–type figures riding dragons and other beasts into battle. It's sort of a cross between *Masters of the Uni-*

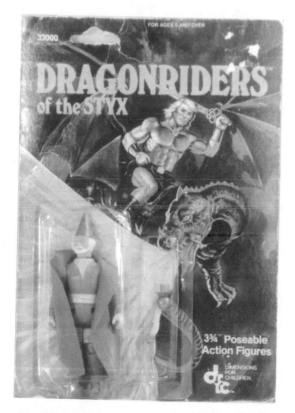

The Wizard, Dragonriders of the Styx (DFC 1984)

verse and Anne McCaffrey's popular science fiction series *The Dragonriders of Pern*. Stick to the originals.

3¾" Figures
The Black Knight $15.00
The Demon Warrior 10.00
Dragon Man 10.00
Guliz the Ogre 10.00
Ragnar the Warrior 10.00
The Wizard 10.00

Horse-like Creatures with Rider
Fantar 12.00
Roozan 12.00

Creatures with Figure in window box with hanging flap
Demon Flyer with figure 12.00
Serpent Rider with figure 12.00

Duelin' Devils, Motorized
The Skull 9.00
The Demon 9.00
The Dragon 9.00
The Spectre 9.00

Vehicles
Mystery Action Dragon (battery operated) 35.00
Skull Sled 8.00

DUKES OF HAZARD
Mego (1981)

You had to be "just a good old boy" in order to really like this line of Mego figures which was based on the late 1970s' CBS television series of the same name. Tom Wopat and John Schneider were Luke and Bo. Catherine Bach played Daisy and Sorrell Brooke played Boss Hogg. Figures were produced in Mego's original 8" size and the new Star Wars 3¾" size.

8" Figures
Bo (#09050/1) $26.00
Bo, with Coy face 28.00
Luke (#09050/2) 26.00
Luke, with Vance face 28.00
Daisy (#09050/3) 50.00
Boss Hogg (#09050/4) 40.00

3¾" Figures
Bo Duke (#09010/1) 16.00
Luke Duke (#09010/2) 16.00
Daisy Duke (#09010/3) 25.00
Boss Hogg (#09010/4) 16.00
Sheriff Rosco Coltrane (#09010/5) 22.00
Uncle Jesse (#09010/6) 22.00
Cooter (#09010/7) 27.00
Cletus (#09010/8) 27.00
Coy on Bo Duke header card 12.00
Vance on Luke Duke header card 12.00

Vehicles with Figures
General Lee Car with **Bo** and **Luke** figures 40.00
Daisy Jeep with **Daisy** figure 30.00
Boss Hogg Caddy with **Boss Hogg** figure 125.00

Baron Harkonnen and Rabban, Dune (LJN 1984)

DUNE
LJN (1984)

Dune, by Frank Herbert, is one of the most highly regarded science fiction novels ever published. Unfortunately, the same cannot be said for the movie, which starred Kyle MacLachlan as Paul, Sting as Feyd and included Jurgen Prochnow as Duke Leto, Max Von Sydow, José Ferrer as the Emperor and Patrick Stewart. It's a complicated story which is much easier to understand in the 45-minute-longer video tape release than in the original theatrical release. The figures owe their popularity to the fame of the source material.

6" Figures with "Battle-Matic" Action
Paul Atreides	$28.00
Stilgar the Freman	28.00

Baron Harkonnen	28.00
Feyd	28.00
Rabban	28.00
Sardaukar Warrior	40.00
Lady Jessica	(not produced)
Gurney Halleck	(not produced)

Vehicles
Spice Scout	30.00
Sandworm monster	40.00
Sand Roller b/o vehicle	30.00
Sand Tracker b/o vehicle	30.00
Sand Crawler b/o vehicle	30.00

DUNGEONS & DRAGONS
SEE: ADVANCED DUNGEONS & DRAGONS

EAGLE FORCE
Mego (1981)

"America's premier strike force to fight world-wide injustice and tyranny." Mego was a lot better off when it stuck to its super hero and Star Trek dolls. But they didn't and so Mego is long gone from the toy industry.

2½" Die-Cast Metal Military Figures
Big Bro', Combat Medic	$6.00
Captain Eagle, The Leader	6.00
The Cat, Escape Artist	6.00
Goldie Hawk, The Blond Bombardier	6.00
Harley, Ace Mechanic	6.00
Kayo, The Judo Fighter	6.00
Stryker, The Sharpshooter	6.00
Turk, The Strongman	6.00
Wild Bill, Cowboy Commando	6.00
Zapper, Electronic Whiz	6.00
Baron Von Chill	6.00
Nemesis	6.00
Red Wing	6.00
Sgt. Brown	6.00

Eagle Force vs. R.I.O.T.
General Mamba, The Ruthless Dictator	6.00
Beta Man, The Arsonist	6.00

R.I.O.T. vs. Eagle Force
Shock Trooper, Soldier of Tyranny	6.00
Savitar, The Assassin	6.00

Eagle Force Vehicles, Accessories and Playsets
The "Eliminator" Jeep with Eagle Mascot	20.00
The "Talon" Tank	22.00
V.T.O.L. Fighter Plane	30.00
Eagle Island Giant Playset	35.00

EARTHWORM JIM
Playmates (1995)

From the 1995 animated series. "The adventure began on a faraway planet where an evil and facially challenged queen, known as Queen Slug-for-a-Butt, commissioned a mad scientist, Professor Monkey-for-a-Head, to deliver a super power suit that would make her all-powerful. As luck would have it, while the suit was on its way to the queen, it fell to Earth and landed right on top of a poor defenseless worm. That worm became Earthworm Jim—super hero to the downtrodden, defender to the Earth, the Cosmos and everything in between! With his newfound powers, Earthworm Jim

Earthworm Jim, Earthworm Jim (Playmates 1995)

battles against Queen Slug-for-a-Butt and her inept henchmen—all for the glory of the greater good, and possibly to save the queen's beautiful and good twin sister, Princess What's-Her-Name."

The figures are whimsical and fun and should appeal to collectors of the Teenage Mutant Ninja Turtles. If they have, we couldn't prove it, and some of them are red tag specials at the moment.

5" Figures
Earthworm Jim (#8601)	$7.00
Battle Damage EWJ (#8602)	7.00
Earthworm Jim in Special Deep Sea Mission Suit (#8603)	9.00
Peter Puppy (#8605)	7.00
Psycrow (#8607)	7.00
Hench Rat & Evil the Cat (#8608)	7.00

Bob & #4 (#8609) 9.00
Princess What's-Her-Name (#8611) 12.00

Vehicles
Earthworm Jim's Pocket Rocket (#8644) 10.00

EMPIRE STRIKES BACK
SEE: STAR WARS

E.T. THE EXTRA-TERRESTRIAL
LJN (1982–83)

From one of the most entertaining (and top grossing) movies of all time, directed by Steven Spielberg and starring Dee Wallace, Henry Thomas and Drew Barrymore. But nobody made action figures out of any of them because the real star was E.T.

Figures
Talking figure (#1253) $30.00
Talking figure, dressed 30.00
Walking figure, glowing heart 18.00
Walking figure, scarf (#1210) 18.00
Walking figure, dress and hat 18.00
Walking figure, robe 18.00
Action figure, glowing heart 10.00
Action figure, scarf with Speak & Spell (#1209) 10.00
Action figure, dress and hat 10.00
Action figure, robe 10.00
E.T. & Elliott-powered Bicycle (#1245) 15.00

EVEL KNIEVEL
"KING OF THE STUNTMEN"
Ideal (1973–74)

Ride into adventure with the self-proclaimed "King of the Stuntmen" in this series of bendy-styled figures and accessories. In 1976, Ideal advertised a Super Jet Cycle for two-man stunts and a Funny Car, but neither has been seen by us.

7" Figures
Evel Knievel, white outfit $45.00
Evel Knievel, red outfit 45.00
Evel Knievel, blue outfit 45.00
Robby Knievel, Teenage Daredevil, 6" 50.00

Vehicles with Figures
Stunt Cycle with figure 80.00
Stunt and Crash Car with figure 100.00
Canyon Sky Cycle with figure 120.00
Formula 1 Dragster with figure 90.00

Vehicles, Accessories and Playsets
Arctic Explorer Set 25.00
Chopper 65.00
Explorer Set 25.00
Racing Set 25.00
Rescue Set 25.00
Road & Trail Adventure Set with figure and Trail Bike 90.00
Scramble Van 70.00
Skull Canyon playset 150.00
Stunt Stadium 125.00
Trail Bike 40.00

EXOSQUAD
Playmates (1993–95)

The ExoSquad figures feature Shawn Napier and his Police Enforcer E-Frames battling to save the earth from Neosapien oppressors. They are based on the animated television series from Universal which starred the voice of Robbie Benson as J.T. Marsh. The series was set in the 22nd century where civilization is threatened by its own greatest achievement—the "genetically engineered perfect race of Neosapiens, led by the ruthless Phaeton, who have turned on their creators." Exo-Frames are "battle-ready exo-skeletal war machines."

The E-Frames look a lot like scaled-up versions of the power-loader used by Ripley to battle the queen alien in the movie *Aliens*. The human figures are small, while the E-Frames vary in size from tiny to gigantic. This is reflected in the packages, which for the larger items are a full 12" cube! Original retail prices varied with size from $3.00 for the smallest figures to $30.00 or more for the largest. These large size differences, rather than scarcity or collector interest, account for much of the price variation in our listing.

General Purpose 5" E-Frame with 3" Figures (Asst. #6300, 1993) in window box with fold-over flap
J.T. Marsh with Aerial Attack E-Frame (#6301) $18.00
   Reissue in hanging window box (#6301, 1995) . 12.00
Alec DeLeon with Field Communications E-Frame
   (#6303) 18.00
   Reissue in hanging window box (#6303, 1995) . 12.00
Phaeton with Command E-Frame (#6304) 18.00
   Reissue in hanging window box (#6304, 1995) . 12.00
Typhonus with High Speed Stealth E-Frame (#6306) . 20.00
   Reissue in hanging window box (#6306, 1995) . 12.00

General Purpose 5" E-Frame with 3" Figures (Asst. #6300, 1994) in window box with fold-over flap
Sean Napier with Police Enforcer E-Frame (#6302) . . 15.00
   Reissue in hanging window box (#6302, 1995) . 12.00
Wolf Bronski with Ground Assault E-Frame (#6305) . 15.00
   Reissue in hanging window box (#6305, 1995) . 12.00
Nara Burnes with Reconnaissance E-Frame (#6307) . 15.00
   Reissue in hanging window box (#6307, 1995) . 12.00
Rita Torres with Field Sergeant E-Frame (#6308) . . . 15.00
   Reissue in hanging window box (#6308, 1995) . 12.00

General Purpose 5" E-Frame with 3" Figures (Asst. #6300, 1995) in hanging window box
General Draconis with Interrogator E-Frame (#6309) . 12.00
Jonas Simbacca with Pirate Captain E-Frame (#6310) 12.00
Peter Tanaka with Samurai E-Frame (#6311) 12.00
Jinx Madison with Fire Warrior E-Frame (#6312) 12.00
Marsala with Sub-Sonic Scout E-Frame (#6313) 12.00

Light Attack 8" E-Frames with 3" Figure (Asst. #6320, 1993–94) battery powered in large try-me box
Maggie Weston Field Repair Light Attack E-Frame
   (#6321, 1994) 28.00
Livanus Troop Transport Light Attack E-Frame (#6322,
   1994) Neosapien 28.00
General Shiva with Amphibious Assault Light Attack E-
   Frame (#6323, 1993) 28.00
Marsala with Rapid Assault Light Attack E-Frame
   (#6324, 1993) 28.00

Jumptroops with Ultralight E-Frame Battle Machines (Asst. #6380, 1994–95) on header card
Gunnery Sergeant Ramon Lightfeather (Heavy Gravity) (#6381) 7.00
Lance Corporal Vince Pellegrino (Fireboss) (#6382) . . 7.00
Second Lieutenant Colleen O'Reilly (Rapid Recon) (#6383) 7.00
Captain Avery F. Butler (Command) (#6384) 7.00

Special Mission 5" E-Frames (1995) in box with flap
J.T. Marsh with Deep Space Special Mission E-Frame (#6861) 14.00
Alec DeLeon with All-Terrain Special Mission E-Frame (#6862) 14.00
Typhonus with Deep Submergence Special Mission E-Frame (#6863) 14.00
Wolf Bronski with Subterranean Special Mission E-Frame (#6864) 14.00

Neosapien Warriors (1995) on header card
Neo Lord with Metallic Assault Armor (#6392) 10.00
Neo Cat with Metallic Predator Armor (#6393) 10.00

Exoconverting E-Frame (1995) in box with hanging flap
J.T. Marsh with Exoconverting Aerial Attack E-Frame (#6871) 15.00

Real Walking Series (1995) in huge cubical box
Marsala with Exowalking Light Attack E-Frame (#6351) 22.00
Livia with Neo Sapien Walking Light Attack E-Frame (#6352) 28.00

Mini Exo-Command Assortment (1996)
Phaeton and J.T. Marsh with Olympus Mons Command Ship Bridge Battleset (#16342) 7.00
J.T. Marsh and Typhonus with Resolute II Hangar Battleset (#16341) 7.00
Alec DeLeon and Phaeton with Vesta Space Port Battleset (#16343) 7.00

Space Series E-Frames, in large cubical box
Kaz Takagi with Exo-fighter Space E-Frame (#6361) . 28.00
Thrax with Neo-fighter Space E-Frame (#6362) 28.00

Vehicle
Exocarrier Resolute II (#6372) 27.00

EXOSQUAD ROBOTECH SERIES
"THE ORIGINAL BATTLE MACHINES"
Playmates (1995)

In 1995, Robotech Defense Force war machines have come to reinforce mankind's final hope, the ExoSquad! They get there through a space fold, since they have different backgrounds. While this sounds like the robot version of free-agency, it was actually a trade with Playmates acquiring the Robotech toy license for a utility infielder, two draft choices and, most importantly, some cash.

3" Attack Mecha Figures (1995)
Excaliber MK VI Battloid Tactical Corps Assignment (#6851) $3.00

Spartan Battloid, Exosquad, Robotech Series (Playmates 1995)

Raidar X Battloid Tactical Corps Assignment (#6852) . 3.00
Gladiator Battloid Tactical Corps Assignment (#6853) . 3.00
Spartan Battloid Tactical Corps Assignment (#6854) . . 3.00
Excaliber MK VI Battloid Civil Defense Unit (#6855) . . 3.00
Raider X Battloid Civil Defense Unit (#6856) 3.00
Gladiator Battloid Civil Defense Unit (#6857) 3.00
Spartan Battloid Civil Defense Unit (#6858) 3.00

7" Robotech Defense Force Attack Mecha (1995)
Excaliber MK VI Destroid (#6331) 9.00
Gladiator Destroid (#6332) 9.00
Spartan Destroid (#6333) 9.00
Raidar X Destroid (#6334) 9.00

7" Invid and Zentraedi Attack Mecha (1995)
Zentraedi Power Armor Botoru Battalion (#6335) 9.00
Zentraedi Power Armor Quadrona Battalion (#6336) . . 9.00
Invid Scout Ship (#6337) 9.00
Bioroid Invid Fighter (#6338) 9.00

Battlepod Class E-Frames (1995) on header card
Zentraedi Tactical Battlepod (#6354) 18.00
Invid Shock Trooper (#6355) 18.00
Officer's Battlepod (#6356) 18.00

Vehicles (1995) boxed
VeriTech Hover Tank (#6357) 25.00
VeriTech Fighter (#6358) 20.00

FAMOUS MONSTERS OF LEGEND
Tomland/Combex (1977)

The Cyclops is from a famous old legend and the Abominable Snow Man legend may be equally old, but Morlock's are from H.G. Wells' *The Time Machine* and the Fly is from the 1958 movie starring Vincent Price. Anyway, they are all legendary here.

Figures

Cyclops	$225.00
The Fly	200.00
Morlock	250.00
Abominable Snow Man	200.00

FANTASTIC FOUR
Toy Biz (1994–96)

In 1994 Toy Biz (and Marvel) broke out the Fantastic Four (plus Iron Man, Ghost Rider, etc.) into their own line of action figures. This made sense, considering the huge number of figures they produced in this period. Almost all of the figures were over-produced and could be found at red-tag prices at the end of 1996. Most of the collecting interest centered on Invisible Woman and Human Torch, both of which appeared in the second batch and went through feature changes. Both versions of Invisible Woman and the "Glow-in-the Dark" Human Torch were scarce. The number of figures from this series that fell onto toy store floors while collectors looked for these scarce figures would have made a good sized mutant army.

5" Figures

The Thing "Clobberin' Time Punch" (#45101)	$7.00
Black Bolt with "Flight Ready Wings" (#45102)	7.00
Silver Surfer "Space Surfing" (#45103)	8.00
Mole Man with "Twirling Combat Staff" (#45104)	7.00
Terrax with "Space Soaring Meteor" (#45105)	7.00
Dr. Doom with "Shooting Arm Action" (#45106)	7.00
Mr. Fantastic with "Super Stretch Arms" (#45107)	7.00

Second Batch (1995)

Invisible Woman (blue costume) with "Invisible Force Shield and Rolling Platform" (#45108)	30.00
Human Torch with "Glow-in-the-Dark Flames with Catapult Launcher" (#45109)	20.00
Human Torch with "Flame-On Sparking Action" (#45111)	6.00
Invisible Woman (clear) with "Invisible Force Shield and Rolling Platform" (#45112)	12.00
Gorgon with "Hoof Stompin' Action" (#45113)	6.00

Mr. Fantastic, *Fantastic Four (Toy Biz 1994)*

Firelord with "Cosmic Flame Launcher" (#45114)	6.00
Thanos with "Pulverizing Gauntlet Action" (#45115)	6.00
Dragon Man with "'Fire' Breathing Action" (#45116)	6.00
Blastaar with "Power Blast Action" (#45117)	6.00

Third Batch (1995)

The Thing II with "Undercover Disguise" (#45121)	6.00
Namor, Power Punch with "Undersea Trident and Shield" (#45122)	6.00
Annihilus with "Cosmic Control Rod Transforming Mutant" (#45123)	6.00
Attuma with "Sword Slashing Action" (#45125)	6.00
Super Skrull with "Super Extending Power Punch Action" (#45126)	6.00
Triton with "Swimming Action with Attack Shark and Sea Trumpet" (#45127)	6.00

Fourth Batch (April 1996)

The Thing with "Rock Breaking Action Platform" (#45131)	6.00

The Thing, Fantastic Four (Toy Biz 1996)

Human Torch (Johnny Storm) with "Firestorm Action
    Platform" (#45132) 6.00
Wizard with "Disc Firing Action Platform" (#45134) ... 6.00
Psycho-Man with "Emotion Detector Action" Platform
    (#45136) 6.00
Medusa with "Hair Snare Action Platform" (#45137) . 10.00

Vehicles and Accessories
Galactus 14" electronic figure (#45310) 18.00
Fantasticar, Cosmic Modular Space Vehicle (#45320) 30.00
The Thing's Sky Cycle (#45325) 10.00
Mr. Fantastic's Sky Shuttle (#45330) 10.00

10" "Fantastic Four" Figures
Silver Surfer (#45501) 10.00
Human Torch (#45502) 10.00
Dr. Doom (#45503) 10.00
The Thing (#48125) 10.00
Johnny Storm (#48406) 10.00

FANTASTIC FOUR/IRON MAN
Toy Biz (1995)

These special "Collector's Edition" two-figure packs
were WalMart exclusives. They came with a collector pin.
The same figures were available individually in Toy Biz's
regular figure assortments.

Collector's Editon Two-Packs with collector pin
Dr. Doom vs. Iron Man (#45511) $20.00
The Thing vs. War Machine (#45512) 20.00

Silver Surfer vs. Mandarin (#45513) 20.00
Mr. Fantastic vs. Iron Man, Hydro Armor (#45514) .. 30.00

FANTASY WORLD
Arron's (1986)

Fantasy World was a series of Masters of the Universe
and He-Man knockoffs. There are eight figures in all, worth
about $4.00 each.

FIGHTING YANK
Mego (1974)

A typical Mego-type doll, this time designed to
compete with G.I. Joe. It didn't work and no one collects
him, and even if someone collects him it's because he is a
Mego doll, not because of his military prowess.

12" Figure
Fighting Yank figure (#3360) $25.00

Outfits
Frog Man (#3363) 12.00
MP Outfit (#3364) 12.00
Flight Outfit (#3365) 12.00
Air Force (#3366) 12.00
Marine Dress (#3367) 12.00
Special Forces (#3368) 12.00
Navy Dress (#3369) 12.00
West Point Cadet (#3370) 12.00
Snowbound (#3371) 12.00
Ski Patrol (#3372) 12.00

FILMATION'S GHOSTBUSTERS
Schaper (1986)

Based on the 1980s animated series by Filmation which
was based on the 1970s live-action television kids show
starring Forrest Tucker and Larry Storch. It has nothing to do
with the Dan Aykroyd movie. Figures from the movie are
listed later under Real Ghostbusters.

5" Figures
Belfry and Brat-A-Rat $12.00
Eddie 12.00
Fangster 14.00
Fib Face 12.00
Futura 16.00
Haunter 12.00
Jake 12.00
Jessica 16.00
Mysteria 18.00
Prime Evil 14.00
Scared Stiff 12.00
Tracy 12.00

Vehicles and Accessories
Bone Troller 12.00
Ghost Command set 28.00
Ghost Buggy 40.00
Scare Scooter 18.00
Time Hopper 15.00

FLASH GORDON
Mego (1976)

Flash Gordon was originally a 1934 comic strip by Alex Raymond which was designed to compete with the highly popular Buck Rogers. His spaceship, ray gun and heroism became necessary components of just about every subsequent science fiction series. There were three black and white serials from the late 1930s starring Buster Crabbe as Flash and Charles Middleton as Ming. These were shown on television in the 1950s, keeping the series alive.

9½" Figures on header card
Flash Gordon (#4400/1)	....	$68.00
Ming the Merciless (#4400/2)	....	68.00
Dr. Zarkov (#4400/3)	....	80.00
Dale Arden (#4400/4)	....	75.00

Playset
Flash Gordon Playset	....	150.00

FLASH GORDON
"THE GREATEST ADVENTURE OF ALL"
Mattel (1979)

Based on the animated television series, not the lousy live-action film from 1980. Flash Gordon remains one of the classics of early adventure science fiction to this day.

3¾" Figures
Flash Gordon (#1525)	....	$15.00
Ming (#1526)	....	15.00
Lizard Woman (#1527)	....	28.00
Thun, the Lion Man (#1528)	....	20.00

Second Series
Dr. Zarkov (#1529)	....	32.00
Beastman (#1530)	....	35.00

Third Series
Captain Arak (#1531)	....	90.00
Vultan (#1532)	....	100.00

Vehicle/Spaceship
Flash Gordon Rocketship, 30" inflatable (#1535)	....	25.00

FLASH GORDON
Playmates (1996)

The figures are from an updated animated television series. "The moons of Mongo cast desperate shadows across a desolate planet. The world of Mongo lay devastated, a hopeless vessel of slavery, adrift under the rule of a mighty emperor, Ming the Merciless." Nothing can save the universe except Flash Gordon, in this version "a hip, flip skateboardin' teenager with an attitude." We don't know about you, but we'd put our money on Ming.

The press release says, "He's back ... but he sure isn't the same Flash Gordon Dad remembers." They were right about that, which was too bad, because the one these dads remember was a lot better. Both the characters and figures looked like teenagers and didn't appeal to collectors. They bought the babes—Dale Arden and Princess Thundar—but had no interest in the other figures. Ming showed more mercy for Flash than the kids did, and the figures all had red tags by December. That's when the vehicles were first spotted.

Ming the Merciless and Princess Thundar, Flash Gordon (Playmates 1996)

Crash Test Barney, Flintstones (Mattel 1994)

5" Figures (Aug. 1996)
Flash Gordon in Flight Suit (#12401) $6.00
Flash Gordon in Mongo Outfit (#12402) 6.00
Dale Arden (#12403) 12.00
Prince Talon (#12404) 6.00
Princess Thundar (#12405) 15.00
Ming the Merciless (#12406) 6.00
General Lynch (#12407) 6.00
Kobalt the Mercenary (#12408) 6.00

Vehicles
Triphibian (#12453) 16.00
Flash Gordon Rebel AirBike (#12461) 10.00
Ming's Jaws of Death Throne (#12462) 10.00

FLINTSTONES
Mattel (1994)

These figures are based on the live-action Flintstones movie starring John Goodman as Fred, Rosie O'Donnell, Rick Moranis, Elizabeth Perkins and Kyle MacLachlan. The movie was heavily promoted as "The Event" of the summer of 1994, but the truth was that the 1960s' cartoon series was better, and it was loosely based on Jackie Gleason's Honeymooners from the 1950s, which was a classic. Toy series like this are not popular with collectors unless the movie turns out to be a winner (or perhaps a colossal turkey). Even then, success is not guaranteed and we suspect that figures based on the television cartoon might be more collectible. The collector's verdict on these figures so far is, "Yabba Dabba Don't!"

The faces are sculpted to look like the actors, not the cartoon. Collectors, if any, looked for the second batch of figures, which are less common than the various versions of Fred and Barney. We picked up a free box of stuff called *"R" Treat* from Toys "R" Us, created by Market Source, which was given away to anyone who bought a Flintstones action figure. For the record, the box contained some Puffs tissues; small bags of Crunch 'n Munch, Gummy Bears, Teddy Grahams and Rain-Blo; a container of Hawaiian Punch and some Mother's Day coupons, none of which had anything to do with the Flintstones, except the box. We decided to collect the box.

First Batch
Hard Hat Fred (#11654) $5.00
Big Shot Fred (#11655) 5.00
Lawn Mowin' Barney (#11656) 5.00
Fillin' Station Barney (#11657) 5.00

Second Batch
Evil Cliff Vandercave (#11658) 6.00
Licking Dino (#11659) 6.00
Wilma & Pebbles (#11660) 6.00
Betty & Bamm-Bamm (#11661) 6.00

Boxed Figures
Bowl-O-Rama Fred (#11663) 4.00
Big Bite Fred (#11664) 4.00
Crash Test Barney (#11665) 4.00
Dyno-Drilling Barney (#11666) 4.00
Yabba-Dabba-Doo Fred (#11667) large figure 4.00

Vehicles
The Flintmobile (#11668) 10.00
Le Saber Tooth 5000 (#11669) 15.00

THE FLINTSTONE KIDS
Coleco (1987)

It has worked before, so Hanna Barbera tried to make a new "Flintstone Kids" cartoon series in the mid 1980s. It was shown on ABC, but didn't last too long. The figures, and the show, were designed for younger kids and this will probably keep the collector interest down.

5" Figures
Freddy Flintstone (#6701) $13.00
Barney Rubble (#6702) 13.00
Wilma Slaghoople (#6703) 15.00
Betty Jean Bricker (#6704) 18.00
Dino (#6705) 12.00
Fang (#6706) 12.00

Second Series (1988) "Hanna Barbera's The Flintstone Kids"
Rocky Ratrock with Stalagmutt (#6707) 30.00
Dreamchip Gemstone 25.00
Philo Quartz (#6709) 25.00
Nate Slate (#6711) 25.00
Cavey, Jr. (#6712) 25.00
Micki 25.00

Vehicles and Playsets
Bedrock Fire Fighter (#6721) 18.00
Bedrock Airlines (#6722) 30.00
Dreamchip Limo (#6723) 18.00
Town of Bedrock Prehistoric Play Town with Mailman
 (#6731) 45.00
Bedrock Elementary School with Girl (#6732) 40.00

THE FLINTSTONES IN ACTION
Irwin (1985)

This is a Canadian series, based on the original, and still popular television show. "Yabba Dabba Doo!"

4" Figures
Fred $25.00
Barney 25.00
Wilma 30.00

Betty 30.00
Pebbles & Bamm-Bamm 35.00
Dino 25.00
Fred Policeman 30.00
Barney Policeman 30.00

Vehicles
Flintmobile 50.00
Barney's Car (#060) 45.00
Motorbike (#063) 20.00
Police Car 60.00

FOOD FIGHTERS
Mattel (1988–89)

A borderline series, at best. There were 10 figures, with names like Private Pizza, and three vehicles. The figures are worth about $5.00 each.

FORT APACHE FIGHTERS
SEE: BEST OF THE WEST

FOX'S PETER PAN & THE PIRATES
THQ, Inc. (1991)

From the FOX network animated television series. Not very many people collect this series and whatever interest it has generated comes from the enduring fame of Peter Pan and not from the television show.

Figures
Peter Pan $7.00
Captain Hook 7.00
Robert Mullins 7.00
Alf Mason 7.00
Smee 7.00
Wendy 9.00
Tinker Bell 9.00
The Mermaid 12.00

GALAXIE GIRL
GALAXY ADVENTURE GIRL
GALAXY FIGHTER
GALAXY WARRIORS
Various Manufacturers (1980s)

All of these series came out in the mid 1980s as knock-offs of the *Masters of the Universe* and *Princess of Power* toy lines. The first and last were Woolworth's exclusives and the other two are drug store series. There is nothing wrong with these series, but collectors have found nothing interesting in them either. There are about six to eight figures in each series and they are worth from $3.00 to $7.00 apiece.

GARGOYLES
Kenner (1995–96)

"Frozen in stone by day, flesh and blood winged warriors by night. Awaking after a thousand years, a band of powerful Gargoyles find themselves transported to a time and place not their own—New York City." They come from a Scottish castle by means of a 1994 animated movie, which was pretty good. They also have an animated television series and a comic book series. Not bad for flying stones.

Collectors have shown particular interest in Elisa Maza, an NYPD cop who helps the Gargoyles fight crime and evil. She and Demona are the female figures in the line. The series is still being shown on television and at the 1997 Toy Fair, Hasbro/Kenner still had these figures on display, but no new figures were offered. That probably means they will be red tag specials by the summer of 1997.

5" Figures

Quick Strike Goliath with Leaping Attack Action (#65521) $7.00
Stone Armor Goliath (#65522) 7.00
Lexington (#65523) 8.00
Broadway (#65524?) 7.00
Brooklyn with "Striking Horns and Snapping Jaw" (#65525) 7.00
Xanatos, with "Gargoyle Disguise Armor and Battle Wings" (#65531) 8.00
Demona, with "Firing Stungun and Wing Flap Action" (#65532) 10.00
Steel Clan Robot with "Exploding Body Power" (#65533) 7.00

Elisa Maza, Gargoyles (Kenner 1996)

Second Batch

Claw Climber Goliath with "Highrise Climbing Gear" (#65526) 7.00
Battle Goliath with "Blasting Combat Mace and Spear" (#65527) 7.00
Hudson with "Sword Thrusting Body Blow" (#65528) .. 8.00
Bronx (#65529) 8.00
Strike Hammer MacBeth with "Pounding Stone Blaster Weapon" (#65534) 7.00

Third Batch

Elisa Maza with "Rocket Wing Jet Pack" (#65538) .. 12.00
Rainstorm Hudson (#65542) 7.00
Flamestorm Goliath with "'Fireball' Throwing Action" (#65543) 7.00
Icestorm Brooklyn with "'Icicle' Blasting Power" (#65544) 7.00

Deluxe Figures

Power Wing Goliath with "Deluxe Wingblast Mechanized

Action" (#65516) 10.00
Mighty Roar Goliath with "Deluxe Electronic Battle Roar
  and Light-Up Eyes" (#65517) 10.00

Vehicles and Playset
Rippin' Rider Cycle (#65536) 9.00
Night Striker Action Vehicle (#65545) 12.00
Gargoyle Castle playset (#65514) 35.00

Series 2 Figures
Stone Camo Broadway with "Overhead Throw Battle
  Axe" (#65556) 7.00
Stone Camo Lexington with "Power Bow Blaster"
  (#65557) 7.00
Xanatos with "Steel Clan Battle Armor and Poseable
  Wings" (#65576) 7.00

Deluxe Battle Doubles (Oct. 1996)
Lion Bronx with "Winged Beast Combat Armor"
  (#65572) 12.00
Minotaur Goliath with "Raging Bull Battle Armor"
  (#65573) 12.00
Griffin Goliath with "Fearsome Predator Attack Armor"
  (#65574) 12.00

Hard-Wired Broadway, Gargoyles (Kenner 1996)

Hardwired Figures (Fall 1996)
Hard-Wired Goliath with "Holo-Blast Wings and Attack
  Gauntlet" (#65581) 8.00
Hard-Wired Broadway with "Spinning Battle Claw"
  (#65582) 8.00
Hard-Wired Lexington with "Power-Attack Wings and
  Rocket Blast-Pack" (#65583) 8.00
Hard-Wired Xanatos with "Blast-Damage Chest Plate
  and Energy Pulse Weapon" (#65584) 8.00

Hard-Wired Coldstone with "Blasting Robo-Arm"
  (#65586) 8.00

Large Figure
Ultimate Goliath (#65541, 1996) 28.00

Banshee, Generation X (Toy Biz 1995)

GENERATION X
Toy Biz (1995)

Generation X Marvel figures are supposed to be the next class of young mutants in training at Professor Xavier's school. They got their own comic book series in October 1994 and a television movie on Fox in 1996.

When the first Generation X figures arrived just before Christmas 1995, collectors were surprised to find two females in the group—Jubilee and Penance. The entire previous Marvel, X-Men, Spider-Man, Iron Man and Ghost Rider lines had only produced a total of 12 versions of 7 other female characters.

The second batch, called "Sophomores" in Toy Biz's 1996 catalog, also had two female figures—White Queen and Marrow. By the time they appeared, collector interest in Marvel Comics female characters was falling quickly. The vast oversupply of figures in general, coupled with the fact that the females were not being short-packed in the five figure assortments, meant that none of the 1995 and 1996 females were scarce.

Generation X figures were discounted by the end of 1996, along with most other Marvel figures. When prices will rebound is anybody's guess.

5" Figures
Chamber with "Sparking Energy Portal" (#43117) ... $6.00
Penance with "Claw Slashing Action" (#43118) 7.50
Skin with "Growing Fingers" (#43119) 6.00
Jubilee with "Plasma Hurling Action" (#43120) 7.50
Emplate with "Arm Extending Action" (#43121) 6.00
Phalanx with "Live Captive Heads" (#43122) 6.00

Second Batch (Aug. 1996) "X-Men Generation X"
Marrow with "Detachable Bone Weaponry" (#43141) .. 7.50
Mondo with "Organic Armor Plating" (#43142) 6.00
White Queen with "Psychic Energy Spear" (#43143) .. 9.00
Banshee with "Portable Cerebro Blaster" (#43144) ... 6.00
The Protector with "Hidden Chest Blast" (#43146) 6.00

GEN. PATCH
Galoob (1983)

These are fully poseable figures, with 10 points of articulation. With the figures you got a mini comic book and weapons with the "smell of battle." However, collectors want G.I. Joe figures and nothing else, so these are not collected.

GHOSTBUSTERS
SEE: FILMATION'S GHOSTBUSTERS
OR SEE: REAL GHOSTBUSTERS

GHOST RIDER
Toy Biz (1995)

"The deafening howling of two-wheeled fury and a blinding flash of spiritfire signals the arrival of Ghost Rider, roaring onto the scene to protect the lives of innocent beings everywhere!" Marvel's Ghost Rider dates back over 20 years to his first comic book in Sept. 1973. The first batch of figures is sub-titled "Midnight Sons" and the second is called "Siege of Darkness" in the Toy Biz catalog. A couple of series of cycles and riders also appeared.

The Ghost Rider series of figures was part of Marvel and Toy Biz's efforts to expand and divide the Marvel characters line into separate groups. The Ghost Rider comics are fairly popular, but this line of toys didn't catch on and was one of the first to be discounted. The figures came with a mini comic and first appeared in November 1995, although Skinner did not show up until early 1996.

5" Figures with mini comic
Ghost Rider with "Chain Whipping Action" (#52301) . $6.00
Blaze with "Mystical Flame Firing Action" (#52302) ... 6.00
Vengeance with "Rib Clawing Action" (#52303) 6.00
Skinner with "Extending Rib Action" (#52305, 1996) . 12.00
Blackout with "Vampire Attack Action" (#52306) 6.00
Ghost Rider II with "Transforming Action" (#52307) ... 6.00

Second Batch (July 1996) with mini comic
The Original Ghost Rider with "Exploding Ghostfire Chest" (#52311) 6.00

Armored Blaze, Ghost Rider (Toy Biz 1995)

Exploding Ghost Rider with "Exploding Torso Action" (#52312) 6.00
Armored Blaze with "Light-Up Ghostfire Chest" (#52313) 6.00
Outcast with "Claw-Ripping Action" (#52314) 6.00
Zarathos with "Ghostfire Hurling Action" (#52316) 6.00

10" "Ghost Rider" Figures with Glow-in-the-Dark Features
Ghost Rider (#52401) 10.00
Blaze (#52402) 10.00
Vengeance (#52403) 10.00

Flamin' Stunt Cycle Vehicles with Figure
Ghost Rider's "Ghost Fire" Cycle (#52436) 12.00
Blaze's Dark Cycle (#52437) 12.00
Vengeance's Steel Skeleton Cycle (#52438) 12.00

Spirits of Vengeance Cycle and 5" Rider, boxed
Ghost Rider (#52431) 9.00
Blaze (#52432) 9.00
Vengeance (#52433) 9.00

12" Ghost Rider (Oct. 1996)
Ghost Rider Special Collectors Edition 12" figure with costumes (Toy Biz #48417, 1996) 28.00

G.I. Joe Action Soldier, G.I. Joe (Hasbro 1964)

G.I. JOE
"AMERICA'S MOVEABLE FIGHTING MAN"
Hasbro (1964–76)

In short, the best known, best loved and most collectible action doll ever made. G.I. Joe spans a history of over 33 years and is still going strong into 1997 with many new dolls scheduled. Even though there were some tough times during the mid to late 1970s and a couple of mishaps in the mid 1990s, nothing can stop G.I. Joe's incredible popularity. Vietnam war hostility turned him into an adventurer, the OPEC oil embargo shrank him and he was "extreme"ly embarrassed recently, but he won the hearts and minds of collectors long ago and he's still going strong. This is due to some caring and intelligent individuals within Hasbro and to the many collectors and fans across the country who have helped bring him to the renaissance he is experiencing today!

11½" G.I. Joe Dolls with 21 points of articulation

G.I. Joe Action Soldier with fatigues, jump boots, cap, dog tags, insignias and Army Manual (#7500, 1964) $400.00

G.I. Joe Action Sailor with work shirt and pants, boots, cap, dog tags, insignias and Navy Manual (#7600, 1964) 450.00

G.I. Joe Action Marine with fatigues, assault jump boots, green cap, dog tags, insignias and Marine Manual (#7700, 1964) 400.00

G.I. Joe Action Pilot with work clothes, flight boots and cap, insignias, dog tags, Pilot Manual (#7800, 1964) 600.00

G.I. Joe Action Soldier Negro with same equipment as original G.I. Joe (#7900, 1965) 1,900.00

G.I. Joe Action Green Beret with fatigue jacket, jungle fatigue pants, M-16 rifle, beret, pistol belt, .45 pistol, holster, boots, grenades, camouflaged scarf and field-comunication set (#7536, 1966) . . . 2,500.00

11" G.I. Nurse Doll (1967)

G.I. Nurse Action Girl, with nurse uniform, cap, shoes, stockings, shoulder bag, crutches, bandages, splints, stethoscope, plasma bottle and arm band (#8060) white shoulder bag 3,500.00

G.I. Nurse with green shoulder bag (#8060) 2,100.00

Talking G.I. Joe 11½" Dolls (1967)

G.I. Joe Talking Action Soldier with fatigues, boots, dog tag, insignias, manuals and comic booklet (#7590) 700.00

G.I. Joe Talking Action Sailor with cap, work clothes, boots, dog tag, insignias, manuals and comic booklet (#7690) 1,400.00

G.I. Joe Talking Action Marine with cap, camouflage clothes, boots, dog tag, insignias, manuals and comic booklet (#7790) 850.00

G.I. Joe Talking Action Pilot with cap, flight clothes, boots, dog tag, insignias, manuals and comic booklet (#7890) 1,400.00

G.I. JOE EQUIPMENT
Hasbro (1964–69)

While the original G.I. Joe action dolls are highly collectible, the essence of this and many other 1960s' figures is the equipment. G.I. Joe had uniforms, equipment, weapons and vehicles in abundance. These came on header cards for smaller items and in window boxes for larger or deluxe equipment sets. Boxes and header cards were color coded to match the branch of service: Light wood and red for the Army and Marines, blue and green for the Navy and blue and yellow for the Air Force. Each service branch's equipment is listed separately below, in code number order, which corresponds roughly with the order of release.

ACTION SOLDIER

Action Soldier Equipment

Combat (Field Jacket) set with field jacket, M-1 rifle, bayonet, grenades, cartridge belt and Army Field Manual in window box (#7501, 1964–65) . . . $375.00

Combat (Field Pack) set with field pack, pistol belt, canteen, canteen cover, first-aid pouch, mess kit, knife, spoon, fork, entrenching shovel, entrenching cover and Army Field Manual in window box (#7502, 1964–65) 425.00

Combat Fatigue Shirt (#7503) 160.00

Combat Fatigue Pants (#7504) 160.00

Combat Field Jacket (#7505) 200.00

Combat Field Pack with entrenching tool and cover (#7506, 1964–65) 90.00

Combat Helmet with strap, netting and foliage (#7507, 1964–65) 80.00

Combat Sandbags, three bags (#7508, 1964–65) . . . 60.00

Combat Mess Kit with plate, fork, knife, spoon, canteen and cover (#7509, 1964–65) 70.00

Combat Rifle with M-1 rifle, bayonet, belt, 6 grenades (#7510, 1964–65) 90.00

Combat Rifle and Helmet set with M-1 rifle, bayonet, belt, 6 grenades and helmet (#7510, 1967) . . 175.00

Combat Camouflage Netting, foliage and poles, stakes

and rope (#7511, 1964–65) 90.00

Bivouac (Sleeping Bag) set with sleeping bag, knife, spoon, fork, mess kit, canteen, canteen cover, M-1 rifle, bayonet, cartridge belt and Army Field manual in window box (#7512, 1964–65) 225.00

Bivouac (Deluxe Pup Tent) set with tent, tent posts and pegs, camouflage, entrenching shovel, entrenching cover, machine gun, ammo box and Army Field manual in window box (#7513, 1964–65) 240.00

Bivouac Machine Gun with ammo box (#7514, 1964–65) 95.00

Bivouac Machine Gun reissue (#7514, 1967) 110.00

Bivouac Sleeping Bag, zippered (#7515, 1964–65) . . 90.00

Bivouac Sleeping Bag reissue (#7515, 1967) 110.00

Sabotage set with life raft, oar, binoculars, signal light, flare gun, detonator, TNT, stocking cap, radio set, gas mask and cal .45 submachine gun (#7516, 1967) 425.00

Sabotage set in reissue photo box (#7516, 1968) . . 575.00

Command Post (Poncho) set with poncho, .45 pistol, holster, pistol belt, wire roll, field radio, field telephone, map case, map, and Army Field Manual in window box (#7517, 1964–65) 250.00

Command Post Small Arms set, .45 and holster, belt, grenades (#7518, 1964–65) 140.00

Command Post Poncho (#7519, 1964–65) 90.00

Command Post Field Radio and Telephone set with wire roll, map and case (#7520, 1964–65) 120.00

Command Post Field Radio and Telephone reissue (#7520, 1968) 145.00

Military Police set with Ike jacket, Ike pants, duffle bag, dress scarf, police club, pistol belt, .45 pistol and holster, arm band and Army Field Manual in window box (#7521, 1964) 400.00

Jungle Fighter set with machete, knife and sheath, entrenching tool, mess kit (#7522, 1966) 165.00

Jungle Fighter set reissue (#7522, 1968) 180.00

MP Duffle Bag (#7523, 1964–65) 95.00

MP Ike Jacket, red scarf and arm band (#7524, 1964–65) 120.00

MP Ike Pants (#7525, 1964–65) 90.00

MP Helmet and Small Arms set with .45 and holster, white belt and club (#7526, 1964–65) 115.00

MP Helmet and Small Arms set, reissue (#7526, 1968) 140.00

Ski Patrol set with white belt, helmet, M-1 rifle and grenades (#7527, 1965) 115.00

Ski Patrol set reissue (#7527, 1968) 135.00

Rocket Firing Bazooka with 2 projectiles (#7528, 1965)145.00

Rocket Firing Bazooka reissue (#7528, 1968) 170.00

Snow Troop set with show shoes, goggles, and pick ax and rope (#7529, 1966) 125.00

Snow Troop set reissue (#7529, 1968) 140.00

Mountain Troops set with snow shoes, ice axe, field pack, grenades, climbing rope, web belt and Army Field Manual in window box (#7530, 1964–65) 200.00

Ski Patrol set with skis and ski poles, snow parka and pants, ski boots, sun goggles, mittens and Army Field Manual in window box (#7531, 1964–65) 500.00

Special Forces set with bazooka, green beret, fatigue jacket, jungle fatigue pants, camouflaged scarf, bazooka rockets, grenades, and special forces insignia (#7532, 1966) 620.00

Green Beret set, with beret, M-16 rifle, radio and headset (#7533, 1967) 220.00

Green Beret set reissue (#7533, 1968) 200.00

Green Beret set with fatigue jacket, jungle fatigue pants, M-16 rifle, beret, pistol belt, .45 pistol, holster,

G.I. Joe Action Soldier Equipment, G.I. Joe (Hasbro 1965–66)

Mountain Troops Set, G.I. Joe (Hasbro 1964–65)

boots, grenades, camouflaged scarf and field communication set (#7536) 2,100.00
West Point Cadet set with parade dress jacket, parade dress pants, dress shoes, belt, parade hat and plume, chest and belt sashes, dress rifle, sword and scabbard (#7537, 1967) 750.00
West Point Cadet reissue set in reissue photo box (#7537, 1968) 1,200.00
Heavy Weapons set with bullet-proof vest, 81mm mortar, mortar shells, M-60 machine gun, belted ammo, and grenades (#7538, 1967) 1,800.00
Heavy Weapons set in reissue photo box (#7538) . . 575.00
Military Police set with dress jacket, dress pants, dress scarf, arm band, helmet, boots, pistol belt, holster, .45 pistol, police club, and hand radio (#7539, 1967) 1,800.00
Military Police set in reissue photo box (#7539, 1968) 2,100.00
Combat equipment set with helmet, camouflage netting, jacket, cartridge belt, bazooka, rocket shells, machine gun, hand grenades and radio set (#7540, 1968) 700.00
Army Bivouac Adventure Pack "Special Value" "with 20 items" including G.I. Joe figure (#7549.83, 1968) 1,000.00
Mountain Troop Adventure Pack "Introductory Offer" "with 23 items" including Talking G.I. Joe figure (#7557.83, 1968) 1,750.00
Combat Engineering set with tripod and tommy gun (#7571, 1967) 350.00
Combat Construction set with helmet, gloves and jackhammer (#7572, 1967) 320.00
Combat Demolition set with pick, shovel and demolition plunger (#7573, 1967) 295.00

Talking G.I. Joe Accessories

Talking G.I. Joe and Bivouac accessories "15 items" (#90513, 1967) 1,750.00
Talking G.I. Joe and Command Post accessories "16 items" (#90517, 1967) 1,750.00
Talking G.I. Joe and Special Forces accessories "13 items" (#90532, 1967) 1,750.00

Sears Exclusives

Machine Gun Emplacement set with **G.I. Joe** figure, machine gun and tripod, combat boots, dog tag, fatigue suit, fatigue cap, helmet, M-1 rifle, bayonet, hand grenades, cartridge belt, first-aid pouch, sand bags and ammo box, Sears exclusive (#5931, 1965) 800.00
Forward Observer set with **G.I. Joe** figure, fatigue shirt, fatigue pants, camouflaged helmet, camouflage netting, dog tag, rubberized poncho, M-1 rifle, hand grenades, field telephone, field radio, field case, wire roll, boots, map and map case, Sears exclusive (#5969, 1966) 875.00
Green Beret Machine Gun Outpost set with 2 **G.I. Joe** figures, 2 camouflaged fatigue pants, 2 camouflaged fatigue shirts, 2 pair boots, 2 dog tags, 2 green berets, hand grenades, camouflage netting, 2 cartridge belts, machine gun, machine gun base, bazooka gun, 6 rocket shells, ammo box, automatic rifle, field telephone and earphone set, Sears exclusive (#5978, 1966) 1,325.00

Action Soldier Vehicles

G.I. Joe Five Star Army Combat Jeep featuring Moto-rev sound with trailer, 106mm rifle and mount, 4 rocket projectiles, searchlight and tripod (#7000, 1965–67) 600.00
G.I. Joe Army Combat Jeep without Moto-rev sound (#7000, 1968–75) 675.00
Desert Patrol Attack Jeep with **G.I. Joe** driver figure in desert campaign hat, uniform boots, 45 pistol holster, goggles, webb belt, 50-caliber machine gun, tripod, antenna, spare tire (#8030, 1967) 2,750.00
Desert Patrol Jeep without driver 1,600.00

ACTION SAILOR

Action Sailor Equipment

Sea Rescue set with life raft, oar, flare gun, anchor, rope, knife and scabbard, first-aid kit and Navy Manual in window box (#7601, 1964) 290.00
(Navy) Frogman set with 3-piece scuba suit, swim fins, face mask, scuba tanks, depth gauge, dynamite, knife, scabbard and Navy Manual in window box (#7602, 1964–65) 475.00
(Navy) Frogman set in reissue photo box (#7602, 1968) 550.00
(Navy) Frogman Scuba Top and headpiece (#7603, 1964–65) 95.00
(Navy) Frogman Scuba Bottoms (#7604, 1964–65) . . 85.00
(Navy) Frogman (Scuba) Accessories, face mask and swim fins, depth gauge, knife and scabbard (#7605, 1964–65) 185.00
(Navy) Frogman Scuba Tanks (#7606, 1964–65) 85.00
Navy Attack set with life preserver, blinker light, binoculars, semiphore flags and Navy Manual in window box (#7607, 1964–65) 225.00
Navy Attack Work Shirt (#7608) 100.00
Navy Attack Work Pants (#7609) 90.00
Navy Attack Helmet set, blinker light and binoculars

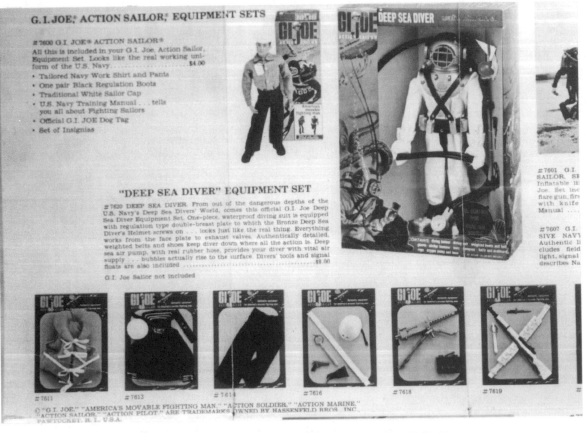

G.I. Joe Action Sailor Equipment, G.I. Joe (Hasbro 1965–66)

(#7610, 1964–65) 110.00
Deck Commander set with helmet, blinker light and
    binoculars (#7610) 110.00
Navy Attack Life Jacket (#7611, 1964–65) 90.00
Shore Patrol set with dress jumper, dress pants, sea
    bag, kerchief, arm band, pistol belt, pistol and
    holster, billy stick and Navy Manual in window box
    (#7612, 1964–65) 475.00
Shore Patrol set reissue (#7612, 1967) 1,200.00
Shore Patrol (Dress) Jumper with arm band, kerchief,
    sailor cap (#7613, 1964–65) 125.00
Shore Patrol Dress Pants (#7614, 1964–65) 100.00
Shore Patrol Navy Sea Bag (#7615) 90.00
Shore Patrol Helmet set, pistol belt, pistol and holster,
    billy stick and helmet (#7616, 1964–65) 125.00
(Navy) Machine Gun with ammo (#7618, 1965) . . . 100.00
(Navy) Dress Parade set, white rifle, billy stick, cartridge
    belt and bayonet (#7619, 1965) 130.00
Deep Sea Diver set with diving helmet, diving suit,
    weighted boots and belt, gloves, sledge hammer,
    buoy, compass, knife and scabbard, rope, oxygen
    pump and hose in window box (#7620, 1964–65)575.00
Deep Sea Diver set in reissue photo box (#7620,
    1968) 650.00
Landing Signal Officer set with landing signal suit, signal
    paddles, flight deck hat, earphones, binoculars,
    clipboard, pencil, flare gun and goggles (#7621,
    1966) 575.00
Sea Rescue set with life raft, oar, anchor rope, knife and
    scabbard, first-aid kit, knife and scabbard and
    Navy Manual (#7622, 1966) 300.00
Deep Freeze set with fur parka, pants, snow boots, ice
    axe, snow sled and rope and flare gun (#7623,

1967) 650.00
Deep Freeze set reissue (#7623, 1968) 720.00
Annapolis Cadet set with parade dress pants, parade
    dress jacket, garrison cap, shoes, sabre, scabbard
    belt, buckle and rifle (#7624, 1967) 1,000.00
Annapolis Cadet set in reissue photo box (#7624,
    1968) 1,700.00
Breeches Buoy set with slicker pants, slicker jacket,
    breeches buoy, pulley, flare gun and blinker light
    (#7625, 1967) 800.00
Breeches Buoy set reissue (#7625, 1968) 925.00
Navy LSO set with helmet, earphones, paddles and flare
    gun (#7626, 1966) 120.00
Navy Life Ring with recovery cord (#7627, 1965) . . 100.00
Navy Basics with white sailor hat, boots and dog tag
    (#7628, 1965) 140.00
Navy Scuba Adventure Pack "Special Value" "with 24
    items" and G.I. Joe (#7643.83) 1,350.00

Talking G.I. Joe Accessories
Talking G.I. Joe Adventure Pack and Shore Patrol
    accessories "16 items" (#90612, 1967) 2,000.00
Talking G.I. Joe Adventure Pack and Landing Signal
    Officer accessories "15 items" (#90621, 1967) 2,000.00

Action Sailor Vehicles
G.I. Joe Official Sea Sled and Frogman set with figure in
    scuba outfit, face mask, swim fins, undersea cave,
    Sears exclusive (#5957, 1966) 800.00
G.I. Joe Sea Sled without frogman (#5979?, 1966) . 650.00
Navy Jet Fighter 975.00
G.I. Joe Sea Sled and Frogman set with figure in orange
    scuba suit, fins, mask, tanks (#8050, 1966) . . 525.00

G.I. Joe Action Marine Equipment, G.I. Joe (Hasbro 1965–66)

ACTION MARINE

Action Marine Equipment

Communications (Poncho) set with poncho, carbine, wire roll, field radio, field telephone, field glasses, map case, map and Marine Field Manual in window box (#7701, 1964–65) 275.00

Communications Poncho (#7702, 1964–65) 140.00

Communications Post Field set, radio, telephone with wire roll, map and case (#7703, 1964–65) ... 120.00

Communications Field set reissue (#7703, 1967) .. 150.00

Communications Flag set with Flags for Army, Air Corps, Marines and Navy plus Old Glory in window box (#7704, 1964–65) 375.00

Combat Paratrooper (Parachute) set with parachute, carbine, pistol belt, canteen, canteen cover, first-aid pouch, grenades, knife, scabbard and Marine Field Manual in window box (#7705, 1964–65) 320.00

Paratrooper Small Arms set, carbine, grenades, knife and scabbard, canteen and first-aid pouch (#7706, 1964–65) 125.00

Paratrooper Small Arms set reissue (#7706, 1967) . 150.00

Paratrooper Helmet set with netting and leaves (#7707, 1964–65) 90.00

Paratrooper Camouflage set, netting for tent and foliage (#7708, 1964–65) 75.00

Paratrooper Parachute set (#7709, 1964–65) 175.00

Marine Dress (Parade) set with dress jacket, dress pants, garrison cap, pistol belt, M-1 rifle and Marine Field Manual in window box (#7710, 1964–65) 350.00

Marine Dress set reissue (#7710, 1968) 650.00

Beachhead Assault (Tent) set with tent, tent poles and pegs, flame thrower, first-aid pouch, pistol belt,

mess kit, knife, spoon, fork and Marine Field Manual in window box (#7711, 1964–65) 250.00

Beachhead Assault (Field Pack) set with field pack, M-1 rifle, bayonet, cartridge belt, entrenching shovel, entrenching cover, canteen, canteen cover, granades and Marine Field Manual in window box (#7712, 1964) 300.00

Beachhead Assault Field Pack (#7713, 1964–65) .. 110.00

Beachhead Assault Fatigue Shirt (#7714, 1964–65) 150.00

Beachhead Assault Fatigue Pants (#7715, 1964–65) 150.00

Beachhead Assault Mess Kit set (#7716, 1964–65) .. 90.00

Beachhead Assault Rifle set, M-1 rifle, bayonet, cartridge belt, 6 hand grenades (#7717, 1964–65) 125.00

Beachhead Assault Rifle set reissue (#7717, 1967) . 145.00

Beachhead Assault Flamethrower (#7718, 1964–65) 125.00

Beachhead Assault Flamethrower reissue (#7718, 1967) 140.00

(Marine) Medic set with stretcher, medic bag, arm bands, crutch, hospital flag, plasma bottle, stethoscope, splints and bandages and Marine Field Manual in window box (#7719, 1965) ... 375.00

(Marine) Medic set, stethoscope, crutch, plasma bottle, bandage and splint package (#7720, 1965) .. 190.00

(Marine) Medic set reissue (#7720, 1967) 210.00

First-Aid set, first-aid pouch, arm band and helmet (#7721, 1965) 120.00

First-Aid set reissue (#7721, 1967) 00

Marine Basics set (#7722, 1966) 175.00

Bunk Bed (#7723, 1966) 275.00

Bunk Bed reissue (#7723, 1967) 300.00

Mortar set with 81mm mortar, 3 shells and tripod (#7725, 1967) 275.00

Mortar set reissue (#7725, 1967) 00

Automatic Machine Gun with M-60, tripod, ammo belt
and box (#7726, 1967) 300.00
Marine Weapons Rack set (#7727, 1967) 400.00
Demolition set with mine detector, carrying case, head
set, voltometer, battery pack, detection light and
land mines (#7730, 1966) 375.00
Demolition set in reissue photo box (#7730, 1968) . 420.00
Tank Commander set with tanker's jacket and helmet,
machine gun and tripod, pistol and holster, ammo
box, pistol belt, radio and tripod in window box
(#7731, 1967) 675.00
Tank Commander set in reissue photo box (#7731,
1968) 900.00
Jungle Fighter set with jungle fatigue shirt and pants, M-
16 rifle, flamethrower, pistol belt, .45 pistol, holster,
canteen and cover, machete and sheath, jungle
knife and field telephone in window box (#7732,
1967) 1,325.00
Jungle Fighter set in reissue photo box (#7732,
1968) 1,500.00
G.I. Joe Marine Medic Adventure Pack "Special Value"
"18 items" and G.I. Joe figure (7733.83, 1967) 1,275.00

Talking G.I. Joe Accessories
Talking G.I. Joe Adventure Pack and Tent set
accessories "15 items" (#90711, 1967) 1,850.00
Talking G.I. Joe Adventure Pack and Field Pack
accessories "16 items" (#90712, 1967) 1,850.00

ACTION PILOT

Action Pilot Equipment
Survival set with life raft, oar, air vest, flare gun, sea

anchor, rope, first-aid kit, knife and scabbard and
Air Force Manual in window box (#7801,
1964–65) 300.00
Survival Life Raft with oar, sea anchor and rope (#7802,
1964–65) 220.00
Dress Uniform set with dress jacket, dress pants, dress
shirt, necktie, Garrison cap, boots, insignia and Air
Force Manual in window box (#7803, 1964–65) 925.00
Dress Uniform Blue Jacket (#7804) 200.00
Dress Uniform Blue Pants (#7805) 175.00
Dress Uniform Shirt and accessories (#7806) 190.00
Scramble set with flight suit, air vest, belt, holster, .45
pistol, clip board with pad and pencil and Air Force
Manual in window box (#7807, 1964–65) 475.00
Scramble Flight Suit, on card (#7808, 1964–65) . . . 275.00
Scramble Flight Suit reissue (#7808, 1967) 300.00
Scramble Air Vest and Accessories with vest, flare gun,
knife and scabbard (#7809, 1964–65) 150.00
Scramble Air Vest reissue (#7809, 1967) 170.00
Scramble Crash Helmet, face mask and hose, tinted
visor (#7810, 1964–65) 175.00
Scramble Crash Helmet reissue (#7810, 1967) 190.00
Scramble Parachute Pack (#7811, 1964–65) 150.00
Scramble Communications set with map and case, clip
board, field radio and binoculars (#7812, 1965) 175.00
Scramble Communications set reissue (#7812, 1967) 200.00
Air Police field phone, carbine, bayonet and white
helmet (#7813, 1965) 175.00
Air Force Police set reissue (#7813, 1967) 190.00
Pilot Basics set with combat boots, fatigue hat, dog tag
(#7814, 1966) 175.00
Pilot Basics set reissue (#7814, 1967) 190.00
Air Force Security set with field telephone and case, .45
pistol, holster, billy club, helmet, cartridge belt

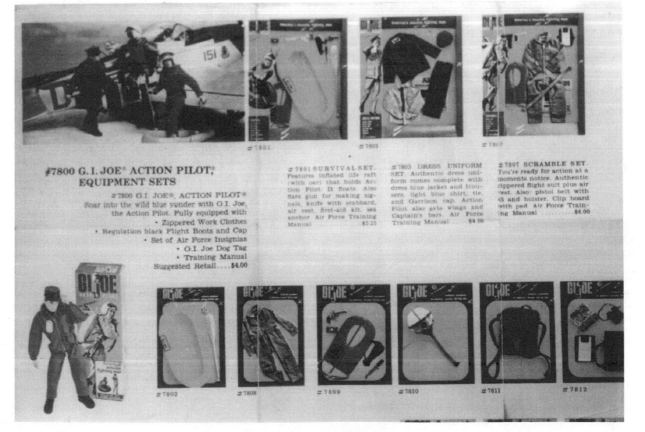

G.I. Joe Action Pilot Equipment, G.I. Joe (Hasbro 1965–66)

(#7815, 1966) 450.00
Air Force Security set reissue (#7815, 1967) 475.00
Mae West Life Vest with vest, flashlight, flare gun, knife
　　and sheath (#7816) 275.00
Mae West reissue (#7816, 1967) 00
Crash Crew set with fireproof jacket and pants,
　　protective hood, gloves, fire extinguisher, crash
　　belt, ax, strap cutter, pliers and flashlight in window
　　box (#7820, 1966) 390.00
Crash Crew set in reissue photo box (#7820, 1968) 00
Air Cadet set, dress parade jacket, dress parade
　　trousers, shoulder and waist sash, M-1 rifle, dress
　　shoes, sabre and scabbard and garrison cap in
　　window box (#7822, 1967) 1,000.00
Air Cadet set in reissue photo box (#7822, 1968) . 1,250.00
Fighter Pilot set with flight suit, Mae West, G-suit, flight
　　helmet, working parachute, flashlight and boots in
　　window box (#7823, 1967) 1,100.00
Fighter Pilot set in reissue photo box (#7823, 1968) 1,250.00
Astronaut set with space suit and helmet, tether cord,
　　space boots and gloves, camera, oxygen chest
　　pack and propellant gun in window box (#7824,
　　1967) 1,250.00
Astronaut set in reissue photo box (#7824, 1968) . . 900.00
Air Sea Rescue set with scuba suit, headpiece, fins,
　　mask, tanks, flare gun, first-aid pouch, rescue life
　　ring and marker buoy in window box (#7825,
　　1967) 975.00
Air Sea Rescue in reissue photo box (#7825, 1968) 1,150.00

Action Pilot Vehicles
Official Space Capsule and Authentic Space Suit set
　　with figure and Mercury Control recording,
　　astronaut helmet (#8020, 1966) 675.00
Astronaut Suit and Space Capsule set without figure 500.00
Crash Crew Fire Truck vehicle with figure, water-
　　pumping truck, nozzle and hoses, extension
　　ladder, working siren, blinking light, fire axe, crash
　　crew suit and boots (#8040, 1967) 3,200.00
Crash Crew Fire Truck without figure 1,800.00

Exclusive Vehicle
Space Capsule and Space Suit set with figure, plus
　　flotation collar, inflatable raft and oar, Sears
　　exclusive (#5979, 1966) 725.00

ACTION SOLDIERS OF THE WORLD
G.I. JOE FIGHTING MEN
Hasbro (1966–67)

Large Boxed Sets with Figures
German Storm Trooper with helmet, jacket, pants, boots,
　　field pack, cartridge belt, holster, lugar pistol,
　　grenades, 9mm schmeisser pistol, Iron Cross
　　Medal and Counter Intelligence Manual (#8100,
　　1966) $2,300.00
Japanese Imperial Soldier with helmet, jacket, pants,
　　boots, field pack, nambu pistol, holster, cartridge
　　belt, arisaka rifle, bayonet, The Order of the Kite
　　Medal and Counter Intelligence Manual (#8101,
　　1966) 2,500.00
Russian Infantry Man with fur hat, jacket, pants, machine
　　gun, bi-pod, field glasses, case, ammo box, boots,
　　belt, anti-tank grenades, The Order of Lenin Medal
　　and Counter Intelligence Manual (#8102, 1966) 2,250.00
French Resistance Fighter with beret, sweater, pants,
　　boots, shoulder holster, knife, Lebel revolver

grenades, radio set, 7.65mm submachine gun, The
　　Croix de Guerre Medal and Counter Intelligence
　　Manual (#8103, 1966) 2,175.00
British Commando with helmet, jacket, pants, boots, gas
　　mask, gas mask case, belt, canteen, canteen
　　cover, Sten submachine gun, The Victoria Cross
　　Medal and Counter Intelligence Manual (#8104,
　　1966) 2,200.00
Australian Jungle Fighter with campaign hat, jacket,
　　shorts, high socks, boots, grenades, flame thrower,
　　jungle knife, entrenching tool, bush machette,
　　sheath, The Victoria Cross Medal and Counter
　　Intelligence Manual (#8105, 1966) 2,275.00

Regular Boxed Sets with Figures
German Storm Trooper with uniform, boots, helmet
　　(#8200, 1966) 1,200.00
Japanese Imperial Soldier with uniform and stockings
　　(#8201, 1966) 1,400.00
Russian Infantry Man with uniform, fur-lined cap with red
　　star, knee boots (#8202, 1966) 1,300.00
French Resistance Fighter with turtleneck, sweater, dark
　　pants, beret (#8203, 1966) 1,250.00
British Commando with uniform and chevrons, battle
　　ribbons, and commando designations (#8204,
　　1966) 1,275.00
Australian Jungle Fighter with uniform, campaign hat,
　　knee socks (#8205, 1966) 1,250.00

"Authentic Equipment" on Cards
German Storm Trooper equipment with field pack, luger
　　pistol, holster, cartridge belt, 9mm schmeisser
　　pistol, grenades and The Iron Cross Medal
　　(#8300) 300.00
Japanese Imperial Soldier equipment with field pack,
　　holster, nambu pistol, bayonet, cartridge belt,
　　arisaka rifle and The Order of Kite Medal
　　(#8301) 350.00
Russian Infantry Man equipment with case, D.P. light,
　　machine gun with bi-pod uniform belt, ammo box,
　　anti-tank grenades and The Order of Lenin Medal
　　(#8302) 250.00
French Resistance Fighter equipment with shoulder
　　holster, Lebel revolver, 7.65 Mas submachine gun,
　　hand grenades, radio, earphones, knife and The
　　Croix de Guerre Medal (#8303) 200.00
British Commando equipment with gas mask, gas mask
　　case, canteen, canteen cover, Sten submachine
　　gun and The Victoria Cross Medal (#8304) . . . 250.00
Australian Jungle Fighter Equipment with flame thrower,
　　jungle knife, grenades, bush machete, sheath,
　　entrenching tool and The Victoria Cross Medal
　　(#8305) 300.00

Specials
The Uniforms of Six Nations, with 6 complete uniforms,
　　medals, weapons, equipment and Counter
　　Intelligence Manual, Sears exclusive (#5038,
　　1967) 1,150.00
Mountie Gift Set (Hasbro Canada #5904,
　　1967) . . . . no price found
Dress Uniform set with 37 items (#8009.83) 1,200.00
Talking G.I. Joe Foreign Soldiers of the World Adventure
　　Pack "Introductory Offer" "with 39 items" including
　　figure (#8111.83, 1968) 2,800.00

Irwin Toys Vehicles (licensed by Hasbro)
Amphibious Duck (Irwin #5693) 675.00

Jet Helicopter (Irwin #5395) 750.00
Motorcycle with Sidecar (Irwin #5651) 475.00
Military Staff Car (Irwin #5652) 875.00

Foot Lockers
G.I. Joe Foot Locker with wood tray (#8000, 1964) . 150.00
　　Variation, with plastic tray 90.00
G.I. Joe Foot Locker Adventure Pack "16 items"
　　(#8000.83, 1968) 250.00
G.I. Joe Foot Locker Adventure Pack "15 items"
　　(#8001.83, 1968) 250.00
G.I. Joe Foot Locker Adventure Pack "22 items"
　　(#8002.83, 1968) 275.00
G.I. Joe Foot Locker Adventure Pack "17 items"
　　(#8000.83, 1969) 250.00
G.I. Joe Foot Locker Adventure Pack "16 items"
　　(#8001.83, 1969) 250.00
G.I. Joe Foot Locker Adventure Pack "18 items"
　　(#8002.83, 1969) 250.00

Four Services Adventure Packs
4 Services in 1 Special Adventure Pack, "with 12 items"
　　(#8005.83) 240.00
4 Services in 1 Special Adventure Pack, "with 14 items"
　　(#8006.83) 250.00
4 Services in 1 Special Adventure Pack, "with 16 items"
　　(#8007.83) 275.00
4 Services in 1 Special Adventure Pack, "with 14 items"
　　(#8008.83) 250.00

THE ADVENTURES OF G.I. JOE
Hasbro (1969)

After a run of over four years, Hasbro had changed America's Fighting Man into a non-military soldier to respond to public outcry. This was to be the first in a series of changes for the popular toy. We always wondered why he still came with a set of dog tags. The packaging was altered to reflect the big change.

11½" Figures (1969)
Adventurer (#7905) $1,050.00
Negro Adventurer (#7905) 1,600.00
Aquanaut (#7910) 1,800.00
Talking Astronaut (#7915) 900.00

Basic Adventure Sets (1969)
Aquanaut: Danger of the Depths with 3-piece scuba suit, swim fins, face mask, oxygen tanks, spear gun, shark knife, scabbard, scuba sled, shark, marker buoy and comic book (#7920) 300.00
Firefighter: The Mysterious Explosion with fireproof jacket, fireproof pants, protective hood, boots, fire extinguisher, crash belt, first-aid bag, axe, pliers, flashlight, strap cutter, stretcher, crutch, plasma bottle and comic book (#7921) 275.00
Secret Agent: The Secret Mission to Spy Island with life raft and oar, binoculars, signal light, flare gun, detonator, TNT, boots, camera, camouflage shirt, camouflage pants, black knit cap, radio and earphones, code sender, .45 submachine gun, wire roll and comic book (#7922) 350.00
Rescue Diver: The Perilous Rescue with 3-piece scuba suit, face mask, swim fins, life ring, marker buoy, flare gun, first-aid kit, breeches buoy, blinker light, stethoscope and comic book (#7923) 350.00

Deluxe Adventure Sets (1969)
Underwater Diver: The Eight Ropes of Danger with diving suit, diving helmet, oxygen pump and hose, map, compass, octopus, weighted belt and boots, treasure chest, treasure coins and comic book (#7950) 400.00
Test Pilot: The Fantastic Free Fall with flight suit, flight helmet, working parachute, flashlight, signal light, boots, Mae West vest and comic book (#7951) 450.00
Spaceman: The Hidden Missile Discovery with space suit and helmet, space boots, missile detector, land mines, propellant gun, camera, oxygen chest pack, tether cord and comic book (#7952) 450.00
Jungle Explorer: The Mouth of Doom with jungle jacket, shorts, socks, pith helmet, canteen and cover, machete and sheath, hunter's rifle, boots, raft, pole, trunk, crocodile and comic book (#7953) 300.00

Super Deluxe Adventure Sets with vehicles (1969)
Frogman: Shark's Surprise with **Adventurer** figure, sea sled, 3-piece scuba suit, swim fins, oxygen tanks, face mask, spear gun, shark, treasure chest, treasure coins and comic book (#7980) 650.00
Frogman: Shark's Surprise without figure (#7980.83) 500.00
Spaceman: Spacewalk Mystery with **Adventurer** figure, space capsule with glow-in-the-dark cockpit, sliding canopy, sound recording, space suit and helmet, space boots, propellant gun, oxygen chest pack, camera, tether cord and comic book (#7981) . 725.00
Spaceman: Spacewalk Mystery without figure (#7981.83) 600.00
Polar Explorer: Fight For Survival with **Adventurer** figure, dog sled, husky dogs, harness, arctic jacket, arctic pants, thermal boots, snow pack, snow shoes, ice axe, polar chests and comic book (#7982) 750.00
Polar Explorer: Fight For Survival without figure (#7982.83) 600.00

Foot Lockers (1969)
Adventure Locker (#7940) 420.00
Aqua Locker (#7941) 500.00
Astro Locker (#7942) 575.00

G.I. JOE ADVENTURE TEAM
Hasbro (1970–73)

The Adventures of G.I. Joe series came and went quite quickly and what took its place was the Adventure Team. This was the period that introduced the figures with "life-like hair" and in the case of some figures, life-like "beards" as well! In the early stages of the Adventure Team, the packaging didn't reflect the change all that much, and some still carried the tag-line "The Adventures of G.I. Joe," while others had the "G.I. Joe Adventure Team" logo. The figures, however, had a change of dog tags, from the regular military style issue to those with the Adventure Team logo. A comic book style adventure booklet was also enclosed. Joe was more of a freelance mercenary type now.

11½" Figures (1970)
Talking Adventure Team Commander, with "Life-Like Hair and Beard," boxed (#7400) $325.00
Land Adventurer, with "Life-Like Hair and Beard," boxed (#7401) 250.00
Sea Adventurer, with "Life-Like Hair and Beard," boxed

#7402) 275.00

Air Adventurer, with "Life-Like Hair and Beard," boxed (#7403) 290.00

Adventurer (Black), with "Life-Like Hair," boxed (#7404) 320.00

Talking Astronaut, with "Life-Like Hair," boxed (#7405) 400.00

Talking Adventure Team Commander (Black), with "Life-Like Hair," boxed (#7406?, 1973) 500.00

Man of Action, with "Life-Like Hair," boxed (#7500) . 250.00

Talking Man of Action, with "Life-Like Hair," boxed (#7590) 350.00

Adventure Team Vehicles (1970–74)

Official Adventure Team Vehicle (ATV) (#7005, 1970) 250.00

Space-A-Matic (#7010, 1970) 500.00

Secret of the Mummy's Tomb with figure, pith helmet, shovel, pick ax, tan trousers, fatigue shirt, mummy, secret mummy case, jewels, ATV vehicle with winch and net (#7441, 1970) 400.00

The Shark's Surprise with figure, sea sled, 3 piece scuba suit, swim fins, mask, spear gun, shark, gold and silver coins, treasure chest, booklet (#7442, 1970) 400.00

Space Walk Mystery with figure, space capsule, canopy, silver suit, boots, propellent gun, camera, tether cord (#7445, 1970) 475.00

Search For the Stolen Idol featuring Adventure Helicopter, with working winch, jeweled idol and hooded cobra snake, booklet (#7418, 1971) .. 250.00

Recovery of the Lost Mummy Adventure, Sears exclusive (#79-59092, 1971) 300.00

Mobile Support Vehicle (Search for the Radioactive Satellite) with detachable canopy with headquarters, maps, viewscreen, swivel chair, control panel, radar, recon camera and storage drawers (#7499, 1972) 400.00

Helicopter (#7380, 1973) 165.00

Devil of the Deep featuring Turbo Swamp Craft with pontoons, storage compartment, working propeller, capture snare, Hammerhead Stingray and booklet (#7439, 1974) 200.00

Fate of the Trouble Shooter featuring Delta 7-X communications vehicle with talking communication center, adjustable viewing screen, tracked wheels for all-terrain travel, rotating antenna, vulture and booklet (#7450, 1974) 225.00

Adventure Team Uniform and Equipment Sets

Secret Mission to Spy Island (for Land Adventurer) with life raft and oar, binoculars, signal light, pants, sweater, boots, camera, black cap, radio and earphones, submachine gun, wire roll and comic booklet (#7411, 1970) 150.00

Danger of the Depths (for Sea Adventurer) with 3-piece scuba suit, swim fins, face mask, oxygen tanks, spear gun, shark, shark knife and scabbard, scuba sled, marker buoy and comic booklet in window box (#7412, 1970) 150.00

Hidden Missile Discovery (for Astronaut) with silver astro suit, boots, helmet, mine detector, land mines, camera, propellant gun, chest pack, backpack and comic booklet in window box (#7415, 1970) .. 200.00

Eight Ropes of Danger (for Sea Adventurer) with diving suit, diving helmet, weighted boots, weighted belt, compass, oxygen pump and hose, treasure chest, coins, Octopus and comic booklet in window box (#7422, 1970) 250.00

Fantastic Freefall (for Air Adventurer) with flight suit, flight helmet, working parachute, flashlight, signal light, boots, Mae West vest and comic booklet in window box (#7423, 1970) 250.00

Flying Space Adventure (for Astronaut) with space chair, space rocket, pack, pickup arm, camera, space suit, astro boots, booklet (#7425, 1970) 375.00

Fight For Survival (for Land Adventurer) with dog sled, 2 dogs, arctic parka, arctic pants, arctic boots, snow shoes, arctic expedition chests, ice axe and rope (#7431, 1970) 350.00

White Tiger Hunt (for Land Adventurer) with hunters jacket and pants, hat, rifle, tent, white tiger, tiger cage and chain, campfire and comic booklet in window box (#7436, 1970) 250.00

Capture of the Pygmy Gorilla (for Land Adventurer) with camouflage shirt and pants, supply chest, rifle, pontoon boat, outboard motor, gun camera, pygmy gorilla, net and comic booklet in window box (#7437, 1970) 250.00

Exclusives

Search For the Abominable Snowman (for Sea Adventurer) Sears exclusive (#7430.16, 1973) 225.00

Mystery of the Boiling Lagoon set, with pontoon boat, diver's suit, diver's helmet, weighted belt, weighted boots, oxygen pump and hose, buoy, nose cone, pincer arm, comic booklet and instructions, Sears exclusive (#7431.16, 1974) 200.00

"Authentic Equipment For Adventure Team" with Adventure Team symbol

Blue Window Box

Missile Recovery with scuba jacket, short pants, face mask, fins, nose cone and missile detector (#7340, 1971) 90.00

Radiation Detection with jumpsuit, belt, simulated uranium rock, container, goggles and pincer arm (#7341, 1971) 90.00

High Voltage Escape with net jumpsuit, hat, wrist meter, wire cutters, 36" wire and warning sign (#7342, 1971) 90.00

Hurricane Spotter with slicker suit, rain measure, portable radar, binoculars, map and case (#7343, 1971) 90.00

Volcano Jumper with jumpsuit, head hood, belt, nylon string, chest pack and volcanic flow detector (#7344, 1971) 90.00

Aerial Recon with jumpsuit, helmet and aerial recon vehicle (#7345, 1971) 90.00

Yellow Window Box

Demolition with armored suit, face shield, bomb disposal box, bomb and extension grippers (#7370, 1971) 90.00

Reissued as Dangerous Removal with armored suit, face shield, disposal box, extension grippers and gas canister (#7370, 197?) 90.00

Smoke Jumper with jumpsuit, helmet, fire extinguisher, equipment belt, chain saw, wire cutters, pliers, flashlight and axe (#7371, 1971) 90.00

Karate with karate uniform, break apart brick and board, rank belts, practice mat and manual (#7372, 1971) 90.00

Jungle Survival with shirt and pants, radio, survival belt, machete and case, canteen, snake bite kit, animal trap, water purification kit, compass and first-aid kit (#7373, 1971) 90.00

Emergency Rescue with shirt and pants, rope ladder

and hook, walkie talkie, oxygen tank, safety belt,
flashlight, axe and first-aid kit (#7374, 1971) . . . 90.00
Secret Agent with trench coat, bullet-proof vest, attaché
case with hidden gun, tape recorder, mask and
shoulder holster (#7375, 1971) 100.00

"Action Pack!"
Rescue Raft (#7350, 1971) 100.00
Fire Fighter (#7351, 1971) 100.00
Life-Line Catapult (#7352, 1971) 100.00
Windboat (#7353, 1971) 100.00
Underwater Explorer (#7354, 1971) 100.00

Escape Car (#7360, 1971) 100.00
Flying Rescue (#7361, 1971) 100.00
Signal Flasher (#7362, 1971) 100.00
Turbo Copter (#7363, 1971) 100.00
Drag Bike (#7364, 1971) 100.00

"Action Outfits" boxed, with Adventure Team symbol
Hidden Treasure with shirt, pants and folding shovel
(#7300, 1973) 50.00
    Reissue, no symbol, carded 30.00
Fight For Survival with shirt, pants and bush hat (#7301,
1973) 50.00
    Reissue, no symbol, machete instead of bush
    hat, carded 30.00
Copter Rescue with flight suit and camera (#7302,
1973) 50.00
    Reissue, no symbol, binoculars instead of
    camera, carded 30.00
Secret Rendevous with parka, pants and flare gun
(#7303, 1973) 50.00
    Reissue, no symbol, carded 30.00
Dangerous Mission with shirt, pants and hunter's rifle
(#7304, 1973) 50.00
    Reissue, no symbol, carded 30.00
Desert Survival with shirt, pants, belt and canteen
(#7305, 1973) 50.00
    Reissue, no symbol, carded 30.00
Secret Mission with jacket, pants and pistol (Asst.
#7309, 1973) 50.00
    Reissue, new logo, no symbol, carded 30.00
Dangerous Climb with jumpsuit, climbing pick and rope
(Asst. #7309, 1973) 50.00
    Reissue, new logo, no symbol, carded (#8202) . 30.00
Jungle Ordeal with camouflage jumpsuit, jungle knife
(Asst. #7309, 1973) 50.00
    Reissue, no symbol, carded 30.00
Winter Rescue with hooded jumpsuit, belt and first-aid
kit (Asst. #7309, 1973) 60.00

Replaced by
Desert Explorer with bush jacket, shorts and belt (Asst.
#7309, 1973) 50.00
    Reissue, new logo, no symbol, carded 30.00
Undercover Agent with trench coat, belt and walkie talkie
(Asst. #7309, 1973) 50.00
    Reissue, no symbol, carded 30.00
Photo Recon with jumpsuit and camera (#8201) . . . 480.00

Adventure Team Equipment (1073-74) on triangle top
header cards, with Adventure Team symbol
Underwater Demolition (#7310) 50.00
Laser Rescue (#7311) 50.00
Sonic Rock Blaster (#7312) 50.00
Chest Winch (#7313) 50.00
Solar Communicator (#7314) 50.00

Rocket Pack (#7315) 50.00

Square Cards (Asst. #7319, 1973)
Escape Slide 50.00
Magnetic Flaw Detector 50.00
Sample Analyzer 50.00
Thermal Terrain Scanner 50.00
Equipment Tester 50.00
Seismo-Graph 50.00

Playsets
Adventure Team Headquarters with map room, storage
    room, staging area, radio shack, signal beacon,
    buzzer, elevator, booklet (#7490, 1972) 200.00
Training Center with tower, crane, winch, training slide,
    rope ladder, support arch, obstacle course, tires,
    barrels, coiled wire, 2 logs, rifle rack, 2 targets, 2
    rifles, 2 pistols, first-aid kit, tent, cave, snake,
    booklet (#7495, 1972) 250.00

Footlocker
Adventure Team Footlocker (#8000, 1974) 120.00

Exclusive Accessories
Helicopter/Ampicat set, Sears exclusive (1972) 175.00
Mobile Support Unit set, Sears exclusive (1972) 90.00

G.I. JOE ADVENTURE TEAM
WITH KUNG-FU GRIP
Hasbro (1974–76)

Beginning in 1974, G.I. Joe had another change, this
time to his hands. In an effort to respond to many requests,
Hasbro altered Joe's hands from the stiff, unmoving variety
to hands with more flexibility. Now Joe could actually hold
onto his equipment without dropping it, like he had in the
past. This new change was echoed on the boxes for the
figures, while the vehicles and accessory packages ran just
the Adventure Team notice on them. During 1975, the body
sculpting on G.I. Joe was altered giving him a body that was
called "Life-Like" on the packaging. The figures were now
offered two ways—in the standard box, available only at
Sears, or a new "cost effective" header card. The year 1976
also saw the introduction of the "Eagle-Eye" (moving eyes)
Man of Action and Land Commander G.I. Joes.

11½" Kung Fu Grip Figures (1974) boxed
Adventurer with Kung Fu Grip (Land) with uniform,
    boots, insignia, rifle (#7280) $275.00
Adventurer with Kung Fu Grip (Sea) with uniform, boots,
    insignia, rifle (#7281) 290.00
Adventurer with Kung Fu Grip (Air) with uniform, boots,
    insignia, rifle (#7282) 300.00
Adventurer with Kung Fu Grip (Black) with fatigue
    uniform, boots, insignia, rifle (#7283) 350.00
Man of Action with Kung Fu Grip with fatigue uniform,
    boots, insignia, rifle (#7284) 320.00

Kung Fu Grip Series carded (1975)
Life-Like Land Adventurer (#7270) 150.00
Life-Like Sea Adventurer (#7271) 175.00
Life-Like Air Adventurer (#7272) 190.00
Life-Like Black Adventurer (#7273) 200.00
Life-Like Man of Action (#7274) 175.00

New Life-Like Land Adventurer (#7280) 170.00
New Life-Like Sea Adventurer (#7281) 190.00
New Life-Like Air Adventurer (#7282) 210.00
New Life-Like Black Adventurer (#7283) 225.00
New Life-Like Man of Action (#7284) 220.00

Boxed Adventure Team Figures
New Life-Like Talking Commander (with Kung Fu Grip)
    with uniform, boots, insignia, rifle (#7290, 1976) 350.00
New Life-Like Talking Commander (Black, with Kung Fu
    Grip) with uniform, boots, insignia, rifle (#7291,
    1976) 575.00
New Life-Like Talking Man of Action (with Kung Fu Grip)
    with uniform, boots, insignia, rifle (#7292, 1976) 425.00

Eagle Eye Figures
Eagle Eye Land Commander with moving eyes (#7276,
    1976) 200.00
Eagle Eye Man of Action with moving eyes (#7277,
    1976) 200.00
Eagle Eye Commando (Black) with moving eyes (#7278,
    1976) 250.00

Adventure Team Uniform and Equipment Sets
Revenge of the Spy Shark with raft, oar, spear gun, flag
    buoy with 15" rope, knife, scabbard, camera, sonar
    detector, black shark, color booklet (#7413,
    1975) 150.00
Black Widow Rendevous with black jacket, pants, helmet
    with visor, boots, map, case, machine gun, knife,
    scabbard, walkie-talkie, holster, revolver, turbo
    copter, booklet (#7414, 1975) 175.00
Peril of the Raging Inferno with fire suit, head gear and
    boots, camera, breathing apparatus, fire
    extinguisher, detection meter, replacement gaskets
    (#7416, 1975) 140.00
Attack at Vulture Falls with jumpsuit, rope ladder,
    grappling hook, raft, backpack, holster, revolver,
    life vest, vulture, booklet (#7420, 1975) 140.00
Jaws of Death with 2-piece wet suit, undersea explorer
    vehicle, diving fins, knife and sheath, face mask,
    spear gun, diving tanks, spy cam, booklet (#7421,
    1975) 140.00

Sky Dive to Danger with parachute, jumpsuit, helmet
    with visor, breathing apparatus, backpack, airman's
    boots, spider, web, booklet (#7440, 1975) . . . 150.00
Trouble at Vulture Pass, Sears exclusive (#59289) . 175.00

Carded Adventures
Secret Courier with jacket, pants, boots, attaché case,
    shoulder weapon (Asst. #7328, 1975 . . . . 75.00
Thrust Into Danger with hooded pullover, pants, radio,
    compass, holster, revolver (Asst. #7328, 1975) . 75.00
Long Range Recon with shirt, pants, boots, holster,
    revolver, map case, binoculars, canteen (Asst.
    #7328, 1975) 75.00
Green Danger with jacket, pants, storage chest,
    machete, snake (Asst. #7328, 1975) 75.00
Buried Bounty with jacket, pants, storage box, map,
    entrenching tool, underground detector (Asst.
    #7328, 1975) 75.00
Diver's Distress with swim trunks, fins, spear gun,
    oxygen tanks, face mask, knife, scabbard, squid
    (Asst. #7328, 1975) 75.00
Magnum Power (Asst. #7328, 1975) . . . . . no price found

Boxed Adventures
Danger Ray Detection with shirt, pants, magnetic ray
    detector, solar communicator (Asst. #7338, 1975)90.00
Night Surveillance with hooded pullover, pants, map and
    case, infrared scanner, submachine gun (Asst.
    #7338, 1975) 90.00
Shocking Escape with jumpsuit, gloves, belt, escape
    slide, high voltage sign, chest pack (Asst. #7338,
    1975) 90.00
Raging River Dam Up with jumpsuit, helmet, chain saw,
    canteen, binoculars, flashlight, shovel, axe,
    campfire, seismograph (Asst. #7339, 1975) . . . 90.00
Jettison to Safety with shirt, pants, mobile terrain
    scanner, rocket pack (Asst. #7339, 1975) 90.00
Mine Shaft Breakout with shirt, pants, sonic rock blaster,
    winch net (Asst. #7339, 1975) 90.00

Vehicle Adventures
Sandstorm Survival Adventure featuring Official G.I. Joe
    Jeep with tent, pith helmet, blinker light, knife and

Sandstorm Survival Adventure, G.I. Joe Adventure Team (Hasbro 1974)

scabbard, supply chest, canteen and cover, mess
kit, rifle, shovel, pick axe, life raft and paddle, net,
crocodile, poncho, flare gun, map and case
(#7493, 1974) 300.00
Sea Wolf Submarine with detachable conning tower,
telescopic periscope, remote control, adjustable
valve, pincer arms, camera, trim tabs, rudder, 12"
hose, face mask, decals, squid, booklet (#7460,
1975) 225.00
Sky Hawk with glider, 100 ft. of nylon string, bobbin,
booklet (#7470, 1975) 130.00

Vehicles
Combat Jeep Vehicle and Trailer set featuring Moveable
Recoilless Rifle and detachable trailer (#7000,
1976) 250.00
Helicopter (#7380, 1976) 175.00
Capture Copter featuring snap-together copter with rotor
blade action, working capture claws, detachable
flotation pontoons, working winch plus net (#7480,
1976) 200.00
Capture Copter with **Adventure Team** figure (#7481,
1976) 250.00
Big Trapper Adventure with **Intruder** figure (#7494,
1976) 250.00
Big Trapper Adventure without figure (#7498, 1976) 175.00

Exclusives
Avenger Pursuit Craft vehicle, Sears exclusive 300.00
Trapped in the Coils of Doom, Sears exclusive
(#7959301) 200.00

MIKE POWERS
Hasbro (1975)

Atomic Man Mike Powers, based on a certain bionic
television series, was the first in a series of superhero-styled
characters which Hasbro introduced. He had a clear see-
through left arm and right leg that allowed you to look at his
inner workings! He "flew" with the aid of a helicopter blade
that attached to his atomic arm and had an "atomic flashing
eye" as well! Mike had his own series of adventure sets and
even his own headquarters. A year later, Hasbro produced
what could be another part of this series, but wasn't marked
as such—Bulletman, The Human Bullet. In the most superhero styled costume ever, Bulletman could fly on his own
and had a bullet shaped helmet and silver arms as well. The
two of them, together with "Eagle Eye" formed what was
known for a brief period of time as "The Super Adventure-
Team." And what better enemies for them to fight than The
Invaders? These looked like human apes, had less articulation
than the Joes and were a bit shorter in height. Two styles
were available: Intruder Commander and Intruder Warrior.

Figures
Atomic Man Mike Powers, with Zoom lens eye,
transparent atomic limbs, rotating flexible gripping
hand, trunks, jacket (#8025, 1975) $100.00
Bullet Man with silver arms and helmet, red boots
(#8026, 1976) 125.00
The Intruders (Commander) boxed or carded (#8050,
1976) 150.00
The Intruders (Warrior) boxed or carded (#8051,
1976) 150.00

Mike Powers Adventure Assortment (#8028)
Race for Recovery with camera, compass, jumpsuit, pick
axe and rope, walkie talkie, chest pack, storage
chamber, rope ladder, grappling hook, boots, etc.
(Asst. #8028, 1975) 75.00
Fangs of the Cobra with jumpsuit, boots, map and case,
snake, belt with snake bite and water purification
kits, machete, sheath, etc. (Asst. #8028, 1975) . 75.00
Special Assignment with jumpsuit, rifle, surveillance
gear, headphones, power source, etc. (Asst.
#8028, 1975) 75.00
Secret Mission with life raft, oar, clothing, binoculars,
signal light, flare gun, camera, radio, machine gun,
etc. (#8030, 1975) 90.00
Dive to Danger with mini sled, shark, buoy, rope, scuba
equipment, spear gun, etc. (#8031, 1975) 90.00
Challenge of Savage River with Adventure Team raft,
outboard motar, life vest, map and case, storage
box, canteen, machete, etc. (#8032, 1975) 90.00
Command Para Drop with parachute, crate, binoculars,
walkie talkie, pistol, canteen and mess kit,
machete, etc. (#8033, 1975) 90.00

Playset
Atomic Man Secret Mountain Outpost with base, walls,
door, log barricade, treadmill, radar screen, viewing
glasses, clothing, etc. (#8040, 1975) 150.00

THE DEFENDERS
Hasbro (1976)

The Defenders figure looks like a cheap drug store
knock-off of G.I. Joe and comes, without equipment, on a

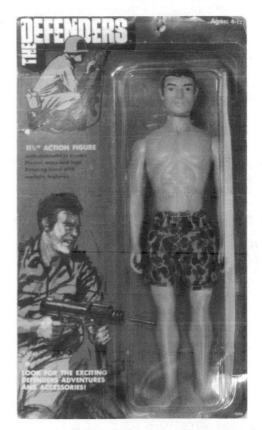

The Defender Figure, Hasbro (1976)

header card which does not say "G.I. Joe." Only a small line of text on the side identifies it as a Hasbro product. It is customarily listed with real G.I. Joe figures to embarrass Hasbro personnel, so they will never do it again!

11½" Figure
Untitled figure $15.00

Uniforms
Ambush 10.00
Commando Assault 10.00
Counter Attack 10.00
Forward Observer 10.00
Point Man 10.00
Sniper Patrol 10.00

Vehicles and Playsets
Command Post with figure (#9020) 50.00
Strong Point with figure (#9021) 50.00
Sea Recovery with figure (#9022) 50.00
Combat Jeep (#9030) 40.00
"Iron Knight" Tank (#9031) 40.00

SUPER JOE
Hasbro (1977–78)

Joe was shrunk down to an eight inch size in this incarnation, due to the problems with the oil embargo of the late 1970s. In this version, Joe was more of a science fiction adventure character and was available with a power vest that accessories could be plugged into and came with a new fighting action called the "1-2 Punch." Adding to this sci-fi theme were villains with names like Terron, Gor, Luminos and Darkon all looking like B-film space aliens. Not much to worry about though as this line lasted only a year and was quickly put out of its misery. Most Joe collectors only vaguely remember it and only as the end of the line for the 1970s.

8" Figures
Super Joe Commander and the Power Vest (#7501) $90.00
Super Joe with the 1-2 punch in red outfit (#7503) . . 65.00
Super Joe (Black) with the 1-2 punch in yellow outfit
    (#7504) 65.00
Night Fighters: The Shield (#7505) 140.00
Night Fighters: Luminos (#7506) 150.00
Darkon (#7508, 1978) 200.00
Terron (#7509?, 1978) 225.00
Gor, King of the Terrons (#7510, 1978) 150.00

Uniform and Equipment, carded
Edge of Adventure (#7511) 40.00
Invisible Danger (#7512) 40.00
Path of Danger (#7513) 40.00
Emergency Rescue (#7514) 40.00

Equipment Sets (Asst. #7528)
Aqua Laser 40.00
Treacherous Dive 40.00
Fusion Bazooka 40.00

Power Packs for G.I. Joe Commander with power vest, boxed
Helipack (#7530) 50.00
Magna Tools (#7531) 50.00
Sonic Scanner (#7532) 50.00

Vehicles and Playsets
Rocket Command Center (#7570) 175.00
Rocket Command Center Super Adventure set with **Gor**
    figure (#7571) 250.00
Super Joe Equipment case (#8000) 55.00

G.I. JOE: A REAL AMERICAN HERO
Hasbro (1982–92)

The Vietnam war was over, Ronald Reagan was President, and there seemed to be a new surge of patriotism following the American olympic hockey team's trouncing of the Soviet players. The folks at Hasbro felt that the time was right to launch a new series of G.I. Joe figures. Well, that's the way we heard it, anyway. If so, it took them two years to get the message, because both the election and the olympics were in 1980 and the figures didn't come out until 1982. The new 3¾" line was quite successful too, aided by animated television programming and comic books from Marvel. Involved in the Joe overhaul project were people such as Kirk Bozigian, Vinnie D'Alleva, Kurt Groen, Greg Berndstadt, and Ron Rudat, whose enthusiasm and concern for top quality-oriented products kept Joe going for over 12 years. It probably would have continued past that point if it weren't for some meddling by the new big brass, resulting in poor decisions and changes in format that brought about the Sgt. Savage and G.I. Joe Extreme lines. It only takes one word to tell how popular they turned out to be—*NOT*! During the later years, the G.I. Joe Hall of Fame series was introduced, starting out as 12" versions of the more popular 3¾" characters. Unfortunately, the popular female characters were dismissed as items which would not have as much sales power! Riigghht! The good news is the 3¾" Joes will be returning in 1997 as a special series of four-pack collectors' items, in order to test the waters before possibly re-launching a new series in this size again! **Yo Joe!**

3¾" Figures
SERIES ONE

First release figures, called "straight arms" bend at the elbow but do not swivel.

Series One ("Straight Arms") (spring 1982)
Ranger Code Name Stalker (#6401) $95.00
Mortar Soldier Code Name Short Fuse (#6402) 85.00
Communications Officer Code Name Breaker (#6403) 85.00
Commando Code Name Snake Eyes (#6404) 165.00
Bazooka Soldier Code Name Zap (#6405) 85.00
Laser Rifle Trooper Code Name Flash (#6406) 85.00
Counter Intelligence Code Name Scarlet (#6407) . . 165.00
Machine Gunner Code Name Rock 'N Roll (#6408) . . 80.00
Infantry Trooper Code Name Grunt (#6409) 70.00

Cobra Enemy (Straight Arms) (fall 1982)
Cobra (Soldier) (#6423) 135.00
Cobra Officer (#6424) 135.00

Mail-in Figure (1982)
Cobra Commander, hooded, bagged 75.00

Vehicles and Accessories, with Figures (1982)
Motorized Battle Tank (MOBAT) battery powered vehicle
    with **Steeler** driver figure (#6000) 150.00

Amphibious Personnel Carrier (APC), G.I. Joe: A Real American Hero (Hasbro 1983)

Attack Vehicle (VAMP) with **Clutch** driver figure
(#6050) 110.00
Heavy Artillery Laser (HAL) with **Grand Slam** figure
(#6052) 110.00
Mobile Missile System (MMS) with **Hawk** figure
(#6054) 110.00

Vehicles and Accessories, without figures (1982)
Jet Pack (JUMP) with platform (#6071) 40.00
Rapid Fire Motorcycle (RAM) vehicle (#6073) 40.00
Attack Cannon (FLAK) (#6075) 40.00

Exclusive
(Cobra) Missile Command Headquarters with **Cobra
Commander, Officer** and **Trooper** figures, Sears
exclusive (#6200) 400.00

SERIES TWO

Swivel-arm figures bend at the elbow and also rotate
360 degrees just above the elbow.

Series Two ("Swivel-Arm Battle Grip") (1983)
Reissue Figures (1982–83)
Ranger Code Name Stalker (#6401) 50.00
Mortar Soldier Code Name Short Fuse (#6402) 50.00
Communications Officer Code Name Breaker (#6403) 50.00
Commando Code Name Snake Eyes (#6404) 150.00
Bazooka Soldier Code Name Zap (#6405) 50.00
Laser Rifle Trooper Code Name Flash (#6406) 50.00
Counter Intelligence Code Name Scarlet (#6407) . . 125.00
Machine Gunner Code Name Rock 'N Roll (#6408) . . 50.00
Infantry Trooper Code Name Grunt (#6409) 50.00

Cobra Enemy Reissues (1982–83)
Cobra (Soldier) (#6423) 50.00
Cobra Officer (#6424) 50.00
Cobra Commander (#6425) 150.00

Reissue Vehicles with Swivel-Arm Reissue Figures
Motorized Battle Tank (MOBAT) vehicle with **Steeler**
driver figure (#6000) 90.00
Attack Vehicle (VAMP) with **Clutch** driver figure
(#6050) 90.00
Heavy Artillery Laser (HAL) with **Grand Slam** figure, red
and black (#6052) 90.00
Mobile Missile System (MMS) with **Hawk** figure
(#6054) 90.00

Mail-in Figure (1982–83)
Mercenary Code Name Major Bludd (swivel arm)
bagged 70.00

New Figures (1983)
Mine Detector Code Name Tripwire (#6410) 70.00
Helicopter Assault Trooper Code Name Airborne
(#6411) 70.00
Arctic Trooper Code Name Snowjob (#6412) 70.00
Seal (Sea, Air and Land) Code Name Torpedo (#6413) 70.00
Marine Code Name Gung Ho (#6414) 70.00
Medic Code Name Doc (#6415) 70.00

Enemy New Figures (1983)
Mercenary Code Name Major Bludd (#6426) 70.00
Enemy Weapons Supplier Code Name Destro (#6427) 70.00

Mail-in Figure (1983)
First Sergeant Code Name Duke, bagged 75.00

New Vehicles and Accessories, with figures (1983)
Combat Jet Skystriker (XP-14F) with **Ace** figure
(#6010) 100.00
Assault Copter Dragonfly (XH-1) with **Wild Bill** figure
(#6025) 150.00
Armored Missile Vehicle Wolverine with **Cover Girl**
figure (#6048) 150.00
Cobra H.I.S.S. (High Speed Sentry) vehicle with **Cobra
H.I.S.S. Driver** figure (#6051) 150.00
Jet Pack (JUMP) with new **Grand Slam** figure, silver

and black (#6065) 250.00

Gliders, with figures (Asst. #6097)
G.I. Joe Attack Glider Falcon with **Grunt** pilot figure   200.00
Cobra Command Attack Glider Viper with **Viper** pilot
figure 200.00

Vehicles and Accessories, without figures (1983)
Polar Battle Bear (skimobile) (#6072) 20.00
Twin Battle Gun Whirlwind (#6074) 20.00
Cobra F.A.N.G. (Fully Armed Negator Gyro) helicopter
(#6077) 20.00
Battle Armor S.N.A.K.E. set (#6083) 60.00
Battle Gear Accessory Pack (#1) (#6088) 20.00
Amphibious Personnel Carrier (APC) (#6093) 75.00

Pac/Rat Accessories (Asst. #6086)
Machine Gun 15.00
Missile Launcher 15.00
Flame Thrower 15.00

Playsets
Headquarters Command Center (#6020) 130.00

Exclusive
Attack Vehicle (VAMP) and Heavy Artillery Laser (HAL)
vehicle, Sears exclusive (#6680) 175.00
Cobra's Sentry and Missile System (S.M.S.), Sears
exclusive (#6686) 100.00

SERIES THREE

Series Three "Swivel-Arm Battle Grip" (1984)
Dog Handler Code Name Mutt with Junkyard (#6416)   40.00
Tracker Code Name Spirit (#6417) 40.00
Halo Jumper Code Name Rip Cord (#6418) 45.00
Heavy Machine Gunner Code Name Roadblock
(#6419) 35.00
Jungle Trooper Code Name Recondo (#6420) 45.00

Flame Thrower Code Name Blowtorch (#6421) 35.00
First Sergeant Code Name Duke (#6422) 55.00

Cobra Enemy (1984)
Cobra Intelligence Officer Code Name Baroness
(#6428) 150.00
Cobra Ninja Code Name Storm Shadow (#6429) . . . 80.00
Cobra Anti-Armor Specialist Code Name Scrap-Iron
(#6431) 40.00
Cobra Saboteur Code Name Firefly (#6432) 75.00

Vehicles and Accessories, with figures (1984)
Hovercraft (Killer W.H.A.L.E.) with **Cutter** figure
(#6005) 100.00
Cobra Rattler (Ground Attack Jet) with **Wild Weasel**
figure (#6027) 150.00
Flying Submarine (S.H.A.R.C.) with **Deep Six** figure
(#6049) 50.00
Attack Vehicle (VAMP Mark II) with **Clutch** figure (Asst.
#6055) 75.00
Cobra Night Attack 4-WD Stinger with **Enemy Cobra
Officer** driver figure (Asst. #6055) 75.00
Self-Propelled Cannon (Slugger) with **Thunder** figure
(#6056) 55.00
Cobra Water Moccasin with **Copperhead** figure
(#6058) 75.00
Zartan the Enemy with **Swamp Skier** (Chameleon) color
changing figure (#6064) 100.00

Vehicles and Accessories, without figure (1984)
Cobra A.S.P. (Assault System Pod) (#6070) 15.00
Sky Hawk One Man V.T.O.L. Jet (#6079) 20.00
Cobra C.L.A.W. (#6082) 10.00
Battle Armor S.N.A.K.E. (#6083) 10.00
Battle Gear Accessory Pack #2 (#6092) 10.00

Battle Stations
Bivouac (Asst. #6125) 12.00
Mountain Howitzer (Asst. #6125) 20.00
Watch Tower (Asst. #6125) 12.00

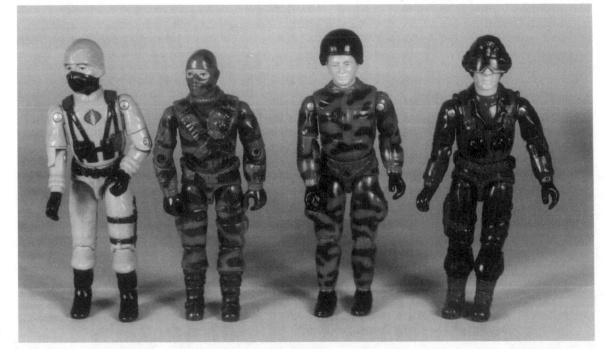

Cobra 4-WD Driver, Cobra Saboteur, Halo Jumper and Cobra Anti-Armor Specialist, G.I. Joe: A Real American Hero (Hasbro 1984)

*Mission Specialist, Infantry Trooper, Sailor and **Cobra Polar Assault**, G.I. Joe: A Real American Hero (Hasbro 1985)*

Battlefield Accessories
Missile Defense Unit (Asst. #6150) 12.00
Machine Gun Defense Unit (#6151) 10.00
Mortar Defense Unit (Asst. #6152) 10.00

Mail-in Vehicle
Manta Windsurfer vehicle (1984) 30.00

Exclusives
Motorized Crimson Attack Tank (C.A.T.), Sears
    exclusive (#6687) 150.00

SERIES FOUR

The G.I. Joe animated television series debuted in fall 1985.

Series Four (1985) Head now moves up and down
Warrant Officer Code Name Flint (#6436) 30.00
Commando Code Name Snake Eyes (with wolf and new
    outfit) (#6437) 90.00
Missile Specialist Code Name Bazooka (#6438) 30.00
Hostile Environment Code Name Airtight (#6439) . . . 30.00
Covert Operations Code Name Lady Jaye (#6440) . . 50.00
Silent Weapons Code Name Quick Kick (#6441) 35.00
Desert Trooper Code Name Dusty (#6442) 40.00
Mountain Trooper Code Name Alpine (#6443) 40.00
Infantry Trooper Code Name Footloose (#6444) 30.00
Fire Fighter Code Name Barbecue (#6445) 35.00
Sailor Code Name Shipwreck (#6446) 40.00

Cobra Enemy
Cobra Communications Code Name Tele-Viper
    (#6447) 25.00
Cobra Frogman Code Name Eel (#6448) 40.00
Cobra Polar Assault Code Name Snow Serpent
    (#6449) 35.00
Cobra Elite Trooper Code Name Crimson Guard

(#6450) 45.00

Dreadnoks
Dreadnok Code Name Buzzer (#6433) 30.00
Dreadnok Code Name Ripper (#6434) 30.00
Dreadnok Code Name Torch (#6435) 30.00

Two-Pack
Crimson Guard Commanders Code Names Tomax and
    Xamot (2-figure pack) (#6063) 60.00

Figure and Tape
Listen 'N Fun with Mine Detector Code Name **Tripwire**
    figure (new colors) . . . . no price found

Vehicles and Accessories, with figure (1985)
Aircraft Carrier USS Flagg with **Keel-Haul Admiral**
    figure, 7½' playset (#6001) 500.00
Mauler M.B.T. Tank with **Heavy Metal** figure (#6015)   60.00
Bridge Layer (Toss 'N Cross) with **Toll Booth** figure
    (#6023) 75.00
Cobra Hydrofoil (Moray) with **Lampreys** figure (#6024) 50.00
A.W.E Striker with **Crank Case** figure (#6053) 40.00
Snow Cat with **Frostbite** figure (#6057) 40.00

Vehicles and Accessories, without figure (1985)
Transportable Tactical Battle Platform (#6021) 50.00
Cobra Ferret (#6069) 20.00
Silver Mirage Motorcycle (#6076) 30.00
Mini Tank Armadillo (#6078) 20.00
Cobra Flight Pod (Trubble Bubble) (#6081) 15.00
Battle Gear Accessory Pack #3 (#6092) 10.00

Battlefield Vehicles (Asst. #6085)
Bomb Disposal vehicle 15.00
Cobra Night Landing raft 15.00
Weapon Transport 15.00

Mauler M.B.T. Tank, G.I. Joe: A Real American Hero (Hasbro 1985)

Battle Stations (Asst. #6125)
Air Defense 15.00
Check Point Tower 15.00
Cobra Bunker 20.00

Battlefield Accessories (Asst. #6129)
Ammo Dump Unit 15.00
Forward Observer Unit 15.00
Cobra Rifle Range Unit 15.00

SERIES FIVE

Actually appeared in late 1985, but listed as "new" in 1986 catalog. Distributed, along with Series Four figures, in three assortments. The figure's "Code Name" now comes first on the header card and in our listings.

Series Five (1986)
B.A.T. (Cobra Android Trooper) (#6456) 18.00
Zandar (Zartan's Brother) (#6457) 18.00
Leatherneck (Marine) (#6458) 20.00
Low Light (Night Spotter) (#6459) 20.00
Monkeywrench (Dreadnok) (#6460) 18.00
Dr. Mindbender (Master of Mind Control) (#6461) ... 18.00
Mainframe (Computer Specialist) (#6462) 18.00
Beach Head (Ranger) (#6463) 20.00
Lifeline (Rescue Trooper) (#6465) 22.00
Iceberg (Snow Trooper) (#6466) 18.00
Roadblock (Heavy Machine Gunner) (#6467) 22.00
Hawk (G.I. Joe Commander) (#6468) 20.00
Sci-Fi (Laser Trooper) (#6469) 18.00
Wet-Suit (Seals) (#6470) 25.00
Dial-Tone (Communications) (#6471) 18.00
Zarana (Zartan's Sister) with earrings, first issue (#6472) 115.00
   Variation, with no earrings, different head (#6472) 18.00
Viper(s) (Cobra Infantry) (#6473) 20.00

Mail-In Figure
Sgt. Slaughter (Drill Instructor) 30.00

Vehicles and Accessories, with figure (1986)
Cobra Terror Drome with Firebat playset with **A.V.A.C.** figure (#6003) 250.00
Cobra Night Raven S³P plane with **Strato-Viper** figure (#6014) 60.00
Tomahawk helicopter with **Lift-Ticket** figure (#6022) . 75.00
H.A.V.O.C. Heavy Articulated Vehicle Ordnance Carrier vehicle with **Cross-Country** figure (#6030) ... 30.00
Conquest X-30 jet plane with **Slip Stream** figure (#6031) 60.00
Cobra Stun vehicle with **Motor Viper** figure (#6041) . 30.00
Dreadnok Thunder Machine with **Thrasher** figure (#6042) 35.00
Sgt. Slaughter with Triple 'T' (Tag Team Terminator) vehicle (#6061) 40.00
Serpentor, Cobra Emperor with Air Chariot vehicle (#6062) 45.00

Vehicles and Accessories, without figure (1986)
Devilfish vehicle (#6066) 18.00
L.C.V. Recon Sled (Low Crawl Vehicle) (#6067) 12.00
Dreadnok Swampfire vehicle (#6068) 18.00
Vehicle Gear Accessory Pack #1 .... 8.00
Cobra Battle Gear Accessory Pack #4 (#6096) 8.00
Cobra Jet Pack (Asst. #6099) 8.00
Cobra Hydro-Sled (Asst. #6099) 10.00

Battle Stations (Asst. #6130)
Cobra Surveillance Port 12.00
Outpost Defender 13.00
L.A.W. (Laser Artillery Weapon) 9.00

Exclusives
Dreadnok Ground Assault, Sears exclusive (#6688) . 75.00
Dreadnok Air Assault, Sears exclusive (#6689) 75.00
Special Mission: Brazil with **Dial-Tone**, **Main Frame**,

Wet-Suit, **Leatherneck** and **Claymore** figures with new outfits and mission tape, Toys "R" Us exclusive (#6691) 75.00

SERIES SIX

Actually appeared in late 1986, but listed as "new" in 1987 catalog. Distributed, along with Series Five figures, in three assortments

Series Six (1987)
Cobra Commander with Battle Armor (#6474) 22.00
Crazylegs (Assault Trooper) (#6475) 12.00
Falcon (Green Beret) (#6476) 12.00
Psyche-Out (Deceptive Warfare) (#6477) 12.00
Law & Order (MP & K-9) (#6478) 18.00
Crystal Ball (Cobra Hypnotist) (#6479) 10.00
Jinx (Ninja/Intelligence) (#6480) 20.00
Tunnel Rat (L.O.D.) (#6481) 20.00
Chuckles (Undercover) (#6482) 18.00
Outback (Survivalist) (#6483) 12.00
Big Boa (Cobra Trainer) (#6484) 20.00
Raptor (Cobra Falconer) (#6485) 20.00
Gung Ho (Marine Dress Blues) (#6486) 18.00
Croc Master (Cobra Reptile Trainer) (#6487) 25.00
Fast Draw (Mobile Missile Specialist) (#6488) 12.00
Techno-Viper (Cobra Battlefield Technician) (#6490) . 12.00
Sneak Peek (Advanced Recon) (#6491) 8.00

Mail-in Figure
The Fridge (Physical Training Instructor) 20.00

Three-Packs
Sgt. Slaughter's Renegades (Taurus, Red Dog and Mercer figures) Toys "R" Us exclusive (#6153, 1987) 60.00
Cobra-La team (Golobulus, Nemesis Enforcer and Royal Guard) (#6154, 1987) 65.00

Vehicles and Accessories, with figure (1987)
Defiant: Space Vehicle Launch Complex playset with **Payload** astronaut and **Hardtop** driver figures (#6002) 375.00
Mobile Command Center vehicle/playset with **Steam-Roller** operator figure (#6006) 80.00
Cobra Mamba vehicle with **Gyro-Viper** figure (#6026) 30.00
Cobra Maggot vehicle with **W.O.R.M.S.** figure (#6029) 40.00
Persuader with **Back Stop** driver figure (#6038) 35.00
Cobra Wolf with **Ice Viper** driver figure (#6039) 45.00
Cobra Sea Ray with **Sea Slug** navigator figure (#6040) 40.00
Zanzibar, Dreadnok Pirate with Air Skiff vehicle (#6060) 25.00

Vehicles and Accessories, without figure (1987)
Vehicle Gear Accessory Pack #1 (#6098) 7.50
Cobra Pogo Ballistic Battle Ball (#6170) 10.00
Dreadnok Cycle (#6171) 13.00
S.L.A.M. (Strategic Long-Range Artillery Machine) (#6172) 12.00
Battle Gear Accessory Pack #5 (#6677) 7.50

Battlefield Vehicles (Asst. #6087, 1987)
Cobra Buzz Boar vehicle 8.00
Costal Defender vehicle 10.00
Road Toad (B.R.V.) vehicle 10.00

Motorized Action Packs (Asst. #6133, 1987)
G.I. Joe
Anti-Aircraft Gun 5.00
Helicopter 5.00
Radar Station 5.00
Rope Walker 5.00

Cobra
Earth Borer 5.00
Mountain Climber 5.00
Pom-Pom Gun 5.00
Rope Crosser 5.00

SERIES SEVEN

Actually appeared in late 1987, but listed as "new" in 1988 catalog. Distributed, along with Series Six figures, in three assortments

Series Seven (1988)
Blizzard (Arctic Attack Soldier) (#6505) 12.00
Iron Grenadiers (Destro's Elite Troopers) (#6506) ... 15.00
Storm Shadow (Ninja) (#6507) 20.00
Repeater (Steadi-Cam Machine Gunner) (#6508) .. 12.00
Shockwave (S.W.A.T. Specialist) (#6509) 15.00
Charbroil (Flame Thrower) (#6510) 12.00
Lightfoot (Explosives Expert) (#6512) 12.00
Toxo-Viper (Cobra Hostile Environment Trooper) (#6513) 13.00
Hardball (Multi-Shot Grenadier) (#6513) 12.00
Spearhead & Max (Point Man & Bobcat) (#6514) ... 14.00
Astro Viper (Cobranaut) (#6515) 15.00
Muskrat (Swamp Fighter) (#6516) 13.00
Budo (Samurai Warrior) (#6517) 12.00
Hit & Run (Light Infantryman) (#6517) 18.00
Hydro-Viper (Cobra Underwater Elite Trooper) (#6519) 14.00
Voltar (Destro's General) (#6520) 14.00
Road Pig (Dreadnok) (#6521) 14.00

Mail-in Figures
Life Line (Rice Krispies mail-in) 12.00
Starduster (Jet Pack Trooper (#6253) ..... no price found

Vehicles and Accessories, with figure (1988)
Rolling Thunder with **Armadillo** (#6012) 100.00
Phantom X-19 Stealth Fighter with **Ghostrider** figure (#6016) 75.00
Cobra Bugg with **Secto-Viper** figure (#6018) 120.00
Mean Dog with **Wildcard** driver figure (#6028) 50.00
Warthog A.I.F.V. with **Sgt. Slaughter** figure (#6032) . 45.00
D.E.M.O.N. with **Ferret** driver figure (Iron Grenadiers) (#6033) 60.00
Skystorm X-Wing Chopper with **Windmill** pilot figure (#6045) 40.00
Destro's Despoiler with **Destro** figure (#6059) 40.00
Cobra Stellar Stiletto with **Star-Viper** pilot figure (#6252) 20.00
Desert Fox 6-W.D. with **Skidmark** driver figure (#6253) 60.00

Vehicles and Accessories, without figure (1988)
Swampmasher vehicle (#6161) 8.00
Cobra Imp vehicle (#6165) 10.00
Cobra Battle Gear Accessory Pack #6 (#6191) 7.00
R.P.V. (Remote Piloted Vehicle) (#6285) 7.50
Cobra Adder vehicle (#6287) 10.00

Astro Viper, Hydro Viper, Road Pig and Storm Shadow, G.I. Joe: A Real American Hero (Hasbro 1988)

Cobra Weapon Assortment (Asst. #6299, 1988)
Cobra Battle Barge 10.00
Cobra Jet Pack 12.00

Radio-Control Vehicles
Crossfire radio-control Fast Attack Vehicle with Rumbler
    (Alpha 27) 150.00
Crossfire radio-control Fast Attack Vehicle with Rumbler
    (Delta 49) 150.00

Motorized Action Packs (1988)
G.I. Joe
Mine Sweeper (Asst. #6133) 7.00
Mortar Launcher (Asst. #6133) 7.00
Double Machine Gun (Asst. #6133) 7.00
A.T.V. (Asst. #6135) 7.00
Scuba Pack (Asst. #6135) 7.00
Tank Car (Asst. #6135) 7.00

Cobra
Cobra Twin Missile Launcher (Asst. #6133) 7.00
Cobra Machine Gun Nest (Asst. #6133) 7.00
Cobra Gyrocopter (Asst. #6133?) 7.00
Cobra Rocket Sled (Asst. #6133?) 7.00
Dreadnok Battle Axe (Asst. #6133) 7.00

Exclusives
Hit & Run (Airborne Assault Parachute Pack) Target
    exclusive .... no price found

BATTLE FORCE 2000 (1987–89)

Battle Force 2000 (1987–89)
Avalanche (Snow Vehicle Driver) (#6522) 22.00
Blaster (Hovercraft Pilot) (#6522) 22.00
Blocker (Four-Wheeled Vehicle Driver) (#6523) 22.00
Maverick (Jet Fighter Pilot) (#6523) 22.00
Dodger (Half-Track Driver) (#6524) 22.00

Knockdown (Anti-Aircraft Driver) (#6524) 22.00
Dee-Jay (Comm-Tech Trooper) (#6531, 1989) 10.00

Battle Force 2000 "Special 2-in-1 Packs"
Avalanche and Blaster (2-pack) (#6522–6696) 30.00
Maverick and Blocker (2-pack) (#6523–6696) 30.00
Knockdown and Dodger (2-pack) (#6524–6696) 30.00

Ultimate Enemies Two-Pack
Muskrat (Swamp Fighter) and Voltar (Destro's
    General) .... no price found

Battle Force 2000 Vehicles (1988)
Marauder (Motorcycle-Tank) (#6643) 25.00
Sky Sweeper (Anti-Aircraft Tank) (#6644) 25.00
Vindicator (Hovercraft) (#6645) 25.00
Dominator (Snow Tank) (#6646) 25.00
Eliminator (4WD) (#6647) 25.00
Vector (Jet) (#6648) 25.00
A.G.P. (Anti-Gravity Pod) with **Nullifier** figure (Iron
    Grenadiers) (#6649) 22.00
Pulverizer (#6286, 1989) 10.00

TIGER FORCE (1988–89)

Tiger Force (Asst. #6697, 1988–89)
Duke (First Sergeant) 17.00
Lifeline (Medic) (#6637) 17.00
Flint (Warrant Officer) 17.00
Dusty (Desert Trooper) 17.00
Bazooka (Missile Specialist) (#6640) 17.00
Roadblock (Heavy Machine Gunner) (#6641) 17.00
Tripwire (Mine Detector) (#6642) 17.00

Mail-In Figures
Super Trooper 20.00
Steel Brigade You Name Joe with patch and certificate 13.00

Tiger Force Vehicles (1988–89)
Tiger Paw (#6669) 16.00
Tiger Shark (#6670) 16.00
Tiger Cat with **Frostbite** figure (#6671) 40.00
Tiger Fly with **Recondo** figure (#6672) 35.00
Tiger Rat with **Skystriker** figure (#6673) 45.00
Tiger Fish (#6674, 1989) 14.00
Tiger Sting (#6675, 1989) 14.00

NIGHTFORCE (1988–89)

Nightforce "Special 2-in-1 Packs" (Asst. #6709, 1988) Toys "R" Us exclusive
Sneak Peek and Lt. Falcon 40.00
Tunnel Rat and Psyche-Out 40.00
Outback and Crazylegs 40.00

Nightforce "Special 2-in-1 Packs" (Asst #6710, 1989) Toys "R" Us exclusive
Charbroil and Repeater 50.00
Lightfoot and Shockwave 50.00
Muskrat and Spearhead & Max 50.00

Nightforce Vehicles (1988) Toys "R" Us exclusives
Night Blaster (#6704) 30.00
Night Storm (#6705) 30.00
Night Raider (#6706) 30.00
Night Shade (#6707) 30.00
Night Striker (#6708) 45.00
Night Ray 40.00
Night Boomer 50.00

Nightforce Vehicles (1989) Toys "R" Us exclusives
Night Scrambler (#6709) 35.00
Three-Vehicle Set: Night Ray, Night Boomer, Night
   Scrambler .... no price found

SERIES EIGHT

Series Eight (1989)
Recoil (Long Range Recon Patrol) (#6525) 7.00
Scoop (Combat Information Specialist) (#6526) 9.00
Countdown (Astronaut) (#6527) 9.00
Snake Eyes (Commando) (#6528) 22.00
Alley Viper (Cobra Urban Assault Trooper) (#6529) .. 12.00
T.A.R.G.A.T. (Trans Atmospheric Rapid Global Assault
   Trooper) (Iron Grenadiers) (#6530) 12.00
Rock & Roll (Gatling Gunner) (#6532) 9.00
Stalker (Tundra Ranger) (#6533) 9.00
H.E.A.T. Viper (High Explosive Anti-Tank) (Cobra
   Bazooka Man) (#6534) 9.00
Gnawgahyde (Dreadnok Poacher) (#6535) 9.00
Back Blast (Anti-Aircraft Soldier) (#6543) 9.00
Downtown (Mortar Man) (#6544) 9.00
Deep Six (Deep Sea Diver) (#6545) 12.00
Frag-Viper (Cobra Grenade Thrower) (#6546) 12.00
Night Viper (Cobra Night Fighter) (#6547) 12.00
Annihilator (Destro's Elite Trooper) (Iron Grenadiers)
   (#6548) 12.00

Vehicles and Accessories, with figure (1989)
Crusader Space Shuttle with Avenger Scout Craft with
   Payload figure (#6220, 1989) 75.00
Cobra Condor Z25 with **Aero-Viper** figure (#6222) .. 50.00
Cobra Battle Copter with **Heli-Viper** figure . no price found
Thunderclap with **Long Range** figure (#6233, 1989) . 85.00
Raider with **Hot Seat** figure (#6240, 1989) 50.00
Destro's Razorback vehicle with **Wild Boar** figure (Iron
   Grenadiers) (#6242) 38.00
Cobra H.I.S.S. II vehicle with **Track Viper** figure (#6246,
   1989) 42.00
Arctic Blast with **Windchill** figure (#6254, 1989) 30.00
Mudfighter plane with **Dogfight** figure (#6255, 1989) . 25.00
Darklon's Evader with **Darklon** figure (Iron Grenadiers)
   (#6271, 1989) 25.00

Downtown, Gnawgahyde, H.E.A.T. Viper and Rock & Roll, G.I. Joe: A Real American Hero (Hasbro 1989)

Vehicles and Accessories, without figure (1989)
Cobra Fang II (#6281, 1989) 12.00

Battlefield Robots
(Cobra) Devastator (#6633) 9.00
(Cobra) Hovercraft (#6637) 9.00
Tri-Blaster (#6638) 9.00
Radar Rat (#6639) 9.00

Two-Vehicle Pack
Mudfighter and Cobra H.I.S.S. II (#6852) 180.00

SLAUGHTER'S MARAUDERS

Slaughter's Marauders (Asst. #6560, 1989)
Sgt. Slaughter (Slaughter's Marauders Commander) . 12.00
Mutt (Animal Control Utilization Technician) 12.00
Low-Light (Night Spotter) 13.00
Spirit (Tracker) 12.00
Barbecue (Firefighter) 13.00
Footloose (Infantry Trooper) 12.00

Slaughter's Marauders Vehicles
Slaughter's Marauders Armadillo vehicle (#6717) ... 14.00
Slaughter's Marauders Lynx vehicle (#6718) 14.00
Slaughter's Marauders Equalizer tank vehicle (#6719) 14.00

PYTHON PATROL

Python Patrol (Asst. #6623, 1989)
Python Officer (Python Patrol Officer) 11.00
Python Viper (Python Patrol Assault Trooper) 11.00
Python Tele-Viper (Python Patrol Communications) .. 11.00
Python Crimson Guard (Python Patrol Elite Trooper) . 11.00
Python Copperhead (Python Patrol Swamp Fighter) . 11.00
Python Trooper (Python Patrol Infantry) 11.00

Python Patrol Vehicles
Asp (#6618) 14.00

STUN vehicle (#6619) 12.00
Conquest (#6620) 35.00

SERIES NINE

Series Nine (1990)
Undertow (Destro's Frogman) (Iron Grenadiers)
    (#6137) 12.00
Captain Grid-Iron (Hand-to-Hand Combat Specialist)
    (#6561) 12.00
Night-Creeper (Cobra Ninja) (#6562) 12.00
Topside (Navy Assault Seaman) (#6563) 12.00
Rock-Viper (Cobra Mountain Trooper) (#6564) 13.00
Sub-Zero (Winter Operation Specialist) (#6565) 10.00
Ambush (Concealment Specialist) (#6566) 13.00
Salvo (Anti-Armor Trooper) (#6567) 13.00
Free Fall (Paratrooper) (#6568) 12.00
Laser-Viper (Cobra Laser Trooper) (#6569) 15.00
S.A.W. Viper (Cobra Heavy Machine Gunner) (#6570) 13.00
Metal Head (Destro Anti-Tank Specialist) (Iron
    Grenadiers) (#6571) 13.00
Range-Viper (Cobra Wilderness Troopers) (#6573) .. 15.00
Rampart (Shoreline Defender) (#6574) 13.00
Stretcher (Medical Specialist) (#6575) 13.00
Bullhorn (Intervention Specialist) (#6576) 13.00
Pathfinder (Jungle Assault Specialist) (#6577) 12.00

Figure with Video Tape
Rapid-Fire with Video Tape "Revenge of the Pharohs" 18.00

Sky Patrol (Asst. #6200, 1990) with "Soaring Silver
Parachute"
Airborne 18.00
Drop Zone 18.00
Sky Dive 18.00
Airwave 18.00
Altitude 18.00
Static Line 18.00

Salvo, Metal Head, Night-Creeper and *Bullhorn, G.I. Joe: A Real American Hero (Hasbro 1990)*

Sky Patrol Vehicles
Sky Havoc (#6110) 35.00
Sky Sharc (#6116) 30.00
Sky Raven (#6118) 40.00
Sky Hawk (#6361) 28.00

Vehicles, with figure (1990)
General with **Major Storm** driver figure (#6320) 50.00
Hammerhead with **Decimator** driver figure (Cobra)
    (#6335) 35.00
Retaliator with **Updraft** driver figure (#6339) 38.00
Avalanche with **Cold Front** driver figure (#6343) 30.00
Hurricane VTOL with **Vapor** driver figure (#6357?) . . 50.00
Cobra Overlord's Dictator with **Overlord** driver figure
    (#6380) 30.00

Vehicles and Accessories, without figure (1990)
Cobra Rage (#6112) 15.00
Destro's Dominator (Iron Grenadiers) (#6368?) 13.00
Hammer vehicle (#6369?) 13.00
Mobile Battle Bunker, Missile Firing Defense Tank
    (#6372) 16.00
Cobra Piranah (#6385) 11.00
Locust vehicle (#6388) 12.00

SERIES TEN

Series Ten (1991)
Dusty & Sandstorm (Desert Trooper & Coyote)
    (#6580) 16.00
Low-Light (Night Fighter) (#6581) 19.00
Big Ben (SAS Trooper) (#6582) 17.00
General Hawk (G.I. Joe Commander) (#6583) 16.00
Crimson Guard Immortal (Cobra Elite Trooper) (#6584) 17.00
Desert Scorpion (Cobra Desert Trooper) (#6585) . . . 20.00
Heavy Duty (G.I. Joe Heavy Ordnance Trooper)
    (#6586) 12.00
Sci-Fi (Directed Energy Expert) (#6587) 20.00
Red Star (Oktober Guard) (#6588) 12.00
    Variation, on Cobra header card 40.00
Snow Serpent (Cobra Snow Trooper) (#6589) 10.00
Incinerator (Flamethrower) (#6590) 18.00
Grunt (Infantry Squad Leader) (#6591) 18.00
Snake Eyes (Commando) (#6592) 17.00
Tracker (Navy S.E.A.L.) (#6593) 20.00
Mercer (Mercenary) (#6594) 20.00
B.A.T. (Battle Android Trooper) (#6595) 10.00
Cobra Commander (Cobra Leader) (#6596) no
    eyebrows 20.00
    Variation, with eyebrows 40.00
Rapid Fire with "Revenge of the Pharoahs" Video Tape
    (Toys "R" Us) 15.00

Mail-in Figures
Life-Line (Rice Krispies mail-in) 20.00
Rampage . . . . no price found

Talking Battle Commanders (1991)
General Hawk (G.I. Joe Commander) (#6751) 14.00
Stalker (Ranger) (#6752) 10.00
Cobra Commander (Cobra Leader) (#6753) 14.00
Overkill (B.A.T. Leader) (#6754) 14.00

Vehicles and Accessories, with figure (1991)
Battle Copter (Asst. #6219)
Battle Copter (Cobra) with **Interrogator** driver figure
    (#6325) 20.00

Battle Copter with **Major Altitude** driver figure (#6326) 20.00

Vehicles and Accessories, without figure (1991)
Badger (#6215) 10.00
Paralyzer (Cobra) (#6217) 9.00
Ice Sabre (Cobra) (#6221) 14.00
Attack Cruiser (#6226) 12.00
Brawler (#6321, 1991) 22.00
Motorized Battle Wagon (#6344) 36.00

Air Commandos Fighters with Glider (1991–92)
Skymate glider with **Skymate** glider trooper driver
    (#6811) 20.00
Cloudburst glider with **Cloudburst** glider trooper driver
    (#6812) 20.00
Sky Creeper glider with **Air Recon Leader** driver
    (#6813) 18.00
Night Vulture glider with **Air Recon Trooper** driver
    (#6814) 18.00
Spirit glider with **Air Commando Leader** driver (#6737,
    1992) 18.00
Cobra Air Devil glider with **Acrobatic Aerial Assault**
    driver (1992) 18.00

SONIC FIGHTERS (1991–92)

Sonic Fighters with "4 Electronic Battle Sounds" (1991)
Tunnel Rat (E.O.D.) (#6311) 16.00
Law (M.P.) (#6312) 16.00
Dial-Tone (Communications) (#6313) 16.00
Dodger (Heavy Ordnance Operator) (#6314) 16.00
Viper (Cobra Infantryman) (#6315) 16.00
Lampreys (Amphibian Assault Troopers) (#6316) . . . 16.00

Sonic Fighters (1992)
Lt. Falcon (Green Beret) (#6597) 10.00
Zap (Ground Artillery Soldier) (#6598) 10.00
Major Bludd (Mercenary) (#6599) 10.00
Road Pig (Dreadnok) (#6630) 10.00
Rock 'N Roll (Machine Gunner) (#6631) 10.00
Psyche-Out (Deceptive Warfare) (#6632) 10.00

Sonic Fighters Vehicles
Fort America (#6241) 35.00
AH-74 Desert Apache 30.00

ECO-WARRIORS (1991–92)

Eco-Warriors (1991)
Clean-Sweep (Anti-Tox Trooper) (#6814) 7.00
Flint (Eco-Warriors Commander) (#6815) 7.00
Ozone (Ozone Replenisher Trooper) (#6817) 7.00
Cesspool (CEO Chief Environmental Operative)
    (#6818) 7.00
Toxo-Viper (Hostile Environmental Trooper) (#6819-1) 10.00
Toxo-Viper II (Maintenance Antarb Trooper) (#6819-2) 10.00
Sludge Viper (Hazardous Waste Viper) (#6820) 10.00

Eco-Warriors (Series 2) (1992)
1. Deep-Six (Deep Water Specialist) and gray dolphin 10.00
    Variation with black dolphin, scarce 600.00
2. Barbecue (Firefighter) (#6822) 10.00
3. Toxo-Zombie (Toxic Disaster Trooper) (#6823) . . . 10.00

Eco-Warriors Vehicles and Playset
Septic Tank (Cobra) vehicle (#6144) 16.00

Eco Striker vehicle (#6145) 16.00
Toxo-Lab (Cobra) playset (#6146) 20.00

SERIES ELEVEN

Series Eleven (1992)
1. Duke (Master Sergeant) (#6725) 8.00
2. Wet-Suit (S.E.A.L.) (#6726) 8.00
3. Roadblock (Heavy Machine Gunner) (#6727) scarce 125.00
4. Big Bear (Oktober Guard Anti-Armor Specialist) (#6728) 8.00
5. Destro (Enemy Weapons Supplier) (#6729) .. 8.00
6. Flak-Viper (Cobra Anti-Aircraft Trooper) (#6730) ... 8.00
7. General Flagg (G.I. Joe General) (#6739) ... 8.00
8. Gung-Ho (U.S. Marine) (#6740 .... 8.00
9. Barricade (Bunker Buster) (#6741) 8.00
10. Wild Bill (Air Cavalry Scout) (#6742) 8.00
11. Firefly (Cobra Saboteur) (#6743) 8.00
12. Eel (Cobra Underwater Specialist) (#6744) 8.00

Vehicles and Accessories, without figure (1992)
Patriot, Armored Missile Launcher Transport (#6232)   18.00
Rat (Cobra) High-Speed Attack Hovercraft (#6228) .. 12.00
Parasite (Cobra) Armored Personnel Carrier (#6234)   18.00
Liquidator, Cobra's Advanced Tactical Fighter Jet (#6237) 15.00
Storm Eagle, High Powered Advanced Tactical Fighter (#6238) 15.00
Earthquake (Cobra) Ground-Ripping Construction and Combat Vehicle (#6239) 18.00
Headquarters, The Fully Armed, Multi-Deployable, G.I. Joe Command Station (#6243) 20.00
Barracuda, One-Man Attack Sub (#6277, 1991?) ... 12.00

Battle Copter (Cobra) with **Heli-Viper** pilot figure (1992) .... .00
Battle Copter with **Ace** pilot figure (1992) .... .00

D.E.F.

Drug Elimination Force (and Headhunters) (1992)
1. Bullet-Proof (D.E.F. Leader) (#) 7.00
2. Shockwave (S.W.A.T. Specialist) (#) 7.00
3. Mutt & Junkyard (K-9 Officer & Attack Dog) (#) ... 7.00
4. Headman (Headman Drug Kingpin) (#) 7.00
5. Cutter (Vehicle Operations Specialist) (#) 7.00
6. Headhunter (Headman's Narcotics Guards) (#) ... 7.00

NINJA FORCE

Ninja Force (Series 1) (1992)
1. Storm Shadow (Ninja Force Leader) (#6731) 15.00
2. Dojo (Silent Weapons Ninja) (#6732) 12.00
3. Nunchuk (Nunchaku Ninja) (#6733) 12.00
4. T'Jbang (Ninja Swordsman) (#6734) 12.00
5. Slice (Cobra Ninja Swordsman) (#6735) red 13.00
6. Dice (Cobra Bo-Staff Ninja) (#6736) 13.00

Ninja Force (Series 2) (Asst. #6770, Jan. 1993)
1. Snake-Eyes (Covert Mission Specialist) (#6871) . 15.00
2. Zartan (Master of Disguise) (#6872) 6.00
3. Night Creeper (Cobra Ninja) (#6873) 7.00
4. Scarlett (Counter Intelligence Specialist) (#6874) . 15.00
5. Banzai (Rising Sun Ninja) (#6875) 9.00
6. Bushido (Snow Ninja) (#6876) 9.00

Scarlet (Ninja Force),
G.I. Joe: A Real American Hero (Hasbro 1992)

7. Slice (Cobra Ninja Swordsman) (#6877) 6.00

Ninja Force Vehicles
Ninja Lightning cycle (#6888, 1993) 12.00
Ninja Raider Battle Axe vehicle with **Red Ninja** figure (1993) 14.00
Ninja Raider Pile Driver vehicle with **T'Gin-Zu** figure (1993) 14.00

MEGAMARINES

MegaMarines (Asst. #6680, May 1993)
1. Gung-Ho (Mega Marines Commander) 8.00
2. Clutch (Monster Blaster APC Driver) 8.00
3. Mega-Viper (Mega Monster Trainer) 8.00
4. Mirage (Bio-Artillery Expert) 8.00
5. Blast-Off (Flame Thrower) 8.00
6. Cyber-Viper (Cybernetic Officer) 8.00

MegaMonsters (Asst. #6075, June 1993)
7. Bio Viper (Genetically Enhanced Undersea Monster) 15.00
8. Monstro-Viper (Genetically Enhanced Bio-Beast) . 15.00

MegaMarines Vehicle
Monster Blaster A.P.C., Armored Personnel Carrier (#6889, 1993) 14.00

STREET FIGHTER II

Street Fighter II (Asst. #6238, May 1993)
1. Ryu (Shotokan Karate Fighter) 5.00

2. Ken Masters (Shotokan Karate Fighter) 5.00
3. Guile (Special Forces Fighter) (#81081) 5.00
4. Chun Li (Kung Fu Fighter) 5.00
5. Blanka (Jungle Fighter) 5.00
6. M. Bison (Grand Master) (#81084) 5.00
6. M. Bison (Grand Master) (#81084) with shoulder
   pads 5.00

Second Batch (Asst. #6657, Oct. 1993)
7. Edmond Honda (Sumo Wrestler) 5.00
8. Dhalsim (Yoga Fighter) (#81092) 5.00
9. Zangief (Russian Bear Wrestler) (#81093) 5.00
10. Vega (Spanish Ninja) 5.00
11. Balrog (Heavyweight Boxer) 5.00
12. Sagat (Fighter) 5.00

12" Street Fighter II Hall of Fame Figures (1993)
Guile (#6765) 25.00
Blanka (#6809) 25.00
M. Bison (#6947) 25.00
Ryu (#6695) 25.00

Street Fighter II Vehicles (1993)
Dragon Fortress playset with **Ryu** and **Ken Masters**
   figures (#6455) 30.00
Beast Blaster vehicle with **Blanka** and **Chun Li** figures 20.00
Sonic Boom Tank with **Guile** figure (#6790) 12.00
Crimson Cruiser with **M. Bison** figure 12.00
Street Buffalo with **M. Bison** figure (#6201) 12.00

SERIES TWELVE

Series Twelve, Battle Corps (Asst. #6860, Late 1982)
1. Bazooka (Missile Specialist) 6.00
2. Cross-Country (Transport Expert) 6.00
3. Iceberg (Arctic Assault Trooper) 6.00
4. Beach-Head (Ranger) 6.00
5. H.E.A.T. Viper (High Explosive Anti-Tank Trooper) . 6.00
6. Alley Viper (Urban Assault Trooper) 6.00
7. Roadblock (Heavy Machine Gunner) old colors ... 6.00
   Variation, repaint 6.00
8. Wet-Suit (Navy S.E.A.L.) 6.00

Series Twelve (Asst. #6123, Jan 1993)
9. Flak-Viper (Anti-Aircraft Trooper) (#6776) 6.00
10. Colonel Courage (Strategic Commander) (#6777) . 6.00
11. Leatherneck (Infantry Training Specialist) (#6778) . 6.00
12. Snow Storm (High Tech Snow Trooper) (#6779) .. 6.00
   Variation, with orange helmet 6.00
13. Outback (Survivalist Specialist) (#6780) 6.00
   Variation, with yellow helmet 6.00
14. Night Creeper Leader (Cobra Ninja Supreme Master)
   (#6781) 6.00
15. Dr. Mindbender (Master of Mind Control) (#6782) . 6.00
16. Gung-Ho (U.S. Marine) 6.00
17. Barricade (Bunker Buster) (#6768) 6.00
18A. Firefly (Cobra Saboteur) 6.00

Battle Corps (1993) (Asst. #6770, April 1993)
19. Duke (Battle Commander) 6.00
20. Frostbite (Arctic Commander) 6.00
21. Keel-Haul (Admiral) large logo 6.00
   Variation, with small logo 15.00
22. Backblast (Anti-Aircraft Soldier) 6.00
23. Crimson Guard Commander (Cobra Elite Officer) . 6.00
24. Cobra Commander (Cobra Supreme Leader) 6.00
25. Wild Bill (Aero-Scout) 6.00

Colonel Courage (Battle Corps),
G.I. Joe: A Real American Hero (Hasbro 1993)

26. General Flagg (G.I. Joe General) 6.00
27. Cobra Eel (Underwater Demolitions Specialist) ... 6.00

Battle Corps (1993) (Asst. #6760, April 1993)
28. Law (Military Police) 6.00
29. Mace (Undercover Operative) 6.00
30. Muskrat (Heavy-Fire Specialist) 6.00
31. Long Arm (First Strike Specialist) 6.00
32. Gristle (Urban Crime Commander) 6.00
33. Headhunter Stormtrooper (Elite Urban Crime
   Guard) 6.00
34. Bullet-Proof (Urban Commander) 6.00
35. Headhunter (Cobra Street Trooper) 6.00
36. Mutt & Junkyard (K-9 Officer & Attack Dog) 6.00

Battle Corps Vehicles (1993)
Detonator (Cobra) vehicle with **Nitro-Viper** figure
   (#6162) 42.00
Shark 9000 vehicle with **Cutter** figure (#6867) 35.00
Ghoststriker X-16 with **Ace** figure (#6868) 45.00
Mudbuster vehicle (#6886) 12.00
Ice Snake (Cobra) vehicle (#6887) 12.00

STAR BRIGADE

Armor-Tech Star Brigade (Asst. #6124, Aug. 1993) with
trading cards (20 different)
1. Robo-J.O.E. (Jet-Tech Operations Expert) (#06783) 5.00
2. Duke (Star Brigade Commander) (#06784) 5.00
3. Rock 'N' Roll (Robo-Gunner) (#06785?) yellow
   weapons 5.00
   Variation, with brown weapons 5.00

Countdown (Star Brigade),
G.I. Joe: A Real American Hero (Hasbro 1993)

4. Heavy Duty (Heavy Ordnance Specialist) (#06786)   5.00
5. Destro (Cobra-Tech Commander) (#06787) 5.00
6. Cobra B.A.A.T. (Battle Armored Android Troop) (#06788) 5.00

Star Brigade (Asst. #6195, Aug. 1993)
7. Payload (Astro Pilot) 5.00
    Variation, in white 6.00
8. Countdown (Combat Astronaut) black launcher (#81102) 5.00
    Variation, with brown launcher 5.00
9. Roadblock (Space Gunner) 5.00
10. Ozone (Astro Infantry Trooper) gray outfit 5.00
    Variation, in tan outfit 5.00
11. Astro Viper (Cobranaut) 5.00
12. T.A.R.G.A.T. (Trans Atmospheric Rapid Global Assault Trooper) 5.00

Star Brigade Vehicles (1993)
Armor-Bot with **Hawk** figure (#6166) 25.00
Invader (Cobra) (#6284) 10.00
Starfighter with **Sci-Fi** figure (#6948) 12.00

SERIES THIRTEEN

Series Thirteen, Battle Corps (1994)
1. Flint (Desert Paratrooper) 4.00
2. Dial-Tone (Communications Expert) 4.00
3. Shipwreck (Navy S.E.A.L.) 4.00
4. Metal-Head (Anti-Tank Specialist) 4.00
5. Viper (Cobra Infantry Trooper) 4.00
6. Beach-Head (Ranger) 4.00

7. Alley Viper (Urban Assault Trooper) 4.00

Canadian Cards Only?
8. Lifeline (Rescue Trooper) 4.00
9. Stalker (Ranger) 4.00
10. Ice Cream Soldier (Flamethrower) 4.00
11. Major Bludd (Mercenary) 4.00
12. Snow Storm (High-Tech Snow Trooper) 4.00
13. Night Creeper Leader (Ninja Master) 4.00

Bushido, Shadow Ninjas,
G.I. Joe: A Real American Hero (Hasbro 1994)

SERIES FOURTEEN

Series Fourteen, Battle Corps (Vertical Logo) (1994)
Canadian Bi-lingual Cards Only?
1. Flint (Desert Paratrooper) 6.00
2. Dial-Tone (Communications Expert) 6.00
3. Shipwreck (Navy S.E.A.L.) 6.00
4. Metal-Head (Anti-Tank Specialist) 6.00
5. Viper (Cobra Infantry Trooper) 6.00
6. Beach-Head (Ranger) 6.00
7. Alley Viper (Urban Assault Trooper) 6.00

U.S. and Canada
8. Lifeline (Rescue Trooper) 5.00
9. Stalker (Ranger) 5.00
10. Ice Cream Soldier (Flamethrower Commando) . . . 5.00
11. Major Bludd (Mercenary) 5.00
12. Snow Storm (High-Tech Snow Trooper) 5.00
13. Night Creeper Leader (Cobra Ninja Supreme Master) 5.00

Battle Corps Vehicles (1994)
Manta-Ray (#6132) 15.00

Scorpion (Cobra) (#6134) 15.00
Razor-Blade (#6139) 15.00
Blockbuster (#6147) 15.00

no #14 to #20

Star Brigade (1994) Series 2, Vertical logo
21. Duke (Star Brigade Commander) 5.00
22. Sci-Fi (Star Brigade Pilot) 5.00
23. Space Shot (Combat Freighter Pilot) 5.00
24. Cobra Commander (Cobra Supreme Leader) 8.00
25. Cobra Blackstar (Elite Space Pilot) 5.00
26. Payload (Astro-Pilot) white 6.00
26. Payload (Astro-Pilot) black 6.00
27. Roadblock (Space Gunner) 5.00

no #28 to #36

Shadow Ninjas (1994)
37. Snake-Eyes (Covert Mission Specialist) (#81141) 12.00
38. Storm Shadow (Shadow Ninja Leader) (#81142) . 12.00
39. Bushido (Snow Ninja) (#81143) 12.00
40. Slice (Cobra Ninja Swordsman) (#81144) 12.00
41. Nunchuk (Nunchuka Ninja) (#81145) 12.00
42. Cobra Night Creeper (Cobra Ninja) (#81146) 12.00

no #43 to #48

Star Brigade (1994) Series 2
49. Effects (Explosives Expert) 12.00
50. Lobotomaxx (Stellar Explorer) 18.00
51. Predacon (Alien Bounty Hunter) 20.00
52. Carcass (Alien Destroyer) 20.00
53. Countdown (Combat Astronaut) 15.00
54. Ozone (Astro Infantry Trooper) 15.00

Star Brigade Power Fighters
Power Fighter (Cobra) with **Techno-Viper** figure (Asst.
    #6064, 1994) 20.00
Power Fighter with **Gears** figure (Asst. #6064, 1994) 20.00

Playset
Dino-Hunter Mission Playset with **Low-Light** and
    Ambush figures, Toys "R" Us exclusive 35.00

G.I. Joe Manimals (1994)
Warwolf .... not produced
Vortex .... not produced
Zigzag .... not produced
Slither .... not produced
Iguanus .... not produced
Spasma .... not produced

30TH ANNIVERSARY
COMMEMORATIVE COLLECTION

3¾" Figures (1994) in window box, with flap
Action Soldier (U.S. Army Infantry) (#81045) $15.00
Action Pilot (Air Force Fighter Pilot) (#81046) 15.00
Action Marine (Marine Corps Commando) (#81047) 15.00
Action Sailor (Navy Frogman) (#81048) 15.00
Original Action Team, Soldier, Marine, Sailor, Astronaut
    and Space Capsule (#6857) 50.00

Mail-in
G.I. Joe original figure 20.00

Electronic Battle Command Duke,
G.I. Joe Hall of Fame (Hasbro 1993)

G.I. JOE HALL OF FAME
Hasbro (1991–94)
Numbered Collector's Editions

12" Figures (1991–92)
Duke with "Electronic Sonic Fighter Battle Weapon"
    (Target special) (#6019, 1991) $65.00
Duke with "Electronic Light and Sound Battle Weapon"
    (#6826, 1991–92) 50.00
Cobra Commander with "Electronic Light and Sound
    Battle Weapon" (#6827, 1991–92) 40.00
Snake Eyes with "Electronic Light and Sound Battle
    Weapon" (#6828, 1991–92) 40.00
Stalker with "Electronic Light and Sound Battle Weapon"
    (#6829, 1991–92) 35.00

12" Figures (1993)
Basic Training Grunt (#6111) 10.00
Basic Training Heavy Duty (#6114) 10.00
Electronic Battle Command Duke (#6117) 30.00
Flint (#6127) 25.00
Rock 'N' Roll (tan shirt) (#6128) 25.00
    Variation, in green shirt 40.00
Ace (#6837) 30.00
Destro (#6839) 25.00
Storm Shadow (#6848) 25.00
Gung Ho Dress Marine with silver sword (#6849) ... 30.00
    Variation, with gold sword 40.00

12" Figures (1994)
Combat Camo Duke (#6044, 1994) 15.00

Combat Camo Roadblock (#6049, 1994) 15.00
Karate Choppin' Snake Eyes (#6089, 1994) 18.00
Battle Pack Major Bludd (#6159, 1994) 18.00
Martial Arts Expert (#27527) 16.00
Red Beret Commando (#27528) 16.00
Surveillance Specialist (#27529?) 16.00
Rapid-Fire The Ultimate Command (Toys "R" Us
    special) 45.00

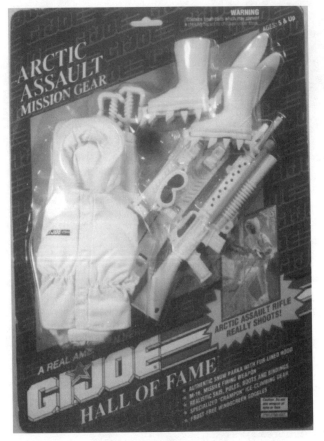

Arctic Assault Mission Gear,
G.I. Joe Hall of Fame (Hasbro 1993)

Hall of Fame Mission Gear Equipment blue blister cards
(1993–94)
Arctic Assault Mission Gear (#27501, 1993) 15.00
Underwater Attack Mission Gear (#27502, 1993) ... 15.00
Light Infantry Mission Gear (#2750?, 1993) 18.00
S.W.A.T. Assault Mission Gear (#2750?, 1993) 10.00
Swamp Fighter Mission Gear (#2750?, 1993) 15.00
Star Brigade Astronaut Mission Gear (#27506, 1993) 15.00
Ocean Enforcer Mission Gear (#27507) 12.00
Desert Camo Mission Gear (1994) 12.00
Jungle Patrol Mission Gear (1994) 20.00
Mountain Assault Mission Gear (1994) 15.00
Red Ninja Mission Gear (1994) 12.00
Air Force Flyer Gear (1994) 13.00
Army Boot Camp Gear (1994) 13.00
Marine Paris Island Gear (1994) 13.00
Navy Shore Patrol Gear (1994) 13.00

G.I. Joe Hall of Fame Equipment (1994)
Arctic Assault Mission Gear (#27501, 1993) 10.00
Red Beret Weapons Arsenal (#27531?) 6.00
Green Beret Weapons Arsenal (#27532) 6.00
High Caliber Weapons Arsenal (#27533) 9.00
Urban S.W.A.T. Weapons Arsenal (#27534) 9.00

Mobile Artillery Assault (#27542) 12.00
Smart Gun Blaster (#27606) 12.00
Backpack Missile Blaster (#27607) 12.00
Underwater Attack Mission Gear 12.00
The Ultimate Arsenal, over 25 pieces, in window box 15.00

Deluxe Mission Gear (1996)
Navy Seal Commando Deluxe Mission Gear 25.00
Cobra Helicopter Attack Deluxe Mission Gear 25.00

Hall of Fame Vehicles
Rhino G.P.V. (#6119, 1993) 35.00
Strike Cycle (#6791, 1994) 25.00
Thunderwing Jet Pack (#27602) 10.00

30th Anniv. Commemorative Collection (1994) in window
box with facsimile original box
Action Soldier 60.00
Action Soldier, black 175.00
Action Sailor 80.00
Action Marine 45.00
Action Pilot 75.00

30th Anniv. Salute Convention, Limited Edition (1994)
WWII Army Aircorp Action Pilot 650.00
Military Police 750.00
Green Beret .... no price found

Limited Edition WWII Commemorative Figures, Target
exclusives (1995)
Action Soldier (#27618) 40.00
Action Sailor (#27617) 50.00
Action Marine (#27615) 40.00
Action Pilot (#27616) 50.00

Target Exclusives (1996)
Army General 40.00
Navy Admiral 40.00
Pilot (African American) 50.00
Soldier 40.00
Marine 40.00
Sailor 40.00

FAO Schwarz Exclusives
Navy Seal with mission raft "Outboard Motor Really
    Works" (#81234) 175.00
Action Astronaut Masterpiece 125.00
F-15 E Pilot 150.00

Mail-in Figures
Lt. Joseph Colton (1994) 200.00
Arctic Lt. Joseph Colton (1994) 175.00

Mission Gear for 12" G.I. Joes
Aussie Outback Mission Gear (#27516) 20.00
Deep Water Salvage Mission Gear (#27517) 20.00
Sniper Patrol Mission Gear (#27518) 20.00

Action Equipment for 12" G.I. Joes
Communications Commando Action Equipment
    (#27535) 16.00
Martial Arts Training Action Equipment (#27536) 16.00
Medic Rescue Action Equipment (#27538) 16.00

WalMart Specials
Home for the Holidays, white (#27498) 30.00
Home for the Holidays, black (#27498) 40.00
Home for the Holidays, Hispanic (#27498) 35.00

G.I. JOE CLASSIC COLLECTION
Hasbro (1996)

12" Figures in window box with flap
U.S. Army Infantry (#81236) four versions:
    White, with blond hair $30.00
    White, with brown hair 30.00
    White, with light brown hair 30.00
    Black 35.00
British S.A.S. with assault helmet, goggles, face mask, camouflage uniform, boots, personal equipment belt, holster, 9mm beretta, grenade pouches, flash back grenades and HK MP5 with silencer (#81237) 30.00
U.S. Airborne Ranger Halo Parachutist with assault helmet, goggles, oxygen mask, oxygen hose, oxygen bottle with pouch, camouflage fatigues, boots, survival knife, parachute backpack and Colt AR-15 assault rifle (#81238) two versions
    White 30.00
    Black 35.00
French Foreign Legion with beret with beret badge, khaki uniform, H-harness, canteen with pouch, personal equipment belt, pouches, bayonet with sheath, 5.56 MM F4-AS rifle and boots (#81252) 35.00
U.S. Marine Corps Sniper with ghillic suit, boots, Remington 7.62 MM A40 A1 sniper rifle, Colt AR-15 assault rifle and binoculars (#81253) 35.00
Australian ODF (Operational Deployment Force) with slouch hat, traditional plain khaki uniform, boots, rucksack, personal equipment belt, pouches, canteen and holder and FN FAL 7.62 (#81344) 35.00
U.S. Army Tank Commander with helmet with communications set, goggles, 9MM beretta, camouflage uniform, holster, tanker boots and .45 M3 submachine gun (#81346) 35.00

Thin Box numbered, "Limited Edition Collector's Special"
Dress Marine (#27596) Toys "R" Us exclusive (50,000 pieces total) two versions:
    White 30.00
    Black 35.00
"Battle of the Bulge" Soldier (#27635) Toys "R" Us exclusive (50,000 pieces total) two versions:
    White 30.00
    Black 35.00
Airborne Military Police, white (#27717) 25.00
Airborne Military Police, black (#27717) 35.00
Airborne Military Police, Hispanic (#27717) 35.00

Convention Issues
WWII Action Pilot FX'95 . . . . 600.00
SWATICC '95, white 250.00
SWATICC '95, black 250.00
UN Peacekeeper ICC '95 . . . . 90.00
French Resistance ICC '95 . . . . 350.00
U.S. Coast Guard 300.00
USN Shore Patrol 300.00
Dress Marine ICC '95 . . . . 450.00

Limited Edition WWII Commemorative Figure
Naval Admiral (#27683, 1996) Target exclusive 35.00

Jungle Camo D-Day, G.I. Joe: Sergeant Savage and His Screaming Eagles (Hasbro 1994)

SGT. SAVAGE AND HIS SCREAMING EAGLES
Hasbro (1994–95)

Deep behind enemy lines, World War II's greatest military hero leads a small platoon of soldiers on a top secret mission. The year is 1944 and Master Sergeant Robert Steven Savage is about to be ambushed by a traitor in his ranks! Fifty years after that fateful ambush, Savage's cryogenically frozen body is discovered among the ruins of a mysterious laboratory dating back to the 1940s. Incredibly, Savage is revived by the G.I. Joe team and given a special DNA formula to maintain his youth and super-enhanced strength. Hawk gives him command of the Screaming Eagles, and the chance to avenge his fallen platoon. Once again, his "blast from the past" is about to show the world what being a hero is all about!

The header card says that these figures play with 4" G.I. Joe figures and accessories. Maybe so, but they are a little bigger than the 4" figures. The figures in the series are articulated at the elbows and knees (along with the shoulder, neck and hips), which is getting less common these days.

4½" Figures, Series One (1994)
1. Commando Sgt. Savage with video (#81121) $8.00
2. Combat Sgt. Savage (#81031) 5.00
3. D-Day (#81033) 5.00
4. Dynamite (#81034) 5.00
5. General Blitz (#81037) 5.00

6. I.R.O.N. Stormtrooper (#81062) 5.00
Battle Bunker and Special Edition Battle Command Sgt.
    Savage (#81201) 12.00
Enemy Battle Bunker and Special Edition Cyborg
    General Blitz (#81203) 12.00

Series 2 (1995)
Cryo-Freeze Sgt. Savage with "Cryo-Freeze Bio-
    Chamber" (#81111) 8.00
Jungle Camo D-Day with "Working Cliff Climber"
    (#81112) 8.00
Urban Attack Dynamite with "Speed Burnin' Attack
    Cycle" (on motorcycle) (#81113) 8.00
Jet-Pack General Blitz with "Spring-Wing Jet Pack"
    (#81114) 8.00
Arctic Stormtrooper with "Shooting Catapult Blaster"
    (#81115) 8.00

Vehicles
Grizzly SS-1 (#6682) 10.00
P-40 Warhawk with **Sgt. Savage** pilot figure (#6937)   15.00
I.R.O.N. Panther with special **I.R.O.N. Anvil** figure
    (#81164) 13.00

Large Figure
12" Sgt. Savage (#81292) 25.00

Deluxe Lt. Stone, G.I. Joe Extreme (Hasbro 1995)

G.I. JOE EXTREME
Hasbro (1995–96)

The package explains that "A terrifying threat no existing combat force has been able to halt is wreaking havoc throughout the world. The evil forces of SKAR—Soldiers of Kaos, Anarchy and Ruin—can only be crushed by extreme measures: new G.I. Joe Extreme, an elite strike force the likes of which have never been seen! Hand-picked for their all-out attitudes, toughness and superior battle skills, their unending mission is to protect humanity from the forces of SKAR."

These are larger, very ordinary action figures without the many points of articulation that distinguish most G.I. Joes from ordinary action figures. That, and the fact that they are treated with utter contempt by G.I. Joe collectors, may be the reason they are all available at red tag prices.

5" Figures (1995)
Lt. Stone with "Semi-Automatic Gattling Firepower"
    (#81161) $4.00
Sgt. Savage with "Power-Launch Catapult" (#81162) . . 4.00
Metalhead with "Heavy Metal Missile Launcher"
    (#81167) 4.00
Ballistic with "Quick-Draw Combat Action" (#81168) . . 4.00
Freight with "Strong-Arm Blocking Power" (#81176) . . . 4.00
Iron Klaw with "Battle-Activated Assault Rocket"
    (#81177) 4.00
Inferno with "Firebolt Flame Thrower" (#81179) 4.00

5" Deluxe Figures with Ultra Slam Firepower
Deluxe Lt. Stone with "Mortar Launcher" (#81207) . . . 5.00
Deluxe Iron Klaw with "Attack Rocket" (#81208) 5.00
Deluxe Ballistic with "Sidearm Blaster" (#81209) 5.00
Deluxe Metalhead with "Shoulder Cannon" (#81211) . . 5.00

Two-Pack
Lt. Stone vs. Iron Klaw (#81295) 13.00

Vehicles
Detonator Combat Cannon with **Sgt. Savage** figure
    (#81213) 10.00
Spitfire Battering Platform with **Inferno** figure (#81214) 10.00
Sand Striker All-Terrain Vehicle (#81216) 8.00
Bone Splitter Armored Tank (#81217) 8.00
Tigerhawk Chopper (#81218) 12.00
Sky Stalker Long Distance (plane) (#81219) 12.00
Road Bullet Assault Vehicle (Missile-Firing Rapid Assault
    Cycle) (#81223) 10.00
Thunderin' Fury Long Distance (tank) (#81224) 12.00

GIL JONES
SEE: MAJOR GIL JONES

GODDESS OF THE ULTRA COSMOS
Agglo (1985)

Considered by most collectors to be knock-offs of the Princess of Power and Golden Girl figure lines and of little interest. Each of the "goddesses" came with a Mystic Mask, a shield, a weapon and lots of hair.

5½" Figures, with Mystic Mask, Shield and Mighty Weapon
Goddess of Bornite $8.00
Goddess of Dyitrite 8.00
Goddess of Gratonite 8.00
Goddess of Microlite 8.00
Goddess of Scheelite 8.00
Goddess of Sodalite 8.00
Goddess of Stibnite 8.00

Battra, Godzilla, King of the Monsters (Trendmasters 1995)

GODZILLA, KING OF THE MONSTERS
Trendmasters (1995)

This series includes the major monster characters from the Godzilla movies, and Rodan, who starred in his own 1956 movie first. Godzilla movies run the gamut from excellent to turkey. In his debut 1956 movie he is a gigantic evil monster, but in later movies he is reduced to a Japanese super hero.

There are a few human action figures, called the "Godzilla Force," but they are definitely secondary characters, even though they were billed as "the ultimate Godzilla fighters." In the movies, Godzilla and the other monsters did most of the fighting. The monsters were prominent features in the action figure aisle at most toy stores during 1995, but they didn't seem to sell all that quickly. So far they haven't attained any collector premium. There were also 10" versions of these monsters which came in an open box and had a motion sensor, so they roared at you when you walked by. This can get tedious.

The figures come with trading cards as a premium. There were only eight Godzilla cards in the series: the six monsters plus Godzilla vs. Ghidorah and Godzilla vs. Rodan. In addition, there are five Godzilla Force cards which come with the human figures. There were also wind-up walkers and small hatchling figures with cracked open eggs, most of which included one of the eight cards, but none of which are action figures, so they are not listed.

In 1996 a 40th Anniversary nine-figure pack was shipped. This included three new figures—Battra, Gigan and Biollante—which were also issued on header cards and in boxes with their own new trading cards. These tail-end figures did not ship to local toy stores and are not well known.

4"–6" Monsters on header card with trading card
Godzilla (#30452) with light-up eyes $5.00
Rodan (#30453) 5.00
Mothra (#30454) 7.00
Mecha-Godzilla (#30455) 5.00
Mecha-Ghidorah (#30456) 6.00
Ghidorah (#30457) 5.00
Gigan (#05938, 1996) 10.00
Biollante (#05939?, 1996) 10.00
Battra (#05940, 1996) 10.00

4"–6" Monsters in open Try-Me box with trading card
Godzilla (#30458) dark green 10.00
 Variation, charcoal black "supercharged" on
 sticker 10.00
Rodan (#30459) 10.00
Mothra (#30460) 10.00
Ghidorah (#30461) 10.00
Mecha-Godzilla (#30462) 10.00
Mecha-Ghidorah (#30463) 10.00
Biollante (1996) 15.00
Gigan (1996) 15.00
Battra (1996) 15.00

10" Monsters, electronic roar and light-up eyes, in open box with trading card
Godzilla (#85109) 9.00
Mothra (#85194) 9.00
Ghidorah (#85195) 9.00
Rodan (#85196) 9.00
Mecha-Godzilla (#85197) 9.00
Mecha-Ghidorah (#85198) 9.00

4½" Godzilla Force with trading card and badge
Dan Easton (#05520) 5.00
Margaret O'Brien (#05521) 6.00
Michael Van Horn (#05522) 5.00
Pete Richards (#05529) 5.00

Godzilla Force Model Vehicle with trading card
Garuda Battleship (#30416) 5.00

4" Godzilla vs. Enemy Collectible Figurines
Godzilla vs. Rodan (#05345) 6.00
Godzilla vs. Mecha-Godzilla (#05346) 6.00
Godzilla vs. Mecha-Ghidorah (#05347) 6.00
Godzilla vs. Ghidorah (#05348) 6.00
Godzilla vs. Mothra (#05349) 6.00

Multi-Pack, 4"–6" Figures
Godzilla, King of the Monsters, 40th Anniversary Collector's Edition, nine figures: Godzilla, Mecha-Godzilla, Ghidorah, Mecha-Ghidorah, Rodan, Mothra, plus new figures Battra, Gigan, Biollante, in window box (#30613) 30.00

Playset
Godzilla Attacks N.Y. giant playset, with **Godzilla** figure (#30628) 25.00

Moguera, Godzilla Wars (Trendmasters 1996)

GODZILLA WARS
Trendmasters (1996)

A continuation of the previous series, with new trading cards and three new figures which appeared previously in the 40th Anniversary Collector's set and as tail-end figures. All of these figures also came with trading cards. There are supposed to be 20 cards in the series, but we don't think all of them were issued. No "Godzilla Force" humans have been found as part of Godzilla Wars, but we can still find most of the original four with a little looking.

4"–6" Monster Figures in Try-Me box with trading card
Space Godzilla (#6250) $12.00
Supercharged Godzilla (#6292) 10.00
Biollante (#6298) 10.00
Gigan (#6299) 10.00
Battra (#6300) 10.00
Moguera (#6301) 12.00

Power-Up Monsters with three Missile Launchers and Snap-on Armor, in window box
Power-Up Supercharged Godzilla 12.00
Power-Up Mecha-King Ghidorah (#6062)
　　　Red weapons, figure on right 12.00
　　　Gray weapons, figure on left 12.00
Supercharged Godzilla . . . . not seen
Cyber Rodan . . . . not seen

10" Motion Activated in open box without trading card
Godzilla (#6302) 15.00
Space Godzilla (#6308) 15.00
Gigan (#6309) 15.00

Multi-Pack
Godzilla, King of the Monsters, 40th Anniversary Collector's Edition, nine figures: Supercharged Godzilla, Mecha-Godzilla, Gigan, Battra, Biollante, Mecha-King Godzilla, Space Godzilla, Moguera and Anguiras, in window box (#30613) 30.00

GOLDEN GIRL AND THE GUARDIANS OF THE GEMSTONES
"ADVENTURE HEROINES AGAINST EVIL"
Galoob (1984–87)

The figures come with "Dazzling die-cast gemstone, cape, headdress, weapon, weapons belt and comb." It's good to know that they can stay well groomed while they protect the gemstones and save the universe.

Figures
Golden Girl (#3020) $18.00
Jade (#3021) 18.00
Rubee (#3022) 18.00
Saphire (#3023) 18.00
Onyx (#3024) 18.00
Vulura (#3025) 18.00
Wild One (#3026) 18.00
Dragon Queen (#3027) 18.00
Moth Lady (#3028) 18.00
Prince Kroma (#3029) 25.00
Ogra (#3030) 18.00

Glorious Glitter Outfits
Golden Girl 8.00
Onyx 8.00
Jade 8.00
Saphire 8.00
Rubee 8.00
Dragon Queen 8.00
Vultura 8.00
Wild One 8.00
Moth Lady 8.00

Forest Fantasy Outfits
Golden Girl 8.00
Onyx 8.00
Jade 8.00
Saphire 8.00
Rubee 8.00
Dragon Queen 8.00
Vultura 8.00
Wild One 8.00
Moth Lady 8.00

Festival Spirit Outfits
Golden Girl 8.00
Onyx 8.00
Jade 8.00
Saphire 8.00
Rubee 8.00
Dragon Queen 8.00
Vultura 8.00
Wild One 8.00
Moth Lady 8.00

Evening Enchantment Outfits
Golden Girl 8.00
Onyx 8.00

Jade	8.00
Saphire	8.00
Rubee	8.00
Dragon Queen	8.00
Vultura	8.00
Wild One	8.00
Moth Lady	8.00

Horses and Accessories

Dream Tents, four different	12.00
Olympia unicorn	35.00
Olympia and Chariot	42.00
Place of Gems playset	48.00
Shadow unicorn	35.00
Shadow and Chariot	42.00

GREATEST AMERICAN HERO
Mego (1981)

This vehicle, with figures, is based on the short-lived television series of the same name starring William Katt. The show was a modest success, but this toy didn't make it. "Believe it or not" a series of 8" figures of Pam, Ralph and Bill got to the prototype stage, but not beyond it.

Vehicle and Figures

Covertible "Bug" vehicle with **Ralph** and **Bill** 3¾" figures	$175.00

GRIFFINS
Kmart (1995)

Two-pack figures seen only at Kmart stores. Collectors have shown no interest in this series and they are only borderline action figures.

GRIZZLY ADAMS
Mattel (1978)

From the television show starring an Indian, a large hairy person and a larger, hairier bear.

12" Figures (1978) in window box

Ben	$45.00
Grizzly Adams (#2372)	45.00
Nakoma	50.00

Two-Pack

Grizzly Adams and Ben	80.00

[THE INCREDIBLE ADVENTURES OF] GUMBY
Trendmasters (1996)

These figures appeared at the very end of 1996. Gumby isn't the type of character to draw a huge collector following, but the kids should like him.

5" Superflex Figures

Cowboy Gumby with Snap-on Cowboy Hat, Vest, Gloves, Belt, Boots and Lasso (#7031)	5.00
Robot Gumby with Snap-on Arm and Leg Bands, Robot Helmet and Chest Plate (#7032)	5.00
Space Gumby with Snap-on Helmet, Chest Plate and Boots (#7034)	5.00
Cowboy Pokey with Snap-on Western Bandana and Saddle (#7036)	5.00
Space Pokey with Snap-on Helmet and Action Spacesuit (#7037)	5.00
GI Gumby with Snap-on Harness, Boots, Helmet, Jacket and Working Parachute (#7061)	5.00

*Convertible "Bug" with **Ralph** and **Bill**, Greatest American Hero (Mego 1981)*

HAPPY DAYS
Mego (1978)

From the television show starring Henry Winkler as the Fonz and Ron Howard as Richie Cunningham. Winkler was the bigger star at the time, but since then Ron Howard has directed more movies than Henry Winkler has appeared in.

The Fonzie figure and the vehicles have a different style logo than the other figures in the series. It is designed to capitalize on the popularity of this character.

8" Dolls
Fonzie, boxed	$60.00
Fonzie, carded	60.00
Richie (#63001/1)	60.00
Potsy (#63001/2)	50.00
Ralph (#63001/3)	50.00

Vehicles and Playset
Fonzie's Motorcycle	40.00
Fonzie's Jalopy	75.00
Fonzie's Garage playset	120.00

HARDY BOYS
Kenner (1979)

From the live-action ABC television show based on the long-running boy's book series of the adventures of two teenage detective brothers. Parker Stevenson and Shaun Cassidy starred as Frank and Joe, respectively. Nancy Drew was the girl's counterpart and her adventures also appeared on television, alternating with the Hardy Boys. She didn't get an action figure series.

12" Figures
Frank Hardy	$30.00
Joe Hardy	30.00

HE-MAN
Mattel (1989–92)

A spin-off or continuation of the Masters of the Universe series, as Mattel tried to keep the toy line and cartoon show alive. It may have satisfied the die-hards, but it was not nearly as successful. The first eight figures had 5¼" x 4"

mini comic books, as did some of the Nocturna figures from the second series.

Just about all of the figures were available as red tag specials at the end of the line.

Flipshot, He-Man (Mattel 1989)

5"–5½" Galactic Guardians Figures (1989) with mini comic
He-Man (#2274)	$10.00
Flipshot (#2275)	9.00
Hydron (#3259)	9.00

5"–5½" Evil Mutants Figures (1989) with mini comic
Skeletor (#2303)	9.00
Flogg (#2314)	9.00
Slushhead (#2315)	9.00

Second Batch (1989) with mini comic
Optikk 5" (#3262)	9.00
Kayo 5½" (#3369)	9.00

Nocturna, He-Man (Mattel 1989)

Foreign Issue with "Master's Action"
Brakk (#2314) same figure as Flogg 15.00
Kalamarr (#2315) same figure as Slushhead 15.00
Lizorr (#3261) 15.00

5"–5½" "New" Figures (1989)
Nocturna with mini comic (#3526) 9.00
Nocturna (#3526) 9.00
Karatti (#3529) 9.00
Hoove (#3530) 30.00
Vizar (#3607, 1989) 9.00

5"–5½" "New" Figures (1990)
Tuskador (#1319) 10.00
Battle Punch He-Man (#1340) 10.00
Artilla (#1639) 10.00
Spinwit (#1683) 10.00
Quakke (#1849) 10.00
Butthead (#2020) 10.00
Disks of Doom Skeletor (#5803) 10.00
Slaghorn (#5804) 10.00

5"–5½" Figures (1991)
Thunder Punch He-Man (#5586) 10.00
Battle Blade Skeletor (#5705) 10.00
Spin-Fist Hydron (#5788) 10.00
Too-Tall Hoove (#7013) 30.00
Missile Armor Flipshot (#7769) 10.00
Hook 'em Flogg (#9309) 10.00

Two-Packs (1989)
He-Man and Slush Head 25.00
He-Man and Skeletor 25.00
He-Man and Flogg 25.00
He-Man and Evil Mutant with mini comic 25.00

Vehicles (1989)
AstroSub vehicle (#1986) 12.00
Starship Eternia large vehicle and battle base (#2133) 65.00
Terroclaw vehicle (#2268) 12.00
Shuttle Pod vehicle (#3336) 10.00
Bolajet vehicle (#3534) 10.00

Vehicles (1990)
Battle Bird (#1262) 10.00
Terrotread vehicle (#1882) 12.00
Sagitar, Galloping Battle Beast (#2145) 12.00
Doomcopter (#9960) 10.00

Xena (brown hair), Hercules (Toy Biz 1995)

HERCULES
"THE LEGENDARY JOURNEYS"
Toy Biz (1995–96)

Based on the 1995–96 live-action television show, or shows, really, since Xena has her own. The original Xena figure had brown hair, which became a very scarce figure when it was changed to black hair to match the television show. Even the black-haired Xena was scarce, but then many turned up at Kay-Bee stores in late summer 1996. She-Demon from the second batch was equally scarce, but a few more were found by late 1996. Xena II appeared separately in Toys "R" Us stores in November 1996.

There are three 10" figures in this series as well. In our area, the first 10" Hercules figure was easy to find through most of 1996. It's just named Hercules on the box, but it is in the same outfit as the 5" Hercules II figure. The second

Hercules, which resembles Hercules I, and the 10" Xena never appeared until 1997, when they were a red tag special. Xena has her own box design, making it appear that she is part of her own series.

5" Figures
Hercules I with Iron Spiked Spinning Mace (#41001) . $5.00
Hercules II with Archery Combat Set (#41002) 5.00
Hercules III with Herculean Assault Blades (#41003) . . 5.00
Iolaus with Catapult Battle Gear (#41004) 7.00
Xena with Warrior Princess Weaponry (#41005) with
    brown hair 25.00
       Variation with black hair 10.00
Minotaur with Immobilizing Sludge Mask (#41006) . . . 7.00
Ares with Detachable Weapons of War (#41007) 7.00

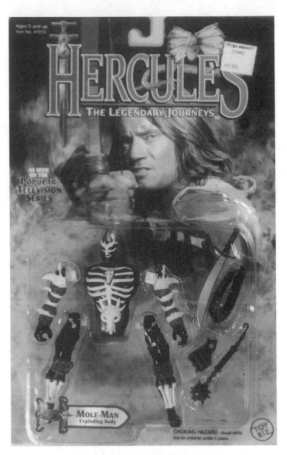

Mole-Man, Hercules (Toy Biz 1996)

Second Batch (Sept. 1996)
Hercules with "Dual Sword Slashing Action" (#41011) . 5.00
Hercules with "Chain Breaking Strength" (#41012) . . . 5.00
Mole-Man with "Exploding Body" (#41013) 7.00
She-Demon with "Stone Strike Tail" (#41014) 10.00
Centaur with "Big Horse Kick" (#41015) 8.00

Third Batch (Nov. 1996)
Xena II with Warrior Disguise (#41016) 9.00

6" Monsters in window box
Hydra (#42201) 10.00
Cerberus (#42202) 10.00
Echidna (#42203) 10.00

Second Batch of 6" Monsters
Labyrinth Snake (#42216) 10.00
Stymphalian Bird (#42217) 10.00
Graegus (#42218) 10.00

10" Figures
Hercules (II) (#42210) 20.00
Hercules (I) (#42221) 20.00
Xena (#42222) 35.00

HISTORY OF THE BATMAN
Kenner (1996)

This is a boxed set of three 12" Mego-style dolls in Bat-outfits representing the original Batman, the 1970s' Batman and the 1990s' Batman. It was a FAO Schwarz exclusive for Christmas 1996, but at its original price of $120.00, i.e. $40.00 per doll, it's overpriced. The similar Batman vs. Catwoman doll set which is in general release in toy stores sells for just $20.00 per doll—the same price as 12" Star Wars dolls.

12" Dolls
Three Batman dolls in window box, FAO Schwarz
    exclusive $140.00

HONEY WEST
"TV PRIVATE EYE-FULL"
Gilbert (1965)

Honey West, the smooth sleuth created by G.G. Fickling, first appeared on the television show "Burke's Law," played by Anne Francis. She got her own ABC television show for the 1965–66 season. She was made into an action doll by the A.C. Gilbert Company when it was also selling James Bond, The Man From Uncle and Moon McDare figures. All of the accessories for these series were interchangeable, which means that Honey could use James Bond's scuba outfit while Illya Kuryakin could have donned Honey's leotards and gold belt and become U.N.C.L.E.'s crossdressed "eyeful"—well, that's what interchangeable means, doesn't it?

Honey West didn't do too well, especially when she was up against that other trendy fashion plate—Barbie. She is highly collectible today, as is Barbie.

12" Figure
Honey West figure $425.00
    Loose, including black judo leotards, cap-firing
      pistol, gold belt and holster and black boots . 225.00

Accessories for "TV's Private Eye-Full"
Equipment Set (Card) 65.00
Formal Outfit (Boxed) 100.00
Karate Outfit (Boxed) 100.00
Pet Set with Ocelot (Boxed) 140.00
Secret Agent Outfit (Boxed) 100.00
Spy Accessory Set (Card) 75.00
Spy Compact Set (Boxed) 100.00

HOOK
Mattel (1991–92)

From the movie starring Robin Williams as Peter Pan and Dustin Hoffman as Capt. Hook, along with Julia Roberts and Bob Hoskins. All eight of the original Hook figures were readily available along with the Lost Boy Attack Raft, and the Strike Tank. Two additions appeared in 1992: **Skull Armor Captain Hook** and **Attack Croc**. These figures are in a package labeled "Deluxe" which means they sold for a couple of bucks more than the earlier figures.

The series was short lived and most of the 1991 figures could be found with red tags, but less of the 1992 "Deluxe" figures.

5" Figures (1991)
Lost Boy Ace (#2817)	$5.00
Lost Boy Rufio (#2818)	5.00
Swashbuckling Peter Pan (#2849)	5.00
Air Attack Peter Pan (#2853)	5.00
Tall Terror Capt. Hook (#2854)	5.00
Multi-Blade Capt. Hook (#2857)	5.00
Pirate Bill Jukes (#2859)	5.00

Second Series (1992)
Pirate Smee (#4094)	7.00
Battle Swing Peter Pan (#4105)	7.00
Food-Fighting Peter Pan (#4152)	7.00
Swiss Army Capt. Hook (#4156)	7.00
Lost Boy Thud Butt (#4719)	7.00

Deluxe Figures (1992)
Lost Boy Attack Croc (#4074)	18.00
Skull Armor Captain Hook (#4075)	15.00
Learn-to-Fly Peter Pan (#4076)	20.00

Vehicles and Accessories (1991)
Lost Boy Strike Tank (#2832)	20.00
Lost Boy Attack Raft (#2833)	20.00

HOW THE WEST WAS WON
Mattel (1978)

These are from the ABC television made-for-TV movie, mini-series, and series starring James Arness, not the 1963 Cinerama epic starring everyone in Hollywood. Jim should have stuck to "Gunsmoke." We still remember him in the title role in *The Thing*.

11" Figures in window boxes
Zeb Macahan (#3587)	$60.00
Lone Wolf	60.00
Dakota	60.00
Dakota and Zeb Macahan	95.00

[DISNEY'S]
THE HUNCHBACK OF NOTRE DAME
Mattel (1996)

From the Disney animated movie based on the Victor Hugo classic featuring prejudice, hypocrisy and obsession. It's quite mature as Disney movies go, but this Quasimodo will never replace Charles Laughton (1939) or Lon Chaney (1923) in our memories, or even Anthony Hopkins in the made-for-TV movie (1982). The figures were not a great success with collectors and could be found easily as red tag specials in late 1996. They are usually racked with the girl's fashion dolls.

Phoebus, The Hunchback of Notre Dame (Mattel 1996)

5" Figures
Esmeralda (#69414)	$5.00
Quasimodo (#69414)	5.00
Gargoyles (#69415)	5.00
Clopin (#69415)	5.00
Phoebus (#69415)	5.00
Frollo (#69415)	5.00

Figures and Horses
Esmeralda with horse	12.50
Phoebus with horse	12.50

Vehicles and Playsets
Carry-Around Bell Tower with PVC figures (#66207)	15.00
Cathedral playset with PVC figures (#66215)	15.00
Quasimodo & Gargoyles Action Figure Gift Set (#66221)	15.00
Esmeralda & Phoebus Action Figure Gift Set (#66221)	15.00
Gypsy Caravan playset with Esmeralda figure (#66223)	15.00
Gypsy Wagon	15.00
Notre Dame Adventure playset	25.00

12" Figures in window box
Esmeralda (#15311)	15.00
Phoebus (#15312)	15.00
Magic View Quasimodo (#15313)	15.00
Gypsy Dancing Esmeralda (#15314)	15.00
True Hearts gift set of Esmeralda and Phoebus	25.00
Gypsy Magic Horse (#15318)	15.00

Alien Attacker Pilot,
ID-4, Independence Day (Trendmasters 1996)

ID 4 (INDEPENDENCE DAY)
Trendmasters (1996)

This movie, starring Wil Smith, Jeff Goldblum and Bill Pullman, opened on July 3, 1996. The advance showing on July 2nd was the biggest in movie history and the movie went on to earn over $300 million. The first batch of figures arrived in May and included no Aliens. The Aliens arrived in June and there were lots available, with none in short supply. The Alien Weapons Expert and Alien Zero Gravity were late additions to the series, but they look a lot like the other Alien figures. Most collectors prefer Trendmaster's Mars Attacks figures, even though they liked this movie better. If a figure of the crazed scientist played by Brent Spinner (*Star Trek*'s Data) or one of the female characters had been included this series might have attracted more interest.

6" Figure (1996) with a Mission Disk, one of 11 disks.
Captain Steven Hiller (#6354) + disk 5 . . . . $8.00
Technical Expert David Levinson (#6355) + disk 6 . . . 8.00
President Thomas J. Whitmore (#6356) + disk 7 . . . . . 8.00

8" Aliens (1996) with Host
Alien Science Officer (#6366) + disk 2 . . . . 10.00
Alien Shock Trooper (#6367) + disk 3 . . . . 10.00
Alien Attacker Pilot (#6368) + disk 4 . . . . 10.00

Second Alien Batch (1996) with Host
Alien Weapons Expert (#6622) + disk 10 . . . . 10.00
Alien Zero Gravity (#6720) + disk 1 . . . . 10.00

Large Alien Figures
Alien Supreme Commander with Host and motion
    sensor (#30663) + disk 1, in window box 20.00
Alien Supreme Commander with Bio-Containment
    Chamber + disk 1 . . . . 15.00

Playsets
Area 51 Micro Playset 12.00
Defend New York City Micro Playset 12.00
Los Angeles Invasion Giant Playset 25.00

Accessory
Bio-Containment Chamber (#30750) 5.00

Vehicles
Electronic F/A-18 Hornet fighter jet (#6369) + disk 9 . 18.00
Electronic Alien Attacker ship (#6365) + disk 8 . . . . . 20.00
Electronic Alien Attack Leader (#7137) 15.00

I DREAM OF JEANNIE
Remco (1978)

From the television show starring Barbara Eden as Jeannie, with Larry Hagman and Bill Daily. The show had a five-year run and is still quite popular in syndication.

6" Figure
Jeannie $40.00
Bottle playset 120.00

[INCREDIBLE CRASH DUMMIES]
VINCE & LARRY
THE CRASH DUMMIES
Tyco (1991)

Initially, this series was licensed by the U.S. Department of Transportation and named after their crash dum-

Vince, Vince and Larry, The Crash Dummies (Tyco 1991)

mies—Vince and Larry. The spoil-sport U.S. government objected to the fact that the figures major play value was that they flew apart on impact, which sent the wrong message to kids. Anyway, Tyco lost the license and changed the name of the series to The Incredible Crash Dummies (listed below). Naturally collectors looked for the early figures, particularly Vince and Larry since their names were changed to Slick and Spin.

5" Figures
Vince (#11701) $15.00
Larry (#11702) 15.00
Daryl (#11703?) 10.00
Spare Tire (#11704) 10.00
Skid the Kid (#11705) 10.00
Hubcat (the Cat) & Bumper (the Dog) (#11706?) 15.00

Vehicles and Accessories (1991)
Crash & Bash Chair 10.00
Crash Cycle 8.00
Crash Test Center 20.00
Crash Car with **Dash** figure 20.00
Student Driver Crash Car with **Axel** figure 20.00

THE INCREDIBLE CRASH DUMMIES
Tyco (1992)

The Department of Transportation withdrew its license for this series and so "Vince & Larry The Crash Dummies" became **"The Incredible Crash Dummies"** and Vince and Larry became **Slick** and **Spin** with new paint jobs but with the same product code numbers. The original names are a service mark (similar to a trademark) of the Department of Transportation. The other characters retain their names with only the logo on the front of the package being changed.

This series continued to be popular, with most stores having large quantities available. Tyco introduced quite a few vehicles, so you could crash your dummies all over the place.

Vehicles (Jan. 1992)
Crash Plane (#11681) 15.00
Crash Cannon (#11682) 15.00
Crash ATV (#11771) 10.00
Crash Lawn Mower (#11772) 10.00
Crash Cab (#11811) 15.00
Crash 'N' Dash Chopper (#21175) 8.00

1992 Figures
Slick 10.00
Spin 8.00
Daryl 6.00
Spare Tire 8.00
Skid the Kid 8.00
Hubcat (the Cat) & Bumper (the Dog) 9.00

Vehicles (1992)
Crash 'N Bash Chair (#1174) 10.00
Crash Cycle (#1175-?) 9.00
Crash Chopper (#1175-?) 12.00
Crash ATV with **Flip** figure (#1176-1) 15.00
Crash Lawn Mower with **Wack** figure (#1176-2) 15.00
Crash Go Kart with **J.R.** figure (#1176-3) 15.00
Crash Test Center playset (#1180) 25.00
Junkyard Playset (#1190) 25.00

THE INCREDIBLE CRASH DUMMIES
Tyco (1993)

Two new types of **Crash Dummies** arrived from Tyco just before Christmas. The **Junkbots** are "powerful robots with only one purpose—to knock Crash Dummies to pieces!" The **Pro-Tek** suit versions of your favorite dummies will help them resist the Junkbots assaults for a while. There are also bendable dummies, probably designed to frustrate the Junkbots. However, the whole point of a crash dummy toy is that it flies apart, so what is the point of a bendable version?

Junkbots (1993)
Junkman with Rocket Tire Launcher (#11731) 10.00
Piston Head with Super-Charged Cam Cover Missile (#11732) 10.00
Sideswipe with Turbo-Powered Dummy Slammer (#11733) 10.00
Jack Hammer with Hydraulic Ram Pump (#11734) . . 10.00

Crash Dummies in Pro-Tek Suits (Asst. #1183, 1993)
Bull in Pro-Tek Suit (#11831) 8.00
Slick in Pro-Tek Suit 8.00
Spin in Pro-Tek Suit 8.00
Chip in Pro-Tek Suit 8.00
Dent In Pro-Tek Suit 8.00
Daryl in Pro-Tek Suit 8.00
Spare-Tire in Pro-Tek Suit 8.00
Ted in Pro-Tek Suit with bonus video 12.00
Junkman with free video 12.00

Vehicles (1993)
Dummy Dirt Digger 10.00
Crash Dummy Flip-Over Truck 18.00
'Bot Hauler vehicle 12.00
JunkBot Wrecker vehicle 20.00
Crash Cannon 12.00

Playset (1993)
Crash Alley Playset (#43710) 25.00

Indiana Jones, 12", The Adventures of
Indiana Jones (Kenner 1982)

[THE ADVENTURES OF]
INDIANA JONES
[IN RAIDERS OF THE LOST ARK]
Kenner (1982–83)

From the movie starring Harrison Ford and Karen Allen, with Paul Freeman as Belloq and John Rhys-Davies as Sallah. The movie series is still highly popular and there are only a few collectibles available, so prices are high. With Kenner's success with the Star Wars action figures, you would have thought there would be more figures and that the other two movies would have seen figure releases as well. As a matter of fact—well, in our opinion—Kenner could probably do pretty well if they made Indiana Jones figures today. Galoob has made Indiana Jones vehicles for its popular micro machines line.

Savage Hulk, The Incredible Hulk (Toy Biz 1996)

INCREDIBLE HULK
Toy Biz (1996)

These figures are 6" tall, while most prior Marvel figures were 5". The larger size and larger header card combined to produce a larger price, but only about $1.00 more. We think they are worth it.

6" Figures
Savage Hulk with "Transforming Action" (#43401) . . . $8.00
Battle Damaged Grey Hulk with "Bombastic Blasters"
    (#43402) 8.00
Leader with "Anti-Hulk Armor" (#43403) 9.00
She-Hulk with "Gamma Cross Bow" (#43406) 9.00
Abomination with "Toxic Blaster" (#43407) 10.00
Rampaging Hulk with "Collapsing Brick Wall" (#43408) 8.00

Playsets
Electronic Hulk Rage Cage playset (#43420, 1996) . . 15.00

12" Figure
Indiana Jones, 12" figure with hat, jacket, shirt, pants,
    boots, holster gun and whip (#46000) in window
    box $250.00
    Loose 100.00

4" Figures
Indiana Jones with whip and pistol (#46060) 150.00
Cairo Swordsman with sword and dagger (#46080) . . 18.00
Toht with trench coat and pistol (#46090) 18.00
Marion Ravenwood with monkey (#46100) 200.00
Sallah (#46150) 45.00
Belloq (#46160) 50.00
German Mechanic (#46170) 45.00

Indiana Jones in German Uniform (#46180) 75.00
Belloq, wearing ceremonial robe (Kenner 1982, mail-
    in) 25.00
Belloq (same as mail-in figure, but carded) 500.00

Vehicles and Accessories
The Map Room Adventure playset with **Indiana Jones**
    in Arab disguise (#46020) 75.00
Streets of Cairo playset with 3 figures (#46040?) ... 60.00
Well of the Souls action playset, with 12 snakes and 2
    torches (#46050) 75.00
Desert Convoy Truck (#46210) 45.00
Arabian Horse (#46220, 1983) 60.00

Loose Figures
Indiana Jones in Arab outfit, from Map Room Adventure
    playset 10.00
Marion Ravenwood figure, from Streets of Cairo
    playset 15.00
Monkey Man, from Streets of Cairo playset 10.00

INDIANA JONES
AND THE TEMPLE OF DOOM
LJN (1984)

From the movie starring Harrison Ford and Kate
Capshaw. Harrison had trouble romancing Kate in the movie,
but director Steven Spielberg had more luck and married her.

5" Figures with Battle-Matic Action (Asst. #4000)
Indiana Jones $120.00
Mola Ram 20.00
Giant Thugee, 6" figure 50.00

INDIANA JONES
Star Toys (1987)

A foreign-issue action figure series, collected in the
United States because of the incredible popularity of the
movie series.

Figures
Indiana Jones, Basic Figure, with whip, gun and hat $75.00
Indiana Jones, Basic Figure with giant snake 75.00
Indiana Jones, Basic Figure with alligator 75.00

THE INFACEABLES
"MYSTIC WARRIORS OF CHANGE"
Galoob (1985)

The faces of these figures "transform from Man to
Beast" when you pull on the figures' legs. Basically, the
flexible head shrinks down to mold around an interior beast
head when you suck the air out.

6¼" Good Warriors
Iron Lion $15.00
Robash 15.00
Sphinx 15.00
War Dog 20.00

6¼" Evil Warriors
Brainor 20.00

Tembo (#5491) 15.00
Torto the Claw 15.00
Tuskus 15.00

Vehicles
Crusher Cruiser, Mobile Command Base 20.00
Horrible Hammer, Roving Attack Tank 20.00
Incredible Thrasher, Wheeling Attack Tank 20.00

Metlar, Inhumanoids (Hasbro 1986)

INHUMANOIDS
"THE EVIL THAT LIES WITHIN"
Hasbro (1986)

"Enter the world of darkness beneath the earth's crust
with the Earth Corps, a group of dedicated scientists ... lead
the fight in their special exploration suits, protecting earth
from the deadly Inhumanoids." There are several types of
Inhumanoids. The Granites are giant 8" rock-like creatures
who hide as a pile of rocks. The Redwoods are petrified
monstrosities who can grow from a few inches to 6¾" tall.
Magnokor is a 7" figure who can split into Crygen, the
iceman and Pyre the fireball. Metlar is their ugly 14" leader.
In addition there are Tendril and D. Compose, who are both
14" tall and don't take orders.

6½" Earth Corps Scientist Figures (Asst. #7540, 1986) on
header card
Dr. Derek Bright, Earth Corps $18.00
Auger, Earth Corps 18.00
Herc Armstrong, Earth Corps 20.00
Liquidator, Earth Corps 20.00

The Granites 8" boxed (Asst. #7520)
The Granites 25.00
Granok 32.00

The Redwoods 6¾" boxed (Asst. #7521)
The Redwoods 25.00
Redsun 30.00
Redlen, Mutore 25.00

Magnokor 7" boxed (#7522)
Magnokor, Mutore (splits into Crygen and Pyre) 30.00

14" Figures boxed
Metlar, Inhumanoid Ultimate Enemy (#7500) 50.00
Tendril (#7503) 50.00
D. Compose (#7505) 50.00

Vehicles
Terrascout Earth Corps Vehicle (#7570) 45.00
Trappeur Vehicle (#7575) 30.00

INSECT MAN
Unknown Manufacturer (1990s)

A group of five cheap fantasy figures made in China. These figures may just possibly be worth the $1.00 we saw them selling for.

INSPECTOR GADGET
Galoob (1984)

From the European animated television series, starring Don Adams as the voice of Inspector Gadget. The series ran in syndication from 1983 to 1985. Gadget has a fantastic, whimsical device for every occasion. There were also PVC figures and wind-ups from Galoob as part of this series.

12" Figure
Inspector Gadget with "8 Magic Action Features" and "20

Moving Parts" (#7505) $65.00
Loose figure with all accessories 35.00

INSPECTOR GADGET
Tiger (1992–94)

Tiger's Inspector Gadget figures are attractive versions of the character and each figure depicts Gadget with one of his trademark fantastic devices. It's pretty much a one-character toy line, even with the three other figures, and we were not surprised that it did not sustain interest for long.

Inspector Gadget's Gadget Mobile from Tiger Toys transforms from a police car to a van and features a villain-grabbing claw on the front–Wowsers! It holds two figures from the series.

5¼" Figures
Go Go Gadget with Snap Open Hat! (#84601) $9.00
Go Go Gadget with Expanding Arms! 9.00
Go Go Gadget with Expanding Legs! 9.00
Go Go Gadget with Telescopic Neck! 9.00
Go Go Gadget with Squirting Water Action 9.00
Go Go Gadget with Fall Apart Action 9.00
Penny and Brain (#84608) 12.00
M.A.D. Agent with Bazooka 18.00
Dr. Claw with Dropping Hand and M.A.D. Cat 25.00

Vehicles
Gadget Mobile (#84705) 20.00
Gadget Windsurfer with **Inspector Gadget** figure and
    top secret mission packet 12.00
Gadget with Copter Pack and top secret mission
    packet 15.00

Go Go Gadget and Gadget Mobile, Inspector Gadget (Tiger 1992)

THE INTER-CHANGEABLES
Hourtoy (1982)

These figures were made from molds for the Micro-nauts and sell for $7.50 to $12.00. It's not really a knock-off, but collectors who are interested in figures of this type want the original series.

Grey Gargoyle, Iron Man (Toy Biz 1995)

IRON MAN
Toy Biz (1995–96)

"When millionaire industrialist Tony Stark dons his cutting-edge suit of technological combat armor, he is transformed into a juggernaut of titanic strength and power—the invincible Iron Man!"

Marvel Comics strategy in 1995 was to group its many comic book titles into lines. In keeping with this strategy, Toy Biz made Iron Man and his related characters into a separate line of toys. One result of this was that the various versions of Iron Man made up 40 percent of the whole line. Why not? Batman is about 80 percent of his toy line. Of course, if Tony Stark is a mere "millionaire" he might not be able to afford all the high-tech suits. A million is just rounding-off money to rich industrialists these days.

Early collector interest focused on Spider-Woman. The hoarders grabbed them from the first few shipments, but she was not all that scarce and could be found easily after that. So many Toy Biz figures were shipped that almost all of

them have been, and still are, available either at retail prices or as red tag specials.

5" Figures
Iron Man with "Plasma Cannon Missile Launcher" (#46101) $8.00
Iron Man Hydro-Armor with "Deep Sea Weapons" (#46102) 9.00
War Machine with "Shoulder Mount Cannons" (#46103) 8.00
Spider-Woman with "Psionic Web Hurling Action" (#46104) 9.00
Mandarin with "Light Up Power Rings" (#46105) 7.00
Blacklash with Nunchak with "Whip Cracking Action" (#46016) 7.00
Grey Gargoyle with "Stone Hurling Action" (#46107) .. 7.00

Second Batch
Iron Man Space Armor with "Power Lift Space Pack" (#46111) 6.00
Iron Man Stealth Armor with "Fight Action Module" (#46112) 6.00
Iron Man Hologram Armor with "Power Missile Launcher" (#46113) 6.00
Hawkeye with "Bow and Arrow Arsenal" (#46114) ... 13.00
Modok with "Energy Brain Blasts" (#46115) 6.00
Blizzard with "Ice Fist Punch" (#46116) 15.00
Whirlwind with "Whirling Battle Action" (#46117) 15.00

Third Batch
Tony Stark with "Armor Carrying Suitcase" (#46121) .. 6.00
Iron Man Arctic Armor with "Removable Armor and Launching Claw Action" (#46122) 6.00
Hulk Buster Iron Man with "Power Removable Armor" (#46123) 8.00
Century with "Cape and Battle Staff" (#46124) 6.00
Dreadknight with "Firing Lance Action" (#46125) 6.00
Titanium Man with "Retractable Blade Action" (#46127) 8.00

Fourth Batch (Apr. 1996)
Iron Man Samurai Armor with "Multi Blade Arsenal" (#46141) 6.00
Iron Man Subterranean Armor with "Excavation Equipment" (#46142) 6.00
Iron Man Inferno Armor with "Water Firing Arsenal" (#46143) 6.00
War Machine 2 with "Double Barrel Missile Launcher" (#46144) 6.00
Crimson Dynamo with "Blasting Action" (#46145) 8.00

10" "Iron Man" Figures in window box
Iron Man (#46601) 10.00
Mandarin (#46602) 10.00
War Machine (#46603) 10.00
Iron Man Space Armor (#48126) 10.00
Tony Stark Techno Suit (#48407) 10.00

"Iron Man" Dragons in window box
Fin Fang Foom (#46131) 10.00
Aureus Gold Dragon (#46132) 10.00
Argent Silver Dragon (#46133) 10.00

James Bond and Oddjob,
James Bond, Secret Agent 007 (Gilbert 1965)

JAMES BOND
SECRET AGENT 007
Gilbert (1965–66)

The James Bond movies which starred Sean Connery are considered the best and these figures are based on *Goldfinger*, which was one of the best of his movies. Harold Sakata played Oddjob and Gert Fröbe was featured in the title role. "Talk? No, Mr. Bond, I expect you to die!"

The A.C. Gilbert series consisted of boxed action dolls of Bond and Oddjob. Bond came in a t-shirt and swim trunks, which we guess made you want to get the tuxedo accessory set that was sold separately. Oddjob was dressed in a karate outfit. 007's spring arm action enabled him to draw his pistol, while Oddjob's similar action made it look like he was throwing that nasty derby of his at an opponent. A number of accessories were made and additional accessories were sold only in England.

12" Dolls
James Bond (#16101) boxed $325.00
   Loose, including scuba mask, snorkle, swim fins,
    bathing trunks, shirt, masks, cap-firing Baretta
    pistol, binoculars and trenchcoat 150.00

Oddjob (#16111) boxed 575.00

Loose, including karate robe, neckcloth, head
   band, black belt and derby 200.00

Action Apparel and Accessories
Disguise Kit (#16251) boxed 125.00
   Loose, including 2 different masks, hand
    grenade, trench coat, black pants, shoes and
    hat, dark glasses, eye patch and binoculars . . 60.00
Thunderball Set (#16252) boxed 150.00
   Loose, including jump set pack, tommy gun,
    long-sleeve white shirt, black pants and
    shoes 80.00
Deluxe Scuba Outfit (#16253) boxed 125.00
   Loose, including scuba vehicle, action spear gun,
    3 different projectiles, scuba air tanks, orange
    scuba jacket and headpiece with detachable
    decoy duck 65.00
Scuba Outfit #2 (#16254) boxed 125.00
   Loose, including scuba jacket, headpiece with
    decoy duck, spear gun, 3 spears and dagger . 65.00
Diguise Kit #2 (#16255) boxed 125.00
   Loose, including 2 masks, cap-firing pistol with
    rifle conversion kit, grenade belt, 4 grenades
    and ammo pouch 65.00
Scuba Outfit #3 (#16256) on header card 60.00
   Loose, including air tanks, tubes, bracket and
    dagger 30.00
Scuba Outfit #4 (#16257) on header card 60.00
   Loose, including spring-action spear gun, 3
    spears, undrwater propulsion unit 30.00
Ski Outfit (rare, boxed) 175.00
   Loose, including 95.00
Tuxedo Outfit (rare, boxed) 175.00
   Loose, including 90.00

JAMES BOND: MOONRAKER
Mego (1979)

Roger Moore was James Bond in this movie, which is generally considered one of the worst Bond films. But James Bond still lives, so the figures are popular without regard to the reputation of this particular film.

12½ Figures in window box
James Bond $110.00
Drax 140.00
Holly Goodhead 140.00
Jaws 400.00
James Bond, Deluxe Version with space suit 250.00

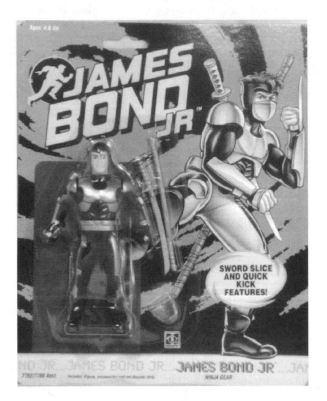

James Bond Jr. Ninja Gear, James Bond Jr. (Hasbro 1992)

JAMES BOND JR.
Hasbro (1992–93)

From the television show which debuted September 1991. Jaws, Dr. Derange and Gordo Leiter arrived somewhat later than the other figures and Buddy Mitchell was the last to appear. The Buddy Mitchell figure is scarce and the James Bond Jr. Ninja Gear figure is even scarcer. This series is not heavily collected today and, since no one watched the show, collectors are not likely to appear in the future.

4½"–5½" Figures (1992)
James Bond Jr. Street Gear with "Spring-Fired Shoot
    from the Hip Action" (#7751) $5.00
James Bond Jr. Ninja Gear with "Sword Slice and Quick
    Kick Features" (#7752) 5.00
IQ with "Undercover Punch Action" (#7753) 5.00
Jaws with "Chomping Jaw-Crushing Action" (#7755) . . 5.00
Walker D. Plank with "Spring-Fired Grappling Hook"
    (#7756) 5.00
Dr. No. with "Pop-Out Weapon Hand" (#7757) 5.00

Second Batch
James Bond Jr. Flight Gear with "Real Working
    Parachute" (#7761) 5.00
James Bond Jr. Scuba Gear with "Real Sink and
    Surface Diving Action" (#7762) 5.00
Gordo Letter with "Pop-Out Skateboard Weapon"
    (#7763) 5.00
Buddy Mitchell with "Spring-Powered Kicking and
    Clubbing Actions" (#7764?) 8.00
Odd Job with "Hat-Flinging Action" (#7765) 5.00
Dr. Derange with "Rotating Head Change Feature"
    (#7766) 5.00

Vehicles (1992)
S.C.U.M. Shark (with pull string motor) (#7791) 12.00
Subcycle (converts to submarine) (#7795) 18.00
Sports Car with ejector seat (#7796) 18.00

JOHNNY APOLLO
Marx (1968)

Figures
Johnny Apollo figure (Space Center box) $125.00
Johnny Apollo Deluxe Set 400.00
Jane Apollo figure 150.00

JONNY QUEST
Galoob (1996)

"In a chaotic world, where madmen plot to melt the polar ice caps and tigers roam free on the streets of New York, Jonny Quest is on a mission to set things right! From Siberia to the Serengeti, travel with Jonny and his intrepid globe-hopping crew. Or take a techno-trip to the virtual reality universe of Questworld and help fight to save the world from parallel-world plunderers and virtual villains."

Jonny Quest started as a Hanna-Barbera prime-time animated television series in 1964. It had been inspired by the *Terry and the Pirates* comic strip. It's about the most respected science fiction cartoon series around.

JQ1, Jonny Quest (Galoob 1996)

Real World Collections
JQ1 Silent Storm Jessie and Night Stryker Jonny Quest
(#74871) $10.00
JQ2 Desert Stealth Hadji and X-Treme Action Jonny
Quest (#74872) 10.00
JQ3 Shuttle Pilot Jonny Quest and Drop Zone Race
(#74873) 10.00
JQ4 Safari Stryker Hadji and Deep Space Race
(#74874) 10.00
JQ5 Jungle Commando Dr. Quest and Evil Ezekial Rage
Villian (#74875) 10.00

Questworld Collections
QW1 Cyber Cycle Jonny Quest (#74923) 15.00
QW2 Cyber Suit Hadji (#74924?) 15.00
QW3 Cyber Jet Race (#74925) 15.00
QW4 Cyber Trax Surd Villian (#74926?) 15.00

Vehicles
Questworld Cyber Copter with Questworld Race figure
(#74844) 17.00
Quest Porpoise with Deep Dive Jonny Quest 17.00
Quest Rover 15.00

Alan Grant, Jurassic Park (Kenner 1993)

JURASSIC PARK
Kenner (1993–94)

From the blockbuster Steven Spielberg movie based on the best-selling book by Michael Crichton starring Sam Niell as Alan Grant, Laura Dern as Ellie Sattler and Jeff Goldblum as Ian Malcolm. The movie grossed over $900 million worldwide.

The first thing to look for in the original figures is the packaging. Some of the figures have a reddish background behind the figure, with black foliage, while most of them have an all black background. Both card variations were used on each of the figures. When these figures first appeared, we couldn't tell which type of package would end up being the more common. We looked at different stores and at different times and saw a mixture. When we asked a spokesman for Kenner, he told us there was no such difference in packaging. The figures haven't gotten much of a collector following, so both types of header card sell for the same price.

4½" Figures with trading card
Alan Grant with "Aerial Net Trap" (#61001) with card
#11 .... $7.00
Tim Murphy with "Retracting Snare" (#61002) with card
#9 .... 7.00
Robert Muldoon with "Firing Tranq Bazooka" (#61003)
with card #2 .... 7.00
Ellie Sattler with "Firing Grappling Hook" (#61004) with
card #15 .... 10.00
Dennis Nedry with "Tranq-Spray Gun and Dino-Damage
Arm" (#61005) with card #14 .... 7.00

Dinosaurs (1993)
Velociraptor with "Dino-Strike Slashing Jaws" (#61006)
with card #8 .... 8.00
Dilophosaurus with "Dino-Strike Venom Spray" (#61007)
with card #1 .... 8.00
Pteranodon with "Dino-Strike Jaws and Wing Flap"
(#61008) with card #7 .... 8.00
Dimetrodon with "Dino-Strike Clamping Jaw" (#61009)
with card #5 .... 8.00
Coelophysis with "Dino-Strike Constrictor Bodies"
(#61010) with card #4 .... 10.00
Young Tyrannosaurus Rex with "'Deadly' Slashing Jaw"
(#61011) with card 15.00
Triceratops with "Head-Ramming Attack" (#61013) with
card 20.00
Stegosaurus with "Whip-Action Spiked Tail" (#61014)
with card 20.00
Tyrannosaurus Rex with "Electronic Roar & Stomping
Sound" (#61015) with card 35.00

Electronic Dinosaurs (Asst. #61021, 1994)
Electronic Velociraptor with "Slashing Claw, Dino
Screams" (#61023) with card 15.00
Electronic Dilophosaurus with "Striking Jaw, Dino
Screams" (#61024) with card 15.00
Electronic Baryonyx "Snapper" with "Head Thrust Attack,
Dino Screams" (#61043) with card #37 ...... 15.00
Electronic Gallimimus "Speeder" with "Leg Kick Attack,
Dino Screams" (#61044) with card #47 ...... 15.00

New Dinosaur Figures (1994) on header card
Pachycephalosarus "Ram Head" with Head-Butting
Attack, "Capture Gear" (#61034) with card #42 . 15.00
Lycaenops "Fang" with Sabre-Strike Teeth "Capture
Gear" (#61035) with card #44 .... 15.00
Tanystropheus "Cobra" with Constrictor Neck Attack
"Capture Gear" (#61036) with card #45 ...... 15.00
Velociraptor "Raptor" with "Slashing Jaws" (#61073) with
card #50 .... 15.00
Dilophosaurus "Spitter" with Venom Spray "Capture
Gear" (#61074) with card #36 .... 15.00

Boxed Dinosaurs (Asst. #61012, 1994)
Young Tyrannosaurus Rex with Slashing Jaws and
  Capture Gear (#61011) 18.00
Carnotaurus "Demon" with "Attacking Jaws and Capture
  Gear" 18.00
Quetzalcoatlus "Fire Beak" with "Attack Beak and Talons
  and Capture Gear" (#61049) 18.00

Vehicles and Playset (1993)
Bush Devil Tracker vehicle (#61016) 12.00
Jungle Explorer vehicle (#61017) 12.00
Capture Copter with Dinosaur Net Trap and Firing
  Tranq-Missile (#61018) 15.00
Electronic Command Compound playset (#61020) . . 65.00

Robert Muldoon, Jurassic Park, Series II (Kenner 1994)

JURASSIC PARK, SERIES II
Kenner (1994)

It took the real dinosaurs over 26 million years to become extinct, so this toy line still has some life to go before it, too, dies. With this in mind, Kenner put out new figures, called **Dino Trackers**, to rejuvenate this line, and they come packed with new trading cards. And it's our scientific guess that Kenner must have planned a whole lot of new figures or new packages, because there are a lot of numbers between card #34 and #51 to fill in.

Several of the old figures now come with the new trading cards as well, which helps to distinguish them from the original versions of these figures. Older cards had lower numbers and individual titles. These cards are numbered 33 and higher and all say "Authentic Movie Collector Card."

Series II figures have a new paint job and a new dino companion. They say "New Series II" on the package. "Dino Trackers" and "Evil Raiders" are new. Series II figures were available in quantity (and at discount) in mid 1996 at Toy Works/Kay-Bee.

Original Characters, new trading cards
Alan Grant (#61001) (Card #53) 6.00
Tim Murphy (#61002) (Card #54) 6.00
Robert Muldoon (#61003) (Card #56) 6.00
Ellie Sattler (#61005) (Card #55) 8.00
Dennis Nedry (#61025) (Card #57) 6.00

Series II, New Dino Companions, new trading cards
Alan Grant with "Double-Barreled Bola Launcher" with
  card #40 . . . . 6.00
Ian Malcolm with "Launching Tranq-Missile Dart"
  (#61057) with card #41 . . . . 6.00
Alan Grant with "Aerial Net Trap" (#61081) with card
  #53 . . . . 6.00
Dennis Nedry with "Tranq-Spray Gun and Dino-Damage
  Arm" (#61082) with card #57 . . . . 6.00
Tim Murphy with "Retracting Snare" (61083) with card
  #54 . . . . 6.00
Ellie Sattler with "Firing Grapling Hook" (#61084) with
  card #55 . . . . 10.00
Robert Muldoon with "Firing Tranq Bazooka" (#61085)
  with card #56 . . . . 6.00

New Evil Raider Figures (Asst. #61080, 1994)
Dr. Snare with "Dino-Stun Gun and Dino-Damage
  Wound" (#61052) with card #33 . . . . 8.00
Skinner with "Tranq Rifle and Dino-Damage Wound"
  (#61053) with card #43 . . . . 8.00

New Dino Trackers Figures (Asst. #61080, 1994)
Sgt. 'T-Rex' Turner with "Launching Compound Bow"
  (#61037) with card #34 . . . . 8.00
"Harpoon" Harrison with "Firing Double Spear" (#61038)
  with card #52 . . . . 8.00
"Jaws" Jackson with "Hair-Trigger Capture Trap"
  (#61039) with card #51 . . . . 8.00

Vehicles (1994)
Dino Trackers Jungle Runner (#61045) 10.00
Evil Raiders Strike Cycle (#61055) 12.00
Dino Trackers Capture Cruiser with Overhead Strike Net
  (#61065) 15.00

Hatchlings in Eggs (Asst. #61070, 1994) + trading card
Triceratops with Breakaway Egg (#61068) 7.00
Raptor Hatchling with Breakaway Egg (#61069) . . . 7.00

JURASSIC PARK: THE LOST WORLD
Kenner (1997)

The Jurassic Park series will be rejuvenated in 1997 by the sequel *The Lost World*. The movie will concentrate on action rather than discovery, which basically means that it will be similar to the last half of the first movie. The book sure was. Jeff Goldblum will be back as Ian Malcolm and Spielberg is directing again, which means that there will be plenty of money available and the movie will probably be good. The first one grossed over $900 million.

THE KARATE KID
Remco (1986)

The Karate Kid opened in 1984 and starred Ralph Macchio and "Pat" Morita. When the second film debuted in 1986 the toy makers were ready.

Figures with Auto Release Tri-Action
Chozen with Breakaway Board $20.00
Daniel, The Karate Kid with Breakaway Ice 20.00
Johnny, Cobra Leader with Breakaway Bamboo Fence 20.00
Kreese, Sensei with Breakaway Chair 20.00
Miyagi, Daniel's Sensei 20.00
Sato with Breakaway Chain 20.00

Vehicles, Accessories and Playsets
Attack Alley & Training Center 40.00
Competition Center with **Karate Referee** figure 30.00
Corner Challenge playset 25.00
Sato's Cannery 27.00

KING ARTHUR & THE KNIGHTS OF JUSTICE
Mattel (1992–93)

Recently released in quantity from Mattel are King Arthur and the Knights of Justice. In case you are unfamiliar with the basic plot of this television show, the package summarizes the story, as follows: "Camelot is torn apart as the evil Morgana imprisons King Arthur and his knights. To save Camelot, Merlin the Wizard uses his magic. He brings the New England Knights football team, including quarterback Arthur King, into the past. Taking on the roles of King Arthur and the Knights of Justice, they battle to rescue the real king and return to the future."

Merlin would have been smarter to fetch any average L.A. street gang. We don't need them here in what's left of the 20th century, and they are better armed for the job. Anyway, they are nice looking figures, with a lot of detail. All of the figures appeared at the same time. There were more items based on this television show scheduled for 1993, but they did not appear.

Figures
Warlord Viper (#4894) $5.00
Warlord Slasher (#4895) 5.00
King Arthur (#5510) 5.00
Sir Darren (#5911) 5.00
Sir Lancelot (#5516) 5.00

Vehicles and Playset
Slime Pit Set (#1248) 10.00
Boulder Basher catapult (#1586) 7.00
Valor the Warhorse (#7687) 10.00

KISS
Mego (1978)

Articulated dolls from the famous rock group with painted faces. If you are a fan of these guys, just wait until you see the 1997 figures from McFarlane toys!

12½" Dolls, boxed
Ace $225.00
Gene 175.00
Peter 250.00
Paul 175.00

KNIGHT RIDER
Kenner (1983–86)

From the television show starring David Hasselhoff which was popular for quite a while in the mid 1980s.

3¾" Figures
Michael Knight $40.00
Knight 2000 Voice Car with **Michael Knight** figure
 (#66550, 1996) 60.00

KOJAK
Excel Toy (1976)

From the television series starring Telly Savalas as the lollipop lovin' bald-headed inspector. "Who loves ya, baby?" Apparently not too many of the action figure collectors!

8" Dolls
Kojak $35.00

Accessories
Police Emergency Set 60.00
Headquarters playset 75.00

L

Christa and Anne Porter, Land of the Lost (Tiger 1992)

LAND OF THE LOST
Tiger (1992–93)

From the live-action television show created by Sid and Marty Krofft—not the beloved first series which debuted in 1974, but the disappointing second series. Our heroes go through a time portal to the age of dinosaurs and look for a way back, while trying to avoid the human-eating lizard men, the Sleestacks.

The Land of the Lost action figures from Tiger appeared about a month ahead of the vehicles. A few months later the line was expanded again with the appearance of talking figures of Annie, Kevin, Christa, Shung and Stink which cost about $3.00 more than the regular figures. Tiger also issued Triceratops & Muttaburrasaurus (#82-613), two dinosaurs packaged together on a card and a battery operated Scarface Tyrannosaurus Rex (#82-300) which comes boxed.

This was a substantial number of figures and vehicles to introduce in such a short period of time. Unfortunately, the series did not survive long enough for later batches to appear.

5" Figures

Annie Porter with Real Bow & Arrow Action (#82-600)	$8.00
Kevin Porter with Karate Kick Action (#82-601)	5.00
Christa with Jungle Battle Action (#82-602)	9.00
Shung with Crystal Power Sword (#82-603)	5.00
Nim Sleestak with Automatic Club Action (#82-604)	5.00
Tom Porter with Karate Punch Action (#82-605)	5.00
Stink with Running Action (#82-606)	5.00
Tasha "Really Walks" (#82-607)	5.00
Triceratops & Muttaburrasaurus (#82-613)	15.00

Talking Figures

Annie (#82-608)	8.00
Kevin (#82-609)	8.00

Christa (#82-610) 8.00
Shung (#82-611?) 10.00
Stink (#82-612) 8.00

Vehicles and Accessories
SS Frisco Sailing Raft (#81-700) 10.00
Land Master Vehicle and Portable Net Cannon (#82-
    701) 20.00
Boulder Bomber Catapult Weapon (#82-702) 10.00
Pterodactyl Glider 15.00

Deluxe Figure, battery powered
Scarface Tyrannosaurus Rex (#82-300) 20.00

Playsets
Dinosaur Watering Hole 11.00
Shung's Lair Villain Playset, with LED lights (#82-400) 20.00
Porters' Treehouse, with battery operated alarm
    system 25.00

LAST ACTION HERO
Mattel (1993)

Arnold Schwarzenegger's super-big summer block-buster movie has led to the Last Action Hero toy line from Mattel. We haven't seen the movie yet, but the show Mattel put on at Toy Fair for these figures was impressive.

Sales on this line seem as slow as the movie receipts. A couple of stores offered ticket promotions and discounts in conjunction with figure purchases.

5" Figures
Heat Packin' Jack (#10666) $8.00
Skull Attack Jack (#10668) 8.00
Dynamite Jack Slater (#10669) 8.00
Axe Swingin' Ripper (#10670) 8.00
Hook Launchin' Danny (#10672) 8.00
Evil Eye Benedict (suitcase open) 18.00
Evil Eye Benedict (suitcase closed) 18.00
Undercover Jack 8.00

Exclusive Figures
Three-figure pack (J.C. Penny exclusive) 18.00

Large Figure
Talking Jack Slater, 15" 50.00

Vehicles
Slater's Convertible 30.00
Evil Eye Roadster (#10673) 20.00

LAVERNE & SHIRLEY
Mego (1978)

From the television show starring Penny Marshall with a large "L" on all her outfits and Cindy Williams. These days Penny Marshall directs movies as well as shilling for Kmart, and Cindy Williams mostly just shills for Jenny Craig.

11½" Figures in Pairs in window box
Laverne & Shirley $90.00
Lenny & Squiggy, 12" 100.00

The Riddler, Legends of Batman (Kenner 1995)

LEGENDS OF BATMAN
Kenner (1994–96)

"The Legends of Batman have always existed and always will, throughout history and into the distant future." This is not just part of the "Batman Syndrome" but a concept created by DC Comics that puts Batman and company in various timelines and fantasy situations known as "Else-worlds." In these stories Batman battles crime throughout time and aspects of his life can be completely changed because he's not Bruce Wayne anymore, but a archetypical mythic hero, while his opponents are timeless mythic villains. Thus Batman and Joker as pirates and Batman and Cat-woman in Egyptian outfits make sense. Robin appears in this line too, so he must be Batman's timeless mythic archetypical teenage companion (if there is such a thing). In one Elseworlds story, Robin is a girl, but his action figure is still a boy in this toy line. Don't hold your breath waiting.

As usual, there are a lot more Batman figures than villains, which doesn't do justice to ancient myths. Heroes don't have much to do if the villains are all gone. None of the figures proved hard to find, except the Catwoman from the first series.

The Batman vs. Catwoman boxed set of 12" Mego-style dolls appeared in stores for Christmas 1996. The cost of $40.00 for the set worked out to a reasonable $20.00 per doll, so we bought one immediately.

Pirate Batman and Pirate Two-Face,
Legends of Batman (Kenner 1995)

4¾" Figures with trading card
Crusader Batman with "Powerful Punching Action"
(#64026) $8.00
Power Guardian Batman with "Real Sword Fighting
Action" (#64027) 8.00
Cyborg Batman with "Light-up Eye and 'Laser' Weapon"
(#64028) 8.00
Nightwing (Robin) with "Super-Strike Rocket Launcher"
(#64029) 8.00
Catwoman with "Quick-Climb Claw and Capture Net"
(#64033) 15.00
The Joker with "Snapping Jaw" (#64034) 12.00
Future Batman with "Pop-Up Aero Power Wings"
(#64037) 8.00
Knightquest Batman with "Battle Wings & Blazing
Missile" (#64041) 8.00

Second Batch (Spring 1995)
Samurai Batman with "Slashing Sword & Spiked Club"
(#64126) 6.00
Knightsend Batman with "Aerial Torpedo Launcher"
(#64127) 6.00
Viking Batman with "Swinging Battle Axe Action"
(#64128) 6.00
The Riddler with "Firing Question Mark Launcher"
(#64130) 15.00

Third Batch (Fall 1995)
Dark Warrior Batman with "Slamming Mace Attack"
(#64038) 6.00
Long Bow Batman with "Arrow Slinging Assault"
(#64043) 6.00
Crusader Robin with "Firing Crossbow and Battle Shield"
(#64057) 6.00
Deluxe Desert Knight Batman with "Whirling Metallic
Swords" (#64058) 12.00
Deluxe Flightpak Batman with "Battle Metallic Armor"

(#64131) 12.00
Deluxe Silver Knight Batman with "Battle Metallic Armor"
(#64132) 12.00

Fourth Batch (1996, back dated 1995)
Buccaneer Batman with "Slamming Mace Action and
Pirate Sword" and Pirate Special Edition sticker
(#64059) 6.00
First Mate Robin with "Blasting Cannon and Cutlass
Sword" and Pirate Special Edition sticker
(#64066) 6.00
The Laughing Man Joker with "Powerful Gatling Gun
Attack" and Pirate Special Edition sticker
(#64067) 9.00
Gladiator Batman with "Spear Launcher" (#64069) ... 6.00
Ultra Armor Batman with "Blasting Battle Cannon"
(#64077) 6.00

Fifth Batch (1996)
Deluxe Energy Surge Batman with "Sonic Stun Blaster"
(#64083) 6.00

Two-Packs with two trading cards
Egyptian Batman and Egyptian Catwoman (#64075) . 15.00
Pirate Batman and Pirate Two-Face (#64078) 11.00

Vehicles
Batmobile with "Missile Detonator and Quick Lift
Canopy" (#64025) 20.00
Dark Rider Batman (on Stallion) (#64042) 20.00
Skybat with Wing-Mount Missile and Menacing Jaw
Attack (#64195, 1996) 15.00
Batcycle (#64981) 10.00

Accessories
Power Spark Accessory Set (#66033) 9.00

Oversize Figures
Batman vs. Catwoman 12" dolls in window box with fold-
over flap (#27821, 1996) 40.00

Batman vs. Catwoman, Legends of Batman (Kenner 1996)

Ultimate Batman, 15" electronic (#64019) 25.00
Ultimate Knightquest Batman 20.00

Special Figure, window box
Limited 100th Edition Batman (#64084) 15.00

Bane, Legends of the Dark Knight (Kenner 1996)

LEGENDS OF THE DARK KNIGHT
Premium Collector Series
Kenner (1996)

"From a horrible nightmare, Batman awakens to a twisted, parallel world where the criminals are in total, tyrannical control. In this apocalyptic vision of Gotham City, the villains are unimaginably deadly and the Dark Knight finds himself surrounded. To fight back and regain control, he develops Neural Suit technology that acts as an integral part of his being, tapping into his thoughts and impulses and automatically reacting to danger without hesitation." He better not let the technology get out, because the thoughts and impulses of ordinary people are dangerous enough. Remember what happened to the Krell in *Forbidden Planet* when they got technology that responded to their thoughts? Monsters from their own subconscious minds destroyed them in a single day.

These figures have been popular with collectors because they are a handsome 7½" tall and contained two prime villains in the first batch. This interest isn't reflected in the price of the figures yet, because you can still get them at retail.

7½" Figures (Dec. 1996)
Neural Claw Batman with "Capture Grip Cape and
    Massive Razor Claws" (#63814) $10.00
Assault Gauntlet Batman with "Neural Pumped Power
    and Spike Strike Missile Gloves" (#63816) 10.00
Spline Cape Batman with "Spiked Assault Cape and
    Arm Swords" (#63817) 10.00
Dive Claw Robin with "Blast Attack Missile and Power
    Glide Wings" (#63818) 10.00
Twister Strike Scarecrow with "Scythe Slash Attack and
    Nightmare Glow Eyes" (#63819) 14.00
Lethal Impact Bane with "Venom-Powered Punch and
    Stinger Gauntlet" (#63821) 14.00

Vehicle
Skywing Street Bike coverts from ground cycle to air
    assault vehicle, includes **Batman** figure 15.00

THE LEGEND BRUCE LEE
LarGo (1983)

This is the only known action figure line featuring the the martial arts superstar.

5" Figures
Bruce Lee with nunchak $30.00
Bruce Lee with stick 30.00

THE LEGEND OF
THE LONE RANGER
Gabriel (1982)

"The Lone Ranger" was a popular television show in the 1950s. It starred Clayton Moore as the silver bullet shooting ex–Texas Ranger and Jay Silverheels as "his faithful Indian companion," Tonto. Those who saw the show can't listen to the "William Tell Overture" without remembering the opening credits of the series. In 1981 "they" decided to do a remake movie. In one of the stupidest publicity moves of all time "they" sued Clayton Moore to prevent him from earning a living appearing in his trademark mask and outfit on college campuses. When this was reported on television and in the press, he put on sunglasses instead of the mask and capitalized on the resulting firestorm of protest.

For less money than their attorney's fees "they" could have given Clayton Moore a walk-on part in the movie and had him promote it instead. True fans wouldn't go near the movie, which turned out to be a turkey anyway.

Neither Custer nor Buffalo Bill had anything to do with The Lone Ranger, but they appeared in the series anyway.

3¾" Figures
The Lone Ranger (#31630) $16.00
Tonto (#31631) 14.00
Butch Cavendish (#31632) 20.00
General George Custer (#31633) 20.00
Buffalo Bill Cody (#31634) 20.00

Horses
Silver, The Lone Ranger's great white stallion
    (#31635) 30.00

Scout, Tonto's Indian pinto pony (#31636) 20.00
Smoke, the wild black stallion of outlaw Butch
　　Cavendish (#31637) 25.00

Horse and Rider
The Lone Ranger & Silver (#32661) 35.00
Tonto & Scout (#32662) 30.00
Butch Cavendish & Smoke (#32663) 40.00

Playset
Western Town playset, mail-in . . . . no price found

9½" Figure and Horse in window box
Lone Ranger & Silver 80.00
Tonto & Scout 65.00
Butch Cavendish & Smoke 65.00

LEGENDS OF THE WEST
Excel Toy Corp. (1973)

"Authentic Replicas" of famous western figures. Their exploits had become legends in novels and on television, but they never trademarked their names, so anyone could use them, and several companies did.

9½" Figures in window box
Jesse James $12.00
Buffalo Bill Cody 12.00
Cochise 12.00
Wyatt Earp 12.00
Wild Bill Hickok 12.00
Davy Crockett 12.00

LEGENDS OF THE WEST
Empire Toys (1979)

The usual suspects, in smaller figures on header cards. The cards have biographical information on the characters and some of the figures are billed as "exact replicas." We doubt that this means they were "anatomically correct, however."

4" Figures
Arrowhead (#0504) $25.00
Bat Masterson 25.00
Billy the Kid 25.00
Buffalo Bill Cody (#0501) 25.00
Cavalry Scout (#0506) 25.00
Cochise 25.00
Davy Crockett (#0165) 25.00
Deadwood Dick 25.00
General Custer 25.00
General Santa Anna (#0507) 25.00
Geronimo 25.00
Jesse James (#0160) 25.00
Wild Bill Hickok 25.00
Wyatt Earp 25.00

Action Horses
Horse, white with dark splotches (#0530) 15.00
Horse, dark with light splotches (#0530) 15.00

Vehicles
Action Covered Wagon, with 2 horses and 1 figure . . 65.00
Action Stage Coach, with 2 horses and 1 figure 75.00

LEGENDS OF THE WILD WEST
Imperial (1991–93)

4" Figures
General Custer $5.00
Billy the Kid 5.00
Wyatt Earp 5.00
Sitting Bull 5.00
Buffalo Bill 5.00
Geronimo 5.00

Horse and Figure Sets
General Custer Action Play Set 10.00
Billy the Kid Action Sound Play Set 10.00
Wyatt Earp Action Play Set (#8352C) 10.00
Sitting Bull Action Play Set 10.00
Buffalo Bill Action Play Set 10.00
Geronimo Action Play Set 10.00

LITTLE DRACULA
DreamWorks (1991)

These were cute figures which came out in time for Halloween. Collectors don't really want cute monsters.

Figures
Deadwood with "Stocks, Balls and Chains" $6.00
Drac Attack with "Light-up Eyes" 6.00
Garlic Man with "Garlic Tank and Blaster" 6.00
Igor with "Handy and Weird Lab Equipment" 6.00
Little Dracula with "Batty and Vampire Gear" 6.00
Maggot with "Garlic Gardening Tools" 6.00
The Man with No Eyes with "Changeable Hand Tools" 6.00
Twin Beaks with "Vulture Dinnerware" 6.00
Werebunny with "Spooky Sports Equipment" 6.00

Vehicles
The Dracster 10.00
The Garlicmobile 10.00

[DISNEY'S]
THE LITTLE MERMAID
Tyco (1989–93)

The 1989 animated film is considered a classic. It's adapted from the famous Hans Christian Andersen fairy tale. The action figure/doll line was kept alive by the animated television series called "Ariel's Undersea Adventures" which ran in the early 1990s for younger viewers. The television series is still around on video tape.

9½" Dolls in window box
Ariel The Little Mermaid, wide box, with clothes (#1801,
　　1989) $50.00
Ariel The Little Mermaid, thin box, with pink seashell
　　(#1801, 1990) 20.00
Holiday Ariel with Holiday Flounder ornament 50.00
Ariel and Her Friends with Flounder, Sebastian, and
　　Scuttle (#1803) 30.00
Ariel The Beautiful Bride (#1804) 50.00
Eric (the Sailor), 12" (#1805) 20.00
Eric 12", casual attire, thin box 40.00
Eric 12", in uniform, thin box with pink seashell 20.00
Ariel's Sister Arista (#1806) 18.00

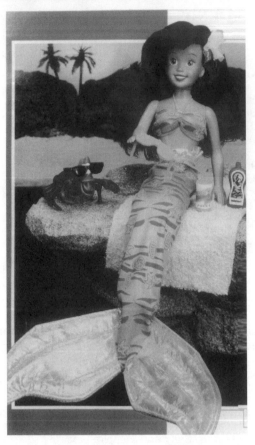

Tropical Ariel, The Little Mermaid (Tyco 1991)

Undersea Party Ariel with accessories (#1807) 15.00
Eric The Handsome Prince, 12" (#1808) 18.00
Tropical Ariel with Sebastian (#1809) 18.00
Ariel, Dressed to Tour the Kingdom (#1812) 20.00
Royal Princess Ariel with gold trimmed fur stole and
     crown (#1816) 25.00
Princess Ariel and Prince Eric: Wedding Couple and
     cake (#1817) 45.00
Calypso Beautiful Hair Ariel, 10½" (#1818-1) 18.00
Springtime Ariel 18.00
Sea Fashion Ariel (#01842) 18.00
Ariel doll, in wedding gown, 9" (#10518) 23.00
Eric doll, in full dress uniform 9½" (#10519) 20.00

Ariel The Little Mermaid series (1993)
Prince Eric (#1808-2) 20.00
Sea Fashion Ariel (#1842) 20.00
Whale of a Tale Ariel with Friend Spot (#1833) 25.00
Cool Teen Ariel (#1864) 15.00
Cool Teen Pearl (#1866) 15.00
Cool Teen Shelly (#1869) 15.00
MerBabysitter Ariel (#1823) 20.00
Beautiful Hair Ariel (Tyco #11802) 25.00

Large Figures (1992)
Talking Ariel 18" (#1828) 40.00
Singing Ariel, 18" with underwater magic (#1829) . . . 40.00

Outfits
Dinner at Eric's Palace, dinner gown place settings,
     "snarfblatt" pipe and Sebastian (Tyco #1825-1,
     1991) 15.00
Ariel's Under-the-Sea Treasures, sparkling fin and top,
     treasure chest, jewels, etc., and Flounder (Tyco

#1825-2, 1991) 15.00
Ariel's Bedtime at the Palace, nightgown, beadsheet and
     pillow, slippers, etc., and Sebastian (Tyco #1825-3,
     1992) 10.00
Ariel's Fin Fashions:
     Ariel fashion fin and bikini top outfits, 7 different,
     (Tyco #1870-1 to 7, 1992), each 10.00
     Eric Funtime Outfit bermuda shorts, shirt and hat
     (Tyco #1870-8, 1992), each 10.00
Ariel's Dress and Fin Fashions:
     Ariel deluxe dress and fin ensembles with bikini top
     & bottom (Tyco #1875-1 to 7, 1992), each 10.00
Eric handsome outfit, Leisure Suit (Tyco #1875-8,
     1992) 10.00

LITTLE RASCALS
SEE: OUR GANG

THE LONE RANGER RIDES AGAIN
Hubley/Gabriel (1979)

This is an attractive and valuable series of Lone Ranger
figures and accessories. The package artwork reminds us of
the original television series, which ran from 1949 to 1965.
We do not know of any comic book or television series in
1979. The "Tarzan/Lone Ranger Adventure Hour" began in
1980 and *The Legend of the Lone Ranger* movie came out in
1981.

Figures (1979)
Butch Cavendish $50.00
Dan Reid 50.00
Little Bear with Nama the hawk 50.00
The Lone Ranger 50.00
Red Sleeves 50.00
Tonto 50.00

Horses
Silver 50.00
Scout 50.00
Banjo 50.00
Smoke 50.00

Horse and Figure Sets
Lone Ranger & Silver 75.00
Tonto & Scout 75.00
Butch Cavendish & Smoke 75.00

Vehicles and Playsets
Prairie Wagon, 4-in-1 set 50.00
Solitary Trapper! with floating canoe 45.00
Carson City playset 75.00
Mysterious Prospector! includes pack burro 75.00

Adventure Sets
The Hidden Rattler Adventure 30.00
The Landslide Adventure 30.00
The Blizzard Adventure 30.00

"The Adventure of ..."
The Hidden Silver Mine 20.00
The Apache Buffalo Hunt 20.00
The Carson City Bank Robbery 20.00
The Lost Calvary Patrol 20.00
The Hopi Medicine Man 20.00

The Tribal Powwow 20.00
The Missing Mountain Climber 20.00
The Red River Floodwaters 20.00

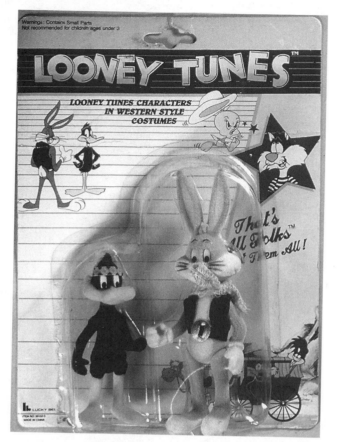

Daffy Duck & Bugs Bunny, Looney Tunes (Lucky Bell 1988)

LOONEY TUNES
Lucky Bell (1988–90)

These are cute little figures but they don't move much so they are borderline as action figures. They come in western-style cloth costumes and have textured squeezable skins, which pick up dirt and lint quickly. The figures that come in the two-packs are not named on the header card, but they are well known.

5" Figures (Asst. #50152) unnamed figures
(Daffy Duck and Bugs Bunny) $30.00
(Tweety and Sylvester) 30.00
(The Road Runner and Wile E. Coyote) 30.00

LOONEY TUNES
Tyco (1994)

These borderline action figures came with a trading card from the "World Cup Toons" series from Pyramid. There were also three larger, talking figures, not to mention radio control cars and other non-action figures produced by Tyco as part of this series. "What's Up Doc?" Not much apparently, since it only lasted one year.

5" Figures (Asst. #1010)
Bugs Bunny with "Carrot Missile" $10.00

Marvin the Martian with "Plutonium 2000 Missile" . . . 10.00
Road Runner "Speeds Away in a Cloud of Dust" 10.00
Tasmanian Devil with "Super Spin Tornado Twist
    Action" 10.00
Wile E. Coyote with "Backfiring Acme Mallet" 10.00

Large, Talking Figures (Asst. #1020)
Bugs Bunny 25.00
Marvin the Martian 25.00
Tasmanian Devil 25.00

LORD OF THE RINGS
Knickerbocker (1979)

From the popular young adult fantasy novel series by J.R.R. (John Ronald Revel) Tolkien, which includes *The Fellowship of the Ring*, *The Two Towers*, *The Return of the King* and its prequel *The Hobbit*. In case you have forgotten, the books begin with the poem "Three Rings for the Elven-kings under the sky, Seven for the Dwarf-lords in their halls of stone, Nine for Mortal Men doomed to die, One for the Dark Lord on his dark throne In the Land of Mordor where the Shadows lie. One Ring to rule them all, One Ring to find them, One Ring to bring them all and in the darkness bind them In the Land of Mordor where the Shadows lie."

The books were first published in the United States by Houghton Mifflin, starting in 1954. College students read them in the 1960s when they were published in paperback by Ballantine Books (and, briefly, Ace). "The Hobbit" was an animated television special and the trilogy was an animated film by Ralph Bakshi, both in 1978. The books are great, but both animated versions were lousy. The figures are popular with collectors.

3" – 5" Figures
Ringwraith the Dark Rider (#0526) $160.00
Aragorn (#0527) 100.00
Samwise 50.00
Gollum (#0529) 40.00
Gandalf the Grey (#0530) 110.00
Frodo (#0531) 50.00

Horses
Charger of the Ringraith 275.00
Frodo's Horse 225.00

THE LOST WORLD OF THE WARLORD/WARRIOR BEASTS
Remco (1983–84)

These figures are based on the DC comic book series "The Warlord." The comics feature heroic fantasy, not super heroes. The toys owe their introduction to the popularity of Mattel's Masters of the Universe figures rather than to any great popularity of the comic books. Mike Grell's Warlord was used to head the line-up. The Warrior Beasts were the enemies of his Warlords. All the figures were designed and marketed as part of a single series, even though their header cards have different titles. Actually, Remco also produced a similar series of Conan figures in 1984, but they are treated as a separate series and were listed previously.

The Lost World of the Warlord (Remco 1983)

5½" The Warlords Figures (from DC comics)
Arak, Son of Thunder, with knife and axe $20.00
Deimos, with crystal orb 15.00
Hercules Unbound, with club 20.00
Machiste, with axe and knife 15.00
Mikola, with staff, bow and arrow 15.00
The Warlord, with sword 20.00
Warpult 15.00

Warteam Horse and Figure Sets
The Mighty Stallion and Warman, white horse and
　　Warlord figure 30.00

The Mighty Stallion and Warman, brown horse and
　　Mikola figure 30.00
The Mighty Stallion and Warman, brown horse and
　　Machiste figure 30.00
The Mighty Stallion and Warman, tan horse and **Deimos**
　　figure 30.00

Playsets
Journey Thru Time playset with **Warlord** figure 80.00

The Warrior Beasts
Craven, with axe and knife 10.00
Guana 10.00
Gecko, with an axe 10.00
Hydraz, with axe and knife 10.00
Ramar 10.00
Skullman, with knife, bow and arrow. 10.00
Snakeman, with axe and knife 10.00
Stegos, with a staff 10.00
Wolf Warrior, with sword 10.00
Zardus 10.00

Beast Team
Fire Dragon and Ramar (#279) 25.00
War Beast and Warrior Beast #1 . . . . 25.00
War Beast and Warrior Beast #2 . . . . 25.00

THE LOVE BOAT
Mego (1981)

From the popular and long-lived television series, starring Gavin McCleod, (previously of the Mary Tyler Moore show) as Captain Stubing and including Fred Grandy as Gopher (later a Congressman from Iowa).

3¾" Figures on header cards
Vicki $25.00
Captain Stubing 25.00
"Doc" 25.00
"Gopher" 25.00
Julie 25.00
Isaac 25.00

The Monster Frankenstein,
The Mad Monster Series (Mego 1974)

[WORLD'S GREATEST SUPER-HEROES]
THE MAD MONSTER SERIES
Mego (1974)

These are highly collectible standard-style Mego 8" dolls, just like the Marvel and DC characters in the "World's Greatest Super-Heroes" series. The packaging contains the logo for that series in addition to the title "The Mad Monster Series," but it's considered a separate series, not a sub-series.

8" Dolls with glow-in-the-dark eyes and hands

The Monster Frankenstein (#51900) boxed	$75.00
Reissue, in window box	95.00
Reissue, on header card	120.00
The Dreadful Dracula (#51901)	220.00
Reissue, on header card	260.00
The Human Wolfman (#51902)	220.00
Reissue, on header card	280.00
The Horrible Mummy ((#51903)	75.00
Reissue, on header card	120.00

Playset

Mad Monster Castle, vinyl	475.00

MAGNUM P.I.
LJN (1983)

LJN saw fit to produce these figures based on the long-running CBS television series starring Tom Selleck.

3¾" Figure and Vehicle

Magnum with Ferarri vehicle	30.00

MAJOR GIL JONES YEAR 2150
Totsy (1995)

These sci-fi 12" action figures have rubbery arms and legs and a plastic torso plus large weapons. They have no story line or scenario on the package, which saves time for fighting.

12" Figures (1995) in open box

Gil Jones (#13350)	$10.00
X Bones, Enemy of All (#13352)	10.00

MAJOR MATT MASON
MATTEL'S MAN IN SPACE
Mattel (1966–71)

There is no fantasy world behind Mattel's Man in Space. It's based on the U.S. space program, which was in full swing in the late 1960s and "all of Major Matt Mason's equipment is based on official space program designs." The figures are "bendies" rather than articulated figures, but this worked well in space suits.

Like G.I. Joe, there were figures, but a lot of the action was in the outfits and vehicles. These were all space-oriented and included space suits, flight suits and lunar vehicles.

Additional figures of Sgt. Storm, Jeff Long and Doug Davis were added later. Captain Lazer is part of the line, but he is a 12" battery powered action figure which is way out of scale with the other figures and vehicles. Callisto was an alien "friend," while the first actual villain didn't appear until 1970 in the form of Scorpio.

Major Matt Mason is one of the premier collectibles for action figure and space/science fiction fans. The series was

Space Station, Major Matt Mason (Mattel 1967)

a mainstay for Mattel for several years and provided children with hours of exciting play during the days when the space program was the hottest. Collectors and dealers are still searching for some pieces which appeared in catalogs but had questionable distribution.

6" Figures
Major Matt Mason with Flight Set (#6300, 1966) . . $175.00
Major Matt Mason with Moon Suit (#6303, 1967) . . 190.00
Sgt. Storm (Flight Set) (#6317, 1968) 250.00
Major Matt Mason with Lunar Trac (#6318, 1968) . . 150.00
Sgt. Storm with Lunar Trac (#6319, 1968) 200.00
Callisto, friend from Jupiter (#6331, 1969)
    Version with big boots, header card green behind
      figure 325.00
    Version with short boots, header card yellow
      behind figure 325.00
Jeff Long with Lunar Trac (#6332, 1969) 400.00
Doug Davis with Lunar Trac (#6333, 1969) 250.00
Major Matt Mason and Space Power Suit (#6336,
    1969) 225.00
Scorpio 7" villain (#6359, 1970) 1,750.00

Uni-Tred Space Hauler, Major Matt Mason (Mattel 1968)

Talking Major Matt Mason (#6362, 1970) 325.00
Talking, Flying Major Matt Mason (#6378, 1970) . . . 375.00

Multi-Figure Set
Space Mission Team, including **Major Matt Mason**, **Jeff Long**, **Doug Davis** and **Calisto** figures (#6337, 1969) 750.00

Large Figure
Captain Lazer, 12" (#6330, 1967) 350.00

Figure and Accessory Sets
Space Discovery Set, with **Doug Davis** and **Calisto** figures, Space Crawler, Space Bubble and Space Power Suit (#1910) 600.00
Space Station & Space Crawler Deluxe Action set with **Major Matt Mason** (#6310, 1967) 450.00
Space Crawler Action Set with **Major Matt Mason**, boxed (#6311, 1967) 220.00
Firebolt Space Cannon Action Set, boxed with **Capt. Lazer** 250.00
Firebolt Space Cannon Super Action Set, boxed with **Capt. Lazer**, **Major Matt Mason**, **Sgt. Storm**, Cannon, Space Sled, Jet Pack, Cat Trak 500.00

Space Power Suit Pak, Major Matt Mason (Mattel 1969)

Orbitor with **Or the Alien** (#6356) . . . . not seen
XRG-1 Reentry Glider with **Major Matt Mason** figure
. . . . no price found

Vehicles and Accessories (1967)
Moon Suit Pak, carded (#6301) 75.00
Astro Trac, boxed (#6302) 120.00
Firebolt Space Cannon, boxed (Asst. #6304) 150.00
Space Crawler, boxed (Asst. #6304) 150.00
Rocket Launch Pak, carded (#6305) 75.00
Satellite Launch Pak, carded (#6306) 75.00
Space Probe Pak, carded (#6307) 75.00
Space Station, boxed (#6308) 190.00

Vehicles and Accessories (1968)
Major Matt Mason Rocket Ship carrying case (#6316) 160.00
Reconojet Pak, carded (#6320) 75.00
Space Shelter Pak (#6321) 50.00
Satellite Locker carrying case (#6322) 80.00
Uni-Tred & Space Bubble, boxed (#6339) 160.00

Vehicles and Accessories (1969)
Talking Command Console, boxed (#5157) 90.00
Gamma Ray-Gard (#6342) 80.00
Supernaut Power-Limbs Pak (#6343) 75.00
Space Power Suit Pak (#6344) 60.00
Space Bubble, boxed (#6345) 60.00
Uni-Tred Space Hauler, boxed (#6346) 130.00
Space Travel Pak (#6347) 60.00
Lunar Base Command Set (#6353) . . . . . . no price found
Star Seeker, boxed (#6357) 140.00
Voyage to Galaxy III set (#6380) . . . . not seen
XRG-1 Reentry Glider 220.00

Exclusives
Astro Trac, Missile Convoy Set (Sears exclusive) 40" x
    24" with Astro Trac, 3 Mobile Launch Pads,
    Sattelite Launcher Space Probe, Rocket
    Launcher 800.00

THE MAN FROM U.N.C.L.E.
Gilbert (1965)

From the very popular television show starring Robert
Vaughn and David McCallum plus Leo G. Caroll. One of
the few action doll series that were produced by the A.C.
Gilbert company, best known for the Erector set. The figures
of Napoleon Solo and Illya Kuryakin were well-dressed spies
in their toy incarnations and were supported with a series of
carded and window boxed accessories. All of the accessories
could be used with Gilbert's James Bond, Moon McDare and
Honey West lines. The instruction sheet which came with the
dolls covered all four series.

12" Dolls "Raises Arm and Shoots Cap-Firing Pistol"
Napoleon Solo (#16120) in 4½" x 12½" x 2½" box $260.00
    Loose, including white shirt, black pants, shoes,
      cap-firing pistol, U.N.C.L.E. Membership Card
      and Identification Badge 125.00
Illya Kuryakin (#16125) in 4½" x 12½" x 2½" box . . 225.00
    Loose, including black sweater, pants and shoes,
      cap-firing pistol, U.N.C.L.E. Membership Card
      and Identification Badge 125.00

Accessories and Apparel
Target Apparel Set (#16271) boxed 140.00
    Loose, including bullet-proof vest, 3 targets with
      stands, action bazooka, 3 shells and working
      binoculars 60.00
Jump Suit Set (#16272) boxed 140.00
    Loose, including jumpsuit with boots and helmet,
      working parachute and pack and cap-firing
      tommy gun with scope 60.00
Armament Set (#16273) boxed 140.00
    Loose, including all-weather jacket, military beret,
      cap-firing pistol with barrel extension, bipod
      stand, rifle butt and telescopic sight, knife,
      working binoculars, accessory belt with utility
      pouch and 4 grenades 60.00
Scuba Set (#16274) boxed 140.00

    Loose, including scuba jacket, swim trunks, air
      tanks, tank bracket, tubes and knife 60.00
Arsenal Set #1 (#16275) boxed 140.00
    Loose, including spring-action bazooka with 3
      shells, cap-firing rifle, cap-firing demountable
      gun with rifle conversion attachments 60.00
Arsenal Set #2 (#16276) on header card 80.00
    Loose, including with cap-firing rifle with
      telescopic sight, grenade belt and 4 grenades 20.00
Pistol Conversion Kit (#16277) on header card 80.00
    Loose, including bipod, rifle butt, barrel
      extension, telescopic sight and working
      binoculars 30.00

MANGLORS
CBS Toys (1983)

Figures
Manglizard $18.00
Manglodactyl 18.00
Manglodemon 18.00
Manglodragon 18.00
Manglord 18.00
Manglosaurus 18.00
Manglor Mountain playset with Manglord 22.00

Martian Spy Girl, Mars Attacks (Trendmasters 1996)

MARS ATTACKS
Trendmasters (1996)

"Puny earthlings! We have no pity for your tiny-brained
species! Nothing shall stop us from completing our mission

of doom. We shall soon rule the entire planet! ... Resistance is futile. Submit to your doom!" From the movie directed by Tim Burton starring Jack Nicholson and the rest of Hollywood. Originally based on the Topps trading card set, which was credited in the movie and on the action figures, with art by Norm Saunders, who wasn't credited in the movie or the action figures. The trading card set featured the Martians in various acts of bizarre torture and gross mayhem along with menacing dogs and kids. Naturally it was a big hit with kids, to the horror of their moms. Most reviewers felt that the Martians in the movie were faithful to the trading cards and current comic book series, but that the bevy of stars didn't have enough funny and satirical things to do.

The figures, in turn, are faithful to the movie and comic book series. Those sent to most retailers have voice chips and come in "Try-Me" packs with a hole cut into the plastic bubble on the header card. The Kay-Bee/Toy Works chain got ones without the chip, in regular packs. Comic book–based figures come on purple header cards, while those based on the movie come on red header cards. Collectors were also impressed with the flying saucers and Brain Disintegrator ray guns. The movie (and the figures) appeared in late 1996. The figures were still available at retail when this book was completed and only the scarce Martian Spy Girl had attained a collector price. Those on red header cards were in shorter supply than those on purple header cards and the non-talking figures from Kay-Bee stores had mostly disappeared. It's too soon to say if this will be the final word on supply.

5" Comic Book Figures on purple header card
Supreme Commander with Power Shield Fires Night
    Glow Missiles (#6692) with voice chip $7.00
    Version without voice chip (#6695) 9.00
Paeec Overlord with Brain Blaster Fires Night Glow
    Missiles (#6693) 7.00
    Version without voice chip (#6696) 9.00
Martian Trooper with Multi-Blaster Fires Disks and Night
    Glow Missiles (#6694) 7.00
    Version without voice chip (#6697) 9.00

Smaller Figures with computer disk
B.A.D.A.A.M.A. Night-Glow Martian Spider with Snap-on
    Armor + disk (#6702) 7.00
Doom Robot with Deadly Grip, Firing Cannon and
    Rotating Cockpit + disk (#6703) 7.00

5" Movie Figures on red header card
Martian Ambassador with Firing Chaos Ray Blaster
    (#6979) 8.00
    Version without voice chip (#7518) 9.00
Martian Trooper with Firing Photon Ray Blaster
    (#6980) 8.00
    Version without voice chip (#7519) 9.00
Martian Leader with Firing Disintegration Ray Staff
    (#6981) 8.00
    Version without voice chip (#7520) 9.00
Martian Spy Girl with Firing Freeze Ray Blaster
    (#6985) 20.00
    Version without voice chip (#7517) 25.00

Large Figures with Throbbing Brain, Evil Voice and Flashing
Lights
Martian Supreme Commander (#6683) 30.00

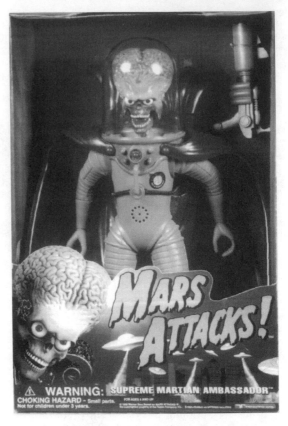

Supreme Martian Ambassador, 12",
Mars Attacks (Trendmaster 1996)

Supreme Martian Ambassador (#6994) 30.00

Vehicles
Doom Saucer (#6719) 19.00
Martian Flying Saucer (#6996) with mission disk 19.00

THE MARTIAN CHRONICLES
Larami (1974)

The Martian Chronicles is a collection of short stories by Ray Bradbury. The stories are from the 1940s and were collected into a book in 1950. They are one of the things that made him famous. The stories are about man's first exploration and colonization of Mars, and encounters with an ancient and enigmatic Martian race. They were made into a television mini series in the 1970s starring Rock Hudson and Darrin McGavin.

The stories and the television adaptation were designed for an older audience, but these Martian figures were made anyway. All three appear on a generic header card, which does not even assign names to them. They have silver masks and white robes, trimmed in different colors. Most of the interest in the figures is from collectors who are familiar with the stories, rather than ones who played with the figures as a child.

8" Figures on generic header card
Pink trim $70.00
Blue trim 65.00
Orange trim 65.00

Wolverine and *Baron Zemo*, Marvel Super Heroes, Secret Wars (Mattel 1984)

MARVEL SUPER HEROES, SECRET WARS
Mattel (1984)

Secret Wars was the title of one of Marvel's periodic 12-issue giant summer crossover comic book series. "The Marvel Super Heroes are forced by the Beyonder, a mighty being from another universe, to fight the Secret Wars against Earth's deadliest Marvel Super Villains. Can secret messages bring the heroes victory?" The figures all came with a secret flasher shield. Everyone was looking for Iceman, Electro and Constrictor to complete their collections, but they were only available in Europe. That didn't keep them from finding their way back to the United States eventually. It seemed that there were a lot of Marvel figures in this line, but these days Toy Biz issues five times as many different figures per year.

Secret Wars figures from Mattel came out at the same time as DC Super Powers figures from Kenner. The mid 1980s were quite a nice period for collectors. You could get new Marvel figures, new DC figures, old and new Masters of the Universe figures and you could still stock up on discounted Star Wars figures. Get us to a time machine, quick.

4¼" Figures with Secret Shields
Captain America (#7205) $20.00
Iron Man (#7206) 20.00
Spider-Man, red outfit (#7207) 30.00
Wolverine (#7208)
　　Version with silver claws 60.00

Version with black claws 90.00
Doctor Doom (#7210) 15.00
Magneto (#7211) 15.00
Kang (#7212) 13.00
Doctor Octopus (#7213) 18.00

Second Batch with Secret Shields (late 1984), "New"
HobGoblin with flying bat (#9138) 50.00
Baron Zemo (#9139) 30.00
Daredevil (#9140) 32.00
Falcon (#9141) 40.00
Spider-Man, black outfit (#9153) 48.00

European Issue Figures
Iceman (#9567) 50.00
Electro (#9569) 65.00
Constrictor (#9631) 55.00

Multi-Packs
Captain America vs. Doctor Doom set 50.00
Doctor Doom, Magneto, Kang set 100.00
Spider-Man (black outfit), Captain America and
　　Daredevil gift set (#9482) 85.00

Vehicles and Accessories
Tower of Doom 15" (#7472) 30.00
Turbo Cycle (#7473) 13.00
　　Reissue with figure 25.00
Doom Roller Command Unit (#7474) 20.00
Secret Messages Pack (#7599) 25.00
Doom Cycle 8" (#7600) 15.00
　　Reissue with **Doctor Doom** figure 25.00
Turbo Copter (#9246) 40.00
　　Reissue with **Captain America** figure 55.00

Freedom Fighter 16" (#9392) 25.00
Doom Copter 16" (#9572) 45.00
   Reissue with **Doctor Doom** figure 55.00
Dark Star flying wing with **Kang** figure (#9692) 30.00
Star Dart flying wing with black-suited **Spider-Man** figure
   (#9693) 45.00
Marvel Super Heroes Machine (#9877) 30.00
Marvel Super Villains Machine (#9880) 30.00

Dr. Doom, Marvel Super Heroes (Toy Biz 1990)

MARVEL SUPER HEROES
Toy Biz (1990–91)

Here's where it all started. After a six-year drought, Marvel Super Heroes were finally returned to the toy stores by Toy Biz in 1990. Toy Biz also had a DC license at first and had issued Batman and other DC figures the previous year. In fairly quick succession, these figures came out, Toy Biz lost or surrendered its DC license to Kenner, lots and lots of Marvel and X-Men figures followed and Toy Biz came under common ownership with Marvel. By 1996, Toy Biz's catalog listed an astounding 105 new figures just for 1996. Don't worry, there won't be any shortage in 1997 either.

The all red Daredevil figure from the first batch has proven to be the most collectible. There is no intriguing story to this figure. It's just scarce and desirable. The reissued Daredevil figure from 1994 is plentiful and cheap.

5" Figures (Asst. #4800, 1990)
Captain America with "Shield Launcher" (#4801) .. $18.00

Spider-Man with "Web-Suction Hands" (#4802) 22.00
Dr. Doom with "Power Driven Weapons" (#4803) ... 18.00
Dr. Octopus with "Suction Cup and Grasping Tentacles"
   (#4804) 18.00
Punisher with "Cap Firing Weapons" (#4806) 18.00
Silver Surfer with "Action Surfboard" (#4807) 25.00
Daredevil with "Extending Billy Club" (#4808) 60.00
Incredible Hulk with "Crushing Arm" (#4809) 18.00

Second Batch (Asst. #4810, 1991)
Incredible Hulk with "Crushing Arm Action" (small logo)
   (#4809) 10.00
Amazing Spider-Man with "Real Web-Shooting Action"
   (#4811) 25.00
Amazing Spider-Man (Web-Shooting) with "New Action"
   sticker (#4811) 20.00
Amazing Spider-Man with "Real Web-Climbing Action"
   (#4812) 35.00
Amazing Spider-Man (Web-Climbing) with "New Action"
   sticker (#4812) 25.00
Punisher with "Real Machine Gun Sounds" (#4813) . 25.00
Punisher (Machine Gun Sounds) with "New Action"
   sticker (#4813) 20.00
Iron Man with "Quick Change Armor" (#4814) 25.00
Green Goblin "Throws Pumpkin Bombs" with lever
   (#4815) 45.00
Green Goblin "Throws Pumpkin Bombs" without lever
   (#4815) 18.00
Venom with "Living Skin Slime Pores" (#4816) 20.00
Thor with "Smashing Hammer Action" with lever
   (#4817) 45.00
Thor with "Smashing Hammer Action" without lever
   (#4817) 25.00
Thor with "Smashing Hammer Action" with short hammer
   (#4817) 30.00

Thor, Marvel Super Heroes (Toy Biz 1991)

Super Size 15" Super Heroes (1991) in open box
Spider-Man (#4823) 35.00
Venom (#4825) 42.00
The Incredible Hulk (#4826) 30.00
The Punisher (mail-in, no box, no gun) 60.00

Vehicles and Playsets (1991)
Spider-Man Dragster (#4861) 25.00
Captain America Turbo Coupe (#4862) 30.00
Punisher Van (#4863) 50.00
Marvel Super Heroes Training Center (#4871) 35.00
Hulk Rage Cage with **Hulk** figure (#4872) 30.00
Punisher Shooting Gallery (#4873) 25.00
Spider-Man Attack Tower (#4874) 30.00

The Thing, Marvel Super Heroes (Toy Biz 1992)

MARVEL SUPER HEROES (Cont.)
Toy Biz (1992–93)

The 1992 Marvel Super Heroes figures are popular collectibles. There seemed to be a lot of Marvel and X-Men figures appearing then and they were new and interesting. What seemed like a lot in 1992 was a paltry few figures by the standards of later years. The Invisible Woman figure with "Vanishing Color" was distributed in very small quantities because the color change feature didn't really work. Every collector was looking for her when the news got out and no one was finding her. More than any other figure, she was responsible for the current practice of toy store stockboys grabbing scarce figures before they were ever put out for sale. Lucky stockboys made good money doing this. In 1996, some of them got even richer selling the three Star Trek limited editon figures.

Invisible Woman remains the most valuable Toy Biz/Marvel figure. If you see one somewhere, look again, because it's almost certainly the 1994 reissue with "Catapult Power Launcher."

5" Figures ("Cosmic Defenders")
Mr. Fantastic with "5-Way Stretch" (#4831) $22.00
The Thing with "Pulverizing Punch!" (#4832) 22.00
Spider-Man with "Multi-Jointed Action Poses" (#4833) 12.00
Deathlok with "Hidden Cyber Strength" (#4834) 18.00
The Silver Surfer (chrome) with "Speed Surfing"
    (#4835) 14.00
Invisible Woman with "Vanishing Color Action" (#4836)
    scarce 165.00
The Human Torch with "Fireball Flinging Action"
    (#4837) 18.00
Amazing Spider-Man with "Enemy Tracking Tracer"
    (#4838) 22.00
Venom with "Flicking Tongue" (#4839) 30.00
Annihilus with "Anti-Matter Wing Thrust" (#4840) 18.00

Reissue Batch (1993) (Asst. #4810E)
Captain America with "Shield Launcher" (#48001)
    reissue 7.00
Dr. Doom with "Power Driven Weapons" (#48003)
    reissue 7.00
Doctor Octopus with "Suction Cup and Grasping
    Tentacles" (#48004) reissue 7.00
Venom "Squirts 'Alien Liquid'" (#48005) 8.00
Incredible Hulk with "Crushing Arm Action" (small logo)
    (#48007) reissue 7.00

Invisible Woman, Marvel Superheroes (Toy Biz 1994)

MARVEL SUPER HEROES (Cont.)
Toy Biz (1994)

Marvel Super Heroes made sense as a series title in 1991, but by 1994 there were too many figures being produced to group them all under one logo. Consequently, beginning in 1994 figures were issued in groups such as Ghost Rider, Iron Man, Incredible Hulk, and Spider-Man. These figures were the last ones under the original title. However, either the kids were buying the other series and ignoring this one or there were way too many made, because these were the figures left over on toy store racks for the next two years. Even half price didn't help all that much. You can probably still find some figures from this assortment at toy stores.

5" Figures ("Cosmic Defenders") (Asst. #4810F)
Invisible Woman with "Catapult Power Launcher"
   (#48101) $10.00
Daredevil with "Exploding Grapple Hook" (#48102)
   reissue 5.00
U.S. Agent with "Shield Launcher" (#48103) 5.00
Punisher with "Full Weapon Arsenal" in Trench Coat
   (#48104) 5.00
Spider-Man with "Multi-Jointed Action Poses" (#48105)
   reissue 5.00

Venom, Marvel Electronic Talking Super Heroes (Toy Biz 1991)

MARVEL ELECTRONIC TALKING SUPER HEROES
Toy Biz (1991)

These figures are from early in the Marvel/Toy Biz partnership. The same 5" figures that Toy Biz was selling in other assortments got a three-phrase voice pack. The header card is bigger and states "Hey, I Can Really Talk!" along with the three phrases that the figure utters. Venom was the hit figure in the group because it said to Spider-Man "I want

to eat your brains!" This was too much for some moms and there were rumors that the figure was being withdrawn. These two factors led public-spirited collectors to snap up the remaining Venom figures. The rumor was basically false, but the controversy made Venom the figure to get anyway. We still see these figures as red tag specials occasionally.

5" Figures
Spider-Man (#4891) $20.00
Punisher (#4892) 20.00
Hulk (#4893) 20.00
Wolverine (#4894) 20.00
Magneto (#4895) 20.00
Cyclops (#4896) 20.00
Venom (#4897) 25.00

Marvel's Classic Super Heroes (Toy Biz 1995)

MARVEL'S CLASSIC SUPER HEROES
MARVEL'S GREATEST SUPER HEROES
Toy Biz (1996)

We found one of these in BJs Club Warehouse Store and the other in Toy Liquidators, late in 1996. These 8-packs seem to be designed for secondary outlets, not toy stores. They are very similar in appearance and seem to be part of the same group or series, despite the difference in titles. The window in the box is clear molded plastic with the Toy Biz logo in raised letters. We have seen them listed as a special giveaway for Marvel stockholders, but obviously there were other ways to get them. Eight figures for the $20.00 to $25.00 we paid for them is a pretty good deal.

5" Figures in 8-Packs
Marvel's Classic Super Heroes, Collector's Signature
   Editon 8-pack: Space Armor Wolverine, Spider
   Armor Spider-Man, War Machine, Iron Man, The
   Thing, Web Glider Spider-Man, Cable, The
   Punisher figures with facsimile signatures of Avi
   Arad and Stan Lee on blue box (#48015) $30.00
Marvel's Greatest Super Heroes, Collector's Signature
   Editon 8-pack: Battle Ravaged Wolverine, Spider-
   Man, Silver Surfer, Hulkbuster Iron Man, The Thing

II, The Incredible Hulk, Venom II and Ghost Rider
I figures with facsimile signatures of Avi Arad and
Stan Lee on black box (#49820) 30.00

Marvel's Famous Couples (Toy Biz 1996)

MARVEL'S FAMOUS COUPLES
Toy Biz (1996)

Mary Jane Watson was introduced in issue #42 of "The
Amazing Spider-Man" comic book and marries Peter Parker
(Spider-Man) in Annual #21. Superheroes have a hard time
with commitment, but Superman took about 30 years longer
to marry Lois (for real that is; DC faked it several times).

This is the first 5" figure of Mary Jane Watson, but she
appeared as a 12" doll in 1995 (listed later, under Spider-
Man). Lois Lane is still waiting. As the series title implies,
there will be more Marvel's Famous Couples in 1997 and the
next happy pair is Gambit and Rogue. None of this will help
Lois, unfortunately, because she's from DC comics.

5" Figures (Nov. 1996) in window box
Spider-Man & Mary Jane, limited to 24,000 sets, with
    exclusive collector's pin (#47060) $20.00

MARVEL HALL OF FAME
Toy Biz (1996)

Puzzle Zoo does an extensive mail-order business and
has arranged three exclusive assortments of Marvel figures
to date. These series have their own Marvel Hall of Fame
header cards and can be purchased from the company in sets.

There are some very interesting figures here and Series
2, called "She Force," appeals to the many female figure
collectors. However, buying figures by mail makes collecting
a pocketbook sport rather than a "dig through the racks for
that scarce figure" treasure hunt. In other words, it takes all
the chest-beating ego boost out of finding the figures.

Series 1 (Asst. #48730) with trading card
Deadpool $10.00

Rhino, repaint 10.00
Daredevil, all red 10.00
Invisible Woman, color change 10.00
Colossus, repaint 10.00

Series 2 She-Force (Asst. #48750) with trading card
Black Queen 12.00
Storm, black costume 12.00
Ms. Marvel 12.00
Jean Gray 12.00
Spider-Woman, new costume 12.00

Invisible Woman, Marvel Hall of Fame (Toy Biz 1996)

Series 3 with trading card
Venom (Flicking Tongue) 10.00
Iceman (Color Change) 10.00
Spider-Man in black costume 10.00
Invisible Woman (repainted Spider-Woman body) . . . 10.00
Wolverine (II) 10.00

MARVEL'S HEAVY HITTERS
Toy Biz (1996)

With Marvel's Heavy Hitters with "Triple Threat
Action" "you and a friend can re-create classic Marvel
battles." The figure keeps one foot on a base with a hang and
thumb control button. The triple threat refers to the three
buttons you have to control punching, kicking and a last
chance projectile. Unfortunately, collectors do their kicking
and punching whenever another collector tries to grab that
scarce action figure that they would have seen hanging on
the toy store rack in another second. Consequently, they have

very few friends and so the whole basis for these toys is lost on them. How dare Toy Biz make toys for kids anyway!

Figures (Asst. #48600) in window box
Slashing Wolverine (#48601) $12.00
Raging Hulk (#48602) 12.00
Amazing Spider-Man (#48603) 12.00
Vicious Venom (#48604) 12.00

MARVEL HEARTS OF DARKNESS
Toy Biz (1996)

A three-figure, FAO Schwarz exclusive, boxed figure set.

Figure Set
Hearts of Darkness including Wolverine, The Punisher and Ghost Rider in open window box (#49020) $40.00

Human Torch and Spider-Man
Marvel Team Up (Toy Biz 1995)

MARVEL TEAM-UP
ToyBiz (1995)

These two-packs were available exclusively at Kmart stores. A bonus Marvel stick-on tattoo came with each two-pack.

Figure Two-Packs
The Thing and Spider-Man (#45521) $18.00
Human Torch and Spider-Man (#45522) 22.00

MARVEL UNIVERSE
Toy Biz (1996)

These are Kay-Bee stores exclusive figures which first appeared in October 1996. The first three groups appeared at

the same time, already "discounted" to three for $10.00. They seem to be designed to sell that way. The header card is a relatively small rectangle and does not contain the name of the figure. The name only appears on a sticker at the bottom of the plastic box holding the figure. About the same time, more expensive Marvel figure assortments, such as Incredible Hulk and Venom: Planet of the Symbiotes appeared with elaborate header cards and 6" figures.

Two more groups appeared at the end of the year. The groupings are our own and are based on the figure's product numbers and the fact that Toy Biz ships figures in assortments of five figures.

Toy Biz's basic strategy is to use this series as inexpensive, entry-level figures. In addition, they will have the regular Spider-Man, X-Men, etc. 5" figures and also slightly more expensive 6" figures geared for collectors. This won't (and shouldn't) stop collectors from checking these figures out. There are some good-looking figures in the series, including the first appearance of characters such as Dark Phoenix. Several more series of these figures will be produced in 1997, along with 10" figures.

Group 1, 5" Figures on generic header card
Spider-Man with "Wall Crawling Action" (#48701) . . . $5.00
The Thing with "Clobberin' Punch Action" (#48702) . . . 5.00
Beast with "Mutant Flipping Action" (#48703) 5.00
Scorpion with "Tail Striking Action" (#48704) 5.00
Wolverine with "Retractable Claw Action" (#48705) . . . 5.00

Group 2
Spider-Man with "Web Swinging Action" (#48711) 5.00

Wolverine, Marvel Universe (Toy Biz 1996)

Silver Surfer with "Space Surfing Action" (#48712) . . . 5.00
Rogue with "Upper Cut Punching Action" (#48713) . . . 7.00
Carnage with "Snap On 'Shape Shifter' Weapons"
   (#48714) 5.00
War Machine with "Missile Launching Action" (#48715) 5.00

Group 3
Venom with "Jaw Chopping Action" (#48721) 6.00
Iron Man with "Missile Launching Action" (#48722) . . . 6.00
Dark Phoenix with "Light Up Hair and Eyes" (#48723) 10.00
Iceman II with "Extending Ice Limbs" (#48724) 8.00
Spider-Man with "Launching Web Shield Action"
   (#48725) 6.00

Group 4
Psycho-Man with "Emotion Detector Action Platform"
   (#48441) 5.00
Iron Man Samurai Armor (#48442) 5.00
Outcast with "Claw-Ripping Action" (#48443) 5.00
Spider-Man Super-Poseable (#48444) 5.00
Cable Cyborg with "Hidden Techno Bionics" (#48445) . 5.00

Group 5
Wizard with "Disk Firing Action Platform" (#48451) . . . 5.00
Iron Man Inferno Armor (#48452) 5.00
Green Goblin with "Missile Firing Action" (#48453) . . . 5.00
Deadpool II "Unmask to Reveal Mutant Form"
   (#48454) 5.00
Wolverine Classic with "Slashing Claws" (#48455) . . . 5.00

(MARVEL) BATTLE ACTION
MEGA ARMOR
Toy Biz (1996)

These are oversized figures in window boxes. Mostly you are buying the armor, so they are somewhat similar to Exo-Squad figures. The figure and armor together are about the size of the Marvel 10" figures and come in a window box.

5" Figures (Sept. 1996) with Exo-Skeleton Armor
Battle Action Mega Armor Wolverine (#46606) $12.00
Battle Action Mega Armor Spider-Man (#46607) 12.00

MARVEL OVERPOWER CARD GAME
POWERSURGE INVINCIBLES
Toy Biz (1996)

Issued to promote the Marvel "Overpower" card game, which was designed to capture some of the gaming market first captured by Magic. The most significant figure in the series is Adam Warlock, which had been scheduled for another Marvel series but was dropped when assortments were reduced to five figures. These figures were becoming hard to find at the end of 1996 and it seems likely that the overall production run was less than Toy Biz's usual number (unless there are a lot of them in some warehouse). Collectors are advised to look for them in stores before paying a premium for them.

5" Figure with Overpower playing card
Scarlet Spider (#48156) $9.00
Bone Claws Wolverine (#48157) 8.00

Night Armor Iron Man (#48158) 8.00
Adam Warlock (#48159) 12.00

*Wolverine, Marvel Interactive
CD-Rom Comic Book (Toy Biz 1996)*

MARVEL
INTERACTIVE CD-ROM
COMIC BOOK

Marvel has put out some "CD-ROM comic books" for kids with computers. They are sold in toy stores, not comic book shops. Some were available packaged with an action figure. We have only seen two, but the package lists several others. The ones we saw had common leftover figures, not exclusives, so they probably won't draw significant collector interest.

CD-ROM Comic with Bonus Figure
Silver Surfer CD-ROM comic with **Silver Surfer** figure
   (#48271) $10.00
X-Men Phoenix Saga CD-ROM comic with **Wolverine**
   figure (#48272) 10.00

M*A*S*H
Durham (1970s)

The figures were based on the television series which was, in turn, based on the popular movie directed by Robert Altman and starring Elliot Gould, Donald Sutherland and Sally Kellerman. These figures are not as well known as the next series. Hot Lips is the hottest figure with collectors.

8" Dolls with "Automatic Push Button Action," on header card

Hawkeye	$25.00
B.J.	25.00
Hot Lips	30.00

M*A*S*H 4077th
TriStar International (1982)

From the long-running television sitcom starring Alan Alda, Loretta Swit, Gary Burghoff, Jamie Farr, etc. These figures appeared toward the end of the series, as can be seen from the line-up, which includes Winchester, who replaced Frank Burns halfway through the show. Klinger wore a dress occasionally earlier in the series in an unsuccessful attempt to get out of the Army. It's the scarcest figure in the series. Today we have Howard Stern, Dennis Rodman and Mayor Rudolph Guillani similarly attired, but none of them have been made into action figures (at least not yet).

3¾" Figures

Hawkeye (#4101)	$16.00
B.J. (#4102)	16.00
Hot Lips (#4103)	20.00
Col. Potter (#4104)	16.00
Klinger (#4105)	16.00
Klinger in Dress	30.00
Winchester (#4106)	16.00
Father Mulcahy	16.00

Multi-Pack

Hawkeye, Hot Lips, Fr. Mulchay and Klinger (#4113)	50.00

Vehicles and Accessories

Jeep with **Hawkeye** figure	20.00
Helicopter with **Hawkeye** figure	20.00
Ambulance with **Hawkeye** figure	20.00
Military Base playset, 63 pieces	50.00

MASK
"ILLUSION IS THE ULTIMATE WEAPON!"
Kenner (1985–87)

The animated television series pits the Mobile Armored Strike Kommand (M.A.S.K.) vs. Venom. The "illusion" in the sub-title comes from the fact that the vehicles transform, a concept that was not exactly new at the time. Each vehicle comes with one or two figures. Starting in 1986, the figures were sold separately. There was also a short-lived comic book series from DC which began in 1985.

Vehicles with Figures (1985)

Rhino vehicle with **Bruce Sato** and **Matt Trakker** figures (#37300)	$35.00
Jackhammer vehicle with **Cliff Dagger** figure (#37330)	32.00
Condor vehicle with **Brad Turner** figure (#37340)	30.00
Piranha vehicle with **Sly Rax** figure (#37350)	30.00
Thunder Hawk vehicle with **Matt Trakker** figure (#37370)	32.00
Gator vehicle with **Dusty Hayes** figure (#37380)	22.00
Switchblade vehicle with **Miles Mayhem** figure (#37390)	40.00

Playset (1985)

Boulder Hill playset with **Alex Sector** and **Buddie Hawks** figures (#37320)	80.00

Two-Packs (1986)

Alex Sector with Jack Rabbit mask and Buddie Hawks with Penetrator mask	12.00
Matt Trakker with Spectrum mask and Miles Mayhem with Viper mask	12.00
Hondo MacLean with Blaster mask and Matt Trakker with Ultra-Flash mask	12.00
Brad Turner with Hocus Pocus mask and Bruce Sato with Lifter mask	12.00
Sly Rax with Stiletto mask and Cliff Dagger with Torch mask	12.00

Adventure Packs (Asst. #37230, 1986)

Rescue Mission with **Bruce Sato** figure	14.00
Jungle Challenge with **Matt Trakker** figure	14.00
Venom's Revenge with **Miles Mayhem** figure	14.00
Coast Patrol with **Matt Trakker** figure	14.00
T-Bob riding vehicle with **Scott Trakker** figure	14.00

Action Vehicles with Figures (1986)

Slingshot vehicle with **Ace Riker** figure (#37210)	32.00
Outlaw vehicle with **Miles Mayhem** and **Nash Gorey** figures (#37220)	40.00
Firecracker vehicle with **Hondo MacLean** figure (#37310)	30.00
Vampire vehicle with **Floyd Malloy** figure (#37400)	30.00
Firefly vehicle with **Julio Lopez** figure (#37410)	30.00

Alex Sector, Matt Trakker, Buddie Hawks and Miles Mayhem, Mask (Kenner 1985)

Raven vehicle with **Calhoun Burns** figure (#37420) . 25.00
Stinger vehicle with **Bruno Sheppard** figure (#37430) 28.00
Hurricane vehicle with **Hondo MacLean** figure
(#37440) 35.00
Volcano vehicle with **Matt Trakker** and **Jacques
LaFleur** figures (#37450) 40.00

Vehicles and Accessories (1987)
Buzzard vehicle with **Miles Mayhem** and **Maximus
Mayhem** figure (#37500) 32.00
Iguana vehicle with **Lester Sludge** figure (#37560) .. 18.00
Manta vehicle with **Vanessa Warfield** figure (#37590) 32.00
Ramp-up accessory with **Hondo MacLean** figure and
Blaster mask 30.00
Thunderball accessory with **Cliff Dagger** figure and
Torch mask 30.00
Pit Stop Catapult with **Sly Rax** figure 15.00
Billboard Blast with **Dusty Hayes** figure 18.00

THE MASK
"FROM ZERO TO HERO"
Kenner (1995)

This series is based on the eye-poppin' movie starring Jim Carrey, who discovers a mask that gives him magical powers. "The mysterious mask has powers beyond belief, powers that take you beyond your wildest dreams! Watch as Stanley becomes an amazing hero as he transforms into the lean, green, crime fighting machine—The Mask!" A lot of collectors would probably settle for just "lean." The movie was based on the Dark Horse Comics series which began in 1991.

The regular 5" figures were produced in abundance, but they were not as popular as the movie and were red tag specials at the end of 1996. The larger figures saw only limited distribution and have attained some "smokin' hot" prices. Toy Island will be making more Mask figures in 1997. We don't know what effect that will have on these figures' values.

5" Figures
Killin' Time Mask with "Pop-Out Eyes and Tongue"
(#81912) $5.00
Heads-Up Mask "Stanley Turns Into the Mask"
(#81913) 5.00
Quick-Draw Mask with "Spring-Action Arms" (#81915) . 5.00
Heads-Up Dorian "Dorian Turns Into the Evil Mask"
(#81910) 5.00
Chompin' Milo with "Chompin' Teeth and Shooting Net
Launcher" (#81918) 6.00
Wild Wolf Mask with "Shocking Surprise Action and
Punchin' Bazooka" (#91919) 6.00
Tornado Mask with "Super-Spinning Tornado Action"
(#81921) 5.00
Belly Bustin' Mask with "Exploding Action and Squirting
Milo" (#81933) 5.00

Oversize Figures
Super Stretch Mask 300.00
14" Talking Mask, poseable talking figure in "Try-me"
window box 250.00
15" Mask, with hat 125.00
Variation without hat 60.00

Vehicles
Mask Mobile with Launching Ejector Seat and Chompin'
Teeth 20.00
Mask Cycle with Detachable Sidecar and Jaw-Chompin'
Action (#81923) 16.00

Comic Waddling Ferbus, Masked Rider (Bandai 1995)
SABAN'S
MASKED RIDER
Bandai (1995–96)

From the live-action FOX television show which debuted in the fall of 1995. "Teen hero, Dex, has been sent from another planet to protect Earth from the powerful galactic warlord, Count Dregon. Using his super human powers, Dex transforms from a teenager into the Masked Rider, with powerful weapons." From the same people who brought you the Mighty Morphin Power Rangers.

5" Figures (1995)
Masked Rider (#3602) $7.00
Masked Rider Super Gold (#3603) 7.00
Mutant Marauder Cyclopter (#3604) 7.00
Slashing Skull Reaper (#3607) 7.00
Disk Throwing Robosect (#3608) 7.00
Double Face (#3609) 7.00
Commanding Count Dregon (#3610) 7.00

Second Batch (1996)
Karate Kicking Dex (#3665) 7.00
Sabre Flipping Masked Rider (#3666) 7.00
Fast Draw Masked Rider Super Gold (#3667) 7.00

Ecto Accelerating Masked Rider, Masked Rider (Bandai 1995)

Water Blasting Masked Rider Super Blue (#3668) 7.00
Comic Waddling Ferbus (#3669) 7.00

Ecto Accelerating Figures
Ecto Accelerating Masked Rider "Ecto Phase Activate"
    (#3630) 7.00
Ecto Accelerating Masked Rider Super Gold "Ecto
    Phase Activate" (#3631) 7.00
Ecto Accelerating Masked Rider Super Gold "Ecto
    Phase Activate" (#3632?) 7.00

Figure and Vehicle Sets
Masked Rider and Combat Chopper set (#3626) 13.00
Masked Rider Super Gold and Combat Chopper set
    (#3627) 13.00

Vehicles (1995)
Cyclopter's Cannon Wheels motorcycle (#3605) 15.00
Masked Rider's Combat Chopper motorcycle (#3606?) 15.00

Vehicles in window box and CardZillion card
Mutating Combat Chopper (#3681) 8.00
Mutating Magno (#3682) 8.00

MASTER WARRIORS
Lido (1984)

Die-cast figures with a fantasy theme designed to compete with Masters of the Universe. These figures have not interested collectors. There are six different figures which are worth about $7.50 each.

Evil-Lyn, Masters of the Universe (Mattel 1983)

MASTERS OF THE UNIVERSE
Mattel (1982–89)

Long-running toy series based on a fantasy theme. "He-man is the strongest man in the universe. His allies are Man at Arms and Teela, a warrior goddess. Their enemies are Skeletor and Beastman." The characters battle over Castle Greyskull and others such as Mer-Man, Stratos and Zodac join in. And that's only the first year!

The animated television show and comics were based on and coordinated with the toy line. The figures were highly creative and very popular. The movie, starring Dolph Lundgren as He-Man with Frank Langella, Courteney Cox, James Tolkand and Meg Foster came later (1987), and was reasonably successful.

The toys had action features, as well as poseability, and are the most interesting heroic fantasy (sword and sorcery) figures ever made. At the time, they were also the largest action figures on the market as they dwarfed rivals such as Star Wars and G.I. Joe. The major factor holding down prices is the large supply and large number of figures available. However, Zodac, Mer-Man and Stratos were discontinued after the first year of the series and King Randor, Scare Glow and Sorceress were tail-end figures, with the usual low distrubution. The series was continued, more or less, as He-Man, which was listed previously.

Bull Alien, Scorpion Alien, and Gorilla Alien, *Aliens* (Kenner 1992)

Clay Face, *Batman: The Animated Series* (Kenner 1994)

Bob, The Joker's Goon, *Batman* (Toy Biz 1989)

Catwoman, *Batman Returns* (Kenner 1992)

Bane, *Batman: The Animated Series* (Kenner 1995)

Shipwreck Beetlejuice, *Beetlejuice* (Kenner 1989)

Vinnie, 12" figure, *Biker Mice from Mars* (Galoob 1994)

Kragen, *Clash of the Titans* (Mattel 1981)

Ming the Merciless, *Defenders of the Earth* (Galoob 1985)

Superman, *DC Comics Super Heroes* (Toy Biz 1989)

Dick Tracy, 15" figure, *Dick Tracy* (Playmates 1990)

Rita Torres with Field Sergeant E-Frame, *Exo-Squad* (Playmates 1994)

Dale Arden, *Flash Gordon* (Playmates 1996)

Demona, *Gargoyles* (Kenner 1995)

Skinner, *Ghost Rider* (Toy Biz 1995)

Rip Cord, Firefly, and Scrap-Iron, *G.I. Joe: A Real American Hero,* Series Three (Hasbro 1984)

Night Storm Vehicle, *G.I. Joe: A Real American Hero,* Nightforce Series (Hasbro 1988)

Slice, *G.I. Joe Shadow Ninjas* (Hasbro 1994)

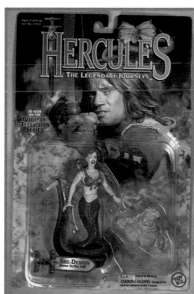

Mobile Artillery Assault, equipment, *G.I. Joe Hall of Fame* (Hasbro 1994)

She-Demon, *Hercules* (Toy Biz 1996)

The Map Room Adventure playset, *Indiana Jones* (Kenner 1993)

Supreme Martian Ambassador, 12" figure, *Mars Attacks* (Trendmasters 1996)

Spider-Man and Mary Jane, *Marvel's Famous Couples* (Toy Biz 1996)

Daredevil, *Marvel Super Heroes* (Toy Biz 1990)

Doctor Octopus, *Marvel Secret Wars* (Mattel 1984)

Yellow Ranger, Trini Doll, *Mighty Morphin Power Rangers* (Bandai 1995)

Lava Planet Predator, *Predator* (Kenner 1994)

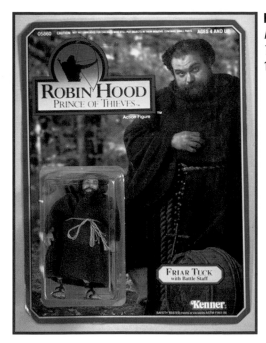

Friar Tuck, *Robin Hood, Prince of Thieves* (Kenner 1991)

Robocop, 12" Audiotronic figure, *Robocop* (Toy Island 1993)

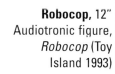

Spawn, unmasked, *Spawn* (Todd Toys 1994)

Angela, 13", *Spawn* (McFarlane 1996)

Tiffany, repaint, *Spawn* (McFarlane 1996)　　**Bridge playset with Klingon, Mr. Scott, and Uhura,** *Star Trek* (Mego 1974)

Captain James T. Kirk, 9" figure, *Star Trek* Command Edition (Playmates 1995)

Lieutenant Thomas Riker, *Star Trek: The Next Generation* (Playmates 1994)

Counselor Deanna Troi as Durango, *Star Trek: The Next Generation* (Playmates 1995)

Classic Star Trek Classic Collector Figure Set, *Star Trek* (Playmates 1993)

Bib Fortuna, Jabba the Hutt playset with Salacious Crumb, Han Solo, and Carbonite Chamber, Princess Leia Organa in Boushh Disguise, *Return of the Jedi* (Kenner 1983)

Han Solo, 12" figure, *Star Wars* (Kenner 1979)

Sy Snootles and the Rebo Band, *Return of the Jedi*
(Kenner 1983)

**Luke Skywalker and Obi Wan Kenobi in Landspeeder,
surrounded by three Stormtroopers,** *Star Wars* (Kenner 1978)

Firestorm, the Nuclear Man,
Super Powers (Kenner 1985)

Numa, the Golden Lion,
Tarzan, The Epic Adventures
(Trendmasters 1995)

Ray Fillet, *Teenage Mutant
Ninja Turtles* (Playmates 1991)

Evil Tongue Thrakkorzog,
The Tick (Bandai 1995)

Wolfman, *Universal Studios Monsters* (Playco 1992)

Fantastic Four (The Thing, Invisible Girl, Mister Fantastic, and Human Torch), *World's Greatest Super Heroes* (Mego 1975)

Zealot, *WildC.A.T.s* (Playmates 1995)

Conan, *World's Greatest Super Heroes* (Mego 1975)

Cannonball, pink outfit, *X-Force* (Toy Biz 1993)

Storm, *Uncanny X-Men* (Toy Biz 1991)

Shaft and Mother-One, *Youngblood* and *Wetworks* (McFarlane 1995)

5½" Figures, First Batch (Asst. #5050, 1982)
Original He-Man (#5040) $35.00
Man-At-Arms (#5041) 30.00
Original Skeletor (#5042) 35.00
Beast Man (#5043) 25.00

Second Batch (Asst. #5334, 1982)
Zodac (#5044) 25.00
Teela (#5045) 35.00
Mer-Man (#5046) 25.00
Stratos (#5047) 30.00

Second Series (1983)
Tri-Klops (#4301) with Ring 22.00
Trap Jaw (#4302) with Ring 22.00
Evil-Lyn (#4712) 40.00
Mekaneck (#4919) 20.00
Man-E-Faces (#5879) "New" 25.00
Ram Man (#5896) 30.00
Faker, blue skin 30.00

Buzz-Off, Masters of the Universe (Mattel 1984)

Third Series (1984)
Webstor (#4895) 15.00
Buzz-Off (#4923) 15.00
Jitsu (#4924) 15.00
Whiplash (#4935). 18.00
Fisto (#7015) 15.00
Clawful (#7016) 20.00
Kobra Khan (#7098) 15.00
Battle Armor Skeletor (#7301) 25.00
Battle Armor He-Man (#7302) 25.00
Prince Adam (#7353) 32.00
Orko (#7354) 15.00

Fourth Series (1985)
Spikor (#7985) "New" 15.00
Sy-Klone (#7997) 15.00

Mantenna, Masters of the Universe (Mattel 1985)
Dragon Blaster Skeletor (#9017) 20.00
Two Bad (#9040) 15.00
Roboto (#9041) 15.00
Thunder Punch He-Man (#9056) 20.00
Moss Man (#9219) 15.00
Stinkor (#9236) 15.00

Evil Horde (1985–87)
Mosquitor (#1191, 1987) "New" 15.00
Buzz-Saw Hordak (#1732, 1987) 30.00
Hurricane Hordak (#2139, 1986) "New" 20.00
Multi-Bot, Transforming Robot (#2312, 1986) "New" . 15.00
Dragstor (#2313, 1986) "New" 15.00
Horde Trooper (#2549, 1986) 15.00
Mantenna (#9168) 20.00
Leech (#9169) "New" 17.00
Grizzlor (#9171) "New" 18.00
Hordak (#9172) 16.00
Modulok, Transforming Creature (#9174) 15.00

Fifth Series (1986)
Rio Blast (#2792) 15.00
Extendar (#2797) 15.00
Snout Spout (#2803) 15.00
Stonedar (#9862) "New" 10.00
Rokkon (#9863) "Comet Warrior" 10.00

Snake Men, Evil Warriors (1986–87)
Snake Face (#1987, 1987) 20.00
Rattlor (#2036) 15.00
Tung Lashor (#2331) 15.00
King Hiss (#2420) "New" 15.00

5th Anniversary Collector's Edition (1986)
Flying Fists He-Man (#9695) "New" 35.00
Terror Claws Skeletor (#9696) "New" 35.00

Extendar, Masters of the Universe (Mattel 1986)

Tyrantisaurus Rex, Masters of the Universe (Mattel 1987)

Sixth Series (1987)
Sssqueeze (#1417) "New"	20.00
Blast-Attak (#1710)	15.00
Sorceress (#1787) "New"	35.00
Twistoid (#3025) "New"	40.00
Rotar (#3034) "New"	50.00
King Randor (#3068) "New"	15.00
Ninjor (#3069)	15.00
Scare Glow (#3072) "New"	15.00
Clamp Champ (#3073) "New"	15.00
Faker, 2nd edition (#4462)	20.00

Motion Picture Figures
Blade (#3275, 1986?)	30.00
Saurod (#3670?, 1986?)	30.00
Gwildor (#3724, 1986?)	25.00
Laser Power He-Man (1988?)	60.00
Laser-Light Skeletor (1988)	60.00

Meteorbs (1986)
Astro Lion	18.00
Comet Cat	18.00
Tuskor	18.00
Ty-Grrr (#1404)	18.00
Dinosorb	18.00
Crocobite	18.00
Gore-illa (#1408)	18.00
Rhinorb (#1412)	18.00
Cometroid (#1414)	18.00
Orbear (#1415)	18.00

Steeds (and Riders)
Zoar (Fighting Falcon) figure (#4014, 1983)	18.00
Panthor and **Skeletor** figure set (#4710, 1983)	30.00
Screeech (Barbarian Bird) (#4713, 1983)	18.00
Panthor (Savage Cat) figure (#4714, 1983)	20.00
Night Stalker 5¾" (Evil Armored Battle Steed) (#4965, 1985)	18.00
Stridor (Heroic Armored War Horse) (#4966, 1984)	18.00
Battle Cat 5½" (Fighting Tiger) (#5048, 1982)	26.00
Battle Cat and **He Man** set (#5049, 1983)	45.00

Powers of Greyskull Cybernetic Dinosaurs (1987)
Bionatops	80.00
Tyrantisaurus Rex (#1273)	140.00
Turbodactyl	40.00

Vehicles
Fright Fighter (Evil Dragonfly Attack Vehicle) (#1053, 1986)	18.00
Jet Sled (#2084, 1986) "New"	12.00
Mantisaur (Evil Insectoid Steed) (#2085, 1986)	18.00
Monstroid (The Ultimate Battling Monster) "Evil Horde" (#2418, 1986)	18.00
Blasterhawk (Heroic Land and Sky Disk Launcher) vehicle (#2607, 1986)	18.00
Beam-Blaster & Artilleray (#3139, 1986)	18.00
Battle Ram (Mobile Launcher) 26" (#3990, 1983)	25.00
Roton (Evil Assault Vehicle) 8½" (#4892, 1984)	15.00
Dragon Walker (Sidewinding Beast/Vehicle) 14" (#4902, 1984)	15.00
Road Ripper warrior carrier 9¼" (#4903, 1984)	17.00
Wind Raider (Assault Lander) 10½" vehicle (#5117, 1983)	20.00
Wind Raider with **He-Man** figure (#5118, 1983)	30.00
Attak Trak (Battle Machine) 10½" (#5470, 1983)	18.00
Land Shark (Evil Monster vehicle) 10" (#7892, 1985)	15.00
Bashasaurus (Heroic Combat Vehicle) 11½" (#9039, 1985) "New"	22.00
Spydor (Evil Stalker) vehicle (#9055, 1985)	18.00
Laser Bolt (Heroic Road Rocket) (#9602, 1986)	18.00

Playsets
Eternia playset (#2855, 1986)	250.00

Castle Grayskull fortress, 27" (#3991, 1982) 80.00
Snake Mountain stronghold 19" tall (#4949, 1984) . . 75.00
Fright Zone "Evil Horde" playset (#9410, 1985) 45.00
Slime Pit "Evil Horde" playset (#9989, 1986) 22.00

Accessories
Stilt Stalkers (#2082, 1986) 16.00
Megalaser weapon (#2083, 1986) "New" 12.00
Slime Gel (#2487, 1986) 7.50
Weapons Pak (#7303, 1984) 4.00
Battle Bones Carrying Case (#9173, 1985) 17.00

Triple Threat, Maximum Carnage (Toy Biz 1994)

MAXIMUM CARNAGE
Toy Biz (1994)

Carnage is part of the Spider-Man family of characters. He appeared initially in "Amazing Spider-Man" #361. In May 1993, Marvel began one of its big crossover story arcs called Maximum Carnage, and these figures presumably derive from that.

We have no idea why Carnage was issued with his own logo. It's not a series—there is only the one 5" figure, along with three multi-packs and a 10" figure. It's not included in Toy Biz's 1994 catalog. Both Venom and, of course, Spider-Man had previously been included in Marvel Super Heroes assortments. Spider-Man got his own series later in 1994 and Carnage was included in the first batch of those figures, along with Venom.

5" Figures
Carnage with "Weapon Arms" (#44100) $10.00

Two-Packs (Asst. #44400, 1994) with collectors pin
Carnage and Spider-Man Battle Pack (#44401) 18.00
Carnage and Venom Battle Pack (#44402) 18.00

Three-Pack in window box
Triple Threat: Spider-Man, Carnage, Venom (#44300) 22.00

Deluxe 10" Figure
Carnage, Deluxe Edition (#44200) 18.00

MAXX FX
Matchbox (1989)

Maxx FX stands for Maximum Special Effects. This one-shot figure was supposed to be part of a series where Maxx would come with the costume of other stars of horror movies, and, no doubt costumes would have been sold separately as well. It didn't work out.

8" Figure
Freddy (from *A Nightmare on Elm Street*) 35.00

MCDONALDLAND CHARACTERS
Remco (1976)

Gee, we wonder if you can figure out where these figures came from. They have a golden arches logo along with Remco's. They are probably more popular with advertising figure collectors than with action figure collectors.

Figures
Ronald McDonald $50.00
Big Mac 50.00
Hamburglar 50.00
Grimace 50.00
Mayor McCheese 50.00
Captain Crook 50.00
Professor 50.00

Playset
McDonaldland wind-up train playset 150.00

MEGA MAN
"SUPER HERO OF THE 21ST CENTURY"
BanDai (1995)

Mega Man, Capcom's "super hero of the 21st century" had a syndicated television show for three years. "For many years the renowned scientist, Dr. Thomas Light, dreamed of creating robots that could handle jobs too dangerous for humans. In a twist of fate, his coworker, Dr. Wily, stole the plans for the industrial robots and disappeared. Several months later, robots—exact replicas of Dr. Light's designs— began to go berserk and took over the city." Dr. Light created Mega Man to fight them. He's supposed to be peaceful by nature, but he spends most of his time fighting and has the ability to copy the weapon from any opponent he defeats. This saves a lot on R & D expenses.

5" Figures (Apr. 1995)
Drillman (#2721) $5.00
Brightman (#2722) 5.00
Snakeman (#2723) 5.00
Eleckman (#2724) 5.00
Mega Man (#2732) 5.00
Proto Man (#2733) 5.00

Cutman (#2734) 5.00
Rush, dog (#2735) 6.00
Gutsman (#2741) 5.00
Bombman 10.00

Vehicles (1995)
Air Raider (#2726) 12.50
Land Blazer (#2740) 12.50

MICRONAUTS
"THE INTERCHANGEABLE WORLD
OF THE MICRONAUTS"
Mego (1976–81)

Micronauts was a popular sci-fi and fantasy based series of figures with Japanese influence. Figures were made of die-cast metal and plastic, and parts were interchangeable, so you could rearrange your figures in many different ways.

There was also a Marvel comic book series which had good art and ran for longer than the toys. The Interchangeables series of figures were based on the same concept. In addition to the figures and vehicles listed, Mego also produced wheeled, battery-powered "robot clowns" called "Trons" and named Alphatron, Betatron and Gammatron.

3¾" Figures (1976)
Time Traveler $18.00
Galactic Warrior 18.00
Space Glider 18.00
Acroyear 18.00
Biotron, boxed 30.00
Microtron, boxed 25.00

Second Series (1977)
Pharoid with Time Chamber, blue and white 18.00
Pharoid with Time Chamber, silver and black 20.00
Acroyear II (#71015) 18.00
Baron Karza, boxed 45.00

Andromeda, boxed 50.00
Force Commander, boxed 55.00
Oberon, boxed 60.00
Giant Acroyear, boxed 35.00

Third Series (1978)
Galactic Defender 18.00
Phobos Robots, boxed 60.00
Nemesis Robots, boxed 50.00

Fourth Series (1979)
Terraphant 130.00
Hornetroid 130.00
Antron 45.00
Membros (1979) 45.00
Repto (1979) 45.00

Fifth Series
Kronos (1980) 90.00
Sentaurus (1980) 115.00
Lobros (1980) 135.00
Emperor (1981) 70.00
Megas (1981) 70.00

Vehicles
Photon Sled with figure (1976) 20.00
Warp Racer, motorized with figure (1976) 20.00
Ultronic Scooter, motorized with figure (1976) 20.00
Crater Cruncher, motorized with figure (1976) 20.00
Hydra (1976) 20.00
Galactic Cruiser (1976) 28.00
Hydro Copter (1976) 30.00
Mobile Exploration Lab (1976) 70.00
Neon Orbiter (1977) 20.00
Rhodium Orbiter (1977) 20.00
Thorium Orbiter (1977) 20.00
Aquatron (1977) 20.00
Micronaut Battle Cruiser (1977) 45.00
Star Searcher (1978) 65.00
Taurion (1978) 42.00
Solarion (1978) 38.00
Battle Cruiser (1977) 45.00

Pharoids with Time Chambers, Micronauts (Mego 1977)

Accessories
Astro Station accessory, boxed (1976)	52.00
Galactic Command Center (1978)	95.00
Interplanetary Headquarters (1978)	90.00
Karrio (carrying case) (1979)	30.00
Mega City (1976)	75.00
Microrail City (1978)	100.00
Micropolis Monorail set	No price found
Rocket Tubes (1978)	100.00
Stratastation accessory, boxed (1976)	60.00
Cosmic Control Base (1976)	not seen
Satellite Survey Station (1978)	not seen

MIGHTY CRUSADERS
Remco (1974)

"The Mighty Crusaders" was a minor comic book super hero series by Archie Comics in the 1960s and was revived with "all new adventures" as a minor comic book series in the 1980s. In between, in the 1970s, they experienced another comeback as a minor action figure series. The only reason anybody collects these figures is because they are the only toy representations of these classic characters! Each one came with a "Secret Sonic Signaling Shield."

5" Figures with Mighty Punch Action
The Shield	$22.00
The Fox	22.00
The Web	22.00
The Comet	22.00
The Evil Sting	20.00
The Evil Eraser	20.00
The Evil Buzzard	20.00
The Evil Brain Emperor	20.00

MIGHTY DUCKS
Mattel (1996)

"They're awesome hockey players and fearless crime fighters. Superhero ducks who traveled to Earth from another dimension to battle the evil Lord Dragaunus." We've seen a number of NHL games, and frankly we'd bet on the average hockey player in a showdown with interdimensionally traveling crime fighters anytime.

This series appeared in the fall of 1996 and continued with new additions in early 1997. Mallory is the girl (or female duck, or whatever) in the series and so the collectors are all interested in her. Ducks aren't even mammals, but female figure collectors aren't very particular about species (or kingdom, order or phylum for that matter). In fact, they don't care if she's alive, dead or undead. As long as the figure has been anthropomorphized with typical female mammalian bodily characteristics, it's a girl, so they collect her. I guess it's only fair, since Howard the Duck had the hots for Lea Thompson.

6" Figures with trading card
Wildwing (Team Leader) (#16069)	$7.00
Nosedive (Weapons Expert) (#16070)	7.00
Mallory (Martial Arts Master) (#16071)	9.00
Grin (Combat Specialist) (#16072)	7.00
Duke L'Orange (Champion Sword Fighter) (#16073)	7.00

Mallory, Mighty Ducks (Mattel 1996)

Lord Dragaunus (Evil Saurian Overlord) (#16074)	7.00

Second Batch
Net Attack Wildwing (#16276)	7.00
Puck Bomber Nosedive (#16277)	7.00
Nitro-Fist Grin (#16279)	7.00
Triple Sword Duke L'Orange (#16280)	7.00
Evil Siege (#16281)	7.00

MIGHTY MORPHIN POWER RANGERS
Bandai (1993–96)

If you aren't familiar with this television show with toy line from Bandai, the basic story line is that five ordinary teenagers are picked by someone named Zordon to save the world from Rita Repulsa, an evil space alien whose interstellar prison cell crash-landed on the moon. She set up shop there and now plans to ravage the earth. Zordon is trapped in a time warp so he naturally picks a few teenagers to do the job for him. They call on the spirits of ancient dinosaurs to "morph" themselves into mighty Power Zords. The ancient dinosaur spirits seem to include a woolly mammoth and a saber-tooth tiger, but why let a little bad science interfere with a good television or toy idea? The Rangers have to work together to morph into the incredibly powerful Mega Zord to have any chance of winning, and working together is not exactly a common teenage virtue, but then saving the world isn't either, now is it?

Yellow Ranger (Trini),
Mighty Morphin Power Rangers (Bandai 1993)

Zord morphing aside, the Power Ranger figures are pretty much the same, except for the different colors. That would normally make the Evil Space Aliens the best figures to collect. They are suitably ugly and repulsive looking, but not very interesting. The first ones included **Squatt, Goldar, Baboo** and **King Sphinx**. Their leader, **Rita Repulsa**, was not released until later.

The Power Rangers best feature is that they are 9" tall, which makes them more interesting than the usual smaller figures. They sell for about $10.00 and reminded us a lot of Ultraman (which was then available at discount). The original Rangers came in triangular boxes, which is different.

It was very difficult to track these toys during 1993 and early 1994 because they disappeared from store shelves immediately and became the number one toy in the country. Spring 1994 brought new 8" aliens—Finster, Bones and Putty Patrol—along with 3½" "collectible figure" versions of the Rangers and the original Aliens.

By late 1994 you could find Power Rangers fairly easily in the space formerly occupied by the Teenage Mutant Ninja Turtle figures, which was too bad because the latter figures were a lot better designed and sculpted. Power Ranger Aliens look really dumb and childish by comparison. But, as Dennis Miller says, that's just our opinion, we could be wrong. By far the best feature of the Power Rangers toy line is the transforming and combining of various Zords to form megazords, ninjazords and thunderzords, etc.

Fall 1994 brought Lord Zedd to the leadership of the Evil Space Aliens, after Rita Repulsa was vanquished. Naturally the Rangers needed more Zords to defeat this new foe. They must have been somewhat successful, because the Evil Space Aliens shrank to 5" tall, except for their deluxe 8" editions.

By 1996 the Rangers had entered a new era, the era of the Zeo Rangers! It seems that the evil Master Vile has turned back time and everybody will have to buy more Rangers to save the earth or something. There has been little collector interest in this line, except for the earliest figures. At the end of 1996, many of the Evil Space Aliens were available at discount. There are a lot of them, and if they ever become valuable there will be a lot of dealers who will be kicking themselves for not grabbing these figures at three for $10.00. The girls' figures are another matter and some collector interest in them can be seen. They are still available at discount too, for the moment.

8" Figures (Asst. #2200, 1993) in triangular window box
Blue Ranger (Billy) $18.00
Black Ranger (Zach) 18.00
Pink Ranger (Kimberly) 25.00
Red Ranger (Jason) 18.00
Yellow Ranger (Trini) 25.00

8" Evil Space Aliens (Asst. #2210, 1993) in window box
Baboo 28.00
Finster 28.00
Goldar 28.00
King Sphinx 28.00
Squatt 28.00
Putty Patrol 28.00
Bones 32.00

Finster, Evil Space Aliens,
Mighty Morphin Power Rangers (Bandai 1993)

Dragonzord,
Mighty Morphin Power Rangers (Bandai 1993)

Battle Bike Vehicles with 4" Figure (Asst. #2230, 1993)
Tyrannosaurus Rex Battle Bike with **Red Ranger**
 figure 25.00
Mammoth Battle Bike with detachable side car and
 Black Ranger figure 25.00
Triceratops Battle Bike with detachable side car and
 Blue Ranger figure 25.00

Zords (1993) last three combine to form Ultrazord
MegaZord (#2220) 25.00
Titanus the Carrier Zord (#2240) 80.00
MegaZord Deluxe Set (#2260) 60.00
DragonZord with **Green Ranger** figure (#2270) 50.00

8" Karate Action Figures (Asst. #2201, 1994) in window box
Karate Kickin' Jason (Red Ranger) (#2202) 8.00
Karate Kickin' Kimberly (Pink Ranger) (#2203) 8.00
Karate Kickin' Zach (Black Ranger) (#2204) 8.00
Karate Choppin' Trini (Yellow Ranger) (#2205) 8.00
Karate Choppin' Billy (Blue Ranger) (#2206) 8.00

5½" "Auto Morphin" Figures (Asst. #2310, 1994)
Red Ranger (Jason) (#2311) 7.00
Pink Ranger (Kimberly) (#2312) 7.00
Black Ranger (Zach) (#2313) 7.00
Yellow Ranger (Trini) (#2314) 7.00
Blue Ranger (Billy) (#2315) 7.00
Green Ranger (Tommy) (#2316) 7.00

5½" Evil Space Aliens (Asst. #2320, 1994) on header card
Slash & Block Minotaur (#2324) 7.00
Devouring Snizard Lips (#2325) 7.00
Eye Popping Eye Guy (#2326) 7.00
Food Gobbling Pudgy Pig (#2327) 7.00
Snatch Attack Spidertron (#2328) 7.00
Sword Slashing Knasty Knight (#2330) 7.00

Sword Slashing Knasty Knight,
Mighty Morphin Power Rangers (Bandai 1994)

Missile Launching Pete & Repeat (#2331) 7.00
Clawing Dramole (#2332) 7.00
Peck Attack Peckster (#2333) 7.00
Stinger Shooting Grumble Bee (#2334) 7.00
Slicing Horns Stag Beetle (#2335) 7.00
Killer Bite Slippery Shark (#2336) 7.00

5½" Series II Evil Space Aliens (Asst. #2350, 1994) on
header card
Evil Light Lord Zedd (#2337) 7.00
Darting Tongue Pythor (#2338) 7.00
Falls Apart Putty Patrol (#2339) 7.00
Sword Slashing Goldar (#2340) 7.00
Snapping Chest Invenusable Fly Trap (#2341) 7.00
Head Butting Robogoat (#2342) 7.00

8" Deluxe Evil Space Aliens (Asst. #2211, 1994) in window
box
Lord Zedd (#2212) 9.00
Rhino Blaster (#2213) 9.00
Pirantus Head (#2214) 9.00
Guitardo (#2215) 9.00
Socadillo (#2216) 9.00
Goo Fish (#2217) 9.00

5½" Evil Space Aliens (Asst. #2450, 1995)
Ivan Ooze (#2451) 10.00
Mordant (#2452) 10.00
Tengu Warrior (#2453) 10.00
Lord Zedd (#2454) 10.00

5½" Evil Space Aliens (Asst. #2460, 1995)
Flap Attack Vampirus (#2461) 7.00

Air Pump Cannon Rito Revolto (#2462) 7.00
Spinning Head Attack Master Vile (#2463) 7.00
Dual-Attack Slotsky (#2464) 7.00
Slicing Action Erik the Barbaric (#2465) 7.00
Rapid-Fire Steamy Meany (#2466) 7.00

Zords (1994)
Red Dragon ThunderZord (#2225) 15.00
Tor the ShuttleZord with Electronic Sound (#2242) . . 45.00
MegaZord Special Edition (#2261) black and gold . . 125.00
ThunderZord Assault Team (#2262) 45.00
Thunder MegaZord (#2263) 40.00
White TigerZord with the **White Ranger** figure (#2271) 40.00
Ultra ThunderZord 60.00

Vehicles and Playset
Thunder Bike with **Red Ranger** figure (#2232) 14.00
Power Cannon 15.00
Saba (White Sword) 15.00
Power Dome Morphin Playset (#2250) 65.00

Exclusives
Mega TigerZord ("Toys "R" Us exclusive, special
    size") 75.00
Red Dragon ThunderZord ("Toys "R" Us exclusive,
    special size") (#2303) 45.00
Tor the ShuttleZord ("Target exclusive, special size") . 50.00
White TigerZord ("Target exclusive, special size") . . . 50.00

8" Talking Figures (1995) in triangular window box
Talking Black Ranger 12.00
Talking Blue Ranger 12.00
Talking Pink Ranger (#2392) 12.00

Talking Red Ranger 12.00
Talking Yellow Ranger (#2394) 12.00
Talking White Ranger 12.00
Talking Lord Zedd in window box 20.00

5½" Ninja Rangers (1995)
Sword Slashing Red Ninja Ranger (#2472) 5.00
Disk Firing Blue Ninja Ranger (#2473) 5.00
One-Two Punch Black Ninja Ranger (#2474?) 5.00
Twirling Action White Ninja Ranger (#2475?) 5.00
Pink Ranger 5.00
Yellow Ranger 5.00

Special Edition Auto Morphin Rangers (Asst. #2420, 1995)
with "Real Morphing Action"
Black Ranger 5.00
Pink Ranger 5.00
Yellow Ranger 5.00
White Ranger (#2564) silver body 5.00
Red Ranger (#2565) metallic body 5.00
Blue Ranger (#2566) 5.00

Series 2 Auto Morphin Rangers (Asst. #2440, 1995) with
"Lightning Tattoo Included"
Red Ranger (#2441) 5.00
Yellow Ranger (#2442) 5.00
Black Ranger (#2443) 5.00
White Ranger (#2444) white body 5.00

Deluxe 8" Evil Space Aliens (Asst. #2521, 1995) in square
window box
Merrick the Barbaric (#2522) 10.00
Calcifire (#2523) 10.00

Darting Tongue Pythor,
Mighty Morphin Power Rangers (Bandai 1994)

Auto Morphin Blue Ranger,
Mighty Morphin Power Rangers (Bandai 1995)

Master Vile (#2524) 10.00
Silent Knight 10.00
Hornitor (#2528) 10.00
Scorpitan (#2529) 10.00

Alien Rangers (1996)
White Ranger 7.00
Red Ranger 7.00
Blue Ranger 7.00
Black Ranger 7.00
Yellow Ranger 7.00

Battle Borgs (1996)
Black Battle Borg (#2663) 7.00
Blue Battle Borg (#2664) 7.00
Yellow Battle Borg 7.00
White Battle Borg 7.00
Red Battle Borg 7.00

Thunder Bikes with 5" Figures
Blue Ranger 9.00
Black Ranger 9.00
Pink Ranger 9.00
Red Ranger 9.00
Yellow Ranger 9.00

Power Rangers for Girls (1994–95) in window boxes
Yellow and Pink Rangers Trini and Kimberly doll set . 30.00
Pink Ranger Kimberly 20.00
Yellow Ranger Trini 20.00
Pink Ranger (signed Kimberly) (1995) 12.00
Yellow Ranger (signed Aisha) (1995) 12.00

Two-Pack (1995)
Special Edition Gold Team including White and Green
    Rangers, 8" (#2687) 15.00

Deluxe Ninja Warriors
Ninja MegaZord (#2491) 30.00
Shogun MegaZord 50.00
White Ranger's Deluxe FalconZord 30.00
Serpentera, Lord Dredd's Power Zord (#2494) 50.00

Vehicles with Figures (Asst. #2480)
White Ranger's Shark Cycle with **White Ranger** figure 10.00
Red Ranger's Shark Cycle with **Red Ranger** figure . 10.00
Black Ranger's Shark Cycle with **Black Ranger** figure 10.00
Blue Ranger's Shark Cycle with **Blue Ranger** figure . 10.00
Yellow Ranger's Shark Cycle with **Yellow Ranger**
    figure 10.00
Pink Ranger's Shark Cycle with **Pink Ranger** figure
    (#2486) 10.00

MOVIE EDITION

8" Movie Figures (Asst. #2430, 1995) with lightning tattoo in triangular window box
Red Ranger (#2431) 9.00
Pink Ranger (#2432) 9.00
Black Ranger (#2433) 9.00
Yellow Ranger (#2434) 9.00
Blue Ranger (#2435) 9.00
White Ranger (#2436) 14.00

5½" Movie Figures (Asst. #2420) with "Movie Power Coin"
Red Ranger (#2421) metallic 6.00
Pink Ranger (#2422) metallic 6.00
Black Ranger (#2423) metallic 6.00

Yellow Ranger (#2424) metallic 6.00
Blue Ranger (#2425) metallic 6.00
White Ranger (#2426) metallic 7.00

8" Evil Space Aliens (movie edition) in window box
Ivan Ooze (#2627) 9.00
Hornitor (#2628) 9.00
Scorpitan (#2629) 9.00

Movie Zords
Ninja MegaFalconZord 40.00
Deluxe Ninja MegaZord 40.00
White Ranger's Deluxe FalconZord 25.00

Power Ranger Girls (movie edition) in window box
Yellow & Pink Rangers 20.00

Super Zeo Megazord, Power Rangers Zeo (Bandai 1996)

POWER RANGERS ZEO
Bandai (1996)

Power Rangers Zeo arrived in the spring of 1996. The television show was in its fourth season and the figures were issued to match the storyline for the new season. "The evil Master Vile has turned back time, leaving the Power Rangers as powerless children in search of the Zeo Crystal—their only hope to restore their power. Zordon, the Alien Rangers and Battle Borgs have failed in their mission to save Earth, and all is destroyed ..." But wait, the five teenage heroes restore the Zeo Crystal and "become an even more powerful team of super heroes." Now, maybe they can finally, once and for all, become powerful enough to defeat Machine Queen.

Since the original toy line has been #1 with kids for several years, these figures sold well too. Collectors are not so excited with the series, or its predecessor for that matter. For one thing, this series continues the past pattern of issuing five Ranger figures which are virtually identical except for colors and emblem. For another, most of the figures can still be found at retail or less.

When the kids who love this series grow up and become collectors, this series may take off. Today, it doesn't show many signs of this.

5½" Figures (Asst. #2530, 1996)
Zeo Ranger I with Shield Spinning Action (#2541) . . . $6.00
Zeo Ranger II with Double Club Action (#2542) 6.00
Zeo Ranger III with Axe Action (#2539) 6.00
Zeo Ranger IV with Hatchet Action (#2540) 6.00
Zeo Ranger V with Sword Action (#2538) 6.00
The Gold Ranger "Staff Whirling" (#2537) 6.00

Drill-Spinning Drill Master, Power Rangers Zeo (Bandai 1996)

5½" Evil Space Aliens (Asst. #2560)
1-2 Punching Action Red Battlezord (#2561) 6.00
Sword Swinging Super Zeo Megazord (#2562) 6.00
Power Sword Action Zeo Megazord (#2563) 6.00
Morphin Action Warrior Wheel (#2597) 6.00
Auric 6.00
Dual Morphing Action Pyramidas, The Carrier Zord (#2599) 6.00

Evil Space Aliens (Asst. #2570, 1996)
Rapid Sword-Swinging Goldar (#2340) 7.00
Air-Pumping Cannon Rito Revolto (#2462) 7.00
Chest-Beating Cogs (#2571) 6.00
Drill-Spinning Drill Master (#2572) 6.00

Missile-Firing Mechanizer (#2573) 6.00
Missile-Launching Quadrafighter (#2574) 6.00
Missile Aiming Silo (#2575) 6.00

8" Deluxe Zeo Rangers (Asst. #2680, 1996) boxed
Zeo Ranger I with "Zeo Laser Blade Action" (pink) (#2681) 10.00
Zeo Ranger II with "Zeo Laser Pistol Action" (yellow) (#2682) 10.00
Zeo Ranger III with "Zeo Laser Blade Action" (blue) (#2683) 10.00
Zeo Ranger IV with "Zeo Laser Pistol Action" (green) (#2684) 10.00
Zeo Ranger V with "Zeo Laser Pistol Action" (red) (#2685) 10.00
The Gold Ranger (#2686?) 10.00

Zeo Rangers with "Real Morphin Action" in window box with top-hanging flap
Zord Morphin Zeo Ranger III (blue) (#2706) 8.00
Zord Morphin Zeo Ranger IV (green) (#2705) 8.00
Zord Morphin Zeo Ranger V (red) (#2704) 8.00

5½" Auto Morphin Rangers (Asst. #2750, 1976)
Zeo Ranger I (pink) (#2751) 6.00
Zeo Ranger II (yellow) (#2752) 6.00
Zeo Ranger III (blue) (#2753) 6.00
Zeo Ranger IV (green) (#2754) 6.00
Zeo Ranger V (red) (#2755) 6.00
Gold Ranger IV (#2756?) 6.00

Cycles with Figure (Asst. #2506, 1996)
Zeo Jet Cycle I (#2511) with **Pink Ranger** 8.00
Zeo Jet Cycle II 8.00
Zeo Jet Cycle III 8.00
Zeo Jet Cycle IV 8.00
Zeo Jet Cycle V 8.00

Deluxe Zords (1996) first 2 combine to form Zeo Mega BattleZord; they combine with last 1 to form Zeo Ultrazord
Deluxe Zeo MegaZord (#2578) consists of 5 Zeo Zords 40.00
Deluxe Red BattleZord (#2588) 40.00
Deluxe Warrior Wheel (#2666) 25.00
Deluxe Super Zeo MegaZord (#2699) consists of 5 Super Zeo Zords 40.00
Auric, The Conqueror Zord (#2715) 30.00
Deluxe Pyramidas, The Carrier Zord (#2717) 35.00

POWER RANGERS TURBO
Bandai (1997)

In 1997 it will be the Power Rangers **Turbo**, the most powerful line of Power Rangers ever. The Blue Senturion will be introduced in May and in September there will be a Rescue MegaZord, while November will bring a mysterious Phantom Ranger to the team! We'll bet they are designing the 1998 Power Rangers Syber line with accompanying GigaZord as you read this.

MIKE HAZARD
Marx (1967)

Besides producing the long-running Best of the West series of 11½" figures, Marx also made smaller lines as well.

This spy was one of them. It was produced during the mid 1960s when spies were the hot ticket in films and television.

12" Figure
Mike Hazard Double Agent, with cloth trench coat, blow-up luggage and over 50 pieces of equipment including disguises, personal gear and weapons, boxed $475.00

MINI MONSTERS
SEE: UNIVERSAL CITY STUDIOS

MISSION: IMPOSSIBLE
Tradewinds (1996)

From the highly successful movie starring Tom Cruise, which was based on the popular 1960s' television series starring Peter Graves and Martin Landau, among others. The figures are not sold in most toy stores, but can be found at the Spencer Gifts chain. We know that because we saw them there when we were looking for Star Trek and Star Wars stuff.

7" Figures
Ethan Hunt "Fireman" (#00016) $12.00
Ethan Hunt "Pointman" (#00017) 12.00
Ethan Hunt "Spy Senator" (#00018) 12.00

MONKEES
Remco (1967 and 1974)

"Hey, Hey, they're the Monkees and they had a television show which featured their slapstick comedy antics. Somebody must have liked it because it lasted for two years and resulted in several successful records and two series of figures from Remco. The zany musicians played themselves—we guess no one else could—hundreds of actors were tested for the roles.

Figures (1967)
Davey Jones $200.00
Peter Tork 200.00
Michael Nesmith 200.00
Mickey Dolenz 200.00

5" Figures (1974)
Davey Jones 160.00
Peter Tork 160.00
Michael Nesmith 160.00
Mickey Dolenz 160.00

MONSTER FORCE
"STRIKING AT THE HEART OF EVIL"
Playmates (1994)

From the cartoon series which debuted in September 1994. "Hollywood's creepiest monsters return with supernatural powers and civilization's only hope is a small band of renegade bounty hunters who roam the streets with a battery of high-tech weapons and vehicles specially designed to subdue supernatural enemies." Doc Reed Crawley leads the Monster Force in their "Emacs (Energized Monster Armed Containment Suits)" and swears that they will prevail against the Creatures of the Night!

Missing from the final figure release were a planned Shelly Frank Frankenstein figure and the Hotep mummy figure. Naturally the collectors looked for the monsters. Luke Talbot (the Wolfman) and Dracula proved easy to find, but Frankenstein and the Creature from the Black Lagoon were tough.

Luke Talbot, Monster Force (Playmates 1994)

5" Figures
Luke Talbot (The Wolfman) (#1601) $9.00
Lance McGruder (#1602)) 6.00
Doc Reed Crawley (#1603) 6.00
Tripp Hansen (#1604) 6.00
Frankenstein (#1605) 22.00
Dracula (#1607) 9.00
Creature from the Black Lagoon (#1608) 15.00

MOON MCDARE
Gilbert (1966)

This A.C. Gilbert action doll wasn't based on any particular character but was just an attempt to cash in on the space race. Moon's accessories are exchangeable with Gilbert's James Bond and Man From Uncle lines. Mr. Main fondly remembers playing with Moon and his Space Mutt and the other two series as well. Now Mr. Main owns a mostly golden retriever mutt, while Mr. Wells owns an overly friendly and distinguished canine of mixed breed.

12" Figure
Moon McDare $95.00

Accessories
Action Communication Set (Boxed) 35.00
Moon Explorer Set (Boxed) 75.00
Space Mutt Set (Boxed) 65.00
Space Suit Outfit (Boxed) 50.00
Space Gun Set (Carded) 35.00
Space Accessory Pack (Card) 30.00

MOONRAKER
SEE: JAMES BOND

MORK & MINDY
Mattel (1980)

The television series brought us Mork (from Ork) played by Robin Williams and brought Robin Williams stardom. Pam Dawber was Mindy, who had the impossible job of keeping up with the wild and wonderful Mork. The show was all Mork, which meant that it couldn't last as long as a series with several comedy talents and it didn't; but it was fun while it lasted.

9" Dolls
Mork, hanging upside down, with Talking Spacepack $50.00
Mindy 9" 45.00
Mork From Ork, 4" with egg 35.00

Vehicle
Jeep 30.00

MORTAL KOMBAT
Kenner (1994)

"Thousands of years ago Mortal Kombat was a noble competition for honor and glory. Today it is a terrifying tournament corrupted by an evil sorcerer who is trying to unbalance the forces of good and evil. If successful, eternal evil will plague our planet and he who falls to defeat has his soul stolen and cast into the outworld ... forever!" Later packages features Real Action Pop-Ups cards with game tips.

5" Figures
Sonya Blade (#81325) $7.00
Sonya Blade with Real Action Pop-Ups (#81325) 6.00
Johnny Cage 7.00
Johnny Cage with Real Action Pop-Ups 6.00
Goro 7.00
Goro with Real Action Pop-Ups 6.00
Lui Kang 7.00
Lui Kang with Real Action Pop-Ups 6.00
Rayden 7.00
Rayden with Real Action Pop-Ups 6.00
Scorpion 7.00
Scorpion with Real Action Pop-Ups 6.00
Shang Tsung 7.00
Shang Tsung with Real Action Pop-Ups 6.00
Smoke 7.00
Smoke with Real Action Pop-Ups 6.00
Sub-Zero 7.00
Sub-Zero with Real Action Pop-Ups 6.00

Sonya Blade, Mortal Kombat (Kenner 1994)

Two-Pack
Goro vs. Johnny Cage (#81349) 15.00

Special Movie Edition Figures
Scorpion with Spring-Action Scorpion Sting (#81301) . 7.00
Sub-Zero with Spring-Action Ice Fist (#81302) 7.00
Rayden with Spring-Action Thunder Punch (#81303) . . 7.00
Shang Tsung with Spring-Action Demon Punch
  (#81304) 7.00
Sonya Blade "Missile Launcher Shoots" (#81305) 7.00
Lui Kang "Spring-Action Double Defender" (#81307) . . 7.00

Movie Two-Pack
Goro vs. Johnny Cage 15.00

12" Figures
Johnny Cage 20.00
Rayden 20.00
Scorpion 20.00

Vehicles
Dragon MK-1, with **Reptile** figure (#81318) 15.00
Dragon Wing, with **Shang Tsung** figure (#81340) . . . 20.00
Kombat Cycle, with **Kano** figure (#81338) 12.00

Jack Skellington, Nightmare Before Christmas (Hasbro 1993)

Oogie Boogie, Nightmare Before Christmas (Hasbro 1993)

[TIM BURTON'S]
NIGHTMARE BEFORE CHRISTMAS
Hasbro (1993)

Hasbro has captured the "feel" of the animated movie with its line of Nightmare Before Christmas toys. These are wonderful figures, but we questioned whether or not they would be all that popular with collectors since action figures from *Beetlejuice*, *Last Action Hero*, *Super Mario Brothers* and *Coneheads* were bathing in cobwebs on toy store shelves at the time these figures appeared. However, the collectors loved the figures and all sell for very high prices.

Figures (Asst. #80101)
Jack Skellington with "Pumpkin Mask and Bendable
   Limbs" (#80102) $30.00

Jack as Santa with "Bendable Limbs" (#80103) 30.00
Sally with "Detachable Arms, Legs & Head" (#80104) 50.00
The Mayor with "Twist 'N' Turn Two-Faced Head"
   (#80105) 60.00
Behemoth with "Shifting Eye Action" (#80106) 35.00
Werewolf with "Ferocious Chomping Action" (#80107) 50.00
Evil Scientist "Flip-Top Skull Reveals Brain" (#80108) 65.00

Figures (Asst. #80111)
Santa with "Sack Full of Surprises Inside" (#80112) . . 65.00
Oogie Boogie with "Creepy Bug Suprises Inside"
   (#80113) 120.00
Lock, Shock & Barrel with "Scary Masks" (Boxed)
   (#80114) 60.00

Captain Kidd, Nightmare Warriors (MTC 1983)

NIGHTMARE WARRIORS
MTC (1983)

A series of skeletal figures which came on a generic header card. The figures had some equipment which matched the name of the historical figure, but were otherwise the same. All you could see were the bones, which glowed in the dark. These pre-dated the Skeleton Warriors from Playmates by over 10 years.

5½" Figures with "Bones That Glow in the Dark"

Captain Kidd	$16.00
Major Bones	16.00
Geronimo	16.00
Sir Lancelot	16.00
Pancho Villa	16.00
Spartacus	16.00

NINJA COMMANDOS
Unknown Manufacturer (1990s)

A group of six cheap figures made in China. These figures may just possibly be worth the $1.00 we saw them selling for.

NINJA WARRIORS
"ENEMIES OF EVIL"
Hasbro (1987)

The Ninja Warriors are masters of the martial art of Ninjutso who use their "mental and physical prowess to avenge the evil that stalks the night!" The evil stalking the night must have won, because these "Enemies of Evil" disappeared with hardly a whimper. According to Hasbro's catalog, each warrior came with three interchangeable weapons and a Ninja wardrobe.

6" Figures (Asst. #5200) with 3 weapons and wardrobe

Scorpia	$9.00
Nunchuka-San	9.00
Lord Taka	9.00
Starcaster	9.00
Dojo Kan	9.00
Dragonmaster	9.00

Figure and Horse (#5210)

Oji San and Windspirit horse (#5210, 1987) with weapon and costume	16.00

NOBLE KNIGHTS
Marx (1968)

A series of soft plastic poseable 12" figures, with molded-on clothing, and horses by Marx. The knights, along with their steeds, had soft molded plastic armor that you could easily (ha!) add onto them to make a full-suited figure ready for battle.

12" Figures

Sir Gordon, The Gold Knight	$190.00
Sir Stuart, The Silver Knight	190.00
The Black Knight	240.00
Valor, The Silver Knight's Horse	140.00
Bravo, The Gold Knight's Horse	140.00
Valiant, The Black Knight's Horse	140.00

O

OFFICIAL WORLD FAMOUS SUPER MONSTERS
AHI/Remco (1973–76)

These Universal Studios monster action figures could be placed "in any gruesome position." Early header cards depict heads of Frankenstein, Wolfman, Mummy and Creature. The first ones say "Official" in black letters rather than white letters. Later header cards have Dracula pictured instead of the Creature. There were many running changes for each figure as well.

8" Figures on pink header cards
Creature from the Black Lagoon with thin waist, "Official" in black on package $1,200.00
   Reissue with thick waist 675.00
Frankenstein with movie-style head, "Official" in black on package 150.00
   Reissue with light green body 100.00
   Reissue with prominent ears 100.00
   Reissue with thick head, Dracula on card 100.00
The Mummy with right arm across body, "Official" in black on package 200.00
   Reissue with right arm at side, some blood . . 100.00
   Reissue with right arm at side, Dracula on card 100.00
Wolfman with fierce face, "Official" in black on package 200.00
   Reissue with long face 100.00
   Reissue with Dracula on card 100.00
Count Dracula with large Dracula picture behind figure, various heads 240.00
   Reissue with four faces on card, including Dracula 120.00

OFFICIAL WORLD'S GREATEST SUPER HEROES
SEE: WORLD'S GREATEST SUPER HEROES

ONE MILLION B.C.
Mego (1976–77)

An action figure set made up of cavemen, dinosaurs and large mammals. Two out of three of them weren't around in One million B.C., but why let bad science get in the way of a toy line.

8" Figures, carded
Grok $42.00
Mada 42.00

Orm 42.00
Trag 42.00
Zon 42.00

Creatures
Dimetrodon, Sailback Dinosaur, boxed 90.00
The Hairy Rhino, boxed 90.00
Tyrannosaurs Rex, boxed 150.00

Playset
Tribal Lair playset 120.00
Tribal Lair giftset with 5 figures 250.00

OTHER WORLD
Arco (1983)

Figures
Antor $12.00
Froggacuda 12.00
Gaifand 12.00
Hondu 12.00
Jipps 4.00
Kamaro 12.00
Kontory 12.00
Kreena 4.00
Mogs 4.00
Raidy 4.00
Ronin 4.00
Sharkoss 12.00
Zendo 4.00

OUR GANG
Mego (1975)

From the 1920s' and 1930s' "Our Gang" comedy shorts directed by Hal Roach starring Jackie Cooper, Spanky McFarland and Oliver Hardy. They were shown extensively on television in the 1970s and are still around on video.

6" Dolls on header card
Alfalfa (#61660/?) $60.00
Spanky (#61660/?) 60.00
Buckwheat (#61660/3) 60.00
Porky (#61660/?) 60.00
Mickey (#61660/?) 60.00
Darla (#61660/?) 70.00

Vehicles and Playset
Orange Crate Cart 90.00
Rowboat 65.00
Playset 120.00

Colossus Rex and *Cyclops* *(Unproduced prototype), The Outer Space Men (Colorforms 1968)*

THE OUTER SPACE MEN
Colorforms (1968–70)

This series of bendy-style action figures was by Colorforms, of all companies. Many found it to be a great companion to the Major Matt Mason space line, which was highly popular at the time. Prices on these figures are out of this world. A second series made it as far as a few handfuls of salesmen's samples. A couple of years ago those samples were sold to a few collectors with much in the way of disposable income.

Figures
Alpha 7 (The Man from Mars)	$600.00
Astro-Nautilus (The Man from Neptune)	600.00
Colossus Rex (The Man from Jupiter)	750.00
Commander Comet (The Man from Venus)	600.00
Electron (The Man from Pluto)	600.00
Orbitron (The Man from Uranus)	600.00
Xodiac (The Man from Saturn)	600.00

OVER THE TOP
LewCo (1986)

Sylvester Stallone made a very forgettable movie called *Over the Top*. We were underwhelmed by it. It's about arm wrestling and a kid and some other plot elements which we forget (see what we mean).

7" Figures with "Real Arm Wrestling Action"
Lincoln Hawks (#6980)	$30.00
Cleve 'Armbender' Dean	25.00
John 'Golden Boy' Brzenk	25.00
John 'The Bear' Grizzly	25.00
Johnny 'Ice Man' Walker	25.00
Bob 'Bull' Hurley	25.00

Large Figure
Lincoln Hawks 20"	60.00
Loose figure	20.00

Accessory
Arm Wrestling Table (#5480)	no price found

Conky and Chairry (blue), Pee-Wee's Playhouse (Matchbox 1988)

PEE-WEE'S PLAYHOUSE
Matchbox (1988)

From the children's television show of the mid 1980s (and a couple of movies). Pee-Wee Herman, a/k/a Paul Reubens, also made some famous appearances on "Saturday Night Live," but his arrest at a XXX-rated movie theater destroyed his career as a children's comedian and the stores couldn't dump his products fast enough. Savvy collectors rushed to do their patriotic duty and bought as many of these items as they could, before they could fall into the hands of unsuspecting children and corrupt their morals.

5" Figures

Pee-Wee Herman (#3561)	$18.00
Miss Yvonne (#3562)	32.00
Cowboy Curtis (#3563?)	26.00
King of Cartoons (#3564)	22.00
Chairry pink card (#3565)	25.00
Chairry blue card (#3565)	25.00
Ricardo (#3566)	24.00
Reba (#3567)	26.00

Pee-Wee Herman with his famous Scooter and favorite Helmet (#3568)	30.00
Conky wacky wind-up (#3571)	30.00
Pterri wacky wind-up (#3572)	24.00
Magic Screen wacky wind-up (#3573)	18.00
Globey and Randy mini characters	30.00
Jambi and Puppet Land Band mini characters	30.00

Playset

Pee-Wee's Playhouse Playset with Scooter, 20" x 28" x 7½" play area	110.00

Large Dolls

Pee-Wee 17"	75.00
Pee-Wee Talking (pull string) 17"	90.00
Bill Baloney 18"	80.00
Chairry 15"	70.00
Pterri 13"	75.00
Pig 12"	45.00
Pig Talking	80.00
Pee-Wee Ventriloquist 25"	140.00
Pee-Wee 36" Limited edition of 2,000 with certificate	520.00
Loose	200.00

PETER PAN
Sears (1988)

These dolls were based on the Walt Disney 1953 animated version of the 1904 classic James M. Barrie children's tale. Mary Martin made a living playing Peter on stage and in a 1960 television special.

6"–8" Dolls in window box

Captain Hook $16.00
Peter Pan 16.00
Tinkerbell 20.00
Wendy 18.00

Phantom Rider, The Phantom (Street Players 1996)

THE PHANTOM
Street Players (1996)

From the live-action movie starring Billy Zane, all muscled up, in the title role as "The Ghost Who Walks" in purple tights, Treat Williams as the villain, plus Kristy Swanson and Catherine Zeta Jones as the good and bad babes, respectively. The movie was based on the comic strips and books by Lee Falk.

Street Players acquired the rights to produce action figures from the movie. This was their first adventure with this type of item. What they did produce were a Phantom on the Skull Throne and a Phantom with his horse Hero. What we didn't get were two Singh Pirates and a 12" Phantom, none of which made it past the prototype stage. Figures of the female characters would have been popular with collectors, but we didn't get them either.

The figures of the Phantom that we did get did not generate much of a collector response, except among die-hards like Mr. Main. Mr. Wells got a couple of buttons and a popcorn bag at the movie instead.

A previous figure of the Phantom was included in the Defenders of the Earth series, and Captain Action had a Phantom costume. Both were listed previously.

6" Figures

The Phantom, with 2 rings, Holster and Guns, Skull
    Buckle and Skull Throne (#43000) $10.00
Phantom Rider, with Skull Buckle and Holster with Guns
    (#43100) 15.00

THE PIRATES OF DARK WATER
Hasbro (1991)

Based on the Hanna-Barbera ABC television series where Ren, the hero of the series, tries to save his home planet of Mer from the Dark Water pirates. The figures are imaginative and well done, but they haven't generated much collector interest to date. The figures and television series lasted only one year, so the pirates must have won.

5" Figures (1991)

1. Ren (#7231) $8.00
2. Ioz (#7232) 8.00
3. Zoolie (#7238) 8.00
4. Mantus (#7239) 8.00
5. Bloth (#7236) 8.00
6. Niddler (#7237) 8.00

Bloth, Pirates of Dark Water (Hasbro 1991)

7. Joat (#7234) 8.00
8. Konk (#7233) 8.00

Vehicles
Wraith, Pirate Attack Ship 20.00

PIRATES OF THE EVIL SEAS, GALAXSEAS, HIGH SEAS AND ALL OTHER SEAS

We like pirates. One of our favorite movies is *The Crimson Pirate* starring Burt Lancaster. But none of the famous pirates of history trademarked his name, so anyone can put out figures named after famous pirates, or other clever pirate terms such as Crossbones or Pegleg. Several companies have done so over the years, but no one collects them. Too bad they didn't do a series of pirate figures from *Cutthroat Island* so collectors could have captured a Geena Davis figure with "Power Punch and Butt-Kicking Action." Would that be a collectible, or what!

Cornelius, Planet of the Apes (Mego 1973)

PLANET OF THE APES
Mego (1973–75)

The original movie starred Charlton Heston, Roddy McDowell, Kim Hunter and Maurice Evans and was based on a book by Pierre Boulle. Five movies were made in the series from 1968 to 1973. A live-action television show followed in 1974, but it only lasted 14 episodes. It starred James Naughton as Peter Burke, Ron Harper as Alan Verdon, Roddy McDowell (again) as Galen and Mark Lenard (more famous as Spock's father, Sarek) as General Urko. The movies are still shown regularly on television, but the series has sunk into oblivion.

Mego's attempt at adapting the movies and the television series to their 8" line of dolls is better received now than it was when the figures were being produced. Budget cutting was in evidence with the figures, as well as with the accessories and playsets, most of which were recycled from previous toy lines. The 1973 figures are based on the movies, while the 1974 figures are from the television show. Collectors don't care. They love both groups, because they are classic Mego figures.

8" Figures (1973)
Cornelius
    Boxed $150.00
    Carded 90.00
    Loose 40.00
Dr. Zaius
    Boxed 150.00
    Carded 90.00
    Loose 40.00
Zira
    Boxed 120.00
    Carded 90.00
    Loose 40.00
Soldier Ape
    Boxed 175.00
    Carded 90.00
    Loose 40.00
Astronaut
    Boxed 180.00
    Carded 125.00
    Loose 60.00

8" Figures (1974)
Galen
    Boxed 120.00
    Carded 90.00
    Loose 40.00
General Ursus
    Boxed 200.00
    Carded 90.00
    Loose 40.00
General Urko
    Boxed 150.00
    Carded 90.00
    Loose 40.00
Peter Burke
    Boxed 150.00
    Carded 90.00
    Loose 50.00
Alan Verdon
    Boxed 150.00
    Carded 90.00
    Loose 50.00

Vehicles, Accessories and Playsets
Treehouse playset (1973) 160.00
Village playset (#51925, 1973) 225.00
Action Stallion (brown) (#51926, 1973) 65.00
Forbidden Zone Trap playset (1974) 90.00
Fortress (#50916, 1974) 200.00
Catapult and Wagon (1975) 45.00

Jail (#50913, 1975) 50.00
Battering Ram (Asst. #50905, 1975) 32.00
Zaius' Throne (Asst. #50905, 1975) 35.00

John Ratcliffe, Pocahontas (Mattel 1995)

[DISNEY's]
POCAHONTAS
Mattel (1995–96)

From the Disney animated movie featuring the voice of Mel Gibson as John Smith. Historical accuracy was not featured, but the songs were winners.

5" Figures
Chief Powhatan $5.00
John Ratcliffe (#66509) 5.00
John Smith 5.00
Kocoum 5.00
Nakoma 7.50
Pocahontas 5.00
Thomas 5.00
Wiggins 5.00

Two-Packs
Pocahontas & Chief Powhatan gift set 15.00
John Smith & John Ratcliffe gift set 12.50
Kocoum & Nakoma gift set 15.00

12" Dolls
Braided Beauty Pocahontas 25.00
Shining Braids Pocahontas 15.00
Bead-so-Pretty Pocahontas 15.00
Spirit of Love gift set (Pocahontas and John Smith) . 20.00
Sun Colors Pocahontas 15.00
Sun Colors John Smith 15.00
Sun Colors Kocoum 15.00

Sun Colors Nakoma 15.00
Color Splash Pocahontas 15.00
Color Splash John Smith 15.00
Color Splash Nakoma 15.00

Accessories and Playsets
Fields of War Playset 20.00
Powhatan Village Playset 20.00
River Rowing featuring 12" Pocahontas (#13333) . . . 35.00

POCKET SUPER HEROES
Mego (1979)

The series combines Marvel and DC characters, since Mego held both licenses. So why did Mego make them in 3¾" instead of their popular 8" doll size? Look at the date. The success of Star Wars figures in 1978 made their size the predominant one for action figures for several years. These figures are definitely collected, but the classic Mego 8" doll is much more popular and the type associated with the name "Mego."

3¾" Figures on header card
Aquaman $90.00
Batman 40.00
Captain America 90.00
Captain Marvel 40.00
General Zod 15.00
Green Goblin 90.00
Hulk 40.00
Joker 40.00
Jor-El 15.00
Lex Luthor 15.00
Penguin 40.00
Robin 40.00
Spider-Man 40.00
Superman 40.00
Wonder Woman 40.00

Accessories
Batmobile, with **Batman** and **Robin** figures 200.00
Batcave 300.00
Spider-Car, with **Spider-Man** and **Hulk** figures 75.00
Spider-Car, with **Spider-Man** and **Green Goblin**
    figures 150.00
Batmachine 100.00
Spider-Machine 100.00
Invisible Jet 125.00

POLICE ACADEMY
Kenner (1989–90)

The first *Police Academy* movie arrived in 1984 and sequels followed every year until 1989, and there was another in 1994. The movies generally starred Steve Guttenberg as Mahoney, Bubba Smith as Hightower with Bobcat Goldthwait, Michael Winslow and David Graf. The action figures appeared as the series was dying.

5" Figures (Asst. #66100) (1989)
Moses Hightower and Meter Reader Scooter
    (#66010) $10.00
Eugene Tackleberry and Armed Flak Vest (#66020) . 10.00
Larvel Jones and Bullhorn (#66030) 10.00

Eugene Tackleberry, Police Academy (Kenner 1989)

Numbskull with Smashing Helmets (#66040) 10.00
Zed and Police Skateboard (#66050) 10.00
Carey Mahoney and Samson Dog (#66060) 10.00
Claw with Mouser Cat (#66070) 10.00
Mr. Sleaze with Foofoo Dog (#66080) 10.00
Captain Harris (mail-in figure) 60.00

Second Series (1990)
S.W.A.T. Eugene Tackleberry with Fistzooka 12.00
Flung Hi with Crazy Karate Gear 12.00
Kingpin with Thief-Trap Safe 12.00
Karate Larvel Jones with Kicker Pack 12.00

Special Assignment Rookie (1990)
Stakeout Sweetchuck with Hide-rant 70.00
Sky Glidin' Zed with Hang Glider 20.00
Undercover Carey Mahoney with Hoodlum Disguise and
　　Sonic Boom Box 15.00
Snack-Attack House with Hoagy Blaster 40.00

Vehicles and Accessories (1989)
Crash Cycle (#66180) 10.00
Crazy Cruiser (#66190) 15.00
The Precinct Police Station (#66210) 35.00

POWER LORDS
"THE EXTRA-TERRESTRIAL WARRIORS"
Revell (1982)

There was a DC comic book based on these toys which ran a whole three issues in late 1983 and early 1984. "Masters of the Universe" figures were available at the same time and were a lot more successful, but these figures have drawn some collector attention.

6" Two-Sided Figures
Adam Power, Leader of the Lords $16.00
Arkus, The Evil Dictator 16.00
Bakatak 18.00
Disguyzor 18.00
Drrench 18.00
Ggripptogg, The Four-Fisted Brute 18.00
Raygoth, Goon of Doom 18.00
Shaya, Queen of Power 18.00
Sydot, The Supreme 18.00
Tork, The Turning Terror 18.00

Vehicles and Playset
Power Ship, Alien Cruiser 22.00
Trigore, The Creature Crusher vehicle 20.00
Volcan Rock, Secret Stronghold of Extra-Terrestrial
　　Power 30.00

POWER MASTERS
Lionel (1987–88)

Figures
Lucky Cooper and Duke $5.00
Red Eye and Cyclops 5.00
Rip McDonald and Digger 5.00
Sean Marshall and Lookout 5.00
Steve Stryker 5.00
Zorn and Scorpion 5.00

POWER RANGERS ZEO
SEE: MIGHTY MORPHIN POWER RANGERS

PREDATOR
Kenner (1994)

There have been two *Predator* movies. The first starred Arnold Schwartzenegger and the second starred Danny Glover. The figures are also based on the Dark Horse Comics series "Aliens vs. Predators" and these figures were marketed with the Aliens figures. The popular Alien and Predator two-packs are listed under Alien.

However, the blister packs have a peel-off offer for a free special edition Predator when you buy any three Aliens or Predators. It's sort of a problem for collectors because you have to "cut out the purchase seals" from the package, making it less collectible.

4¾" Figures (1994)
Cracked Tusk (Predator) with "Firing Pulse Cannon"
　　(#65716) warning left middle [509-176-00] $9.00
Scavage Predator "With Bola Blasting Action" (#65717)
　　dark green [509-178-01] 11.00
　　Light green 20.00
Spiked Tail "Predator Throws Punishing Assault Disks"
　　(#65723) [01] 9.00
　　Reissue, warning re: plastic fasteners behind figure
　　[02] 9.00
Stalker Predator "Glows in the Dark and Shoots Spears"
　　(#65722) [513-489-02] 9.00
Nightstorm Predator with "Twin Turbo Blaster" (#65737)
　　[00] 9.00
Lasershot Predator, Electronic 22.00

***Cracked Tusk**, Predator (Kenner 1994)*

Lava Planet Predator with "Blazing Rocket Launcher"
    (#65729) [01] 9.00
Predator Clan Leader "With Whipping Dreadlocks and
    Power Boots" (#65727) [513-955-00] 14.00
Ambush Predator, clear plastic, with 4 pieces of armor
    and small instruction sheet, mail-in figure 35.00

Large Figure (1995)
Ultimate Predator, 10" (#65882) 18.00

Predator Vehicle (1994)
Predator Blade Fighter with "Capture Jaw & Shooting
    Missile" in 8" x 7" x 3¾" box (#65719) 14.00

PRIMAL RAGE
Playmates (1996)

"In the near future, a great meteor collides into Earth—
a cataclysmic chain reaction causes civilization as we know
it to crumble. From out of the rubble emerge immense dino-
beasts, who have lain dormant for 60 million years deep
within the Earth. It is their fate to battle each other for
control of the new Urth." This unlikely scenario is from a
top-selling video game. There are a few humans around, but
they haven't been made into figures and, even if they are,
they won't include a group of savior teenagers with magical
powers.

Some of these dino-beasts look like King Kong, who
was mammal, but so what! They look like they could eat

***Blizzard**, Primal Rage (Playmates 1996)*

their Jurassic Park counterparts for a mid-morning snack.
Collectors have largely ignored the series since it first
appeared. We don't recall seeing new ones at Toy Fair
either, so maybe the kids have ignored the series too.

5" Figures
Primal Rage Armadon (#12201) $10.00
Primal Rage Blizzard (#12202) 10.00
Primal Rage Chaos (#12203) 10.00
Primal Rage Diablo (#12204) 10.00
Primal Rage Sauron (#12205) 10.00
Primal Rage Talon (#12206) 10.00
Primal Rage Vertigo (#12207) 10.00

9" Prehistoric Beasts
Super Primal Rage Blizzard with Electronic Rage 'n
    Roar (#12232) 15.00
Super Primal Rage Diablo with Primal Crush 'n Crunch
    (#12234) 15.00
Super Primal Rage Sauron with Primal Crush 'n Crunch
    (#12235) 15.00
Super Primal Rage Talon with Primal Crush 'n Crunch
    (#12236) 15.00

PRINCESS OF POWER
Mattel (1985–87)

A spin-off from the Masters of the Universe toys, this
time for girls. It's not a knock-off because Mattel made both
series. Princess Adora spends her time in Etheria putting on
neat outfits, combing her incredibly long hair and playing
with her friends, but when there's trouble, she becomes She-
Ra, the most powerful woman in the universe. Like every
powerful woman, she comes with a sword and a comb. What
good is all that power if you don't look great?

The only guy in the series is Bow and there is a distinct shortage of villains as well. You know this is a fantasy series because with all these beautiful babes and only one guy there would be plenty of trouble.

Most action figure collectors are males and, while they collect the rare female figures in the male-dominated lines, they haven't shown much interest in this girl's fantasy line.

5½" Figures (1985)
She-Ra (#9182) $5.00
Bow (#9183) 10.00
Catra (#9184) 10.00
Double Trouble 10.00
Angella (#9186) 8.00
Castaspella (#9187) 8.00
Glimmer (#9188) 8.00
Frosta (#9189) 8.00
Kowl (#9190) owl 8.00

Castaspella, Princess of Power (Mattel 1985)

5½" Figures (1986)
Starburst She-Ra (#2450) 10.00
Scratchin' Sound Catra (#2451) 25.00
Peekablue (#2452) 25.00
Flutterina (#2453) 25.00

Mermista (#2454) 25.00
Perfuma (#2455) 25.00
Sweet Bee (#2635) 25.00
Entrapta (#2636) 25.00

5½" Figures (1987)
Bubble Power She-Ra 25.00
Loo-Kee 45.00
Netossa 25.00
Shower Power Catra 25.00
Spinnerella 25.00

Fashions (1985)
Rise & Shine fashions (#2824) 5.00
Fit to be Tied fashions (#2825) 5.00
Hold on to Your Hat fashions (#2826) 5.00
Ready in Red fashions (#2827) 5.00
Flight of Fancy fashions (#2828) 5.00
Veils of Mystery fashions (#2829) 5.00
Flower Power fashions (#2835) 5.00
Deep Blue Secret fashions (#2836) 5.00

Horses and Sets
Swift Wind unicorn (#9191, 1985) 16.00
Crystal Castle playset (#9193, 1985) 40.00
Enchanta Swan (#9681, 1985) 20.00
Royal Swift Wind 25.00
Arrow 16.00
Storm 16.00
Silver Storm 16.00
Crystal Swift Wind horse (#2433, 1986) 25.00
Crystal Moonbeam horse (#2434, 1986) 25.00
Crystal Sun Dancer horse (#2435, 1986) 25.00
Crystal Falls playset (#2456, 1986) 40.00
Butterflyer carrying case (#2903, 1986) 25.00
Clawdeen cat (#9627, 1986) 16.00

PULSAR
"THE ULTIMATE MAN OF ADVENTURE"
Mattel (1977–78)

Strange, see-through figures where you could observe your hero's internal organs. You could put mission disks in Pulsar's brain and activate his internal organs, so "no mission is impossible for him." On the other hand, everyone feared the hypnotic powers of Hypnos, which included sparks, sounds and "swirling cosmic colors." The playset gave you additional ways to play doctor with your toys.

12" Figure
Pulsar, The Ultimate Man of Adventure $85.00
Hypnos, The Ultimate Enemy 70.00

Playset
Life Systems Center 60.00

R

Mad Dog and Nomad, Rambo (Coleco 1985)

RAMBO
Coleco (1985–87)

The Rambo movies starred Sylvester Stallone against impossible odds. The first movie (*First Blood*) appeared in 1982, and sequels appeared in 1985 and 1988. However, this series of figures is based on the animated television series which was shown in syndication in 1986 and not the movies.

6¾" Figures (1986)
Rambo (#0801) $12.00
Sergeant Havoc (#0802) 17.00
Colonel Trautman (#0803) 19.00
General Warhawk (#0804) 17.00
Turbo (#0805) 17.00
Mad Dog (#0806) 15.00
Gripper (#0807) 17.00
Fire Power Rambo (#0808) 12.00
K.A.T. (#0809) 22.00
Nomad (#0810) 18.00
Black Dragon (#0811) 17.00
White Dragon (#0813) 19.00

6¾" Figures (1987)
Muscle Power Rambo (#0850) 12.00
T.D. Jackson (#0851) 22.00
Chief (#0852) 22.00
Whip Action Warhawk (#0854) 25.00
X-Ray (#0855) 42.00

Snakebite (#0857) 22.00
Dr. Hyde (#0858) 30.00

Weapons and Accessories
106mm Recoilless Rifle, 10" (#0825, 1987) 5.00
.50 Caliber Machine Gun with Tripod, 5½" (#0826) . . 12.00
81mm Mortar with Bipod, 5" (#0827) 12.00
Twin-Mounted 7.62mm Machine Gun with Bunker, 6"
    (#0831, 1987) 18.00
.50 Caliber Anti-Aircraft Gun with Tripod, 5½" (#0832) 15.00
20mm Automatic Cannon, 12" (#0835) 18.00
Weapons Pack Asst. (#0836) 8.00
Tri-Tracker Heat-Seeking Missile Launcher, 8½"
    (#0861) 8.00

Vehicles and Playset
Defender 6X6 assault vehicle (#0821) 30.00
Skyfire Assault Copter (#0822) 30.00
S.A.V.A.G.E. Strike Cycle (#0824) 20.00
S.A.V.A.G.E. Strike Headquarters (#0828) 45.00
Skywolf assault jet (#0830) 30.00
S.A.V.A.G.E. Stormbomber (#0843) 30.00
Swampdog Assault Boat & ATV, 12" (#0846) 20.00

RAPID DEPLOYMENT FORCE
Time Products (1995)

Time Products produced six action soldiers called the Rapid Deployment Force. These soldiers are the same 12" size as the original G.I. Joe figures and sell for about $15.00 with weapons. You will have to decide whether to collect these figures for yourself, but we are pleased to see more 12" figures on the market. For one thing, 12" figures come in boxes rather than on blister cards, so the figures can be put on display.

12" Figures
Airborne Ranger (#40101?) $15.00
Sky Raider (#40102) 15.00
Scuba (#40103) 15.00
Para Ninja (#40104) 15.00
Night Fighter (#40105) 15.00
Skull (#40106) 15.00

RAT FINK AND THE RAD RODS
Kenner (1990)

Rat Fink was created by car designer Ed "Big Daddy" Roth and the toys are based on an animated television series with his signature character.

Figures
Rat Fink & Rockin' Roadster $10.00
Rat Fink & Sonic Scream 10.00
Drag Lover & Turbo Tank 10.00
Deputy Sludge & Bruiser Cruiser 10.00
Dragnut & Haulin' Hog 10.00
Gearhead & Beach Bomber 10.00
Junkyard Kid & Clod Hopper 10.00

REAL GHOSTBUSTERS
"WHO YOU GONNA CALL?"
Kenner (1987–89)

These figures are from the *Ghostbusters I* and *II* movies starring Bill Murray, Dan Aykroyd, Harold Ramis,

Ernie Hudson and Sigourney Weaver and the "Real Ghostbusters" animated television series. The figures, and the series, lasted several years and have been popular with collectors as well.

The Classic Monsters batch from 1989 are just what the title implies. They are nice, but so far as we know, they have nothing to do with the rest of the series. The Ecto-Glow Heroes were tail-end figures from 1991 and saw only limited distribution.

5¼" Hero Figures (Asst. #80000, 1987) with Proton Pack and Nutrona Blaster, "I Ain't Fraid of No Ghost"
Peter Venkman and Grabber Ghost (#80010) $25.00
Ray Stantz and Wrapper Ghost (#80020) 25.00
Egon Spengler and Gulper Ghost (#80030) 25.00
Winston Zeddmore and Chomper Ghost (#80040) ... 25.00

Action Ghosts (Asst. #80100, 1987)
Stay-Puft Marshmallow Man 6" (#80110) 35.00
Green Ghost (#81020) 40.00
Bug-Eye Ghost (#80130) 20.00
H₂Ghost (#80140) 20.00
Bad-to-the-Bone Ghost (#80210) 28.00

Fright Features Figures (Asst. #80350, 1988)
Peter Venkman and Gruesome Twosome Ghost (#80360) 18.00
Egon Spengler and Soar Throat (#80370) 18.00
Ray Stantz and Jail Jaw Ghost (#80380) 18.00
Winston Zeddmore and Scream Roller Ghost (#80390) 18.00
Janine Melnitz and Tickler Ghost (#80570) 18.00

Haunted Humans (Asst. #80500, 1988)
Granny Gross Ghost (#80510) 10.00
Mail Fraud Ghost (#80520) 10.00
X-Cop Ghost (#80530) 10.00
Hard Hat Horror Ghost (#80540) 10.00
Terror Trash Ghost (#80550) 10.00
Tombstone Tackle Ghost (#80560) 10.00

Real Ghostbusters (Kenner 1987)

Ecto-1 Vehicle, Real Ghostbusters (Kenner 1988)

Screaming Heroes Figures (Asst. #80850, 1989)
Peter Venkman and Ghoulgroan Ghost (#80860) . . . 16.00
Egon Spengler and Squidsqueal Ghost (#80870) . . . 16.00
Winston Zeddmore and Houndhowl Ghost (#80880) . 16.00
Ray Stantz and Vermoan with Radar Ray (#80890) . . 16.00
Janine Melnitz and Swinewhine Ghost (#80900) 16.00

Super Fright Feature Heroes (Asst. #81060, 1989)
Peter Venkman and Snake Head Ghost (#81070) . . . 16.00
Egon Spengler and Slimy Spider Ghost (#81080) . . . 16.00
Ray Stantz and Monster Mouth Ghost (#81090) 16.00
Winston Zeddmore and Meanie Wienie Ghost
    (#81100) 16.00
Janine Melnitz and Boo Fish Ghost (#81110) 16.00

Power Pack Heroes (1989)
Peter Venkman with Bouncin' Bazooka and Lightning
    Ghost (#81160) 14.00
Ray Stantz with Grabbin' Grappler and Snatcher Ghost
    (#81170) 14.00
Egon Spengler with Crazy Copter and Twister Ghost
    (#81180) 14.00
Winston Zeddmore with Cyclin' Slicer and Spitting Ghost
    (#81190) 14.00
Janine Melnitz with Racin' Wringer and Stretch Ghost
    (#81210) 14.00
Louis Tully with Power Pincher and Vapor Ghost
    (#81400) 14.00

Classic Monsters (Asst. #80800, 1989)
The Wolfman Monster (#80810) 13.00
The Frankenstein Monster (#80820) 13.00
The Dracula Monster (#80830) 13.00
The Mummy Monster (#80840) 13.00
The Quasimodo Monster (#80930) 13.00
The Zombie Monster (#80940) 13.00

Slimed Heroes (1990)
Peter Venkman and Tooth Ghost (#81550) 10.00
Egon Spengler and Brain Ghost (#81560) 10.00

Ray Stantz and Vapor Ghost (#81570) 10.00
Winston Zeddmore and Sucker Ghost (#81580) 10.00
Louis Tully and Four-Eyed Ghost (#81590) 10.00

Ecto-Glow Heroes with Nutrona Blasters (1991)
Peter Venkman and Spider Ghost (#81690) 23.00
Ray Stanz and Gulper Ghost (#81710) 25.00
Egon Spengler and Jail Jaw Ghost (#81720) 20.00
Winston Zeddmore and Wrapper Ghost (#81730) . . . 30.00
Louis Tully and Meanie Wienie Ghost (#81740) 30.00

Gooper Ghost Figures (1987–88) with Exto-Plazm
Sludge Bucker, Gooper Ghost (#80260) 7.00
Banshee Bomber Gooper Ghost (#80270) 7.00
Squisher, Gooper Ghost (#80280) 7.00
Green Ghost, Gooper Ghost (#80320, 1988) 20.00

Action Ghosts (1988)
Pull Speed Ahead Ghost (#80610) 10.00
Brain Blaster Ghost (#80620) 9.00

Gobblin' Goblins Ghost Figures, boxed (1989)
Nasty Neck (#81220) 9.00
Terror Tongue (#81230) 9.00
Terrible Teeth (#81240) 9.00

Mini Ghosts (Asst. #80400, 1988)
Mini Goopers 9.00
Mini Shooter Boo-zooka with Boo-lets 9.00
Mini Traps 9.00

Accessories
Fearsome Flush (#80920, 1989) 4.00
Ecto-Plazm play gel with Ecto-Ghost (#80240, 1987)
    4 different colors, each 4.00

Haunted (Transforming) Vehicles (Asst. #80680, 1988)
Wicked Wheelie cycle and driver (#80690) 10.00
Air Sickness plane and pilot (#80700) 10.00

Vehicles

Ecto-1 Ambulance Vehicle with Ambu Ghost (#80230,
　1987) 80.00
Ecto-1A Vehicle (#80230, 1987–88) 25.00
Ecto-2 Vehicle (#80450, 1988) 10.00
Ecto-3 Vehicle (#81050, 1989) 10.00
Ecto-500 Vehicle (#81120, 1989) 10.00
Ecto-Bomber Vehicle (#81470) 14.00
Ghost Sweeper Vehicle (#81390) 10.00
Highway Haunter Vehicle (#80600, 1988) 16.00

Playset

Fire House Headquarters playset (#80580, 1987) . . . 60.00

Plush Ghosts (Asst. #80150, 1987)

Green Ghost 13" plush 35.00
Stay-Puft Marshmallow Man 13¾" plush 30.00

REAL MONSTERS
SEE: AAAHH!! REAL MONSTERS

Dot, ReBoot (Irwin 1995)

REBOOT
Irwin (1995)

"Welcome to our world—the world inside Mainframe City. Enzo, his sister, Dot and Bob, the Guardian, all live here along with the other computer Sprites. Mostly it's a mega-binary place to file serve, except for the few nasty virus types known as Megabyte and Hexadecimal. Incoming games from the User can appear at anytime and anywhere

and when they do, you better be ready to ReBoot, or run your escape sequence!" Wow! With a thrilling, action-packed premise like that, it's simply shocking that these television show figures weren't a mega hit. Anyway, they weren't, but Hexadecimal, "Mainframe's queen of chaos and malfunction," who comes all in red with four white face masks, has been popular with collectors. We didn't have to look on the Internet for her; we got ours the old fashioned way—as a red tag special. A lot of new toys were supposed to appear in 1996, but didn't.

5" Figures

Bob (#30011) $7.00
　Special edition repaint 9.00
Dot (#30012) 10.00
Enzo (#30013) 7.00
Megabyte (#30014) 7.00
Hexadecimal (#30015) 18.00
Hack "Pop Apart Head & Body with Extendable Arms"
　(#30016) 7.00
Slash "Pop Apart Head & Body with Extendable Arms"
　(#30017) 7.00

REN AND STIMPY SHOW
Mattel (1993)

These figures have articulated limbs and a working mechanism that allows you "to activate hilarious actions made popular from *The Ren & Stimpy Show*." For example, Bathtub Ren Hoek has "underleg bubbling action." If you have seen the show, you should have gotten the idea long ago. Collector interest, based on the popularity of the show, has been reasonably good.

Figures

Army Ren Hoek $15.00
Boot Camp Stimpy 15.00
Bump-a-Riffic Stimpy 15.00
Commander Ren Hoek 15.00
Deluxe Ren 25.00
Deluxe Stimpy 25.00
Slap Happy Ren Hoek 20.00
Space Cadet Stimpy 40.00
Bath Tub Ren Hoek (Suncoast Video exclusive) 20.00
Gritty Kitty Stimpy (Suncoast Video exclusive) 20.00

Large Figures

Belching Stimpy 10" 40.00
Farting Ren 10" 45.00
Talking Ren 14" 75.00
Talking Stimpy 14" 75.00

ROBIN HOOD
AND HIS MERRY MEN
Mego/Marx (1974)

There was a Disney animated movie of Robin Hood in 1973, but this series seems to be based on the continuing fame of the story.

8" Dolls, boxed

Friar Tuck $70.00
　Loose 30.00

Little John	100.00
Loose	40.00
Robin Hood	90.00
Loose	40.00
Will Scarlet	110.00
Loose	40.00

Long Bow Robin Hood (#05810)	8.00
Crossbow Robin Hood, original non-Costner head (#05820)	18.00
Crossbow Robin Hood (#05820)	8.00
Little John with Quarterstaff (#05830)	14.00
Azeem with Scimitar (#05840)	12.00
Sheriff of Nottingham with Sword (#05850)	8.00
Friar Tuck with Battle Staff (#05860)	30.00
Will Scarlett with Crossbow (#05870)	20.00
The Dark Warrior with Pike Scythe (#05880)	20.00

Vehicles and Accessories

Net Launcher (#05890)	10.00
Bola Bomber (#05910)	10.00
Battle Wagon (#05920)	20.00
Sherwood Forest playset (#05930)	60.00

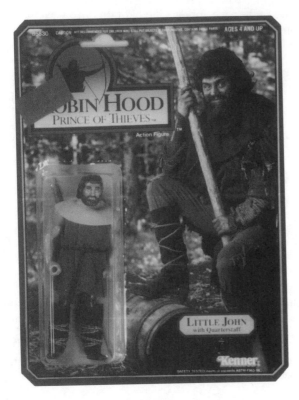

Little John, Robin Hood, Prince of Thieves (Kenner 1991)

ROBIN HOOD
PRINCE OF THIEVES
Kenner (1991)

From the movie starring Kevin Costner in tights, Morgan Freeman as Azeem, Christian Slater as Will Scarlett and Alan Rickman as the Sheriff of Nottingham. Maid Marion, played by Mary Elizabeth Mastrantonio, had a prominent part in the movie and kicked a lot of butt herself, but was not included in the action figure release.

In order to ship the figures on time, Kenner made the two Robin Hood figures with a generic head. These early versions were quickly replaced by ones with Costner's likeness (more or less) or maybe the head was just larger on account of the success of his previous film, *Dances With Wolves*. Anyway, that was the joke line at the time. The second series of figures was to include Sean Connery's King Arthur, but sadly it was never produced. Friar Tuck was the short-packed (and also short) figure in the line and everybody was looking for him, along with the early headed versions of Robin Hood. This series continues to have a respectable collector following.

4½" Figures

Long Bow Robin Hood, original non-Costner head (#05810)	$18.00

"Torpedo" Thompson,
Robocop and the Ultra Police (Kenner 1988)

ROBOCOP
AND THE ULTRA POLICE
Kenner (1988–90)

The *Robocop* movie series starred Peter Weller as the 90 percent robot, 10 percent human and Nancy Allen as his partner. Robocop in animation began in 1988 as part of the Marvel Action Universe.

Ultra Police (1989) with rapid repeat cap firing

Robocop (#64210)	$16.00
"Birdman" Barnes (#64250)	18.00
"Ace" Jackson (#64290)	12.00
Sergeant Reed (#64360)	20.00
Ann Lewis (#64370)	20.00
"Wheels" Wilson	20.00

*Robocop figure with **Robo-I** vehicle, Robocop and the Ultra Police (Kenner 1988)*

Second Batch (1990)
RoboCop Nightfighter (#64430) 20.00
Gatlin' Blaster Robocop 22.00
"Claw" Callahan (#64480) 15.00
"Torpedo" Thompson (#64490) 20.00

Vandals (1989)
Headhunter (#64220) 16.00
Nitro (#64330) 16.00
Chainsaw (#64340) 16.00
Dr. McNamara (#64350) 16.00
ED-260 Droid, boxed (#64390) 30.00

Second Batch (1990)
Toxic Waster (#64460) 20.00
Scorcher (#64510) 20.00

Vehicles (1989)
Robo-1 vehicle, boxed (#64280) 38.00
Robo-Command vehicle 30.00
Robo-Cycle vehicle, boxed (#64310) 20.00
Skull Hog cycle vehicle (#64320) 14.00
Robo-Copter vehicle, boxed (#64330) 42.00
Robo-Jailer vehicle (#64420) 50.00

ROBOCOP/
ROBOCOP THE SERIES
Orion/Toy Island (1993–95)

Toy Island has put out a line (or maybe several lines) of toys to correspond with the return of Robocop to the silver screen (*Robocop III*). There are several small versions of Robocop and his friends, but these have proved hard to collect because distribution has been so spotty. The product numbers given for the smaller figures are from Toy Island's catalog. Only the assortment number appears on the header card.

The most interesting figure for collectors is the 12" electronic figure. It is nicely detailed, says three phrases, and comes with an attachable weapon arm which has a separate battery and makes weapon noises. There are two different boxes shown in the catalog. We have seen the wide box but not the narrow one.

4" Electronic Robocop Figures (Asst. #39010) on "Try-me" header card
Electronic Robocop with weapon arm, M-16 and assault
    rifle (#39001) $5.00
Electronic Robocop with recharging repair station
    (#39002) 5.00
Electronic Robocop with flight pack (#39003) 5.00

4½" Robocop The Series "Police Detroit" (Asst. #39410)
(Battle Damaged) Robocop with interchangeable armor
    and pistol (#39401) 8.00
Stan Parks, Robocop's Sergeant with pistol and field
    transmitter (#39402) 8.00
Madigan, Robocop's Partner with shield, pistol and
    bazooka, pictured in cap (#39403) 8.00
    Variation, pictured in police helmet (#39403) . . . 8.00
Pudface, Robocop's Arch Enemy with super rifle and
    missile launcher (#39404) 8.00
Commander Cash, OCP's Superhero with working
    parachute and pack (#39405) 25.00

4½" Special Forces (Asst. #39710, 1995)
Fire Patrol Robocop with fire protective helmet and fire
  fighting arm (#39711) 5.00
Deep Sea Robocop with deep sea helmet and grappling
  retrieval arm (#39712) 5.00
Sky Patrol Robocop with rocket droid, removable chest
  armor, Robocop helmet and pistol (#39713) 5.00
Pudface, the Arch Enemy with virtual reality mask,
  missile launcher and sniper rifle 10.00

4½" Figures (Asst. #39810, 1995)
Power Glow Robocop with real illuminating armor 5.00

3¾" "Future of Law Enforcement" Mini Classic Figure
Robocop with M-16 Battle Rifle (#50103, 1995) 4.00

8" Talking Robocop Figures (Asst. #39110, 1994) on "Try-
me" header card
Talking Robocop with weapon arm and rifle (#39101) . 7.00
Talking Robocop with removable flight pack (#39102) . 7.00
Talking Robocop with working bazooka (#39103) 7.00

8" Emergency Response Figures (#39730)
Robocop Tactical Chemical Response with Vega droid
  (#39731) 10.00
Robocop Tactical Undersea Command with Triton droid
  (#39732) 10.00
Robocop Tactical Space Command with Cygnus droid
  (#39733) 10.00

Large Figures (1993)
Robocop 12" Audiotronic figure with "Light & Sound
  Weapon Arm" (#39201) in wide box 20.00
Robocop 12" Audiotronic figure with "Light & Sound

Weapon" Arm (#39202) in narrow box 20.00
Robocop Super Classics 15" (Super Classics Collection
  Series) with 9 play pieces (#50102) 30.00

Vehicles with siren and flashing lights, in "Try-Me" open box
OCP Interceptor 11" (#39501) 15.00
Tactical Command Vehicle (#39502) 15.00
Tactical Field Ambulance 11" (#39503) 15.00
Mobile Armored Detention Vehicle 13" (#39504) 15.00

ROBOT DEFENDERS/RENEGADES
Remco (1984)

The good robots are the "Robot Defenders" and the bad
guys are the "Robot Renegades." The robots are on the same
scale as Remco's other series of the time—Conan and the
Lost World of the Warlord/Warrior Beasts. Those two series
were based on comic books, but this one wasn't. Remco was
sure trying hard with all these series, but they were up
against Masters of the Universe at the time.

6" Figures
Diotrax Renegade $10.00
Epaxion Defender 10.00
Mazrak Defender 10.00
Wargor Renegade 10.00
Zebok Renegade 10.00
Zonton Defender 10.00

Vehicles
Marauder Renegade Ship 15.00
Strike Cruiser Defender Ship 15.00

Electronic Robocop, Robocop (Orion/Toy Island 1993)

Sky Patrol Robocop, Robocop the Series (Orion 1995)

ROBOTECH
Matchbox (1986)

"Robotech" was a very popular Americanized Japanese animated space saga. A damaged alien spaceship lands on Earth containing advanced technology. The evil Zentraedi want the ship and the Robotech Defense Force of young warriors is determined to keep it for Earth. There were several related comic book series from Comico, starting in 1985. Later the comics appeared from Eternity. The comics are reasonably popular as independent, non–super hero series go and have had an extensive run with continuations in "The Macross Saga" and "Robotech Genesis," etc.

The Zentraedi figures are a lot bigger than the Robotech figures. Two figures appear in both groups. Miriya defected to the Zentraedi during the series and was enlarged by them and the Zentraedi micronized a warrior in an attempt to infiltrate the Robotech Defense Force. Both sides made "mecha," basically armored walking vehicles, to fight with. The series is popular with both boys and girls and the figures have generated significant collector interest. There were also four 12" dolls.

3¾" Robotech Defense Force Figures
Rick Hunter (#7210) $18.00
Scott Bernard (#7211) 30.00
Lisa Hayes (#7212) 16.00
Dana Sterling (#7213) 26.00
Rand (#7214) 9.00

Second Batch
Roy Fokker (#7220) 16.00
Lunk (#7221) 22.00
Max Sterling (#7222) 17.00
Rook Bartley (#7223?) 50.00
Miriya (#7225)(red outfit) 20.00
Miriya (black outfit) 60.00

Robotech Masters Enemy Figures
Robotech Master (#7215) 10.00
Micronized Zentraedi Warrior (#7216) 8.00
Bioroid Terminator (#7217) 12.00
Corg, Invid Enemy (#7218) 12.00
Zor Prime (#7219) 8.00

Vehicles for 3¾" Figures
Armoured Cyclone (#7351) 20.00
Bioroid Hover Craft (#7352) 14.00
Veritech Fighter 40.00
Veritech Hover Tank 32.00

Battle Pods for 3¾" Figures
Tactical Battle Pod (#7254) 30.00
Invid Shock Trooper (#7258?) 30.00
Zentraedi Officer's Battle Pod (#7259) 30.00

Playset for 3¾" Figures
SDF-1 Action Playset 135.00

6" Zentraedi Figures
Breetai (#7261) 18.00
Exedore (#7262) 18.00
Khyron (#7263) 18.00
Dolza (#7264) 18.00
Armoured Zentraedi Warrior (#7265) 18.00

Miriya (#7266) 22.00

7" Robotech Defense Force Attack Mecha
Excaliber MkVI 35.00
Gladiator 35.00
Spartan 40.00
Raidar X 40.00

7" Zentraedi Attack Mecha
Invid Bioroid Fighter 30.00
Invid Scout Ship 30.00
Zentraedi Power Armour Botoru Batallion 45.00
Zentraedi Power Armour Quadrono Batallion 45.00

Lisa Hayes, 11½", Robotech (Matchbox 1986)

11½" Dolls (1986) in window box
Lynn Minmei in Chinese dress 30.00
Lisa Hayes (#5102) in dress uniform 30.00
Dana Sterling in flight uniform 30.00
Rick Hunter in flight uniform 40.00

Vehicles and Accessories
Dana's Hover Cycle (#5410) 30.00

Fashion Outfits carded
Exercise Outfit (#5201) 12.00
Star Disguise (#5202) 12.00
Street Clothes (#5203) 12.00
Party Dress (#5204) 12.00
Nightgown (#5205) 12.00
Stage Dress (#5251) 12.00
Fancy Dress Clothes (#5252) male 12.00
Miss Macross Outfit (#5253) 12.00
Evening Gown (#5254) 12.00
Fashion Accessories Pack 12.00

Lisa Hayes, Harmony Gold (1991)

ROBOTECH
Harmony Gold (1991–94)

Harmony Gold reissued the Robotech figures, along with Lynn Minmei, which was never produced by Matchbox in the 3¾" size. Harmony Gold licensed the various 1990s' comic books as well. After 1994, the action figures were licensed to Playmates and incorporated into their Exo-Squad action figure series, despite some logical inconsistences. The two series had similar armored walking "vehicles" but completely different story lines.

3¾" Robotech Defense Force, reissues
Lynn Minmei	$18.00
Rick Hunter	10.00
Scott Bernard	10.00
Lisa Hayes	12.50
Dana Sterling	18.00
Rand	10.00
Roy Fokker	10.00
Lunk	15.00
Max Sterling	12.50
Rook Bartley	18.00
Miriya (red outfit)	12.00
Miriya (black outfit)	10.00
Miriya (purple outfit)	10.00

Robotech Masters Enemy Figures
Robotech Master	10.00
Micronized Zentraedi Warrior	12.50
Bioroid Terminator	10.00
Corg	10.00
Zor Prime	10.00

ROCK LORDS
"POWERFUL LIVING ROCKS"
Tonka (1986–87)

These are die-cast metal and plastic figures, each with a weapon and comic book. The "Rock Lords conceal themselves as stones and reveal themselves as warriors." They don't seem to have attracted much interest among collectors.

Heroic Rock Lords (Asst. #7500, 1986)
Crack-Pot, Good Rock Warrior	$9.00
Boulder, Leader of Good Rock Lords	9.00
Nuggit, Heroic Rock Warrior	9.00
Granite, Heroic Rock Warrior	9.00
Marbles, Good Rock Warrior	9.00
Pulver-Eyes, Good Rock Warrior	9.00

Second Batch (1987)
Solitaire, Queen of the Jewel Lords	9.00
Flamestone, Good Jewel Lord	9.00
Sunstone, Good Rock Warrior	9.00

Evil Rock Lords (Asst. #7501, 1986)
Slimestone, Evil Rock Warrior	10.00
Tombstone, Evil Rock Warrior	10.00
Stoneheart, Evil Rock Warrior	10.00
Magmar, Evil Rock Lords Leader	10.00
Sticks 'N Stones, Evil Rock Warrior	10.00
Brimstone, Evil Rock Warrior	10.00

Second Batch (1987)
Saberstone, Evil Rock Warrior	10.00
Spearhead, Evil Rock Warrior	10.00

Rock Lords: Fossil Lords (Asst. #7510, 1987) with unique weapon and comic book, they combine to form Rockasaurus Rex
Jawbone, Lord of the Fossile Lords	9.00
Ribcage, Fossile Warrior	9.00
Hipbone, Fossile Warrior	9.00
Tailbone, Fossile Warrior	9.00
Rockasaurus Rex gift set (#7509, 1987)	9.00

Rock Lords: Shock Rocks (Asst. #7511, 1987) with powered-action feature and comic book
Blast Rock, Leader, Good Rock Warrior	9.00
Dragon Stone, Evil Rock Warrior	9.00
Rock Shot, Evil Rock Warrior	9.00
Stun Stone, Good Rock Warrior	9.00
Stone Hook, Evil Rock Warrior	9.00
Rock Roller, Evil Rock Warrior	9.00

Monster Rocks (Rockasaurus) (Asst. #7506, 1987)
Terra-Roc, Monstrous Rockasaurs	20.00
Spike Stone, Monstrous Rockasaurs	20.00

Rock Lord Narlies (Asst. #7503, 1987)
Narliphant, Good Rock Lord Work Horse (1986)	9.00
Narlihog, Good Rock Lord Watch Animal (1986)	9.00
Narlizard, Evil Rock Lord Attack Animal (1986)	9.00
Narligator, Evil Rock Lord Attack Animal (1986)	9.00
Narlibat, Evil Rock Lord Attack Animal (1987)	9.00
Narlibaboon, Evil Rock Lord Attack Animal (1987)	9.00
Narlirhino, Evil Rock Lord Attack Animal (1987)	9.00
Narlilion, Evil Rock Lord Attack Animal (1987)	9.00

Vehicles
Rock Pot Vehicle, Boulder's Battle Car with comic book
(#7504, 1986) 15.00
Stone Wing Vehicle, Magmar's Mean Machine with
comic book (#7505, 1986) 15.00
Rock Lords Snarlie Narlie, King of the Evil Narlies,
battery powered (#7507, 1987) 25.00

ROGER RABBIT
SEE: WHO FRAMED ROGER RABBIT

ROM, THE SPACE KNIGHT
Parker Bros. (1979)

Rom was battery powered and had light-up Rocket
Pods and a Respirator which made breathing noises. His
accessories included an Energy Analyzer, a Translator and a
Neutralizer weapon. There was also a Marvel comic book
series based on the toy which ran for an impressive 75
issues.

Game and Figure
Rom, The Space Knight, in box $140.00
Loose figure 45.00

RONIN WARRIORS
Playmates (1995)

"The malevolent forces of the Dynasty have crushed the
megapolis and now threaten to bring the rest of mankind to
its knees. Enter the mighty Ronin Warriors, bringing hope,
faith and a ton of armor to take on the dark Shogun masters
of the Dynasty." The figures are based on the animated
television show of the same name and feature "Power Coil"
articulation, which allows the figures to snap back into
battle-ready stances.

Nine 4½" "Create a Ronin" figures were included in
Playmates 1996 catalog, but we have not seen them and
don't recall them being on display at Toy Fair either.

5½" Figures
Ryo (#8801) $6.00
Sage (#8802) 6.00
Rowen (#8803) 6.00
Kento (#8804) 6.00
Cye (#8805) 6.00
Hariel (#8806) 6.00
Dais (#8807) 6.00
Cale (#8808) 6.00

Hariel, Ronin Warriors (Playmates 1995)

Sekhmet (#8809) 6.00
Anubis (#8810) 6.00
Talpa (#8811) 6.00

ROOKIES
LJN (1973)

LJN took a cue from Mego and made a series of
figures from this 1970s' cop action ABC television series.
The series starred Michael Ontkean as Willie Gillis, Georg
Stanford Brown as Terry Webster, Sam Melville as Mike
Danko and Bruce Fairbairn as Chris Owens. Kate Jackson
(later one of Charlie's Angels) played Jill Danko, but, sadly,
no figure of her was produced.

8" Doll Figures on header card
Mike $40.00
Willie 40.00
Terry 40.00
Chris 40.00

SAILOR MOON
Bandai (1995)

Sailor Moon is supposed to be the first, true action adventure heroine for girls. It's a popular television show in Europe and Japan and it made its U.S. debut in the fall of 1995. Sailor Moon and her sailor planet friends are school girls who save the world from the evil Queen Beryl and Rubeus, and look great too. You could find most of them discounted at the end of 1996.

6" Dolls in window box
Sailor Moon (#03401)	$10.00
Sailor Mars (#03402)	10.00
Sailor Venus (#03403)	10.00
Sailor Jupiter (#03404)	10.00
Sailor Mercury (#03405)	10.00
Queen Beryl (#03406)	12.00

11½" "Deluxe Adventure" Dolls in window box
Sailor Moon (#3426)	15.00
Sailor Mars (#3427?)	15.00
Sailor Venus (#3428)	15.00
Sailor Jupiter (#3429)	15.00
Sailor Mercury (#3430?)	15.00
Queen Beryl (#3431?)	20.00

Vehicle for 6½" figure
Moon Cycle (#3420)	7.50

THE SAVAGE DRAGON
Playmates (1995)

From the Image comic book by Erik Larsen. These figures came in the same assortment with the three Jim Lee Teenage Mutant Ninja Turtles figures. The She-Dragon figure comes with two different hair styles and is very hard to find in either.

Sailor Moon (Bandai 1995)

Battle Damage Dragon, The Savage Dragon (Playmates 1995)

6" Figures with special comic
The Savage Dragon (#03045)	$7.00
Battle Damage Dragon (#03046)	7.00
She-Dragon (#03047) mohawk hair style	20.00
She-Dragon (#03047) full hair	20.00
Barbaric (#03048)	7.00

SCHWARZENEGGER COMMANDO
Diamond (1985–86)

In the movie *Commando*, Arnold Schwarzenegger plays John Matrix. As with most of his action movies, he kicks butt and takes names when his daughter is kidnapped by some dictator with a death wish. With all that action, it's not surprising that there were also action figures. Matrix has always drawn some collector interest because of Arnold, but the others haven't, until recently.

3¾" Figures (1985)
Blaster	$18.00
Chopper	18.00
Lead Head	18.00
Matrix	90.00
Psycho	18.00
Sawbones	18.00
Spex	18.00
Stalker	18.00

7" Figures with comic book
Blaster	28.00
Chopper	28.00
Lead Head	28.00

Matrix	70.00
Loose, with removable vest, uzi, pistol, leg holster and knife	25.00
Psycho	28.00
Sawbones	28.00
Spex	28.00
Stalker	28.00

Large Figure
Matrix, in black box	130.00
Variation, in red box	180.00
Ninja Claw	95.00

SEA DEVILS
Mattel (1970–71)

The Sea Devils could "play on land or water" and came with a "motorized sea jet" which was battery powered and towed the figure underwater. It dived when you operated a hand compressor.

Figures
Sea Devils with Commander Carter	no price found
Sea Devils with Rick Riley	no price found
Kretor	no price found
Zark	no price found

Vehicle and Playset
Aqualander, battery powered	no price found
Search & Rescue Set with **Commander Carter** figure and Aqualander	no price found

SEAQUEST DSV
Playmates (1994)

SeaQuest DSV (Deep Submergence Vehicle) figures are based on the live-action television show of the same name starring Roy Scheider as Captain Nathan Hale Bridger. Along with his multi-national crew, the seaQuest submarine saved the world every week from an assortment of undersea and earthbound invaders. The series was created by Steven Spielberg and showed some promise, at first anyway. At least it made it to a second season, with a lot of new cast members and to a third season as *seaQuest 2032* with even more new actors.

The figures are individually numbered for collectors and come with a display base. Playmates did their usually excellent job of making them. They are all modeled after the human characters in the original series, which limits the creativity of the model artists, but they do come with a lot of accessories.

Darwin (the Dolphin), Dr. Z and The Regulator appeared in the second batch. What collectors wanted were the vehicles (ships) which we liked a lot when we saw them at Toy Fair. Unfortunately, the line was cancelled and they never appeared. Still, the line is collected.

5" Figures
Captain Nathan Hale Bridger (#1501)	$10.00
Commander Ford (#1502)	13.00
Lucas Wolenczak (#1503)	10.00

"The Regulator" Leslie Ferina, seaQuest DSV (Playmates 1993)

Lt. Commander Katherine Hitchcock (#1504) 15.00
Lt. J.G. O'Neill (#1505) 13.00
Dr. Z (#1506) 10.00
"The Regulator" Leslie Ferina (#1507) 10.00
Darwin (the Dolphin) (#1508, 1994) 20.00
Chief Manilow Crocker (#1510) 18.00

SECRET OF THE NINJA
"ACTIONIZED MARTIAL ARTS MASTERS"
Remco (1984)

The six figures in this series have not drawn much collector interest.

SECTAURS
"WARRIORS OF SYMBION"
Coleco (1984)

In this series, telepathically bonded Sectaur Warriors and their oversized insect companions do battle with each other on the planet Symbion, "a world where insects grow to frightening proportions ... where the inhabitants have taken on the awesome characteristics of insects" and "where the good of the Shining Realm is locked in mortal combat with the evil of the Dark Domain." Fortunately, the good guys have the bad guys outnumbered three to two in the basic assortment. The toys spawned a short-lived Marvel comic book series which began in 1985, and there was an animated television series by Ruby Spears as well.

Zak and Bitaur, Sectaurs (Coleco 1984)

Coleco was best known for sports and children's toys, but some of its action figure lines, like this one, were not bad at all. Sectaurs were humanoid insect types, divided into different factions, who commanded larger bug-type creatures that they used as transportation and as weapons.

Sectaur and insect were packaged together in a window box with weapons, a mini comic book and instructions. There were also four larger, riding insects sold with Sectaurs and a playset.

Figure and Insect
Commander Waspax and Wingid $20.00
Dargon and Parafly 20.00
Mantor and Raplor 20.00
Skito and Toxcid 20.00
Zak and Bitaur (#00924) 20.00

Figures Riding Insects with "hands-in action"
Dargon and Dragonflyer 30.00
General Spidrax and Spiderflyer 30.00
Pinsor and Battle Beetle 25.00
Skulk and Trancula 20.00

Playset
The HYVE Action Play Set with "two hands-in action
    monsters Naurr and Vypex" 60.00

SGT. ROCK
Remco (1982–83)

"Tough Action Soldiers, combat ready with weapon and gear" from the DC comic book series. The figures came with dog tags with your own serial number. The only trouble with this series is that Remco kept recycling it over and over again as generic military figures.

3¾" Figures
Airman	$8.00
Chutes	8.00
Cowboy	8.00
Dock	8.00
Gunner	8.00
Gyrene	8.00
The Instructor	8.00
Leatherneck	8.00
Mack	8.00
Marksman	8.00
MP	8.00
Raider	8.00
Sgt. Rock	8.00
Snow Force	8.00
Special Forces	8.00
Tanker	8.00

Accessories and Playsets
Action Machine Gun Nest	10.00
Action Playcase	10.00
Airborne Parachute Invader	10.00
A.T.A. (Anti-Tank Anti-Aircraft) Weapon	12.00
A.T.C. (Amphibious Armored Troop Carrier)	12.00
Climbing Assault Unit	10.00
Forward Recon Post	10.00
L.E.M. Attack Command Vehicle	12.00
L.E.M. Attack Vehicle	10.00
River Commando Patrol	10.00
Track Attack Cat	10.00

THE SHADOW
Kenner (1994)

From the July 1994 movie starring Alec Baldwin as Lamont Cranston, the enigmatic Shadow, and featuring John Lone as Shiwan Khan, the last descendent of Genghis Khan. The Shadow originated in the 1930s as a pulp magazine hero and the 1940s as a radio hero. "Who knows what evil lurks in the hearts of men? The Shadow knows!"

Many of the figures and vehicles could still be found discounted at the end of 1996.

4½" Heroes (#65200)
Lightning Draw Shadow with "Silver Heat 45s" (#65201)	$5.00
Transforming Lamont Cranston with "Snap-on Shadow Armor" (#65202)	5.00
Ambush Shadow with "Quick Draw Action" (#65203)	7.00
Ninja Shadow with "Rapid Strike Chopping Action" (#65204)	6.00
Electronic Bullet-Proof Shadow, battery powered (#65246)	12.00

Electronic Bullet-Proof Shadow, The Shadow (Kenner 1994)

Villains (#65220)
Battle Shiwan Khan with "Red Demon Armor" (#65221)	5.00
Mongul Warrior with Firing Crossbow and Power Slice Action (#65222)	6.00
Shiwan Khan with Rapid Strike Chopping Action and Striking Serpent Staff (#65223)	6.00
Dr. Mocquino with Mace and Attacking Claw Staff (#65226)	6.00

Vehicles
Nightmist Cycle with Surprise Attack Missile (#65240)	10.00
Shiwan Khan Serpent Bike (#65252)	18.00
Mirage SX-100 Car with Blasting Missile and Armored Roof (#65260)	25.00
Thunder Cab (#65270)	30.00

SHOGUN CYBER WARRIORS
TrendMasters (1994)

These early TrendMasters figures are not as interesting as some of their later series. Each figure had snap-on armor and came with a trading card. A few were still available with red tags at the end of 1996.

5" Figures (Asst. #30401) with trading card
Jason Stealth	$5.00
Lord Tyrantus	5.00
Michael Titan	5.00
Mitch Talon	5.00
Scragg	5.00
Sean Velociraptor	5.00

Vehicles

Raptor's Powercycle	6.00
Stealth's Powercycle	6.00
Talon's Powercycle	6.00
Titan's Powercycle (#30403)	6.00

Heli-Capter	50.00
Danguard Launcher	50.00
Nessar	50.00
Kargosaur	50.00
Grand Car	50.00

SHOGUN WARRIORS
"INVINCIBLE GUARDIANS OF WORLD FREEDOM"
Mattel (1977–80)

These giant figures were based on the "Mazinger Z" animated series from Japan, which aired in the United States as "Force Five." They were made by Bandai and sold by Mattel. There is also a comic book series, which began in February 1979 and ran for 20 issues.

24" Warrior Figures

Dragun (#9858, 1977)	$175.00
Raydeen (#9859, 1977)	175.00
Mazinga (#9860, 1977) with red V-shaped chest plate	175.00
Gaiking (#2441, 1978)	175.00
Godzilla 20" (1978)	225.00
Daimos (1979)	175.00
Godzilla (2nd) 19½" (1979)	175.00
Great Mazinga (1979)	175.00

5" Die-Cast Warrior Figures (1978)

Great Mazinga (#2103)	45.00
Poseidon (#2104)	45.00
Raider (#2105)	45.00
Dragun (#2106)	45.00

5½" Two-in-One Figures

Raydeen	75.00
Gaiking	75.00
Daimos	75.00
Dangard	75.00
Voltus V	75.00

3" Die-Cast Metal Figures

Dragun (1978)	25.00
Grandizer (1978)	25.00
Gaiking (1978)	25.00
Poseidon (1978)	25.00
Great Mazinga (1978)	25.00
Combatra (1978)	25.00
"17" (1979)	30.00
Voltus V (1979)	30.00
Dangard (1979)	30.00
Leopaldon (1979)	30.00

Vehicles (1978–79)

Varitank (#2519)	50.00
Solar Saucer (#2520)	50.00
Vertilift (#2521)	50.00
Sky Arrow (1979)	50.00
Shigon Jet (1979)	50.00
Shigon Tank (1979)	50.00
Liabe (1979)	50.00
Daimos Truck (1979)	50.00
Ballozer	50.00
Kondar	50.00
Rydoto	50.00
Jet Car	50.00
Sky Jet	50.00

Windhammer with Tuning Fork, SilverHawks (Kenner 1988)

SILVERHAWKS
Kenner (1987–88)

"SilverHawks" was an animated television series distributed by Lorimar-Telepictures which began in the fall of 1986. In the story, the peaceful 26th-century galaxy of Limbo is under attack from "the galaxy's foulest, most diabolical villain," Mon*Star, free after 100 years of imprisonment. Five volunteers from Earth "undergo a transformation, becoming incredibly powerful super beings—partly metal, partly real." Our heroes, the SilverHawks, soar through space to the Limbo galaxy and get weapon birds and go forth to battle Mon*Star and his mob.

5" Figures (Asst. #49200, 1987)

Copper Kidd with May-Day	$35.00
Quicksilver with Tally-Hawk (#49060)	12.00
Steelwill with Stronghold (#49070)	12.00
Steelheart with Rayzor (#49080)	25.00
Bluegrass with Sideman (#49090)	10.00
Hotwing with Gyro	12.00
Stargazer with Sly-Bird (#49110)	12.00
Flashback with Backlash (#49130)	12.00

Bluegrass, SilverHawks (Kenner 1988)

Villains (Asst. #49250, 1987)
Mon*Star with Sky-Shadow (#49140) 12.00
Mo-Lec-U-Lar with Volt-Ure (#49150) 12.00
Mumbo-Jumbo with Airshock (#49160) 12.00
Buzz-Saw with Shredator (#49170) 12.00

Second Series, Asst. 1 (Asst. #49200, 1988)
Condor with Jet Stream (49230) 15.00
Quicksilver with "New! Ultrasonic Suit" and Tally-Hawk
    Launcher 42.00
Copper Kidd with Laser Discs 12.00
Windhammer with Tuning Fork (#49410) 18.00

Second Series, Asst. 2 (Asst. #49300, 1988)
Steelwill with Steamer 12.00
Moon Stryker with Tail-Spin (#49220) 12.00
Hardware with Prowler (#49240) 12.00
Mon*Star with Laser Lance 12.00
Steelwill with "New! Ultrasonic Suit" and laser spark
    action (#49390) 12.00
Bluegrass with "New! Ultrasonic Suit" and Hotlicks
    Amplifier (#49400) 25.00

Vehicles and Playset
Tally-Hawk attack bird, 25" wing span (#49010, 1987) 25.00
Stronghold attack bird, 20" wing span (#49020, 1987) 15.00
Sky-Shadow attack bird, 20" wing span (#49030,
    1987) 20.00
Maraj vehicle (#49040, 1987) 30.00
Sprinthawk vehicle (#49190, 1988) 18.00
Sky-Runner vehicle (#49290, 1988) 15.00
Copper Racer vehicle (#49450, 1988) 20.00

Bartman, Simpsons (Mattel 1990)

SIMPSONS
Mattel (1990)

Matt Groening's long-running Fox television animated series, which really caught on in 1990. The figures came with plastic word balloons.

Figures
Bart with "5 cool things to say" $25.00
Bartman with "5 warnings for evil doers" 20.00
Homer with "5 fatherly phrases" 25.00
Lisa with "5 phrases to bug brothers" 30.00
Maggie with "5 thoughts to suck on" 30.00
Marge with "5 things moms say" 25.00
Nelson with "5 wisecracks" 20.00

Accessory
Sofa & Boob Tube 28.00

THE SIX MILLION DOLLAR MAN
Kenner (1975–78)

From the popular television series starring Lee Majors as Colonel Steve Austin. The series was originally based on the novel *Cyborg* and its sequels by Martin Caidin. **See also The Bionic Woman,** listed previously.

The basic doll has a "Bionic Eye" which you can look through, a "Bionic Power Arm" which can lift up to two pounds and is fully articulated.

13" Figures

The Bionic Man, 13" (with Engine Block) (#65000 1975) $60.00
The Bionic Man with Bionic Grip, 13" (with Steel Beam) (#65010 1977) 75.00
The Bionic Man, with Biosonic Arm, 13" (with Blocks and Boards) (#65030 1978) 95.00
Oscar Goldman with Exploding Briefcase, 13" (#65100, 1977) 70.00
Maskatron 13" (#65600, 1976) 100.00
Bionic Bigfoot, The Sasquatch Beast, 15" (#65170, 1977) 160.00

Vechicles and Accessories

O.S.I. Headquarters playset (#65150, 1976) 70.00
Back Pack Radio (#65200, 1975) 20.00
Bionic Mission Vehicle, 20" (#65290, 1977) 60.00
Bionic Transport and Repair Station, 17½" tall (#65300, 1975) 30.00
Venus Space Probe (#65310 1978) 180.00
Critical Assignment Arms (#65500, 1976) 20.00
Critical Assignment Legs (#65520, 1976) 20.00
Mission Control Center playset (#65700, 1976) 65.00
Bionic Cycle (#86040, 1976) 20.00

Adventure Sets (1977)

Mission to Mars (#65050) 30.00
O.S.I. Undercover Assignment (#65060) 30.00
Test Flight at 75,000 Feet (#65070) 30.00

SKELETON WARRIORS
"THEY'RE BAD TO THE BONE"
Playmates (1994)

From the animated CBS television series, pitting Prince Lightstar, heir to the throne of Luminaire, against the evil Baron Dark and his henchmen, villains "so wicked the very flesh has burned from their bones." "The peaceful world of Luminaire becomes the final battleground for the forces of light and dark. When Baron Dark attempts to steal the legendary Lightstar Crystal, he causes the all-powerful stone to split, dividing the forces of good and evil."

These toys looked great at Toy Fair in 1994. Sales to kids must have been slow in 1995 because no second-batch figures appeared and existing figures were available in quantity and at discount. The humans were the scarce figures and collectors were waiting for Talyn, Prince Lightstar's hot looking sister. Unfortunately, she was scheduled for the second batch and was never produced.

5½" Figures (Sept. 1994) with mini comic and poster

Prince Lightstar, Courageous Leader of the Legion of Light (#8501) $14.00
Urshak: The Guardian (#8502) 14.00
Grimskull, Shadow-Jumping Warrior of the Legion of Light (#8504) 14.00
Baron Dark (#8505) 9.00
Shriek (#8506) 9.00
Dagger (#8507) 9.00
Aracula (#8508) 9.00
Dr. Cyborn (#8509) 9.00

Vehicles

Skeleton Legion Warhorse (#8521) 12.00
Skeleton Legion Skullcycle (#8541) 12.00

SKY COMMANDERS
Kenner (1987–88)

"It happened suddenly, without warning. The sea exploded—and the world was changed forever. A terrifying new continent emerged from the earth's core—deadly and everchanging. Hurricane-force winds and tornadoes of poisonous gas veil the bizarre new continent." Mankind can survive only on the "High Frontier" of the mountain tops, by using incredible, new, high-altitude battle technology on roadways in the sky, all supplied by the military industrial complex of Kenner for a few bucks each. Each figure comes with either battle track roadway or transport cable plus clamps to attach to furniture.

The figures don't seem to have attracted very much collector interest. More figures were scheduled for 1988, but we have never seen them and assume they were never made.

3¾" Figures (Asst. #35800, 1987) on header card

Ascender backpack with **Commander Jack Reily** (#35850?) $6.00
Rollerball backpack with **General Summit** (#35860) .. 6.00
Geyser Attack backpack with **Commander R.J. Scott** (#35870) 6.00
Search & Rescue backpack with **Commander Rex Kling** (#35880) 6.00

Aracula, Skeleton Warriors (Playmates 1994)

Battle Track Dispatch, Sky Commanders (Kenner 1987)

Deception Raider backpack with **General Plague**
(#35890) 6.00
Cable Raider backpack with **Raider Rath** (#35900) ... 6.00

Figure and Vehicle Sets (1987) boxed
Locust Raider mini vehicle with **Raider Rath** (Asst.
#35820) 10.00
Cable Cannon mini vehicle with **Commander Pete
Crane** (Asst. #35820) 10.00
Bomb Blast mini motorized vehicle with **Commander
Pete Crane** (Asst. #35760) 10.00
Track Patrol mini motorized vehicle with **Commander
Cliff Baxter** (Asst. #35760) 10.00
Jackal Raider vehicle with **General Plague** (#35830) 10.00
Motorized Battle Track Protector vehicle with
Commander Jack Reily (#35840) 10.00
Outrider vehicle with **Commander Rex Kling** (#35940)10.00
Flex Wing vehicle with **Commander R. J. Scott**
(#35950) 10.00
Rapid Deployment Vehicle with **Commander Pete
Crane** (#35970) 10.00
Battle Track Dispatch (mail-in) 10.00

Playsets
Vector Command Playset with **General Summit**
(#35810) 20.00

SLAMMERS
Mattel (1990)

The package describes the Slammers as "Totally righteous dudes that shred the edge of cool! Their bods are ultra-flexible! Tweak 'em! Twist 'em! Bend 'em into rip ridin' poses for incredible board action!" The collector market decided that it didn't care whether you could tweak these skateboard-riding flexie figures or not.

5" Figures
Tin Head (#1320) $3.00
Gnash (#1322) 3.00
Ripster (#1368) 3.00
Lip Slide (#1369) 3.00
Ding Dang (#1385) 3.00

Zombod, Slammers (Mattel 1990)

Jive Guy (#1431) 3.00
Ollie Grab (#1480) 3.00
Zombod (#1581) 3.00

Playset
Ramp Grinder stunt set (#9109) 7.00

SOCKET POPPERS
Ertl (1991)

Socket Poppers by Ertl came in "Two Figure" assortments and "Gift Sets" of five figures. All arms, legs and heads on all figures are interchangeable, making zillions of different combinations possible! According to the Ertl catalog the Mummy, Cyclops, Wrestler, Mutant, Soldier and Indian were only available in the gift sets with two packed in each set along with three regular figures. That makes the three gift sets the most collectible items along with the Monster Fly and Football Player two-pack, which contains characters not found in the gift sets, all assuming that anyone wants to collect these figures.

Two-Figure Assortments (1991)
Dinosaur & Rock Star (#748) $6.00
Monster Fly & Football Player 6.00
Vampire & Swamp Monster 6.00
Skateboarder & Pterodactyl 6.00
Sheriff & Robot 6.00

Gift Set Assortments (1991)
Mummy, Dinosaur, Vampire, Swamp Monster and

Indian 10.00
Mutant, Sheriff, Soldier, Robot and Swamp Monster . 10.00
Cyclops, Pterodactyl, Wrestler, Robot and Dinosaur . 10.00

SOUND FORCE/SOUND TEAM
Toy Island (1989)

Better than average drug store figures which came with two "Electronic Gun Sounds" on a "Try-me" header card. Toy Island made a lot of these types of figures. **See also Space Attack, Voice Squad, Voice Patrol and Voice Rangers**. Some of these series even made it into toy stores.

6¾" Figures (#30307)
Captain Adam, Special Tactics Expert $7.00
Agent Zebra 7.00
Red Top 7.00

SPACE: 1999
Mattel (1976)

From the syndicated television series starring husband and wife acting team of Martin Landau and Barbara Bain with Barry Morse. The series ran for two years, pretty good for something ranked among the worst science fiction shows of all time. The problem with the series logic was that the moon had to wander around the universe from episode to episode without propulsion or guidance, dropping into the next space hole or whatever to take the actors to the next adventure.

9" Dolls
Commander Koenig $70.00
Doctor Russell 70.00
Professor Bergman 70.00
Zython 150.00

Vehicles and Accessories
Moonbase Alpha Control Room & Launch Monitor
  Center 90.00
Eagle 1 Spaceship with 3" action figures of **John Koenig**, **Dr. Russell** and **Prof. Bergman** 175.00

SPACE: 1999
Palitoy (1977)

British-manufactured figures which made it to this hemisphere. They are obviously based on the same television show as the previous series.

Alan Carter $375.00
Captain Zantor 100.00
Capt. Koenig 200.00
Mysterious Alien 100.00
Paul Morrow 150.00

SPACE ACADEMY
Hasbro (1977)

A Woolworth stores exclusive, based on a CBS television series set at a training school for space explorers.

"Lost in Space's" Jonathan Harris was Issac Gampu, the three-hundred-year-old head of the Space Academy. The series starred Ric Carrott as Chris, Brian Tochi as Tee Gai and Eric Greene as Loki, all cadets at the Academy.

Figures
Issac Gampu $45.00
Chris 45.00
Tee Gai 45.00
Loki 45.00

Com Link Orbit Command Saucer,
Space Attack (Toy Island 1991)

SPACE ATTACK
Toy Island (1991)

These figures appeared in 1991 from Toy Island. They are 6¾" talking action figures and were available primarily in drug stores. Toy Island also made the Voice Rangers, Voice Squad, etc., figures, which you may have seen in toy stores. Most drug store items are cheap knock-offs, but these figures are up to toy store quality. They aren't based on a television show or comic book and don't seem to be collected today, but maybe they should be. This science fiction series would have the most potential of any of Toy Island's talking figures. Small figures named Drac, Fang and Boomer are listed on the packages, but their availability is unknown.

6¾" Talking Figures
K.C. Knox Special Z-force (#31001) $5.00
Crossbones Lunar Security 5.00
Cap-Com-1 Outpost Commander (#31003) 5.00
Tanec-3 Mission Control (#31101) 5.00
Oma-Ba Battalion Commander 5.00
Delta-6 Assault Leader (#31103) 5.00

Vehicles
Com Link Orbit Command Saucer (#30614) 6.00
Mach-9 Strike Leader Space Plane (#30615) 6.00
TK-5 Battle Shield 6.00

SPACE JAM
Playmates (1996)

From the live-action and animated feature film starring Michael Jordan and the Looney Tunes gang playing basketball for the future of mankind. The movie opened with much fanfare and the kids went to see it, but the stores must have over-ordered the toys because modest discounts were available at year's end—only a couple of months after the toys (and the movie) appeared.

Figures
Michael Jordan/Bugs Bunny with Hyper Lane Surfer
(#17651) $9.00
Michael Jordan/Sylvester with Sky Stilts and Plunger
Stuffer (#17652) 9.00
Michael Jordan/Elmer Fudd with Flight School Flinger
(#17653) 9.00
Charles Barkley/Wile E. Coyote 8.00
Swackhammer vs. Tweety with Hang Time Hoop Cage
(#17655) 8.00
Yosemite Sam vs. Bupkus with 3-Point Ball Blaster
(#17656) 8.00
Lola Bunny vs. Bang with Jumpin' Jam Hoop (#17657) 8.00
Daffy Duck vs. Pound with Sky Duck Bouncer
(#17658) 8.00
Marvin the Martian vs. Nawt with Slammin' Saucer
(#17659) 8.00
Tasmanian Devil vs. Blanko with Twist and Roll Cyclone
(#17667) 8.00

9" Dolls
Michael Jordan in Baseball uniform 15.00
Michael Jordan in Basketball uniform 15.00
Michael Jordan in Golf outfit 15.00

SPAWN
Todd Toys (1994–95)

From the very popular comic book created by Todd McFarlane, we have a line of toys created by Todd McFarlane, and manufactured and distributed by a company first called Todd Toys and later McFarlane Toys. Every five minutes, Todd McFarlane doesn't like something on the figures, so he changes them. Every ten minutes Todd McFarlane paints them a different color and reissues them. He also made a deal with Kay-Bee/Toy Works and reissued a lot of the early ones, all painted gold.

Todd McFarlane became famous in the comic-book industry as an artist for Marvel on comics such as "The Incredible Hulk" and "The Amazing Spider Man." He struck out on his own with his own comic book line, "Spawn," in 1992, forming Image Comics in the process (along with six other prominent comics artists).

His toys are large, detailed and imaginative. Their best feature is that quality isn't sacrificed just for short-term

Angela, Spawn (Todd Toys 1995)

profits. The worst feature is all the variations. There are so many of these that collectors have gone crazy trying to find them and given up on the line. The essence of the problem is as follows: If there is one variation in a figure during its production run, such as hair color, that one version of the figure is scarce and desirable and becomes worth more money. Everybody figures this out immediately and looks for the scarce figure and feels good when they find one at retail price, and not quite so good when they pay more for one from a dealer. Ten variations on the same figure means that no one knows which figures are really scarce and desirable. Ten figures must be found, and bought, and paid for, to have a complete collection, with no assurance that there isn't an eleventh variation which is even scarcer. The result is that prices on all variations converge, since none is more desirable than any other. Prices fall overall, because collectors get annoyed and don't bother with the series.

The first Spawn figures arrived in late 1994 in an all-plastic pack with a comic book serving for header card art. These figures were repackaged the following spring with a blue lightning bolt header card and no comic. A second batch of figures arrived about the same time.

Angela caused a lot of controversy. She had a couple of different spear shafts and came with or without a ribbon painted on her staff and with or without painted-on panties. Jaded collectors named the later figure "Party Angela" and she, along with Cosmic Angela and Mother-One from the Wetworks series, made it into first place on the annual "Top

10 Warped Toy List" by Episcopal Reverend Christopher Rose of Hartford, Connecticut. Most collectors had already had their minds warped by comic books, rock and roll, horror movies, toy guns, violent cartoon shows, satanic role-playing games and MTV, so they didn't care.

McFarlane Toys continues to pump out action figures, make variations and repaint them all within moments. Mr. Main gets all excited about this and hates Spawn figures, but Mr. Wells remains calm and takes the philosophical view that it's nice to wake up in the morning and know that some things are constant in the universe—like the sunrise, the bureaucratic mind and Spawn variations.

Medieval Spawn (#10103)	15.00
Violator (#10104)	9.00
Clown (#10105)	10.00
Overtkill (#10106)	14.00

Second Series (1995) with lightning bolt package

Commando Spawn, speckled gun (#10111)	10.00
Variation, with plain silver gun	20.00
Chapel (#10112)	9.00
Angela (#10113) most variations	15.00
Unnotched spear shaft, and other variations (if actually scarce)	up to 50.00
Badrock (#10114)	10.00
Malebolgia, deluxe figure (#10115) any variation	60.00
Pilot Spawn, deluxe figure (#10116)	15.00

Malebolgia, Spawn (Todd Toys 1995)

Cy-gor, Spawn (McFarlane Toys 1996)

McFarlane Toys (1995)

6" Figures with comic in plastic pack

Spawn (#10101)	$8.00
Spawn, unmasked (#10101)	18.00
Tremor (#10102)	12.00
Medieval Spawn (#10103) pewter armor	10.00
Variation, with black armor	35.00
Violator (#10104) with green-border or orange-border trading card, or no card	10.00
Variation, with chrome card	20.00
Clown (#10105) Alien head	13.00
Variation, with Clown head showing	15.00
Overtkill (#10106) 5¢/10¢ on meter, turquoise or dark green	15.00
Variation, with 5¢ on meter (scarce)	100.00

Reissue Figures (1995) lightning bolt plastic package

Spawn (#10101)	8.00
Spawn, unmasked (#10101)	18.00
Tremor (#10102)	12.00

Second Series Repaints

Commando Spawn, gold guns (#10111)	9.00
Chapel, olive drab (#10112)	10.00
Angela, navy and silver (#10113)	12.00
Badrock, brown chest (#10114)	10.00
Pilot Spawn, white outfit (#10116)	17.00

Third Series

Spawn II (#10121)	9.00
Violator II (#10122)	9.00
Vertebreaker (#10123)	9.00
The Curse (#10124)	9.00
Ninja Spawn (#10125)	9.00
Cosmic Angela (#10126)	14.00
Redeemer (#10127)	9.00

Fourth Series (March, 1996)
Exo-Skeleton Spawn (#10131) black body 9.00
   Repaint, white body 14.00
She-Spawn (#10132) 16.00
   Repaint, black mask 16.00
Clown II (#10133) 9.00
   Clown II repaint, with red weapon 9.00
Cy-Gor (#10134) purple trim 25.00
   Repaint, gold trim 15.00
Shadowhawk (#10135)
   Black body, gray armor 9.00
   Shadowhawk repaint, Bronze body, gray armor 10.00
The Maxx (#10136) with black Izz 30.00
   Variation, with white Izz 25.00
Violator II with Cybernetic Parts (#10137) 10.00

Series Five (July 1996)
Overtkill II with "Spin Action Hand & Weapons" (#10141)
   tan and black with putty colored hardware 10.00
   Repaint, gray and silver with black and tan
   hardware 9.00
Tremor II "Pumps Vital Body Fluid" (#10142) brown and
   black flesh with red blood 12.00
   Repaint, purple and black flesh, green blood. . . 9.00
Nuclear Spawn with "Giant Weapon Fires Rat Missiles"
   (#10143) tan skin 10.00
   Repaint, green skin and silver shirt 9.00
Widow Maker with 20 points of articulation (#10144) . 18.00
   Repaint, black and red outfit on flesh-tone body 15.00
Vandalizer "Ready-For-Battle Phlebiac" (#10145) . . . 12.00
   Repaint, yellowish tan with copper-tone armor . 10.00
Viking Spawn with "Ax Chopping Arm Action" (#10146)
   tan with black beard 10.00
   Repaint, gray with brown beard 9.00

Series Six (Sept. 1996)
Alien Spawn with "Catapult Launcher Bomb" (#10151) 13.00
   Reissue on header card with diagonal white
   bands 10.00
   Repaint 9.00
Tiffany the Amazon "Wings and Sword Turn Into Sled"
   (#10152) gold sword 18.00
   Reissue on header card with diagonal white
   bands, silver sword 15.00
   Repaint 15.00
Superpatriot with "Cybernetic Snap-On Arm Cannons"
   (#10153) name on package in flag design 12.00
   Reissue with name in yellow 10.00
   Reissue on header card with diagonal white
   bands 9.00
   Repaint 9.00
Battleclad Spawn with "Removable Body Armor"
   (#10154) 10.00
   Reissue on header card with diagonal white
   bands 9.00
   Repaint 9.00
The Freak with "A Nasty Bag of Tricks" (#10155) . . . 10.00
   Reissue on header card with diagonal white
   bands 9.00
   Repaint, purple 9.00
Sansker with "Huge Swinging Bendy Tail" (#10156) . . 12.00
   Reissue on header card with diagonal white
   bands 10.00
   Repaint with white underside 10.00

Special Figures
Future Spawn, boxed (#10161) 15.00
   Repaint 10.00

Widow Maker, Spawn (McFarlane Toys 1996)

Spawn, blue, limited promo figure 85.00
Limited Edition Violator, red (mail-in) 25.00
Red Angela (Spawn collector club mail-in) 25.00
Mutant Spawn with Transforming Action, black tongue
   and highlights and 2 chest tentacles, in window
   box (#10162) 15.00
   Repaint, purple tongue, blue highlights and 4
   long chest tentacles (#10152) 13.00

Kay-Bee Special Figures
Violator, gold, numbered (#90104) 12.00
Tremor, gold, numbered (#90106) 12.00
Spawn, gold, numbered (#90109) 18.00
Overtkill, gold, numbered (#90111) 12.00
Medieval Spawn, gold, numbered (#90112) 12.00
Clown, gold, numbered (#90113) 12.00

Exclusive Figures
Spawn, 50th issue (Diamond Distributors exclusive) 100.00
Medieval Spawn vs. Malebolgia (Kmart exclusive)
   (#90119) 60.00
Violator vs. Spawn PVC 2-pack (FAO Schwarz
   exclusive) 15.00
The Maxx with 4 Izzs (FAO Schwarz exclusive) 30.00
Vertebreaker (Puzzle Zoo exclusive) (#90123) 14.00
Vertebreaker (Hill's stores exclusive) (#90125) 13.00
Exo-Skeleton Spawn (Target exclusive) (#90131) . . . 14.00
Cy-Gor (Target exclusive) (#90134) white body 14.00
Spawn vs. Violator, double size (Target exclusive) . . . 40.00

15" Figures in window box
Super Size Spawn (#60101) 30.00
Super Size Angela (#60103) 45.00

Vehicles
Spawn Mobile (#10201) 20.00
Violator Monster Rig (#10202) 18.00
Pilot Spawn Air Cycle (#10211) 30.00
    Reissue with figure (McFarlane Toys #10211) . . 25.00
Violator Chopper (#10212) 20.00
    Reissue with figure (McFarlane Toys #10212) . . 25.00
Spawn Battle Horse with figure (McFarlane Toys
    #10220) 25.00
Spawn Alley playset (#10300) 30.00

Smythe, Spider-Man (Toy Biz 1994)

SPIDER-MAN
Toy Biz (1994–96)

This series is based on the "Spider-Man" animated
FOX television show, which is obviously based on the long-
running *Spider-Man* comic book titles. Spider-Man was
originally known to the world as Peter Parker, but in 1962
(in *Amazing Fantasy* #15) he was bitten by a radioactive
spider and acquired super powers. He also got stuck with the
responsibility of saving the world from various villains, both
in the comics and on various television series.

All of the figures in these toy series turned out to be
easy to find, except the original version of Rhino, in the third
batch of figures. When this news got around, the great Rhino
hunt of 1995 was on. Ultimately a few turned up here and
there and most serious collectors eventually found one. Prices
have fallen somewhat from their high, but Rhino remains the
most expensive (actually, the only expensive) figure in the
series.

By the middle of 1996, Toy Biz stopped putting out
unnamed series and gave new series their own title and
distinctive header card. This helps the stock boys to sort the
figures out on store shelves.

5" Figures (Asst. #47100, 1994)
Spider-Man Web Racer (#47101) $5.00
Spider-Man Web Shooter (#47102) 5.00
Smythe with "Punching Power" (#47103) 7.00
Venom with "Jaw Chomping Action" (#47104) 9.00
Carnage with "Weapon Arms" (#47105) 7.00
Dr. Octopus with "Tentacle Whipping Action" (#47106) . 7.00
Hobgoblin with "Hurling Pumpkin Bomb" (#47107) 7.00

Second Batch (Asst. #47110, 1994)
Spider-Man with "Web Parachute" (#47111) 5.00
Peter Parker with "Camera Accessory" (#47112) 9.00
Alien Spider-Slayer with "Twin Torso Spider Pincers"
    (#47113) 9.00
KingPin with "Grab and Smash Action" (#47114) 10.00
Kraven with "Spear Throwing Action" (#47115) 10.00
The Lizard with "Lashing Tail Action" (#47116) 10.00
Vulture with "Spreading Wing Action" (#47117) 10.00

Scorpion, Spider-Man (Toy Biz 1995)

Third Batch (1995)
Spider-Man Multi-Jointed with "Super Poseable Action"
    (#47121) 5.00
Spider-Man Spider Armor with "Super Web Shield"
    (#47122) 5.00
Shocker with "Shooting Power Blasts" (#47124) 7.00
Green Goblin with "Goblin Glider Attack" (#47125) . . . 7.00
Scorpion with "Tail Striking Action" (#47126) 9.00
Rhino with "Head Ramming Action" (#47127) scarce . 35.00

Fourth Batch (1995) with pin
Spider-Man Black Costume with "Web-Climbing Action"
   (#47131) 6.00
Spider-Man Web Glider with "Air Assault Action"
   (#47132) 6.00
Mysterio with "Mist Squirting Action" (#47133) 11.00
The Chameleon with "Transforming Identity" (#47134) . 9.00
The Prowler with "Extending Claws" (#47135) 9.00
Venom II with "Removable Symbiotic Mask" (#47136) . 8.00
Spider-Man Night Shadow with "Web Swinging Gear"
   (#47137) 6.00

Six Arm Spider-Man, Spider-Man (Toy Biz 1995)

Fifth Batch (1995) with pin
Six Arm Spider-Man with "Six Arm Arachnid Battle
   Attack" (#47141) 5.00
Battle Ravaged Spider-Man with "Secret Storage
   Backpack" (#47142) 5.000
Nick Fury with "Missile Launching Jet Pack" (#47143) . 8.00
Morbius with "Transforming Vampire Action" (#47144) . 8.00
Punisher with "Immobilizing Arsenal" (#47146) 8.00
Spider-Sense Spider-Man with "Wall Crawling Action"
   (#47147) 5.00

Sixth Batch (March 1996) with pin
Man-Spider with "Immobilizing Restraints" (#47161) . . 5.00
Octo-Spidey with "Poseable Tentacles" (#47162) 5.00
Web Cannon Spider-Man with "Web Blast Action"
   (#47163) 5.00
Carnage Unleashed with "Removable Symbiotic Limbs"
   (#47164) 7.00
Tombstone with "Double Punch Action" (#47166) 9.00

Seventh Batch (The Amazing Spider-Man, Special Collector
Series) (Asst. #47250, Aug. 1996)

Spider-Man 2099 with "Spider Assault Weaponry"
   (#47251) 8.00
New Spider-Man with "Venom Containment Gear"
   (#47252) 5.00
Total Armor Rhino with "Anti-Spider Armor" (#47253) . 8.00
Spider-Woman with "Black Widow Assault Gear"
   (#47254) 10.00
Stealth Venom (Sneak Attack Symbiote) (#47255) . . . 9.00

Kay-Bee/Toy Works Exclusive Figures (1995)
Spider-Man Web Trap (#47046) 12.00
Spider-Man Web Lair (#47047) 12.00

Sam's Club Exclusive 4-Pack Figures
Spider-Man The Venom Saga 4-pack of Octo Spider-
   Man, Venom II, Kingpin and Black Costume
   Spider-Man 25.00

Vehicles
Smythe Battle Chair Attack Vehicle (#47310, 1994) . . 17.00
Plush Spider-Man doll (#47320, 1994) 30.00
Tri-Spider Slayer (#47330, 1994) 25.00
Daily Bugle Playset (#47400, 1994) 30.00
Hobgoblin Wing Bomber (#47410, 1994) 15.00
Spider-Man Wheelie Cycle, Motorized (#47456, 1995) 15.00
Hobgoblin Pumpkin Bomber (#47457, 1995) 12.00
Venom Assault Racer (#47458, 1995) 12.00
Spider-Man Radio Control Spider Cycle (#47460,
   1995) 30.00
Rip 'N Rev Cycle (#47495) 22.00

Playsets and Figures
Scorpion Spider Slayer with full size **Spider-Man** figure,
   boxed (#47335) 9.00
Sky Scraper Stunt Set Skyline Web-Runner with small
   Spider-Man figure (#47481, 1996) 9.00
Daily Bugle Sky-Dive Spidey (#47482, 1996) 9.00
Kingpin's Crime Central with small **Spider-Man** figure
   (#47484, 1996) 9.00

LARGE FIGURES
10" Figures (Asst. #47700, 1994) in window box
Spider-Man "Web Hanging" (red chest) (#47701) . . . 10.00
Venom (#47702) 18.00
Hobgoblin (#47703) 10.00

Second Batch (Asst. #47710, 1994) in window box
Spider-Man "Wall Hanging" (black chest) (#47711) . . 10.00
Dr. Octopus (#47712) 10.00
The Lizard (#47713) 10.00

Third Batch (Asst. #47720, 1995) in window box
Carnage (#47721) 10.00
Kraven (#47722) 10.00
Vulture (#47723) 10.00

Other 10" Figures
Super Poseable Spider-Man (#48408, 1995) 10.00
The Punisher (#48411, 1995) 10.00
Spider-Man Spider Armor (#48123, 1995) 16.00
   Reissue repainted blue and silver (1996) 10.00
Mysterio (#48124, 1995) 10.00
Sensational Spider-Man (#48173, 1996) 10.00

14" Electronic Talking Figures (1994)
Spider-Man (#47361) 20.00
Venom (#47362) 20.00
Spider-Man Projectors . . . . **See X-Men Projectors**

Hydro-Man, *Spider-Man Spider Wars (Toy Biz 1996)*

SPIDER-MAN SPIDER-WARS
Toy Biz (1996)

The scenario for this series is that "Spider-Man and Dr. Strange team-up to rescue Black Cat from the clutches of the evil Hydro-Man!" His water blasting powers are too much for them to handle so, Dr. Strange uses his magical powers to summon forth the Doppelganger Spider to fight Hydro-Man, leaving them free to rescue the Black Cat.

These figures were to form the eighth or ninth Spider-Man assortment, but got their own series title instead. The title is only on a strip inside the plastic blister on the header card and the series comes with a "Bonus Collector Pin," both of which are similar to prior Spider-Man batches. Nevertheless, this is the first of the separately titled series, which is in keeping with Toy Biz's strategy for the last half of 1996. We like having separate titles for each group because it forces the designers to come up with more interesting packaging. Black Cat is "the first female super hero in the Spider-Man collection," according to the press release. Don't believe everything you read, because Spider-Woman came out in the seventh assortment, three months earlier.

5" Figures (Nov. 1996) with bonus collector pin
Hydro-Man with "Aquatic Arsenal" (#47181) $7.00
Cyborg Spider-Man with "High Tech Armor" (#47182)
    Variation 1, thick stitches and head bandana tail
      on the figure's left 7.00
    Variation 2, thin stitches and head bandana tail
      on the figure's right 7.00

Doppleganger with "Living Alien Spider-Trap" (#47183) 7.00
Black Cat with "Cat Scratching Crossbow" (#47184) . . 10.00
Dr. Strange with "Mystical Morphing Cape" (#47185) . . 7.00

[THE SPECTACULAR]
SPIDER-MAN TECHNO-WARS
Toy Biz (1996)

The ninth series of Spider-Man figures appeared hot on the heels of the eighth series, Spider-Wars, listed previously. The header card now has the title, but the individual picture for each character is gone and all five figures sport the same Spider-Man art work. The figures are still from the "Spider-Man" animated television series.

5" Figures (Asst. #47270, Nov. 1996)
Vault Guardsman with "Riot Control Unit" (#47271) . . $8.00
Anti-Symbiote Spidey with "Sonic Containment Unit"
    (#47272) 7.00
Radioactive Spider Armor with "Radiation Containment
    Weaponry" (#47273) 7.00
Hyper Tech Spider-Man with "Giant Gamma Gun"
    (#47274) 7.00
Ultimate Octopus with "Spider Squashing Gear"
    (#47275) 8.00

SPIDER-MAN VAMPIRE WARS
Toy Biz (1996)

This is the tenth series of Spider-Man figures and the third to have its own title. There are some very attractive

Morbius Unbound, *Spider-Man, Vampire Wars (Toy Biz 1996)*

pointed ears in this batch, lots bigger than Spock's. Even a Ferengi would be proud to sport a set of lobes like these guys.

5" Figures (Dec. 1996)
Vampire Spider-Man with "Bat Launching Action" (#47191) $6.00
Morbius Unbound with "Blood Pumping Action" (#47192) 7.00
Blade-Vampire Hunter with "Spear Launching Action" (#47193) 7.00
Air Attack Spider-Man with "Wing Attack Back Pack with Missile Launcher" (#47194) 6.00
Anti-Vampire Spider-Man with "Spinning Sunlight Blaster" (#47195) 6.00

Man-Lizard, Spider-Man Arachniphobia (Toy Biz 1996)

SPIDER-MAN ARACHNIPHOBIA
Toy Biz (1996)

Arachniphobia figures are "wind-up mutations of two characters who have been genetically fused together." I think that this makes sense, but it didn't generate much interest. Most oversized figures have been passed-up by collectors due to the large number of 10" Marvel and X-Men figures which are available at discount.

6" Figures (Sept. 1996), in window box
Vampider with "Chomp and Flap Action" (#47171) ... $9.00
Spider-Goblin with "Swinging Tongue and Arm Attack Action" (#47172) 9.00
Man-Lizard with "Creepy Crawly Action" (#47173) 9.00

SPIDER-MAN
SPECIAL COLLECTORS EDITION
12" DOLLS
Toy Biz (1995–96)

Toy Biz has been testing the water with these 12" Mego-style dolls, which come in large slant-sided boxes and sell for $25.00 to $30.00 retail. The Mary Jane Watson doll is the first doll or action figure of this character, who is Peter (Spider-Man) Parker's wife in the comic book series. She comes with costumes and is billed as a 12" fashion doll, but toy stores put her in the action figure aisle with the other Marvel figures, where she belongs. There were also several X-Men dolls in the same type of package.

12" Dolls (1995) in window box.
Mary Jane Watson with costumes (#48428) 60.00
Wolverine with costumes (#48426) 35.00
Spider-Man with costumes (#48427) 30.00

12" Collector Hero
The Spectacular Spider-Man, changes from Scarlet Spider into New Spider-Man (#48419, 1996) .. 30.00

SPIRAL ZONE
"EARTH'S MOST POWERFUL SOLDIERS!"
Tonka (1987–88)

Spiral Zone doll/action figures come with interchangeable accessories including a uniform, helmet, armor, boots, backpacks and guns. The figures have many points of articulation and several weapons, and several outfits and vehicles were also available. The figures came in window boxes which also included an adventure cassette. They might have been popular with kids and collectors, but they weren't.

Spiral Zone Zone Raiders assortment (#7040, 1987)
Col. Dirk Courage, Zone Rider Leader $25.00
Sgt. Tank Schmidt 20.00
Lt. Hiro Taka 20.00
Lt. Max Jo 20.00

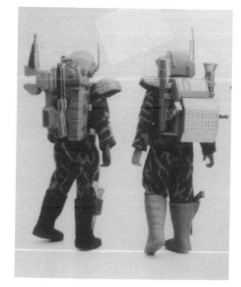

Spiral Zone (Tonka 1987)

Spiral Zone Black Widows assortment (#7041, 1987)
Overlord, Black Widow Leader 25.00
Bandit, Black Widows Master of Disquise 20.00
Reaper 20.00
Duchess Dire 20.00
Razor Back 20.00

Spiral Zone Action Weapon Packs assortment (#7048, 1987)
Snapper claws, Zone Riders 10.00
Zone Blaster, Zone Riders 10.00
Zone Runner, Zone Riders 10.00
Grappler, Black Widows 10.00
Spin Shot, Black Widows 10.00
Zone Drone, Missile Launcher Backpack, Black
    Widows 10.00

Spiral Zone Outfits assortment (#7042, 1987)
Jet Pilot 10.00
Frogman Suit 10.00
Paratrooper 10.00
Ninja Warrior 10.00
Flame Suit 10.00
Desert Fighter 10.00

Spiral Zone Scout Vehicles assortment (#7043, 1987)
Zone Rider Cycle, Heroic 30.00
Sledge Hammer Tank, Evil 40.00

Weapons (1987)
Spiral Zone Rim Fire Cannon (#7044) 25.00
Spiral Zone Bullwhip Cannon (#7045) 25.00

STARCOM
Coleco (1986–87)

The good guys are the U.S. Space force. They are opposed by the Shadow Force. All of the figures had Magna Lock feet.

2¼" Magna Lock Magnetic Figures
Sgt. Kramer $5.00
Sgt. Baker 5.00
Capt. Yablonsky 5.00
Pfc. Caldwell 5.00
Pfc. Evans 5.00
Sgt. Travers 5.00
Pfc. Jefferson 5.00
Col. Derringer 5.00
Lt. Rogers 5.00
Col. Griffin 5.00
Pfc. Reed 5.00
Col. Corbin 5.00
Sgt. Rivera 5.00
Sgt. Morales 5.00

Evil Figures
General Torvek 5.00
Cpl. Argon-6 . . . . 5.00
General Vondar 5.00
Sgt. Von Rodd 5.00
Sgt. Ramor 5.00
Sgt. Borek 5.00
Cpl. Storn 5.00
Sgt. Hack 5.00
Cpl. Slash 5.00

Vehicles and Accessories (1986)
Laser Rapid Assault Tracker, with **Capt. Vic Hayes**
    figure (#1321) . . . . no price found
M-6 Railgunner ground attack vehicle, with **Capt. Rick
    Ruffing** figure (#1322) . . . . no price found
Shadow Invader rapid strike vehicle, with **Maj. Romak**
    figure . . . . no price found
F-1400 Starwolf flexwing astro fighter, with **Lt. Tom
    Waldron** figure (#1331) . . . . no price found
Battlecrane combat cargo lifter, with **Sgt. Bob Anders**
    figure (#1332) . . . . no price found

Vehicles and Accessories (1987)
Shadow Parasite attack fighter, with **Lt. Magg** figure
    (#1333) . . . . no price found
H.A.R.V.-7 heavy armed recovery vehicle, with **Staff
    Sgt. Champ O'Ryan** figure (#1341) . . no price found
Shadow Raider sneak attack vehicle, with **Capt.
    Battlecron-9** figure (#1342) . . . . no price found
SF/B Starhawk Strategic Fighter/Bomber with **Lt. Jeff
    Carver** figure (#1352) . . . . no price found
Starmax Bomber transport missle cruiser, with **Capt. Rip
    Malone** figure (#1361) . . . . no price found
Shadowbat battle cruiser, with **Maj. Klag** figure
    (#1362) . . . . no price found
Starbase Station strategic deployment platform, with
    Sgt. Maj. Bull Gruff figure (#1392) . . no price found

STARGATE
Hasbro (1994)

From the summer 1994 "blockbuster" movie starring Kurt Russell as O'Neil, Jaye Davidson as Ra and James Spader as Daniel. The movie was okay, but not as big as its hype, and all of the figures and vehicles were discounted in due course.

Ra, Stargate (Hasbro 1994)

3¾" Figures
Daniel (Archaeologist) (#89001) $5.00
Ra (Ruler of Abydos) (#89102) 5.00
Horus (Attack Pilot) (#89003) 5.00
Skaara (Rebel Leader) (#89004) 5.00
Col. O'Neil (Team Leader) (#89011) 5.00
Anubis (Chief Guard) (#89012) 5.00
Horus (Palace Guard) (#89013) 5.00
Lt. Kowalsky (Weapons Expert) (#89014) 5.00

Vehicles
Winged Glider (Alien Attack Craft) (#89026) 10.00
Mastadge (Beast of Burden) (#89024) 8.00
All-Terrain Cruiser (#89022) 8.00

STARRIORS
Tomy (1984)

In the far flung future, Earth is devastated by deadly solar flares. Mankind goes into suspended animation after creating the Starriors—Protector robots to repair the earth and Destructor robots to kill mutated monsters. With nobody else around, the robots start fighting each other, just like people would.

These figures featured detachable arms, legs and heads that were interchangeable with the other figures in the series. The names of the figures don't match the characters in the mini comic books.

Wastors–Protectors with Marvel mini comic book
Flashfist $5.00
Ripsaw 5.00
Twinblade 5.00

Wastors–Destructors with Marvel mini comic book
Clawgut 5.00
Bolar 5.00
Slice (#6304) 5.00

Starrunner 5.00
Strazor 5.00
Cosmittor 5.00

Accessories with Marvel mini comic book
Transfer Rings, each 5.00
Trashors, each 5.00
Rammors, each 5.00

Vehicles with Marvel mini comic book
Vultor Windstorm (#5313) 9.00
Stalkors Twinhorn (#5319) 9.00

STARSKY & HUTCH
Mego (1976–78)

This upbeat 1970s' television show starred David Soul and Paul Michael Glaser in the title roles. The show emphasized the "super cops" theme, which was a staple of police shows at the time. Soul had previously played a vigilante cop opposite Clint "Dirty Harry" Eastwood in *Magnum Force*. This, and Mego's other police figure lines, such as "CHiPS," were not nearly as successful as their earlier Star Trek and Super Heroes lines, but they are still collected today.

8" Figures on header card
Starsky (#62900/1) $45.00
Hutch (#62900/2) 45.00
Huggy Bear (#62900/3) 45.00
Captain Dobey (#62900/4) 50.00
Chopper (#62900/5) 50.00

Vehicles
Starsky & Hutch Car with "Twist-Out Action" (#62812) 60.00

STAR TEAM
Ideal (1978)

The figures have a science fiction theme and include some new figures and some recycled Zeroids robots. The package pictures a space battle and two robots who look a lot like C-3PO and R2-D2, but this is undoubtedly just a coincidence and had nothing to do with the *Star Wars* movie which opened in June 1977 and made hundreds of millions of dollars.

Figures
Knight of Darkness $40.00
Zem 21 . . . . 40.00
Blue Zeroid 40.00
Star Hawk vehicle with red Zeroid 40.00
Kent and his Cosmic Cruiser 40.00

(ORIGINAL) STAR TREK
Mego (1974–76)

The first Star Trek action figures were 8" dolls produced by Mego Corporation in 1974. At first there were just four crew members and a Klingon. These earliest figures

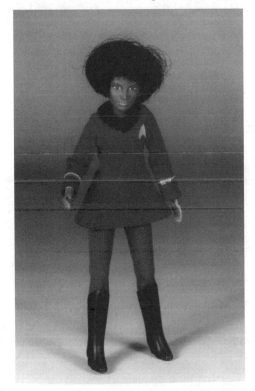

Uhura, Star Trek (Mego 1974)

came on a header card which had only five characters' heads pictured. Dolls on these cards command a premium price. The much more common second version header card adds a picture of Uhura, and her doll made a total of six figures in the first series. Captain Kirk, Mr. Spock and the Klingon were produced in large numbers by Mego, and remaining stocks were being distributed to comic shops as late as 1994.

8" Dolls, First Series, 1974
Capt. Kirk, with phaser, communicator and belt
    (#51200/1, 1974) original header card $60.00
    Reissue on second header card, adding Uhura 50.00
    Loose figure 25.00
Mr. Spock, with phaser, communicator, tricorder and belt
    (#51200/2, 1974) original header card 60.00
    Reissue on second header card, adding Uhura 50.00
    Loose figure 25.00
Dr. McCoy (*Bones*), with tricorder (#51200/3, 1974)
    original header card 150.00
    Reissue on second header card, adding Uhura 125.00
    Loose figure 50.00
Lt. Uhura, with tricorder (#51200/4, 1974) 100.00
    Loose figure 45.00
Mr. Scott (*Scottie*), with phaser, communicator and belt
    (#51200/5, 1974) original header card 150.00
    Second header card, adding Uhura 125.00
    Loose figure 50.00
Klingon, with phaser, communicator and belt (#51200/7,
    1974) original header card 90.00
    Reissue on second header card, adding Uhura 50.00
    Loose figure 20.00

Vehicles and Accessories
Enterprise Transporter Room playset (Mego/Palitoy
    #22608, 1974) 150.00
Star Trek Enterprise "Action Playset" (Bridge) (#51210,
    1975) 150.00
Star Trek Mission to Gamma VI playset (#51226,
    1976) 500.00
Star Trek Telescreen Console playset (#51232, 1976) 150.00

STAR TREK ALIENS
Mego (1975–76)

Later, Mego produced eight aliens, in two series, which were distributed overseas. These are all extremely valuable, especially the last series figures: Andorian, Mugato, Romulan and Talosian. The most popular (and valuable) alien from the second series is the Gorn. He battled Kirk in "Arena," an episode adapted from a short story by Fredric Brown. Charon is from a less popular episode, and The Neptunian and the Keeper are not actually from the television series at all.

Second Series (1975) Foreign issue
Neptunian (#51203/1) $300.00
    Loose figure 125.00
The Keeper (#51203/2) 240.00
    Loose figure 125.00
The Gorn, with phaser (#51203/3) 240.00
    Loose figure 125.00
Cheron (#51203/4) 160.00
    Loose figure 100.00

Third Series (1976) Foreign issue
The Romulan, with helmet and phaser (#51204/1) . 800.00

The Keeper, Star Trek Aliens (Mego 1975)

    Loose figure 400.00
Talos, with belt and boots (#51204/2) 275.00
    Loose figure 150.00
Andorian (#51204/3) 400.00
    Loose figure 225.00
Mugato (#51204/4) 375.00
    Loose figure 200.00

STAR TREK:
THE MOTION PICTURE
Mego (1979)

In 1979, Mego produced seven figures based on the first movie, *Star Trek: The Motion Picture.* They were 12½" dolls. The Arcturian is not from the movie or the television series. Mego also produced 3¾" figures of the crew from this movie and six unrelated aliens. These later were sold mostly overseas.

3¾" Figures (1979)
Capt. Kirk (#91200/1) $20.00
Mr. Spock (#91200/2) 25.00
Decker (#91200/3) 25.00
Ilia (#91200/4) 25.00
Scotty (#91200/5) 20.00
Dr. McCoy (#91200/6) 25.00
Klingon (#91200/7) 25.00
Zaranite (#91200/8) 150.00
Betelgeusian (#91200/9) 150.00
Arcturian (#91201/1) 125.00
Megarite (#91201/2) 150.00
Rigellian (#91201/3) 140.00

12½" Dolls
Capt. Kirk, with phaser (#91210/1) 50.00

Ilia, 12½" Doll, Star Trek: The Motion Picture (Mego 1979)

Mr. Spock, with phaser (#91210/2) 50.00
Decker, with phaser (#91210/3) 75.00
Ilia, with necklace and white shoes (#91210/4) 50.00
Klingon (#91210/5) 60.00
Arcturian (#91210/6) 75.00

Vehicles and Accessories:
U.S.S. Enterprise Bridge (#91233, 1980) 135.00

STAR TREK III
Ertl (1984)

In 1984, Ertl produced 3¾" action figures of Kirk, Spock, Scotty and the Klingon Kruge (along with his dog) based on *Star Trek III: The Search For Spock.*

3¾" Die-Cast Figures
Kirk $30.00
Spock 35.00
Scotty 30.00
Klingon Leader 45.00

STAR TREK V:
THE FINAL FRONTIER
Galoob (1989)

These are borderline action figures which we listed primarily because they are from an action figure manufacturer. Each figure is individually numbered and has a display base and a backdrop scene. They came in a 9½" x 10½" x 5" window box with a sticker that says "Limited Edition." They were originally priced at $30.00 through distributors or at $20.00 in some retail stores.

8" Figures (Asst. #5350, 1989) in window box
Captain James T. Kirk $40.00
Mr. Spock 40.00
Dr. Leonard "Bones" McCoy 40.00
Sybok 40.00
Klaa 40.00

Lieutenant Tasha Yar,
Star Trek: The Next Generation (Galoob 1988)

STAR TREK:
THE NEXT GENERATION
Galoob (1988)

The return of Star Trek to television in the form of "The Next Generation" produced one set of 3¾" action figures in 1988 from Galoob. They only made six crew members and four aliens. Data was the most popular character and a variation in his figure has increased collector interest. The Tasha Yar figure was also scarce. No figure of Deanna Troi was made. Q, the popular alien from the pilot episode "Encounter at Farpoint," and a Ferengi, a new race of villains, were also included in this series. These two figures are more valuable than the other two aliens because of their popularity as continuing characters in the Star Trek saga.

The Selay and the Antican were really generic aliens since they didn't appear in the series. Galoob quit making Next Generation action figures and there were no more produced for four long years.

3¾" Figures (Asst. #5340)

Captain Jean-Luc Picard	$15.00
Commander William Riker	15.00
Lieutenant Geordi LaForge	18.00
Lieutenant Worf	18.00
Lieutenant Tasha Yar	25.00
Lieutenant Commander Data, speckled face	30.00
Variation with blue face	150.00
Q	75.00
Ferengi	75.00
Selay	75.00
Antican	75.00

Vehicles

Shuttlecraft Galileo (#5362)	60.00
Ferengi Fighter (#5364)	60.00

Gowron the Klingon,
Star Trek: The Next Generation (Playmates 1992)

STAR TREK:
THE NEXT GENERATION
Playmates (1992–96)

Playmates, flush with cash from the success of their Teenage Mutant Ninja Turtles figures, acquired the Star Trek figures license in 1992 and isn't about to give it up over 150 figures later! They are now producing more new action figures each year than were produced in the entire 25 prior years. Their figures are 5" tall and are extremely well detailed, with weapons and accessories plus a logo base. The Ferengi in this first batch of figures is based on their first appearance in the television series when they were portrayed

as warlike. In later years they became greedy capitalists.

The figures did not appear all at the same time. Deanna Troi was delayed several months after the others. In the meantime, collectors were looking everywhere for her and listening to the latest rumor about where she could be found or when she would appear. The first ones to appear were quickly purchased by collectors, but in the long run she turned out to be only slightly scarcer than the others.

The package back of the original version of this figure shows Geordi with his visor removed. The later, more common and less valuable version has a non-removable visor figure and the picture on the back shows LaForge with his visor on. The only way to tell the difference, without removing the figure and destroying its value, is to look for this picture.

5" Figures, 1992 Series, no trading card or Space Cap

Captain Jean-Luc Picard, with Type I Hand Phaser, Tricorder with Holster, Personal View Screen, Padd and Captain's Log Adventure Booklet (#6011)	$25.00
Lieutenant Commander Data, with Type II Hand Phaser, Diagnostic Testing Unit with Monitor, Tricorder with Holster and Android Access Panels (#6012)	25.00
Lieutenant Worf, with Type II Hand Phaser, Tricorder with Holster, Ceremonial Bat'telh Sword, Klingon Combat Blade and Klingon Sword (#6013)	25.00
Commander William Riker, with Type II Hand Phaser, Tricorder with Holster, Directional U.V. Source and Field Kit with Detachable Analyzer (#6014)	25.00
Lieutenant Commander Geordi LaForge, with Type II Hand Phaser, Tricorder with Holster, Bio Engineering Tools, Dilithium Crystals, Away Team Portable Computer Gear and V.I.S.O.R. (#6015) original version, with removable visor	45.00
Variation without removable visor (#6015)	25.00
Lieutenant Commander Deanna Troi, with Tricorder, Padd, Portable Computer Gear and Desktop Viewer (#6016)	25.00
Romulan with Phaser Rifle, Disruptor Pistol and Romulan Padd (#6051)	35.00
Ferengi with Energy Whip, Hand Blaster, Ferengi Rifle and Dilithium Crystals (#6052)	35.00
Variation with no black on boots (#6052)	50.00
Gowron, the Klingon with Ceremonial War Club, Klingon Disruptor with Holster, Targ and Pain Stick (#6053)	25.00
Variation without gold trim (#6053)	45.00
Borg, Mechanically-enhanced Cybernetic Humanoids with Mechanical Manipulation Arm, Bionic Plasmic Laser and Cutting Ray Arm and Shield Generator Coils (#6055)	25.00
Variation with reversed photo on back of header card	50.00

Vehicle

Shuttlecraft Goddard vehicle, electronic, dual light-up thrusters, two sounds and blueprint, battery powered in 16" x 10" x 6" "Try-me" box (#6101, 1992)	25.00

Playmates second batch of figures appeared in 1993. These figures all came with a special edition SkyBox Trading Card. There were 23 figures in this batch. These figures did not appear at the same time.

K'Ehleyr, Star Trek: The Next Generation (Playmates 1993)

Guinan came out later than most of the other figures in this series, much like Deanna Troi in the first series. Collectors looked high and low for her and mostly found rumors. Once she appeared in quantity this all died down. Female action figures are more popular with collectors than with kids, in part because they are often produced in lower quantity.

Lore was the last figure to appear with a trading card, but enough were produced so that this did not increase his price. Then all of the above 23 figures were reissued in 1994 with Space Caps, under the same product numbers and with only slight packaging changes. Many of these are scarce and more valuable than the original versions.

5" Figures, 1993 Series with 3½" SkyBox trading card
　Reissue Figures (1994) with Space Cap
Dr. Beverly Crusher, with Portable Medical Monitor, Medical Tricorder, Portable Medical Kit and Hypospray (#6019) with trading card 15.00
　Reissue (#6019) with Space Cap #2 . . . . 20.00
Guinan, with Drinking Glasses, Chess Set and Ten-Forward Tray (#6020) with trading card 20.00
　Reissue (#6020) with Space Cap #4 . . . . 30.00
Cadet Wesley Crusher, with Type II Hand Phaser, Portable Tractor Beam, Tricorder with Holster and Starfleet Carrying Case (#6021) with trading card 20.00
　Reissue (#6021) with Space Cap #3 . . . . 25.00
Locutus, Captain Jean-Luc Picard as a Borg, with Borg Cybernetic Hand, Mechanical Cybernetic Borg Manipulator and Shield Generator Coils (#6023) with trading card 25.00
　Reissue (#6023) with Space Cap #1 . . . . 35.00
Klingon Warrior Worf, with Klingon Pain Stick, Klingon Spiked Club, Klingon Disruptor and Ceremonial

Robe (#6024) with trading card 20.00
　Reissue (#6024) with Space Cap #11 . . . . 30.00
Lt. Commander Geordi LaForge, in Dress Uniform, with Type II Hand Phaser, Desktop Viewer, Tricorder and Plaque of Medals (#6026) with trading card 15.00
　Reissue (#6026) with Space Cap #23 . . . . 25.00
Mordock the Benzite, with Type II Hand Phaser, Tricorder with Holster, Scanner and Monitor (#6057) with trading card 20.00
　Reissue (#6057) with Space Cap #6 . . . . 35.00
(Ambassador) K'Ehleyr, with Spiked Glove, Life Support Mask and Ceremonial Klingon Sword (#6059) with trading card 15.00
　Reissue (#6059) with Space Cap #12 . . . . 25.00
Captain Jean-Luc Picard, in First Season Uniform, with Type I Hand Phaser, Tricorder with Holster, Personal View Screen and PADD (#6071) with trading card 15.00
　Reissue (#6071) with Space Cap #16 . . . . 35.00
Lieutenant Commander Data, in First Season Uniform with Type II Hand Phaser, Diagnostic Testing Unit with Monitor, Tricorder with Holster and Android Access Panel (#6072) with trading card 15.00
　Reissue (#6072) with Space Cap #18 . . . . 30.00
Lieutenant (JG) Worf, in First Season Uniform, with Type II Hand Phaser, Tricorder with Holster, Ceremonial Bat'telh Sword, Klingon Combat Blade and Klingon Sword (#6073) with trading card 15.00
　Reissue (#6073) with Space Cap #20 . . . . 30.00
Commander William T. Riker, in Second Season Uniform, with Type II Hand Phaser, Tricorder with Holster, Directional U.V. Source and Field Kit with Detachable Analyzer (#6074) with trading card . 20.00
　Reissue (#6074) with Space Cap #17 . . . . 40.00
Lieutenant (J.G.) Geordi LaForge, in First Season Uniform, with Type II Hand Phaser, Tricorder with Holster, Bio-Engineering Tools, Dilithium Crystals, Away Team Portable Computer Gear and V.I.S.O.R. (#6075) with trading card 15.00
　Reissue (#6075) with Space Cap #19 . . . . 35.00
Counselor Deanna Troi, in Second Season Uniform, with PADD, Portable Computer Gear, Desktop Viewer and Tricorder (#6076) with trading card 15.00
　Reissue (#6076) with Space Cap #21 . . . . 25.00
Borg, with Multi-functional Rotation Arm, Hydraulic Mechanical Ram Arm and Shield Generator Coils (#6077) with trading card 15.00
　Reissue (#6077) with Space Cap #22 . . . . 35.00

1993 Series, Second Batch with 3½" trading card
Ambassador Spock, with Klingon Monitor, Romulan Padd, Romulan Phaser Rifle and Vulcan Book (#6027) with trading card 15.00
　Reissue (#6027) with Space Cap #13 . . . . 15.00
Admiral (Leonard H.) McCoy, with Medical Monitor, Medical Tricorder, Portable Medical Kit and Hyposprayer (#6028) with trading card 10.00
　Reissue (#6028) with Space Cap #14 . . . . 15.00
Captain (Montgomery) Scott, with Dilithium Crystal, Engineering Monitor, Bio-Engineering Tools and Multi-range Light Source (#6029) with trading card 10.00
　Reissue (#6029) with Space Cap #15 . . . . 15.00
Commander Sela, Half-Human/Half Romulan Commander, with Romulan Padd, Romulan Phaser Rifle, Romulan Knife and Romulan Phaser (#6056) with trading card 15.00
　Reissue (#6056) with Space Cap #5 . . . . 20.00

"Q" (Mischievous Omniscient Being), with Miniature *U.S.S. Enterprise*, Miniature Earth, Dilithium Crystal and Sceptre (#6058) with trading card . 15.00
   Reissue (#6058) with Space Cap #9 . . . . 20.00
(Captain) Dathon, A Tamarian Captain, with Dagger, Log Book, Flaming Branch and Tamarian Knife (#6060) with trading card 15.00
   Reissue (#6060) with Space Cap #7 . . . . 75.00
Vorgon, A Mysterious Alien Race From the Future, with Tox Uthat Artifact, Dilithium Crystal, Hex and Vorgon Scanner (#6061) with trading card 15.00
   Reissue (#6061) with Space Cap #8 . . . . 50.00

Lore, Star Trek: The Next Generation (Playmates 1993)

Lore, Data's Evil Twin Brother, with Type II Hand Phaser, Hand-Held Laser, Field Kit and Tricorder (#6022) with trading card 15.00
   Reissue (#6022) with Space Cap #10 . . . . 20.00

Playsets
Star Trek: The Next Generation *Enterprise* **Bridge Playset**, battery powered with technical blueprints in box (#6103, 1993) 75.00
Star Trek: The Next Generation **Transporter** playset, battery powered with technical blueprints in 14" x 11" x 9½" box (#6104, 1993) 40.00
Star Trek Generations **Engineering** playset, battery powered in box (#6108, 1994) 35.00

Playmates' third batch of figures appeared in 1994. These figures all came with a special "SkyCap," which is a card-sized frame with a center punch-out pog. These pogs are numbered and the frame provides a checklist. The figures from 1993 were repackaged with a Space Cap as well. Ones which appeared late in 1993 (such as Lore) are somewhat scarce with their original trading card, but more common with a Space Cap.

The Space Cap frame was revised as the figure assortments changed throughout the year. Originally, only the 23 reissue figures were listed. Most of the later figures have a Space Cap frame that lists 40 figures, but eventually Picard as Dixon Hill was listed for a total of 41 figures. Not all of these figures were actually produced and some others that did appear did not have Space Caps.

The first four figures listed in this series seem to have been overproduced (or underbought) because they were available everywhere with red tags when all other figures from 1994 had long disappeared. You might still be able to find one in some drug store near you.

Captain Picard as a Romulan,
Star Trek: The Next Generation (Playmates 1994)

5" Figures, 1994 Series with Space Cap
Lieutenant Commander Data as a Romulan, with Romulan Rifle, Klingon Monitor, Starfleet Type II Phaser and Romulan Padd (#6031) with Space Cap #25 . . . . 8.00
Captain Picard as a Romulan, with Romulan Bowl, Romulan Disguise Kit, Romulan Phaser and Romulan Padd (#6032) with Space Cap #24 . . . 8.00
LaForge as a Tarchannen III Alien, with Searchlight, Field Kit, UV Source and Medical Monitor (#6033) with Space Cap #27 . . . . 8.00
Commander Riker as a Malcorian, with Malcorian Medical Scanner, Malcorian Syringe, Starfleet Type II Phaser and Malcorian Monitor (#6034) with Space Cap #26 . . . . 8.00
Lieutenant Commander Deana Troi, in 6th Season Uniform with Starfleet Monitor, Portable Computer Gear, Padd and Tricorder (#6035) with Space Cap #30 . . . . 10.00

Lieutenant Worf, in Starfleet Rescue Outfit with Backpack, Klingon Spear and Ring, Explosive Charge and Homing Device (#6036) with Space Cap #28 . . . . 12.00

Hugh Borg, with Mechanical Telescoping Arm, Power Regulator and Scanner Device (#6037) with Space Cap #31 . . . . 15.00

Lieutenant Barclay, with Engineering Tool, Anti-Gravity Pallet, Fencing Foil and Cryo Canister (#6045) with Space Cap #29 . . . . 10.00

There were six 1994 figures which came without trading card or Space Cap. The last three have turned out to be very scarce and quite valuable.

Lieutenant Commander Data, As Seen in "Redemption," Star Trek: The Next Generation (Playmates 1994)

1994 Series, Second Batch without Space Cap or card

Lieutenant Commander Data in Dress Uniform, with Tricorder, Starfleet Monitor, Starfleet PADD and Plaque (#6941) 12.00

Captain Picard in Duty Uniform, with Type II Phaser, Mug, Starfleet Monitor and Tricorder with Holster (#6942) 8.00

Ensign Wesley Crusher, with Engineering Scanner, Monitor, Starfleet PADD and Dilithium Crystal (#6943) 8.00

Gowron in Ritual Klingon Attire with Bat'telh, Klingon Combat Blade, Klingon Combat Sword and Klingon Painstick (#6945) 50.00

Lieutenant Thomas Riker, A Transporter Clone of Commander Riker, with Type II Phaser, Portable Computer Gear, Duffel Bag and Tricorder with Holster (#6946) 250.00

Lieutenant Commander Data, As Seen in "*Redemption*" with Portable Tractor Beam, Tricorder with Holster, Starfleet Science Kit and Hand Laser (#6947) 300.00

Q, Star Trek: The Next Generation (Playmates 1994)

1994 Series, Third Batch with Space Cap

Dr. Noonian Soong, Cyberneticist and Creator of the Android Data, with Human Motion Simulacrum, Sub-Processor Surgical Tool and Crystalline Test Tubes (#6038) with Space Cap #31 . . . . 15.00

Q in Judge's Robe, with Ceremonial Gavel, Lion Statue, Scroll and Scepter (#6042) with Space Cap #31 20.00

Ensign Ro Laren, Former Bajoran Freedom Fighter with Type II Phaser, Tricorder, Starfleet Monitor and Starfleet Duffle Bag (#6044) with Space Cap #36 25.00

Esoqq, a Member of the Chalnoth Race, with Knife, Knife Leg-Sheath, Food Ration and Chalnoth Communicator (#6049) with Space Cap #38 . . . 70.00

Captain Jean-Luc Picard as Dixon Hill, with Pistol, Rotary Telephone and Floor Lamp (#6050) with Space Cap #41 . . . . 15.00

Note: Canadian release figures come on a generic blister card without the figure name. The name appears only on a strip, in blue, on the plastic bubble which covers the figure.

Ambassador Sarek, with Space Cap #35, Canada release 150.00

Lwaxana Troi, with Space Cap #40, Canada release 150.00

Note: Natasha Yar, Dr. Katherine Pulaski and the Nausican were on the Space Cap checklist and were listed on package backs, but they were not issued until later series.

In 1995, Playmates came out with another new group of figures, along with a new package design, and a different style of trading card. Many of the packages have a "7th Season" sticker, but many figures can be found both with and without this sticker. Natasha Yar was included in this batch even though she had been killed, i.e. left the show, after its first season.

Ambassador Sarek,
Star Trek: The Next Generation (Playmates 1995)

Playmates seemed to be searching for a way to organize its figure releases into groups based on particular episodes. It started with Star Trek: The Next Generation packaging, added Episode and Series designations, then changed to generic Star Trek packaging and finally dropped the Episode and Series designations. Since it kept changing its mind, Captain Picard ended up being the only character from the "All Good Things Series." Two other figures from this show were produced later, on different header cards. These changes mean that there is no completely satisfactory way to group these figures.

5" Figures, 1995 Series with 3½" trading card
Lieutenant Commander Geordi LaForge in Movie Uniform with Engineering Tools, Engineering Monitor, Multi-Range Light Source and Isolinear Chips (#6960) 10.00
Dr. Beverly Crusher in Starfleet Duty Uniform, with Medical Tricorder, Medical Kit, Type II Phaser and Starfleet Container (#6961) 10.00
Lieutenant Commander Data, in Movie Uniform with Type II Phaser, Tricorder, Starfleet Monitor and Isolinear Chips (#6962) 10.00
Lieutenant Natasha Yar, Security Chief of the *U.S.S. Enterprise* NCC-1701-D with Type II Phaser, Tricorder, Starfleet Issue Flashlight and PADD (#6965) 10.00
Lwaxana Troi, Ambassadress to Betazed and Mother of Deanna Troi, with Wine Glass, Crystal Gong, Intergalactic Suitcase and Talking Gift Box (#6967) 10.00
Ambassador Sarek, Vulcan Ambassador to United

Federation of Planets with Vulcan Gong, Vulcan Harp, Vulcan Book and IDIC Medallion (#6968)   10.00
The Nausicaan, with Nausicaan Knife, Telescoping Dom-jot Cue, Alien Bottle and Alien Mug ("Tapestry!") (#6969) 10.00
Ensign Ro Laren, reissue (#6981) 10.00
Dr. Noonian Soong, reissue (#6982) 10.00

Jean-Luc Picard, Star Trek: The Next Generation,
"All Good Things" Series (Playmates 1995)

"ALL GOOD THINGS" SERIES

5" Figures (1995) on The Next Generation header card with The Next Generation trading card
Jean-Luc Picard, Retired Starfleet Captain with Gardening Tool, Scanner and Metal Carrying Case (#6974) 18.00
Note: This series was not continued, and other characters from this episode were packaged as part of other series.

HOLODECK SERIES

5" Figures (1995) on The Next Generation header card with The Next Generation trading card
Lieutenant Worf in Ritual Klingon Attire, featuring metallic armor, with Klingon Disruptor, Klingon Painstik and Spiked War Club (#6985) 25.00
Captain Jean-Luc Picard as Locutus, featuring metallic armor, with 2 Electronic Enhancement Hoses and 2 Cybernetic Borg Hands (#6986) 25.00
Lieutenant Commander Data in 1940s' Attire, with Manual Typewriter, Champagne Bottle, Glass and Pistol (#6979) 20.00

Starting in late 1995 and continuing into 1996, most of the Star Trek figures were produced on a generic header card. This header card reflects the fact that figures are being produced from several series, including the classic television series. In many ways, these are the most fun ones, because so many characters from the classic television series have never been seen on a collectible before.

NO SERIES

5" Figures (1995) on generic Star Trek header card with Next Generation trading card

Sheriff Worf in Western Attire, with Six Shooter Pistols, Shot Glass and Alexander in Western Attire mini action figure ("A Fist Full of Datas") (#6434) . . . 12.00

Dr. Beverly Crusher in 1940s' Attire, with Pistol, Handbag, Parasol and Compact ("The Big Goodbye") (#6435) 10.00

Counselor Deanna Troi as Durango in Western Attire, with Sure-Shot Rifle, Shooter Revolver, Ring of Jail Keys and Showdown Time Clock, ("A Fist Full of Datas") (#6438) 15.00

Borg, Star Trek,
Interstellar Action Series (Playmates 1995)

INTERSTELLAR ACTION SERIES

5" Figures (1995) on generic Star Trek header card with no trading card

Borg, with Firing Cybernetic Arm, Laser Scanner and Borg Entity Hoses (#6441) 22.00

Lieutenant (J.G.) Geordi LaForge, with Firing Phaser Rifle and Away Team Gear (#6443) 22.00

The Traveler, Star Trek (Playmates 1995)

THE NEXT GENERATION SERIES

5" Figures (1995–96) on generic Star Trek header card, with 3½" The Next Generation trading card

Dr. Katherine Pulaski, Chief Medical Officer of the *U.S.S. Enterprise* with Medical Scanner, Starfleet Monitor, Medical Tricorder and Medical Case (#6428, Nov. 1995) 12.00

Vash, Mysterious Galactic Archaeologist with Duffle Bag, Statue, Crystal Egg with Protective Encasement and Dagger (#6429) 25.00

Note: The package backs list Vash *as part of the Deep Space Nine series, but her trading card and packaging appear to place her in this series.*

Captain Picard as Galen, an Intergalactic Pirate with Stone of Gol, Alien Desktop Science Monitor, Hand Disruptor and Alien PADD ("The Gambit") (#6432) 8.00

Geordi LaForge, Retired Starfleet Officer and Journalist with Cup of Tea, Handheld Recorder, Starfleet Monitor and Book ("All Good Things") (#6433) . 10.00

The Traveler, The Mysterious Interdimensional Explorer of Mind and Space with Engineering Monitor and Engineering Stool (#6436) 13.00

(Governor) Worf, Governor of H'Atoria, with Bat'Telh, Klingon Knife, Klingon Disruptor and Klingon Monitor (#6437, 1996) 10.00

In 1996, figures continued to be produced on a generic Star Trek header card, but now they had a larger, 4" 30th Anniversary Star Trek trading card. Most of them are listed in the next group, because they were from the Classic Star

Trek series, but Admiral Riker, listed below, belongs with Star Trek: The Next Generation figures.

1996 Series with 4" "30th Anniversary" Star Trek: The Next Generation trading card
Admiral William T. Riker, Commanding Officer of the Futuristic Starship *Enterprise* with Starfleet Type II Phaser, Padd, Desk Top Monitor and Starfleet Tricorder ("All Good Things") (#16034) 8.00

Vina as Orion Animal Woman,
Star Trek, Original Series (Playmates 1996)

ORIGINAL STAR TREK SERIES
Playmates (1996)

Vina is one of four figures from the original pilot episode for "Star Trek." She has disappeared from the toy stores quickly as hot-blooded collectors grabbed her just as quickly as Captain Pike did in the original show.

5" Figures (1996) on generic Star Trek header card, with 4" "30th Anniversary" Star Trek trading card
(Nurse) Christine Chapel, with Medical Tricorder, Anabolic Protoplaser, Hypospray and Medical Scanner (#6447) 8.00
Captain Christopher Pike, with Starfleet Hand Laser, Starfleet Communicator, Warrior's Shield and Rigelian Spear ("The Cage") (#6448, Aug. 1996) 8.00
(Yeoman) Janice Rand, with PADD, Tricorder, Communicator and Phaser (#6449) 8.00
Captain James T. Kirk, wearing Captain's Casual Attire, with Starfleet Tricorder, Starfleet Communicator, Captain's Log and Starfleet Phaser (#16031) . . . 8.00
Mister Spock, with Starfleet Hand Laser, Communicator, Landing Party Case and Desktop Monitor ("The Cage") (#16038) 8.00

The Talosian Keeper, with Nourishment Vial, Talosian Viewscreen and Gas Sprayer ("The Cage") (#16039) 13.00
Vina as Orion Animal Woman, with Torch and Fountain ("The Cage") (#16040) 25.00

LIMITED EDITION FIGURES

In 1996, Playmates issued three limited edition figures. The theory was that kids and collectors would have to buy all the figures in any new batch because one of them might be a limited edition and they wouldn't know right away which one. This drew a firestorm of criticism from collectors because the figures were limited to such a small number and because every one of Playmates' assumptions was wrong. Collectors did know which figures to look for because news travels faster than boxes of toys and because two of the three limited edition figures had a sticker on them identifying them as limited editions. However, the figures never reached the display racks in toy stores because the stock boys bought them first. Collectors couldn't find them and so they had to buy them from the stock boys (who made a killing) or from dealers. They were so scarce that most collectors couldn't afford them, and many were so mad that they couldn't complete their collections that they gave up on the series.

Limited (1,701 of Each Figure) (1996) no trading card
Captain Jean-Luc Picard, with Dom-Jot Rod, Chess Set, Duffel Bag and Drinking Mug, ("Tapestry") (#6442) with limited edition sticker 750.00
Tasha Yar, with Isolinear Optical Chips, Starfleet Type II Phaser, Enterprise-C Phaser and Starfleet Tricorder, ("Yesterday's Enterprise") (#16043) no limited edition sticker 450.00

Limited (3,000 of Each Figure) (1996) no trading card
Lt. Reginald Barclay, with Type II-B Phaser, Medical Tricorder, Desktop Monitor and Personal Access Display Device (PADD) ("Projections") (#16044) with limited edition sticker 200.00

30th Anniversary Convention Special 5" Figures no trading card, limited to 10,000 figures (Spencer Gifts exclusive) (Sept. 1996)
Lt. Commander Montgomery Scott with Classic Starfleet Phaser, Classic Starfleet Communicator and Classic Starfleet Tricorder (#16045) 50.00
Lt. Hikaru Sulu with Classic Starfleet Phaser, Classic Starfleet Communicator and Classic Starfleet Tricorder (#16046) 50.00

CLASSIC STAR TREK
—MOVIE SERIES
Playmates (1995)

Martia is a shape-shifter and can transform herself into any desired shape. Kirk meets her while he is imprisoned during *Star Trek VI*. It was nice of her to stay in this highly desirable shape long enough to pose for her action figure. Khan is the most famous Star Trek villain, returning from an original television series episode to the title role in the second movie. This figure from the Classic Movie Series of action figures captures him in all his wrath!

Commander Spock, Classic Star Trek–
Movie Series (Playmates 1995)

Montgomery Scott, Star Trek: Generations (Playmates 1994)

5" Figures with 4½" trading card

Admiral Kirk (*Star Trek: The Motion Picture*) with Type
II Phaser, Starfleet Wrist Communicator, PADD
and Mini V'GER Spacecraft Component (#6451) $8.00

Commander Spock (*Star Trek: The Motion Picture*) with
Starfleet Tricorder, Engineering Tool, Vulcan
Kolinahr Necklace and V'GER Spacecraft Section
(#6452) no trading card 8.00

Dr. McCoy (*Star Trek: The Motion Picture*) with Starfleet
Medical Tricorder, Starfleet Medical Kit,
Neurological Scanner and V'GER Spacecraft
Section (#6453) 8.00

Lieutenant Sulu (*Star Trek: The Motion Picture*) with
Starfleet Wrist Communicator, Starfleet Tricorder
and V'GER Spacecraft Section (#6454) 8.00

Lieutenant Uhura (*Star Trek: The Motion Picture*) with
Tricorder, Starfleet Wrist Communicator, PADD
and V'GER Spacecraft Section (#6455) 9.00

Khan (*Star Trek II, The Wrath of Khan*) with Starfleet
Phaser, Bowl of Ceti Eels, Genesis Torpedo and
Genesis Control Box (#6456) 10.00

Martia (*Star Trek VI, The Undiscovered Country*) with
Laser Drill, Flare, Drilling Mask and Leg Irons
(#6457) 10.00

General Chang (*Star Trek VI: The Undiscovered
Country*) with Klingon Communicator, Glass of
Romulan Ale, Klingon Disruptor and Klingon Staff
(#6458) 10.00

Commander Kruge (*Star Trek III, The Search for Spock*)
with Klingon Communicator, Klingon Tricorder,
Klingon Disruptor and Klingon Rifle (#6459) . . . 10.00

Lieutenant Saavik (*Star Trek II: The Wrath of Khan*) with
Starfleet Tricorder, Starfleet Phaser, Starfleet
Communicator and Starfleet Duffel Bag (#6460) 12.00

STAR TREK: GENERATIONS
Playmates (1994)

There were 17 figures in this series, including the first
ones of B'Etor and Lursa in Klingon outfits showing a lot of
cleavage. This certainly hasn't detracted from their collectibility. This series includes the first separate action figure of
Chekov available for collectors, although he was included in
the Classic (Bridge) figure set from 1993.

5" Figures

Admiral James T. Kirk, with Classic Phaser, Classic
Communicator and Classic Tricorder (#6911) . $20.00

Montgomery Scott, with Classic Phaser, Classic
Communicator and Classic Tricorder (#6914) . . 35.00

Pavel A. Chekov, with Classic Phaser, Classic
Communicator and Classic Tricorder (#6916) . . 40.00

Captain Jean-Luc Picard, with Type I Phaser, Tricorder,
Starfleet Monitor and Family Album (#6918) . . . 10.00

Lieutenant Commander William Riker, with Type II
Phaser, Isolinear Chips, Starfleet Scanner and
Field Science Kit (#6919) 12.00

Commander Deanna Troi, with Portable Computer Gear,
Tricorder, Starfleet Monitor and PADD (#6920) . 15.00

Lieutenant Commander Data, with Type II Phaser,
Tricorder, Starfleet Monitor and Isolinear Chips
(#6921) 12.00

Lieutenant Commander Worf, with Type II Phaser, UV
Light Source and Tricorder (#6922) 10.00

Lieutenant Commander Geordi LaForge, with
Engineering Tools, Engineering Monitor, Multi-
Range Light Source and Isolinear Chips (#6923) 15.00

Doctor Beverly Crusher, with Medical Tricorder, Medical Kit, Type II Phaser and Medical Monitor (#6924) 18.00

Guinan, with Tray, Glasses and Starfleet Monitor (#6927) 15.00

Dr. Soran, El Aurian Nemesis of Starfleet, with Pocketwatch, Klingon Disruptor, PADD and Multi-Range Light Source (#6925) 13.00

B'Etor, Notorious Klingon Warrior and Youngest Daughter of the House of Duras, with Ceremonial War Club, Klingon Disruptor, Klingon Knife and Klingon Combat Sword (#6928) 18.00

Lursa, Notorious Klingon Warrior and Eldest Daughter of the Huse of Duras with Ceremonial Klingon Sword, Klingon Disruptor, Ceremonial Bat'telh and Isolinear Chip (#6929) 18.00

Captain James T. Kirk in Space Suit, with Champagne Bottle, Engineering Tools, Light and Space Helmet (#6930) 15.00

Lieutenant Commander Worf in 19th-Century Outfit, with Secret Scroll, Swashbuckler's Pike, Hand Shackle and Pirate Sword (#6931) 12.00

Zefram Cochrane, Star Trek: First Contact (Playmates 1996)

STAR TREK: FIRST CONTACT
Playmates (1996)

The movie opened in November 1996 and was generally well received. The figures appeared a month or so before the picture, although the new characters—Zephram Cochrane and Lilly—were in the second batch, which arrived a few weeks after the first eight. Actually Cochrane is not a new character, since he appeared in an episode from the original series, but he is played by a new actor—James Cromwell,

made famous by his role in *Babe*, where he played second banana to a pig.

6" Figures (Oct. 1996) with mini poster

Captain Jean-Luc Picard of the *U.S.S. Enterprise*, with Starfleet Type II Phaser, Compression Phaser Rifle, Borg Scanner, and Personal Access Display Device (PADD) (#16101) $7.00

Commander William T. Riker, First Officer, *U.S.S. Enterprise*, with Starfleet Type II Phaser, Compression Phaser Rifle, Starfleet Tricorder and Sims Beacon (#16102) 7.00

Lt. Cmdr. Geordi LaForge, Chief Engineer, *U.S.S. Enterprise*, with Engineering Case, Engineering Monitor, Engineering Tools and Starfleet Type II Phaser (#16103) 7.00

Lt. Commander Data, Operations Officer, *U.S.S. Enterprise*, with Starfleet Tricorder, Starfleet Type II Phaser, Laser Drill and Test Cylinder (#16104) 7.00

Lt. Commander Worf, Strategic Operations Officer, *Deep Space Nine*, with Starfleet Type II Phaser, Compression Phaser Rifle, D'k tahg and Desktop Monitor (#16105) 7.00

Commander Deanna Troi, Counselor, *U.S.S. Enterprise*, with Away Team Case, Shot Glass, Personal Access Display Device (PADD) and Starfleet Type II Phaser (#16106) 9.00

Dr. Beverly Crusher, Chief Medical Officer, *U.S.S. Enterprise*, with Medical Tricorder, Hyposfor, Biological Scanner and Medical Tool (#16107) .. 8.00

The Borg, Member of the Borg Collective, with Borg Scanner and Surgical Grafting Tool (#16108) ... 8.00

Second Batch (Nov. 1996)

Zefram Cochrane, Inventor of Warp Drive Technology with Engineering Kit, Maintenance Tool, Liquid Refreshment and Flashlight (#16109) 8.00

Lily, Zefram Cochrane's Assistant with Starfleet Type II Phaser, DNA Scanner, Searchlight and Biosample Collector (#16110) 9.00

Picard in Starfleet Space Suit with Starfleet Type II Phaser and Compression Phaser Rifle (#16115) . 9.00

STAR TREK
COLLECTOR SERIES—9" DOLLS
Playmates (1994–96)

Just 20 years after Mego introduced the original 8" Star Trek dolls, Playmates came out with a 9" series which seemed to out-Mego Mego. The initial three figures were called the "Command Edition" and included the captains of the three television shows then in existence. The Kirk doll is the most valuable figure among the 9" Star Trek dolls, all of which have proved highly collectible. Sisko and Picard round out this group and all three come with a trading card as well.

COMMAND EDITION

9" Command Edition Dolls (1994) with base and 3½" trading card

Captain Jean-Luc Picard, with Type I Phaser, PADD and Tricorder (#6066, 1994) $20.00

Commander Benjamin Sisko, with Type II Phaser, PADD and Tricorder (#6067, 1994) 25.00

Captain James T. Kirk, with Classic Type II Phaser,

Classic Communicator and Classic Tricorder
(#6068, 1994) 60.00

STAR TREK: GENERATIONS, MOVIE EDITION

Only four 9" dolls were released in the Generations
series—Kirk, Picard, Data and LaForge. All were regular
characters who had been or would be produced as other
dolls. Collectors would have liked to see the new characters
such as Dr. Soran, B'Etor and Lursa. There were no Space
Caps or trading cards with this series.

9" Movie Edition Dolls (1994) with base, no card or cap
Captain Jean-Luc Picard, with Type II Phaser, Isolinear
     Chips and Family Photo Album (#6141) $20.00
Captain James T. Kirk, with Type II Phaser, Multi-Range
     Light Source and Champagne Bottle (#6142) . . 60.00
Lieutenant Commander Data, with Tricorder, Type II
     Phaser and Ultraviolet Light Source (#6143) . . . 30.00
Lieutenant Commander Geordi LaForge, with
     Engineering Kit, Engineering Tools and Tricorder
     (#6144) 30.00

*Captain James T. Kirk in Dress Uniform, 9" Doll,
Star Trek, Starfleet Edition (Playmates 1995)*

STARFLEET, ALIEN AND FEDERATION EDITIONS

The females in the 9" doll series have turned out to be
very hard to find. Most disappear within a few weeks of their
release, as this one did. The only one that can be found
easily is Guinan, and she came out in 1996.

A total of 15 of the 9" dolls have appeared to date in
the ongoing Starfleet/Federation/Alien series. The Next
Generation crew members have all come out and the original
series crew is now appearing. Worf in his Deep Space Nine
uniform was the first one from this series, and O'Brien
followed just at the end of 1996. No Voyager crew members
have been made into 9" dolls—yet.

9" Starfleet Edition Dolls (1995–96) with base and Space
Cap
Commander Deanna Troi, with PADD, Portable
     Computer Gear and Tricorder (#6281) with Space
     Cap #13 . . . . $45.00
Doctor Beverly Crusher, with Hypospray, Medical Tri-
     corder and Medical Kit (#6282) with Space Cap
     #10 . . . . 50.00
Lieutenant Commander Data with Tricorder, Laser Light
     and Isolinear Chips (#6284) with Space Cap #8   30.00
Commander William Riker, with Phaser Rifle, UV Light
     Source and Type II Phaser Gun (#6285) with
     Space Cap #7 . . . . 30.00
Lieutenant Commander Geordi LaForge, with Tricorder,
     Padd and Multi-Range Light Source (#6287) with
     Space Cap #9 . . . . 30.00
Captain James T. Kirk in Dress Uniform, with Classic
     Phaser, Classic Communicator and Classic
     Tricorder (#6288) with Space Cap #1 . . . . 45.00
Captain Jean-Luc Picard in Dress Uniform, with Phaser,
     Tricorder and PADD (#6289) with Space Cap #6 35.00
Lieutenant Uhura, with Classic Phaser, Classic
     Communicator and Classic Tricorder (#6294, 1996)
     with Space Cap #5 . . . . 40.00

*Commander Deanna Troi, 9" Doll,
Star Trek, Starfleet Edition (Playmates 1995)*

Lieutenant Commander Worf in Deep Space Nine
Uniform, with Bat'telh, Starfleet Phaser Rifle and
Tricorder (#6295, 1996) no Space Cap 25.00

9" Alien Edition Dolls (1995–96) with base
Borg, with Collective Connector Tubes (#6069) with
Space Cap #14 .... 45.00
Lieutenant Worf in Ritual Klingon Attire with Klingon
Disruptor, Klingon Knife and Bat'telh (#6286) with
Space Cap #11 .... 35.00
Romulan Commander, with Romulan Dirsuptor Rifle,
Romulan Disruptor and Romulan Personal Access
and Display Device (PADD) (#16181, 1996) ... 20.00

9" Federation Edition Dolls (1996) with base
Guinan, with Serving Tray and 2 Glasses (#6283) with
Space Cap #12 .... 40.00
Commander Spock, with Vulcan Harp, Classic Phaser
and Classic Tricorder (#6291) with Space Cap
#2 .... 30.00
Lt. Commander Montgomery Scott, with Classic Phaser,
Multi-Range Light Source and Engineering Tool
(#6293) 25.00
Chief Medical Officer Dr. Leonard McCoy, with Classic
Communicator, Medical Tricorder and Test Tubes
(#6292) 25.00
Captain Christopher Pike, with Starfleet Hand Laser,
Starfleet Communicator and Starfleet Tricorder
(#16183) 25.00
Chief Engineer Miles O'Brien, with Type II Phaser, Multi-
Range Light Source and Engineering Tricorder
(#16182 .... 25.00

*Mr. Spock, 9" Doll, "Where No Man Has
Gone Before" Series, Star Trek (Playmates 1996)*

"WHERE NO MAN HAS GONE BEFORE" SERIES

This group of four 9" Classic Star Trek dolls was a
Target Stores exclusive. The dolls came out in September,
but our contact in the Midwest was able to get all four of
them easily in December at a retail price of $20.00, so there
were enough of them produced to go around. Their initial
collector value is largely due to their regional distribution
rather than their inherent scarcity. They will be more
common and less expensive in regions served by Target
Stores.

9" Collector Edition Dolls (Sept. 1996) with base
Captain James T. Kirk, with Starfleet Phaser, Starfleet
Communicator and Starfleet Tricorder (#16096) $35.00
Mr. Spock, with Starfleet Phaser, Starfleet
Communicator and Vulcan Harp (#16097) 35.00
Lt. Commander Montgomery Scott, with Starfleet
Phaser, Multi-Range Light Source and Engineering
Diagnostic Tool (#16098) 35.00
Lieutenant Hikaru Sulu, with Starfleet Phaser, Starfleet
Communicator and Starfleet Tricorder (#16099)   35.00

STAR TREK: FIRST CONTACT, MOVIE FIGURES

Collectors would have preferred a figure of Lilly or the
Borg Queen, the one who tries to seduce Data, instead of a
second Picard figure in this series. At least Playmates made
one new 9" figure. For the previous movie there were only
four figures, all regular cast members.

*Dr. Leonard McCoy, 9" Doll,
Star Trek, Federation Edition (Playmates 1996)*

Captain Jean-Luc Picard in 21st Century Civilian Outfit,
9" Dolls, Star Trek: First Contact (Playmates 1996)

9" Movie Figure Dolls (Nov. 1996) with base and mini poster
Captain Jean-Luc Picard, with Starfleet Compression
    Phaser Rifle, Borg Scanner and Laser Light
    (#16131) $17.50
Cmdr. William T. Riker with Starfleet Type II Phaser,
    Sims Beacon and Starfleet Tricorder (#16132) . 17.50
Lt. Commander Data with Away Team Gear, Starfleet
    Type II Phaser and Personal Access Display
    Device (PADD) (#16133) 17.50
Zefram Cochrane with Engineering Kit, Warp Propulsion
    Diagnostic Tool and Liquid Refreshment
    (#16134) 20.00
Captain Jean-Luc Picard in 21st-Century Civilian Outfit
    with Starfleet Type II Phaser, Starfleet Tricorder
    and Personal Access Display Device (#16135) . 17.50

STAR TREK:
DEEP SPACE NINE
Playmates (1994–96)

    Appropriately, there were nine figures in the first Deep
Space Nine figure series. All the regular cast was included.
Gul Dukat was the only villain in the first Deep Space Nine
figure series. At least he was everybody's favorite villain.
The only other character who wasn't drawn from the regular
cast was the Morn.

5" Figures First Series (1994) with 3½" trading card
Commander Benjamin Sisko, with Type II Hand Phaser,
    Starfleet PADD, Deep Space Nine Monitor and
    Bajoran Orb Case (#6201) $12.00

Odo, Deep Space Nine (Playmates 1994)

(Security Chief) Odo, with Bajoran PADD, Bajoran
    Tricorder, Bucket Sleeping Chamber and Deep
    Space Nine Monitor (#6202) 15.00
Quark, Ferengi Bar and Casino Proprietor of Deep
    Space Nine, with Ferengi Head Cane, Reptilian
    Pet, Gold Press Latinum Bars, Exotic Beverage
    Bottle and Ferengi Hand Blaster (#6203) 20.00
Chief Miles O'Brien, with Type II Hand Phaser,
    Engineering Kit, Laser Drill and Fire Extinguisher
    (#6204) 18.00
Lieutenant Jadzia Dax, with Starfleet Tricorder, Trill, Bio
    Sample Collector, Field Hypospray and Portable
    Computer Gear (#6205) 22.00
Major Kira Nerys, with Bajoran Pistol, Bajoran Tricorder,
    Duffle Bag and Bajoran PADD (#6206) 20.00
Commander Gul Dukat, Former Cardassian Prefect of
    Deep Space Nine, with Cardassian Pistol,
    Cardassian Rifle, Cardassian Field Control Unit
    and Cardassian PADD (#6207) 23.00
Dr. Julian Bashir, with Medical Kit, Medical Tricorder,
    Starfleet PADD, DNA Scanner and Type II Phaser
    (#6208) 30.00
Morn, Frequent Visitor of Deep Space Nine, with Laser
    Pistol, Pyramid Dice, Gold Press Latinum Bars and
    Exotic Beverage Glass (#6210) 20.00

Vehicle
Star Trek Deep Space Nine **Runabout Orinoco**, battery
    powered, holds 2 figures, with blueprint and
    Certificate of Authenticity in 16" x 10½" x 5" "Try-
    me" box (#6252, 1994) 20.00

    The second series of Deep Space Nine figures came
with Space Cap premiums instead of trading cards. This was

the first Star Trek show with regular cast members in their early teens and both Jake Sisko and Rom were made into action figures.

Second Series (1995) with Space Cap
Commander Benjamin Sisko in Starfleet Dress Uniform, with DS9 Monitor, 3-D Chess Set, Salah'na Clock and Starfleet Carrying Case (#6220) with Space Cap #15 .... 10.00
Chief Miles O'Brien in Starfleet Dress Uniform with Type I Phaser, Pattern Enhancer, Cello and Starfleet Carrying Case (#6226) with Space Cap #16 ... 10.00
Jake Sisko, Son of Commander Benjamin Sisko with Book Bag, Baseball Mitt, Jum Jum Stick and DS9 Monitor (#6235) with Space Cap #7 .... 15.00
Vedek Bareil, Bajoran Spiritual Leader, with Orb Case, Snake in Ceremonial Encasement and Candleholder (#6236) with Space Cap #9 .... 25.00
(The) Tosk, Reptilian Alien from the Gamma Quadrant, with Rifle, Collar and Leash, and Mug (#6237) with Space Cap #10 .... 18.00
Rom, Ferengi Brother of Quark, with Nog Mini Action Figure, Lock Pick and Magnesite Drops (#6241) with Space Cap #12 .... 18.00
Note: Two versions: Nog under, or on top of trading card. There is no difference in price.
Lieutenant Jadzia Dax in Starfleet Duty Uniform, with Starfleet Tricorder, Trill, Bio Sample Collector and Field Hypospray (#6242) with Space Cap #4 .. 15.00
Dr. Julian Bashir in Starfleet Duty Uniform, with Medical Kit, Medical Tricorder, PADD, DNA Scanner (#6243) with Space Cap #5 .... 15.00
Chief Miles O'Brien in Starfleet Duty Uniform, with Type II Hand Phaser, Engineering Kit, Laser Drill and

Protable Fire Extinguisher (#6244) with Space Cap #6 .... 15.00
Captain Picard in Deep Space Nine Starfleet Uniform, with Type II Phaser, Tricorder, Directional UV Light Source and Field Kit (#6245) with Space Cap #1 8.00
Lieutenant Thomas Riker in Deep Space Nine Uniform, with Tricorder, Scanner, Type II Phaser and Deep Space Nine Monitor (#6246) with Space Cap #2 18.00
Q in Deep Space Nine Starfleet Uniform, with Orb Case, Type II Phaser, PADD and DS9 Monitor (#6247) with Space Cap #3 .... 15.00
Vash (with Space Cap #7) .... not released, **see TNG**

In 1995 figures from all the television series (except "Voyager") began appearing on generic Star Trek header cards. The only distinction between the three series is in the Space Cap or trading card premium and the listing on the package back.

Third Series (1995–96) on generic Star Trek header card with Deep Space Nine Space Cap
The Hunter of Tosk, Agressive Predator from the Gamma Quadrant with Rifle, Helmet and Scanner (#6439, 1995) with Space Cap #11 .... 15.00
Lieutenant Jadzia Dax from "Blood Oath" in Ritual Klingon Attire with Bat'Telh, D'K Tahg Knife, Cup of Bak'Dule and Starfleet Duffle Bag (#6440, 1995) with Space Cap #17 .... 20.00
Grand Nagus Zek, Ferengi Grand Master of Commerce, with Ferengi Cane, 2 Gold Latinum Pieces and Ferengi Refreshment Bottle (#6444, 1996) with Space Cap #13 .... 10.00
Commander Benjamin Sisko with Klingon Disruptor, Type II Phaser, Alien Knife and Bottle of Liquid

Lieutenant Thomas Riker, Deep Space Nine (Playmates 1995)

Lieutenant Jadzia Dax, Deep Space Nine (Playmates 1996)

Nutriment ("Crossover") (#6445, 1996) with Space
Cap #14 . . . . 8.00
Security Chief Odo from "Necessary Evil" with List of
Bajoran Traitors, Bajoran Padd, Bajoran Tricorder
and Deep Space Nine Monitor (#6446, 1996) with
Space Cap #18 . . . . 10.00

In 1996, playmates switched to 4" trading cards—halfway between the standard 3½" trading card and the 4½" wide-screen movie size. This is the first appearance of these villains on a collectible.

Fourth Series (1996) on generic Star Trek header card, with 4" "30th Anniversary" Deep Space Nine trading card
The Jem'Hadar, Soldiers of the Dominion, with
Jem'Hadar Hand Gun, Jem'Hadar Rifle and
Jem'Hadar Knife (#16032) 12.00
Lt. Commander Worf, Strategic Operations Officer, Deep
Space Nine with Starfleet Type II Phaser, Klingon
Battle Blade, D'K Tahg and Starfleet Duffel Bag
(#16033) 10.00
Elim Garak, with Tailor's Tape Measure, Obsidian Order
Isolinear Rods, Cardassian Padd and Cardassian
Phaser (#16035) 9.00

Neelix the Talaxian, Star Trek Voyager (Playmates 1995)

STAR TREK VOYAGER
Playmates (1995–96)

Figures from the Voyager series began appearing on their own separate style of header card in late 1995. They also have their own series of premium trading cards. The first series of Voyager figures came out in two distinct batches. Kes, Chakotay, Paris and Kim were in the second batch. The header cards don't distinguish between these batches This is the first action figure made from a holograph-

ic projection and the first time such a character has been a featured member of the crew.

The second series of Voyager figures included villains such as the Vidiian, a Kazon and the Cardassian spy/traitor Ensign Seska. Crew members in the second Voyager series included Lt. Carey, Torres as a Klingon and Chakotay in a Maquis outfit.

5" Figures First Series (1995) with 3½" Voyager trading card
Captain Kathryn Janeway, Commanding Officer, *U.S.S.
Voyager* with Type II-B Phaser, Starfleet Tricorder,
Personal Access Display Device and Desktop
Monitor (#6481) $10.00
Lieutenant B'Elanna Torres, Chief Engineer, *U.S.S.
Voyager* with Type II-B Phaser, Engineering Case,
Test Cylinder and Trajector Device (#6485) . . . 15.00
The Doctor, Emergency Medical Hologram with
Hypospray, Personal Access Display Device,
Desktop Monitor and Medical Tool (#6486) 9.00
Lieutenant Tuvok, Tactical/Security Officer, *U.S.S.
Voyager* with Type II-B Phaser, Starfleet Tricorder,
Sims Beacon and Compression Phaser Rifle
(#6487) 6.00
Neelix the Talaxian, Delta Quadrant Guide, *U.S.S.
Voyager* with Starfleet Tricorder, Talaxian Phaser,
Sims Beacon and Cooking Pan (#6489) 9.00

Second Batch (1995) with 3½" Voyager trading card
Commander Chakotay, First Officer, *U.S.S. Voyager* with
Type II-B Phaser, Sims Beacon, Medicine Bundle
and Starfleet Tricorder (#6482) 6.00
Lieutenant Tom Paris, CON Officer, *U.S.S. Voyager* with
Type II-B Phaser, Away Team Gear, Personal
Access Display Device and Compression Phaser
Rifle (#6483) 6.00
Ensign Harry Kim, OPS Officer, *U.S.S. Voyager* with
Starfleet Tricorder, Field Kit, Polaric Generator and
Anti-Polaric Armband (#6484) 6.00
Kes the Ocampa, Medic Intern, *U.S.S. Voyager* with
Medical Tricorder, Personal Access Display
Device, Desktop Monitor and Biological Scanner
(#6488) 12.00

Third Batch (1996) with 3½" Voyager trading card
Ensign Seska, Cardassian Agent with Type II Phaser,
Starfleet Tricorder, Engineering Tools and Trajector
Device (#16460) 7.00
Lt. Carey, Engineer *U.S.S. Voyager* with Type II Phaser,
Personal Access Display Device, Text Cylinder and
Engineering Diagnostic (#16461) 6.00
The Kazon, Delta Quadrant Nomad with Kazon Rifle,
Kazon Canteen and Kazon Hand Gun (#16462) . 9.00
Vidiian, with Vidiian Bioscanner/Phaser, Medical
Tricorder, Hypospray and Medical Tool (#16463) . 9.00
B'Elanna Torres the Klingon, from "Faces" with Vidiian
Bioscanner/Phaser, Bat'leth, D'K Tahg and Klingon
Ceremonial Sword (#16465) 9.00
Chakotay The Maquis, Freedom Fighter Against the
Cardassian Occupation with Type II Phaser,
Tricorder and Medicine Bundle (#16466) 6.00

STAR TREK SPACE TALK
Playmates (1995)

Space Talk figures are larger than the normal Star Trek action figures and say three phrases each. The Borg from this

Commander William Riker,
Star Trek Space Talk Series (Playmates 1994)

series is hard to find, but Picard, Riker and Q are available. There is also a *U.S.S. Enterprise NCC 1701-D* in this series and it says over 100 phrases.

7" Figures
Captain Jean-Luc Picard, with Federation Type I Phaser
    and PADD (#6081) with Adventure booklet . . . $10.00
Commander William Riker, with Federation Type II
    Phaser and Tricorder (#6082) with Adventure
    booklet 10.00
(Hugh) Borg, with Borg Scanner and Borg Connector
    Tubes (#6085) with Adventure booklet 20.00
Q, with Q Continuum Scepter and Ceremonial Graver
    [sic] (#6086) with Adventure booklet 15.00

STARFLEET ACADEMY
Playmates (Sept. 1996)

Starfleet Academy figures came with a CD-Rom adventure, along with the usual equipment. Collectors don't have much use for a CD-Rom, especially when it's inside the plastic bubble on the header card and can't be removed without destroying the mint-in-package value of the figure.

5" Figures with CD-Rom
Cadet Jean-Luc Picard in Standard Issue Flight Training
    Suit with Starfleet Phaser, Subspace Beacon,
    Protective Flight Vest, Eye Visor and Padd
    (#16001) $7.00
Cadet William Riker in Starfleet Geo-Hazard Suit with
    UV Light Source, Starfleet Phaser, Temperature

Regulator, Survival Pack and Eye Visor (#16002) 7.00
Cadet Geordi LaForge in Starfleet Radiation Protection
    Suit, with Isolinear Chips, Carrying Case, Chest
    Protector and Diagnostic Tool (#16004) 7.00
Cadet Worf in Starfleet Night Reconnaissance Suit with
    Starfleet phaser, Survival Knife, Chest Protector,
    Tricorder and Searchlight (#16005) 7.00

MULTI-PACKS
Playmates (1993–94)

These two multi-packs are not really a series, but then they aren't part of any of the other series of figures either. The Classic Figure set included the first Playmates action figures from the original Star Trek series. The set was discounted in early 1996, but all that stock has been sold, so the set is becoming more valuable by the week. The Officers set was a Toys "R" Us exclusive. It was discounted in early 1996 and was quite a bargain at $14.95.

5" Figures in window box
Classic Star Trek Classic Collector Figure Set, 7 original
    crew: Captain James T. Kirk, First Officer Spock,
    Dr. Leonard McCoy, Ensign Pavel Chekov,
    Lieutenant Sulu, Lieutenant Uhura and Lieutenant
    Commander Montgomery Scott, each figure with a
    Classic Communicator, Classic Type II Phaser and
    Classic Starfleet Action Base, on Enterprise Bridge
    playset. Limited edition of 150,000 in 17" x 10½" x
    8½" window box (#6090, 1993) $40.00
Star Fleet Officers Collectors' Set, 6 officers:
    Commander Benjamin Sisko with DS9 Monitor and
    Phaser Rifle; Major Kira Nerys with Bajoran Phaser
    and Bajoran Tricorder; Captain James T. Kirk with
    Classic Phaser and Classic Communicator; Mr.
    Spock with Classic Phaser and Classic
    Communicator; Captain Jean-Luc Picard with
    Tricorder and Type I Phaser; and Commander
    William Riker with Starfleet Monitor and Type II
    Phaser, all on action display stand in window box,
    Toys "R" Us exclusive (Playmates #6190, 1994) 25.00
Classic Star Trek 30th Anniversary Galileo Shuttlecraft
    with Kirk figure (#16087, 1996) 30.00

STAR TREK SPACESHIPS
Playmates (1992–96)

The many Star Trek spaceships are not vehicles or playsets (both of which have been previously listed) since they are not made to the same scale as the action figures. However, they are popular collectibles and are sold in the same line of toys, so we have included a short list.

Spaceships
Star Trek The Next Generation **Starship Enterprise**
    model, 15" with battery powered dual light-up
    engines, 4 authentic starship sounds and blueprint
    (but no stand) in 17" x 12" x 3½" try-me box
    (#6102, 1993) $37.00
    *Note: Box variation: Small parts warning in one line at
    top (earlier) or two lines bottom left (later).*
Star Trek **Space Talk Series** U.S.S. **Enterprise NCC
    1701-D** with over 100 commands and sound
    effects, battery powered with blueprint in 17" x 12"
    x 3½" try-me box (#6106, 1995) 25.00

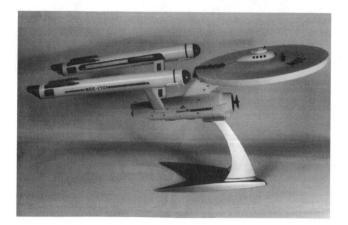

Classic Star Trek U.S.S. Enterprise NCC-1701 (Playmates 1995)

7th Anniversary Special Collector's Edition gold-decorated **U.S.S. Enterprise**, with base and Certificate of Authenticity (50,000 made) (#6112, 1993) 40.00

Classic Star Trek U.S.S. Enterprise NCC-1701, battery powered in 17" x 11¾" x 4" try-me box (#6116, 1995) 35.00

U.S.S. Excelsior NCC-2000, Star Trek The Movie Collection in 17?" x 12?" x 3½?" try-me box (#6127, 1994) 25.00

Star Trek The Next Generation **Klingon Bird-of-Prey**, battery powered with technical blueprint in 17?" x 12?" x 3½?" try-me box (#6128, 1995) 25.00

Star Trek The Next Generation **Romulan Warbird**, battery powered with technical blueprint in 17" x 12" x 3½" try-me box (#6154, 1993) 27.00

Star Trek The Next Generation **Klingon Attack Cruiser**, battery powered with technical blueprint in 17" x 12" x 3½" try-me box (#6155, 1993) 27.00

Star Trek The Next Generation **Borg Ship**, 7½" cube plus display stand, battery powered in 10" x 10" x 7" try-me box (#6158, 1994) 25.00

Star Trek Generations **Starship Enterprise NCC 1701-D** with Blow Apart Battle Damage, mini poster,

Starship U.S.S. Voyager, Star Trek: Voyager (Playmates 1996)

blueprints plus display stand, battery powered in 17" x 11¾" x 3½" box (#6171, 1994) 50.00

Star Trek Generations **Starship Enterprise NCC 1701-B** battery powered in 17?" x 12?" x 3½?" try-me box (#6172, 1994) 50.00

Star Trek Generations **Klingon Bird-of-Prey**, battery powered in 17?" x 12?" x 3½?" try-me box (#6174, 1995) 25.00

Star Trek Deep Space Nine **Space Station DS9**, 13" diameter, including miniature docking Starship Enterprise, battery powered with rotating display stand, technical blueprint and Certificate of Authenticity in 15½" x 13½" x 4" try-me box (#6251, 1994) 27.00

Star Trek Voyager Starship **U.S.S. Voyager NCC-74656**, battery powered with pivoting engine nacelles in 17" x 12" x 3½" try-me box (#6479, 1996) 27.00

Star Trek First Contact **Phoenix Warp Drive Ship** (#16147, 1996) 27.00

Star Trek First Contact **Starship Enterprise NCC 1701-E**, battery powered in try-me box (#16148, 1996) 27.00

Star Trek First Contact **Borg Ship** (#16149, 1996) .. 27.00

U.S.S. Enterprise NCC-1701-D,
Star Trek Space Talk Series (Playmates 1995)

Romulan Warbird
Star Trek: The Next Generation (Playmates 1993)

Princess Leia Organa, Star Wars (Kenner 1978)

STAR WARS
Kenner (1977)

Most *Star Wars* fans and collectors saw this George Lucas film many times and probably have the script committed to memory along with the credits, even though it seems that the movie came out "a long time ago in a galaxy far, far away." In the unlikely event that the force was *not* with you, the film starred Mark Hamill as the young Luke Skywalker, Harrison Ford as the handsome rogue Han Solo, Carrie Fisher as Princess Leia, the brains of the outfit, Alec Guinness as the old coot Ben Kenobi, Anthony Daniels as the prissy C-3PO, and the giant body of David Prowse plus the giant voice of James Earl Jones as the heavy breathing Darth Vader.

Time magazine picked *Star Wars* as the best picture of the year in a two-page feature when it opened in early summer 1977. It played to packed houses for about a year, but it has been off the big screen since 1980. The special edition, with added scenes and improved special effects, opened on January 31, 1997, and the other two films followed a few weeks later.

Star Wars action figures are heavily collected, both on their original header cards and loose. Every tiny variation in the figure or the packaging makes a difference in the price and Star Wars figures have many of both kinds of variations. The chief variation comes about because Kenner continued to produce the original figures for many years, but changed the movie logo to "*The Empire Strikes Back*" and then to

"*Return of the Jedi*" as each of those new movies premiered. After the movies, figures were issued on *Power of the Force* header cards with a collectible coin as a premium.

In addition, most of the figures were available in the United States on foreign "Tri-Logo" header cards which had *Return of the Jedi* movie logos in three languages. There are variations among Tri-Logo header cards as well, but all are lumped together for pricing purposes. This means that there are four or five different packages for most figures, before you even consider the normal variations that occur in any action figure line, such as hair color or other changes to the figure and photo or text changes to the card.

The most significant of the header card changes involves the first group of figures to be produced, which includes all of the major characters. The cards for these figures have a picture and list on the back which shows just the original 12 figures and are called "12 backs." When more figures were produced later, their cards reflected all 20 or 21 then existing figures and the cards for the original 12 got new backs as well, called "20/21 backs." Original figures on 12 back cards are scarce and desirable, so they are worth a lot more money—$75.00 to $100.00 more at current prices.

The most significant of the figure variations was with the Jawa, where the original version had a vinyl cape. This was quickly changed to cloth, which was used for all the rest of the figures. The few vinyl-caped Jawas are the most valuable of all the Star Wars figures and currently sell in the $1,500.00 range, with loose figures going for $250.00 to $300.00. Care in buying is essential, because a loose Jawa in cloth cape is only worth $15.00 and a fake vinyl cape is not hard to make.

All Star Wars action figure prices are volatile and generally increasing. This will almost certainly continue with the forthcoming release of another movie in the series.

Early Bird "Figures" (1977)
Early Bird Package, 19" x 9½" flat envelope with certificate to purchase soon-to-be released figures and scenes to be used with them (#38140) Star Wars logo $300.00
Early Bird figures **R2-D2**, **Luke Skywalker**, **Princess Leia** and **Chewbacca**, in box . . . .

3¾" Figures (1978)
Luke Skywalker (#38180) **blond hair**
   Original *Star Wars* "12 back" header card . . . 300.00
   Reissue on *Star Wars* "20/21 back" header card 200.00
   Reissue on *Empire Strikes Back* header card . 175.00
   Reissue on *Return of the Jedi* header card . . 100.00
   Reissue on Tri-Logo header card 90.00
   Loose, with lightsaber 30.00
Luke Skywalker (#38180) **brown hair**
   Original *Star Wars* "12 back" header card . . . 375.00
   Reissue on *Star Wars* "20/21 back" header card 275.00
   Reissue on *Empire Strikes Back* header card . 180.00
   Reissue on *Return of the Jedi* header card . . 100.00
   Reissue on Tri-Logo header card 150.00
   Loose, with lightsaber 25.00
Princess Leia Organa (#38190) 3½" figure

Original *Star Wars* "12 back" header card ... 300.00
Reissue on *Star Wars* "20/21 back" header
card 245.00
Reissue on *Empire Strikes Back* header card . 275.00
Reissue on *Return of the Jedi* header card .. 350.00
Reissue on Tri-Logo header card 120.00
Loose, with pistol 30.00

Artoo-Detoo (R2-D2), Star Wars (Kenner 1978)

Artoo-Detoo (R2-D2) (#38200) 2¼" figure
Original *Star Wars* "12 back" header card ... 125.00
Reissue on *Star Wars* "20/21 back" header
card 80.00
Reissue on *Empire Strikes Back* header card .. 45.00
Reissue on *Return of the Jedi* header card ... 35.00
Reissue on Tri-Logo header card 35.00
Loose, no accessories 10.00
Chewbacca (#38210) 4¼" figure
Original *Star Wars* "12 back" header card ... 180.00
Reissue on *Star Wars* "20/21 back" header
card 100.00
Reissue on *Empire Strikes Back* header card .. 60.00
Reissue on *Return of the Jedi* header card ... 40.00
Reissue on *Return of the Jedi* header card with
new package, head and shoulders photo 45.00
Reissue on *Power of the Force* header card ... 80.00
Reissue on Tri-Logo header card 35.00
Loose, with rifle 10.00
See-Threepio (C-3PO) (#38220)
Original *Star Wars* "12 back" header card ... 120.00
Reissue on *Star Wars* "20/21 back" header
card 80.00
Reissue on *Empire Strikes Back* header card .. 45.00
Reissue on *Return of the Jedi* header card ... 35.00
Reissue on Tri-Logo header card 45.00
Loose, no accessories 10.00
Darth Vader (#38230) 4¼" figure
Original *Star Wars* "12 back" header card ... 200.00
Reissue on *Star Wars* "20/21 back" header
card 90.00
Reissue on *Empire Strikes Back* header card .. 60.00
Reissue on *Return of the Jedi* header card ... 40.00
Reissue on Tri-Logo header card 30.00
Reissue on *Return of the Jedi* header card, new
package 40.00

Reissue on *Power of the Force* header card ... 80.00
Loose, with lightsaber 10.00
Stormtrooper (#38240)
Original *Star Wars* "12 back" header card ... 200.00
Reissue on *Star Wars* "20/21 back" header
card 130.00
Reissue on *Empire Strikes Back* header card .. 75.00
Reissue on *Return of the Jedi* header card ... 40.00
Reissue on *Power of the Force* header card as
Imperial Stormtrooper 150.00
Reissue on Tri-Logo header card, new package 30.00
Loose with weapon 12.00
Ben (Obi-Wan) Kenobi (#38250) **white hair**
Original *Star Wars* "12 back" header card ... 200.00
Reissue on *Star Wars* "20/21 back" header
card 130.00
Reissue on *Empire Strikes Back* header card .. 75.00
Reissue on *Return of the Jedi* header card ... 40.00
Reissue on Tri-Logo header card 30.00
Reissue on *Power of the Force* header card ... 50.00
Loose, with lightsaber 12.00
Ben (Obi-Wan) Kenobi (#38250) **gray hair**
Original *Star Wars* "12 back" header card ... 200.00
Reissue on *Star Wars* "20/21 back" header
card 130.00
Reissue on *Empire Strikes Back* header card .. 75.00
Reissue on *Return of the Jedi* header card ... 40.00
Reissue on *Return of the Jedi* header card new
package 40.00
Reissue on *Power of the Force* header card .. 100.00
Reissue on Tri-Logo header card 30.00
Loose, with lightsaber 12.00
Han Solo with **small head** (#38260) brown hair
Original *Star Wars* "12 back" header card ... 500.00
Reissue on *Star Wars* "20/21 back" header

Chewbacca, Star Wars (Kenner 1978)

card 400.00
Reissue on *Empire Strikes Back* header card . 275.00
Reissue on *Return of the Jedi* header card .. 150.00
Reissue on *Return of the Jedi* header card, new
package .... no price found
Reissue on Tri-Logo header card 125.00
Loose, with pistol 25.00

Han Solo with **large head** (#38260) dark brown hair
Original *Star Wars* "12 back" header card ... 575.00
Reissue on *Star Wars* "20/21 back" header
card 400.00
Reissue on *Empire Strikes Back* header card . 225.00
Reissue on *Return of the Jedi* header card, new
package 100.00
Reissue on Tri-Logo header card 90.00
Loose, with pistol 25.00

Jawa (#38270) **vinyl cape**, 2¼" figure
Original *Star Wars* "12 back" header card .. 1,500.00
Loose, with weapon 300.00

Jawa (#38270) **cloth cape**
Original *Star Wars* "12 back" header card ... 200.00
Reissue on *Star Wars* "20/21 back" header
card 80.00
Reissue on *Empire Strikes Back* header card .. 50.00
Reissue on *Return of the Jedi* header card ... 35.00
Reissue on *Power of the Force* header card ... 65.00
Reissue on Tri-Logo header card 35.00
Loose, with weapon 13.00

Sand People (#38280)
Original *Star Wars* "12 back" header card ... 225.00
Reissue on *Star Wars* "20/21 back" header
card 150.00
Reissue on *Empire Strikes Back* header card as
Sandpeople (#38280) 90.00

Reissue on *Return of the Jedi* header card as
Tusken Raider (Sand People)" (#38280) ... 60.00
Reissue on Tri-Logo header card 45.00
Loose, with cloak and weapon 15.00

Death Squad Commander (#38290)
Original *Star Wars* "12 back" header card ... 200.00
Reissue on *Star Wars* "20/21 back" header
card 100.00
Reissue on *Empire Strikes Back* header card as
Star Destroyer Commander 85.00
Reissue on *Return of the Jedi* header card ... 65.00
Reissue on Tri-Logo header card 55.00
Loose, with pistol 15.00

Second Release (1978–79)

Greedo (#39020)
Original *Star Wars* header card 140.00
Reissue on *Empire Strikes Back* header card . 115.00
Reissue on *Return of the Jedi* header card ... 65.00
Reissue on Tri-Logo header card 40.00
Loose, with pistol 10.00

Hammerhead (#39030) 4" figure
Original *Star Wars* header card 130.00
Reissue on *Empire Strikes Back* header card .. 90.00
Reissue on *Return of the Jedi* header card ... 60.00
Reissue on Tri-Logo header card 40.00
Loose with pistol 12.50

Snaggletooth (**red**) (#39040) 2¾" figure
Original *Star Wars* header card 120.00
Reissue on *Empire Strikes Back* header card .. 90.00
Reissue on *Return of the Jedi* header card ... 60.00
Reissue on Tri-Logo header card 40.00
Loose, with pistol 10.00

Snaggletooth (**blue**) (Sears Exclusive) 3¾" figure
loose only, from Cantina Adventure Set 125.00

Walrus Man (#39050)
Original *Star Wars* header card 150.00
Reissue on *Empire Strikes Back* header card . 130.00
Reissue on *Return of the Jedi* header card ... 60.00
Reissue on Tri-Logo header card 40.00
Loose, with pistol 12.50

Luke Skywalker X-Wing Pilot (#39060)
Original *Star Wars* header card 150.00
Reissue on *Empire Strikes Back* header card as
Luke Skywalker (X-Wing Pilot) 110.00
Reissue on *Return of the Jedi* header card as
Luke Skywalker (X-Wing Fighter Pilot) 50.00
Reissue on *Power of the Force* header card ... 90.00
Reissue on Tri-Logo header card 40.00
Loose, with pistol 15.00

R5-D4 (#39070) 2½" figure
Original *Star Wars* header card 130.00
Reissue on *Empire Strikes Back* header card .. 90.00
Reissue on *Return of the Jedi* header card ... 60.00
Reissue on Tri-Logo header card 40.00
Loose, no accessories 10.00

Death Star Droid (#39080)
Original *Star Wars* header card 150.00
Reissue on *Empire Strikes Back* header card . 130.00
Reissue on *Return of the Jedi* header card ... 60.00
Reissue on Tri-Logo header card 40.00
Loose, no accessories 10.00

Power Droid (#39090) 2¼" figure
Original *Star Wars* header card 115.00
Reissue on *Empire Strikes Back* header card . 100.00
Reissue on *Return of the Jedi* header card ... 60.00
Reissue on Tri-Logo header card 40.00
Loose, no accessories 10.00

Greedo, *Star Wars (Kenner 1978)*

Boba Fett and ***Darth Vader***, *Star Wars (Kenner 1978–79)*

Boba Fett (#39250)
    Original *Star Wars* header card 550.00
    Reissue on *Empire Strikes Back* header card . 250.00
    Reissue on *Return of the Jedi* header card . . 150.00
    Reissue on *Return of the Jedi* header card new
        package 150.00
    Reissue on Tri-Logo header card 150.00
    Loose, with pistol 30.00
Boba Fett with Rocket Launcher (mail-in offer) unpainted
    blue/gray with red missile, with mailer box and
    letter 200.00

STAR WARS:
THE EMPIRE STRIKES BACK
Kenner (1980–82)

In the second movie of the series we learn the secret of Luke's parentage and meet Yoda, played by a puppet, and Lando Calrissian played by Billy Dee Williams. There are lots of new figures. Luke looses his hand, C-3PO gets chopped into pieces, Han Solo gets to cool off on the way to Jabba's palace and Lando gets his ship and favorite Wookie back. Not to worry, though, because before the movie is over Luke gets a new hand, C-3PO gets put back together and Lando turns out to be a good guy and not a traitor.

Lots of neat figures and vehicles got produced. They are cheap by the standards of the first series, but valuable by any other standard.

3¾" Figures (1980)
Leia Organa (Bespin Gown) (#39720)

Original *Empire Strikes Back* header card, **crew
    neck** version $115.00
Original *Empire Strikes Back* header card, crew
    neck, new package 90.00
Reissue on *Return of the Jedi* header card . . . 60.00
Loose, in cloak with pistol 18.00
Leia Organa (Bespin Gown) (#39720)
    Original *Empire Strikes Back* header card, **turtle
    neck** version 115.00
    Original *Empire Strikes Back* header card, turtle
      neck, new package 90.00
    Reissue on *Return of the Jedi* header card . . . 60.00
    Reissue on Tri-Logo header card . . . . no price found
    Loose, in cloak with pistol 18.00
FX-7 (Medical Droid) (#39730)
    Original *Empire Strikes Back* header card 40.00
    Reissue on *Return of the Jedi* header card . . . 30.00
    Reissue on Tri-Logo header card 30.00
    Loose, no accessories 10.00
Imperial Stormtrooper (Hoth Battle Gear) (#39740)
    Original *Empire Strikes Back* header card 45.00
    Reissue on *Return of the Jedi* header card . . . 35.00
    Reissue on Tri-Logo header card 30.00
    Loose, with rifle 10.00
Rebel Soldier (Hoth Battle Gear) (#39750)
    Original *Empire Strikes Back* header card 35.00
    Reissue on *Return of the Jedi* header card . . . 30.00
    Reissue on Tri-Logo header card 25.00
    Loose, with pistol 10.00
Bossk (Bounty Hunter) (#39760)
    Original *Empire Strikes Back* header card 55.00
    Reissue on *Return of the Jedi* header card . . . 35.00
    Reissue on Tri-Logo header card 50.00
    Loose, with rifle 10.00

IG-88 (Bounty Hunter) *The Empire Strikes Back (Kenner 1980)*

IG-88 (Bounty Hunter) (#39770) 4½" figure
    Original *Empire Strikes Back* header card 65.00
    Reissue on *Return of the Jedi* header card . . . 40.00
    Reissue on Tri-Logo header card 60.00
    Loose, with rifle and pistol 15.00
Luke Skywalker (Bespin Fatigues) (#39780)
    Original *Empire Strikes Back* header card . . . 100.00
    Reissue on *Return of the Jedi* header card, new
      package, yellow hair 120.00
    Reissue on Tri-Logo header card . . . . no price found
    Loose, with pistol and lightsaber 15.00
    Reissue on *Return of the Jedi* header card, new
      package, brown hair 60.00
    Reissue on Tri-Logo header card . . . . no price found
    Loose, with pistol and lightsaber 18.00

Han Solo (Hoth Outfit), The Empire Strikes Back *(Kenner 1980)*

Han Solo (Hoth Outfit) (#39790)
    Original *Empire Strikes Back* header card 45.00
    Reissue on *Return of the Jedi* header card . . . 30.00
    Reissue on Tri-Logo header card 30.00
    Loose, with pistol 15.00
Lando Calrissian (#39800) **no teeth** version
    Original *Empire Strikes Back* header card 40.00
    Loose, with pistol 10.00
    white teeth version
    Original *Empire Strikes Back* header card 50.00
    Reissue on *Return of the Jedi* header card . . . 30.00
    Reissue on Tri-Logo header card 25.00
    Loose, with pistol 15.00
Bespin Security Guard (#39810) white
    Original *Empire Strikes Back* header card 50.00
    Reissue on *Return of the Jedi* header card . . . 30.00
    Reissue on Tri-Logo header card 25.00
    Loose, with pistol 10.00

Second Release (1981)
Yoda (with **orange snake**) (#38310)
    On original *Empire Strikes Back* header card . . 55.00
    Loose, with snake 16.00
Yoda (with **brown snake**)
    Original *Empire Strikes Back* header card . . . 100.00
    Reissue on *Return of the Jedi* header card . . . 60.00
    Reissue on *Return of the Jedi* header card as
      Yoda, The Jedi Master 50.00
    Reissue on *Power of the Force* header card . . 200.00
    Reissue on Tri-Logo header card 30.00
    Loose, with snake 16.00
Ugnaught (#39319)
    Original *Empire Strikes Back* header card 35.00
    Reissue on *Return of the Jedi* header card . . . 25.00
    Reissue on Tri-Logo header card 25.00
    Loose, in blue smock with case 10.00
Dengar (#39329)
    Original *Empire Strikes Back* header card 30.00
    Reissue on *Return of the Jedi* header card . . . 28.00
    Reissue on Tri-Logo header card 25.00
    Loose, with rifle 10.00
Han Solo (Bespin Outfit) (#39339)
    Original *Empire Strikes Back* header card 60.00
    Reissue on *Return of the Jedi* header card . . . 50.00
    Reissue on Tri-Logo header card 30.00
    Loose, with pistol 12.50
Lobot (#39349)
    Original *Empire Strikes Back* header card 30.00
    Reissue on *Return of the Jedi* header card . . . 20.00
    Reissue on Tri-Logo header card 25.00
    Loose, with pistol 8.00
Leia Organa (Hoth Outfit) (#39359)
    On original *Empire Strikes Back* header card . . 40.00
    Reissue on *Return of the Jedi* header card . . . 30.00
    Reissue on *Return of the Jedi* header card, new
      package 30.00
    Reissue on Tri-Logo header card 35.00
    Loose, with pistol 13.00
Rebel Commander (#39369)
    Original *Empire Strikes Back* header card 20.00
    Reissue on *Return of the Jedi* header card . . . 20.00
    Reissue on Tri-Logo header card 25.00
    Loose, with rifle 10.00
AT-AT Driver (#39379)
    Original *Empire Strikes Back* header card 25.00
    Reissue on *Return of the Jedi* header card . . . 20.00
    Reissue on *Power of the Force* header card,
      foreign release only 175.00
    Reissue on Tri-Logo header card 25.00
    Loose, with rifle 10.00
Imperial Commander (#39389)
    Original *Empire Strikes Back* header card 25.00
    Reissue on *Return of the Jedi* header card . . . 20.00
    Reissue on Tri-Logo header card 25.00
    Loose, with pistol 10.00
2-1B (#39399)
    Original *Empire Strikes Back* header card 35.00
    Reissue on *Return of the Jedi* header card as
      Too-Onebee (2-1B) (#71600) 30.00
    Reissue on Tri-Logo header card 45.00
    Loose, with weapon 10.00

Third Release (1982)
Artoo-Detoo (R2-D2) (with Sensorscope) (#69590)
    Original *Empire Strikes Back* header card 25.00
    Reissue on *Return of the Jedi* header card
      (#69420) 23.00

Reissue on Tri-Logo header card 28.00
Loose, with scope 10.00
C-3PO (Removable Limbs) (#69600)
   Original *Empire Strikes Back* header card 30.00
   Reissue on *Return of the Jedi* header card as
     See-Threepio (C-3PO) (#69430) "now with
     removable arms, legs and back pack" 25.00
   Reissue on *Power of the Force* header card as
     See-Threepio (C-3PO) with removable limbs
     (#69430) 25.00
   Reissue on Tri-Logo header card 25.00
   Loose, with back pack and limbs 10.00
Luke Skywalker (Hoth Battle Gear) (#69610)
   Original *Empire Strikes Back* header card 30.00
   Reissue on *Return of the Jedi* header card . . . 30.00
   Reissue on Tri-Logo header card 25.00
   Loose, with rifle 10.00
AT-AT Commander (#69620)
   Original *Empire Strikes Back* header card 25.00
   Reissue on *Return of the Jedi* header card . . . 20.00
   Reissue on Tri-Logo header card 25.00
   Loose, with pistol 10.00
Cloud Car Pilot (Twin Pod) (#69630)
   Original *Empire Strikes Back* header card 35.00
   Reissue on *Return of the Jedi* header card . . . 30.00
   Reissue on Tri-Logo header card 30.00
   Loose, with pistol and light 15.00
Bespin Security Guard (#69640) black
   Original *Empire Strikes Back* header card 40.00
   Reissue on *Return of the Jedi* header card . . . 35.00
   Reissue on Tri-Logo header card 30.00
   Loose, with pistol 10.00
4-LOM (#70010)
   Original *Empire Strikes Back* header card . . . 100.00

Reissue on *Return of the Jedi* header card . . . 20.00
Reissue on Tri-Logo header card 25.00
Loose, with weapon 10.00
Zuckuss (#70020)
   Original *Empire Strikes Back* header card 30.00
   Reissue on *Return of the Jedi* header card . . . 22.00
   Reissue on Tri-Logo header card 20.00
   Loose, with rifle 10.00
Imperial Tie Fighter Pilot (#70030)
   Original *Empire Strikes Back* header card 50.00
   Reissue on *Return of the Jedi* header card . . . 40.00
   Reissue on Tri-Logo header card 35.00
   Loose, with pistol 15.00

Princess Leia Organa (Boushh Disguise),
Return of the Jedi (Kenner 1983)

STAR WARS:
RETURN OF THE JEDI
Kenner (1983)

The third movie in the series had the distinct advantage of being able to tie up all the loose ends and have the Rebels win. Solo is rescued, Jabba gets his just deserts, the new, improved, even bigger Death Star is blown up and the Ewoks steal the show. Everybody went home happy.

Collectors were happy too, with plenty of figures and vehicles to collect. They were even happier a couple of years later when the series had finally run its course with kids and the figures finally became red tag specials. Super Powers figures were red tag specials around the same time. You just couldn't go wrong, no matter what you bought.

Zuckuss, The Empire Strikes Back (Kenner 1982)

3¾ Figures (1983)

Luke Skywalker (Jedi Knight Outfit) with **green lightsaber** (#70650)

Original *Return of the Jedi* header card $60.00
Reissue on *Power of the Force* header card . . 175.00
Reissue on Tri-Logo header card 50.00
Loose, with cloak, pistol and green lightsaber . . 30.00

With **blue lightsaber**, scarce

Original *Return of the Jedi* header card 150.00
Reissue on Tri-Logo header card 80.00
Loose, with cloak, pistol and blue lightsaber . . . 50.00

Princess Leia Organa (Boushh Disguise) (#70660)

Original *Return of the Jedi* header card 40.00
Reissue on Tri-Logo header card 25.00
Loose, with helmet and weapon 15.00

Gamorrean Guard (#70670)

Original *Return of the Jedi* header card 15.00
Reissue on *Power of the Force* header card,
  foreign release only 130.00
Reissue on Tri-Logo header card 18.00
Loose, with axe 10.00

Emperor's Royal Guard (#70680)

Original *Return of the Jedi* header card 25.00
Reissue on Tri-Logo header card 20.00
Loose, with staff 10.00

Chief Chirpa (#70690)

Original *Return of the Jedi* header card 20.00
Reissue on Tri-Logo header card 17.00
Loose, with long club 10.00

Lograv (Ewok Medicine Man)

Original *Return of the Jedi* header card 20.00
Reissue on Tri-Logo header card 15.00
Loose, with mask, staff and pouch 10.00

Klaatu, Return of the Jedi (Kenner 1983)

Weequay

Original *Return of the Jedi* header card 15.00
Reissue on Tri-Logo header card 17.00
Loose, with spear 10.00

Klaatu (#70730) with **tan arms** or **gray arms**

Original *Return of the Jedi* header card 20.00
Reissue on Tri-Logo header card 15.00
Loose, with apron and spear 10.00

Rebel Commando (#70740)

Original *Return of the Jedi* header card 20.00
Reissue on Tri-Logo header card, new package 15.00
Loose, with rifle 10.00

Squid Head (#70770)

Original *Return of the Jedi* header card 20.00
Reissue on Tri-Logo header card 15.00
Loose, with pistol and cloke 10.00

General Madine (#70780)

Original *Return of the Jedi* header card 20.00
Reissue on Tri-Logo header card 15.00
Loose, with staff 10.00

Bib Fortuna (#70790)

Original *Return of the Jedi* header card 20.00
Reissue on Tri-Logo header card 15.00
Loose, with brown cloak and staff 10.00

Ree-Yees (#70800)

Original *Return of the Jedi* header card 20.00
Reissue on Tri-Logo header card 15.00
Loose, with weapon 10.00

Admiral Ackbar (#70310?)

Original *Return of the Jedi* header card 20.00
Reissue on Tri-Logo header card 15.00
Loose, with staff 10.00

Biker Scout (#70820)

Original *Return of the Jedi* header card 25.00

Lograv (Ewok Medicine Man), Return of the Jedi (Kenner 1983)

Reissue on *Power of the Force* header card . . . 50.00
Reissue on Tri-Logo header card 15.00
Loose, with pistol 12.00
Lando Calrissian (Skiff Guard Disguise) (#70830)
    Original *Return of the Jedi* header card 35.00
    Reissue on Tri-Logo header card 20.00
    Loose, with spear 15.00
Nien Nunb (#70840)
    Original *Return of the Jedi* header card 25.00
    Reissue on Tri-Logo header card 20.00
    Loose, with pistol 9.00

Han Solo (in Trench Coat), Return of the Jedi (Kenner 1984)

Second release (1984)
Nikto (#71190)
    Original *Return of the Jedi* header card 16.00
    Reissue on *Power of the Force* header card,
      foreign release only 230.00
    Reissue on Tri-Logo header card 15.00
    Loose, with staff 10.00
8D8 (#71210)
    Original *Return of the Jedi* header card 20.00
    Reissue on Tri-Logo header card 15.00
    Loose, no accessories 10.00
Princess Leia Organa (in Combat Poncho) (#71220)
    Original *Return of the Jedi* header card 40.00
    Reissue on *Power of the Force* header card . . . 90.00
    Reissue on Tri-Logo header card 20.00
    Loose in poncho with pistol 15.00
Wicket W. Warrick (#71230)
    Original *Return of the Jedi* header card 20.00
    Reissue on *Power of the Force* header card . . 130.00
    Reissue on Tri-Logo header card 15.00
    Loose, with spear 12.00

The Emperor (#71240)
    Original *Return of the Jedi* header card 25.00
    Reissue on *Power of the Force* header card . . . 50.00
    Reissue on Tri-Logo header card 15.00
    Loose, with cane 10.00
B-Wing Pilot (#71280)
    Original *Return of the Jedi* header card 15.00
    Reissue on *Power of the Force* header card . . . 20.00
    Reissue on Tri-Logo header card 12.00
    Loose, with pistol 8.00
Klaatu (in Skiff Guard Outfit) (#71290)
    Original *Return of the Jedi* header card 20.00
    Reissue on Tri-Logo header card 15.00
    Loose, with weapon 10.00
Han Solo (in Trench Coat) (#71300)
    Original *Return of the Jedi* header card 45.00
    Reissue on *Power of the Force* header card . . 300.00
    Reissue on Tri-Logo header card 25.00
    Loose, with camo coat and pistol 15.00
Teebo (#71310)
    Original *Return of the Jedi* header card 20.00
    Reissue on *Power of the Force* header card . . 130.00
    Reissue on Tri-Logo header card 16.00
    Loose, with club, mask and pouch 12.00
Prune Face (#71320)
    Original *Return of the Jedi* header card 17.00
    Reissue on Tri-Logo header card 15.00
    Loose, with cloak and rifle 10.00
AT-ST Driver (#71330)
    Original *Return of the Jedi* header card 16.00
    Reissue on *Power of the Force* header card . . . 50.00
    Reissue on Tri-Logo header card 14.00
    Loose, with pistol 10.00
Rancor Keeper (#71350)
    Original *Return of the Jedi* header card 18.00
    Reissue on Tri-Logo header card 15.00
    Loose, with prodd 10.00
Paploo (#93680)
    Original *Return of the Jedi* header card 30.00
    Reissue on *Power of the Force* header card . . . 35.00
    Reissue on Tri-Logo header card 25.00
    Loose, with staff 15.00
Lumat (#93760)
    Original *Return of the Jedi* header card 30.00
    Reissue on *Power of the Force* header card . . . 45.00
    Reissue on Tri-Logo header card 25.00
    Loose, with bow 15.00

Multi-Pack
Sy Snootles and the Rebo Band
    Original *Return of the Jedi* header card 60.00
    Reissue on Tri-Logo header card 50.00
    Loose: Sy Snootles, Droopy McCool or Max
      Rebo, each 15.00

STAR WARS:
THE POWER OF THE FORCE
Kenner (1985)

The Power of the Force figures were produced after all three movies had come and gone. Without a new movie to pump-up sales, less of these figures were ordered and many that were scheduled were never made. As sales slowed, collector interest waned and the figures became red tag specials. When the collectors finally realized that they didn't have these figures, it was too late and so now they are among the most valuable of Star Wars figures. Several were released only overseas.

The 22 figures which were reissued in this series with their original product numbers are listed above. All of them came with coins, too, making a total of 37 figures that came with coins. However, two foreign release figures (AT-AT Driver and Nikto) came with coins from other figures, so only 35 different coins came with these 37 figures. Two other foreign Power of the Force figures (Imperial TIE-Fighter Pilot and FX-7) are claimed to exist in some publications and denied in others.

However, coins were also available as a mail-in premium with a proof of purchase from some prior *The Empire Strikes Back* and *Return of the Jedi* figures and so there are actually 62 coins in the series to collect.

Anakin Skywalker reissue, *Tri-Logo header card (Kenner 1986)*

3¾" Figures (1985) with silver colored aluminum coin
Luke Skywalker (in Battle Poncho) (#93710)
    Original *Power of the Force* header card 75.00
    Reissue on Tri-Logo header card 50.00
    Loose, with poncho and pistol 30.00
Artoo-Detoo (R2-D2) with Pop-up Lightsaber (#93720)
    Original *Power of the Force* header card 150.00
    Reissue on Tri-Logo header card 125.00
    Loose, with lightsaber 75.00
Romba (#93730)
    Original *Power of the Force* header card 40.00
    Reissue on Tri-Logo header card 30.00
    Loose, with spear 20.00
Amanaman (#93740) 5"
    Original *Power of the Force* header card 160.00

    Reissue on Tri-Logo header card 90.00
    Loose, with something 65.00
Barada (#93750)
    Original *Power of the Force* header card 75.00
    Reissue on Tri-Logo header card 50.00
    Loose, with staff 30.00
Imperial Gunner (#93760)
    Original *Power of the Force* header card 120.00
    Reissue on Tri-Logo header card 100.00
    Loose, with pistol 70.00
Han Solo (in Carbonite Chamber) (#93770)
    Original *Power of the Force* header card 200.00
    Reissue on Tri-Logo header card, figure on top 150.00
    Loose, with carbonite sheet 90.00
Luke Skywalker, Imperial Stormtrooper Outfit (#93780)
    Original *Power of the Force* header card 300.00
    Reissue on Tri-Logo header card 180.00
    Loose, with removable helmet and pistol 125.00
Anakin Skywalker (#93790) foreign release
    Original *Power of the Force* header card 600.00
    Reissue on Tri-Logo header card 50.00
    Loose, no accessories 30.00
EV-9D9 (#93800)
    Original *Power of the Force* header card ... $110.00
    Reissue on Tri-Logo header card 80.00
    Loose, no accessories 50.00
Warok (#93810)
    Original *Power of the Force* header card 40.00
    Reissue on Tri-Logo header card 30.00
    Loose, with bow and pouch 20.00
Lando Calrissian (General Pilot) (#93820)
    Original *Power of the Force* header card 90.00
    Reissue on Tri-Logo header card 60.00
    Loose, with cape and pistol 40.00

Yak Face, *Star Wars: The Power of the Force (Kenner 1985)*

A-Wing Pilot (#93830)
    Original *Power of the Force* header card 80.00
    Reissue on *DROIDS* header card 145.00
    Reissue on Tri-Logo header card 55.00
    Loose, with pistol 35.00
Yak Face (#93840) foreign release
    Original *Power of the Force* header card 650.00
    Reissue on Tri-Logo header card 180.00
    Loose, with staff 100.00
Imperial Dignitary (#93850)
    Original *Power of the Force* header card 60.00
    Reissue on Tri-Logo header card 45.00
    Loose, no accessories 20.00

(THE TV ANIMATED SERIES)
DROIDS
"THE ADVENTURES OF R2-D2 and C-3PO"
Kenner (1985)

The real movies were gone from the theaters, but there was still money to be made, so a couple of Ewok movies (*The Ewok Adventure* and *Ewoks: The Battle For Endor*) were produced, along with both an Ewoks and a Droids animated ABC television series. We didn't see any of them when they came out and they put us to sleep when we try to watch them on television. They must do the same to just about everybody, because the figures haven't attained much of a collector following. This may be undeserved, because, judged on their own, the figures are not too bad. So far, anyway, these figures haven't gotten much of a boost in value from the incredible popularity of the Star Wars series and the current re-releases and hype. Maybe they will, or

King Gorneesh, Ewoks (Kenner 1985)

maybe all the money will chase the huge pile of new figures and other collectibles and these will be completely over-looked.

3¾" Figures (1985) with copper or gold colored coin
See-Threepio C-3PO (#71770) $30.00
    Loose 12.00
Artoo-Detoo R2-D2 (#71780) with pop-up lightsaber . 30.00
    Loose 15.00
Thall Joben (#71790) 15.00
    Loose 10.00
Kea Moll (#71800) 15.00
    Loose 10.00
Jord Dusat (#71810) 20.00
    Loose 10.00
Sise Fromm (#71820) 45.00
    Loose 20.00
Tig Fromm (#71830?) 45.00
    Loose 15.00
Jann Tosh (#71840) 15.00
    Loose 10.00
Kez-Iban (#71850) 20.00
    Loose 10.00
Uncle Gundy (#71880) 15.00
    Loose 9.00
Boba Fett (#39260) 125.00
    Loose 25.00
See also A-Wing Pilot, listed previously.

EWOKS
Kenner (1985)

3¾" Figures (1985) with copper or gold colored coin
Dulok Shaman (#71150) $15.00
    Loose 9.00
Dulok Scout (#71160) 15.00
    Loose 9.00
Urgah Lady Gorneesh (#71170) 15.00
    Loose 9.00
King Gorneesh (#71180) 15.00
    Loose 9.00
Wicket W. Warrick (#71250) 20.00
    Loose 10.00
Logray (Ewok medicine man) (#71260) 15.00
    Loose 9.00

TWO PACKS, THREE PACKS
AND SIX PACKS

In addition to all the different versions of the figures previously listed, Kenner also produced various multi-packs from time to time. "Action Figure Sets" of three figures were issued for each of the three movies. They were subtitled "Hero Set," "Villain Set," "Rebel Set," etc. They are quite scarce, and worth about $400.00 to $500.00 each, regardless of movie. Some *Star Wars* sets came with a back-drop scene and they are worth about $100.00 extra.

Two six-pack sets of figures were issued for *The Empire Strikes Back* movie. They are worth about $300.00 today. Last, and least, *Return of the Jedi* two-packs were issued with leftover figures. They are worth the price of the two loose figures contained in the pack (if they have their weapons) and maybe an additional dollar or two for oddity.

IG-88, 15", The Empire Strikes Back (Kenner 1980)

LARGE SIZE ACTION FIGURES
Kenner (1979–80)

Between 1979 and 1980 Kenner produced a dozen "Large Size Action Figures," i.e. dolls in window boxes with a flap. All the figures were made to the same 12" scale, but R2-D2 and the Jawa were small characters and so their dolls are about 8" tall, while Chewbacca, Darth Vader and IG-88 were about 15" tall. These are highly prized collectibles, both in and out of box (loose). The final item listed in this section is the Radio Control R2-D2, which isn't part of the same series, or of any series, but was made to the same scale as the other listed figures.

Large Figures, *Star Wars* logo (1979)
Princess Leia Organa (#38070) 11½" tall $220.00
   Loose, in Alderaanian cape and royal belt with
     comb, brush and booklet 130.00
Luke Skywalker (#38080) 11¾" tall 325.00
   Loose, in Tattooine desert costume with light-
     saber, grappling hook and utility belt 160.00
Chewbacca (#38600) 15" tall 125.00
   Loose, with ammunition belt with removable
     cartridges and crossbow laser rifle 75.00
Darth Vader (#38610) 15" tall 200.00
   Loose, with lightsabre and removable cloth
     cape 85.00
See-Threepio (C-3PO) (#38620) 12" tall 100.00
   Loose, issued without equipment 50.00
Artoo-Detoo (R2-D2) (#38630) 7½" tall 100.00
   Loose, with removable Death Star Plans 50.00

Han Solo (#39170) 11¾" tall 450.00
   Loose, with shirts, pants, vest, boots, laser pistol
     and Rebel Alliance Medal of Honor 180.00
Stormtrooper (#39180) 12" tall 250.00
   Loose, with laser rifle 120.00
Ben (Obi-Wan) Kenobi (#39340) 12" tall 290.00
   Loose, in hooded cloak with lightsaber 145.00
Jawa (#39350) 8" tall 140.00
   Loose, with laser rifle, ammunition belt and
     hooded cloak 75.00
Boba Fett (#39140) 13" tall 350.00
   In *Empire Strikes Back* box 310.00
   Loose, with cape, Wookie scalps, utility belts,
     laser pistol, grappling hook and backpack . . 145.00

Large Figure, *Empire Strikes Back* logo (1980)
IG-88 (Bounty Hunter) (#39960) 15" tall 525.00
   Loose, with rifle, pistol and cartridge belt 250.00

Radio Controlled R2-D2, Star Wars (Kenner 1979)

Radio-Controled Figure, *Star Wars* logo (1979)
Radio Controlled R2-D2, 8" (#38430) 125.00
   Loose 65.00

VEHICLES AND ACCESSORIES

Vehicles are much more important in Star Wars than in most other action figure lines. The 3¾" size of the figures allowed the production of vehicles which were large enough to accommodate several figures, and so the larger vehicles became virtual playsets for the figures.

Vehicles were released over the period of all three movies and many which originally came out in "Star Wars" boxes can be found in boxes from one or both of the later movies. As with the figures, vehicles are listed first in their original box, followed by information and values for later issues.

Star Wars Vehicles, Accessories and Playsets (1978)
Landspeeder, rolls on spring-loaded wheels, holds 2
  figures plus 2 more on rear deck (#38020)
    Original *Star Wars* box $60.00
    Star Wars Collector's Series Land Speeder
     (1983) 35.00
    Loose 20.00
X-Wing Fighter, 14" long, electronic light and sound,
  cockpit canopy opens, wings open and close
  (#38030)
    Original *Star Wars* box 100.00
    Reissue in *Empire Strikes Back* box 150.00
    Loose 40.00
Imperial TIE Fighter, 12" wide, battery light and sound,
  red laser cannon, 2 "solar panels" can be released
  to simulate "battle damage," escape hatch
  (#38040)
    Original *Star Wars* box 110.00
    Reissue in *Empire Strikes Back* box 150.00
    Loose 40.00

Millennium Falcon Spaceship, Star Wars (Kenner 1979)

Star Wars Vehicles, Accessories and Playsets (1979)
Death Star Space Station, 23" high, three-story playset,
  manual elevator, exploding laser cannon, light
  bridge, trash compactor with garbage and Trash
  Monster (#38050)
    Original *Star Wars* box 200.00
    Loose 60.00
Darth Vader TIE Fighter, 11" across, pop-off solar
  panels, battery light and sound in 13" x 11½" x
  6½" box (#39100, 1977)
    Original *Star Wars* box 100.00
    Loose 60.00
    Original *Star Wars* box with Battle Scene
     Setting 500.00
    Loose, with Battle Scene 150.00
    Star Wars Collector's Edition (1983) 60.00
    Loose 40.00
Millenium Falcon Spaceship, 21" long, 18" wide, with
  "Battle Alert Sound" in 22" x 17" x 6" box (#39110)
    Original *Star Wars* box 275.00
    Reissue in *Empire Strikes Back* box 200.00
    Reissue in *Return of the Jedi* box 125.00
    Star Wars Collector Series Millenium Falcon
     (1983) 125.00
    Loose 80.00

Creature Cantina (Cafe) Action Playset, with lever-
  activated functions, no figures in 14" x 8" x 3½"
  box (#39120)
    Original *Star Wars* box 125.00
    Loose 40.00
Land of the Jawas Action Playset (#39130)
    Original *Star Wars* box 125.00
    Reissue in *Empire Strikes Back* box 175.00
    Loose 30.00

Droid Factory, Star Wars (Kenner 1979)

Droid Factory with 31 plastic robot parts, plastic base
  and movable crane, in 13" x 11" x 3" box (#39150)
    Original *Star Wars* box 80.00
    Reissue in *Empire Strikes Back* box 140.00
    Loose 30.00
Patrol Dewback, 10¼" long, with reins and saddle in 11"
  x 6" x 4½" box (#39240)
    Original *Star Wars* box 50.00
    Reissue in *Empire Strikes Back* box 75.00
    Star Wars Collector Series Patrol Dewback
     (1983) 40.00
    Loose 25.00
Radio-Controlled Jawa Sandcrawler, 17" long, in 17½" x
  9" x 7" box (#39270, 1978)
    Original *Star Wars* box 450.00
    Reissue in *Empire Strikes Back* box 525.00
    Loose 175.00
Imperial Troop Transporter, compartments for figures, 6
  different battery operated sounds (#39290, 1979)
    Original *Star Wars* box 85.00
    Reissue in *Empire Strikes Back* box 115.00
    Loose 45.00

Exclusive Figures (1979)
Sonic-Controlled Land Speeder (battery operated,
  mechanical clicker shaped like R2-D2) (J.C.
  Penny) (#38540)
    Original *Star Wars* box 450.00
    Loose 150.00
Cantina Adventure Set (Sears promotional set) 4 figures,
  including: Greedo, Hammerhead, blue
  Snaggletooth and Walrusman (#38861)
    Original *Star Wars* box 500.00
    Loose 150.00

The Empire Strikes Back Vehicles, Accessories and Playsets (1980)
Tauntaun, 8" tall, with saddle and reins in 9" x 7" x 4" box (#39820)
    Original *Empire Strikes Back* box 60.00
    Loose 25.00
Imperial Attack Base, Hoth scene, in 18" x 10¼" x 3¾" box (#39830)
    Original *Empire Strikes Back* box 90.00
    Loose 30.00
Darth Vader's Star Destroyer, 20" long (#39850)
    Original *Empire Strikes Back* box 125.00
    Loose 30.00

Twin-Pod Cloud Car, The Empire Strikes Back (Kenner 1980)

Twin-Pod Cloud Car, 10" wide, orange plastic, in 11" x 9½" x 4" box (#39860)
    Original *Empire Strikes Back* box 70.00
    Reissue in *Empire Strikes Back* box with **Bespin Security Guard** (white) figure 125.00
    Loose, no figure 40.00
Hoth Ice Planet Adventure Set (1980)
    Original *Empire Strikes Back* box 130.00
    Reissue in *Empire Strikes Back* box, with **Imperial Stromtrooper (Hoth Battle Gear)** figure 200.00
    Loose, no figure 50.00

Exclusive Vehicle (1980)
Imperial Cruiser (similar to Imperial Troop Transporter) (#93351)
    Original *Empire Strikes Back* box (Sears exclusive) 150.00
    Loose 40.00

The Empire Strikes Back Vehicles, Accessories and Playsets (1981)
Turret/Probot Playset, with Probot (#38330)
    Original *Empire Strikes Back* box 100.00
    Loose 40.00
AT-AT All-Terrain Armored Transport, 17½" tall, posable legs, movable control center (#38810)
    Original *Empire Strikes Back* box 200.00
    Reissue in *Return of the Jedi* box 150.00
    Loose 80.00

Dagobah Action Playset, lever-operated functions (#38820)
    Original *Empire Strikes Back* box 55.00
    Loose 25.00
Rebel Command Center Adventure Set, including **R2-D2**, **Luke Skywalker** and **AT-AT Commander** figures (#69481)
    Original *Empire Strikes Back* box 250.00
    Loose 120.00

Cloud City Playset, The Empire Strikes Back (Kenner 1981)

Exclusive Playset
Cloud City Playset (Sear's exclusive) including 4 figures: Han Solo in Bespin outfit, Ugnaught, Lobot and Dengar, and Boba Fett (#38781)
    Original *Empire Strikes Back* box 325.00
    Loose 130.00

The Empire Strikes Back Vehicles, Accessories and Playsets (1982)
Rebel Armored Snowspeeder, 12" long, 10¾" wide, battery light and sound (#39610)
    Original *Empire Strikes Back* box 90.00
    Reissue in *Empire Strikes Back* box with **Rebel Soldier (Hoth Battle Gear)** figure 175.00
    Loose 40.00
Slave I, Boba Fett's Spaceship, 12" long, including Simulated Frozen Han Solo (#39690)
    Original *Empire Strikes Back* box 80.00
    Reissue in *Empire Strikes Back* box with Battle Scene Setting 275.00
    Loose 40.00
Hoth Wampa, 6¼" tall, movable arms and legs (#69560)
    Original *Empire Strikes Back* box picturing Rebel Commander 60.00
    Reissue in *Empire Strikes Back* box picturing Luke 35.00
    Reissue in *Return of the Jedi* box 40.00
    Loose 15.00
Rebel Transport, 20" long, including accessories (#69740)
    Original *Empire Strikes Back* box 60.00
    Loose 35.00
"Battle Damaged" X-Wing Fighter, battery powered, "Labels Create Battle-Damaged Look" in 14" x 12½" x 4¼" box (#69780, 1981)

Original *Empire Strikes Back* box 150.00
Reissue in *Return of the Jedi* box 125.00
Loose 35.00
Scout Walker, 10" tall, hand-operated walking
mechanism (#69800)
Original *Empire Strikes Back* box 70.00
Reissue in *Return of the Jedi* box 60.00
Loose 25.00
Tauntaun, with Open Belly Rescue Feature (#93340)
Original *Empire Strikes Back* box 45.00
Loose 30.00

The Empire Strikes Back Accessories (1983)
Imperial TIE Fighter (Battle Damaged, same mold as
original TIE but in blue with "damage" decals)
(#71490)
Original *Empire Strikes Back* box 150.00
Reissue in *Return of the Jedi* box 125.00
Loose 40.00
Vehicle Maintenance Energizer in 6" x 4½" x 3¾" box,
(#93430)
Original *Empire Strikes Back* box 15.00
Reissue in *Return of the Jedi* box 15.00
Loose 9.00
Radar Laser Cannon (#93440)
Original *Empire Strikes Back* box 20.00
Reissue in *Return of the Jedi* box 15.00
Loose 7.50
Tri-Pod Laser Cannon, 4½" x 6" box (#93450)
Original *Empire Strikes Back* box 15.00
Reissue in *Return of the Jedi* box 15.00
Loose 9.00

Return of the Jedi Vehicles and Playsets (1983)
Jabba the Hutt Action Playset, including Jabba figure,
Salacious Crumb molded figure (#70490, 1983)
Original *Return of the Jedi* box 50.00
Reissue in *Return of the Jedi* box (Sears) 40.00
Loose 30.00
Speeder Bike 8" long (#70500)
Original *Return of the Jedi* box 20.00
Reissue in *Power of the Force* box 20.00
Loose 12.00
Y-Wing Fighter with Laser Cannon Sound in 21" x 11½"
x 3¾" box (#70510)

Ewok Village, Return of the Jedi *(Kenner 1983)*

Original *Return of the Jedi* box 90.00
Loose 40.00
Ewok Village Action Playset, 12" high, 2-story playset
(#70520)
Original *Return of the Jedi* box 60.00
Loose 20.00

Exclusives
The Jabba the Hutt Dungeon Action Playset (2 different
variations)
Variation #1, including Klaatu, Nikto and 8D8
action figures, red box, Sear's exclusive
(#71381?, 1983)
Original *Return of the Jedi* box 130.00
Loose 60.00
Variation #2, including EV-9D9, Amanaman, and
Barada figures, green box, Sear's exclusive
(#59262?, 1984)
Original *Return of the Jedi* box 290.00
Loose 160.00

Mini Rig 1-Figure Vehicles, 6" x 4½" boxes (1981-83)
MTV-7 Multi-Terrain Vehicle (#40010, 1981)
Original *Empire Strikes Back* box 25.00
Reissue in *Empire Strikes Back* box with **AT-AT
Driver** figure 60.00
Reissue in *Return of the Jedi* box 18.00
Loose, without figure 9.00
MLC-3 Mobile Laser Cannon, 6" x 4½" x 1" box + flap
(#40020, 1981)
Original *Empire Strikes Back* box 25.00
Reissue in *Empire Strikes Back* box with **Rebel
Commander** figure 60.00
Reissue in *Return of the Jedi* box 15.00
Loose, without figure 9.00
PDT-8 Personnel Deployment Transport (#40070, 1981)
Original *Empire Strikes Back* box 25.00
Reissue in *Empire Strikes Back* box with **2-1B**
figure 60.00
Reissue in *Return of the Jedi* box 15.00
Loose, without figure 9.00
INT-4 Interceptor (#69750, 1982)
Original *Empire Strikes Back* box 25.00
Reissue in *Empire Strikes Back* box with **AT-AT
Commander** figure 60.00
Reissue in *Return of the Jedi* box 15.00
Loose, without figure 9.00
CAP-2 Captivator (#69760, 1982)
Original *Empire Strikes Back* box 20.00
Reissue in *Empire Strikes Back* box with **Bossk**
figure 60.00
Reissue in *Return of the Jedi* box 15.00
Loose 9.00
AST-5 Armored Sentinel Transport (#70880, 1983)
Original *Return of the Jedi* box 15.00
Loose 7.00
ISP-6 (Imperial Shuttle Pod) (#70890, 1983)
Original *Return of the Jedi* box 18.00
Loose 9.00

Return of the Jedi Vehicles and Accessories (1984)
Ewok Assault Catapult, 4½" x 6" box (#71070)
Original *Return of the Jedi* box 12.00
Loose 8.00
B-Wing Fighter, 22" long, battery operated sound
(#71370)
Original *Return of the Jedi* box 75.00
Loose 40.00

Rancor Monster, Return of the Jedi (Kenner 1984)

TIE Interceptor, with Battle Sound and Flashing Laser
   Light, battery powered, 12" wide (#71390)
      Original *Return of the Jedi* box 90.00
      Loose 45.00
Rancor Monster, 10" high
      Original *Return of the Jedi* box 70.00
      Reissue in *Power of the Force* box 60.00
      Loose 30.00
Ewok Combat Glider, 4½" x 6" box (#93510)
      Original *Return of the Jedi* box 12.00
      Loose 8.00
Desert Sail Skiff (#93520) mini rig
      Original *Return of the Jedi* box 18.00
      Loose 10.00
Endor Forest Ranger (#93610) mini rig
      Original *Return of the Jedi* box 18.00
      Loose 9.00
Imperial Shuttle, 18" tall, wings folded, battery sound
   (#93650)
      Original *Return of the Jedi* box 175.00
      Loose 80.00

Power of the Force Vehicles and Playsets (1984–85)
Ewok Battle Wagon, 12" long with Star Wars Planetary
   Map (#93690, 1984)
      Original *Power of the Force* box 90.00
      Loose 35.00
Imperial Sniper Vehicle, 1-figure vehicle with overhead
   wings (Asst. #93920, 1984)
      Original *Power of the Force* box 80.00
      Loose 30.00
Security Scout, camouflage colored, 1-figure vehicle
   (Asst. #93920, 1984)
      Original *Power of the Force* box 80.00
      Loose 30.00
One-Man Sand Skimmer, small 1-figure vehicle (Asst.
   #93920, 1984)
      Original *Power of the Force* box 80.00
      Loose 25.00
Tattoine Skiff, 12" long (#71540, 1985)
      Original *Power of the Force* box 500.00
      Loose 200.00

Ewok Battle Wagon,
Star Wars: The Power of the Force (Kenner 1984)

Ewoks Vehicles, Accessories and Playsets (1984–85)
Ewok Family Hut, 12" high, Hut plus 15 accessories and
   4 non-poseable figures (Kenner Preschool, 1984)
      Original *Ewoks* box 50.00
      Loose 15.00
Ewok Fire Cart, accessories plus 2 non-poseable figures
   (Kenner Preschool, 1984)
      Original *Ewoks* box 40.00
      Loose 15.00
Ewok Woodland Wagon, covered wheel cart, horse and
   accessories (Kenner Preschool, 1985)
      Original *Ewoks* box 75.00
      Loose 20.00

Droids Vehicles, Accessories and Playsets (1985)
A-Wing Fighter, 12" long, battery operated sound, with
   planetary map (#93700)
      Original *Droids* box 200.00
      Loose 120.00
ATL Interceptor Vehicle (#93900)
      Original *Droids* box 30.00
      Loose 15.00
Side Gunner with Star Wars Planetary Map (#94010)
      Original *Droids* box 40.00
      Loose 10.00

Display Stands and Carry Cases
Display Arena, 4 L-shaped plastic stands for figures,
   mail-order item (1981)
      Original *Empire Strikes Back* box 40.00
      Reissue in *Return of the Jedi* box . . .   no price found
      Loose 15.00
Action Display Stand for Star Wars Figures (#38990)
Action Stand (mail-in)
      Original *Star Wars* box 350.00
      Reissue in *Empire Strikes Back* box 350.00
      Loose 40.00
Darth Vader (head) Collector's Case
      Original *Empire Strikes Back* package, no
         figures 35.00

with **IG-88**, **Bossk** and **Boba Fett** figures in original *Empire Strikes Back* package (#39330?) 350.00
    Loose, without figures 15.00
See-Threepio (head) (C-3PO) Collector's Case (#70440, 1983)
    Original *Return of the Jedi* package 25.00
    Loose, without figures 15.00
Chewbacca Bandolier Strap (#70480)
    Original *Return of the Jedi* box 5.00
    Loose, without figures 2.00

Ben (Obi-Wan) Kenobi, Star Wars (New) (Kenner 1995)

STAR WARS (NEW):
THE POWER OF THE FORCE
Kenner (1995–96)

The reintroduction of Star Wars action figures was a resounding success and hooked many collectors who had played with Star Wars figures as kids when they first came out. Collector interest in the original figures—always strong—got even stronger. Princess Leia was the hot early figure. She did not appear on the back of the header cards and many collectors thought she had not been released. Actually, she had been part of the original shipments and the only reason she was scarce was that every collector bought her as soon as she was spotted. Then she was not shipped for a while and prices increased still further. In the fall of 1996 she appeared again, along with Lando Calrissian from the second batch, who had also been scarce, and prices fell. Some collectors must have taken this personally, because we have seen these figures in stores with their header cards broken intentionally. We only hope that these irate collectors

don't turn to gun collecting. Some of those paranoids really take things personally.

In the meantime, collectors were hot on the trail of variations in the other figures and in the packaging. The light sabers were shortened, yielding variations for Darth Vader, Luke Skywalker and Ben (Obi-Wan) Kenobi. The later figure also had a packaging change with his original head photo being replaced by a full-figure photo. If short lightsabers were not enough, some figures were found with short lightsabers in the plastic slots designed for long sabers.

The last two figures, Jedi Knight Luke and Han Solo in Carbonite, shipped with the Shadows of the Empire figures. A wording variation was detected on the back of the Han Solo in Carbonite package, providing some collector interest.

Except for a few popular variations, all of the figures were shipped (and purchased) in enormous quantity, keeping the price for most figures at or near the retail level.

3¾" Figures
Luke Skywalker with "Grappling-Hook Blaster and Lightsaber" (#69571) with long lightsaber $25.00
    Loose, with long lightsaber 12.50
    Short lightsaber version 7.50
    Loose, with short lightsaber 3.00
Darth Vader with "Lightsaber and Removable Cape" (#69572) with long lightsaber 17.50
    Loose, with long lightsaber 10.00
    Short lightsaber in long package slot 12.50
    Short lightsaber version 7.50
    Loose, with short lightsaber 3.00
C-3PO with "Realistic Metalized Body" (#69573) 7.50
    Loose 4.00
R2-D2 with "Light Pipe Eye Port and Retractable Leg" (#69574) 6.00
    Loose 3.00
Stormtrooper with "Blaster Rifle and Heavy Infantry Cannon" (#69575) 10.00
    Loose 5.00
Ben (Obi-Wan) Kenobi with "Lightsaber and Removable Cloak" (#69576) head photo, long lightsaber . . 45.00
    Full-figure photo on package, long lightsaber . . 50.00
    Loose, with long lightsaber 12.50
    Full-figure photo, short lightsaber 7.50
    Loose, with short lightsaber 3.00
Han Solo with "Heavy Assault Rifle and Blaster" (#69577) 7.50
    Loose 3.00
Chewbacca with "Bowcaster and Heavy Blaster Rifle" (#69578) 6.00
    Loose 3.00
Princess Leia Organa with "'Laser' Pistol and Assault Rifle" (#69579) 10.00
    Loose 4.00
Mail-in Han Solo in Stormtrooper disguise, with box . 25.00

Second Batch (March 1996)
Luke Skywalker in X-Wing Fighter Pilot Gear with "Lightsaber and Blaster Pistol" (#69581) with long lightsaber 19.00
    Loose, with long lightsaber 6.00
    Short lightsaber in long package slot 12.50
    Short lightsaber 7.00
    Loose, short lightsaber 3.00

Yoda, Star Wars (New) (Kenner 1996)

Boba Fett with "Sawed-Off Blaster Rifle and Jet Pack"
(#69582) with full circle on hand 7.00
Loose, full circle on hand version 3.00
Half circle on hand version 30.00
Loose, with half circle on hand 10.00
Lando Calrissian with "Heavy Rifle and Blaster Pistol"
(#69583) 7.50
Loose 3.00
TIE Fighter Pilot with "Imperial Blaster Pistol and Rifle"
(#69584) with small-parts warning printed on
sticker 30.00
Warning printed on header card 6.00
Loose 3.00
Yoda with "Jedi Trainer Backpack and Gimer Stick"
(#69586) 7.50
Loose 3.00
Han Solo in Hoth Gear with "Blaster Pistol and Assault
Rifle" (#69587) closed hand 6.00
Loose, with closed hand 3.00
Variation with open hand 18.00
Loose, with open hand 8.00
Luke Skywalker in Dagobah Fatigues with "Lightsaber
and Blaster Pistol" (#69588) with long lightsaber 17.50
Loose, with long lightsaber 6.00
Short lightsaber in long package slot 12.50
Short lightsaber 6.00
Loose, with short lightsaber 3.00

Third Batch (Sept. 1996 with first Shadows of the Empire
figures)
Jedi Knight Luke Skywalker with "Lightsaber and
Removable Cloak" (#69596) with brown tunic . . 35.00
Loose, with brown tunic 12.00
Black tunic 8.00
Loose, with black tunic 3.00

Han Solo in Carbonite with "Carbonite Freezing
Chamber" (#69613) back says "Carbonite freezing
chamber" 9.00
Variation, back says "Carbonite Block" 18.00
Loose 3.00

The Classic Edition 4-Pack caused quite a bit of controversy when it first appeared because the figures were very
close to being identical to the original Luke Skywalker, Han
Solo, Darth Vader and Chewbacca from 1978. These original
loose figures sell for over $25.00 each and there was some
fear that collectors could be duped. Just enough difference
between new and old was discovered so that these fears
proved groundless. Now the four-pack has risen considerably
in value, so it is even less likely that someone will open one
and try to pass off the new figures as the old ones.

Star Wars Power of the Force Classic Edition 4-Pack,
including Luke Skywalker, Han Solo, Darth Vader
and Chewbacca with 4 Topps "Star Wars"
widevision special cards (#69595, 1995) 55.00

Power of the Force Vehicle with Figure
Imperial Speeder Bike with **Biker Scout Stormtrooper**
figure (#69765) 18.00

Power of the Force Vehicles (1995–96)
Electronic Rebel Snowspeeder with Topps "Star Wars"
widevision trading card (#69585) 25.00
Landspeeder (#69770) 10.00
TIE Fighter (#69775) 20.00
Imperial AT-ST (Scout Walker) (#69776) 20.00
Electronic X-Wing Fighter (#69780) 30.00
Electronic Millennium Falcon (#69785) 50.00

Fourth Batch (Dec. 1996)

The fourth batch of Power of the Force figures appeared in December 1996 with the captions "Collection 1" or
"Collection 2" at the top. The two collections appeared at the
same time, and the earliest versions came on a header card
with an orange laser blast, the same color used on the other
"Power of the Force" figures from 1995–96. Later header
cards had a green laser blast on the header card. The new
green cards appeared with some of the first figures to arrive
in the northeast and rumor and collector magazines placed a
high price on the orange cards. A month later, a supply of
the orange-carded figures turned up at another toy store chain
and all the local collectors grabbed some.

The Tatooine Stormtrooper (orange-carded) and the
Sandtrooper (green-carded) are identical—only the name had
been changed to confuse the weary collector. That figure, and
most of the other figures in collections 1 and 2, also had
changes in the name of their weapon. Just as collectors were
digesting these changes, holographic sticker pictures were
added to the cards, making a third or forth version of some
figures. The holographic pictures can be removed, so green
cards without them won't attain a premium price as long as
the original picture is still printed under the sticker. (No, we
didn't remove a sticker on one of our figures to check—we
peeled one back at a local toy store when no one was
looking.) All this was happening at the end of 1996 and early
in 1997 as this book was being completed so we don't know
how it will turn out. More figures are scheduled for 1997.

Jawas, Collection 2, Star Wars (New) (Kenner 1996)

Collection 1 Figures (Asst. #69570, Dec. 1996)
Tatooine Stormtrooper with "Concussion Grenade Cannon" (#69601)
    On original orange laser blast header card 25.00
    Reissue as **Sandtrooper**, with "Heavy Blaster Rifle" (#69601) on green laser blast header card 6.00
    Reissue with holographic picture on green laser blast header card 6.00
Greedo, with "Rodian Blaster Pistol" (#69606)
    On original orange laser blast header card 25.00
    Reissue, now with "Blaster Pistol" on green laser blast header card 6.00
    Reissue with holographic picture on green laser blast header card 6.00
Death Star Gunner with "Radiation Suit and Blaster Pistol" (#69608)
    On original orange laser blast header card 25.00
    Reissue, now with "Imperial Blaster and Assault Rifle" on green laser blast header card 6.00
    Reissue with holographic picture on green laser blast header card 6.00

Collection 2 Figures (Asst. #69605, Dec. 1996)
R5-D4 with "Concealed Photon Missile Launcher" (#69598)
    On original orange laser blast header card, no small parts warning 20.00
    Reissue on orange card, with small parts warning 15.00
    Reissue, now with "Concealed Missile Launcher" on green laser blast header card, with warning 6.00
    Reissue with holographic picture on green laser blast header card, with warning 6.00

Tusken Raider with "Gaderffi Stick Battle Club" (#69603)
    On original orange laser blast header card 20.00
    Reissue, now with "Gaderffii Stick" on green laser blast header card 6.00
    Reissue with holographic picture on green laser blast header card 6.00
Luke Skywalker in "Stormtrooper Disguise with Imperial Issue Blaster" (#69604)
    On original orange laser blast header card 20.00
    Reissue on green laser blast header card 6.00
    Reissue, with holographic picture on green laser blast header card 6.00
Jawas with "Glowing Eyes and Ionization Blasters" (#69607)
    On original orange laser blast header card 20.00
    Reissue, now with "Glowing Eyes and Blaster Pistols" on green laser blast header card 6.00
    Reissue with holographic picture on green laser blast header card 6.00
Momaw Nadon "Hammerhead" with "Double-Barreled Laser Canon" (#69629)
    On original orange laser blast header card 20.00
    Reissue, now with "Double-Barreled Blaster Rifle" on green laser blast header card 6.00
    Reissue, with holographic picture on green laser blast header card 6.00

Dash Rendar, Star Wars: Shadows of the Empire (Kenner 1996)

STAR WARS
SHADOWS OF THE EMPIRE
Kenner (1996)

Shadows of the Empire figures appeared in September 1996 and were very popular. All the collectors bought them and then looked at every minute detail in an effort to spot some valuable variation. Unfortunately, none were found and the figures are all available at retail prices. All come with a holographic or reflective picture on a sticker pasted on the card. They are based on the book series, not any of the movies.

3¾" Figures (Sept. 1996)
Dash Rendar, with "Heavy Weapons Pack" (#69561) $7.00
Chewbacca in Bounty Hunter Disguise, with "Vibro Axe
    and Heavy Blaster Rifle" (#69562) 7.00
Luke Skywalker in Imperial Guard Disguise, with "Taser
    Staff Weapon" (#69566) 7.00
Prince Xizor, with "Energy Blade Shields" (#69594) . . . 7.00
Leia in Boushh Disguise, with "Blaster Rifle and Bounty
    Hunter Helmet" (#69602) 8.00

Two-Packs, with special comic book
Darth Vader vs. Xizor (#69567) 15.00
Boba Fett vs. IG-88 (#69568) 15.00

Shadows of the Empire Vehicles
Boba Fett's Slave I (#69565) 30.00
Dash Rendar's Outrider, with Topps "Star Wars"
    widevision trading card (#69593) 20.00

Vehicle with Figure
Swoop vehicle with **Swoop Trooper** figure (#69591) . 10.00

Deluxe Boba Fett, Star Wars (New), (Kenner 1996)

Deluxe
Deluxe Crowd Control Stormtrooper with "Flight-Action
    Thruster Pack and Capture Claw" (#69609) . . . 12.00
Deluxe Luke Skywalker's Desert Sport Skiff with
    "Blasting Rocket Launcher and Rapid-Deploy
    Wing" (#69611) 12.00

Deluxe Han Solo with Smuggler Flight Pack plus "Battle-
    Pivoting Blaster Cannons and Cargo Claw"
    (#69612) 12.00

Luke Skywalker, 12" doll, Star Wars (New), (Kenner 1996)

STAR WARS:
COLLECTOR SERIES—12" DOLLS
Kenner (1996)

The first dolls to appear had a dark blue inside package card. In December, light blue cards appeared. Obi-Wan Kenobi was scarce and almost impossible to find in stores from the very first. Chewbacca is also pictured on the back of the boxes, but he was not included in the first series of dolls. He is now scheduled for 1997, along with Luke Skywalker in Bespin Fatigues, Lando Calrissian and a Tusken Raider.

12" Dolls (Aug. 1996) in window box with flap cover
Obi-Wan Kenobi (#27719)
    On original dark blue package card $50.00
    Reissue, on light blue package card 35.00
    Loose, with lightsaber 25.00
Luke Skywalker (#27724)
    On original dark blue package card 25.00
    Reissue, on light blue package card 20.00
    Loose, with lightsaber 12.50
Han Solo (#27725)
    On original dark blue package card 25.00
    Reissue, on light blue package card 20.00
    Loose, with pistol and rifle 12.50
Darth Vader (#27726)

On original dark blue package card 25.00
Reissue, on light blue package card 20.00
Loose, with red lightsaber 10.00

STAR WARS
Kenner (1997)

Sixty figures and vehicles are scheduled for release in 1997. Highlights among these are four more 12" figures including Princess Leia, the first figure of Grand Moff Tarkin, large creature figures of Jabba the Hutt, Dewback, Tauntaun and the new Ronto plus the one 3¾" figure every red-blooded collector will want—the Enslaved Princess Leia, brass bikini and all. Don't let this figure corrupt the morals of our children .... Buy five for your collection! It's your patriotic duty.

Steel Monsters (Tonka 1987)

STEEL MONSTERS
"THE ONLY SURVIVORS"
Tonka (1986–87)

Tonka is best known for its metal toy trucks. In the middle 1980s they were trying to broaden their toy line by adding action figures. Usually the action figures are produced first and then a few vehicles are added. Tonka did it the other way. The early Steel Monsters figures came only with the trucks and were not released separately until later. The trucks and figures have a "survivalist" theme which reminds us somewhat of the *Mad Max* movies. For instance, the catalog says that "Viking drives his battle-scarred vehicle on his quest to help others." There was no cartoon series so these figures didn't really make it as collectibles, but Tonka ended up in the action figure business anyway—they merged with Kenner.

4" "Secret Society" Figures
Survivors (Asst. #2608)
Wheel Boss, Leader of the Survivors (1986) $7.00
Half Trak, Survivor (1986) 7.00
Tygress, Survivor (1987) 9.00
Viking, Survivor (1987) 7.00

Marauders (Asst. #2608)
Talon, Leader of the Marauders (1986) 7.00
Metal Face, Marauder Lieutenant (1986) 7.00

Punk, Marauder (1987) 7.00
Retread, Marauder (1987) 7.00

Figures and Vehicles
Steel Monster Enforcer jeep vehicle with **Wheel Boss** figure and comic (#2600, 1986) 20.00
Steel Monsters Blaster pick-up vehicle with **Talon** figure and comic (#2601, 1986) 20.00
Steel Monsters Destroyer vehicle with **Half Trak** figure and comic (#2602, 1986) 20.00
Steel Monsters Bomber, battery powered jeep with **Metal Face** figure (#2604, 1986) 25.00
Steel Monsters Barbarian with **Retread** figure and comic (#2606, 1987) 20.00
Steel Monsters Wrecker with **Viking** figure (#2607, 1987) 20.00
Steel Monsters Masher with **Metal Face** figure 20.00
Steel Monsters Pulverizor with **Tygress** figure 25.00

Steel Monsters Small Vehicles (1986)
Lil' Destroyer 10.00
Top Gunner 10.00
Mud Dog 10.00
Metal Maniac 10.00

Gift Set
Steel Monsters Gift Set of Long-Haul truck, Chop-Top Pickup, Pick-up with trailer and 2 Motorcycles (#1043, 1986) 30.00

***Marina**, Stingray (Matchbox 1992)*

STINGRAY
Matchbox (1992)

"In the year 2065, the World Aquanaut Security Patrol (W.A.S.P.) operates to insure world security. Operating from their Marineville base, the Stingray team under Commander Sam Shore comes under constant attack from the underwater world of Aquaphibians and Titan."

This is a very good line of figures which adapts the Gerry Anderson syndicated television series to G.I. Joe and Star Wars size. Marina and Phones are highly collectible.

3¾" Figures
Commander Sam Shore $10.00
Captain Troy Tempest 10.00
Marina (#SR253) 20.00
Phones 35.00
Titan 10.00

Vehicle
Stingray Craft 75.00

Maxwell the Accelerator, Stone Protectors (Ace Novelty 1993)

STONE PROTECTORS
Ace Novelty (1993)

Ace Novelty Co. was responsible for the Stone Protectors action figures. They are five trolls who were originally an unsuccessful rock and roll singing group called the Rock Defectors. They discovered "five glistening Power Stones" and were transformed into dazzling musicians and crimefighters. Zok and Stink, the Predators, hate loud music and want to put an end to the Stone Protectors. They seem to have been completely successful in this endeavor—the figures, the animated television series on which they appeared, and the company that made them have all disappeared.

Stone Protectors
Chester the Wrestler $5.00
Angus the Soldier 5.00
Clifford the Rock Climber 5.00

Cornelius the Samurai 5.00
Maxwell the Accelerator (#76011) 5.00

Predators
Zok the Evil Leader (#76015) 5.00
Stink the Horrible Hatchetman 5.00

Vehicles
Anti-Aircraft Barbeque 9.00
Hang Glider Bomber 9.00
Mortar-Launching Golf Cart 9.00
Mow 'N' Surf Attack Scooter 9.00

STONY SMITH
Marx (1960s)

This army figure by Marx was another short-lived series in the same format as Mike Hazard and Johnny West (Best of the West).

Figure
Stony Smith figure $300.00

[CAPCOM] STREET FIGHTER
(OFFICIAL MOVIE FIGHTERS)
Hasbro (1993–94)

From the movie starring Jean-Claude Van Damme, Raul Julia and Wes Studi, based on the video game.

4" Figures
Edmond Honda, Sumo Wrestler with "Spring Action
 Head Butt Bash" (#81029) $4.00
Chun Li Xiang with "Spring Action Whirlwind Punch"
 (#81049) 6.00
Blanka, Bio Warrior with "Spring Action Missile Shop" . 4.00
Vega, Spanish Ninja with "Spring Action Flying Fist"
 (#81064) 4.00
Dhalsim, Yoga Fighter with "Shooting Bio Blaster"
 (#81065) 5.00
Balrog, Heavyweight "Mega Cannon Shoots" (#81066) 5.00
Zangief, Russian Wrestler "Terror Cannon Shoots"
 (#81067) 5.00
Sonic Boom Guile with "Spring Action Sonic Boom
 Punch" (#81073) 5.00
Ken Masters, Shotokan Karate Fighter, with "Spring
 Action Fireball Fists" (#81074) 4.00
General M. Bison, Evil Grand Master, with "Spring
 Action Terror Twister" (#81075) 2 versions
 Version with black cape 4.00
 Version with red cape 5.00
Viktor Sagat, Evil Warlord Gangster with "Spring Action
 Thai Chop" (#81129) 5.00
Arctic Assault Guile (#81242, 1993) 5.00
Arctic Assault Guile with "Arctic Bazooka Blaster Shoots"
 (#81242, 1994) 5.00
Rock Trooper Guile (#81243, 1993) 5.00
Rock Trooper Guile with "Artillery Cannon Shoots"
 (#81243, 1994) 5.00
Nightfighter Guile (#81244, 1993) 5.00
Nightfighter Guile with "Bow and Arrow Shoots" (#81244,
 1994) 5.00
Navy S.E.A.L. Guile (#81246, 1993) 5.00
Navy S.E.A.L. Guile with "Squirting Water Blaster"
 (#81246, 1994) 5.00

Chun Li Xiang, Street Fighter (Hasbro 1993)

Paratrooper Guile (#81247, 1993) 5.00
Paratrooper Guile with "Parachute Really Works"
(#81247, 1994) 5.00

Large Figure
Colonel Guile 12" figure 20.00

Two-Pack
Colonel Guile vs. General M. Bison (#06157) 10.00

Vehicles and Playsets
Street Striker, Official Movie Vehicle with "Striker Missile
Launcher Shoots" (#84001) 12.00
Devastator, Official Movie Fighter with **Viktor Sagat**
figure (#84002) 15.00
Heli-Fighter, The World Warior with **Colonel Guile**
figure 15.00
Karate Chopper, Official Movie Vehicle (#6164) 10.00
Shadowloo Headquarters, Official Movie Fortress with
General M. Bison figure 35.00

STREET FIGHTER II
SEE: G.I. JOE

STREET SHARKS
Mattel (1994–96)

Street Sharks are a fun concept for a toy, but action
figure collectors have shown little interest in this series so
far. The figures come in open hanging boxes.

First Series (1994) with cage
Jab with "Jackhammer Head Butt" (#12253) $13.00
Ripster with "Power Punching Action" (#12254) 13.00
Blades with "Extending Claws and Fin Line Skates"
(#12255) 13.00
Big Slammu with "Super Slam Fist" (#12256) 13.00
Slobster with "Seize & Slice Claw" (#12257) 13.00
Slash with "Chilling Drilling Action" (#12258) 13.00
Dr. Piranoid with "Spring-Fired Speargun" (#12259) . 13.00

Second Series (1995)
Ravenous Ripster "Chews Guns Into Scrap" (#13437) 10.00
Rox with "Rock & Roll Moves and Heavy Metal Gear"
(#13438) 10.00
Streex with "Real Fighting Action and Battle Gear"
(#13439) 10.00
Moby Lick with "Tongue Twisting, Water Blasting Action"
(#13440) 10.00
Tentakill (#13441?) 10.00
Killamari with "Dart-Spitting, Tentacle Gripping Action"
(#13442 . . . . 10.00

Third Series (1995)
Slugger Slammu with "Knock-Out Punching Action"
(#14037) 10.00
Jet Pack Jab with "Flip-Up Wing Action" (#14038) . . . 10.00
Power Bite Piranoid with "Biting Mask and Blasting Gun"
(#14039) 10.00
Radical Bends with "Ripcord Propeller Pack" (#14040) 10.00
Evil Repteel "Fires Fanged Serpent Missiles" (#14041) 10.00

Fourth Series (1996)
Pool Shark Ripster "Cue Stick Really Shoots" (#15034)10.00
Moto Streex with "'All Terrain' Moto Action" (#15035) 10.00
Mantaman 10.00
Turbo Jab "Turns Into Racing Car" (#15038) 10.00
Super Slammu "Fires Super Shield" (#15039) 10.00

Vehicles
Sharkruiser 4X4 (#12330) 18.00
Rip Rider Motorcycle (#13448) 13.00
Slobster-Zooki Motorcycle (#13449) 13.00
Sharkforce Jet (#15028) 13.00
Sharkforce Tank (#15029) 13.00

SUN-MAN
Olmec (1989)

Scarce, black and Hispanic-oriented figures which have
not attracted much collector interest. There are 10 different
ones in all.

SUPERHUMAN SAMURAI
SYBER-SQUAD
Playmates (1994–95)

Another entry in the suddenly crowded Robot/Trans-
former/Power Ranger market is the Superhuman Samurai
Syber-Squad from the syndicated, live-action television series
starring Matthew Lawrence as video game whiz Sam.
According to the package, "Sam, rock 'n roller and computer
genius in the real world, crashes the portal into the digital
world and Samurizes into ... Superhuman Samurai Servo!"
He picks up some other teen heros—Amp, Syd and Tank-

er—and battles the evil "Kilokhan and his electro havoc-wreaking Megavirus Monsters." Instead, how about a show where some old, retired monsters get back their super powers .and save the world from electro havoc-wreaking teen-agers! If any of you turn this idea into a real show we want royalties.

The monsters look like a cross between dinosaurs and various Godzilla characters. We liked Kilokhan, the evil overlord of the Megavirus Monsters who comes in a jet black robe and a purple helmet and sholder pads. We always look for the villains because usually a lot more of the good guys are produced. In addition, most of the groups of heroes are the same, except for colors, while each of the monsters is unique.

5¼" Servo and the Syber-Squad Figures (1994)
Servo (#1701) $5.00
Zenon (#1702) 5.00
Superhuman Samurai Synchro (#1703) 5.00
Drago (#1704) 5.00
Superhuman Samurai Phormo (#1705) 5.00
Tanker in Samurizing Battle Unform (#1720) 8.00
Amp in Samurizing Battle Uniform (#1721) 8.00
Digital Night Servo (#1722) 8.00
Eletro Grid Servo (#1723) 8.00
Neutron Armor Servo (#1724) 8.00
Syd in Samurizing Battle Uniform (#1725) 10.00

5¼" Kilokhan Megavirus Monsters (1994)
Kilokhan (#1706) 5.00
Sybo (#1708) 5.00
Troid (#1710) 5.00
Hock (#1711) 5.00
Skorn (#1715) 5.00

5¼" Special Mission Series Figures (1994)
Special Mission Drago (#1907) 5.00
Special Mission Synchro (#1908) 5.00
Special Mission Zenon (#1906) 5.00
Special Mission Phormo (#1909) 5.00

5¼" Basic All-Tech Adventure Figures (1995)
Circuit Safari Servo in Compu Jungle Camouflage
    (#1901) 5.00
Polarized Servo in Data Freeze Camouflage (#1902) . 5.00
Hot Wire Servo in Electro Desert Camouflage (#1903) 5.00
Current Wave Servo in Hydro-Surge Camouflage
    (#1904) 5.00
Anti-Gravity Tanker in Syber Space Camouflage
    (#1905) 5.00

5¼ Circuit Protector Series (1995)
Circuit Protector Servo in Re-digitized Battle Uniform
    (#1916) 5.00
Circuit Protector Tanker in Re-digitized Battle Uniform
    (#1917) 5.00
Circuit Protector Syd in Re-digitized Battle Uniform
    (#1918) 5.00
Circuit Protector Lucky in Re-digitized Battle Uniform
    (#1919) 5.00

5¼" Digital Crasher Series (1995) with removable helmets
Digital Crasher Servo (#1911) 5.00
Digital Crasher Tanker (#1912) 5.00
Digital Crasher Syd (#1913) 5.00
Digital Crasher Amp (#1914) 5.00

7½" Superhuman Samurai Phormo Samurizing Sets (1994–95)
Superhuman Samurai Phormo Amp Samurizing Set, with Jamb, Torb and exclusive 5½" Syber-Squad figure (Asst. #1791) 15.00
Superhuman Samurai Phormo Polarized Servo Samurizing Set, with Jamb, Torb and exclusive 5½" Syber-Squad figure (Asst. #1791) 15.00
Superhuman Samurai Phormo Digital Night Servo Samurizing Set, with Jamb, Torb and exclusive 5½" Syber-Squad figure (Asst. #1791) 15.00

7½" Superhuman Samurai Synchro Samurizing Sets (1994–95)
Superhuman Samurai Synchro Tanker Samurizing Set, with Borr, Tracto, Vitor and exclusive 5½" Syber-Squad figure (Asst. #1792) 15.00
Superhuman Samurai Synchro Electro Grid Servo Samurizing Set, with Borr, Tracto, Vitor and exclusive 5½" Syber-Squad figure (Asst. #1792) 15.00
Superhuman Samurai Synchro Neutron Armor Servo Samurizing Set, with Borr, Tracto, Vitor and exclusive 5½" Syber-Squad figure (Asst. #1792) 15.00
Superhuman Samurai Synchro Amp Samurizing Set, with Borr, Tracto, Vitor and exclusive 5½" Syber-Squad figure (Asst. #1792) 15.00

9" Metal Samurai Figures (1994–95)
Ion Array Servo (#1751) 12.00
Data Matrix Servo (#1752) 12.00
Supercharged Syd (#1753) 12.00
Supercharged Tanker (#1754) 12.00
Supercharged Amp (#1755) 12.00

Deluxe Figures (1994)
Servo 9" (#1794) 10.00
Zenon 10½" includes 3 vehicles: Borr, Tracto and Vitor
    (#1795) 20.00
Drago 9½" (#1796) 25.00

9" Deluxe All-Tech Adventure Figures (1995)
Circuit Safari Servo in Compu Jungle Camouflage
    (#1757) 10.00
Polarized Servo in Data Freeze Camouflage (#1758) 10.00
Hot Wire Servo in Electro Desert Camouflage (#1759) 10.00
Current Wave Servo in Hydro-Surge Camouflage
    (#1768) 10.00
Anti-Gravity Tanker in Syber Space Camouflage
    (#1769) 10.00

3" Miniature figures (1995)
Servo (#1731) 4.00
Servo in Syber-Action Pose (#1732) 4.00
Zenon (#1733) 4.00
Superhuman Samurai Synchro (#1734) 4.00
Drago (#1735) 4.00
Superhuman Samurai Phormo (#1736) 4.00
Sybo (#1737) 4.00
Hock (#1739) 4.00
Manfu (#1740) 4.00
Plexton (#1741) 4.00
Gramm (#1742) 4.00
Skorn (#1743) 4.00

Superboy, *Superman* and *Steel*, *Superman: Man of Steel (Kenner 1995)*

SUPERMAN: MAN OF STEEL
Kenner (1995)

The amazing thing is that there never was a Superman action figure line prior to 1995. Superman and various villains have appeared as part of other series, but never, until now, did they have a scrics of their own. Unfortunately, the figures don't fly, have actual X-ray vision or other super powers, so they have accessories—just like Batman.

Lex Luthor from the second batch of figures proved very hard to find. This made the lucky collectors who found one quite happy, because they feared that he might become common like the Batman villains Bane, Pogo Stick Joker and Rā's Al Ghūl which came out at about the same time. Some of the figures listed in catalogs and on package backs do not seem to have been made. They are listed as "not seen" in the list.

5" Figures with Joe Jusko trading card
Power Flight Superman with "Take-off Force Arm Action"
 (#62901) $7.00
Laser Superman with "Super-charged 'Laser' Cannon"
 (#62902) 7.00
Superboy with "Mammoth Capture Claw and Taser
 Missiles" (#62903) 7.00
Steel (a.k.a. John Henry Irons) with "Pounding Hammer
 Blows" (#62904) 7.00
Conduit with "Spinning Kryptonite Attack Cables"
 (#62906) 7.00

Vehicles
Superboy "VOTL" Cycle (#62921) 10.00
Matrix Conversion Coupe with exclusive **Clark Kent**
 figure (#62923) 25.00

Two-Packs (Jan. 1996)
Hunter-Prey Superman vs. Doomsday with comic book
 (#62911, 1995 i.e. 1996) 12.50
Massacre vs. Full Assault Superman with comic book
 (62912, 1995 i.e. 1996) 12.50

Second Batch (April 1996) with Joe Jusko trading card
Solar Suit Superman with "Space Probe Launcher
 Backpack" (#62907) 7.00
Ultra Shield Superman with "Kryptonite Shield Armor
 and Blasting Rocket" (#62908) 7.00
Street Guardian Superman with "Swinging Battle Chain
 and Armor Shield" (#62917) 7.00
Lex Luthor with "Squirting Hornet Attack Jetpack"
 (#62918) 20.00
Street Guardian Superboy with "Karate Kicking Action"
 (#62924) 7.00

Deluxe Figures with trading card
Deluxe Ultra Heat Vision Superman with "Electronic
 Light, Electronic Sound, and 'Metallic' Chest Plate"
 (#62926) 10.00
Deluxe Blast Hammer Steel with "'Full Metallic' Lock,
 Firing Hammer, & 'Rivit' Ratchet Sounds"
 (#62927) 10.00

Two-Packs (Oct. 1996)
Cyber-Link Superman and Cyber-Link Batman (#62953,
 1996) with 2 cards, WalMart exclusive 15.00
Cyber-Link Superman and Cyber-Link Batman (#62953,
 1996) with comic, Toys "R" Us exclusive 15.00

Large Figure
Ultimate Superman, 10" in open box (#62940, 1996) . 20.00

Quick Change Superman,
Superman: From the Animated Show (Kenner 1996)

SUPERMAN: FROM THE ANIMATED SHOW
Kenner (1996)

This is basically a continuation of the previous series. Brainiac and Lex Luthor from this series were scarce as of the end of 1996 and had already attained a collector price which was significantly above retail. Since the series is still being shipped, it's impossible to say if this will change with future deliveries.

5" Figures (Oct. 1996)
Capture Net Superman with "S-Shield Snare Shooter"
    (#62928) $7.00
Deep Dive Superman with "Underwater Rocket Blaster"
    (#62929) 7.00
Quick Change Superman with "Instant Reveal Action"
    (#62931) 7.00
Neutron Star Superman with "Galactic Armor and
    Rockets" (#62932) 7.00
Evil Alien Brainiac with "Blasting Space Sled" (#62934) 12.00
Lex Luthor with "Kryptonite Armor and Launcher"
    (#62937) 12.00

Deluxe Figure
Deluxe Vision Blast Superman with Light-Up S-Shield,
    Power Glow Eyes and Power Disc Launcher
    (#62952) 9.00

Vehicles and Playset
Superman Conversion Coupe 15.00
Metropolis Playset (#62941) 10.00

SUPERMAN MOVIE
SEE: WORLD'S GREATEST SUPER HEROES

SUPER MARIO BROS.
Ertl (1993)

From the live-action movie starring Bob Hoskins and John Lequizamo as the plumbers who save the world from Dennis Hopper and friends. Based on the popular Nintendo video game.

5" Figures
Mario with "Action Plunger Lunger & Tool Belt"
    (#7789) $5.00
Luigi with "Action Wrench Shipper & Tool Belt" (#7790) 5.00
The Subterranian Koofa with "Action Devo Gun"
    (#7791) 5.00
The Lethal Goomba with "Action Flame Thrower &
    Removable Coat" (#7792) 5.00
The Cowardly Iggy with "Action Flame Thrower"
    (#7793) 5.00
The Cowardly Spike with "Action Devo Gun" (#7794) . 5.00

Playset
Devo Chamber with **Goomba** figure 15.00

SUPER NATURALS
Tonka (1987)

Described in Tonka's catalog as Ghost Warriors with double-channel holograms. The head and body holograms

Snakebite, Super Naturals (Tonka 1987)

change between images as the viewing angle changes. An interesting idea, but collectors have shown little interest in the series.

6" Figures "Release Their Hologram Powers" (Asst. #6580)
LionHeart, Heroic Leader $8.00
Eagle Eye, Heroic Warrior 8.00
Thunder Bolt, Heroic Warrior 8.00
BurnHeart, Evil Warrior 8.00
Snakebite, Evil Warrior 8.00
Skull, Evil Leader 8.00

3" Ghostlings, warriors with holograms (#6570)
Spooks, Heroic Ghostling 5.00
Hooter, Heroic Ghostling 5.00
Mr. Lucky, Heroic Ghostling 5.00
See-Thru, Heroic Ghostling 5.00
Vamp-Pa, Evil Ghostling 5.00
Scary Cat, Evil Ghostling 5.00
Rags, Evil Ghostling 5.00
Weird Wolf, Evil Ghostling 5.00

Vehicles and Playset
Dark Dragon Evil Battle Beast (#6585) 20.00
Lionwings Heroic Battle Creature (#6585) 12.00
Ghost Finder Heroic Vehicle (#6590) 20.00
Bat Bopper Evil Ghost Riders vehicle . . . . not seen
Super Naturals Tomb of Doom Ghostworld playset
　(#6591) 20.00

[DC] SUPER POWERS COLLECTION
Kenner (1984–86)

This is one of the classic super hero action figure lines. It incorporated unique action features into each figure, great graphics and lots of your favorite DC characters. Most of these figures have not reappeared in the 1990s, at least not yet. There were many other Super Powers products in addition to action figures, but the action figures are the key to them all. They were based on the mid 1980s cartoon series and, of course, on DC comics. The only criticism from collectors was "Why did they stop?"

Action features are commonplace now, but they were an innovation in 1984. Each figure had a different power, which was activated by squeezing the legs together. These features were incorporated into the graphics, which were different for each character. Several of the 1986 figures received only limited distribution and have correspondingly high prices. Some of the figures were also issued on narrow header cards and many of the figures were sold overseas on header cards as well. Only the El Acertijo (Riddler) figure was sold overseas, but not in the United States.

5" Figures, (1984) with mini comics
Superman with "Power Action Punch" and mini comic #1
　(#99610) 38.00
Batman with "Power Action Bat Punch" and mini comic
　(#99620) 57.00
Robin with "Power Action Karate Chop" and mini comic
　#9 (#99630) 40.00
Green Lantern with "Power Action Ring Thrust" and mini
　comic (#99640) 62.00
Aquaman with "Power Action Deep Sea Kick" and mini
　comic #8 (#99650) $37.00

Hawkman, Super Powers Collection (Kenner 1984)

Flash with "Power Action Lightning Legs" and mini comic
　#4 (#99660) 18.00
Lex Luthor with "Power Action Nuclear Punch" and mini
　comic #10 (#99670) 13.00
The Joker with "Power Action Madcap Mallet" and mini
　comic #7 (#99680) 30.00
The Penguin, 4", with "Power Action Umbrella Arm" and
　mini comic (#99690) 38.00
Braniac with "Power Action Computer Kick" and mini
　comic #5 (#99700) 30.00
Hawkman with "Power Action Flight Wings" and mini
　comic #13 (#99710) 58.00
Wonder Woman with "Power Action Deflector Bracelets"
　and mini comic #3 (#99720) 25.00
Steppenwolf mail-in (1984) 15.00

Second Series (1985) with mini comic
Parademon with "Power Action Battle Flight" and mini
　comic (#99870) 30.00
Mantis with "Power Action Pincer Thrust" and mini comic
　(#99880) 30.00
Desaad with "Power Action Shock Squeeze" and mini
　comic (#99890) 22.00
Dr. Fate with "Power Action Mystic Spell Cast" and mini
　comic (#99900 . . . . 68.00
Martian Manhunter with "Power Action Martian Punch"
　and mini comic #14 (#99910) 37.00
Green Arrow with "Power Action Archery Pull" mini
　comic (#99920) 42.00
Firestorm with "Power Action Atomic Punch" and mini
　comic #16 (#99930) 32.00
Red Tornado with "Power Action Tornado Twist" and
　mini comic (#99940) 70.00
Kalibak with "Power Action Beta-Club Swing" and mini
　comic #10 (#99950) 18.00

Darkseid 5¾" with "Power Action Raging Motion and Power Action Omega Effect Eyes" and mini comic #19 (#99960) 28.00
Steppenwolf with "Power Action Electro-Axe Chop" and mini comic (#99970) 60.00

Third Series (1986)
Orion with "Power Action Astro-Punch and Changing Face" (#67130) 45.00
Shazam with "Power Action Thunder Punch" (#67140) 40.00
Cyborg with "Power Action Thrusting Arms" (#67150) 280.00
Cyclotron with "Power Action Cyclo-Spin" (#67160) .. 60.00
Plastic Man with "Power Action Stretching Neck" (#67170) 110.00
Mister Miracle with "Power Action Wrist Lock Escape" (#67180) 150.00
Tyr with "Power Action Rocket Launch" (#67190) ... 52.00
Mr. Freeze with "Power Action Cold-Blast Punch" (#67200) 40.00
Samurai with "Power Action Gale-Force Spin" (#67220) 85.00
Golden Pharoah with "Power Action Soaring Wings" (#67230) 130.00
Clark Kent (mail-in offer or free with Superman figure from Sears) 60.00

Figures on small header card
Batman 30.00
Firestorm 20.00
Green Lantern 30.00
Martian Manhunter 22.00
Red Tornado 40.00
Robin 20.00
Superman 20.00
Wonder Woman 12.00

Note: Super Powers figures on Canadian header cards are worth 25 percent less than on American header cards.

Super Amigos Foreign Figure
El Acertijo (Riddler) 60.00
Note: Other Super Amigos figures are the same as their American counterpart and are worth about 10% less.

Vehicles
Kalibak Boulder Bomber, "The Cruel Crusher's Massive Machine" (#67020) 20.00
Darkseid Destroyer, "Flying Flagship of the Ultimate Evil" (#67040) 25.00
Batcopter, "Batman's Air-Pursuit Chopper" (#67270, 1986) 80.00
Justice Jogger, "Overland Villain Chaser," wind-up (#67280, 1986) 25.00
Lex-Soar 7, "Lex Luthor Assault Ship" (#99730, 1984) 15.00
Supermobile, "Shields Superman From Kryptonite" (#99760, 1984) 25.00
Batmobile, "The 'Caped Crusader's' Action Vehicle" (#99780, 1984) 90.00
Hall of Justice plastic playset, 34" x 10½" (#99830, 1984) 100.00
Delta Probe One, "Battling Spaceship of the Super Powers Heroes," 8" (#99850) 20.00

SUPER STARS
Ertl (1981)

In addition to the movie and television "stars" listed, this series included two stock car racing stars as well. Colt was Lee Majors and Bandit was Burt Reynolds, but they aren't identified by name on the header cards, only by picture. I guess Stallone wasn't as big a star, because he had to sign his name.

2½" Die-Cast Metal Moveable Figures
Sylvester Stallone as seen in *Rocky III* (#236) $25.00
Colt as seen on "The Fall Guy" (#237) 20.00
Bandit as seen in *Smokey and the Bandit* (#239) ... 25.00

S.W.A.T.
LJN (1976)

Another set of figures where LJN tried the Mego approach to a cop-based ABC television series. S.W.A.T., which stands for Special Weapons and Tactics, was criticized

Hall of Justice, Super Powers Collection (Kenner 1984)

for its violence. It featured Steve Forrest as Hondo, Rod Perry as Deacon, Robert Urich as Street Mark Shera as Luca and James Coleman as McCabe.

8" Figures
Deacon	$35.00
Hondo	35.00
Luca (#6850)	35.00
McCabe	35.00
Street	35.00

Two-Pack
Boxed set of Hondo and Street	50.00

Vehicles and Accessories
S.W.A.T. Van	60.00
S.W.A.T. Pack (accessories)	15.00
S.W.A.T. Action Set playset	90.00

SWAMP THING
Kenner (1990–91)

More from the FOX network animated television show than the USA network live-action series or the DC comic book series and not at all from the 1982 Wes Craven –directed movie starring Louis Jourdan and Adrienne Barbeau. Mr. Main likes them anyway and claims to have a complete collection. Big deal—he got them as red tag specials in 1992 and you can still get almost all of them for less than 10 bucks each.

4½" Swamp Thing Figures
Camouflage Swamp Thing with "Vine Snare" (#41430)	$9.00
Variation with paint on arm (#41430)	18.00
Snap Up Swamp Thing with "Log Bazooka" (#41470)	9.00
Snare Arm Swamp Thing with "Vine Winch Arm & Monster Trap" (#41480)	9.00
Bio-Glow Swamp Thing (#41490)	9.00
Capture Swamp Thing with "Organic Net and Cypress Club" (#41680, 1991)	7.00
Climbing Swamp Thing with "Bayou Staff & Shield of Reeds" (#41690, 1991)	7.00

Evil Un-Men Villains
Dr. Deemo with "Serpent BioMask" (#41310)	9.00
Weed Killer with "Bogsucker BioMask" (#41320)	9.00
Skinman with "Fangbat BioMask" (#41330)	9.00
Anton Arcane with "Spidery BioMask" (#41340)	9.00

Heroes
Bayou Jack with "Swamp Water Blaster" (#41440)	9.00
Tomahawk with "Swift Shot Crossbow" (#41450)	12.00

Vehicles and Playsets
Bog Rover vehicle (#41350)	10.00
Marsh Buggy vehicle (#41370)	10.00
Bayou Blaster (#41390)	10.00
Transducer playset (#41400)	25.00
Swamp Trap playset (#41410)	15.00

Swamp Thing (Kenner 1990)

SWANS CROSSING
Playmates (1991–92)

Only a few series designed for girls have enough of the characteristics of action figures to qualify as such. One such series was Swan's Crossing, based on the syndicated television series that was a soap-opera for teenage girls. According to the Playmates catalog, the series consists of the figures listed below. We didn't check the entire rack of the figures carefully when they first appeared, but we did see figures from each of the four series, so the whole line was produced. However, we did not see any of the male figures, so they are probably scarce (which would normally be the case with girl's action figures).

Sometimes a figure or a series can generate interest in two groups of collectors, such as 1996's Barbie and Ken in Star Trek outfits. However, sometimes the figure or series just falls between the cracks and no one is interested. This was the case with the Wonder Woman series of action figures, which was heavily promoted at Toy Fair in 1994, but was never made. The market value of Swans Crossing figures is limited because most action figure collectors have too many things to collect already and are not interested in a girls' series, and most doll collectors have too many dolls to collect and are not interested in an action figure series.

Girls 5" Figures (1991)

Rock Concert Mila (#5801, 1991)	$7.00
Rock Concert Glory (#5802, 1991)	7.00
Rock Concert Sandy (#5803, 1991)	7.00
Rock Concert Owen (#5804, 1991)	7.00
Rock Concert Jimmy (#5805, 1991)	7.00
Slumber Party Sydney (#5821, 1991)	7.00
Slumber Party Mila (#5822, 1991)	7.00
Slumber Party Glory (#5823, 1991)	7.00
Slumber Party Callie (#5824, 1991)	7.00
Hangin' Out Sydney (#5841, 1991)	7.00
Hangin' Out Mila (#5842, 1991)	7.00
Hangin' Out Glory (#5843, 1991)	7.00
Hangin' Out Callie (#5844, 1991)	7.00
Hangin' Out Garrett (#5845, 1991)	7.00
Dance Party Mila (#5851, 1991)	7.00
Dance Party Sydney (#5852, 1991)	7.00
Dance Party Glory (#5853, 1991)	7.00
Dance Party Garrett (#5854, 1991)	7.00

Vehicles and Playsets

Callie's Motor Bike (#5861, 1992)	10.00
Mayor Rutledge's Mercedes Car (#5862, 1992)	15.00
Swan's Crossing Rock Concert playset (#5863, 1992)	25.00
Mila's Slumber Party playset (#5864, 1992)	25.00

Dr. Viper, Swat Kats (Remco 1994)

SWAT KATS
Remco (1994–95)

From the animated television show by Hanna-Barbera, which takes place in Mega City. The heroes have been easy to find as red tag specials, but the villains are harder to come by and rather attractive.

6" Hero Figures

T-Bone	$4.00
Razor	4.00

6" Villain Figures (Asst. #00366)

"Dr. Viper"	9.00
"Dark Kat"	9.00

TALES FROM THE CRYPTKEEPER
Ace Novelty (1994)

They banned the comic book in the '50s, but it was too late! All the kids who loved the *Tales from the Crypt* stories were already corrupted and so when they grew up, the Cryptkeeper got to host its own television show. He even got a Saturday-morning cartoon show on ABC. Ace Novelty made the expected action figures and they are nice versions of the usual monsters, plus the cryptkeeper in formal attire and monk's robe. The figures lingered around in the usual vaults for a while and haven't acquired any collector following.

You may want to look for the two 12" versions of the Cryptkeeper. We particularly like the version in the striped shorts, Hawaiian shirt and straw hat! The other version has your favorite storyteller in formal attire, although it doesn't wear shoes in either version.

5" Figures (Asst. #55300)
Werewolf $4.00
Vampire 4.00
Cryptkeeper (formal) 4.00
Mummy 4.00

Second Batch (Asst. #55305)
Gargoyle 4.00
Cryptkeeper (yellow, in monk outfit) 4.00
The Frankenstein 4.00
The Zombie 4.00

Large Talking Cryptkeeper Figures (Asst. #55310)
Talking Cryptkeeper in formal attire 25.00
Talking Cryptkeeper in Hawaiian shirt and shorts ... 25.00

TALESPIN
Playmates (1991)

From the animated television series with Walt Disney characters. Six new figures were announced for 1992, but never produced.

3¾" Figures
Baloo (#2701) $8.00
Kit Cloudkicker (#2702) 8.00
Rebecca Cunningham (#2703) 8.00
Molly Cunningham (#2704) 8.00

Baloo, Talespin (Playmates 1991)

Louie (#2705) 8.00
Don Karnage (#2707) 8.00
Colonel Spigot (#2708) 8.00
Dumptruck (#2709) 8.00

Vehicles
Baloo's Sea Duck (#2761, 1991) 30.00
Don Karnage's Tri-Wing Terror (#2762, 1991) 30.00
Don Karnage's Air Pirate Kit (#2764, 1991)   no price found

Large Figure
Giant Baloo collector figure 12" (#2751, 1992) 25.00

TARZAN
Mattel (1978)

These figure were based on the "Tarzan, Lord of the Jungle," "The Batman/Tarzan Adventure Hour," and "Tarzan and the Super 7" CBS television series.

Figure with Jungle Animal
Tarzan and the Giant Ape $200.00
Tarzan and the Jungle Cat 200.00

TARZAN
"KING OF THE APES"
Dakin (1984)

The year 1984 saw the premier of the heavily promoted *Greystroke: The Legend of Tarzan, Lord of the Apes* movie which starred Christopher Lambert and Andie MacDowell. While these figures are not based on the movie, they were released in time to take advantage of the publicity.

Figures
Tarzan, 7" $40.00
Tarzan, 4" 20.00
Young Tarzan, 3½" bendable 20.00
Kala (ape) 25.00
Young Tarzan with Kala 30.00

TARZAN: THE EPIC ADVENTURES
Trendmasters (1995–96)

Edgar Rice Burroughs' three most famous continuing series are Tarzan, Mars and Pellucidar. The first to see print was the Mars series (*Under the Moons of Mars*, All Story Magazine, beginning Feb. 1912), published in book form in 1917 as *A Princess of Mars*. Tarzan came next, later the same year (*Tarzan of the Apes*, All Story Magazine, beginning Oct. 1912) and was the most popular by far, being adapted into more than 24 books and many movies. The Pellucidar or Earth's Core series was third and somewhat less popular, although it also saw movie adaptation. Tarzan got to Pellucidar in *Tarzan at the Earth's Core* and this book is part of both series. He never made it to Mars in the novels, except in an unauthorized sequel titled *Tarzan on Mars* by "John Bloodstone," which has never been published in book form. Trendmasters gets him to Mars though, to join John Carter, Dejah Thoris, Tars Tarkas and the other Martians.

Additional figures in all three sub-series were planned, along with a couple of vehicles, but they now appear unlikely as the Tarzan series seems to have died out. We doubt that this will be the last attempt to bring Tarzan to the world, but so far he has never been adapted into a successful toy line.

6" Tarzan, Lord of the Jungle Figures, with badge
Tarzan, Lord of the Jungle $6.00
Tarzan City of Gold (#06029) 6.00
Numa the Golden Lion, with riding harness (#06053)   10.00
Tarzan the Hunter, with bow and snake (#06239) 6.00

Tarzan of Mars,
Tarzan: The Epic Adventures (Trendmasters 1995)

6" Tarzan at the Earth's Core Figures, with badge
Horib the Snakeman (#06051) 6.00
Tarzan Dino Armored (#06241) 6.00

6" Tarzan, Conqueror of Mars Figures, with badge
Tars Tarkas, The Green Martian (#06028) 6.00
Tarzan of Mars (#06050) 6.00
Nolach the Kaldane (#06052) 6.00

6" Talking Figures, in window box
Tars Tarkas, The Green Martian (#06032) 10.00
Tarzan City of Gold (#06033) 10.00
Horib the Snakeman (#06055) 10.00
Tarzan the Warrior with spear, shield and chimp
    (#06232) 10.00
Tarzan Dino Armored (#06235) 10.00

4" Two-Pack Bendie Figures
Harbenite Tarzan vs. The Mahar (#06016) 6.00
Deja Thoris vs. Nolach the Kaldane (#06017) 6.00
Tarzan of Mars vs. The Plantman (#06018) 6.00
John Carter vs. O Mad Zad (#06019) 6.00
Jungle King Tarzan vs. The Leopard Man (#06020) .. 6.00

4" Bendie Figures (Kmart exclusives), with badge
City of Gold Tarzan with "Action Battle Sword" (#6337)   4.00
Dino-Armor Tarzan with "Action Battle Sword" (#6339)   4.00
Horib the Snakeman with "Action Battle Sword"
    (#6340) 4.00
Tars Tarkas with "Action Battle Sword" (#6341) 4.00
Leopard Man with "Action Battle Claws" (#6342) 4.00
Plantman, Vicious Martian Monster (#6343) 4.00

Tars Tarkas, Tarzan: the Epic Adventures (Trendmasters 1995)

Tarzan: The Epic Adventures (9-pack)
Special Collector Edition of nine 4" figures: Dino-
    Armored Tarzan, Nolach the Kaldane, O Mad Zad,
    The Mahar, The Plantman, King Kerchak, Dejah
    Thoris, John Carter and the Leopard Man (#30719,
    1996) 24.95

14" Figures, with CDS Light Motion Sensor and computer disk
Jungle King Armor Tarzan (#06118) 20.00
City of Gold Armor Tarzan (#06125) 20.00
Kerchak (#06243) 20.00

TEAM AMERICA
Ideal (1982)

There was a 12-issue Marvel comic book series
released in conjunction with this toy series and the Team also
appeared in Captain America comics for a while. The figures
came with a special edition comic book as well. Captain
America's fans were not impressed.

7" Figures
R.U. Reddy $12.00
Marauder 12.00
Honcho 12.00
Wolf 12.00

Vehicles
Super Stunt Dirt Buggy 18.00
Super Stunt Dirt Bike 18.00
Super Stunt Chopper 18.00
Scramble Rig 30.00
Energizer 20.00

TEENAGE MUTANT
NINJA TURTLES
Playmates (1988–96)

The Teenage Mutant Ninja Turtles figures are based on
Kevin Eastman and Peter Laird's black and white comic
books published originally by Mirage in the mid 1980s. They
became the action figure phenomenon of the late 1980s and
early 1990s, with more figures, more vehicles and more toy
store shelf space than any other series. Over 250 million
figures were sold in just five years.

Most collectors ignored the series as too juvenile for
their tastes and too plentiful for future appreciation. Many of
the early assortments of figures could still be found in 1992,
four years after they first appeared.

However, the collectors were wrong on both counts.
Compare any of the non-Turtle figures with the aliens from
the Mighty Morphin' Power Rangers—the most recent hot
juvenile series. The TMNT figures are quite imaginative,
highly detailed and clever, while the MMPR figures are
kiddie fare. Despite the huge number of Turtle figures
produced, many have appreciated substantially in value.

While later Turtle figure assortments had themes and
special header cards, early assortments were all part of the
same general series. The only way to tell the original figures
from the more common early figure reissues is to look at the
back of the header card, where the number of figures
pictured reveals the vintage—similar to early Star Wars
header cards. The first cards (Type A, 1988) picture 10

Type A Pack Back,
Teenage Mutant Ninja Turtles (Playmates 1988)

figures, while the second series cards (Type B, 1989) picture 14 figures and the third series cards (Type C, 1989) picture 19 figures. After that it gets complicated, so we have described the card backs under the particular group below.

Except for April O'Neil and Leatherhead, the figures on types A, B and C header cards were shipped in great quantity for several years. We found almost all of them in local toy stores in late 1991. Shipments of figures on original types B and C cards continued into 1992. In 1993, many of the original figures were reissued with new product numbers on "Pizza Back" header cards.

April, the Ninja Newscaster,
Teenage Mutant Ninja Turtles (Playmates 1992)

The April O'Neil story

The original April O'Neil figure is quite valuable. The earliest April has no stripes on the side or front of her outfit and appears on a type A header card with a turtle shell and character name imprint (on the left) which covers the top of her head in the accompanying picture. (The shell and name are in the same place for the four Turtles and Splinter, but they are shorter, so their heads are not covered.) On April's later type A header cards the shell and name imprint was moved up, near the "T" in Turtles and off her head. Second-version April figures had a blue stripe on each side. Some original Aprils appeared on second-version cards and some second-version Aprils appeared on first-version cards. After all this, April was dropped from the line for a while and redesigned.

When April reappeared in 1991, she had orange boots, shirt collar and breast pockets, with a small blue stripe on the pockets. Most say "Press" over her left pocket, but a very valuable few omit this word. Then the header card was changed, so that, among other things, her name appeared

centered above the figure rather than in the middle of the turtle shell on the left.

The other April O'Neil figures are popular with collectors. Our favorite is **April, The Ninja Newscaster**, where she is wearing a very hot one-piece leopard-skin bathing suit. Collectors should also look for the **Channel 6 News Van**, which comes with a special edition April figure and **Cave Woman April with Radical Raptor**, where she comes with a dinosaur. Monster collectors should look for the **Bride of Frankenstein April** from the second Universal Studios Monsters group.

The Leatherhead Story

Leatherhead was included in the general assortment in 1989 but, unlike the other figures from that year, could not be found in later shipments. It was pictured on the package backs and in Playmates catalogs as late as 1992, but was nowhere to be found. At least it appeared for a while. **Scratch**, from the 1993 assortment, hardly appeared at all. Other figures which are unaccountably scarce are **Hot Spot** from the same 1993 assortment as Scratch and Black Belt Boxer Mike from the 1993 "Ninja Action" assortment.

The Ray Fillet Story

The original Ray Fillet changed color with differences in temperature. This feature was expensive and didn't do well, so it was dropped. This led to several figure and package variations. The earliest figures had a purple torso with a red "V" on the chest or a red torso with a maroon

Michaelangelo,
Teenage Mutant Ninja Turtles (Playmates 1989)

"V." Later figures had a yellow torso with a blue "V" and did not change color. The earliest header card said "Awesome Mutant Color Change" in a yellow starburst and showed Ray's chest changing color. The second card dropped the starburst, but kept the color changing picture. The final card eliminated this picture.

Bebop, Teenage Mutant Ninja Turtles (Playmates 1988)

4½" to 5" Figures
Earliest Turtles (1988) on type A header card, with fan club flyer in pack

Leonardo (#5001)	$40.00
Donatello (#5002)	40.00
Michaelangelo (#5003)	40.00
Raphael (#5004)	40.00

Type A Header Card (1988–89) picturing 6 Turtle and 4 "Foot Clan" figures on the back and with a turtle shell or foot symbol on the front showing the character's affiliation.

Turtle Group

Leonardo (#5001) no flyer	20.00
Donatello (#5002) no flyer	20.00
Raphael (#5003) no flyer	20.00
Michaelangelo (#5004) no flyer	20.00
April O'Neil (#5005, 1988) no stripes on earliest type A header card	160.00
All other versions on type A header card (#5005, 1989)	20.00
Splinter (#5006, 1988)	25.00
Reissue on type F header card (#5006, 1990)	10.00

Foot Clan

Shredder (#5007, 1988)	25.00
Foot Soldier (#5008, 1988)	25.00
Rocksteady (#5009, 1988)	25.00
Reissue on type F header card (#5009, 1990)	12.00
Bebop (#5010, 1988)	25.00
Reissue on type F header card (#5010, 1990)	10.00

Type B Header Cards (1989) picturing 8 Turtle and 6 "Foot Clan" figures on the back, and no group affiliation symbol on the front.

Genghis Frog (#5051) with black belt	12.50
Variation with black belt and weapons bagged	30.00
Variation with yellow belt	75.00
Ace Duck (#5055) with hat on	12.50
Variation with hat off	40.00
Krang (#5056)	12.50
Baxter Stockman (#5057) with brown swatter	35.00
Variation with blue-green swatter	30.00

Type C Header Cards (1989) picturing 10 Turtle and 9 "Foot Clan" figures.

Leatherhead (#5052) scarce	60.00
Metalhead (#5053)	10.00
Usagi Yojimbo (#5054)	12.00
Reissue on type F header card	6.00
Casey Jones (#5058)	15.00
Rat King (#5059)	12.50
General Traag (#5061)	10.00

Note: Many of the figures on type B and type C header cards were still being shipped on their original cards in 1992.

Type D Header Cards (1990) picturing 4 Wacky Action figures at top plus 24 (type D1) or 27 (type D2) other figures, and

Type E Header Cards (1991) picturing 7 Wacky Action figures at top plus 30 (type E1) or 32 (type E2) other figures.

April with orange pockets, blue stripe, says "Press" (#5005) on type A header card	20.00
Reissue on later header cards (#5005)	15.00
April with orange pockets, blue stripes, but no "Press" (#5005) scarce	125.00
Muckman and Joe Eyeball (#5101) on type D1 header card	10.00
Scumbug (#5102) on type D1 header card	10.00
Wingnut and Screwloose (#5103) on type D1 header card	10.00
Triceraton (#5104) on type D2 header card	10.00
Reissue on type F header card	5.00
Slash (#5105) on type E1 header card with black belt	15.00
Variation with purple belt	45.00
Mondo Gecko (#5106) on type D1 header card, with blue eyebrow	10.00
Variation with green eyebrow	25.00
Mutagen Man (#5107) on E1 header card	10.00
Panda Khan (#5108) on E1 header card	12.00
Reissue (#5108, 1991) on F header card	4.50
Fugitoid (#5109) on E2 header card	10.00
Ray Fillet (#5110)	
Original purple torso, red V or red torso, maroon V with "Awesome Mutant Color Change" on type E2 header card	30.00
Variation with purple torso, red V or red torso, maroon V with color-change drawings on type F header card	25.00
Reissue, with yellow torso, blue V, color-change drawings on type F header card (does not change color)	20.00

Reissue, with yellow torso, blue V, no color-
change drawings on header card 12.50
Pizzaface (#5111) on E2 header card 10.00
Napoleon Bonafrog (#5113) on E2 header card 10.00

Type F Header Cards (1990) with 7 Wacky Action figures,
initially 22 turtles (in 3 rows) and 15 Foot Clan (in 2 rows) on
the back. Many reissues of figures listed above came on these
cards. For new figures, the front of the card says "New" in a
starburst. As additional figures appeared, the card back was
adjusted—usually by adding the new figure to front of its
affiliation group.
Leo, the Sewer Samurai (#5112) 4.50
Don, the Undercover Turtle (#5114) 3.50
Mike, the Sewer Surfer (#5115) 4.50
Raph, the Space Cadet (#5116) 3.50
*Note: See 1993 following for later reissues of many early
figures on "Pizza Back" header cards.*

Wacky Walkin' Mouser,
Teenage Mutant Ninja Turtles (Playmates 1990)

Wacky Action Figures (1989–91) with joke book on header
cards which are larger than normal. The card back changed as
figures were added in 1990 and 1991. The figures initially cost
about $1.50 more than normal.
Sword Slicin' Leonardo (#5611) 12.00
Sewer-swimmin' Donatello (#5612) 12.00
Breakfightin' Raphael (#5613) 12.00
Rock 'n' Roll Michaelangelo (#5614) 12.00
Wacky Walking Mouser (#5615) 15.00
Creepy Crawlin' Splinter (#5616, 1990) 18.00
Slice 'n' Dice Shredder (#5617, 1990) 18.00
Headspinnin' Bebop (#5618, 1991) 15.00
Machine Gunnin' Rocksteady (#5619, 1991) 15.00

Sewer Sports All-Stars Turtles (1991)
Skateboardin' Mike (#5142) 8.00
Reissue (#5441, 1993) 4.00

T.D. Tossin' Leo (#5143) 8.00
Reissue (#5338, 1993) 4.00
Grand Slammin' Raph (#5144) 8.00
Reissue (#5337, 1993) 4.00
Reissue + card (#5337, 1994) 5.00
Slam Dunkin' Don (#5145) 8.00
Reissue (#5339, 1993) 4.00
Shell Slammin' Mike (#5146) 8.00
Reissue (#5444, 1993) 4.00
Slap Shot Leo (#5147) 8.00
Reissue (#5443, 1993) 4.00
Shell Kickin' Raph (#5148) 8.00
Reissue (#5442, 1993) 4.00
Reissue + card (#5442, 1994) 4.00

Storage Shell Turtles (1991)
Donatello, with Storage Shell (#5122) 6.00
Raphael, with Storage Shell (#5123) 6.00
Leonardo, with Storage Shell (#5124) 6.00
Michaelangelo, with Storage Shell (#5125) 6.00

Rock 'n' Rollin' Turtles (1991)
Rappin' Mike (#5155) 6.00
Punker Don (#5156) 6.00
Heavy Metal Raph (#5157) 6.00
Classic Rocker Leo (#5158) 6.00

Headdroppin Turtles (1991)
Headdroppin' Leo (#5171) 6.00
Headdroppin' Mike (#5172) 6.00
Headdroppin' Raph (#5173) 6.00
Headdroppin' Don (#5174) 6.00

Talkin' Turtles (1991)
Talkin' Michaelangelo (#5180) 7.00
Talkin' Leonardo (#5181) 7.00
Talkin' Donatello (#5182) 7.00
Talkin' Raphael (#5183) 7.00

Mutant Military Turtles (1991)
Lieutenant Leo (#5149) 6.00
Midshipman Mike (#5150) 6.00
Pro Pilot Don (#5151) 6.00
Raph, the Green Teen Beret (#5152) 6.00

1991 Figures
Super Shredder (#5128) 10.00
Rahzar (#5129) 10.00
Tokka (#5130) with dark green shell 10.00
Variation with orange shell 15.00
Tattoo (#5131) 9.00
Dirtbag (#5132) 9.00
Groundchuck (#5133) 9.00
Wyrm (#5134) 8.00
Zak, the Neutrino (#5135) 9.00
Chrome Dome (#5136) 9.00
Space Usagi (#5137) 9.00
Walkabout (#5139) 8.00
Sergeant Bananas (#5141) 9.00
Make My Day Leo (#5153) 8.00
Hose 'em Down Don (#5154) 8.00

Movie Star Turtles (1992)
Movie Star Leo (#5201) 7.00
Movie Star Don (#5202) 7.00
Movie Star Raph (#5203) 7.00
Movie Star Mike (#5204) 7.00
Movie Star Splinter (#5295, 1992) 8.00

Reissue, on Pizza Back card (#5295, 1993) 4.50
Reissue, on new card + card (#05295) 5.00
Movie Star Foot Soldier (#5296, 1992) 8.00
Reissue on Pizza Back card (#5296, 1993) ... 4.50
Reissue with trading card (#05296, 1994) ... 4.50
Reissue with card and coin (#05296, 1995) 4.50

Mutatin' Splinter,
Teenage Mutant Ninja Turtles (Playmates 1992)

Mutatin' Turtles (1992–93)
Mutatin' Leonardo (#5221) 9.00
Mutatin' Donatello (#5222) 9.00
Mutatin' Raphael (#5223) 9.00
Mutatin' Michaelangelo (#5224) 9.00
Mutatin' Splinter (#5225) 11.00
Mutatin' Bebop (#5226) 11.00
Mutatin' Rocksteady (#5227) 11.00
Mutatin' April (#5235, 1993) 20.00
Mulatin' Shredder (#5236, 1993) 11.00
Mutatin' Foot Soldier (#5237, 1993) 11.00
Mutatin' Rahzar (#5238, 1993) 11.00
Mutatin' Tokka (#5239, 1993) 11.00

Wacky Wild West Turtles (1992)
Sewer Scout Raph (#5297) 7.00
Chief Leo (#5298) 7.00
Bandito-Bashin' Mike (#5299) 7.00
Crazy Cowboy Don (#5300) 7.00

Sewer Spittin' Turtles (1992)
Spike 'n' Volley Don (#5251) 6.00
Beachcombin' Mike (#5252) 6.00
Sewer-Cyclin' Raph (#5253) 6.00
Lifeguard Leo (#5254) 6.00

Bodacious Birthday Turtles (1992)
Classic Party-Reptile Leo (#5261) 7.00

Crazy Clownin' Mike (#5262) 7.00
Raph, The Magnificent (#5263) 7.00

Mutant Military 2 Series (1992)
Kookie Kavalry Leo (#5271) 6.00
Delta Team Don (#5272) 6.00
Yankee Doodle Raph (#5273) 6.00
Navy Seal Mike (#5274) 6.00
Private Porknose Bebop (#5275) 6.00
Dim Wit Doughboy Rocksteady (#5276) 6.00

Turtle Games (1992)
Track 'N Field Leo (#5211) 5.00
Powerliftin' Don (#5212) 5.00
Super-Swimmin' Raph (#5213) 5.00
Hot Doggin' Mike (#5214) 5.00

Smash 'Em Bash 'Em Series (1992)
Kowabunga Kickboxin' Leo (#5241) 6.00
Karate Choppin' Mike (#5242) 6.00
Ninja Knockin' Bebop (#5243) 6.00
Power-Punchin' Rocksteady (#5244) 6.00

1992 Figures
Leo 5th Anniversary limited edition Collector Turtle
(#5231) in window box 10.00
April, The Ravishing Reporter (#5281, 1992) 15.00
Reissue, on Pizza Back card (#5281, 1993) ... 10.00
April, The Ninja Newscaster (#5282, 1992) 16.00
Reissue, on Pizza Back card (#5282, 1993) ... 12.00
April (II) (#5283, 1992) 15.00
Reissue, on Pizza Back card (#5283, 1993) ... 12.00
Scale Tail (#5284, 1992) 10.00
Reissue, on Pizza Back card (#5284, 1993) 4.50
Hothead (#5285, 1992) 10.00
Reissue, on Pizza Back card (#5285, 1993) 4.50
Reissue, with trading card (#05285, 1994) 5.00
Antrax (#5286, 1992) 10.00
Reissue on Pizza Back card (#5286, 1993) 4.50
Doctor El (#5288, 1992) 10.00
Reissue, on Pizza Back card (#5288, 1993) 4.50
Monty Moose of the Royal Mutant Mounted Police
(#5289, 1992) 10.00
Reissue, on Pizza Back card (#5289, 1993) 4.50
Merdude (#5290, 1992) 10.00
Reissue, on Pizza Back card (#5290, 1993) 4.50
King Lionheart (#5291, 1992) 10.00
Reissue, on Pizza Back card (#5291, 1993) 4.50
Rock 'n' Roll Mondo Gecko (#5293, 1992) 9.00
Reissue, on Pizza Back card (#5293, 1993) 4.50

Sewer Heroes (1993)
Super Mike (#5421) 7.00
Reissue with trading card (#5421, 1994) 4.50
Reissue + card and coin (#5421, 1995) 4.50
Super Don (#5422) 7.00
Reissue, with trading card (#5422, 1994) 5.00
Mighty Bebop (#5423) 9.00
Rhinoman (#5424) yellow accessories 9.00
Variation, with red accessories 9.00
Reissue, with trading card (#05424, 1994) 4.50
Reissue, with card and coin (#05424, 1995) 4.50

Toon Turtles (1993) with "Real Toon Texture Feel"
Toon Dask (#5401) 9.00
Toon Kala (#5402) 9.00
Toon Burne (#5403) 9.00
Toon Leo with Bulgin' Eye Action (#5404) 7.00

Toon Mike with Tacky Tongue Action (#5405) 7.00
Toon Don with Spinnin' Bandana Action (#5406) 7.00
Toon Raph with Head Spinnin' Action (#5407) 7.00
Toon Irma (#5408) 9.00
Toon Vernon (#5409) 9.00
Toon Zak (#5410) 9.00
Toon Shredder (#5411) 9.00

Movie Star Turtles (1993)
Movie Star Don, rubbery (#5366) 6.00
Movie Star Mike, rubbery (#5368) 6.00

Movie III Turtles (1993)
Movie III Samurai Leo (#5471) 6.00
Movie III Samurai Mike (#5472) 6.00
Movie III Samurai Don (#5473) 6.00
Movie III Samurai Raph (#5474) 6.00
Movie III Princess Mitsu (#5475) 9.00
Movie III Warlord (#5476) 8.00
Movie III Splinter (#5478) 8.00
Movie III April (#5479) 12.00
Movie III Walker (#5481) 8.00
Movie III Kenshin (#5482) 8.00

Night Ninja Turtles (1993)
Night Ninja Leo (#5461) 8.00
Night Ninja Mike (#5462) 8.00
Night Ninja Don (#5463) 8.00
Night Ninja Raph (#5464) 8.00
Night Ninja Rocksteady (#5465) 10.00
Night Ninja Bebop (#5466) 10.00

Ninja Action Turtles (1993) in window box with hanging flap.
When you push one down and then release it, you can watch
it "jump off the ground, into the air and perform a midair attack
flip and kick!"
Somersault Samurai Leo (#5446) 10.00
Black Belt Boxer Mike (#5447) scarce 50.00
Cartwheelin' Karate Don (#5448) 10.00
Jump Attack Jujitsu Raph (#5449) 10.00

Universal Studios Monsters Turtles (1993)
Leo as The Wolfman (#5451) 15.00
Mike as Frankenstein (#5452) 15.00
Don as Dracula (#5453) 15.00
Raph as The Mummy (#5454) 15.00

Universal Studios Monsters Turtles (1994) with trading card
Invisible Man Michaelangelo (#5425) 15.00
Creature from the Black Lagoon Leonardo (#5426) . . 15.00
The Mutant Raphael (#5427) 15.00
Bride of Frankenstein April (#5428) 25.00

Turtle Trolls (1993)
Turtle Troll Leo (#5486) 8.00
Turtle Troll Don (#5487) 8.00
Turtle Troll Raph (#5488) 8.00
Turtle Troll Mike (#5489) 8.00

Road Ready Turtles (1993)
Road Ready Leo (#5371) 10.00
Road Ready Don (#5372) 10.00
Road Ready Splinter (#5374) 10.00
Road Ready Shredder (#5375) 10.00

1993 Figures
Sandstorm (#5491) 12.00
Halfcourt (#5492) 12.00

Hot Spot, Teenage Mutant Ninja Turtles (Playmates 1993)

Hot Spot (#5493) scarce 50.00
Scratch (#5494) very scarce 100.00
Mona Lisa (#5495) 12.00
Robotic Bebop (#5496) 12.00
   Reissue, with trading card (#05496, 1994) 4.50
   Reissue, with coin (#05496, 1995) 4.50
Robotic Rocksteady (#5497) 12.00
   Reissue, with trading card (#5497, 1994) 5.00

In 1993, most of the early TMNT figures were reissued
with new product numbers on new header cards which we
call "Pizza Backs" because the back contains the heads of the
figures in the series looking like so many pepperonis on a
giant pizza. Many of the later TMNT figures also appeared
on these header cards, but with their original product numbers. These reissues are listed immediately after the listing
for the original figure

1993 Reissues of Early Figures, on Pizza Back header card
and with new product numbers (Asst. #5000.50)
Movie Star Super Shredder, reissue (#5128) 4.50
   Reissue, with trading card (#05128, 1994) 4.50
   Reissue, with card and coin (#05128, 1995) 4.50
   Reissue, with coin (#05128, 1995) 4.50
Rahzar, reissue (#5129) 4.50
   Reissue, on new card, with trading card
   (#05129) 5.00
Tokka, reissue (#5130) 4.50
Dirtbag, reissue (#5132) 4.50
Chrome Dome, reissue (#5136) 4.50
   Reissue, with trading card (#05136, 1994) 4.50
Space Usagi, reissue (#5137) 4.50
Sergeant Bananas, reissue (#5141) 4.50
Krang's Android Body, reissue (#5160) 6.00
   Reissue, with trading card (#5160, 1994) 7.50
   Reissue, with card and coin (#5160, 1995) 5.00

Reissue, with coin (#05160, 1995)	4.50
Robotic Foot Soldier, reissue (#5161)	4.50
Reissue, with trading card (#05161, 1994)	5.00
Hose 'em Down Don, reissue, with trading card (#5168, 1994)	4.00
Make My Day Leo, reissue, with trading card (#5169, 1994)	4.50
Hot Doggin' Mike, reissue (#5336)	4.00
Casey Jones, reissue (#5377)	5.00
Reissue, on new card + trading card (#05377) . .	5.00
Reissue, with card and gold coin (#05377, 1995)	5.00

April O'Neil reissue, with trading card,
Teenage Mutant Ninja Turtles (Playmates 1993)

April O'Neil, reissue + trading card (#5378)	6.00
Splinter, reissue (#5379)	4.50
Reissue, with trading card (#05379, 1994)	4.50
Reissue, with card and coin (#05379, 1995) . . .	4.50
Reissue, with coin (#05379, 1995)	4.50
Usagi Yojimbo, reissue (#5380)	4.50
Ace Duck, reissue (#5381)	4.50
Mondo Gecko, reissue (#5382)	4.50
Reissue, with trading card (#05382, 1994)	4.50
Wingnut, reissue (#5383)	4.50
Ray Fillet, reissue (#5384)	10.00
Metalhead, reissue (#5385)	4.50
Napoleon Bonafrog, reissue (#5386)	4.50
Muckman and Joe Eyeball, reissue (#5387)	4.50
Rat King, reissue (#5388)	4.50
Shredder, reissue (#5389)	4.50
Bebop, reissue (#5390)	4.50
Rocksteady, reissue (#5391)	4.50
Reissue, with trading card (#05391, 1994)	4.50
Reissue, with card and coin (#05391, 1995)	4.50
Krang, reissue (#5392)	4.50

Reissue, with trading card (#05392, 1994)	5.00
Foot Soldier, reissue (#5393)	4.50
Reissue, with trading card (#05393, 1994)	4.50
Reissue, with card and coin (#05393, 1995)	4.50
Baxter Stockman, reissue (#5394)	10.00
Reissue on new card, with trading card (#05394, 1994)	6.00
General Traag, reissue (#5395)	4.50
Reissue, with trading card (#05395, 1994)	4.50
Mutagen Man, reissue (#5396)	4.50
Triceraton, reissue (#5397)	4.50
Pizzaface, reissue (#5398)	4.50
Scumbug, reissue (#5399)	4.50

1994–95

In 1994, many reissue figures and some new figures appeared with exclusive trading cards as an in-pack premium. In 1995, the premium was changed to a "coin." Not all of the trading cards had been distributed when the coins were first produced and some figures were issued with both for a while. Ones which we observed have been noted, but others may well exist.

Construction Mutations Turtles "mutate into actual construction vehicles." Pizza Tossin' Turtles could "shoot pizzas into the air by pulling back on their right arms." Cyber Samurai Turtles come "outfitted in Turtle-tech titanium suits of mutant metal." Star Trek Turtles are just what you think they are. Popular with trekkers, too.

Apollo 11 25th Anniversary Astronaut Turtles (July 1994) with trading card

Lunar Leonardo (#5256)	15.00
Touchdown Donatello (#5257)	15.00
Retro Rocket Raphael (#5258)	15.00
Moon Landin' Michaelangelo (#5259)	15.00

Cyber Samurai Turtles (1994)

Cyber Samurai Leo (#3001)	8.00
Cyber Samurai Raph (#3002)	8.00
Cyber Samurai Mike (#3003)	8.00
Cyber Samurai Don (#3004)	8.00
Cyber Samurai Bebop (#3006, 1994)	9.00
Cyber Samurai Shredder (#3008, 1994)	9.00

Kowabunga Crackin' Turtle Eggs (1994)

Kowabunga Crackin' Turtle Egg Don (#3481)	12.00
Kowabunga Crackin' Turtle Egg Mike (#3482)	12.00
Kowabunga Crackin' Turtle Egg Leo (#3483)	12.00
Kowabunga Crackin' Turtle Egg Raph (#3484)	12.00

Kung Fu Turtles (1994)

Kung Fu Leo (#3021)	6.00
Kung Fu Don (#3023)	6.00
Kung Fu Raph (#3024)	6.00
Kung Fu Rocksteady (#3026, 1994)	9.00

Mighty Mutations (1994) in window box

Construction Mutation Leonardo (#3081)	12.00
Construction Mutation Michaelangelo (#3082)	12.00
Construction Mutation Donatello (#3083)	12.00
Airforce Mutation Raphael (#3084)	12.00
Airforce Mutation Donatello (#3085)	12.00

Pizza Tossin' Turtles (Feb. 1994)

Pizza Tossin' Don (#3070)	6.00

Pizza Tossin' Leo (#3071) 6.00
Pizza Tossin' Mike (#3072) 6.00
Pizza Tossin' Raph (#3074) 6.00

Shogun Ninja Fighters (Feb. 1994)
Shogun Triceraton with card (#5162) 9.00
Shogun Shoate with card (#5163) 8.00
Shogun Turtle Leo + card (#5431) 7.00
Shogun Turtle Don + card (#5432) 7.00
Shogun Turtle Mike + card (#5433) 7.00
Shogun Turtle Raph + card (#5434) 7.00
Shogun Shredder with card (#5435) 9.00
    Reissue, with card and coin (#05435, 1995) 4.50
Shogun Splinter with card (#5436) 9.00
    Reissue, with coin (#5436, 1995) 5.00
Shogun April with card (#5437) 9.00

Storage Shell Turtles (1994)
Storage Shell Mike, + card (#5164) 6.00
Storage Shell Don + card (#5165) 6.00
Storage Shell Raph + card (#5166) 6.00
Storage Shell Leo + card (#5167) 6.00

Captain Leonardo, Star Trek Turtles,
Teenage Mutant Ninja Turtles (Playmates 1994)

Star Trek Turtles (June 1994) with trading card
Captain Leonardo (#3451) 18.00
Chief Engineer Michaelangelo (#3452) 18.00
Chief Medical Officer (Raphael) (#3453) 18.00
First Officer Donatello (#3454) 18.00

Undercover Turtles (1994) with trading card
Undercover Leonardo (#5176) 8.00
    Reissue, with coin (#5176, 1995) 5.00
Undercover Donatello (#5177) 8.00

Undercover Michaelangelo (#5178) 8.00
Undercover Raphael (#5179) 8.00

"Warriors of the Forgotten Sewer" Turtles (April 1994) with
color comic book
Savage Leo (#5264) 7.00
Dwarf Don (#5265) 7.00
Knight Mike (#5266) 7.00
Warrior Bebop (#5267) 7.00
Gatekeeper Rocksteady (#5268) 9.00
Spellcaster Splinter (#5269) 9.00

Adventuers Turtles (1995)
Safari Michaelangelo with coin (#5118) 7.00
Deep Sea Diver Leonardo with coin (#5119) 7.00

Metal Mutant Turtles (1995)
Donatello with Lion Spirit Armor (#3031) 7.00
Leonardo with Dragon Spirit Armor (#3032) 7.00
Raphael with Phoenix Spirit Armor (#3033) 7.00
Michaelangelo with Beetle Spirit Armor (#3034) 7.00
Shredder with Tiger Spirit Armor (#3035) 9.00
Bebop, with Fish Spirit Armor (#3036) 10.00
Rocksteady, with Serpent Spirit Armor (#3037) 10.00

Sumo Turtles (1995)
Sumo Raphael with coin (#5127) 4.50
Sumo Donatello (#5128?) with coin 4.50
Sumo Michaelangelo with coin (#5138) 4.50

Supermutant Turtles (1995)
Supermutant Raphael (#3010) 7.00
Supermutant Donatello (#3011) 7.00
Supermutant Michaelangelo (#3012) 7.00
Supermutant Leonardo (#3013) 7.00
Supermutant Shredder (#3015) 8.00
Supermutant Rocksteady (#3016) 8.00
Supermutant Bebop (#3017) 8.00
Supermutant Splinter (#3018) 8.00

Warrior Turtles (1995)
Warrior Metalhead Michaelangelo + coin (#5206) 5.00
Warrior Chrome Dome + coin (#5207) 5.00
Warrior Winged Donatello + coin (#5249) 5.00
Warrior Winged Leonardo + coin (#5249) 5.00

1996–97

    The turtles were still alive in 1996. Obviously they do not draw the shelf space they once did, but new figures are still being introduced. Collecting them can be somewhat of a challenge, but they're out there if you look for them. One line that did see wide distribution in 1996 was the Jim Lee Turtles, which were packed with the Savage Dragon figures.

    In addition to April O'Neil and some scarce and/or early figures, collectors have shown the most interest in the action figure/vehicle combinations and in the two crossover collectibles—Star Trek Turtles and Universal Studios Monsters Turtles. For other figures, supply probably exceeds demand for the near future. In about five years, collector interest may pick up. This has been the pattern for the Masters of the Universe figures, which were the previous action figure phenomenon.

    "Ninja Turtles: The Next Mutation" will premiere as a

live-action series in the fall. Look for the introduction of the first female Turtle, **Venus de Milo**. She will probably be the brains of the outfit and will definitely give the original four turtles something to fight about. More to the point, she should interest female figure collectors.

Jim Lee Turtles, with mini comic (1996)
Donatello (#3041) 7.00
Michaelangelo (#3042) 7.00
Raphael (#3043) 7.00

Muta Force Turtles (1996)
Robotation Michaelangelo, The Roudy Robotic Rouster
    (#13051) 8.00
Dynatronic Donatello, The Cyber-Dynamic Destroyer
    (#13052) 8.00
Robomatic Raphael, The Ragin' Ruckus Raiser
    (#13053) 8.00
Andro Skeleton-Leonardo, The Awesomely-Armed
    Attacker (#13054) 8.00

Mutatin' Shredder, Ninja Power,
Teenage Mutant Ninja Turtles (Playmates 1996)

Ninja Power Turtles (1996) from catalog. Not sure if all have been produced.
Pizza Tossin' Michaelangelo (#15101) . . . . not seen
Pizza Tossin' Leonardo (#15102) . . . . not seen
Pizza Tossin' Raphael (#15103) 5.00
Pizza Tossin' Donatello (#15104) . . . . not seen
HeadDroppin' Michaelangelo (#15105) 5.00
HeadDroppin' Leonardo (#15106) . . . . not seen
HeadDroppin' Donatello (#15107) . . . . not seen
HeadDroppin' Raphael (#15108) . . . . not seen
Lifeguard Leo (#15109) 5.00

Spike 'n Volley Donatello (#15110) . . . . not seen
Sewer-cyclin' Raphael (#15111) 5.00
Beachcombin' Michaelangelo (#15112) 5.00
Mutatin' Michaelangelo (#15113) . . . . not seen
Mutatin' Donatello (#15114) . . . . not seen
Mutatin' Raphael (#15115) . . . . not seen
Mutatin' Leonardo (#15116) 5.00
Mutatin' April (#15117) . . . . not seen
Mutatin' Splinter (#15118) 5.00
Mutatin' TOKKA (#15119) 5.00
Mutatin' Rahzar (#15120) . . . . not seen
Mutatin' Shredder (#15121) 5.00
Mutatin' Foot Soldier (#15122) . . . . not seen
Mutatin' Rocksteady (#15123) 5.00
Mutatin' Bebop (#15124) 5.00
Cartwheelin' Karate Don (#15125) 5.00
Jump Attack Jujitsu Raph (#15126) 5.00
Somersault Samurai Leo (#15127) 5.00
Kung Fu Rocksteady (#15145) 5.00
Kung Fu Michaelangelo (#15147) 5.00

Coil Force Turtles (1996)
Coil Cool Donatello (#15151) 7.00
Mighty Mech Michaelangelo (#15152) 7.00
Rapid Recoilin' Raphael (#15153) 7.00
Lickety-Split Leonardo (#15154) 7.00

Ninja Shooter Figure Assortment (1996) from catalog, not sure any were produced.
Ninja Shooter Donatello (#3091) . . . . not seen
Ninja Shooter Raphael (#3092) . . . . not seen
Ninja Shooter Leonardo (#3093) . . . . not seen
Ninja Shooter Michaelangelo (#3094) . . . . not seen

13" Giant Turtle Figures (1989–93)
Donatello (Asst. #5623, 1989) 30.00
Leonardo (Asst. #5623, 1989) 30.00
Michaelangelo (Asst. #5623, 1989) 30.00
Raphael (Asst. #5623, 1989) 30.00
Bebop (#5521, 1991) 30.00
Rocksteady (#5522, 1991) 30.00
Krang's Android Body (#5526, 1991) 30.00
Giant Movie Star Leo (#5513, 1992) 25.00
Giant Movie Star Raph (#5514, 1992) 25.00
Giant Movie Star Don (#5515, 1992) 25.00
Giant Movie Star Mike (#5516, 1992) 25.00
Giant Movie III Samurai Leo (#5506, 1993) 20.00
Giant Movie III Samurai Don (#5507, 1993) 20.00
Giant Movie III Samurai Raph (#5508, 1993) 20.00
Giant Movie III Samurai Mike (#5509, 1993) 20.00
Giant Mutatin' Leo (#5561, 1993) 25.00
Giant Mutatin' Don (#5562, 1993) 25.00
Giant Mutatin' Raph (#5563, 1993) 25.00
Giant Mutatin' Mike (#5564, 1993) 25.00

Combinations: Turtle and Vehicle or Beast, boxed
(Original) Cave-Turtle Leo with Dingy Dino (#5301,
    1993) i.e. late 1992 . . . . 15.00
Movie III Samurai Evil War Horse with **Castle Guard**
    figure (#5304, 1993) 15.00
Movie III Samurai Rebel War Horse with **Rebel Soldier**
    figure (#5305, 1993) 15.00
Movie III Turtlepult with **Whit** figure (#5306, 1993) . . 10.00
Farmer Mike and His Turtle Tractor (#5307, 1993) . . 10.00
Channel 6 News Van with **April** figure (#5322, 1992) 60.00
Farmer Donatello and His Modern Mutant Tractor
    (#5326, 1994) 10.00
Channel 6 News Van with **April** figure (#5346, 1993) 15.00

Toon Cycle with Toon Raph,
Teenage Mutant Ninja Turtles (Playmates 1993)

Toon Cycle with Toon Raph (#5347, 1993) 10.00
Cave-Woman April with Radical Raptor (#5358, 1994) 20.00
Cave-Beast Bebop with Bodacious Brontosaurus (#5359,
    1994) 12.00
Cave-Turtle Mike with Silly Stegosaurus (#5361, 1993) 12.00
Cave-Turtle Don with Trippy Tyrannosaurus (#5362,
    1993) 15.00
Cave-Turtle Raph with Tubular Pterodactyl (#5363,
    1993) 12.00
Cave-Turtle Leo with Dingy Dino (#5364, 1993) 12.00
Road Racin' Mike with Kowabunga Bike (Bodacious
    Biker) (#3401, 1994) pull-cord powered 12.00
Cruisin' Leo with Classic Bike (Bodacious Biker) (#3402,
    1994) pull-cord powered 12.00
Savage Leo with Sewer Warcat (#3477, 1994) 12.50
Scuba Divin' Raph with Psych-Out Spin-Out Scuba Tube
    (#3491, 1994) 12.50
Surfer Leo with Mondo Mutant Surfer Tube (Surfin'
    Ninja) (#3492, 1994) 12.50

Vehicles and Equipment
Bubble Bomber (Mutant Military) (#5312, 1992) 30.00
Cheapskate Skateboard (#5017, 1988) 11.00
Cheapskate II Skateboard (#5017-2) 10.00
Don's Krazy Carnival Car (#5553, 1991) 15.00
Don's Pizza-Powered Parachute (#5314, 1992) 12.00
Don's Telephone Line Rider Backpack (#5574, 1991)
    . . . . no price found
Double Barreled Plunger Gun (#5662, 1990) 10.00
Flushomatic (#5661, 1990) 15.00
Foot Cruiser (#5625, 1989) 35.00
Footski (#5632, 1989) 11.00
Killer Bee, Mega Mutant (#5635, 1990) 10.00
Knucklehead (#5018, 1988) 11.00
Leo's Jolly Turtle Tubboat (#5554, 1991) 15.00
Leo's Turtle Trike (#5698, 1991) 10.00
Lieutenant Leo's Bodacious Buggy (Mutant Military)
    (#5316, 1992) 20.00
Macho Mutant Module (#3412, 1994) 10.00
Needlenose, Mega Mutant (#5634, 1990) 20.00
Michaelangelo's Sidewalk Surfer (#5317, 1992) 15.00
Mike's Kowabunga Surf Buggy (#5556, 1991) 10.00
Mike's Pizza Chopper Backpack (#5575, 1991)
    . . . . no price found
Muta-Party Wagon (#5325, 1993) 20.00
Mutant Module (#5624, 1990) 25.00
Mutant Sewer Cycle with Sidecar (1989) 15.00

Mutations Muta-Bike (#5331, 1992) 10.00
Mutations Muta-Carrier (#5324, 1992) 30.00
Mutations Muta-Raft (#5303, 1992) 10.00
Mutations Muta-Ski (#5332, 1992) 10.00
Ninja Grapplor, battery powered (#5318, 1993) 20.00
Ninja Newscycle (#5557, 1991) 10.00
Oozey (#5602, 1990) . . . . no price found
Party Hearty Wacky Wagon (#3411, 1994) 20.00
Pizza Powered Sewer Dragster (#5692, 1990) 15.00
Pizza Powered Turtle Prop (#3498, 1994) 15.00
Pizza Skimmin' Jetboat (#3496, 1994) 10.00
Pizza Thrower (#5621, 1989) 35.00
Psycho Cycle (#5691, 1990) 25.00
Raph's Pizza-Powered Parachute (#5314, 1992) 10.00
Raph's Sewer Speedboat (#5559, 1991) 10.00
Raph's Turtle Dragster (#5699, 1991) 10.00
Retrocatapault (#5663, 1990) 11.00
Rock N' Roll Muta-Bus (#5321, 1992) 30.00
Rocksteady's Pogocopter (Mutant Military) (#5558,
    1991) 10.00
Samurai Scooter (#5302, 1992) 8.00
Sewer Army Tube (#5651) 10.00
Sewer Dragster (#5692, 1990) 15.00
Sewer Party Tube (#5652, 1990) 10.00
Sewer Playset (#5685, 1990) 50.00
Sewer Sandcruiser (Mutant Military) (#5313, 1992) . . 25.00
Sewer Seltzer Cannon (#5601, 1990) 15.00
Sewer Sub (Mutant Military) (#5572, 1991) 25.00
Sewer Subway Car (#3099, 1994) 20.00
Shell Top 4X4 (#5576, 1991) 25.00
Shreddermobile (#5555, 1991) 20.00
Slugemobile (Wacky Action) (#5551, 1991) 15.00
Supermutant Cyclone Cycle (#3019, 1994) 11.00
Talkin' Turtle Communicator (#3495, 1994) 20.00
Technodrome, 22", (#5684, 1988) 60.00
Technodrome (#5684, 1990) 15.00
Technodrome Scout Vehicle (#5308, 1993) 18.00
Toilet Taxi (Wacky Action) (#5552, 1990) 7.00
Turtle Blimp, 30", vinyl (#5020, 1988) 30.00
Turtle Blimp II (#5050-2) 25.00
Turtle Communicator (#5682, 1993) 15.00
Turtle Cycle with sidecar (#5631) . . . . no price found
Turtle Party Wagon (#5622, 1989) 40.00
Turtle Popcan Racer (#5315, 1992) 20.00
Turtle Tank (Mutant Military) (#5571, 1991) 25.00
Turtle Trooper, 22", parachute (#5019, 1988) 10.00
Turtlecopter (Mutant Military) (#5626, 1991) 25.00
Turtlemobile (#5323, 1992) 25.00

TEEN TITANS
Mego (1976)

Closely related to the World's Greatest Super-heroes
series from Mego, these four DC Comics teen-age super
heroes came on a header card with their own logo. They are
all very scarce.

6½" Figures
Aqualad (#51316/1) $300.00
Aqualad (loose) 100.00
Kid Flash (#51316/2) 400.00
Kid Flash (loose) 150.00
Wondergirl (#51316/3) 250.00
Wondergirl (loose) 100.00
Speedy (#51316/4) 500.00
Speedy (loose) 250.00

Cyber Grip, Terminator 2 (Kenner 1992)

TERMINATOR 2
Kenner (1991–92)

From the movie starring Arnold Schwarzenegger, Linda Hamilton, Robert Patrick and Joe Morton. The movie had excellent special effects and a good story. Both it and its predecessor are rated among the top science fiction movies of all time by *Cinescape* magazine.

The first four figures appeared around Christmas 1991, while the second batch appeared the following summer. The back of the header cards was updated to show the new figures. The backs pictured only four figures.

A lot of collector interest focused on the **John Connor** figure from the third batch. He was not shipped to many of the large toy stores and the only ones we found were at a drug store chain. John comes with a motorcycle, which is more elaborate and larger than he is. He remains more valuable than the other figures.

The Ultimate Terminator originally cost about $25.00. The arms rotate at the shoulder, but otherwise it's not an action figure. Most other oversize figures sold for around $20.00, but for about $7.00 more you got a machine gun, dark glasses, together with battery powered light-up eyes, and the ability to say "I'll be Back" and "Hasta La Vista Baby." This is a very attractive figure and has been an excellent collectible.

The final two figures in this line shipped in late 1992. The **Damage Repair Terminator** comes with an extra arm and an extra head so you can replace the damaged ones. Arnold always needed a spare head and now he has one. **Cyber Grip** came with a big gripping claw and was recycled as the Cyber Grip Villain in the subsequent *T2 Future War* series. Third and fourth batch were not available at any of the local Toys "R" Us stores, which had still not sold off their supply of the original figures. You had to find them in Drug Stores and Discount Stores which ordered smaller quantities of the original figures. This made them scarcer (and more collectible) than the first figures.

5" Figures (Dec. 1991)
Battle Damage Terminator with "Blow-Open Chest Damage" (#56410, 1992) $12.00
Power Arm Terminator with "Missile Launcher and Grabbing Claw" (#56420, 1992) 12.00
Techno-Punch Terminator with "Super Smashing Action" (#56430, 1992) 12.00
Blaster T-1000 with "Rapid Deploy Missles" (#56440, 1992) 12.00

Second Batch (Summer 1992)
Secret Weapon Terminator with "Hidden Chest Cannon" (#56480, 1992) 15.00
Exploding T-1000 with "Blast Apart Action" (#56490, 1992) 15.00

Third Batch (Fall 1992)
John Connor, with Motorcycle (#56550, 1992) 28.00
Meltdown Terminator with "White-Heat Bazooka Sprayer" (#60202) 20.00
Endoglow Terminator with "Flame-Thrower Blaster" (#60203) 20.00
White Hot T-1000 with "Arrow Blaster" (#60204) with White missile 20.00
Reissue, with red missile 20.00

Fourth Batch (Nov. 1992)
Damage Repair Terminator with "Battle Repair Tools" (#60205) 17.00
Cyber Grip with "Crushing Claw Action" (#60206?) . . 17.00

Oversize Figure (1992)
Ultimate Terminator, 13½" figure with Battle Noises and Light-Up Eyes (#56530) 35.00

Vehicles (1992)
Mobile Assault Vehicle (#56450) 18.00
Heavy Metal Cycle (#56460) 13.00
Bio-Flesh Regenerator playset (#56470) 30.00

TERMINATOR 2: FUTURE WAR
Kenner (1993)

Hidden Power Terminator, Battle Ready Terminator and Kromium followed the other five figures in this series by a month or so. **Kromium** is a skull-faced villain who "Grows into a Towering Foe!" He also seems to have large horns on his head, wear body armor and be a Cyborg. We guess the idea is to make Arnold handsome by comparison. Cyber-Grip Villain was recycled from the Cyber Grip tail-end figure from the previous series. This has lead to some confusion in price listings.

Rapid Repair Terminator,
Terminator 2: Future War (Kenner 1993)

5" Figures (1993)

Battle Ready Terminator with "Dual Swing-Down Cannons" (#60208) $6.00
Hidden Power Terminator with "Hidden Grappling Hook That Really Fires" (#60209) 6.00
Kromium "Expands to Nearly Double Size" (#60210) . . 6.00
Metal-Mash Terminator with "Punch Action and Arrow Blaster" (#60213) 12.00
Hot Blast Terminator with "Bazooka Sprayer" (#60214) 6.00
Rapid Repair Terminator with "Field Repair Tools" (#60215) 12.00
Cyber-Grip Villain with "Crushing Claw Action" (#60216) 6.00
3-Strike Terminator with "3 Weapon Arms, Missile Really Fires" (#60217) 6.00

TERMINATOR 2
JUDGMENT DAY
Toy Island (1995)

Toy Island continued both this series and the Robocop series when Kenner was done with them. The figures are cheaper looking than those from the major toy companies and designed to sell at a modest price. They are not really collected in themselves, but fans of the two series will probably want one if they can find one cheap, which they were at the end of 1996.

4" Figures
Endoskeleton, with "Phase Plasma Rifle" (#50106) . . $7.00
T-1000 with "Special Weapon Accessory" (#50107) . . . 7.00

TERRAHAWKS
Bandai (1983)

"Terrahawks" is another Gerry Anderson (& Christopher Burr) British television series, like "The Thunderbirds," "Captain Scarlet" and "Stingray." These series have their fans, so the figures are collectible. They never saw extensive distribution in the United States, where the cartoon series played in syndication, starting in 1985.

4" Figures
Doctor Ninestein (#0988721) $10.00
Lieutenant Hiro (#0988722) 10.00
Captain Kate Kestrel (#0988723?) 15.00
Lieutenant Hawkeye (#0988724) 10.00
Captain Mary Falconer (#0988725?) 15.00
Zelda (#0988726) 10.00
Sergeant Major Zero (#0988727) 10.00
Space Sergeant 101 (#0988728) 10.00

THUNDERBIRDS
Matchbox (1994–95)

"The Thunderbirds" are based on the most popular of the Gerry Anderson television programs, which were done in "Super-Marionation." The original 1967 programs spawned two feature-length films as well. The 1994 program, which appeared on FOX, was a redubbed and re-edited rerun of the 1967 show. In the show, Jeff Tracy is the father of the five Tracy boys: Scott, Virgil, Gordon, Alan and John. The Tracy clan love their vehicles, the largest of which is Thunderbird 2, which is 250' long and can fly 5,000 miles per hour, and carries the smaller vehicles on rescue missions. We'd hate to

Lady Penelope, Thunderbirds (Matchbox 1994)

see their fuel bill. Brains is the genius scientist that builds everything on Tracy Island, while the Hood is the bad guy in the series. Lady Penelope and her limo driver, Parker, are a powerful international rescue team.

Matchbox and Matchbox UK had their action figure lines shipping the same figures just a few months apart from each other. The only really significant difference is in the header cards. The Thunderbirds were a top-selling toy line in Britain, but in the United States the figures could only be found here and there. Most collectors were not aware of them and they have received little coverage in the collector magazines.

British figures get to Canada quickly, and some collectors and dealers have connections in both places. Consequently, we are not certain if all of the figures and vehicles listed were actually distributed in the United States or whether some of them are British issue. That wouldn't make them any less popular or valuable, but we have generally included only figures distributed in the United States in the rest of this book. The rarer figures from the series are those of Lady Penelope and Parker.

4" Figures
Lady Penelope (#41750)	$20.00
Scott Tracy (#41751)	5.00
Virgil Tracy (#41752)	5.00
Alan Tracy	5.00
Gordon Tracy	5.00
John Tracy	5.00
Jeff Tracy	5.00
Brains	10.00
Parker	15.00
The Hood	8.00

Die-Cast Vehicles
Thunderbird 1	10.00
Thunderbird 2 with Thunderbird 4 (#41702)	25.00
Thunderbird 3	10.00
Thunderbirds Rescue Pack, with all Thunderbird vehicles including Lady Penelope's Fab1, boxed	40.00

Playset
Tracy Island Electronic Playset	40.00

THUNDERCATS
LJN (1985–87)

This syndicated animated television series by Ruby-Spears was based on the toy line, rather than the other way around. It pits the Evil Mutants against the Lion-O led ThunderCats, in a fantasy series with a view to the Masters of the Universe figures and show, which were then highly popular.

6" Figures (1985) with "Battle-Matic Action"
Lion-O "Eyes Light-Up"	$25.00
Panthro	25.00
Mumm-Ra "Eyes Light-Up"	25.00
Monkian	25.00

Second Batch (1986) with "Battle-Matic Action"
Tuska Warrior	25.00

Lion-O, Thundercats (LJN 1985)

Hachiman	25.00
Vultureman	25.00
Grune the Destroyer	25.00
Safari Joe	25.00

Third Batch with "Battle-Matic Action" (Asst. #3545, 1986)
S-S-Slithe	20.00
Jackalman	20.00
Ratar-O	20.00
Tygra	30.00
Cheetara	30.00

Fourth Batch (1986)
Tygra and Wilykat	35.00
Variation, with older face	no price found
Cheetara and Wilykit	35.00
Lion-O with Sanrf	15.00
Mumm-Ra with Ravage	15.00

"New!" Figures (1987) with "Battle-Matic Action"
Ben Gali	100.00
Capt. Shiner	25.00
Capt. Cracker	25.00
Jaga	75.00
Lynx-O	30.00
Mongor	35.00
Pumyra	30.00

Other Figures
Astral Moat Monster (#3535, 1985)	20.00
Snowman of Hook Mountain	25.00
Mumm-Ra, mummified, mail-in	15.00

Companions (1987)
Berbil Belle companion	25.00
Berbil Bert companion	25.00
Berbil Bill companion	25.00

Ravage companion 25.00
Snarf companion 25.00
Willykat companion 25.00
Willykit companion 25.00

Berserkers (1986)
Cruncher Berserker 15.00
Hammerhand Berserker 15.00
Ramrider Berserker 15.00
Top-Spinner Berserker 15.00
Tornado Berserker 15.00

Vehicles
Blue Stalker vehicle 12.00
Electronic Cats' Lair fortress with mutant vehicle
    (#3550) 24.00
Energy Pack (2 color variations) 6.00
Flying Claw vehicle 12.00
Luna-Lasher Battling Coat of Weapons (#3590) 12.00
Mumm-Ra's Tomb Fortress with **Mumm-Ra** figure
    (#3565) 40.00
Mutant Fistpounder vehicle (#3563) 20.00
Mutant Skycutter Air and Ground Attack vehicle
    (#3530) 14.00
Mutant Fistpounder Evil Earthshaking Combat Machine 20.00
Mutant Nose Diver Land and Sea Attack Vehicle . . . 16.00
Stilt Runner Ground Transporter Craft (#3590) 8.00
Thundertank vehicle (#3540) 24.00
Thunderwings 22.00
Tongue-A-Saurus Deadly, Devouring Monster (#3561) 18.00

THE TICK
Bandai (1995)

These figures are from the comic book and FOX animated television super hero spoof created by Ben Edlund. The original black and white comic book debuted in 1988 from New England Comics Press. The animated television show began in September 1994 on the Fox Children's network. Now it plays on the Comedy Channel. "Entirely committed, but barely coordinated, The Tick is a 400-pound blue crime fighter .... He bounces across the rooftops of The City, a determined, well-intentioned force of nature who succeeds by accident and meets failure with denial .... Together with his trusty sidekick Arthur (an ex-accountant in a shimmering white moth suit), they overcome crime by taking on the world's most 'unusual' super villains."

The Man Eating Cow and Pose Striking Die Fledermaus were very scarce for most of the time the figures were for sale, but some of them showed up when the series went to red tag specials at Kay-Bee and Toys Works stores. The other figures have generally been available. Series two figures did not ship to local toy stores and were largely unknown until the series was cancelled and Kay-Bee got them all as red tag specials. This made a lot of collectors happy. As our hero would say, "Spoon!"

6" Figures, Good Doers
Bounding Tick (#02601) $10.00
Fluttering Arthur (#02602) 10.00
"Man Eating" Cow (#02603) 40.00
"Pose Striking" Die Fledermaus (#02604) 40.00
Sewer Spray Sewer Urchin (#02605) 10.00
Projectile Human Bullet (#02606) 10.00

Evil Doers
Growing Dinosaur Neil (#02607) 10.00
Death Hug Dean (#02608) 10.00
Exploding Dyna-Mole (#02609) 10.00
Grasping El Seed (#02610) 10.00

Wacky Wind-Up Action
Hard Drivin Tick (#02614) 4.00
Wing Flutterin Arthur (#02615) 4.00
Submarine Sewer Urchin (#02616) 4.00
Cannon Human Bullet (#02617) 4.00
Crop Dustin' El Seed (#02618) 4.00
Time Bomb Dyna-Mole (#02619) 4.00

Series II, Good Doers (Fall 1995)
Twist and Chop American Maid (#02631) 20.00
Hurling Tick (#02633) 10.00
Color Changing Crusading Chameleon (#02635) 15.00

Evil Doers
Skippy the Propellerized Robot Dog (#02632) 10.00
Mucus Tick (#02634) 10.00
Evil Tongue Thrakkorzog (#02636) 10.00

Tick Talkers
Tourist Tick (#02641) 12.00
"I Love Wheat" Tick (#02642) 12.00
"I Dig Dinosaur Neil" Tick (#02643) 12.00
Natural Tick (#02644) 12.00

Large Figure
Talking Tick, 16" (#02611) 20.00

Other Item
The Steel Box (#02645) 20.00

The Tick Seated in The Steel Box, The Tick (Bandai 1995)

TIGERSHARKS
LJN (1987)

This fine line of figures was based on guess what? That's right, a cartoon series, by Ruby-Spears. They are the aquatic equivalent of the Thundercats, which were also produced by LJN at this time.

6" Figures

Dolph	$20.00
Doc Walro, with Gup, his loyal pet	20.00
Mako	20.00
Lorca	20.00
Bronc	20.00
T-Ray, Evil Leader of the Mantanas	20.00
Bizarrly, Leader of the Evil Pirates	20.00
Spike Marlin, Nasty First Mate Pirate	20.00

Vehicle

Sharkhammer vehicle	40.00

TIM BURTON
SEE: NIGHTMARE BEFORE CHRISTMAS

Droopy, Tom and Jerry (MultiToy 1989)

TOM & JERRY
MultiToy (1989)

Tom and Jerry are well-known comic strip and cartoon characters. The header cards don't name them.

Figures (Asst. 08500) unnamed

(Tom)	$10.00
(Jerry)	10.00
(Droopy)	10.00
(Spike)	10.00
(Tyke)	10.00
(Quackers)	10.00

Large Figures

Tom and Jerry boxed set

Version with Jerry, mouth open	25.00
Version with Jerry, mouth closed	35.00
Spike 'n' Tyke boxed set	25.00

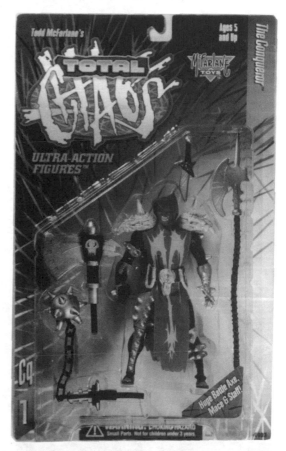

The Conqueror, Total Chaos (McFarlane Toys 1996)

TOTAL CHAOS
McFarlane Toys (1996)

This is another series of toys from the overworked mind of Todd McFarlane, featuring characters not yet involved in his comic book series. According to the package, "In a far off sector of the galaxy, there is a battle of good vs. evil. This conflict is not fought by armies, but by a handful of warriors picked from throughout the eons of time. Chosen for their distinctive skills they are then adapted to fight in the war know as Total Chaos."

Thresher was chosen for her "experience in marine warfare," but collectors chose her because she was the only female figure in the assortment and thus the hardest figure to find. Gore was scarce at first, but later boxes remedied the imbalance. Right away, collectors started looking for the usual McFarlane Toys variations and repaints and they were not disappointed. We also found an unusual figure, The

Conqueror, which has the same product number as Gore, is not pictured on the back of the header card, and has no character biography. It seems to have replaced Gore in an early 1997 batch of repaint figures.

6" Figures, Series One (Oct. 1996)
Dragon Blade "Battle Armor with Real Cloth Tunic" (#10171) long dragon on tunic $8.00
   Reissue, with short dragon on tunic chest 8.00
Gore "Launches Harpoon! Parrot Drops Bomb!" (#10172) 12.00
The Conqueror with Huge Battle Axe, Mace & Staff (#10172) 20.00
Thorax "Multipositional Turret Fires Spear" (#10173) . . 8.00
Thresher with "Trident Claw Fires All Around" (#10174) 16.00
   reissue, green armor 16.00
Hoof "Rotating Launcher Fires Bomb" (#10175) blue arm pads 8.00
   Reissue, with brown arm pads 8.00
Al Simmons "Fires Missiles from Launcher on Arm" (#10176) 8.00
   Reissue, dark body 8.00

Aquaman, Total Justice (Kenner 1996)

TOTAL JUSTICE
Kenner (1996)

The package describes the mission of this group of super heroes as follows: "On a distant planet, an evil being known as Darkseid prepares for his invasion and destruction of Earth. Batman learns of this diabolical plan and recruits the world's mightiest super heroes in an all-out assault on

Darkseid's forces. Armed with amazing new Fractal Tech-gear defenses created from a mix of Martian science and Batman's technology, the heroes are ready to fight back with increased powers and auto-morphing armor that appears when danger arises. Prepared for the ultimate battle, this special team committed to Total Justice soars off to cosmic combat!"

5" Figures (Sept. 1996)
The Flash with "Velocity Power Suit" (#63801) $9.00
Aquaman with "Blasting Hydro Spear" (#63802) 9.00
   Variation, with gold armor (#63802) 10.00
Green Lantern with "Ring-Energy Disk Launcher" (#63803) 12.00
Batman with "Flight Armor and Glider Cape" (#63804) . 9.00
Robin with "Spinning Razor Disc and Battle Staff" (#63806) 9.00
Darkseid with "Omega Effect Capture Claw" (#63807) . 9.00

Second Batch (Nov. 1996)
Hawkman with "Massive Grip Talons" (#63808) 15.00
Fractal Armor Batman with "Optical Shoulder Cannon System" (#63809) 10.00
Superman with "Kryptonite Ray Emitter" (#63811) . . . 12.00
Despero with "Galactic Body Blow Attack" (#63812) . 15.00

TOXIC CRUSADERS
Playmates (1991)

The figures are based on the humorous, anti-pollution themed animated series. The concept is very loosely based on the really really ridiculous *Toxic Avenger* film series from the Troma Films outfit.

5" Figures
Toxie (#2001) $7.00
Major Disaster (#2003) 7.00
Nozone (#2004) 7.00
Junkyard (#2005) 7.00
Headbanger (#2002) 7.00
Dr. Killemoff (#2006) 7.00
Bonehead (#2007) 7.00
Psycho (#2010) 7.00
Radiation Ranger (#2009) 7.00

Vehicles
Hideous Hovercraft (#2504) 18.00
Apocalypse Attackcopter (#2507) 25.00
Toxic Turf Surfer 9.00
Crusaderskater 9.00
Toxie's Toxic Waste 4.00

TOY STORY
Thinkway Toys (1996)

From the Disney all-computer-animated movie starring the voices of Tim Allen as Buzz and Tom Hanks as Woody. It's considered a kiddie movie and the figures are quite juvenile as well. This may restrict the collectibility of the figures. The kids love it, though, so Thinkway has a hit on their hands and the movie was pretty good, so you never know.

Boxer Buzz Lightyear, Toy Story (Thinkway 1996)

5" Figures
Buzz Lightyear with "Flying Rocket Action" $6.00
Quick-Draw Woody with "Quick-Draw Action" (#62801) 6.00
Buzz Lightyear with "Karate Chop Action" (#62802) . . . 6.00
Hamm with "Pop-Up Coin and Auto Deposit Action"
 (#62820) 6.00
Kicking Woody with "Kicking Leg Action" (#62863) . . . 6.00
Rex with "Moving Legs, Clamping Jaws and Glow in the
 Dark Parts" 6.00

Series Two Figures (1996)
Baby Face with "Blinking Eye and Pull Back Action"
 (#62876) 7.50
Chrome Buzz with "Flying Rocket Action" (#62879) . . . 6.00
Super Sonic Buzz Lightyear with "Rocket Boosters and
 Pop-Out Wings" (#62882) 6.00
Boxer Buzz Lightyear with "Swinging Fist Action"
 (#62883) 6.00
Fighter Woody with "Punching Fist Action" (#62884) . . 6.00
Alien with "Turning Head and Rotating Hands"
 (#62886) 6.00
Knock-Down Woody with "Collapsible Rag Doll Action"
 and stand 6.00

Series Three Figures (1996)
Karate Buzz with "Chopping Arm Action" 6.00
Solar Buzz Lightyear with "Rocket Action" 6.00
Infrared Buzz Lightyear with "Laser and Dome Light" . 6.00
Fighter Woody with "Punching Cactus" 6.00

Large Figures (1996)
Talking Buzz Lightyear, original box 50.00
 Reissue, in second box 20.00
Talking Woody 25.00

TROLL WARRIOR
Applause (1992)

Another entry in the Troll sweepstakes are the Troll Warriors from Applause Toys. Each comes with a tatoo and a weapon or other accessory. Twelve trolls were listed on the package, but only the first five ever appeared.

Figures
Thorbjorg the Trapper (#65020) $5.00
Fanta the Rascal (#65021) 5.00
Vegar the Champion (#65022) 5.00
Oddvar the Wizard (#65023) 5.00
Sven the Freedom Fighter (#65024) 5.00

TRON
Tomy (1982)

From the Disney live-action and computerized movie starring Jeff Bridges, David Warner and Bruce Boxleitner. "Denied access to a program he created, computer expert Alan Bradley seeks out Flynn, a video game virtuoso who is the only man clever enough to outwit the powerful Master Control Program." Instead, the MCP zaps Flynn into a bizarre electronic world where video games are life and death and the players race around on light cycles and are chased by tanks, etc. Flynn and Bradley's alter ego, Tron, join up to defeat the MCP.

The story was novelized by the late Brian Daley and published by Del Rey books. The figures were produced by Tomy, which was more famous for kiddie toys. They are hard to find, but not too many collectors are looking for them either.

4" Figures
Tron $10.00
Flynn 10.00
Sark 10.00
Warrior 10.00

Vehicles
Red Light Cycle (#5030) 25.00
Yellow Light Cycle (#5030) 25.00

U

Prototype, Ultra Force (Galoob 1995)

ULTRA FORCE
Galoob (1995)

From the Malibu comic book series and animated television series comes the Ultra Force! About 40,000 years ago, an alien spacecraft crash landed on the moon. Aboard the ship was "The Entity," which periodically sends a message across the universe hoping for a rescue. Sending the message causes strange effects on the Earth. "Rising from the chaos on Earth are Ultras, humans endowed with awesome powers greater than any known science can duplicate." In addition, the Fire People are released from deep within the Earth, having been mutated into Ultra bad guys. NM-E and Atalon are the Ultra Villains, while the rest, including Topaz the obligatory babe in the series, are Ultra Heroes.

The figures were numbered to make it easier to collect them. This was a good idea, but it didn't help this toy line. Figures 1 through 4 and 6 through 9 were released at the same time and were generally available. Other figures were planned, but not produced.

"Ultra 5000" figures came on a black header card and were included randomly as "chase figures" in cases with the regular figures, but different ones went to different retail chains. "Ultra 5000" figures, which went to toy store chains, could occasionally be found on the racks, but many were grabbed by stock boys. We found figures #11, #15, #16, #20 and #25 at local Kay-Bee and Toys "R" Us stores, some of them at red tag prices! Figure #0 went to the direct market, i.e. comic shops, and it was immediately priced higher by the shop owners.

We have also seen figures #5 and #10 at comic stores. We have seen pictures of the others, but we have never seen them for sale and so we are not sure if they were distributed. That's why we don't have prices listed for them. Even if they never appeared, there are still more different Ultra 5000 figures than regular figures, which is pretty strange for a "chase figure," until you realize that several of them are just repackaged original figures. It's possible that these missing Ultra 5000 figures are packed in the left-over cases, in which case they will eventually appear in Kay-Bee stores and other places where tail-end figures are distributed. Check those bargain bins thoroughly!

5" Figures

0. Prime (Ultra 5000) (#76596)	$35.00
1. Prime (#75597)	7.00
2. Prototype (#75598)	7.00
3. Hardcase (#75599)	7.00
4. Atalon (#75600)	7.00
5. All-American Prime (Ultra 5000) (#75596)	25.00
6. Ghoul (in coffin) (#75603)	7.00
7. NM-E (#75604)	7.00
8. Topaz (#75605)	9.00
9. The Night Man (#57601)	7.00
10. NM-E (Ultra 5000) (#75642)	25.00
11. Night Strike Prime (Ultra 5000) Bionic Helmet with Rocket Launcher (#75646)	25.00
12. Polar Prime (Ultra 5000)	20.00
13. Solar Prototype (Ultra 5000)	not seen
14. Radiation Hardcase (Ultra 5000)	not seen
15. Hardcase (Ultra 5000) (#75643)	25.00
16. Red Slayer NM-E (Ultra 5000) Ammo Arms Fire Electro Missiles (#75648)	25.00
18. Shadowfire The Night Man (Ultra 5000)	not seen
19. Queen Topaz (Ultra 5000)	not seen
20. The Night Man (Ultra 5000) (#75644)	25.00
21. Desert Heat The Night Man (Ultra 5000)	not seen
25. Topaz (Ultra 5000)	25.00

Vehicles
Ultra Rage Rover vehicle (#76161) 10.00

ULTRAMAN
Dreamworks (1991)

This interesting hero from *Dreamworks* is 8¼" tall and comes in a box with a 3" Jack Shindo figure for about $8-10.00. He battles five very weird looking '60s' Japanese movie-style monsters named Barrangas (sort of a winged dinosaur), Majaba (a giant insect), Gerrukadon (a four-armed dragon), Bogun (a two-headed I-don't-know-what), and Kilazee (a long-necked, winged reptile). We discovered that the later Jack Shindo figures have a red costume, while the early releases were a blue costumed figure. Our reports from local toy stores indicate that Ultraman sold faster than the monsters.

Figures
Ultraman with Jack Shindo (blue) (#5025) $10.00
Ultraman with Jack Shindo (red) (#5025) 10.00
Barrangas 12.00
Majaba 12.00
Gerrukadon 12.00
Bogun 12.00
Kilazee 12.00

Vehicle
Hummer with pilot figure (#5043) 25.00

THE UNCANNY MASTER
Unknown Manufacturer (1990s)

A group of cheap X-Men knock-off figures made in China. These figures may just possibly be worth the $1.00 we saw them selling for. Their only appeal is that they look a lot like your favorite X-Men super heroes and might amuse you or your friends.

UNIVERSAL CITY STUDIOS (MONSTERS)
"MINI-MONSTERS"
Remco (1979)

These monsters are as well known as any monster can be, but how many of their original appearances can you name and date? *Creature from the Black Lagoon* (1954) starred Richard Carlson and Julie Adams. *Dracula* (1931) starred Bela Lugosi. *Frankenstein* (1931) starred Boris Karloff as the monster. In later films he played Frankenstein, which is the name of the Doctor. *The Wolf Man* (1941) starred Lon Chaney Jr. with Claude Rains and Bela Lugosi. Frankenstein met the Wolf Man in 1943. *The Mummy* (1932) starred Boris Karloff. *Phantom of the Opera* (1925) starred Lon Chaney, Sr. in the silent film. Claude Rains played him in 1943.

Remco took up the torch (or cross) to produce monster action figures in the 1980s and started with two versions of 3¾" figures: glow-in-the-dark and non-glow. The Mummy

and The Wolfman are the rarest, but the entire series is great to collect.

3¾" Figures
Creature from the Black Lagoon $47.00
   Reissue, with Glow in the Dark 30.00
Dracula 30.00
   Reissue, with Glow in the Dark 22.00
Frankenstein Monster 32.00
   Reissue, with Glow in the Dark 20.00
Mummy 110.00
   Reissue, with Glow in the Dark 75.00
Phantom of the Opera 36.00
   Reissue, with Glow in the Dark 22.00
Wolfman 63.00
   Reissue, with Glow in the Dark 40.00

Accessories
Mini Monster Monsterizer 100.00
Mini Monster Play Case 25.00

[OFFICIAL]
UNIVERSAL STUDIOS (MONSTERS)
Remco (1980)

These are basically larger, doll versions of the previous Remco series. The Creature and The Wolfman are the high-priced notables here, but as with the smaller series, the whole line is worth collecting!

8" Dolls, boxed, with ring and Iron-on patch
Creature From the Black Lagoon $210.00
Dracula 90.00
Frankenstein Monster 45.00
The Mummy 40.00
Phantom of the Opera 20.00
The Wolfman 115.00

UNIVERSAL STUDIOS MONSTERS
Playco (1992)

These four figures don't have much action, but they are nicely sculpted. They come in window boxes and have molded-on clothing.

10" Figures
Dracula, 60th Anniversary limited edition $25.00
Frankenstein, 60th Anniversary limited edition 25.00
Wolfman (#2203) 30.00
Mummy (#2204) 25.00

U.S. FORCES DEFENDERS OF PEACE
U.S. MILITARY
Remco (1986–90)

Drug store military figures in which collectors have shown little interest. Remco has been making these same basic figures (with different colors, etc.) for years. Before this, they were called American Defense. After this they were called Desert Patrol and Desert Storm. I guess our heroic conquests of Grenada and Panama didn't rate a series.

V
LJN (1985)

Based on the popular NBC television mini series and the unpopular 1984–85 regular television series. Several other lizard/human-headed figures were planned but only the one 12" figure was produced. Robert Englund played Willie, the alien Visitor who defected to the human resistance. He went on to fame as Freddy Krueger.

12" Figure in window box
Enemy Visitor (#4500) $60.00

[SPIDER-MAN]
VENOM
PLANET OF THE SYMBIOTES
Toy Biz (1996)

These are the first of the Marvel 6" figures. The header cards are almost ornate.

6" Figures, First Batch (Sept. 1996)
Venom, The Madness with "Surprise Attack Heads and Symbiotic Wall-Crawler" (#47241) $9.00
Hybrid, with "Pincer Wing Action and Symbiotic Wall-Crawler" (#47242) 9.00
Lasher, with "Tentacle Whipping Action and Symbiotic Wall-Crawler" (#47243) 9.00
Scream, with "Living Tendril Hair and Symbiotic Wall-Crawler" (#47244) 9.00
Riot, with "Launching Attack Arms and Symbiotic Wall-Crawler" (#47245) 9.00

VIDEO COMMAND
Toy Island (1992)

While the figures talk, their faces change. This is one of the better series of drug store figures.

6" Figures on header cards
Lizard (#32006) $5.00
Max 5.00
Stinger 5.00

13" Figures in window box
Lizard 10.00
Max (#32011) 10.00
Stinger 10.00

Lasher, Venom, Planet of the Symbiotes (Toy Biz 1996)

VISIONARIES
"KNIGHTS OF THE MAGIC CIRCLE OF LIGHT"
Hasbro (1987)

"Enter a land where magic is more powerful than science—a futuristic world filled with magical power and spellbinding intrigue. Travel to a distant planet where the evil Darkling Lords, armed with dark, ominous powers and devastating weapons, threaten to unravel the existence of this once prosperous world. Only the Spectral Knights, worthy men of great courage and ability, can stop them with the aid of magic spirit crystals called totems that give them strange and mysterious power." The totems were holographic images and each Visionary came with two of them—one chest-mounted shield and a double image power staff. The holograms were expensive to produce and even the figures' "strange and mysterious power" couldn't keep this line alive for a second year.

Cindarr, Visionaries (Hasbro 1987)

4½" Spectral Knights Figures (Asst. #7800)
Leoric (#7901) $10.00
Arzon (#7903) 10.00
Cryotek (#7904) 10.00
Witterquick (#7905) 10.00

Darkling Lords
Darkstorm (#7907) 8.00
Cravex (#7909) 8.00
Lexor (#7910) 8.00
Cindarr (#7912) 8.00

Vehicles and Playset (1987)
Spectral Knights Lancer Cycle with **Ectar** figure
  (#7820) 12.00
Darkling Lords Sky Claw vehicle with **Mordred** figure
  (#7830) 16.00
Spectral Knights Capture Chariot vehicle with **Feryl**
  figure (#7840) 12.00
Darkling Lords Dagger Assault vehicle with **Reekon**
  figure (#7850) 28.00
Holodrome Iron Mountain playset (#7860) . . . . . .not made

VOICE PATROL
VOICE RANGERS
VOICE RAIDERS
VOICE SQUAD
Toy Island (1991)

Toy Island's Voice Patrol (Police), Voice Raiders (Pirates), Voice Rangers (Cowboys) and Voice Squad (Military) figures are 6¾" to 7" tall and feature electronic voices. They all come on "Try-me" header cards and are really one line of toys, despite the slight differences in title. Toy Island figures were most often found in drug stores, but some of these figures made it into toy stores as well. Unfortunately, these talking figures aren't based on a television show or comic book and aren't collected today, but maybe they should be. Toy Island's Space Attack series would probably be the place to start.

Voice Patrol
Emergency Control (#30801) $5.00
Contact Leader 5.00
Tactical Commander 5.00

Voice Rangers
U.S. Marshal Roy Star 5.00
Sheriff Tom Rider 5.00
Deputy Butch Cody 5.00

Voice Raiders
Capt. Claw 5.00
Red Beard 5.00
Evil Eye McGrub 5.00

Dragon King, Voice Squad (Toy Island 1991)

Voice Squad
Dragon King Rebel Commander Leader (#30731) 5.00
Eagle One Front Assault 5.00
Fire Bird Tactical Options 5.00
Tiger Chief Sneak Attack 5.00
Wizard Search and Destroy 5.00
Red Raven First Strike Leader (#30732) 5.00

VOLTRON
"DEFENDER OF THE UNIVERSE"
Matchbox (1985–86)

From a syndicated children's television series, naturally. It was an English language version of a Japanese cartoon series about a super-robot. The first five pilot figures came with a "Clip-On Lion Key" so that you could start your own lion to pilot. The next three figures commanded, rather than piloted, so they each came with a clip-on badge.

3¾" Figures

Keith, Pilots the Black Lion	$16.00
Hunk, Pilots the Yellow Lion	12.00
Lance, Pilots the Red Lion	14.00
Pidge, Pilots the Green Lion	12.00
Princess Allura, Pilots the Blue Lion	16.00
Doom Commander, Commands the Doom Blaster	10.00
Skull Scavenger, Commands the Skull Tank	10.00
Prince Lotor, Commands the Zarkon Zapper	16.00
Haggar the Witch	10.00
King Zarkon	10.00
Robeast Mutilor	10.00
Robeast Scorpious, Commands the Coffin of Doom	10.00

Vehicles and Accessories

Coffin of Darkness vehicle	18.00
Coffin of Doom vehicle	18.00
Doom Blaster vehicle	25.00
Skull Tank vehicle	20.00
Zarkon Zapper vehicle	25.00
Giant Commander	45.00
Green and Yellow Lion	25.00
Gift Set 1	150.00
Gift Set 2	150.00
Gift Set 3	200.00

Robot Figure

Voltron I, Miniature Warrior Space Robot (#700002)	30.00

VOLTRON
LJN (1986)

LJN picked up this series in 1986. The Motorized Lion Force consisted of a total of five vehicles that could be combined to from Voltron, a concept that hit it big in the 1990s with the Power Rangers.

Figures

Motorized Lion Force, Black Lion	30.00
Motorized Lion Force set, Blue Lion and Red Lion	35.00
Motorized Lion Force set, Green Lion and Yellow Lion	35.00

VOR-TECH UNDERCOVER
CONVERSION SQUAD
Kenner (1996)

"Be a part of the VOR-Tech Undercover Conversion Squad, where things are not always as they seem! Enter a world where a team of ordinary people in ordinary vehicles use amazing computer technology to convert themselves and their vehicles into an incredible fighting force, dedicated to saving Earth from an evil power spreading a deadly plague.

Join in this titanic struggle of human against cyborg, brother against brother, and machine against machine."

This struggle was just beginning at the end of 1996, so we don't know how it, or the toys will make out.

Conversion Action Vehicles and Small Figures

Battle Tracker ATV with Brad Logan (#37301)	$7.00
Road Head Cycle with Jason King (#37302)	7.00
Desert Striker Dune Buggy with Jeremy "Mac" MacMasters (#37303)	7.00

Rattler Off-Roader, Vor-Tech (Kenner 1996)

Larger Vehicles with Figure

Thunderwing Fighter with Hudson Roarke (#37307)	11.00
Sonic Singer Sports Car with Rick Rhodes (#37308?)	11.00
Rattler Off-Roader with Damian Roarke (#37309)	11.00

Larger Vehicle, boxed

Blazin Fury 4X4, with Tate Osborne (#37316)	23.00

(SABAN'S) VR TROOPERS
Kenner (1994–96)

VR (for Virtual Reality) Troopers is a live-action television series. The story centers on three teenagers "who, with the help of Professor Hart, a brilliant aging scientist existing solely as a holographic, virtually intelligent computer image, are able to transform into crime-fighting superheroes." (We have reread this promo copy several times and it still says that Professor Hart is "virtually intelligent.") The teenagers also have a sarcastic talking dog companion. They have to save the real world and the virtual world from "the evil megalomaniac Karl Zitko." In the real world we hire police to save us from teenagers.

Kaitlin Star, VR Troopers (Kenner 1994)

Deluxe Hyper-Tech Kaitlin Star, VR Troopers (Kenner 1995)

All of the first series figures were available as red tag specials in early 1996. Kaitlin Star is the girl, but she hasn't gotten much collector attention so far.

5" Figures
Ryan Steele with "Edge-Glow 'Laser' Blade and Snap-
    On Pistol" (#65941) $5.00
J.B. Reese with "Interlocking Edge-Glow 'Laser' Lances"
    (#65942) 5.00
Kaitlin Star with "Connectable Edge-Glow Trident Sword
    and Ray Gun" (#65943) 5.00
Tankotron with "Shoulder Turrets and Double-Barreled
    Bazooka" (#65944) 5.00
Skug with "Battle Hatchet and Pistol" (#65947) 5.00

Second Series (1996)
Air Striker with "Spinning Propeller and Blitz Bomb"
    (#65954) 20.00
Dark Heart with "Dual Assault Cannons" (#65955) . . . 5.00
Virtual Armor J.B. Reese with "Snap-on Battle Gear"
    (1996) 20.00
Virtual Armor Ryan Steel with "Snap-on Battle Gear"
    (1996) 20.00

Deluxe Figures (1995) with "Laser" Light Eyes
Deluxe Mega-Tech Ryan Steele with "Firing Power
    Spear Launcher" (#65934) 8.00
Deluxe Turbo-Tech J.B. Reese with "Firing VR Techno
    Bazooka" (#65936) 8.00
Deluxe Hyper-Tech Kaitlin Star with "Sword-Firing Jet
    Pack" (#65937) 8.000

Deluxe Figures (1996) with "Battle Grid"
Deluxe Ryan Steel with "Lightning Strike Punch"
    (#65921) 10.00
Deluxe J.B. Reese with "Turbo Spinning Weapons"
    (#65922) 10.00
Deluxe Kaitlin Star with "Powerful Ninja Kick" (#65923) 10.00

Other Deluxe Figure
Deluxe The Decimator with "Suprise-Attack Sword
    Launcher" (#65927) 12.00

Vehicles
VR Turbo Cycle with "Blasting VR Missile and
    Breakaway Sidecar" (#65982) 8.00
VR Pursuit Jet with "Drop & Lock Wings and Rapid-Fire
    VR Missiles" (#65981) 16.00
Skyborg Jet "Fires Assault Missile and Drops Mega
    Bombs" (#65992) 10.00
VR Fighter Bike with "Firing VR Missile and Flip-Up
    Delta Wings" 10.00
VR Battle Cruiser with "VR Interceptor Jet" (#65937,
    1996) 20.00

Large Figures
Ultimate Ryan Steele, 14" (#65325) 14.00

THE WALTONS
Mego (1975–76)

From the television show which ran from 1972 to 1981. Richard Thomas played John-Boy most of the time and Judy Norton-Taylor played his sister Mary Ellen. Ralph Waite and Michael Learned were John and Olivia (Mom and Pop) Walton and Will Geer and Ellen Corby were Grandpa and Grandma. It was a sweet, homespun and thoroughly middle-American show full of family values so we didn't watch it. The toys didn't do too well either, although they are collected because they are Mego figures. "Goodnight, John-Boy!"

8" Two-Pack Figures in window boxes
Johnboy and Ellen	$50.00
Grandma and Grandpa	45.00
Mom and Pop	45.00

Vehicles and Playsets
Barn	150.00
Country Store	150.00
Farmhouse playset, vinyl	125.00
Farmhouse playset with Waltons	175.00
Truck	125.00

WARRIOR BEASTS
SEE: LOST WORLD OF THE WARLORD

WARRIOR NUN AREALA
Antarctic Press (1996)

Based on the comic book of the same name. The figure was issued independently by the comic book publisher and sold direct to comic stores. While it was late in shipping and there were some problems, the entire 25,000 figure production run was sold out. More figures are scheduled for 1997.

5" Figure
Warrior Nun Areala (#0001)	$15.00

WATERWORLD
Kenner (1995)

Based on the 1995 movie starring Kevin Costner, Jeanne Tripplehorn and Dennis Hopper. On a future earth, the polar icecaps have all melted and the earth is covered by water. The survivors live in floating villages and look for land, rumored to be somewhere. The first problem with this scenario is that if all the ice in the world melted, the oceans would only rise a few hundred feet. Lots of land would be left. The second problem is that a map is worthless unless you know where you are on it and the characters are all floating in the middle of an ocean and don't have a clue. Still, an interesting concept for a movie, but it was panned by the critics, especially because of its reported $200 million cost.

The figures came out in mid 1995, just before the movie. No one bought them, and by spring of 1996 all of the figures were three for $5.00 at local stores.

5" Figures
Bola Attack Mariner with "Double Claw Launcher and Mutant Eel" (#62811)	$5.00
Deacon with "Disc Firing Helmet and Mutant Hunter Shark" (#62806)	5.00
Hydro Stinger Mariner with "Blasting Aqua Spear and Mutant Manta Ray" (#62802)	5.00

Hydro Stinger Mariner, Waterworld (Kenner 1995)

Atoll Enforcer with "Launching Capture Web and Mutant
    Squid" (#62804) 5.00
Power Bow Mariner with "Shooting Combat Bow and
    Mutant Moray Eel" (#62812) 5.00
Nord with "Firing Bazooka Bomber and Mutant Crab"
    (#62807) 5.00

Vehicles
The Trimaran, 21" mast (#62811) .: 18.00
Smoker Thunder Ski with "Berserker Rider" (#62808) 10.00
Wave Ripper with "Warrior Mariner" (#62809) 10.00

WELCOME BACK, KOTTER
Mattel (1976)

Based on the popular television series with Gabriel
Kaplan as Mr. Kotter and a young John Travolta as Barbarino. Now that Travolta has a career again, his figure has
risen in value a little.

Figures
Mr. Kotter (#9770) $40.00
Horshack (#9771) 40.00
Barbarino (#9772) 60.00
Washington (#9773) 40.00
Epstein (#9774) 40.00

Vehicles and Playsets
Sweathogs Bike 20.00
Welcome Back, Kotter Classroom playset, includes
    record and booklet 80.00
Deluxe Classroom playset 125.00

WETWORKS
McFarlane Toys (1995–96)

WetWorks figures are based on the comic book series
of the same name created by Whilce Portacio. The first series
figures come on blue lightning bolt header cards which are
identical to Spawn header cards. Second series figures have
the same design cards, but in purple. They were all repainted
within a few months. Werewolf from the first series and
Blood Queen from the second series are scarce and desirable.

6" Figures
Dane with "Removable Combat Jacket and Belt; Flip-Up
    Head Gear" (#12101) $9.00
Dozer with "Heavy Fire Power Guns; Twin Ammo Belts"
    (#12102) 9.00
Mother-One with "Multi-Function Interchangeable
    Cybernetic Arms" (#12103) 20.00
Vampire with "Removable Leg Armor; Stands 7¾" Tall"
    (#12104) 15.00
Werewolf "Stands Up on Both Feet or Drops to All
    Fours" (#12105) scarce 22.00
Grail with "Back Pack Battle Weapons and Ammo Belt"
    (#12106) 9.00

Series Two (June 1996)
Mendoza "Telescoping Cannon Fires Missile" (#12111) 9.00
Frankenstein "Battle Staff with Wolf Skull" (#12112) .. 9.00
Blood Queen "Ceremonial Staff & Real Cloth Cape"
    (#12113) 25.00
Assassin One with "Cross Bow Fires Missile Arsenal"
    (#12114) 9.00

Dozer, WetWorks (McFarlane 1995)

Pilgrim "Assault Rifle Fires Missile" (#12115) 18.00
Delta Commander "Launches Tactical Missile"
    (#12116) 9.00

Third Batch Repaints (1996)
Mendoza (#12111) flesh tone 11.00
Frankenstein (#12112) green body 11.00
Blood Queen (#12113) red highlights 20.00
Assassin One (#12114) red body 11.00
Pilgrim (#12115) flesh tone 12.00
Delta Commander (#12116) flesh tone 11.00

WHERE'S WALDO?
Arco Toys Ltd., A Mattel Company (1991)

This was a popular book series, but if you haven't
already found Waldo several times you probably won't be all
that excited about looking for these figures. We are sure
someone, somewhere still looks for Waldo, but it doesn't
seem to be action figure collectors. Where's Waldo? Try the
discount bins in the bargain aisles.

5" Figures (Asst. #9102)
Norseman bendie $5.00
Waldo and Woof 5.00
Crusader 5.00
Wizard 5.00
Wenda and Woof 5.00
Pirate 5.00

WHO FRAMED ROGER RABBIT
LJN (1988)

Based on the 1988 movie starring Bob Hoskins and Christopher Lloyd and the voices of Charles Fleischer and Joanna Cassidy as toons Roger Rabbit and the sexy ("I'm not bad; I'm just drawn that way") Jessica. The movie was based on the book *Who Censored Roger Rabbit?* by Gary Wolf and included an all-star cast of toons in addition to Roger and Jessica.

Animates Figures (Asst. #8610)
Benny the Cab	$35.00
Eddie Valiant	8.00
Judge Doom	8.00
Roger Rabbit	8.00
Smart Guy (Boss Weasel)	8.00

Flexies Poseable Figures (Asst. #8638)
Baby Herman	30.00
Jessica	40.00
Judge Doom	15.00
Roger Rabbit	10.00
Smart Guy (Boss Weasel)	12.00
Eddie Valiant	12.00
Super Flexie Roger Rabbit	15.00

WILD WEST
Mattel (1976)

Mattel made these figures during the time westerns were trying to make a comeback on television. They are *not* based on the television show "The Wild, Wild West" which ran in the late 1960s.

12" Figures
Bloody Fox	$45.00
Old Firehand	45.00
Old Surehand	45.00
Indian Guide	45.00
Mexican Guerrero	60.00
Old Shatterhand	45.00
Prospector	50.00
Medicine Man	60.00
Wagon Driver	40.00

WILD WEST
C.O.W. BOYS OF MOO MESA
Hasbro (1991)

This is a series of figures from Hasbro which remind us of Barnyard Commandos. The mostly bovine characters are styled to represent various western characters more or less along the lines of their clever names. We saw all ten of the figures when they first appeared and none were short-packed. We didn't collect any Barnyard Commandos either, even though they were available on red tag sale and there doesn't seem to be a lot of collector interest in this series either, although we actually know a couple of adults who admitted that they watched the ABC animated television show.

5" Figures
Moo Montana (#7081)	$7.00
The Cowlorado Kid (#7082)	7.00
Geronimoo (#7083)	7.00
Sheriff Terrorbull (#7084)	7.00
Saddlesore (#7085)	7.00
The Dakota Dude (#7087)	7.00
Colonel Cudster (#7088)	7.00
Buffalo Bull (#7089)	7.00
Five Card Cud (#7090)	7.00
Boot Hill Buzzard (#7091)	7.00

Vehicle
Wild West Iron Horse vehicle with Spring-Fired Can O' Beans Cannon (#7093)	15.00

Zealot, WildC.A.T.s (Playmates 1995)

WILDC.A.T.S.
Playmates (1995)

Based on the popular comic books by Jim Lee starring the Wild Covert Action Team or WildC.A.T.s, which became a "mega-hit CBS animated show" (according to the catalog, anyway). "For millennia, two opposing cabals of aliens have conducted secret wars in the midst of human society, in search of the omnipotent Orb .... On the dark side, the Daemonites plan to plunder Earth, capture the Orb and commence a Reign of Galactic Terror! On the side of mankind, the Kherubim stand in the way of the Daemonites' evil plans. The Kherubim, joined by humans and crossbreeds, together form the WildC.A.T.S Covert Action Teams" to save the earth, the universe and whatever.

The first several batches of figures came with one of two different exclusive trading cards. They were not as successful as other super hero action figures, were not included in Playmates' 1996 line and were discounted at local Toys "R" Us and other stores starting in March 1996. Third-batch figures became available in quantity at this time at Caldor's and other stores at red-tag prices. Fourth-batch figures were not available in local stores until August 1996, when Kay-Bee and Toy Works stores began to offer them. This is a common occurrence, as Kay-Bee often buys up large quantities of the tail-end of toy lines which are first seen as red-tag specials.

6" Figures, with one of two trading cards
Spartan (#01801) with card #1 or #2 . . . . $9.00
Zealot (#01802) with card #3 or #4 . . . . 15.00
    Variation, autographed by Jim Lee 30.00
Grifter (#01803) with card #9 or #10 . . . . 15.00
    Variation, autographed by Jim Lee 30.00
Maul (#01804) with card #7 or #8 . . . . 10.00
Warblade (#01805) with card #5 or #6 . . . . 9.00
Helspont (#01806) with card #13 or #14 . . . . 15.00
Daemonite (#01807) with card #11 or #12 . . . . 15.00

Second Batch, all say "New" with one of two trading cards
Spartan in ECM Stealth Suit (#01816) 9.00
Zealot in Classic Coda Uniform (#01817) 12.00
WarBlade in Bio-Flexon Armor Suit (#01818) 9.00
Helspont in Daemonite Ceremonial Battle Gear
    (#01819) 10.00
Maul in Flexon All-Weather Combat Suit (#01820) . . 10.00

Mr. Majestic, WildC.A.T.s (Playmates 1995)

Third Batch, with one of two trading cards
Void (#01808) with card #20 or #21 . . . . 10.00
Voodoo (#01809) with card #22 or #23 . . . . 11.00
Pike (#01810) with card #24 or #25 . . . . 9.00

Fourth Batch "Image Universe" with trading card
Mr. Majestic (Maverick Kherubim Master) (#11801) . . 15.00
Slag (Chemically-Created Volcanic Villain) (#11802) . 15.00
Black Razor (Max Cash, Member of ETR Squad)
    (#11803) 15.00
Pike in ECM Stealth Suit (#11804) 15.00

Vehicle with trading card
Bullet Bike vehicle (#01851) 10.00

10" Figures
Giant Spartan (#01831) 17.00
Giant Maul (#01832) 17.00
Giant Grifter (#01835) 20.00

Two-Packs, limited editions with two trading cards and comic
Spartan vs. Helspont (#01841) with cards #1 and #2 . 16.00
The Grifter vs. Daemonite (#01842) with cards #3 and
    #4 . . . . 16.00

WILLOW
"THE MAGIC LIES WITHIN!"
Tonka (1988)

From the live-action fantasy movie directed by Ron Howard and starring Val Kilmer, Joanne Whalley, Jean Marsh, Warwick Davis (as Willow) and Billy Barty. The movie was fairly popular and had some decent special effects. The figures are only borderline action figures and haven't gone up in value.

3" Figures
Airk Thaughbaer, Heroic Commander $5.00
Death Dog, Evil Beast 5.00
General Kael, Evil Commander 5.00
High Aldwin, Heroic Wise Man 5.00
Madmartigan, Heroic Swordsman 5.00
Nockmaar Lieutenant, Evil Trooper 5.00
Nockmaar Warrior, Evil Soldier 5.00
Queen Bavmorda, Evil Sorceress 10.00
Rebel Trooper, Heroic Soldier 5.00
Sorsha, Heroic Warrior 5.00
Troll, Evil Creature 5.00
Willow Ufgood, Heroic Protector 5.00
Willow Ufgood, Heroic Protector (with baby) 10.00

Exclusives and Mail-in Figures
Willow (Nestle premium, loose figure) 15.00
Catapult (Sears exclusive) 60.00
Chariot (Sears exclusive) 60.00
Mangonel (Sears exclusive) 70.00

Figure and Horse Sets (Asst. #6610)
Airk Thaughbaer and Horse, Heroic Commander . . . 10.00
General Kael and Horse, Evil Commander 10.00
Madmartigan and Horse, Heroic Swordsman 10.00
Nockmaar Warrior and Horse, Evil Soldier 10.00
Sorsha and Horse, Beautiful Warrior 10.00

Collector Sets (Asst. #6620)
Evil Collector Set #1, including Nockmaar Warrior, Death

Dog, and General Kael, with Horse 20.00
Evil Collector Set #2 (Sears exclusive) 90.00
Heroic Collector Set #1, including Willow Ufgood,
    Sorsha, and Madmartigan, with Horse 20.00
Heroic Collector Set #2, including Madmartigan, Rebel
    Trooper, and Airk Thaughbaer, with Horse 20.00

Large Figure, in window box
Eborsisk Dragon (#6650) 40.00

WIZARD OF OZ
Mego (1974)

In case you slept through your entire prior life and aren't familiar with *The Wizard of Oz* movie you should know that it starred Judy Garland, Ray Bolger, Bert Lahr, Jack Haley and Margaret Hamilton. The movie came out in 1939 and was based on a series of children's books by L. Frank Baum.

The movie was still popular in 1974, its 25th anniversary, but Mego found that they weren't in Kansas anymore either and didn't do too well getting Munchkins to buy these figures. They are a lot more collectible today.

8" Figures in window box
Cowardly Lion $40.00
Dorothy and Toto 40.00
Glinda, The Good Witch 40.00
Scarecrow 30.00
Tin Woodsman 30.00
Wicked Witch 80.00
Winged Monkey 60.00
The Wizard (of Oz) 300.00

Munchkins
Flower Girl 115.00
Mayor 115.00
Dancing Girl 115.00
General 115.00
Lolly Pop Kid 115.00

Playsets
Emerald City playset, with **Wizard** figure 90.00
Enchanted City of Oz playset 150.00
Munchkinland playset, with **Mayor** figure 300.00
Witches Castle (Sears exclusive) 425.00

THE WIZARD OF OZ
Multi-Toys (1989)

The movie was made in 1939 and was 50 years old when these figures were made. They are collected more by movie collectors than by action figure collectors. The larger figures are mostly interesting to doll collectors, but there are better ones available in the Barbie doll line.

3¾" "50th Anniversary" Figures
Dorothy $10.00
Scarecrow 10.00
Tinman 10.00
Cowardly Lion 10.00
Wicked Witch 10.00
Glinda 10.00

Multi-Pack
Boxed set of 6 figures 30.00

6" Figures
Mayor Munchkin 15.00
General Munchkin 15.00
Flower Girl Munchkin 15.00
Dancer Munchkin 15.00
Lolly Pop Kid Munchkin 15.00
Witch's Monkey 15.00

12" "50th Anniversary" Figures, in window box
Dorothy and Toto 20.00
Scarecrow 20.00
Tin Man 20.00
Cowardly Lion 20.00
Wicked Witch 20.00
Glinda 20.00
Wizard 25.00

Boxed Set
Boxed set of 6 figures 60.00

WONDER WOMAN
Mego (1978–79)

From the television series which starred Lynda Carter as Wonder Woman, in the role originated by Cathy Lee Crosby in a 1974 made-for-TV movie. Wonder Woman worked for the government as a secretary or something for Major Steve Trevor who was played by Lyle Waggoner. In the 1980s, the government tried unsuccessfully to lasso Linda's husband and get him to tell the truth about his part in the BCCI bank scandal. Lynda, on the other hand, still looked good doing television info-mercials, not, sadly, in her low-cut Wonder Woman outfit.

12" Wonder Woman TV Figures (1976)
Wonder Woman, with Diana Prince outfit, Lynda Carter
    photo box 150.00
Wonder Woman, with "Fly-Away Action" (second-issue
    box without Lynda Carter picture) (1979) 90.00
Nubia 120.00
Queen Hippolyte 100.00
Steve Trevor 80.00

Playset
Wonder Woman playset 140.00

(OFFICIAL) WORLD'S GREATEST SUPER HEROES
Mego (1972–79)

Mego super heroes are the most famous action figures in existence. They weren't the first—that title goes to G.I. Joe; they aren't the most valuable—that prize goes to Captain Action. However, in both of those series the collecting action is in the outfits and accessories. Mego super heroes came complete in their own box and there were dozens of characters to choose from. Every boy had them.

This line of figures put Mego on the map. In addition to DC and Marvel super heroes figures, Mego also produced

Spider-Man, Green Goblin, Iron Man and Captain America, World's Greatest Super Heroes (Mego 1972–74)

figures of Robert E. Howard's Conan and Edgar Rice Burrough's Tarzan. The figures came in many different packages over the years, including boxes, window boxes, header cards and Kresge exclusives. Popular figures were produced for several years after their initial release. This makes it difficult to place the figures in meaningful groups or series, so all are listed alphabetically. Dates given below are for the first year of release.

Figures on **Kresge** cards are from 1972–74 and are worth *as much or more* than the boxed figures from these years. Listed prices for carded figures are for the 1976–79 figure releases. Prices on all these figures have increased steadily over the years and this entire series is considered a very good investment.

The popularity of the line was so great that several of Mego's series of monsters, western heroes, etc., also carry the "Official World's Greatest Super Heroes" logo. Each of these groups has its own listing elsewhere in the book.

8" Action Figures

Aquaman (1972) in solid box	550.00
Aquaman in window box	150.00
Aquaman (1976) on header card	175.00
Aquaman (loose)	35.00
Batgirl (1973) in window box	250.00
Batgirl (1976) on header card	275.00
Batgirl (loose)	100.00
Batman (removable mask) (1972) in solid box	1,000.00
Batman (removable mask) in window box	375.00
Batman, removable mask (loose)	130.00
Batman without removable mask, in window box	225.00
Batman without removable mask (1976) on header card	100.00
Batman, non-removable mask (loose)	45.00
Batman (Fist Fighting (1976) in window box	400.00
Batman (Fist Fighting, loose)	100.00
Bruce Wayne (Mont. Ward's exclusive) (1974)	525.00
Captain America (1972) in window box	250.00
Captain America (1976) on header card	150.00
Captain America (loose)	60.00
Catwoman (1973) in window box	300.00
Catwoman (1976) on header card	275.00
Catwoman (loose)	100.00
Clark Kent (Mont. Ward's exclusive) (1974)	525.00
Conan (1975) in window box	400.00
Conan (1976) on header card	350.00
Conan (loose)	100.00
Dick Grayson (Mont. Ward's exclusive) (1974)	525.00
Falcon (1974) in window box	120.00
Falcon (1976) on header card	575.00
Falcon (loose)	45.00
Green Arrow (1973) in window box	300.00
Green Arrow (1976) on header card	490.00
Green Arrow (loose)	75.00
Green Goblin (1974) in window box	250.00
Green Goblin (1976) on header card	600.00
Green Goblin (loose)	120.00
Human Torch (1975) in window box	145.00
Human Torch (1976) on header card	90.00
Human Torch (loose)	35.00
Incredible Hulk (1974) in window box	90.00
Incredible Hulk (1976) on header card	40.00
Incredible Hulk (loose)	18.00
Invisible Girl (1975) In window box	135.00
Invisible Girl (1976) on header card	45.00
Invisible Girl (loose)	35.00
Iron Man (1974) in window box	240.00
Iron Man (1976) on header card	480.00
Iron Man (loose)	60.00
Isis (1976) in window box	300.00

Isis (1976) on header card 160.00
Isis (loose) 75.00
Joker (1973) in window box 160.00
Joker (1976) on header card 120.00
Joker (loose) 50.00
Joker (Fist Fighting) (1976) in window box 350.00
Joker (Fist Fighting, loose) 100.00
Lizard (1974) in window box 220.00
Lizard (1976) on header card 480.00
Lizard (loose) 80.00
Mr. Fantastic (1975) in window box 180.00
Mr. Fantastic (1976) on header card 90.00
Mr. Fantastic (loose) 45.00
Mr. Mxyzptlk (with smirk) (1973) in window box . . . 160.00
Mr. Mxyzptlk (with smirk, loose) 60.00
Mr. Mxyzptlk (with mouth open) (1973) in window box 100.00
Mr. Mxyzptlk (carded, with mouth open) 160.00
Mr. Mxyzptlk (with mouth open, loose) 30.00
Penguin (1973) in window box 130.00
Penguin (1976) on header card 130.00
Penguin (loose) 45.00
Peter Parker (Mont. Ward's exclusive) (1974) 525.00
Riddler (1973) in window box 300.00
Riddler (1976) on header card 400.00
Riddler (loose) 90.00
Riddler (Fist Fighting) (1976) in window box 350.00
Riddler (Fist Fighting, loose) 100.00
Robin (removable mask) (1972) in solid box 1,375.00
Robin (removable mask) in window box 600.00
Robin (removable mask, loose) 380.00
Robin (without removable mask) in window box . . . 135.00
Robin (without removable mask) (1976) on header
    card 85.00

Robin (without removable mask, loose) 50.00
Robin (Fist Fighting) (1976) 350.00
Robin (Fist Fighting, loose) 100.00
Shazam (1972) in window box 175.00
Shazam (1976) on header card 175.00
Shazam (loose) 60.00
Spider-Man (1972) in window box 130.00
Spider-Man (1976) on header card 60.00
Spider-Man (loose) 30.00
Supergirl (1973) in window box 375.00
Supergirl (1976) on header card 450.00
Supergirl (loose) 115.00
Superman (1972) in solid box 625.00
Superman in window box 150.00
Superman (1976) on header card 90.00
Superman (loose) 40.00
Tarzan (1972) in window box 90.00
Tarzan (1976) on header card 300.00
Tarzan (loose) 50.00
The Thing (1975) in window box 175.00
The Thing (1976) on header card 90.00
The Thing (loose) 50.00
Thor (1975) in window box 410.00
Thor (1976) on header card 425.00
Thor (loose) 100.00
Wonder Woman (1973) in window box 375.00
Wonder Woman (carded) (Kresge only) 480.00
Wonder Woman (loose) 110.00
See Also: Teen Titans series

Note: Batgirl, Catwoman, Supergirl and Wonder Woman packages say "World's Greatest Super Gals" and Isis package does not say "World's Greatest Super Heroes."

Thor, World's Greatest Super Heroes (Mego 1975)

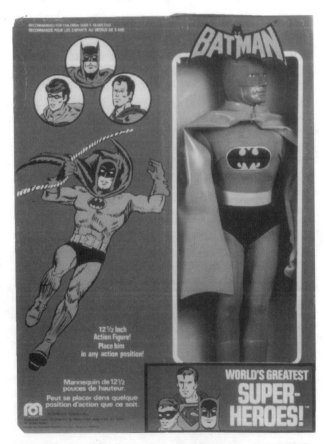

Batman, 12", World's Greatest Super Heroes (Mego 1976)

Vehicles and Playsets

The Amazing Spider Car "Featuring Spidey's Web Trap" (1976)	90.00
Aquaman vs. The Great White Shark	500.00
Batcopter (boxed) (#51326, 1974)	120.00
Batcopter (carded) (1974)	100.00
Batcycle (1974)	200.00
Batmobile (boxed) (1974)	225.00
Batmobile (carded) (1974)	125.00
Captain Americar with "Flip-Out Deflector Shield" (1976)	250.00
Green Arrowcar "Featuring Green Arrow's Flying Missles" (1976)	250.00
Jokermobile (1975)	200.00
Batcave playset (1974)	200.00
Batman's Wayne Foundation (1977)	700.00
Hall of Justice (1976)	150.00
Mobile Bat Lab (1975)	140.00
Supervator (1974)	90.00

Mego (1976–81)

12½" Figures

Batman in window box	90.00
Batman "Fly Away Action"	140.00
Batman with magnetic power	125.00
Captain America "Fly Away Action"	125.00
Incredible Hulk	90.00
Incredible Hulk "Fly Away Action"	100.00
Lex Luthor	150.00
Robin in window box	200.00
Robin "Fly Away Action"	140.00
Robin, with magnetic power	225.00
Spider-Man in window box	90.00
Spider-Man with magnetic power	125.00
Amazing Spider-Man with Spiderweb (#83001, 1977) (carded)	70.00
Spider-Man "Fly Away Action"	125.00
Web-Spinning Spider-Man	150.00
Superman in window box	100.00

WORLD'S GREATEST SUPER HEROES SUPERMAN (MOVIE)
Mego (1979)

These figures have the logo for the "World's Greatest Super Heroes" series, but they are also a separate series based on the *Superman I* and *Superman II* movies, which appeared in 1978 and 1980 respectively. These movies starred Christopher Reeve as Superman, with Margo Kidder as Lois Lane, Gene Hackman as Lex Luthor, Terence Stamp as General Zod and Jackie Cooper as Perry White. Did we forget someone important? Oh yeah, also starring Marlon Brando as Jor-El.

12½" Superman Movie Figures (1979) in movie box

Jor-El (#87003/1)	40.00
Lex Luthor (#87003/2)	40.00
General Zod of the Phantom Zone (#87003/3)	40.00
Superman (#87003/4?)	75.00
Superman with "Fly Away Action"	150.00

WORLD'S GREATEST SUPER HEROES (AMERICAN) (WESTERN HEROES)
SEE: AMERICAN WEST

WORLDS GREATEST SUPER-KNIGHTS
Mego (1975–76)

Knights of legend and lore, in other words, from King Arthur's legendary time.

8" Figures

King Arthur	$100.00
Sir Launcelot	175.00
Sir Galahad	175.00
Ivanhoe	100.00
The Black Knight	300.00

Vehicles and Playset

Jousting Horses	100.00
Castle Playset	200.00

WORLDS GREATEST SUPER PIRATES
Mego (1975–76)

"Aaarrgghh matey!" said the big boss at Mego. "Make me a new series of figures that I don't have to pay another licensing fee for!"

8" Figures

Jean Lafitte	$150.00
Blackbeard	120.00
Captain Patch	90.00
Long John Silver	150.00

Shatterstar (I) with "Dual Sword Action" (#4952) 10.00
Kane (I) with "Snap-Back Living Hand!" (#4953) 18.00
    Variation with blue leg holster 80.00
Warpath with "Thunder Punch Action" (#4954) 12.00
G.W. Bridge with "Rapid-Fire Gun" (#4955) 14.00
Stryfe with "Flip-Up Helmet Reveals Identity" (#4956) 15.00
Deadpool with "Spring Out Dagger" (#4957) 38.00
Forearm with "Four Arm Punching Action" (#4958) . . 22.00
Gideon with "Sword Slashing Thrust" (#4959) 15.00

[THE UNCANNY X-MEN]
X-FORCE
Toy Biz (1993)

The most collectible figure among the X-Force 1993 figures is the pink Cannonball. He is easy to find in purple; the pink outfit is scarce, but not too scarce. We have seen a number for sale from dealers and suspect that a lot of collectors would rather look for a bargain. Still, though, it's *the* figure to have in this series.

Second Series (Asst. #4950C) with SkyBox X-Men 2 card
Cable 2nd Edition with "Deep Space Armor" (#4963) $14.00
Cable 3rd Edition with "Rapid Rocket Firing Action"
    (#4964) 14.00
Kane (II) with "Double Fisted Weapons" (#4965) 15.00
Cannonball with "Catapult Launching Action" (#4966)
    pink, scarce 40.00
Cannonball with "Catapult Launching Action" (#4966)
    purple 20.00
Grizzly with "Crushing Power Hammers" (#4967) . . . 15.00
Krule with "Shrunken Heads" (#4968) 15.00

Forearm, X-Force (Toy Biz 1992)

[THE UNCANNY X-MEN]
X-FORCE
Toy Biz (1992)

The X-Force figures are also part of the X-Men series, but they are generally considered to be a separate group rather than a sub-group. Cable is their leader and they got their own comic book series in 1991.

The first group of figures appeared in the fall of 1992, along with several X-Men figures. All of them originally came with an Impel X-Men series 1 trading card. When these ran out, the figures were shipped with a series 2 card. These reissues are worth a few dollars less than the original issue.

5" Figures, with Impel X-Men (I) card
later shipments, with SkyBox X-Men 2 card
Cable (I) with "Clobber Action" (#4951) $16.00

[X-MEN]
X-FORCE
Toy Biz (1994)

The year 1994 brought two series of X-Force figures. The X-Men series logo changed from "The Uncanny X-Men" to "X-Men" and this change was made on X-Force packaging as well. By the time the second batch arrived, either the kids had too many X-Men already or the total production was increased because that batch hung around a long time in toy stores.

Third Series (Asst. #4950E) with Fleer Ultra X-Men card
Cable 4th Edition with "Air Assault Action" (#49513) $15.00
Rictor with "Seismic Shock Wave Action" (#49514) . . 18.00
Sunspot with "Explosive Power Punch" (#49515) . . . 22.00
Quark with "2-Fisted Quick Draw" (#49516) 15.00

Quark, X-Force (Toy Biz 1994)

Shatterstar 2nd Edition with "Dual Sword Slashing
    Action" (#49518) 13.00
Pyro with "Flame Throwing Action" (#49519) 22.00
Mojo with "Wild Whipping Tail" (#49528) (Toys "R" Us
    exclusive) 9.00

Fourth Series (Asst. #4950F) with Ultra X-Men card with or
without T-shirt offer on header card back
X-Treme with "Axe Attack" (#49520) 10.00
Black Tom with "Power Bio-Blast" (#49521) 10.00
Killspree with "Slashing Blade Arms" (#49523) 12.00
Slayback with "Extending Bio-Mechanical Arms"
    (#49524) 6.00
Cable 5th Edition with "Deep Sea Gear" (#49525) 8.00
Commcast with "Mutant Hunting Hovororaft" (#49526) . 7.00
Warpath 2nd Edition with "Smashing Power Punch"
    (#49527) 6.00

10" X-Force Figures (1994)
Cable (#49550) 11.00
Kane (#49551) 11.00
Shatterstar (#49552) 11.00
Cable (#49510) Venture Stores exclusive 15.00

[X-MEN]
X-FORCE
Toy Biz (1995–96)

In 1995, Toy Biz made the transition to the new, larger
size header cards which also appeared on X-Men figures.
Only one batch of X-Force figures appeared in 1996. None

of the figures has attracted much individual attention except
Domino, the first female figure in the line.

Fifth Series, with Fleer Ultra X-Men card
Mojo with "Wild Whipping Tail Action" (#49528) $5.00
Black Tom with "Power Bio-Blast" (#49529) 5.00
Urban Assault Cable with "Shoulder Cannon Blaster"
    (#49530) 5.00
Avalanche with "Exploding Rock Platform" (#49532) . . 5.00
Commando with "Techno Sludge Liquid Blaster"
    (#49533) 5.00
Exodus with "Plasma Burst" (#49534) 5.00

Sixth Series, with Flair Marvel Annual card or Fleer Ultra X-
Men card
Cable Cyborg with "Hidden Techno Bionics" (#49535) . 6.00
The Blob with "Rubber Blubber Belly" (#49536) 10.00
Domino with "Twin Weapon Arsenal" (#49537) 11.00
Caliban with "Mutant Roaring Attack" (#49538) 6.00
Nimrod with "Mutant Seeking Missiles" (#49539) 6.00
Deadpool with "Mutagenic Hidden Nightmare"
    (#49540) 9.00
Genesis with "Spine Sidekick Feature" (#49543) 6.00

Seventh Series (Sept. 1996)
Killspree II with "Ripping Forearm Blades" (#49566) . . 6.00
Cable Stealth with "Stealth-Tech Armor" (#49567) 6.00
Arctic Armor Cable with "Armor Piercing Weaponry"
    (#49568) 6.00
Shatterstar III with "Twin Slashing Swords" (#49569) . . 6.00

Cable Stealth, X-Force (Toy Biz 1996)

Cyclops, The Uncanny X-Men (Toy Biz 1991)

(THE UNCANNY) X-MEN
Toy Biz (1991)

The first few X-Men figures were greeted with considerable enthusiasm by comic book fans and collectors alike. The first five were Cyclops, Wolverine, Nightcrawler, Colossus and Magneto. The later four included Storm, the first Marvel heroine available in quite a while. She sat around on the shelves for quite a while, as Toy Biz learned the first basic rule of action figures. Boys will not buy many of the girl figures, but collectors will, as long as she is somewhat scarce. There is probably a master's thesis in behavioral psychology in this rule somewhere, but it's pretty well known now.

Storm could have been purchased by the bushel basket when the rest of this series was gone from the shelves. She wasn't, and when she was eventually gone from the shelves, a lot of collectors realized they didn't have one. New collectors didn't have one either and as female figure collecting became more and more common her price finally rose, and now she is the most valuable figure in this group. All the collectors make sure they grab the occasional female figure now, so this phenomenon probably won't occur again.

All of the figures in this first series came with a Marvel Universe One trading card that matched the figure. The cards were a special printing and had a Toy Biz logo in color on the back. This is the first and only time that Toy Biz did this. All other figures that came with trading cards from a card set had a randomly selected card from the set. However, some

other groups had exclusive trading cards, such as the X-Men Classic series.

5" Figures, with Impel Marvel Universe One card
Wolverine with "Snap-Out Claws" (#4901) $20.00
Archangel with "Missile Shooting Wings" (white wings)
    (#4902) 20.00
Colossus with "Power Lift Action" (#4903) 20.00
Nightcrawler with "Super Suction" (#4904) 30.00
Storm with "Power Glow" (#4905) 40.00
Cyclops with "Laser Light Eyes" (#4906) blue and
    white 20.00
Apocalypse with "Extending Body" (#4907) 20.00
Magneto with "Magnetic Hands and Chest" (#4908) . 20.00
Juggernaut with "Power Punch Action" (#4909) 20.00

Vehicles and Accessories
Magneto Magnetron Vehicle (#4961, 1991) 11.00
    Reissue (#04961, 1994) 10.00
Wolverine Mutant Cycle (#4962, 1991) 11.00
    Reissue (#04962, 1994) 10.00
Wolverine Combat Cave (#4971, 1991) 12.00
Cyclops Light Force Arena (#4973, 1991) 12.00

Super-Size 15" Super Heroes (1991) in open box
Magneto (#4921) 20.00
Wolverine (#4922) 20.00

(THE UNCANNY) X-MEN
Toy Biz (1992)

The trickle of figures released in 1991 became a stream of figures in 1992 when 30 new Marvel, X-Men and X-Force

Banshee, The Uncanny X-Men (Toy Biz 1992)

figures were produced. All the X-Men figures had trading cards, but they were randomly selected from the entire X-Men 1 series. There is nothing wrong with this, but it isn't as elegant a premium as the first nine figures had. The original Iceman figure was the one the collectors were looking for. This version changes color when it gets cold. This feature didn't work very well and so not too many were produced.

Later shipments of these figures had an X-Men 2 trading card or a Fleer Ultra X-Men trading card. They are worth a few dollars less than the original versions. Some of these reissues were hanging around for quite a while on toy store shelves.

Second Series, with Impel X-Men (1) card
later shipments: SkyBox X-Men 2 or Fleer Ultra X-Men card and 5-digit code on back, adding a "2"
Wolverine 2nd Edition with "Spring-Out Slashing Claws" (#4931) $19.00
Wolverine 3rd Edition with "Savage Strike Twist Action" (#4932) 25.00
Wolverine "Weapon X" with "High-Tech Training Helmet," green cords (#4933) 13.00
Iceman "Changes Color in Freezer" (#4934) 40.00
Forge with "Quick Draw Action" (#4935) with brown holster 40.00
Forge with "Quick Draw Action" (#4935) with yellow holster, later issue 20.00
Gambit with "Power Kick Action" (#4937) 10.00
Reissue shipments: back (#49492) 8.00
Banshee with "Sonic Scream" (#4938) 12.00
Sabretooth with "Self-Healing Wounds" (#4939) 10.00
Sauron with "Savage Attack Wings" (#4940) yellow belt 9.00
Variation, with gold belt 9.00
Magneto 2nd Edition with "Super Spark Action" (#4941) 9.00
Variation, with red stripe on glove 9.00
Mr. Sinister with "Power Light Eyes" (#4942) 9.00

Sears X-Men Sets, bagged, no card
Classic Heroes 4-Pack, with Spider-Man, Green Goblin, Venom and Punisher (#59501) 20.00
Classic Heroes 4-Pack, with Mr. Fantastic, Thing, Venom and Annihilus (#59506) 20.00
X-Force 4-Pack, with Cable, Stryfe, Forearm and Deadpool (#59505) 20.00
X-Men 4-Pack, with Mr. Sinister, Iceman, Sabretooth and Wolverine II (#59508) 20.00

(THE UNCANNY) X-MEN
Toy Biz (1993)

More figures continued to appear in 1993. There were a lot of these figures shipped and they hung around for quite a while. You can probably still find some reissue figures at your local toy store. There were two different versions of Cyclops available, Archangel had white or gray wings and many of the 1991 figures were reissued.

Third Series reissue figures with Impel X-Men (1) card
later shipments: SkyBox X-Men 2 or Fleer Ultra X-Men card and 5-digit code on back, adding a "6" (Assts. #4900G and #4900H)

Wolverine 5th Edition (Kay-Bee Special),
The Uncanny X-Men (Toy Biz 1993)

Juggernaut with "Power Punch Action" (#4943) reissue $10.00
Cyclops with "Laser Light Eyes," blue and white (#4944) reissue 10.00
Cyclops, yellow and blue (#4944) 10.00
Reissue shipments: back (#49491) 10.00
Magneto with "Magnetic Hands and Chest" (#4945) reissue 10.00
Wolverine (I) with "Snap-Out Claws" (#4946) reissue . 10.00
Archangel with "Missile Shooting Wings," white wings (#4947) reissue 10.00
Archangel, gray wings, back (#49495) 10.00
Apocalypse with "Extending Body" (#4948) reissue . . 10.00
Nightcrawler with "Super Suction" (#4950) reissue . . 12.00
Colossus with "Power Lift Action" (#4903) reissue . . 12.00
Reissue shipments: back (#49494) 10.00

Fourth Series, with Impel X-Men (1) card or SkyBox X-Men 2 card (Asst. #4900E). Figures with "Charan Toy" logo are worth about $3.00 less.
Wolverine 5th Edition with "Thrusting Knife Action" (#4910) 20.00
Wolverine 5th Edition with "Thrusting Knife Action" (#4910) green and copper color (Kay-Bee special) 15.00
Bishop with "Quick-Draw Weapon Release" (#4911) . 15.00
Strong Guy with "Power Punch" (#4912) 10.00
Apocalypse (2nd) with "Transforming Weapon Arms" (#4913) resculpt 10.00
Tusk "Surprise Attack Mutant" (#4914) 13.00
Omega Red with "Whipping Tendril Weapons" (#4916) 10.00
Wolverine "Weapon X" with "High-Tech Training Helmet," red cords (#4933) 15.00

Ahab, The Uncanny X-Men (Toy Biz 1994)

X-MEN
Toy Biz (1994)

Even more X-Men figures were shipped in 1994. The logo on the header card, which said "The Uncanny X-Men" for the first to the fifth series is changed to "X-Men" for the sixth and later series. Rogue, the second female X-Men figure, appeared that year. She was fairly easy to find. Recently, eagle-eyed collectors have spotted variations in her eye make-up and this has increased her price. What you would expect is that one eye variation would be the scarce and valuable one, but what has actually happened is that every female figure collector wants the version he does not own and all versions have increased in price.

The other figure which has attracted collector interest is the Wolverine "Weapon X" figure. The 1994 version with silver cords is quite scarce compared to the 1993 version with red cords.

Fifth Series, with SkyBox X-Men 2 card
later shipments: Fleer Ultra X-Men card (Asst. #4900F). Figures with original card are worth $2.00 more.
Cyclops with "Light-Up Optic Blast" (#4917) blue and
    yellow $8.00
Professor X with "Secret Control Panels" "Uncanny X-
    Men" (#4918) 5.00
Longshot with "Knife Throwing Action" (#4923) 10.00
Sabretooth with "Snarl and Swipe Action" (#4924) 9.00
Ahab with "Harpoon Shooting Gun" (#4925) 7.00
Brood with "Wing Operated Snarl and Tail Whipping
    Action" (#4926) 9.00

Rogue, X-Men (Toy Biz 1994)

Sixth Series, (Asst. #4900I) with Fleer Ultra X-Men card With or without T-shirt offer on back of header card — same price.
Beast with "Mutant Flipping Power" (#49355) 18.00
Robot Wolverine (Albert) 6th with "Robotic Arm
    Weapons" (#49356) 6.00
Random with "Missile Blasting Arm" (#49357) 6.00
Silver Samurai with "Metal Samurai Armor" (#49358)   12.00
Trevor Fitzroy with "Futuristic Crystal Battle Armor"
    (#49360) 6.00
Morph with "Mutant Shape Shifter" (#49361) 10.00

Seventh Series, with Fleer Ultra X-Men card (Asst. #4900J)
Rogue with "Power Uppercut Punch" (#49362) any
    version 25.00
Kylun with "Twin Striking Swords" (#49363) 6.00
Raza with "Swashbuckling Sword Action" (#49364) . . . 6.00
Ch'od with "Double Arm Hurling Action" (#49365) 6.00
Wolverine–Street Clothes 7th Edition "Street Tough"
    (#49366) 6.00
Bonebreaker with "Mutant Attack Tank" (#49368) 6.00

Eighth Series, with Fleer Ultra X-Men card (Asst. #4900K)
Nightcrawler with "Super Suction" (#49369) reissue . . 10.00
Storm (#2) "Power Glow" (#49370) 9.00
Magneto (Super Spark) (#49371) 6.00
Mr. Sinister with "Power Light Blast," with goatee
    (#49372) reissue 6.00
Wolverine "Weapon X" with "High-Tech Training Hel-
    met," silver cords (#49373) scarce 20.00
Sauron with "Savage Attack Wings" reissue with black
    symbol on loincloth (#49374) 5.00
Iceman (#2): "Super Ice Slide" (#49375) clear 12.00
    Variation, clear with blue tint 10.00
Senyaka (#49389) with "Whip Snapping Action" (Toys
    "R" Us exclusive) 4.00

Phoenix, X-Men Phoenix Saga (Toy Biz 1995)

X-MEN
Toy Biz (1995)

Early in 1995, X-Men figures began being issued in named groups of five or six figures. This certainly helped collectors keep track of the figures, since they previously only had slight packaging variations and esoteric assortment numbers to guide them through the hundreds of X-Men and Marvel figures then on toy store shelves. It also helps us a lot in listing them in groups, since we don't have to refer to "batches" or "series" or other names which don't actually appear on the header cards.

Toy Biz also redesigned the header cards for their X-Men line, making it larger and blue rather than smaller and orange. The Phoenix Saga figures were caught in the transition and so there were two different versions of each of those figures. There are weapon and accessory differences, as well, but the product codes were the same.

5" Figures, with Fleer Ultra X-Men card
Phoenix Saga (Summer 1995) With or without T-shirt offer on header card—same price.
Corsair "Swashbuckling Space Pirate" (#49380) $8.00
    Reissue on larger header card 8.00
Gladiator with "Super Strength Power Punch" (#49381)10.00
    Reissue on larger header card 8.00
Space Wolverine, 8th Edition with "Slashing Space
    Armor" (#49383) 8.00
    Reissue on larger header card 8.00
Warstar "Surprise Attack Team" (#49384) 8.00

Reissue on larger header card 8.00
Phoenix with "Fiery Phoenix Power" (#49385) 25.00
    Reissue on larger header card 18.00

Mutant Genesis (August 1995) Faded header card or glossy header card—same price.
Cameron Hodge (Phalanx) with "Water Blasting Bio
    Weapon" (#49386) 5.00
X-Cutioner with "Battle Staff Spinning Action" (#49387) 5.00
Maverick with "Quick-Draw Weapon Action" (#49388) . 5.00
Senyaka with "Whip Cracking Action" (#49389) 5.00
Wolverine Fang with Shi'ar Weapon with "Super
    Slashing Claw Action" (#49390) 5.00
Sunfire with "Removable Solar Armor" (#49399) 5.00

Invasion Series (October 1995)
Captive Sabretooth with "Break-Away Action" (#49392) 5.00
Battle Ravaged Wolverine with "Berserker Rage Action"
    (#49393) 5.00
Havok with "Projectile Throwing Action" (#49394) 5.00
Iceman II with "Extending Ice Limbs" (#49395) 5.00
Archangel II with "Wing-Flapping Action" (#49396) .. 18.00
Spiral with "Arm-Spinning Action" (#49397) 10.00
Eric the Red with "Super Metallic Armor" (#49398) ... 5.00

X-MEN
Toy Biz (1996)

X-Men figures continued to be issued in named group assortments in 1996. Groups were reduced to (generally) five figures from six. The group name moved from a simple line of text at the top of the header card to a larger and more

Bishop II, X-Men Flashback Series (Toy Biz 1996)

prominent sub-title. By the end of the year, with X-Men Ninja Force, the group name was part of the series title itself. Header cards were getting larger and fancier, in an attempt to have the new figures noticed in the sea of older figures hanging in many toy stores.

Age of Apocalypse (Feb. 1996)
Weapon X with "Interchangeable Weaponry" (#49413) $7.00
Sabertooth with "Wild Child Sidekick Figure" (#49414) . 7.00
Magneto with "Removable Helmet and Shrapnel Hand"
    (#49415) 7.00
Gambit . . . . not issued
Apocalypse with "Removable Armor and Transforming
    Limbs" (#49417) 7.00
Cyclops with "Cybernetic Guardian and Laser Blaster"
    (#49418) 7.00

Flashback (Aug. 1996) with trading card
Omega Red II with "Whipping Tendril" (#43211) red
    body 7.00
    Variation with black body 7.00
Polaris with "Power Upper Punch" (#43212) 7.00
Bishop II with "Weapon Release" (#43213) gray body . 7.00
    Variation with red body 7.00
Savage Land Wolverine with "Super Slashing Claw
    Action" (#43214) 7.00

Battle Brigade with card (Nov. 1996)
Wolverine Patch with "Total Assault Arsenal" (#43171) 7.00
Colossus with "Super Punch Gauntlets" (#43172) silver
    and yellow body 7.00
    Variation, with purple and red body 7.00
Post Apocalypse Beast with "Sci-Tech Blaster" (#43174)
    red chest 7.00

Variation with yellow chest 7.00
Lady Deathstrike with "Bio-Morphing Armor" (#43175) 10.00
Archangel with "Wing-Flapping Action" (#43176) 7.00

Mutant Armor Series, with Flair Marvel Annual 1995 trading card
Iceman with "Crystalline Armor" (#43201) 8.00
Quicksilver with "Quantum Speed Sled" (#43202) purple
    body 8.00
    Variation, with purple and white body 8.00
Battle Armor Wolverine with "Anti-Magnetism Armor"
    (#43203) 8.00
Heavy Metal Beast with "Anti-Mutagenic Armor"
    (#43204) 8.00
Professor Xavier with "Astral Plane Armor" (#43205) . 12.00

X-Men Vehicles and Accessories
X-Men Sentinel 14" (#49320, 1994) 25.00
X-Men Blackbird Jet (#49400, 1994) 25.00
X-Men Mini Blackbird Jet (#49690, 1995) 10.00
X-Men Wolverine Jeep (#49685, 1995) 10.00
X-Men Headquarters Playset (#49810, 1995) 35.00

X-MEN NINJA FORCE
Toy Biz (1996)

The header card says that the "X-Men team up with Space Ninja Deathbird to become the Ninja Force and battle to save Japan." Actually Space Ninja Deathbird teams up with Dark Nemesis and the Ninja Force has to stop them! Anyway, interest in this new series has focused on the two female figures, Psylocke and Deathbird. They aren't really

Archangel, X-Men Battle Brigade Series (Toy Biz 1996)

Space Ninja Deathbird, X-Men Ninja Force (Toy Biz 1996)

scarce, but every female figure collector has to have one of each.

5" Figures (Dec. 1996)
Ninja Wolverine with "Warrior Assault Gear" (#43216) $7.00
Ninja Psylocke with "Extending Power Sword" (#43217) 10.00
Space Ninja Deathbird with "Fold-Out Ninja Wings" (#43218) 10.00
Ninja Sabretooth with "Clip-On Claw Armor" (#43219) . 7.00
Dark Nemesis with "Spear Shooting Staff" (#43220) .. 7.00

Silver Samurai and Robot Wolverine, X-Men (Boy Biz 1994)

X-MEN MULTI–PACKS

X-Men Mutant Hall of Fame, 10 figures on collector display stand, numbered (75,000 made) (#49800) $80.00
X-Men Gift Set (Wolverine, blue Iceman, Mr. Sinister and Sabretooth) (#49100) 30.00

WalMart 2-Pack Figures (X-Men/Spider-Man)
Beast vs. Spiderman (Web-Shooter) 25.00
Nightcrawler vs. Spider-Man (Web-Racer) 25.00
Juggernaut vs. Spider-Man (Web-Parachute) 25.00
Civilian Wolverine vs. Peter Parker 25.00

WalMart 2-Packs with 4 cards
Wolverine vs. Sabretooth 20.00
Strong Guy vs. Tusk (#49602) 20.00
Professor X vs. Ahab (#49603) 20.00
Wolverine Spy vs. Omega Red 20.00
Bishop vs. Apocalypse 20.00
Cyclops vs. Mr. Sinister 20.00

F.A.O. Schwarz Special
Trevor Fitzroy, Combat Cable, Forge and Deadpool in mail-order box 50.00
Dark Phoenix Saga 4-pack: Phoenix, Corsair, Ch'od, Wolverine Space (#49050) 45.00

Kay-Bee Collector's Edition
Maverick and Trevor Fitzroy (with Steel Mutants Wolverine) (Maverick sold exclusively at Kay-Bee) (#49640, 1994) 14.00
Silver Samurai and Robot Wolverine (with Steel Mutants Cyclops) (#49641, 1994) 14.00

Beast, 10", The Uncanny X-Men (Toy Biz 1995)

X-MEN DELUXE EDITION—10" FIGURES
Toy Biz (1993–96)

All of Toy Biz's 5" action figures are originally sculpted in a 10" size and mechanically reduced to the 5" size during production. Consequently, they didn't have to have an expensive new sculpt produced to make 10" figures. In 1993 they started making these figures in groups of three and selling them in window boxes for $10.00 to $12.00. The only problem was that they didn't sell all that well.

Toy Biz sold all the remaining stock to the Kay-Bee toy chain, who sold them for $5.00 to $6.00 each. At that price they sold fairly well. Toy Biz also bought the remaining stock of 5" figures and offered them at discount as well. Collectors picked out the female figures, along with the occasional scarce figure and otherwise largely left these figures alone for the kids to buy. Many of the large figures were quite common, which has kept the price down, but a few were hard to find. There are over 50 different 10" figures available if you count X-Force, X-Men, Spider-Man, Marvel and the others.

10" X-Men Figures (1993) in window box
Cyclops (#49755) $20.00
Wolverine (#49765) 20.00
Sabretooth (#49775) 18.00

Second Batch (Asst. #49710, 1994) in window box
Gambit (#49711) 8.00
Mr. Sinister (#49712) 8.00
Bishop (#49713) 8.00

Third Batch (Asst. #49720, 1994) in window box
Beast (#49721) 18.00
Weapon X (Wolverine) (#49722) 14.00
Apocalypse (#49723) 18.00

Fourth Batch (1995) in window box
Beast (#49041) 15.00
Wolverine (#49042) 10.00
Magneto (#49043) 10.00

Fifth Batch (1995) in window box
Wolverine (Battle Ravage) (#48409) 10.00
Archangel II (#48410) 10.00

Sixth Batch (1995) in window box
Wolverine Space (#48121) 10.00
Rogue (#48122) 15.00

Seventh Batch (1996) in window box
Mystique (#48171) 15.00
Wolverine Classic (#48172) 8.00
Spy Wolverine (#48173?) black 20.00

X-MEN METALLIC MUTANTS

10" Metallic Mutant Figures (Asst. #49730, 1994)
Spy Wolverine (#49621) 10.00
Omega Red (#49622) 10.00
Magneto (#49623) 10.00

Second Batch (Asst. #49740, 1994)
Wolverine (#49741) 10.00
Cyclops (#49742) 10.00
Sabretooth (#49743) 10.00

X-MEN MUTANT MONSTERS
Toy Biz (1996)

These are interesting figures, but the jury is still out on whether collectors are interested enough to collect them. They are 6" tall, but seem bigger. Each figure has a "Wind-Up Action."

6" Figures, in window box
Werewolf Wolverine with "Slash and Howl Action"
   (#43191) $12.00
Sugar Man with "Wicked Laugh and Big Bad Bite"
   (#43192) 12.00
Dark Beast with "Growl and Scratch Action" (#43193) 12.00

Wolverine, X-Men Projectors (Toy Biz 1994)

X-MEN PROJECTORS
Toy Biz (1994–95)

The idea behind these figures was to project a picture on your wall using a device in the chest of the figure. If it had worked, you can be certain that more film disks would have been made and sold separately. But the idea didn't work and was dropped and the figures were discounted. Collectors have ignored these figures completely. They may be very hard to find if collectors change their mind in the future. With so many other types and sizes of figures available this may never happen, but you never know.

8" Figure/Projectors with film disks, on header card
Wolverine (#49104) $9.00
Cyclops (#49105) 9.00
Sabretooth (#49106) 9.00
Magneto (#49107) 9.00
Apocalypse (#49108) 9.00
Spider-Man (Spider-Man) (#47221, 1995) 9.00
Venom (Spider-Man) (#47222, 1995) 9.00
Hobgoblin (Spider-Man) (#47223, 1995) 9.00

8" Figure/Projectors (1995) boxed
Civilian Wolverine (X-Men) (#48131) 10.00
Beast (X-Men) (#48132) 10.00
Iron Man (Iron Man) (#48133) 10.00
Lizard (Spider-Man) (#48134) 10.00
Thing (Fantastic Four) (#48135) 10.00
Mr. Sinister (X-Men) (#48211) 10.00
Cable (X-Men) (#48212) 10.00
Dr. Octopus (Spider-Man) (#48213) 10.00
Super Sense Spider-Man (#48214) 10.00
Bishop (X-Men) (#48215) 10.00

black pants (#43153) 6.00
Repaint figure, yellow chest and blue pants
(#43153) 7.00
Nightcrawler with "Light-Up Sword" red highlights
(#43154) 6.00
Repaint figure, silver highlights (#43154) 7.00
Juggernaut (II) with "Light-Up Jewel Weapon" (#43155) 6.00
Repaint figure, black pants and lighter skin
(#43155) 7.00
Elektra with "Light-Up Ninja Blade" repaint of Psylocke
figure, red outfit (#43156) 10.00

X-MEN 2099
Toy Biz (1995–96)

X-Men 2099 figures are based on the comic book series of the same name which began in 1993. It's another way to have a different universe of characters with new stories. Collectors have mostly been interested in La Lunatica, the female figure in the line. She was hard to find at first, but this proved to be a self-fulfilling situation and there was no great problem finding her later.

5" Figures, no trading card
Skullfire with "Glowing Energy Skeleton" (#43106) . . $6.00
Bloodhawk with "Wing Flapping Action" (#43107) 6.00
Meanstreak with "High Speed Action" (#43108) 6.00
Metalhead with "Heavy-Metal Punch" (#43109) 6.00
Brimstone Love with "Back Slash Action" (#43110) . . . 6.00

Second Batch (May 1996)
Shadow Dancer with "Jaw Chompin' Action" (#43164) . 6.00

Skullfire, X-Men 2099 (Toy Biz 1995)

Juggernaut, X-Men Classics (Toy Biz 1996)

X-MEN CLASSICS
Toy Biz (1995)

These figures have their own distinctive header card and the first batch got a special trading card as well, rather than a recycled trading card from one of the many series of Marvel and X-Men cards produced by SkyBox. Collectors have grabbed the female figures and ignored the others, at least so far. The first series figures are based on the X-Men animated television series which debuted on the FOX network in 1992. Second series figures feature a "Light-Up Weapon." They were repainted in late 1996, but only some stores got the repaint figures. The most significant repaint figure is Psylocke—she was repainted into a new figure: *Electra*.

5" Figure, with special trading card. Later shipments with Fleer Ultra X-Men card are worth $1.00 less.
Wolverine with "Spring-Out Slashing Claws" (#43126) $7.00
Gambit with "Power Kick Action" (#43127) 7.00
Cyclops with "Light-Up Optic Blast" (#43128) 7.00
Storm with "Power Glow Action" (#43129) 12.00
Beast with "Mutant Flipping Power" (#43130) 9.00
Magneto with "Super Spark Action" (#43131) 7.00

Second Series (Aug. 1996) no trading card
Woverine (Stealth) with "Light-Up Plasma Weapon"
(#43151) 6.00
Repaint figure, yellow and navy blue (#43151) . . 7.00
Psylocke with "Light-Up Psychic Knife" (#43152) 8.00
Gambit with "Light-Up Energy Weapon" pink chest and

Breakdown with "Dominick Sidekick Figure" (#43166) . 6.00
Halloween Jack with "Super-Poseable Action"
    (#43161) 6.00
Junkpile with "Snap-on Battle Armor" (#43162) 6.00
La Lunatica with "Futuristic Jai-Lai" (#43165) purple
    bikini 9.00
    Repaint figure with black bra under purple bikini . 9.00

X-Men, Alternate-X (Toy Biz 1996)

X-MEN ALTERNATE X
Toy Biz (1996)

So far this is a one-shot two-pack. No line like this was promoted at Toy Fair, so it may simply remain a curiosity. On the other hand, Toy Biz produces a lot of figures and may decide to package others in this manner. Who knows.

Two-Pack, boxed
Weapon X with Interchangeable Weaponry and
    Wolverine with Light-Up Plasma Weapon
    (#49070) $13.00

Rogue, 12" Doll, X-Men (Toy Biz 1995)

X-MEN 12" DOLLS
Toy Biz (1996)

Toy Biz has been making a few of these very doll-like figures in an attempt to appeal to girls or collectors or both. Rogue went only to Kay-Bee stores and comic shops, while Storm was sold to everybody. There are also a couple of Spider-Man dolls and one Ghost Rider doll.

12" Dolls (Oct. 1996)
Storm Special Collectors Edition 12" figure with
    costumes (#48416) $25.00
Rogue 12" Collector Hero, changes from Superhero to
    Civilian (#48418) 30.00

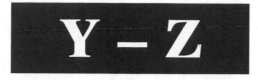

Shaft, Youngblood (McFarlane Toys 1995)

YOUNGBLOOD
McFarlane Toys (1995)

Youngblood figures are based on the Image comic book series by Rob Liefeld. Troll was, and is, scarce. The others have been easy to find. The comic books are popular, but there are a lot of super heroes around in toy stores these days and these figures look a lot like the Spawn series, also produced by McFarlane Toys. The day may come when collectors regret passing this series up.

6" Figures

Troll (#13101) scarce, white abdomine	$20.00
Variation, green abdomine	15.00
Dutch (#13102)	8.00
Die Hard (#13103)	8.00
Shaft (#13104)	8.00
Crypt (#13105)	10.00
Sentinel (#13106)	8.00
Shaft and Mother-One boxed gift set (#92101)	10.00

ZEN INTERGALACTIC NINJA
Just Toys (1992)

Zen Intergalactic Ninja is a comic book with a small following. Just Toys was a manufacturer of bendie figures. Just Toys tried to get into the action figure business with this series and with Fish Police (which never came out). Neither the comic book nor these figures caught on with collectors and they disappeared with barely a trace. This is too bad, because they are perfectly nice figures.

5" Figures

Zen (#14001)	$7.00
Lord Contaminous (#14002)	7.00
Jeremy Baker, battery powered (#14003)	7.00
Garbage Man (#14004)	7.00
Can-It (#14005)	7.00
Lights Out, battery powered (#14012)	7.00

ZORRO
Gabriel (1982)

Zorro dates back to the 1920 silent movie *The Mark of Zorro* starring Douglas Fairbanks. Tyrone Power starred in the 1940 remake with Basil Rathbone. Zorro has also been a movie serial, a television series, more movies and several comic books. These figures were based on the television cartoon series from Filmation. They were also creating The Lone Ranger show at this time. Zorro will be coming around again in 1997 from Playmates based on the new movie starring Antonio Banderas and there will be an animated series as well.

3" Figures

Zorro (#32710)	$20.00
Amigo (#32712)	20.00
Captain Ramon (#32714)	20.00
Sergeant Gonzales (#32716)	20.00

Figure and Horse

Zorro and Tempest	40.00

Horses

Picaro	25.00
Tempest (#32720)	25.00

INDEX

Man from Pluto, 152
Man from Saturn, 152
Man from Uranus, 152
Man from Venus, 152
Man With No Eyes, The, 119
Man-At-Arms, 137
Man-Bat, 16
Man-E-Faces, 137
Man-Lizard, 185
Man-Spider, 183
Mandarin, 61, 109
Mandoom, 4
Mandrake the Magician, 47
Mangler, 44
Manglizard, 125
Manglodactyl, 125
Manglodemon, 125
Manglodragon, 125
Manglord, 125
Manglosaurus, 125
Manta Ray Batman, 19
Mantaman, 227
Mantenna, 137
Mantis, 231
Mantis Alien, 8
Mantor, 172
Mantus, 154
Mara, 29
Marauder, 237
Marbles, 168
Margaret O'Brien, 97
Marge, 175
Marina, 226
Mario, 230
Marion Ravenwood, 106
Marksman, 173
Marrow, 67
Marsala, 58, 59
Marshal BraveStarr, 32
Marshal Roy Star, 257
Marshall LeFors, 33
Martia, 197
Martial Arts Expert, 94
Martial Arts Robin, 19
Martian Ambassador, 126
Martian Leader, 126
Martian Manhunter, 231, 232
Martian Spy Girl, 126
Martian Trooper, 126
Marvel Super Heroes, 128, 129
Marvel – Secret Wars, 127
Marvin the Martian, 121, 179
Mary Jan Watson, 185
Mary Jane, 131
Mask of the Phantasm, 17
Maskatron, 176
Masked Rider, 135
Massacre, 229
Master Sergeant Cornelius
    Cannonfodder, 12
Master Vile, 144, 145
MaTi, 37
Matrix, 171
Matt Trakker, 134, 135
Maul, 263
Maul in Flexon, 263
Mauler, 22
Maverick, 86, 273, 275
Max, 34, 256
Max Ray, 40
Max Sterling, 167, 168
Maximillian, 29
Maximum Carnage, 139
Maximus Mayhem, 135
Maxwell the Accelerator, 226
Maxx, 181
Mayor, 149, 264
Mayor Munchkin, 264

Mazinga, 174
Mazrak Defender, 166
McCabe, 233
McCoy, 188, 191, 197, 200, 204
Mcanstreak, 277
Mech-Wing Batman, 16
Mecha-Ghidorah, 97
Mecha-Godzilla, 97
Mechanic, 28
Mechanizer, 146
Medicine Man, 262
Medieval Spawn, 180
Medusa, 54, 61
Meg, 28
Mega Armor Spider-Man, 133
Mega Armor Wolverine, 133
Mega Man, 139
Mega-Viper, 90
Megabyte, 163
Megarite, 188
Megas, 140
MegaZord, 143
Mekaneck, 137
Mekanicle, 6
Mel, 52, 53
Melf, 3
Meltdown Terminator, 247
Membros, 140
Mendoza, 261
Mer-Man, 137
Mercer, 85, 89
Mercion, 3
Mercury, 49
Merdude, 241
Mermaid, 64
Mermista, 159
Merrick the Barbaric, 144
Metal Face, 225
Metal Head, 88
Metal Mutant Turtles, 244
Metal-Head, 92
Metal-Mash Terminator, 248
Metalhead, 96, 239, 243, 277
Metlar, 108
Mettaflame, 4
Meuton, 29
Mexican Guerrero, 262
Michael Jordan, 179
Michael Knight, 114
Michael Nesmith, 147
Michael Titan, 173
Michael Van Horn, 97
Michaelangelo, 239, 245
Mickey, 151
Mickey Dalens, 147
Micki, 64
Micronized Zentraedi Warrior, 167
Microtron, 140
Mighty Mutations, 243
Mike, 169, 240
Mike as Frankenstein, 242
Mike Hazard, 147
Mike Powers, 79
Mikola, 122
Mila, 234
Miles, 135
Miles Mayhem, 134
Mind-Zei, 49, 50
Mindy, 148
Ming, 62
Ming The Merciless, 47, 62, 63
Minotaur, 102, 143
Minotaur Goliath, 66
Mirage, 90
Miriya, 167, 168
Miss Yvonne, 153
Missile Armor Flipshot, 101
Missing Tomato Link, 10

Mister Miracle, 232
Mister Spock, 196
Mitch Talon, 173
Miyagi, 114
Mo-Lec-U-Lar, 175
Moby Lick, 227
Modo, 27
Modok, 109
Modulok, 137
Mogs, 151
Moguera, 98
Mojo, 269
Mola Ram, 107
Mole Man, 60
Mole-Man, 102
Molt, 31
Moltar, 45
Momaw Nadon "Hammerhead",
    223
Mon-Star, 175
Mona Lisa, 242
Mondo, 67
Mondo Gecko, 239, 243
Mongor, 249
Mongul Warrior, 173
Monkey Man, 107
Monkeywrench, 84
Monkian, 249
Monroe, 44
Monster Fly, 177
Monstro-Viper, 90
Montgomery Scott, 197
Monty Moose, 241
Moo Montana, 262
Moon McDare, 148
Moon Stryker, 175
Morbius, 183
Morbius Unbound, 185
Mordant, 143
Mordock the Benzite, 191
Mork, 148
Morn, 201
Morph, 272
Morticia, 3
Moses Hightower, 156
Mosquitor, 137
Moss Man, 137
Moth Lady, 98
Mother-One, 261
Mothra, 97
Moto Streex, 227
Motor Viper, 84
Movie III April, 242
Movie III Kenshin, 242
Movie III Turtles, 242
Movie III Walker, 242
Movie III Warlord, 242
Movie Star Splinter, 240
Movie Star Super Shredder, 242
Movie Star Turtles, 240, 242
Moze, 34
MP, 173
Mr. Fantastic, 60, 61, 129, 266, 271
Mr. Freeze, 16, 47, 232
Mr. Kotter, 261
Mr. Lucky, 231
Mr. Majestic, 263
Mr. Mxyzptlk, 266
Mr. Scott, 188
Mr. Sinister, 271, 272, 275, 276
Mr. Sleeze, 157
Mr. Spock, 188, 189, 200
Mr. T, 1
Ms. Marvel, 131
Muckman & Joe Eyeball, 239
Muckman and Joe Eyeball, 243
Mucus Tick, 250
Mugato, 188

Muggle Rat, 34
Multi-Bot, 137
Mumbles, 49
Mumbo-Jumbo, 175
Mumm-Ra, 249
Mummato, 10
Mummy, 42, 123, 151, 162, 235,
    255
Murdock, 1, 2
Muscle Power Rambo, 160
Muskrat, 85-87, 91
Mustapha Cairo, 34
Muta Force Turtles, 245
Mutagen Man, 239, 243
Mutant Marauder, 135
Mutant Military 2 Turtles, 241
Mutant Military Turtles, 240
Mutant Raphael, The, 242
Mutatin' Turtles, 241
Mutt, 88
Mutt & Junkyard, 90, 91
Mutt with Junkyard, 82
Mysteria, 61
Mysterio, 183
Mystique, 276
Nakoma, 99, 156
Namor, 60
Napolean Solo, 125
Napoleon Bonafrog, 240, 243
Napoleon Brie, 27
Nara Burnes, 58
Nash Gorey, 134
Natasha Yar, 194
Nate Slate, 64
Natural Tick, 250
Nausicaan, 194
Navy S.E.A.L. Guile, 226
Nawt, 179
Neelix The Talaxian, 203
Nelson, 175
Nemesis, 57
Nemesis Enforcer, 85
Nemesis Robots, 140
Neo Cat, 59
Neo Lord, 59
Neon Armor Batman, 19
Neptul, 29
Neptunian, 188
Netossa, 159
Neural Claw Batman, 118
Neutron Armor Servo, 228
Neutron Star Superman, 230
Nevtrino, 49
New Spider-Man, 183
Nick Fury, 183
Nicolai Malthus, 22
Niddler, 154
Nien Nunb, 213
Night Armor Iron Man, 133
Night Climber Batman, 15
Night Cougar Alien, 9
Night Creeper, 90
Night Creeper Leader, 91, 92
Night Fighter, 161
Night Fighters, 80
Night Flight Batman, 19
Night Hunter Batman, 19
Night Man, 254
Night Man, The, 254
Night Ninja Turtles, 242
Night Strike Prime, 254
Night Viper, 87
Night-Creeper, 88
Nightcrawler, 270-272, 275, 277
Nightfighter Guile, 226
Nightmare, 44
Nightstick, 44

ABOUT THE AUTHORS

STUART W. WELLS III started as a science fiction collector in the 1960s. In the 1990s he served as executive editor of *Toy Values Monthly* (later *Collectible Toys and Values*) for most of its existence and has written for various other collector magazines. He is the author of *Comic Cards and Their Prices* and *The Science Fiction and Heroic Fantasy Author Index*, the coauthor of *Comics Collectibles and their Values*, and, for the last several years, the editor of *Comics Values Annual*. He is also the photographer and script writer for the *House of Collectibles CD-Rom Guide to Star Trek Collectibles*.

JIM MAIN has been involved in writing, publishing, and editing since 1971, beginning with the comic book small press. In toy collecting circles he has written for many magazines and books with articles, interviews, price information, and the like for titles such as *Comics Collector*, *Toy Shop*, *Greenberg's Guide to Super Hero Toys*, and *Collecting Toys* by Richard O'Brien. He co-created *Toy Values Monthly* magazine, which evolved in *Collectible Toys & Values*, for which he served as managing editor for the titles' entire 42-issue run. Main also has self-published his own toy-related titles, most notably *Action Figure Collector*, *Model Scene*, and *Toy Collectors Journal*, one of the earliest toy-related collector publications, in 1984. He has made valuable contacts in the major toy companies and is known by many in the toy collecting community.

BEAM UP A WHOLE UNIVERSE OF STAR TREK COLLECTIBLES!

Explore this phenomenal multi-billion-dollar marketplace for fun and profit—the largest array of collectibles in the history of entertainment!

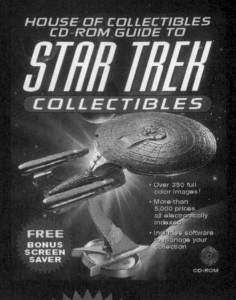

HOUSE OF COLLECTIBLES
CD-ROM GUIDE TO

STAR TREK
COLLECTIBLES

FREE BONUS SCREEN SAVER

- Over 350 full color images!
- More than 5,000 prices all electronically indexed
- Includes software to manage your collection

CD-ROM

With the 30th anniversary of Star Trek upon us, Star Trek is hotter than ever. This new CD-ROM guide boldly goes where none has gone before – to the far reaches of Star Trek collecting. Essential for any Trekker, it takes you on an enterprising voyage with leading-edge technology through the vast universe of Star Trek collectibles, including official items that have boosted Star Trek into a $2 billion phenomenon!

Now discover electronically "what's out there" as well as current prices ... from Star Trek action figures to watches and everything in-between. Passionate Trekkers can plan ahead for the next convention ... and starters can energize their interest. "Make it so" – order the House of Collectibles CD-ROM Guide to Star Trek Collectibles today! (see next page for details)

INSTANT CURRENT PRICE
Track any of over 5,000 prices in a flash on the electronic index.

Introducing the 21st century's way to look at Star Trek collectibles!

SPECTACULAR VIEWS
Beam up over 350 high-resolution full-color photos of important collectibles, including seldom-seen rarities.

COLLECTION COMMAND
Manage your Star Trek collection from your PC screen and keyboard ... fast and easily.

OVER, PLEASE ☞

HOUSE OF COLLECTIBLES CD-ROM GUIDE TO STAR TREK COLLECTIBLES

PRODUCT FEATURES

THE PHOTO GALLERY

View over 350 large, full-color pictures covering the entire universe of Star Trek collectibles.

- The high-resolution photos show all the intricate details of each collectible – an invaluable identification reference.

- All your favorite Star Trek characters are included: Captain Kirk, Mr. Spock, Captain Picard, Doctor McCoy, Mr. Scott, Tasha Yar, Klingons, Cardassians, Vulcans, Romulans and many more ... plus the Starship Enterprise and a full array of insignias, uniforms and symbols.

- In addition to familiar items, see many rarities from private collections. Discover items you never dreamed existed!

- Each photo comes with essential information: full description, date of manufacture, manufacturer, identification markings and current market value.

- Easily search through detailed descriptions for each collectible – it's like an electronic catalog.

- Listen to narrative descriptions and the sounds that some collectibles make!

- Search through the photos by series, movie or type of collectible.

- Get full introductions to Star Trek collecting and each category of collectibles.

- **FREE BONUS:** show off your passion for Star Trek by customizing your PC with screensavers!

COLLECTORWARE

- Instantly check any of over 5,000 current market prices in the huge database – virtually every type of Star Trek treasure is covered.

- Use these prices to spot bargains and get full value for your collectibles.

- Systematically track and plan your collection with interactive access to electronic Star Trek data that no other source provides.

- **BROWSE** from item to item or **SEARCH** by series/movie, character, manufacturer, category of collectible or key word.

- Quickly **FIND** any Star Trek collectible from the most comprehensive and authoritative database.

- **COPY** and **STORE** information under "MY COLLECTION" – your customized inventory of the collectibles you own and their current trading value. It's ideal for insurance purposes – and you can automatically total up your collection's value anytime.

- Print out **WANT LISTS** of collectibles you're looking for – keep them handy when shopping for new items.

- Create **PROFIT AND LOSS STATEMENTS** – your complete record of purchases and sales really organizes your collecting hobby.

- Automatically **SORT** your collection by series, character or price – cross-referencing items shows your collection's strengths and weaknesses.

- **EDIT** as changes occur or add non-listed items – there's also room for your personal comments on any item in your collection.

All data contained in this CD-ROM have been independently researched by experts. This project is not licensed, approved, sponsored or authorized by Paramount Pictures. Star Trek is a trademark of Paramount Pictures ▪ Windows is a trademark of Microsoft Corporation ▪ ©1996 Random House, Inc. All Rights Reserved.

Order Form

❑ **YES, Please send me the House of Collectibles CD-ROM Guide to Star Trek Collectibles. My price direct from the publisher is just $39.95 plus $3.95 shipping and handling. If not satisfied, I may return this software at the end of 30 days for a full refund.**

Name _____

Address _____

City _____ State _____ Zip Code _____

❑ **Check enclosed for $** _____ *(payable to House of Collectibles)
❑ **Charge my**
    ❑ **VISA**   ❑ **MasterCard**   ❑ **American Express**   ❑ **Discover**

_____   _____   _____
Credit Card Number   Expiration Date   Signature(required)

FOR IMMEDIATE DELIVERY, CALL TOLL-FREE • 1-800-800-1462

* Please add applicable sales tax. All orders subject to acceptance.

HOUSE OF COLLECTIBLES
P.O. Box 3580 • Wallingford, CT 06494

Dept. E13-001

HOUSE OF COLLECTIBLES

THE OFFICIAL® IDENTIFICATION AND PRICE GUIDES TO

AMERICAN INDIAN ARROWHEADS
1st edition
John L. Stivers
876-37913-7 $17.50

ANTIQUE AND MODERN FIREARMS
8th edition
Robert H. Balderson
876-37907-2 $17.00

ANTIQUE AND MODERN TEDDY BEARS
1st edition
Kim Brewer and Carol-Lynn Rossel Waugh
876-37792-4 $12.00

ANTIQUE CLOCKS
3rd edition
876-37513-1 $12.00

ANTIQUE JEWELRY (ID) 6th edition
Arthur Guy Kaplan
876-37759-2 $21.00

ARTS AND CRAFTS
The Early Modernist Movement in American Decorative Arts, 1894–1923 (ID)
2nd edition
Bruce Johnson
876-37879-3 $12.95

AUTOMOBILIA
1st edition
David K. Bausch
676-60030-1 $19.95

THE BEATLES
Records and Memorabilia
1st edition
Perry Cox and Joe Lindsay, with an introduction by Jerry Osborne
876-37940-4 $15.00

BEER CANS
5th Edition
Bill Mugrage
876-37873-4 $12.50

BOTTLES
11th edition
Jim Megura
876-37843-2 $14.00

CIVIL WAR COLLECTIBLES
1st edition
Richard Friz
876-37951-X $17.00

COLLECTIBLE TOYS (ID), 5th edition
Richard Friz
876-37803-3 $15.00

COLLECTOR CARS
8th edition
Robert H. Balderson
676-60024-7 $17.00

COLLECTOR HANDGUNS
5th edition
Robert H. Balderson
676-60038-7 $17.00

COLLECTOR KNIVES
11th edition
C. Houston Price
876-37973-0 $17.00

COLLECTOR PLATES
6th edition
Rinker Enterprises
876-37968-4 $17.00

COMPACT DISCS
1st edition
Jerry Osborne
876-37923-4 $15.00

COUNTRY MUSIC RECORDS
1st edition
Jerry Osborne
676-60004-2 $15.00

ELVIS PRESLEY RECORDS AND MEMORABILIA
1st edition
Jerry Osborne
876-37939-0 $14.00

FINE ART
2nd edition
Rosemary and Michael McKittrick
876-37909-9 $20.00

FRANK SINATRA RECORDS AND CDs
1st edition
Vito R. Marino and Anthony C. Furfero
876-37903-X $12.00

GLASSWARE
1st edition
Mark Pickvet
876-37953-6 $15.00

OLD BOOKS
1st edition
Marie Tedford and Pat Goudey
876-37915-3 $15.00

ORIENTAL RUGS
2nd edition
Joyce C. Ware
676-60023-9 $15.00

POSTCARDS (ID)
1st edition
Diane Allmen
876-37802-5 $9.95

POTTERY AND PORCELAIN
8th edition
Harvey Duke
876-37893-9 $15.00

ROCK AND ROLL— MAGAZINES, POSTERS, AND MEMORABILIA (ID),
1st edition
David K. Henkel
876-37851-3 $12.50

STAR TREK COLLECTIBLES
4th edition
Sue Cornwell and Mike Kott
876-37994-3 $19.95

WATCHES
10th edition
Cooksey Shugart & Tom Engle
876-37808-4 $18.00

THE OFFICIAL® BLACKBOOK PRICE GUIDES TO

U.S. COINS
35th Edition, 1997
Thomas E. Hudgeons, Jr.
876-37938-2 $6.99

U.S. PAPER MONEY
29th Edition, 1997
Thomas E. Hudgeons, Jr.
876-37935-8 $6.99

U.S. POSTAGE STAMPS
19th Edition, 1997
Thomas E. Hudgeons, Jr.
876-37932-3 $6.99

COIN COLLECTING

COIN COLLECTOR STARTER KIT/ONE-MINUTE COIN EXPERT
Scott A. Travers
676-60045-X $9.95

HOW TO MAKE MONEY IN COINS RIGHT NOW
Scott A. Travers
876-37997-8 $12.95

ONE-MINUTE COIN EXPERT
The Complete and Easy Guide for Fun and Profit
Second Edition
Scott A. Travers
676-60027-1 $5.99

THE OFFICIAL® GUIDE TO

GUNMARKS
3rd edition
Robert H. Balderson
676-60039-5 $15.00

THE OFFICIAL® DIRECTORY TO

U.S. FLEA MARKETS
5th edition
876-37978-1 $6.99

THE OFFICIAL® BECKETT PRICE GUIDES TO

FOOTBALL CARDS
16th edition, 1997
676-60020-4 $6.99

HOCKEY CARDS
6th edition, 1997
676-60022-0 $6.99

BASKETBALL CARDS
6th edition, 1997
676-60021-2 $6.99

BECKETT GREAT SPORTS HEROES

TROY AIKMAN
676-60035-2 $15.00

WAYNE GRETZKY
676-60032-8 $15.00

ANFERNEE HARDAWAY
676-60033-6 $15.00

MICHAEL JORDAN
876-37979-X $15.00

DAN MARINO
676-60034-4 $15.00

JOE MONTANA
876-37981-1 $15.00

SHAQUILLE O'NEAL
876-37980-3 $15.00

FRANK THOMAS
676-60029-8 $15.00

ORDER FORM

☐ YES. Please send me the following book(s):

_____
_____
_____

My price direct from the publisher is just $_____ plus $2.95 shipping and handling.
If not satisfied, I may return this book at the end of 30 days for a full refund.
Name _____
Address _____
City/State/Zip _____

☐ Check enclosed for $_____* (payable to House of Collectibles).
☐ Charge my
  ☐ VISA   ☐ MasterCard   ☐ American Express   ☐ Discover

_____   _____   _____
Credit Card Number   Expiration Date   Signature (required)

FOR IMMEDIATE DELIVERY, CALL TOLL-FREE • 1-800-800-1462
* Please add applicable sales tax.

HOUSE OF COLLECTIBLES
P.O. Box 3580 • Wallingford, CT 06494

Allow at least 4 weeks for delivery   Dept. AD11-002